Rosebery

Other books by the author

Fit to Govern?

Turning the Tide

Boycs: The True Story

Jack and Bobby: A Story of Brothers in Conflict

Rosebery

Statesman in Turmoil

LEO McKINSTRY

JOHN MURRAY

© Leo McKinstry 2005

First published in Great Britain in 2005 by John Murray (Publishers)
A division of Hodder Headline

The right of Leo McKinstry to be identified as the Author of the Work has been asserted by him
in accordance with the Copyright, Designs and Patents Act 1988.

1 3 5 7 9 10 8 6 4 2

A CIP catalogue record for this title is available from the British Library

ISBN 0 7195 5879 4

Typeset in Monotype Bembo 10.75/13pt
by Servis Filmsetting Ltd, Manchester

Printed and bound by
Clays Ltd, St Ives plc

Hodder Headline policy is to use papers that are natural, renewable and recyclable products and
made from wood grown in sustainable forests. The logging and manufacturing processes are
expected to conform to the environmental regulations of the country of origin.

John Murray (Publishers)
338 Euston Road
London NW1 3BH

To my late mother, Cherith Rosalind Mckinstry, 1928–2004

Contents

Illustrations

Section One

Section Two

Preface and Acknowledgements

> The biography and the subject are the great things. Everything should be tested, solely with reference to them. The biographer should be the unseen wire-puller.
>
> Lord Rosebery to Winston Churchill, 31 October 1905.

THE SUBJECTS OF my two previous biographies were the cricketer Geoffrey Boycott and the World Cup-winning footballers Jack and Bobby Charlton. So it might appear quite a leap to go from living sporting icons to a dead Victorian Prime Minister. But the 5th Earl of Rosebery has fascinated me ever since I first read about him when I was at school in the west of Ulster. I was intrigued by the charisma and contradictions of his enigmatic personality, this strange politician who loathed office but could bewitch the public with his oratory, this richest of aristocrats who was the darling of the urban working-class, this passionate Imperialist who married outside his race. My interest in Rosebery was deepened by my studies in nineteenth- and early twentieth-century British political history at Sidney Sussex College, Cambridge, where I was lucky enough to be taught by the renowned Derek Beales.

For more than a decade after my graduation in 1985, the idea of writing a book about Rosebery was nothing more than an idle daydream. Throughout this period, as I worked for the Labour Party at Westminster and on Islington Council, my literary efforts were confined to a series of unpublishable novels and the occasional po-faced letter to the *Guardian*. Yet even as I toiled in the dreary world of municipal socialism, my life continued to be touched by the 5th Earl. Living in Islington, I constantly cycled down Rosebery Avenue, one of the main roads through the borough and named in tribute to the former Prime Minister, who was not only the first chairman of the London County Council but also sat on the LCC as one of the members for Finsbury. Then, in 1995, my marriage took place at the old Finsbury Town Hall on Rosebery Avenue. Soon afterwards, when I abandoned politics and decided to take the risk of pursuing a career as a writer, we moved to Essex. On my very first visit to Colchester, our nearest large town, I noticed a plaque beside the entrance to the ornate Edwardian town hall which declared that the building had been opened in 1905 by the Earl of Rosebery. Only a few hundred yards away was another 'Rosebery Avenue'. It seemed as if this remarkable man must have left a tangible legacy right across the country. My eagerness to write about him was only quickened.

Though I dreamt about this book for many years, it was only in 2002, when I had finally established myself as an author, that I was able to contemplate seriously the task of writing a new Life of the 5th Earl. In arriving at that point I owe a huge debt to my dear wife Elizabeth, without whose support, faith, wisdom and advice I would have never been able to start this biography, never mind complete it. Throughout the long, lonely months of research and writing, she gave me nothing but support, even when I was sitting at my desk at 3 a.m. trying to fathom out another Balkan crisis or the Edwardian Liberal Party's policy on education. And her genius as a psychotherapist brought me an understanding of the complexities of Rosebery's personality.

There are two other people who gave me uplifting encouragement at the start of the project, when I was doubting whether I should proceed. One was Grant McIntyre, then at John Murray, who had enough faith in me to commission the book on the basis of a shamefully flaccid proposal and a shambling interview; the other was Andrew Roberts, who was not only generous with his time and hospitality but provided invaluable advice about how to begin my research. His magisterial Life of Salisbury, a model for any historical biographer, was a constant inspiration.

Once I had decided to press ahead, a host of people gave me an enormous amount of help. Foremost were the present Earl and Countess of Rosebery, who welcomed me to Dalmeny and could not have been kinder hosts. My time spent working on parts of the Rosebery archive was made much more enjoyable by the warmth and interest they showed me. I know they were, understandably, sometimes wary of my intentions, especially in the light of the continued speculation about the 5th Earl's private life, but I hope I have not betrayed their trust. All I have tried to do is present a balanced portrait of the 5th Earl, based primarily on archive material. In that context, I am indebted to the family for permission to quote from the Rosebery papers, and for allowing me to use many photographs from their own collection. I also wish to place on record my gratitude to the present Lord Dalmeny for his support.

With regard to archive material, I am grateful for all the assistance and courtesy shown to me by the staff of the National Library of Scotland, in which the bulk of the Rosebery collection is housed. My thanks also go to other libraries whose archives I have consulted: the Bodleian Library, the West Sussex Record Office, the British Library, the Norfolk Record Office, the London School of Economics, the Churchill Archive Centre, Cambridge University Library, the Liverpool Record Office, Bristol University Library, the Centre for Kentish Studies, the London Metropolitan Archive, the Public Record Office of Northern Ireland (PRONI), the British Newspaper Library at Colindale, the Liddell Hart Archives at King's College, London, the House of Lords Record Office, the Essex County Archive, Nottingham University Library, the General Register of Births, Deaths and Marriages, Hove Central Library, Imperial College London, Gloucestershire Record Office, Birmingham University Library, Durham County Record Office, the National Library of Wales, Eton College, and King's College, Cambridge.

I am grateful to Her Majesty The Queen for her gracious permission to quote from material in the Royal Archives at Windsor Castle. The staff at the Royal Archives, headed by Pamela Clark, could not have been more helpful or efficient. Jane Anderson, the archivist at Blair Castle in Perthshire, was equally obliging about access to the papers of Sir George Murray and permission to quote from them. I further wish to acknowledge other permissions from the following: the Deputy Keeper of Records at the PRONI, to quote from the papers of the Lord Dufferin; The Honourable Mrs E. A. Gascoigne, to quote from the Harcourt papers; the Bodleian Library, to quote from John Morley's diary; the Rt Hon. Lord Egremont, to quote from the Petworth House archives and to reproduce a copy of the painting of Lord Drumlanrig; Mrs Mary Bennett, to quote from the H.A.L. Fisher papers; the National Library of Scotland, to quote from the Haldane papers; the Norfolk Record Office, to quote from the Massingham and Neville-Rolfe papers; the Centre for Kentish Studies, to quote from the Stanhope papers; London School of Economics, to quote from the Passfield papers; Cambridge University Library, to quote from the Maxse papers; Christopher Osborne, to quote from the Margot Asquith papers; and the Provost and Fellows of Eton College, to quote from papers in the Eton archives.

The present Marquess of Queensberry not only talked to me with frankness about the Wilde case, but also generously provided me with copies of documents from his family's records. Eileen Simpson of the Grosvenor Estate kindly searched through the Wyndham papers for relevant correspondence, while the Historic Manuscripts Commission gave me useful advice about tracking down other papers. One search which proved ultimately fruitless was for the papers of Neville Waterfield, Rosebery's longest-serving private secretary, but I am grateful to the author Giles Waterfield and to Ruth Bell for trying to track down information for me. In the United States, the historian Lee I. Niedringhaus filled in some background about Rosebery's US investments and the sad life of his business associate Ferdinand Van Zandt; and Yale student Nick Baldock went through the papers and diaries of Norman Douglas for me. My brother Jason McKinstry helped me with my research at the British Newspaper Library, and Cambridge University student Stefano Collaca searched out the few mentions of Rosebery in the Italian press and archives in Naples.

Neil McKenna generously informed me of the documentation he had uncovered in his research for his ground-breaking book *The Secret Life of Oscar Wilde*, though I have to admit that I disagree profoundly with his conclusions about Rosebery's private life. My agent Andrew Lownie pointed me in the direction of some vital papers belonging to John Buchan, of whom he has written the standard Life. Peter Thompson kindly sent me part of his manuscript of his biography of the journalist G.E. Morrison. Before his death Robert Rhodes James, the distinguished politican, historian and author of the previous biography of Rosebery, granted me an interview which was full of insights into the 5th Earl.

On the production side, I am sincerely appreciative of the enthusiasm and wise counsel of Roland Phillips at John Murray. In Liz Robinson I had a thoughtful and rigorous editor who carried out invaluable work on the manuscript, correcting a host of errors and infelicities. I am also grateful to the rest of the ever patient, ever efficient John Murray staff, especially Rowan Yapp and Caroline Westmore. For help with the pictures, I must thank the Mary Evans Picture Library, the National Portrait Gallery and the National Library of Scotland.

None of my research would have been possible without the fulsome, unstinting support of my aunt, Anthea Orr, who provided me with week after week of the most wonderful hospitality while I was working in the National Library at Edinburgh. This book was written in the early summer months of 2004, just after I learnt that my mother, Cherith McKinstry, was suffering from terminal cancer. Her stoicism, courage and humour were an inspiration to me as I wrote, and it is to her that this biography is dedicated.

Leo McKinstry
September 2004

Introduction

'WHO IS LORD Rosebery?' It is a question I have been asked time and time again while I have been conducting the research for this book. If Andrew Bonar Law was 'the Unknown Prime Minister' of the early twentieth century, then Archibald Primrose, 5th Earl of Rosebery, has become the forgotten premier of the late nineteenth century. He is now, it seems, little more than a footnote in the history of an age dominated by Gladstone, Disraeli and Salisbury.

Yet to the Victorians and Edwardians, this question would have appeared bizarre. During most of his lifetime Rosebery was one of the most celebrated figures in England, a statesman of enormous glamour, wealth and influence. He was not only a successful politician who had reached the highest office, twice held the Foreign Secretaryship and led the Liberal party, but also a renowned millionaire, orator, writer, art collector and racehorse owner. In a succession of political crises from 1895 right up to the First World War, he was continually portrayed as the potential saviour of the nation. His pronouncements caused a greater sensation than those of any other Parliamentarian; at times his stature almost eclipsed that of Royalty. It is no exaggeration to say that, at the turn of the century, he was the most famous man in the British Empire, his every move exerting a remarkable hold on the public. In 1899, for instance, the marriage of his daughter Peggy brought central London to a standstill, so large were the crowds lining the streets around Westminster Abbey. Margot Asquith, a shrewd if emotional observer, wrote of the wedding, 'When the Prince of Wales went up the aisle, he was a nobody compared to Rosebery.'[1] Many of his speeches aroused such interest that there was a vibrant black market in tickets to hear him. When he addressed a meeting at Chesterfield in 1901 the national mood of excitement was so great that special telegraph services had to be installed by the Post Office to meet the demands of the press. Torchlight parades accompanied his public appearances in places as far apart as Leeds and Norwich. Politicians and press barons from all sides begged for his support. Winston Churchill urged him to lead a centre party coalition in 1903; Alfred Harmsworth, founder of the *Daily Mail*, offered to throw the entire might of his newspaper empire behind him. In 1912 Arthur Balfour wanted him to return as Prime Minister. As late as 1916, Lloyd George sought to add the lustre of Rosebery's name to his war Ministry.

In his native Edinburgh, he was treated as a national hero. The writer J.M. Barrie described him as 'The Uncrowned King of Scotland'. When he spoke once at Aberdeen, a vast throng gathered at the railway station to meet him and then dragged his carriage through the streets as if he were a Roman emperor returning to his people. Rosebery's resonant phrases, such as his reference to the Empire as 'a commonwealth of nations' or his call for the Liberals to adopt 'a clean slate' in making policy, became part of the currency of public debate. His fame was further demonstrated in the popular song *Burlington Bertie* by William Hargreaves, which contained the lines 'Nearly everyone knows me, from Smith to Lord Rosebery.' In the summer of 1900 one magazine reflected on Lord Rosebery's unique popularity: 'The future of Lord Rosebery is one of the things which all England is unanimous in caring about. Great men are not so plentiful in England today that the state can spare them and not miss them and Lord Rosebery, now that Mr Gladstone is dead, is by common consent the most brilliant figure in the British senate. In office or out of office, Lord Rosebery is the most popular, as he is the most fascinating of our public men.'[2]

But on a deeper level, the question 'Who is Lord Rosebery?' was one frequently asked by his puzzled contemporaries. To all of them, even his few confidants, he was a riddle, an enigmatic loner who would never reveal his true emotions or intentions. Indeed, it was this sense of mystery that enhanced his public appeal. No one ever knew what to expect from Lord Rosebery. He exuded a sense of the dramatic, the unpredictable. For all his personal charm, he maintained an aloof, secretive existence. Occasionally he would emerge in a blaze of memorable rhetoric, only to retreat again to his study. He almost appeared to revel in his political isolation, referring on one occasion to 'ploughing his furrow alone'. His sudden absences from the political battlefield were almost as celebrated as his explosive appearances. On platforms and in Parliament, his face was often inscrutable; a wall of reserve permeated his manner. Ian Malcolm, one of his admirers, wrote of him: 'He cultivated, exclusively for the benefit of his colleagues and society, a Sphinx-like attitude, a faintly sarcastic tone, and a gloomy manner which he could put on and off at will.'[3]

The atmosphere of mystery around Rosebery was bound up with the way he exuded paradox. He was so unpredictable, so intriguing because he continually faced in opposite directions. Here was a statesman who spent more than forty years in public life yet always claimed that he hated 'the evil-smelling bog' of politics. Rosebery was once described by Gladstone as the most ambitious man he had ever known, yet his two favourite political activities were refusing to accept office and resigning from it. He was a distinguished peer whose most passionate political campaigns were against the House of Lords. He managed to be both a democrat and an aristocrat, 'the coroneted socialist' as Lord Hartington once dubbed him. One of the greatest orators of his generation, he loathed platform speaking because of his innate shyness. Though a beloved son of Scotland, the only elected office he held was as a London county councillor. He worshipped men of iron like Cromwell and Napoleon, but shrank from decisive action himself. One of the richest men in England and the owner of a series of magnificent homes, he flirted with advanced radicalism, was condemned by Queen Victoria as 'almost communistic', and managed briefly to attract the support of the austere Fabians Sidney and Beatrice Webb, who later turned their hero worship towards Comrade Josef Stalin. Even at the peak of his career in the 1890s, he somehow managed to pose as both Home Ruler and Unionist, as a friend of labour and an anti-socialist, as a progressive and a moderate, as the man of both establishment and reform. The very creed he promulgated, Liberal Imperialism, seemed to many critics to be a contradiction in itself in view of the internationalist ethos of the Gladstonian Liberal party.

The paradoxes continued away from politics. Rosebery was a man of the Turf who owned three Derby winners yet was a poor judge of a horse. He loved scandalous gossip and collected pornography, but was also deeply religious, with what John Buchan called a 'seventeenth century Calvinist' streak. He simultaneously craved solitude and complained of loneliness. A fine writer with an elegant prose style and a rich sense of history, he produced no major book worthy of his talent. The creator of one of the country's finest private collections of paintings and furniture, he admitted that he had little understanding of aesthetics. A devoted husband, admired by some of the most fashionable beauties of his time and, in later life, almost married into Royalty, he was nevertheless the subject of continual whispers about the ambiguity of his sexual nature, these rumours reaching their climax during the 1895 trial of Oscar Wilde, when Rosebery's own government was accused of conspiracy and cover-up.

The personalities of most prime ministers have embodied contradictory elements. Clement Attlee, Haileybury-educated, pipe-smoking cricket lover, presided over the most radical left-wing government of the twentieth century. Winston Churchill, a warrior whose soul quivered with excitement at the trumpet blast of war, was also a sensitive, even lachrymose, individual. Ramsay MacDonald, illegitimate crofter's son and socialist firebrand, delighted in the company of society hostesses. But none carried paradox to such an extreme as Lord Rosebery. So glaring were the contrasts that at times there seemed to be nothing to connect the different facets of his character, whether bookish recluse, gregarious racehorse owner, devout church-goer, municipal radical, or Royal courtier. In his illuminating 1923 study of Rosebery, E.T. Raymond said that 'all men have their incongruities, but it is not often that so many are compressed in a single individual.' Using faintly repellent imagery, Raymond described Rosebery as a 'bundle of separate and often antagonistic personalities, wrapped up in one skin like a mass of writhing snakes in a bag. We seem, in reviewing his actions, to be dealing with several minds rather than one person in his various moods.'[4]

Many of Rosebery's contemporaries were puzzled by this trait. Margot Asquith decided that there were two Lord Roseberies. In a passage in her diary in 1904, she wrote:

> He lies about himself to himself. He wavers between two conceptions of himself – the one: a man suffering from the nerves that go with genius; affectionate, right, strong, morbidly sensitive and isolated, shrinking from public opinion, baffling, complex and charming. The other: a great man cursed with ambition, powerful, independent and indifferent – hating party politics, dreaming of Empire, besought by Kings and armies to put countries and continents right, a man irresistible to his friends and terrible to his enemies, a man whose notice blasts or blesses young men of letters, poets, peers and politicians, a man who at once scares or compels every human being he meets either by his freezing silence, his playful and beautiful smile or the weight of his moral indignation. These are the two men that Lord Rosebery imitates and contemplates every day of his life till he is not sure that he is not one and both at the same time.[5]

Beatrice Webb felt that there were four Roseberies, writing in her diary that he 'might be a great statesman, a Royal Prince, a beautiful woman and an artistic star all rolled into one.'[6] And in a *Spectator* article in October 1894, St Loe Strachey managed to bring the total number of Rosebery personalities to no fewer than seven: the Home Ruler, the Unionist, the Democratic Socialist, the Political Boss, the Man above Party, the Sphinx, and the Man of the Turf. 'I have no option but to treat Lord Rosebery as if he were nothing but a bundle of seven aliases, for that is all I can find in him,' wrote Strachey.

Given the vividness of Rosebery's strange, contradictory personality and the enormous popularity he once enjoyed, it is surprising that so little has been written about him in recent decades. In fact there has not been a biography of him for more than forty years, a record of neglect unique among those who have served as prime minister since the epochal 1867 Reform Act which extended the franchise and ushered in the age of democracy. Every other modern premier, no matter how short his term, has been the subject of at least one study since 1973. The last book on Rosebery was produced as long ago as 1962 by the distinguished historian and long-serving Cambridge MP, Robert Rhodes James. Though highly readable and full of shrewd political analysis and insights into Rosebery's mercurial character, it is inevitably somewhat dated now. The only other full biography was written by his son-in-law, the Marquess of Crewe, in 1931, two years after Rosebery's death. It was described by the late Roy Jenkins as 'pedestrian', which was being generous. Tactful to the point of vapidity, Crewe managed to take more than 650 pages to say almost nothing of interest about Rosebery's career, preferring to give wearisome accounts of his voyages overseas.

The long gap since Rhodes James's volume would perhaps in itself be enough to justify a new biography, especially in view of the large number of recent publications on all aspects of Victorian and Edwardian politics. But there are two other important factors. The first is the wealth of archive material which was either unused or unavailable when Rhodes James was carrying out his research. This documentation, all shedding new light on both Rosebery's politics and his personal life, includes the diaries of Margot Asquith, Beatrice Webb, Lewis Harcourt, and Lord Derby, as well as the papers of Lord Northcliffe, Herbert Gladstone, Lord Dufferin, Princess Victoria, John Buchan, and Sir George Murray (Rosebery's principal secretary during his time in Downing Street). Rosebery's correspondence with his sister Constance Leconfield is now accessible at the West Sussex Record Office, and provides a rich commentary on his family life. Another fascinating item which has recently surfaced is the fragmentary diary of Thomas Gilmour, an earnest young man who worked as Rosebery's secretary and recorded many of his conversations with his master. But probably most rewarding of all has been the private journal of the Liberal politician John Morley, which was donated to the Bodleian Library only in 2003 after lying hidden in an Oxford study for years. Far more frank and detailed than Morley's published *Recollections*, it alters the traditional understanding of Liberal politics during the early 1890s. I believe I am the first biographer to have been able to make use of this wonderful new source. I have also been fortunate in my access to the Rosebery papers themselves. When Crewe and Rhodes James were writing their books, these papers were stored in haphazard fashion in a number of Rosebery's homes; since then, they have been sorted and catalogued superbly by the Rosebery family. Though some of the 5th Earl's papers remain at Dalmeny, the bulk is now in the National Library of Scotland. The excellence of this archive's organisation makes it easy to study material that might have been overlooked in the past.

The second factor is that the central themes of Rosebery's life are far more pertinent now than they were 43 years ago when Rhodes James wrote his book. Politically, the wheel has come full circle. The undemocratic nature of the House of Lords, efficiency in the public sector, nationalism in Ireland, devolution in Scotland and London, and Britain's role within a wider federation (albeit an Imperial rather than European one) were the questions which dominated Rosebery's public life. At the beginning of the 1960s most of them seemed dormant; Scottish Home Rule was an irrelevance in a country where unionism remained a powerful political force; Irish conflict appeared to belong to the past; talk about federalism was confined to university lecture rooms; the post-war consensus had settled the role of the public sector; the Lords and the London County Council had seen only minor alterations to their constitutions over the previous seventy years. But the changing, increasingly divided, nature of the British Isles has reawakened the importance of all these issues, putting them once more at the centre of political debate. In a similar fashion, Rosebery's own personal life mirrors our modern fixations with race and sexuality. Defying convention, he married into a Jewish family, causing much anguished comment on both sides of the religious divide, while his reclusive, artistic temperament left him the target of rumours about his inclinations, an area previous studies have not covered.

Rosebery's reclusive nature also led him to despise the idea of producing his own autobiography. 'I will not give the last proof of senility by writing a memoir, nor am I capable,' he said. He was equally suspicious of plans for any biography. During his own lifetime he was the subject of four rather shallow books, with which he refused to co-operate despite their adulatory content. He told Gladstone's daughter Mary that, because he so hated the idea of a biography, he considered burning all his papers to prevent a full-scale work after his death. But, tellingly, he failed to implement this drastic step. In fact, as in so many other aspects of his life, he was contradictory on this point, for he also informed his former secretary Sir George Murray in 1921 that he did not really care what was written about him after his death. 'What posthumous attacks there may be will not reach me where

I shall be and I cannot anticipate their tendency. When one reflects on the millions of years which comprise the history of this planet, of the million other worlds with their millions of inhabitants, the character of one worm cannot be of much importance.'

Such self-deprecation hardly convinces. Rosebery was a central figure in the history of modern Britain and of our Empire. And his tale is one of the most colourful, absorbing and, ultimately, tragic of any of our prime ministers.

I

'Almost a good genius'

◗━━◖

SUNK INTO MELANCHOLIA by the First World War, Lord Rosebery wrote in the autumn of 1916:

> I look back on my life as a long dark tunnel which I have traversed not with-
> out pleasure but also with pain and anguish. The flowers, the pleasures,
> evanescent at best, have disappeared and I can only see the passage black,
> gloomy with poisonous hissing like snakes, with abysses yawning on each
> side into which I have stumbled, with memories hanging like stalactites from
> the room, the floor a stagnant marsh exhaling pestilence. Sinister memories
> like bats scurry about, past sorrows still alive flap along like owls. I can feel
> nothing but desolation and horror. How was I able to struggle through such
> long drawn agony, I ask myself, for I have said the joys have evaporated like
> will o'the wisp. And as I strain my eyes through the darkness I see at the fur-
> ther end a pretty, smiling, innocent child, in whom I recognise myself.[1]

In this memorandum, remarkable for its nightmarish imagery and despair, Rosebery evoked the picture of happy childhood before the rest of his life became enveloped in gloom. But this was a romanticised ideal of inno-cence. In reality, Rosebery's early years were much less carefree, featuring bereavement, loneliness, poor health and maternal indifference.

Archibald Philip Primrose was born on 7 May 1847 in Charles Street, London. His father was Lord Dalmeny, Liberal MP and heir to the Rosebery title. His mother was Lady Wilhelmina, only daughter of the 4th Earl Stanhope. Many of the traits for which Rosebery later became renowned can be seen in his two parents. From his father he inherited his handsome features, his interest in progressive politics, and his love of sport, as well as a touch of hypochondria. Lord Dalmeny never rose to the heights later achieved by his brilliant son, though he represented Stirling from 1832 until 1847 and was briefly a Lord of the Admiralty under Lord Melbourne. His main political concern, which amounted to something of a fixation, was with the physical and moral fibre of the British people. In an eccen-tric pamphlet published in 1848, entitled *An Address to the Middle Classes On the Subject of Gymnastics*, Lord Dalmeny wrote in lurid tones about the need 'to purge the air of noxious exhalations' and 'banish the hideous family of plagues which have their origin in the accumulations of filth, deleterious effluvia and foul habitations.' Improvements in sanitation might help, but they could never be enough 'to protect any man against that state of debility and disease which is the inevitable consequence of his own luxury and sloth.' While he admitted that there were 'many gentlemen whose sole exercise consists in crawling from their sofa to their dinner table and from their dinner table to their bed', Dalmeny's real target was the behaviour of the ordinary British tradesman. His working day involved eating too much beefsteak and gulping too many cups of tea, but even worse was his leisure. 'Does he brace his nerves, reanimate his spirits or circulate his blood by any gymnastic exercise, any invigorating game? Nothing of the kind.'[2]

The 5th Earl of Rosebery had too strong a sense of humour ever to descend in public to such patronising depths, though he was in later life inclined to occasional outbursts against indulgent conduct, writing privately in 1898 that 'the progress of luxury and the expenditure on luxury are assuming alarming proportions; they are eating into the framework of society. If luxury were confined to those who can afford it, it would matter little. But its curse is to produce emulation. Each must live as the other does. Hence money must be got somehow – by gambling in its various forms, by the sacrifice of honour, nay if necessary by fraud. It is a terrible evil and requires a drastic remedy. There is only one possible one: a realistic effort on behalf of simplicity of life.'[3] Coming from someone who lived in unrivalled opulence, those words would have produced derisive laughter among Rosebery's enemies.

Rosebery's father did not confine his worries about physical fitness to British shopkeepers. He was just as concerned about his own health, filling his correspondence with references to his possible ailments. He had his favourite remedies, believing, for example, that a glass of ice-cold water drunk before breakfast could ward off influenza; in the same way his son, the 5th Earl, came to believe that the only cure for his crippling insomnia was a glass of hot water drunk before bed. 'I cherish a great antipathy to all medicine, particularly to that of a mercurial description,' Lord Dalmeny said in 1847;[4] 'My belief in the art of medicine grows slighter and slighter every day. It was not very robust to begin with but now it is almost nil,' his son Rosebery wrote to the historian Herbert Fisher in 1924.[5]

Rosebery's mother was perhaps an even more interesting figure than his fitness-obsessed father. Born into the illustrious Stanhope family, a ravishing beauty in her youth, she was widely regarded as the most attractive woman at Court at the time of Queen Victoria's accession in 1837, serving as a Maid of Honour at Victoria's coronation and a bridesmaid at her wedding to Prince Albert. Her appearance was so enticing that when, at the age of just nineteen, she met John Lockhart, Sir Walter Scott's son-in-law and later biographer, at the Kent County Ball, she seduced him into dancing until three o'clock in the morning, even though, as he confessed, he was 'the staid father of a family.'[6] Her attributes went far beyond her beauty. She was also a fine artist and, like her son, a dazzling conversationalist. Baroness Bunsen, the English wife of the German ambassador, wrote of a dinner party at the Stanhopes' in 1842, 'Lady Wilhelmina is a very fine creation and also a very agreeable converser, full of intelligence and information, but I was not prepared for the genius which her drawings denote.'[7] Disraeli, later an admirer of her son, claimed that 'she has the quickest and the finest perception of humour I know, with an extraordinary power of expression and the Stanhope wit, her conversation unceasing, but never long or wearying; a wondrous flow of drollery, information, social tattle, taste, eloquence; such a ceaseless flow of contemporary anecdote I never heard. And yet she never repeats.'[8]

But Lady Wilhelmina's clever wit could also be biting. As G.W.E. Russell once put it euphemistically, 'She hardly uttered a sentence without giving it a turn which one remembered; and her inclination to sarcasm was not unduly restrained'[9]: exactly the sort of language that might have been used of her son, who was notorious for his cutting remarks. In a perceptive profile, Rosebery's own daughter Sybil wrote of him: 'He enjoyed a duel of words and enjoyed winning that duel, but often forgot that his sword had a razor-like quality denied to most.'[10] Yet Rosebery himself often tired of his mother's malicious streak. 'Why will our Parent insist on filling her letters with gossip about Prince Eddy's doings, which is not merely ill-natured but is absolutely unfounded?' he once asked his sister.[11] In later life, some in Rosebery's family were repelled by her; 'Oh Grandmama is not a human being, she is just she,' said the young Sybil in 1897 to Margot Asquith, who added a note in her diary, 'This is rather clever and exactly describes the old horror.' A year later, Margot's son Raymond, on a visit to Dalmeny, gave this graphic picture of the ageing mother: 'a painted relic of the first Empire in a marvellous state of preservation: face like a well-bred parrot.'[12]

Breeding was certainly part of Lady Wilhelmina's inheritance, for she counted the two great Pitts, both prime ministers, among her forebears. Her other ancestors included the 1st Earl Stanhope, a leading soldier and Parliamentarian during the reign of George I, and the 3rd Earl, whose chief interests were science and republicanism, an enthusiasm which earned him the nickname 'Citizen Stanhope'. But perhaps the 3rd Earl's most important accomplishment was his marriage to Lady Hester, sister of the younger Pitt. This close familial connection to the great eighteenth-century statesman had a profound influence on Rosebery, not just through his writings but also in the way he perceived his own political career. 'There are few figures in political history which have greater attraction for him than Pitt. I am sure R. has constantly had Pitt before him as his political type,' wrote his close friend Edward Hamilton.[13]

The Rosebery lineage could not claim any figures of the same stature as Pitt, though the family heritage was interesting enough. Scottish landowners for generations, the Primroses first rose to prominence in the sixteenth century, as Archibald Primrose took up the post of King James VI's chief adviser for the collection of Scottish revenue and ran the family estates at Culross, near Dunfermline, while his brother Gilbert became Principal Surgeon to the King. Archibald's eldest son James reinforced the political strength of the family by serving as Clerk to the Privy Council for forty years. James Primrose's son, another Archibald, was an adroit operator who gained a baronetcy and clung to high office in Scotland throughout much of the turbulent mid seventeenth century. He even managed, through his social contacts, to avoid execution when he was arrested by the Parliamentarians during the Civil War, before coming back to power at the Restoration It was this Sir Archibald Primrose who in 1662 purchased the estate at Dalmeny beside the Firth of Forth, which has remained the principal seat of the Rosebery family to this day. In a portrait of Sir Archibald, intriguing for its parallels with the 5th Earl, Bishop Burnet described him thus: 'He was a dexterous man of business: he always had expedients ready at any difficulty. He had an art of speaking to all men according to their sense of things and so drew out their secrets, while he concealed his own. He said everything that was necessary to persuade those he spoke to that he was of their mind; and he did it in so genuine a way that he seemed to speak their heart.'[14]

Sir Archibald had no fewer than eleven children by his two marriages, but none of his immediate successors was as skilful or distinguished as he. His eldest son from his first marriage, Sir William Primrose, died young after proving inadequate and idle in public office. The eldest son from his second marriage was of somewhat higher calibre, serving both as a soldier in Hungary and an MP for Edinburgh. In 1700 he was created Viscount Rosebery, and three years later advanced to an earldom. On his death in 1723 he was succeeded by his son James, a tragic individual whose near insanity and fetish for unsuccessful litigation led to severe money problems. During his father's lifetime he was actually imprisoned in the Old Tolbooth because of his debts. Nor were other Primroses distinguished at this time by their domestic stability. One secretly married a bigamist and had to live on the Continent under an assumed name; another, while fighting in Holland in one of Marlborough's campaigns, was only prevented from committing bigamy with a rich Dutch woman by the armed intervention of his brother-in-law.

Neil, who became 3rd Earl of Rosebery in 1756, was a much shrewder man than his wayward, litigious father, and before inheriting the title had worked in a merchant's business in London. His financial acumen enabled him 'to repair the rather dilapidated family fortunes', in the words of Lord Crewe.[15] His eldest son Archibald, the grandfather of the subject of this biography, became 4th Earl in 1814 and further consolidated the revival of the family. He also presided over the short move from the old, increasingly dangerous castle of Barnbougle on the Dalmeny estate into a magnificent new Gothic revival home, today one of the most beautiful houses in Scotland, with its sweeping views across the Firth of Forth. The 4th Earl experienced some of the same domestic problems that had plagued his ancestors, for his first marriage, to Harriet Bouverie, ended in scandal when she embarked on an affair with Sir Harry Mildmay. The 4th Earl divorced her in 1815, winning £15,000 from Mildmay in damages, and subsequently remarried, much more successfully, in 1819. He lived until 1868 and, like his grandson after him, had a strong sense of public duty and enjoyed great popularity in Edinburgh. He was briefly an MP between 1805 and 1807 before taking his seat in the House of Lords, where he was a powerful advocate of the Great Reform Bill in 1832.

His son, Lord Dalmeny, born in 1809, was thirty-four when he first met Lady Wilhelmina at a ball at Buckingham Palace in July 1843. She immediately fell for the tall Rosebery heir, describing him in her diary as the 'cleverest and most agreeable of all my partners.'[16] They were married within just three months, and a year later their first child was born, Mary Catherine Constance. Three other children followed, Constance Evelyn in 1846, Archibald Philip in 1847, and Everard Henry in 1848. Young Archie was baptized in the Anglican Church of St George's in London's Hanover Square in June 1847; in later life, however, he usually preferred to worship in the established Presbyterian Church of Scotland whenever he was in the north, rather than the Scottish Episcopal Church.

He seems to have been an appealing and intelligent if somewhat sensitive child. In April 1850, shortly before his third birthday, his mother penned this description of him: 'He is a great darling, more affectionate than any child I ever knew: very tall, thin & rather pale, with very fine large blue eyes and the prettiest smile in the world . . . He is so sensitive that a harsh word throws him into a flood of tears: nor is he, like his sisters, one instant crying, the next laughing – he is some time recovering from a burst of sorrow.'[17] Those words about his hurt at any criticism would have certainly struck a chord with his Liberal party colleagues of the 1890s. But he could also be headstrong, as his sister Constance once recalled: 'The nursery party was returning home via Chesterfield Street when Archie became fractious. Our nurse, Mrs Green, threatened to give him up to a soldier who was passing by. Archie ran up to the soldier, took his hand and began walking away.'[18]

Lord Dalmeny's unorthodox ideas on health might seem amusing, but one of them fatally impaired Archie's ability to sleep, later leading to untold anguish. Around the age of three, Archie was regularly put to bed in the middle of the day and instructed to sleep. But the alert child, unable to rest as required, came to associate the bedroom with anxiety and insomnia. 'I was very, very young but I remember with horror those weary, wakeful hours,' he wrote later.[19] Rosebery never fully overcame the problem. He was always one of those 'who go to bed despairing of sleeping, tossing till their pillows are hot, with every muscle extended and every nerve alive, till at last they turn on the light in misery and seek for a book'.[20]

Nor did Lord Dalmeny's mania for health prevent his own early demise. In the autumn of 1850 he became seriously ill with pleurisy, and in January 1851, just when he appeared to have recovered, he had a sudden heart attack, and died almost instantly. He was only forty years old. Commenting on his funeral at Dalmeny, the *Scotsman* said that his death 'left a blank in his family and society which must be long and deeply felt'. His loss was undoubtedly a severe blow to Archie, who had been his favourite child. Sensitive and always prone to psychosomatic reactions, Archie was ill for several weeks after this tragedy, while the family noticed that he became even more reserved. His father's death also had a deep impact on Archie's personal and political fortunes. As the eldest son, he was now Lord Dalmeny, heir to the Rosebery title. With his grandfather already 67, barring some miracle of longevity Archie was almost certain to succeed to the earldom within the next twenty years.

The widow did not overdo her mourning. By 1854 Lady Wilhelmina had married again, this time to Lord Harry Vane, heir to the dukedom of Cleveland. Lord Harry, who succeeded his brother in 1864, had nothing like his new wife's brilliant wit and intellectual power, but he was kind, genial – and hugely rich. The centre of the Cleveland possessions was Raby Castle in Northumberland but he owned property in ten other counties across England, bringing in an income of around £97,400* in 1878. What Lord Harry lacked in brains, he made up for in grandeur. 'A fine specimen of an English aristocrat and as he got older I think his picturesqueness increased. In the evening, when he wore the Ribbon of the Garter, standing up with his tall, erect figure, piercing eyes and snow-white hair, he was always a very striking personage,' was the verdict of Lady St Helier.[21] His great sadness in life was that he was unable to have children of his own, though he never showed any ill-feeling to his wife's four children, as Rosebery later remembered: 'He was a kind step-father. This is all the more meretorious in him as we must hourly have recalled a bitter disappointment.' In an intriguing footnote, Rosebery revealed that Lord Harry had long been attracted to the beautiful Lady Wilhelmina: 'My step-father had been in love with my mother before her first marriage.'[22]

Before inheriting Raby and the Cleveland estates Lord Harry and his new family lived in a series of rented mansions, including Brocket, the home of Lady Palmerston. The children also stayed frequently at the famous Stanhope home, Chevening, today an official Government residence. Archie adored Chevening even more than Dalmeny. A solitary boy, he loved to wander through its parkland or read in its library. He always called it Paradise and, after a visit there in 1924, told Lady Stanhope, 'I hope you realize that as Jerusalem is to a Jew and Mecca to a Mohamedan, so Chevening is to me.'[23]

He was less impressed with Battle Abbey in Sussex, which Lord Harry purchased as the family's permanent home. For all the Abbey's rich history, which made it something of a tourist attraction, he found it a depressing place, as he later recalled when he paid a visit there with his sister Constance in July 1916. 'There was not a twinge of pain, for we both disliked the place, I vehemently, whereas I suppose there is pain in revisiting a beloved lost home. And though we hated the place we had all sorts of pleasant and comical memories of our childhood which occurred at every corner and every turn. Oh heavens! What Battle was every now and then when a gale of three days driving rain before it would afflict us, when looking out we could see nothing to comfort us but that unspeakably dreary ruin, the Refectory, dreary because so vast and lacking a roof. I have hated ruins and living with ruins ever since.'[24] One of the Clevelands' guests was

---

* All sums given in the text are contemporary figures unless otherwise stated.

equally unenthusiastic, writing in the visitors' book at the end of an awkward stay: 'From Battle, murder and death, Good Lord deliver us!'

No motherly affection compensated Archie for the loss of his father – or even for the dreariness of Battle Abbey. He always felt that Lady Wilhelmina favoured his younger brother Everard, a not unjust belief, as some of her private writings testify. 'Everard is different. He is much cleverer, we think,' was one entry in her journal. Of Archie she wrote, 'I cannot conceal from myself that he is a terribly dull little boy – Conny is a genius in comparison.'[25] There can be little doubt that much of the pessimism, insecurity and reserve demonstrated by Rosebery as an adult stemmed from the lack of affection shown him by his mother. As his daughter Sybil later wrote, 'Hardly anyone ever suspected his almost pathetic hunger for affection, only known to his family circle.'[26] This distance between Lady Wilhelmina and her elder son only increased when he went away to boarding school in 1855 at the age of eight. His first establishment was Bayford House in Hertfordshire, which he entered with an excitement that soon turned to trepidation. 'The joy and exultation of going to school so quickly evaporated; the coarse sheets of the bed, the being expected to undress without assistance, and the conversation about myself between my room-mates, when I was believed to be asleep, all these are indelible memories of that lonely evening half a century ago,' he wrote to his sister.[27] He also remembered without fondness an attack of the measles. 'Ten or twelve other patients in the room snoring or talking in their sleep, I feverish, wakeful and utterly miserable. Parched also with thirst which could only be quenched with a thick beverage miscalled barley water which turned to a thick slime in one's mouth.'[28] But he appears to have generally enjoyed his brief spell at this school, and looked back on it with nostalgia. 'To this day a photograph of Bayford always hangs in my room,' he wrote to his old schoolmaster, the Reverend George Renaud, when he was Prime Minister.[29] Less happy, though, was his relationship with his mother. Just as, when he was at Harrow, Winston Churchill sorrowed over his mother's apparent indifference, so Archibald complained bitterly of Lady Wilhelmina's neglect. 'I want to know why you have not written to me. I expect a letter every day.'[30] At one stage, he became so desperate about his mother's failure to contact him that he wrote to his grandmother: 'I want to know where Mama is now for do you know I feel quite uneasy about her because I've not had a letter for a long time because she must have gone somewhere and I can't conceive where she is because I believe you would forward if she was not at Dalmeny.'[31] Even as a child, Rosebery had a dark foreboding about the future, his doom-laden sense of self-pity exacerbated by his pessimistic temperament and precocious literary talent. Shortly before his death he explained to his sister, looking back on his childhood, 'I have found some verses written by me when I was about ten, exactly predicting what I am suffering now. They began, "How long, oh Lord, how long" and went into the various troubles incident to my position. A marvellous prediction.'[32]

While Archie was eleven two incidents occurred which, though apparently minor in themselves, had a major effect on the rest of his life. The first happened when, playing a boyish game, he ran blindfold into an iron gate, gashed his head open, and suffered a concussion. Having been carried home, he was confined to a darkened room, from which he did not emerge for some weeks. The physical consequence was obvious enough, in the permanent scar across his forehead. The psychological effects may have been more serious, since he grew even more introspective. His sister Constance recalled that he 'remained ill for a long time, with fits of deep depression, hating all exercise and conversation, only asking to be left alone.'[33] Indeed, Rosebery's family always believed that this accident at the gate worsened his tendencies towards insomnia and nervous irritability.

Just as serious, but in the long term more beneficial, was a disaster at Chevening during the Christmas of 1858. Archie was among a group of children in the kitchen, admiring the snapdragon, when a foolish servant decided to put a red-hot poker into the large dish of brandy and raisins. Immediately flames shot out of the dish, and in the conflagration the muslin dress of Miss Sykes, daughter of the vicar of Chevening, caught fire. With precocious courage Archie rushed to her rescue and put out the flames but, in his own words, 'I burned myself badly.'[34] Once more, he bore the scars for life. And once more, he went through a drawn-out recovery. But this time his period as an invalid was far more productive. As he later told the historian Sir George Trevelyan, on the night of the accident 'I was introduced to Sir Walter Scott by my mother's reading to me the Legend of Montrose to keep me quiet. A day or two afterwards I was wandering about the delightful Chevening library and quite by chance took down Macaulay's *Essays*. I fell at once under the wand of the enchanter. I began with Milton, and read no other book till I had finished the three volumes. And at the New Year, seeing my absorption, my mother gave me a copy. There was much, of course, that I could not really understand. But I delighted in the eloquences, the grasp and the command of knowledge, the irresistible current of the style. And to that book I owe whatever ambitions or aspirations I have ever indulged in.'[35] It was therefore a flaming snapdragon that sparked in Archie Dalmeny the devotion to literature and history which was one of the abiding passions of his life. Whatever he said to Trevelyan, his admiration for Macaulay diminished greatly as he grew older, however. 'I was bitterly disappointed with his History of England. He is no more a historian than a clodhopper,' he wrote on re-reading one of his favourite childhood texts. [36]

After recovering from these two accidents Archie was sent to a preparatory school in Brighton, the school in Bayford having closed. In 1860, at the age of thirteen, he entered Eton, his intelligence and wide reading winning him a place in the Lower Remove, the highest form for new boys. It was with a sense of pride that he took up his place at the ancient college: 'I am an Etonian, George, there is something great in that name,' he told his friend George Dundas. [37] Already mature for his age, he proved an able pupil, though his traits of aloofness and intolerance of criticism were as apparent as ever. A cutting but not unfriendly profile of Archie Dalmeny at Eton was later provided by a fellow pupil, James Brinsley Richards, who described him as having a

> slight figure and a fresh, prim, young lady-like appearance. His family name of Primrose suited him to a nicety. He was not remarkable for scholarship but he possessed plenty of cool assurance . . . Underneath Dalmeny's dainty appearance there was some Scotch hard-headedness. He kept out of all scrapes. Walking very erect, with a tripping gait and a demure look, he was the pink of neatness and seemed wrapt up in himself until you caught a glance of his shrewd eyes which showed that he thought of weightier things than his personal appearance. Such eyes are like lighted windows, which reveal that a house is not empty. He was not an energetic wet bob or dry bob.★ He read a good deal by himself – books of history and memoirs and newspapers and parliamentary reports in them . . . His patrician hauteur was unmistakable. Not an offensive hauteur but that calm pride by which a man seems to ascend in a balloon out of earshot every time he is addressed by one not socially his equal. [38]

Regy Brett, also an Eton pupil and later one of Archie's closest friends, gave another description of his coolness. 'When he arrived at Eton as a new boy, he used to lie low while others talked and wait for a chance of saying something unexpected . . . He possessed, even then, that capacity for the true adjustment of two dissimilar things which make a spark and is called wit.' [39]

In respect of learning, Archie Dalmeny was fortunate in his tutor. William Johnson was the most erudite schoolmaster of his time, his scholarship so impressive that Lord Palmerston had recommended him for the

---

★ Wet bob is the Eton slang for an oarsman, dry bob for a cricketer.

Chair of Modern History at Cambridge University in 1860 (a choice that was over-ruled by the Prince Consort). The breadth of his knowledge in the Classics, history, philosophy and literature was extraordinary, while he also had an instinctive gift for teaching, making every subject appear exciting. One of his pupils, Herbert Paul, later a Rosebery supporter in Parliament, said 'nothing that he taught could ever for a moment, while he taught it, be dull.'[40] Arthur Coleridge, a fellow Classics teacher, believed that Johnson 'was the wisest master who has ever been to Eton.'[41] Yet he was an eccentric figure, extravagant in his gestures and inclined to outbursts of temper – he once threw a book at Archie's head in fury at his insouciant attitude. He wrote some fine poetry and, in lighter vein, the lyrics to the *Eton Boating Song*, but he also had some literary neuroses, one of them being the quality of novelists' handwriting. Of Charlotte Brontë's, for instance, he regretted that she 'turns her *d* over' but was glad she wrote 'a good *s* and *a* in the Greek manner'.[42] As well as being hard of hearing, he was so short-sighted that he sometimes had to wear three pairs of spectacles, and confessed that he had never seen a bird fly.

Johnson's greatest weakness was his habit of cultivating favourites, and inevitably Archie Dalmeny became one of them. He admired the boy's advanced intellect and romantic love of history, as he told his friend Henry Bradshaw in 1862: 'My friend Dalmeny is looking forward to making your acquaintance with the natural eagerness of a budding bibliomaniac . . . He has the finest combination of qualities I have ever seen . . . The night before I had translated to him most of the beautiful bits of *Agamemnon* and I assure you he enjoyed the old poetry nearly as much as the modern. I am doing all I can to make him a scholar; anyhow, he will be an orator and, if not a poet, such a man as poets delight in.'[43] But Johnson was never blind to Dalmeny's faults, especially his occasional indolence. As another Johnson favourite Charles Wood, later Lord Halifax, put it: 'William Johnson used to say that Rosebery was the cleverest and most brilliant pupil he had ever had but I think with some regrets that he had not, from lack of resolution to do what was a bore and disagreeable, made the most of his talents and opportunities.'[44]

The mixture of approbation and exasperation Archie Dalmeny evoked in him runs through Johnson's correspondence. At Christmas 1860, the end of Dalmeny's first term, Johnson gave Lady Harry (as Lady Wilhelmina now was) a positive report. Describing Dalmeny as 'singularly well-informed' with a 'very considerable' knowledge of history, Johnson continued, 'I thought him at first rather over-educated and almost unnaturally intellectual, and his failures in writing Latin I thought would be wholesome in their humbling effect. On better acquaintance I find him endowed with heart as well as mind, very sociable, friendly and gay. I find he likes nearly everyone in his house, and is liked, apparently by all, certainly those whom I know and like best.' By the end of the next term, however, Johnson was expressing disappointment to Lady Harry, telling her that Dalmeny was 'not much interested in the lessons. He does very short and unsatisfactory exercises.' There was little improvement over the following year, and in April 1862 Johnson had to report 'the entire failure of our attempts to get more work out of him. In all my experience it is the saddest case of the waste of faculties.' He also added the complaint which was to become a familiar accusation, that he was 'gradually becoming frivolous.' That summer Johnson wrote Lady Harry a perceptive analysis of Dalmeny's character in which he highlighted those virtues and flaws that shone through his adult personality. 'He has in himself wonderful delicacy of mind, penetrating sympathy, flexibility, capacity for friendship – all but the tenacious resolution of one that is to be great. He is original all day long; too original to be very popular. He has more affection than tact and quite as much antipathy as sympathy; so that he is not floating with the stream of popularity. All would come right if he were seriously engaged in a course of study, overcoming difficulties and competing with the many worthy rivals of a great school.'[45]

Johnson did not confine his encouragement and disapproval to Lady Harry; he also wrote in these terms to Archie himself. In August 1862 he said, 'I wish you to be one that will not only understand but do justice to what passes in other minds – one that will not merely pick out what pleases but unconsciously attract and imperceptibly check and indirectly stir and elevate the minds of equals no less than inferiors.'[46] Johnson's frustration over Dalmeny's reluctance to fulfil the promise of his talents was even more graphically expressed in a famous letter to another Eton schoolmaster, F. Warre Cornish, who had temporarily taken over Dalmeny's class while Johnson was recovering from an illness: 'I would give you a piece of plate if you would get that lad to work; he is one of those who like the palm without the dust.'[47] It was a phrase inspired by Milton's epic lines 'I cannot forgive a fugitive and cloistered virtue, unexercised and unbreathed, that never sallies out and sees the adversary, but slinks out of the race, where that immortal garland is to be run for, not without dust and heat.' The argument that Rosebery looked for the glory without the struggle was constantly used against him throughout his life, especially during the bitter crises of Gladstone's last administration and the internecine wars within the Liberal party in the early Edwardian period, when Rosebery was frequently condemned for seeking public adulation without accepting less glamorous political responsibilities. To many, Johnson's phrase later came to be seen as the key to the enigma of Rosebery, the explanation for his puzzling moods and avoidance of office. 'Fortune, with cruel irony, gave him the palm without the pursuit. He found it an emblem of nothing and he threw it scornfully aside,' wrote A.G. Gardiner.[48]

But Johnson's chastisement gradually appeared to yield some results. By August of 1863 he was able to write to Dalmeny's mother: 'Now that he has got rid of a certain fastidiousness and peevishness he seems to me singularly enlightened and high minded, with strong affections well regulated. To me personally he is almost a good genius.' He concluded with the prophetic hope that 'he will grow up as an orator and a man of wide influence; if he goes on as he does now, it could not be otherwise; and I think he has passed the crisis of his school life.'[49] But within less than a year, Johnson was again in despair over Dalmeny's work. In a report of July 1864 to Lady Harry, he wrote: 'I am sorry to find that he is, in the main, impregnable in his indifference. He will do nothing worth mentioning except sometimes try to put poetical thoughts into Latin and whenever he tries to do this his want of skill in handling the language causes something like disappointment. Your son is letting year after year drift away without learning what in theory he should be learning, the art of expressing himself like a reasoner in Latin and English, not to say Greek and French.' He was able, however, to strike a more optimistic tone about other aspects of Dalmeny's behaviour. 'He has been gaining in bodily strength, animal spirits, experience, friendship, tact and almost everything else that will eventually make him a happy and influential member of society.'[50]

As Johnson revealed in that report, Dalmeny was no cloistered recluse at Eton. He fully entered into the life of the school, showing a less solitary streak than he had previously, at home. Though not possessed of outstanding sporting ability, he was a useful cricketer, fives player and oarsman. His sense of humour was revealed through other, more domestic activities. In a characteristic letter, he thanked his sister for the birthday present of a coffee pot: 'A chronic fear of explosions is growing up in my mind and I regard the coffee pot as an infernal machine, made on purpose to kill me. But I am devoted to it nevertheless.'[51] His more serious side was illustrated in his veneration of religion. As a spectator at a school confirmation in 1861, he was appalled by the behaviour of one boy who giggled at the moment the bishop laid his hands on him. 'I think this was the most horrible thing ever thought of,' he wrote to his mother. 'Just when God was about to admit him to his table – laughing. I prayed Mother that I never should commit such an enormous sin.'[52]

More important for the future was his election in October 1864 to the Eton Society – 'Pop' – after being twice blackballed, another sign of his lack of universal popularity among his fellow pupils. In a letter to Gladstone written exactly thirty years after he joined Pop, Rosebery was rather disparaging about the institution. 'We had weekly debates – not very good I think but that was because we were a poor generation.' He went on to describe Pop as 'an assembly of the aristocracy of the school – the eleven, the eight and so forth, with almost always the cleverest lads in the sixth form, unless otherwise intolerable.'[53] The Society's records of its debates, which Dalmeny attended regularly, provide an intriguing glimpse not only of his youthful political outlook but also of his early rhetorical gifts. His opening two speeches, for example, presaged several of the abiding interests of his life. The first, described in the records as a 'well-timed oration', was a defence of the greatness of William Pitt, Lord Chatham; the second was an appeal for Canada to remain within the British Empire. In words that he might later have used on any Liberal Imperialist platform, Dalmeny proclaimed that 'while they stick to us, we should stick to them. A country that was gained for us by the sagacity of Chatham, which cost us the blood of Wolfe, ought not to be lightly abandoned.' Then in March 1865 Rosebery showed his early Whig sympathies with an attack on Charles I's minister Stafford, which aroused the ire of some fellow members. 'He wanted to establish in England a complete despotism [oh, oh!]', where 'all justice was subservient to the Crown.' In another liberal attack on dictatorship he argued that Brutus was justified in killing Julius Caesar: 'I believe he acted with true love of his country. The country had fallen into despotism. Caesar had absorbed all the power of the state into his own hands. Brutus held that he had a right to kill the man who crushed the republic and I rather think he was right.' Archie Dalmeny's rhetorical style showed that biting humour for which he later became so famous. In a debate on Sir Robert Walpole he was said to have spoken 'in his usual vein of sarcastic and cutting wit, making several members look very small.' Again just as in later life, he was often at his best on non-serious subjects. Debating a motion on whether 'white flannels should be worn in school or not', he said: 'No doubt some people envy the dazzling purity of the President's trousers and would like to beam on the Society with the same brilliancy. But I would point out that there are such things as coloured trousers and that white has always been the colour of honour.'[54] He easily won the motion.

Dalmeny's burgeoning interest in politics was also demonstrated away from Eton. Like Gladstone, he was initially enthusiastic about the secession of the Confederacy from the United States, telling his friend George Dundas that it was 'a wonderful event'.[55] His enthusiasm for the possibilities of Empire was shown in a letter to one of his aunts in October 1862: 'I have often thought about Australia. I have often thought what a glorious, what a successful career is open to anyone of moderate intelligence and energy, to mould a new country, to bring commerce into ports and merchandise into great cities, to lay open to the colonisation of enterprise the huge tracts of the country.' The budding politician was just fourteen when he was asked to make his first public speech. After a visit of the Linlithgow Rifle Volunteers to Dalmeny in September 1861, Archie had to reply to a toast made to him by the company. According to one account, 'without hesitation he rose and with modesty and clearness of speech which greatly impressed those who listened, he expressed thanks for the honour which had been done to him.' After he sat down, James Dundas, an old friend of the Rosebery family, 'ventured to prophesy that the speaker would become a future Prime Minister.'[56]

Dalmeny found other aspects of life at home more difficult. His relationship with his mother grew ever more fractious as she became increasingly aggrieved by his reserved manner, so different from the more open affection shown by his younger brother, her favourite Everard. At one stage she reproved Archie for his reticence: 'Your letters seem to give you so much trouble from the inability of finding anything to say.' On another occasion she reproached him for his unaristocratic bearing: 'I have only one wish in the world for you: that you should learn to hold up your head and not go about in your present slovenly, slouching way.'[57] Though Archie enjoyed shooting on his various family estates, he was bored by much of the social routine in which he was expected to participate. On New Year's Day in 1861 he wrote mournfully to his sister Constance about a forthcoming servants' ball at Dalmeny at which he dreaded seeing a certain Miss Stuart, 'an odious person who is always being forced upon one for a partner. Last time, whenever I asked who I might dance with next, the answer was always "Miss Stuart". At last I said, "I will not dance with that abominable woman".'[58] Similarly, in May 1862 he told Johnson that he was desperate to break a party engagement in London: 'I hate dancing.'[59]

The truth was that he preferred the company of his friends at Eton. For perhaps the only time in his life, he felt at ease among a close circle of contemporaries, whose number included Edward Hamilton and Lord Randolph Churchill, both of whom always remained loyal friends, whatever their later political differences. Another contemporary was Arthur Acland, who served under Rosebery in his 1894 Cabinet; almost thirty years earlier their roles had been reversed, as Archie fagged for Acland. 'I little thought when I poached your eggs and made your tea that we were destined to meet under these dissimilar circumstances,' Rosebery as the guest speaker later said at a public dinner for Acland.[60] Interestingly, though he and A.J. Balfour were at Eton at the same time, they were never friends despite having a great deal in common, including Scottish ancestry, a penchant for shooting, and a certain elegance of style. The Queen's private secretary Sir Frederick Ponsonby wrote in his memoirs: 'I was always surprised at the way Balfour and Lord Rosebery disliked each other, when they were really so much alike and there seems so little difference in the way they looked at various questions of the day. They were both literary, both very cynical and both lazy. There was always a certain rivalry between them. Rosebery said that for an amateur politician Balfour was wonderful while Balfour told me that he always admired the glib way Rosebery spoke when he knew little or nothing of the subject on which he was speaking.'[61]

It was precisely this kind of glibness that so annoyed William Johnson, who loathed the superficial and the second-rate. Yet all his persistent criticism of Dalmeny cannot disguise the fact that he was infatuated with the young man; in a perverse way, the depth of his frustration only reflected the intensity of his feelings, as expressed in several letters. 'You exerted enough zeal to touch my heart,' Johnson wrote in 1862. After a trip to Scotland that summer he reported: 'I met some excellent Scottish people who talked to me with the greatest affection of your sweet self. I made them quite happy by giving them a glowing account of you.' In the autumn of the following year, he urged Dalmeny 'to take care of your precious limbs. We miss you sadly and wish you to get back.'[62] This is hardly the sort of language that a schoolmaster is usually recommended to use towards a pupil. And in Archie's case such hero-worship from an older man cannot have been good for either his self-discipline or his modesty, never two of his greatest virtues. The very tutor who should have been teaching him reverence for authority was instead gazing upon him in rapture.

Johnson was not fitted by his nature to provide any form of moral guidance to his boys. For he was a pederast who treated his duties as opportunities for romance and his pupil-room as an adolescent harem. Privately Johnson tried to defend his yearnings by reference to the Classical concept known in the nineteenth century as 'Greek Love'. Rooted in Plato's Dialogues, this ideal held that the devotion of an older man to a younger was ennobling, even spiritual, as long as it was not based on degraded lust. As Oscar Wilde famously put it during his second trial in 1895, 'It is beautiful, it is fine, it is the noblest form of affection. There is nothing unnatural about it. It is intellectual, and it repeatedly exists between an elder and a younger man, when the elder man has intellect and the younger man has all the joy, hope and glamour of life before him.' But, as Wilde's own trial proved, beneath this elevated intellectual gloss usually lurked a much stronger, physical impulse. And so it was with William Johnson. It may have been his misfortune to have been born with such questionable inclinations towards adolescents, but it was his great fortune to inhabit a milieu which allowed them to flourish. Eton, like many public schools at the time, was a hothouse of seething passions which someone like Johnson could easily exploit. Though Charles Goodford, the Head Master when Dalmeny first arrived at Eton, had made some attempt at reform, an undercurrent of sexual longing still prevailed in many parts of the school, not least in master–pupil relationships. In Johnson's diary for February 1864 he recounted a conversation with Oscar Browning, a teacher who shared his taste for pederasty and was deeply in love with A.J. Balfour's brother Gerald: 'We agreed in thinking it very satisfactory that there should be sets held together by the more feminine sympathies.'[63] Johnson's set revolved around his room – nicknamed the Mousetrap after one of his favourites, Frederick Wood, known as Mouse – where he would spend long evenings with a group selected for their charms.

In other correspondence Johnson gave full expression to his desires. He wrote for instance to Regy Brett about Charlie, later Sir Charles, Elliott: 'I envy you being kissed by him. If I were dying like Nelson, I would ask him to kiss me. I kissed his dear foot last Tuesday on the grass at Ankerwyke.'[64] In his journal he said of Elliott: 'I can't conceive how anyone can love a son or daughter or wife more than I love him. Day by day his lovely countenance has been getting more expressive and more tender and kind.'[65] The perverted atmosphere of the Mousetrap is shown in another diary entry, for 1868: 'I have been cheered by the inexhaustible charms of Chatterbox [a pupil called Williamson]. After a day in London we dined snugly in the Mousetrap – then did I lament a little that I had to go to pupildom. Chatterbox came prettily, weary and half-silent, having a touch of sore throat and he was altogether in minor key. But I went to bad Latin and he to his bath, the first use of the new bathroom; he looked in upon us when at work, déshabillé.'[66] And Johnson took a voyeuristic pleasure in encouraging physical relationships between boys: 'I have seen young lovers interlacing like honeysuckle, rose and jasmine, romantic chivalrous friendships forming under my eye, to which I am almost admitted as a partner.'

With his dark good looks, Dalmeny could hardly avoid being drawn into Johnson's web. Rather than a tutor, Johnson sometimes sounded like a love-lorn teenager, as demonstrated by one extraordinary letter written when Dalmeny was just fourteen.

> My dear Dalmeny. What is the matter? Wood says you are not coming here any more because I cut you. I don't agree to that. You cut me for four days. You came here on Thursday night and I was very polite, only Mr Day's presence prevented any ordinary conversation. On Friday night I made reasonable overtures, stomaching my pride which is not less than yours: only reason convinces me that it must be subdued, or else I shall lose more than I can afford to lose in this dearth of sympathy. Why could you not be civil enough to come in on Saturday or today? I have been in the whole of both days. Some day you will lose a friend worth much more than me if you do not come to an understanding sooner after something has gone wrong. Come and have it out, if you have any grievance. I have been unhappy for a week without you, though too proud to say so, till the gentle influence of Sunday and the peace-making Mouse prevailed. On Wednesday night I had no companion but the dog Rabe and I was sorely tempted to remonstrate. If I did not show sufficient joy at your appearance on Thursday, it was out of pride which you ought to make allowances for. I was really very glad when you came in and began to romp.[67]

Johnson also derived a vicarious thrill from sending Dalmeny French love poems, and telling him of his other objects of lust. Of one boy, he admitted that he 'really melted with pathetic pleasure at having him here again.' Of another, called Cyril, he said 'I love him better every time I see him.'

It is impossible to know how much Archie reciprocated his tutor's affections, for in his old age he asked Johnson's family to return to him all his letters to his former tutor, and then systematically destroyed them. But it seems likely, since Johnson sometimes complained about his 'impregnable' nature and his 'want of deep feelings', that he maintained his habitual reserve. On the other hand, in 1864 he willingly travelled to Italy with Johnson, who recorded that the boy was 'full of fun'. And Johnson was aware of that almost feminine sensitivity in Archie which later so intrigued his contemporaries. 'It seems to me sometimes as if I were talking to an experienced married lady,' he wrote.[68] Nor was Archie himself entirely immune to the charms of his peers, commenting to his sister of a certain deaf boy, for instance: 'Archie Campbell was down here the other day. He is so handsome.'[69] The same tone was captured in one of his poems written at Eton, which included the lines 'a fair-haired lad and his faithful friend joined hand-in-hand and heart-in-heart'. Looking back on these verses at the age of 70, though he claimed they 'were not amatory',

Rosebery did admit that they were 'mediocre poetry'. 'I read into them the whirl of passion in which they had been produced. I read them over to myself in a sort of ecstasy, feeling in them the ardour and inspiration which, as I thought, I had transfused into them but which were not the least apparent.'[70] Equally redolent of the mood of Eton was a letter from Johnson's beloved Frederick Wood to Archie, written in February 1866. 'L. Gower has contracted a great friendship for Laws. Give my love to Pink, accompanied by a gentle kick, and if you would ruffle his hair over his face, it would please.'[71] Brinsley Richards, in his profile of Archie Dalmeny at Eton, threw in the rather vulgar memory that he had seen him 'running swiftly down the High Street with the breeches of a parson's boy under his arm', and there is little doubt that Archie was besotted with a certain Frederick Vyner, from a distinguished Yorkshire family, of whom he later wrote: 'no one ever saw him without being irresistibly drawn to him. The peculiar and lofty beauty of the face, the pale brow fringed with black curls, the tall and graceful form and, above all, the sweet expression of his countenance were his external extractions.'[72]

Johnson's infatuation would not necessarily have come as a shock to Dalmeny, for he was the subject of advances in his domestic life too, from a family acquaintance, Edward Cheney, an antiquarian of Badger Hall in Shropshire. Cheney's adoration began when Archie was only fourteen, and was perhaps even more explicit than Johnson's. When he saw that poem about the 'fair-haired lad', Cheney wrote to his 'dearest boy' that he had 'read and re-read the verses with feelings that it might be difficult to define but in which tenderness and affection predominate over all.' In attempting just such a further definition, Cheney assured Archie that 'the lines express my feelings towards you in words that I could never have arranged so well', and, further, that the poem 'will remain in my casket of treasures as long as life is granted me.' The smitten tone continued in Cheney's request for a lock of Archie's hair: 'I must beg for a long and thick lock on the first convenient opportunity.' After a visit Archie paid to Badger Hall Cheney appears to have been deceived into thinking that the boy, when wrapping up some papers, would leave some written evidence of his love. It turned out to have been a false hope. 'I suspected they [the papers] contained some expressions in verse or prose that were destined for me and I expected that the packet would be slipped into my hand as we extended our tender farewell.' But Cheney found nothing in either his desk or his pocket book. 'I shall *not* be disappointed again when I open the answer to this letter. I shall find the lines which you know well have a double intent in my eyes.'

Refusing to be downhearted, Cheney then demanded a photograph of the young Dalmeny, setting out in detail his specifications: 'The hair should not be so much smoothed. The neck-cloth should be loosely tied in a sailor's knot; the eyes should look towards the spectator and the lips should not be forcibly closed; your lips are slightly parted when you are making no effort to close them. I despair of ever getting a portrait of you that satisfies me but I should like to make several trials.' When a set of photographs eventually arrived, Cheney was overjoyed. 'You are the best of boys. The photograph is beautiful – extremely like and very pleasing.' In another letter he proclaimed that he had 'never had any photographs which pleased me so well'. But there was always the sense that Archie was not responding to Cheney's ardour: 'Why have you not written? I have been waiting to hear from you every day and every morning I have been disappointed.' He also regretted that the passage of years was taking Archie out of his boyish adolescence. After seeing him soon after he turned fifteen: 'You guessed right in supposing me disappointed at finding you older in appearance but I will tell you the answer. It was not because you looked less well – though this was a reason – but because it reminded me that you were approaching an age when our early friends, however much we are attached to them, become less important.'[73]

Other friends would soon be disappearing. By 1865 Archie was nearing the end of his schooling at Eton; the exact timing of his departure was a source of anger to himself, his choice of university college one of dismay to his tutor. It had been decided by the family that he should go to Christ Church, Oxford, partly because his cousin Edward Stanhope had gone there, partly because Lord Rosebery, Archie's grandfather, argued that Oxford was geographically nearer to Battle Abbey than his own alma mater of Cambridge. But Johnson was appalled by the idea that Archie should go to Christ Church, which he regarded as a place fit only for idlers. As he explained in a letter to the Duchess of Cleveland, as Dalmeny's mother now was, Johnson believed that the more austere, academic regime of Balliol College would have a better influence on the boy. 'If he were going to live at the age of 19 and 22 with jealous, intellectual men, he might well afford to trifle now. But with nothing else to look forward to but a set of fashionable triflers, gamblers, loungers and cricketers, wholly left to themselves so far as the University frightens them into spasmodic cramming for six weeks a year, I have a dismal foreboding of this rare, fine intellect being wasted either on society or the turf.'[74] Another, more dubious voice, that of Edward Cheney, joined the chorus of disapproval. 'I would rather you should have gone to Balliol than to Christ Church. I wish to see you an elegant scholar and I fear at Christ Church there is a very idle set.'[75]

The Duchess was more concerned by Archie's present indolence at Eton than his future conduct at Christ Church. Thinking that he was frittering away his time at the school, she decided that he must leave by Easter 1865, giving up his final summer term in order to attend classes with a private tutor. Such activity, she felt, would be more productive than several more months spent fooling around with his friends. Archie, however, was furious at the prospect of missing what promised to be a glorious climax to his career as an Etonian. And in this he was, predictably, supported by Johnson, who warned the Duchess that her son would gain little from leaving Eton early. Not only would he spend an 'immensely long vacation' in the summer, 'languishing at Hyde Park and wishing he were with his schoolfellows of whom he is so singularly fond' but he would also be hampered academically. 'In order to take honours, boys leave school not till they have had the full benefits of doing the highest school work which is much higher than the work of freshmen in their first two years at University.'[76] Johnson, who believed that 'the life of the last summer months at Eton is probably as happy as any kind of life',[77] could hardly have been more sympathetic to Archie's distress, as he showed in a letter to the boy: 'It is a loss which ladies cannot be expected to understand and not many men of fifty can estimate aright – perhaps no one who has not been at Eton. I never spent such a summer myself, but I have watched many boys in their enjoyment of it, and caught the glow and lustre by reflection. Nor would I preach to the effect that similar and greater enjoyment and companionship will be found at Oxford or elsewhere. Even if it were so, human life is not so long or well-arranged as to spare one such summer. It is the pearl in the crown of years.'[78] He was just as dismissive of the idea of private tutoring. His loyalty lay entirely with the boy rather than with his mother, and he told Archie it was absurd 'to suppose that a country clergyman should be capable of effecting what the disciplines of public school cannot effect.'[79]

Supported by Johnson, Archie refused to accede to his mother's demand, though she threatened to 'wash her hands of him altogether' if he insisted on staying at Eton. But his will proved too formidable for the Duchess, and eventually she capitulated with a bad grace, telling her son that she trusted he would 'not let this half at Eton be an idle one, with Mr Johnson or without him and not let the golden days slip unimproved through your fingers.'[80] She stipulated, however, that he must undertake an autumn of private tutoring before going up to Oxford at the beginning of 1866. Archie might have triumphed over his mother, but the episode only deepened their mutual antagonism. The Duchess saw her son as self-indulgent, disobedient and aloof; he saw her as unreasonable and tyrannical – and he never forgave her for her stance over that last Eton summer. As his sister Constance later revealed, the affair 'of his leaving Eton *did* overshadow all his subsequent relations with my mother.'[81]

After a final flourish, Archie left Eton in August 1865. He could hardly bear the moment of departure, as he confessed in his diary on 4 August. 'God grant that I never have such a wrench again. I cannot take in that I am no longer an Etonian. It must have taken place at some time. Why not now?'[82] Yet in a sense be never left Eton, for he remained devoted to the school for the rest of his life. He sent both his sons there, and was delighted when he was appointed to the school's Governing Body, one of the few offices he ever accepted without hesitation. In his old age he wrote to the Provost to explain that, because he had become so decrepit, he could not attend a ceremony at the school; nevertheless, 'Whether I am there or not, my heart is always at Eton.'[83] In terms of politics, he always had reason to be grateful to the school. It is a tribute either to the effectiveness of Eton's teaching methods or to the narrowness of the Victorian political class that for a quarter of a century, from 1880 to 1905, each one of Britain's four prime ministers – Gladstone, Salisbury, Rosebery and Balfour – was educated there.

As for William Johnson, his end was much sadder. For a time after Dalmeny left he continued to revel in the company of his pupils, as a party invitation he extended to his young hero in June 1870 suggests: 'If you don't come I shall expect a telegram, and I shall probably fill up with boyflesh lacking your soul of wit and mirth; but there are some festive lads still here and some that like ducks and one or two that like me.'[84] But Johnson's delight in 'boyflesh' was to bring about his downfall. In April 1872 the father of a boy there intercepted a typically effusive letter from Johnson to his son. Outraged by its tone, he brought the letter to the attention of the Head Master, Dr Hornby, who demanded Johnson's resignation. Exiled from Eton Johnson took desperate measures to avoid disgrace, changing his name to Cory and marrying. But right up to his death in 1892, his heart always ached for the past.

In an interesting postscript to the Johnson saga at Eton, Rosebery had to deal with a similar problem at the school more than twenty years later, when he became Prime Minister. In July 1894 he was contacted by Mary Lyell, a mother who was concerned about the 'unhealthy influence' exerted on her son by a group of 'thoroughly depraved associates'. Claiming that the school was 'getting rather out of hand', she attacked the Head Master, Dr Warre, for his apathy in the face of this scourge. In a subsequent series of hysterical letters about the moral turpitude of Eton, she urged that Rosebery should seek Dr Warre's resignation. In Rosebery's rather delayed reply, he explained that there was simply no evidence that Dr Warre had acted wrongly or that he was a poor Head Master. As to the particular case of her son, Rosebery said it was not for him to intervene. But he added these lines, which may reflect some doubts about his own experiences of the 1860s: 'It is not easy in a letter or even in a day to discuss the whole system of a great public school. The evils necessarily inherent in that system are so great that I am often doubtful as to whether it is well to send a boy there. There are evils of indolence, ignorance and contamination. A genius like Arnold obviates many of these, though among a much smaller number of boys. Eton has become so vast that more seems to me to depend on the tutors than on the Head Master.'[85] In William Johnson, Rosebery had a tutor who, for all his gifts, was only too thrilled by the thought of 'contamination'.

2

'The emptiness of a life of pleasure'

$\sim$

IN JANUARY 1866 Lord Dalmeny arrived in Oxford, having completed his studies at Revesby Abbey in Lincolnshire under the local vicar Mr Warburton, one of the clerical teachers so despised by William Johnson. Warburton, in his turn, was not overly impressed by the influence of the famous public school. Of the boys who had been pupils there he said, 'It is wonderful how much they have improved since they left Eton.'[1]

On his matriculation at Christ Church Archie Dalmeny was not yet nineteen but seemed extremely self-assured for his age, exuding intellectual confidence. Wealthy, widely read and full of wit, he was not a figure to be easily ignored. The hero-worship of Eton masters and pupils had increased his poise, while his isolation from his mother and the early loss of his father made him appear more mature than many of his more gauche contemporaries. But there was also an air of mystery about him, an aloofness that masked an inner shyness, a certain inscrutability that could appear dismissive, a moodiness that made him unpredictable. For all his charm and dazzling conversation he was reluctant to be drawn into close friendships, partly because of his love of solitude, partly because his very private nature made intimacy difficult for him. It is telling that in the remainder of his life no one except for his relatives and a handful of others ever addressed him as 'Archie'.

Until the political and personal crises of his middle age Rosebery's personality did not alter much; nor did he change physically, apart from a slight tendency to corpulence due to his fondness for fine cuisine and vintage wines. Below medium height and well-built, he had light blue eyes, a large forehead and a deep, rich voice. He never went bald, but his dark hair began to grey at the time of his premiership. Sometimes, when he was in one of his sombre moods, he would deliberately adopt an expressionless face. At other times he could dissolve the most icy atmosphere with a flash of his radiant smile, all the more winning because it was so rarely displayed. Except occasionally during overseas voyages he always remained clean-shaven, though at Oxford he did sprout a pair of fashionable short whiskers. Apart from his insomnia he was generally in good health, helped by his enthusiasm for long-distance walks. Surprisingly for someone who was a follower of 'the Turf', as the Victorians referred to the racing world, he was an awkward horseman and disliked hunting.

When Dalmeny arrived at Christ Church to read history, the college was rife with snobbery and antiquated customs. Dean H.G. Liddell, who had taken up his post in 1855, was trying to institute reforms, but it was proving a slow process. In accordance with medieval regulations which were still in force in 1866, High Table was generally reserved for young noblemen rather than dons. Such noblemen, among them Dalmeny, were a separate order inside Christ Church, known as 'Tufts' because they wore black silk gowns adorned with gold lace. The approach to academic work was just as reprehensible, since greater emphasis was placed on social distinction than on learning. The dullest of young gentlemen were indulged, providing they had the right connections. In one notorious case an undergraduate who had done nothing in Classics was ordered by his tutor to attend a series of lectures on the earth's atmosphere. When the course was over, he was tested by his tutor. 'Of what is the atmosphere composed?' was the first, apparently simple question. After a long pause, the undergraduate replied, 'Zinc.'[2]

It was just this lack of rigour which made William Johnson so worried about Dalmeny's presence at Christ Church. And his doubts soon appeared justified, as Dalmeny savoured the pleasurable joys of Oxford life. He became part of a fast aristocratic set centred on the champagne-fuelled Bullingdon Club, while his closest friend remained the wayward Lord Randolph Churchill, now up at Merton. Contemptuous of both the Oxford curriculum and university discipline, Churchill was regularly in trouble with the authorities for misdemeanours such as drunkenness, smoking in academic dress, and smashing windows at the Randolph Hotel. Though Dalmeny never descended to such behaviour, some of Churchill's rebellious spirit undoubtedly affected him. With an independent outlook and a generous allowance of £600 a year, which his mother thought excessive,[3] he rarely felt the need to show too much respect for college rules. In his first term, for example, he once refused to attend obligatory morning chapel, and was sent for by Dean Liddell. 'Told him it was too cold,' wrote Dalmeny in his diary.

A more serious clash arose over his attitude to public lectures. One of the Christ Church fellows was the Reverend Charles Dodgson, a mathematics lecturer and today more famous as Lewis Carroll, author of *Alice in Wonderland*, written for Dean Liddell's daughter Alice. At the time of his differences with Dalmeny, Dodgson already had reason to be suspicious of him. He had once seen Dalmeny drive a dog-cart recklessly through Oxford and crash into another vehicle, a collision which sent him and his passenger, Prince Hassan of Egypt, tumbling to the ground. Soon afterwards, in May 1867, Dalmeny, again in his carriage, saw Dodgson in the street and offered him a lift. Dodgson responded Biblically, 'Intendest thou to kill me, as thou killedst the Egyptian?'[4]

Dodgson's sense of humour deserted him, however, when Dalmeny failed to attend one of his lectures on the flimsy pretext that he 'had another engagement', connected with his birthday. In response Dodgson wrote him a stiff letter: 'It is to me a simple matter of duty to maintain the discipline of the College and it is my earnest desire that the undergraduates should submit to that discipline as a matter of duty. The College rule as to public lectures has always been that those belonging to them have no right to absent themselves without the permission of the lecturer.' As a punishment, Dodgson ordered Dalmeny to write out a hundred lines of Virgil. Outraged at being treated like a naughty schoolboy, Dalmeny stood on his pride, refused to do the lines and then, still brimming with indignation, boycotted Dodgson's next two lectures. Dodgson increased the number of lines to five hundred, which only reinforced Dalmeny's stubbornness. He objected, he said, 'to the principle' of the punishment. Faced by such a direct challenge to his authority, Dodgson felt he had no alternative but to report him to the Dean. 'On Monday 7 May,' he wrote, 'Lord Dalmeny absented himself from the public Euclid lecture without having asked permission, his reason being one for which I would not have given permission had he asked for it: it was that it was his birthday and he wished to leave Oxford for a few days' pleasure.' Dodgson went on to explain about Dalmeny's obduracy over the lines, though he concluded that his conduct had been 'perfectly courteous and respectful from first to last.' Eventually a compromise was reached, by which Dalmeny agreed to future attendance in addition to writing out 'the last six propositions of the second book of Euclid'.[5] But just as he had demonstrated in his struggle with his mother over leaving Eton, Dalmeny was not a man who easily forgave: one of his most negative characteristics was his enthusiasm for harbouring grudges. Always quick to take offence, keenly aware of his own dignity, he littered his life with feuds and estrangements, often quite obscure in their origin. In the case of Dodgson, for almost thirty years Rosebery refused to speak to him, and avoided reading *Alice in Wonderland*. It was not until November 1893 that the rift was healed, and Rosebery finally agreed to accept a copy of the book from Dodgson. 'I am proud of you as a Christ Church man and I hope we are now reconciled,' said Dodgson.[6]

He was not the only don who tired of Dalmeny's attitude. 'I want to see you about your work. It is not good of you to have waited instead of coming of your own accord' was a characteristic letter from one of his tutors, Edward Stewart Talbot, later Bishop of Winchester.[7] Dalmeny's mother was aggrieved by what she perceived as her son's idleness, scolding him about the dangers of self-indulgence. Yet he was not as indolent as she supposed, or as his enthusiasm for the turf and his poor disciplinary record suggested. His intellect was sharper than ever, his reading still voracious. He switched readily from moments of high gregariousness, drinking noisily with his Bullingdon circle, to times of complete solitude, with only books for company. 'I am here quite alone. Yesterday I had not spoken to a human being, except the house-keeper and the forester, for a week,' he wrote to his sister from Dalmeny in late 1866.[8] He performed well in his first examinations in November 1867 and was predicted to do even better in his finals. An interesting picture of him as a diligent student was provided by the son of Sidney James-Owen, Senior Censor at Christ Church during the 1860s, and Dalmeny's tutor. As James-Owen *fils* recalled, 'It would not be true to say that Lord Rosebery neglected the regular studies of the university. It was far otherwise. Lord Rosebery was no idle aristocrat. He went industriously through the ordinary course of study for the Honours School of Modern History. My father always told me that, for an undergraduate, he read specially widely and brought to my father brilliant and carefully written work in the form of essays and otherwise. It was my father's opinion that if he had been able to enter for the University's examination, Lord Rosebery would certainly have obtained a brilliant first-class.'[9] The evidence of a fellow Christ Church undergraduate, Henry Tollemache, backs up this assertion of Dalmeny's scholarly prowess: 'I saw a good deal of Rosebery at Oxford and was very friendly with him. I should say that whilst he was universally liked, he was not one who at the time had many bosom friends, possibly because he was intellectually so immeasurably superior to all his contemporaries.'[10]

After two years of mixing pleasure and study at Christ Church, Dalmeny's life was suddenly and dramatically changed. On 3 March 1868 he was summoned to London to the bedside of his elderly grandfather, who had fallen into a coma. The 4th Earl of Rosebery died at 10.15 the next morning. His grandson, still only twenty, was now the 5th Earl, inheritor of a great fortune, considerable estates, a distinguished title, and a seat in the House of Lords. The annual income from his property in Scotland

and East Anglia, including 15,000 acres in Midlothian and another 2,000 at Postwick in Norfolk, was estimated to be around £30,000. Unfettered access to this wealth brought Rosebery not only an absolute freedom denied to most young men, but also made him a significant figure in society, a man of interest to prime ministers and fashionable hostesses alike.

But there was also a less positive side to this transformation in Rosebery's status, for it also meant he had no need to make his own way in the world. He was therefore denied the chance to experience the usual setbacks that are part of most young lives. He had, in effect, gained the palm without the dust. As the author T.H.S. Escott wrote of him in 1898, 'The one great misfortune which has dogged Rosebery through his life is the absence, at each successive stage, of difficulties at once bracing and chastening.'[11] Though his financial independence enabled Rosebery to take a higher view of the national interest, as he never had to indulge in the grubby place-seeking and ditching of principles that drove other party politicians, it also made him treasure his freedom perhaps too zealously, and to see in almost every proposal of office a potential affront to his self-respect. Even more negatively, it ensured that Rosebery, used to having his own way, became inconsiderate of the feelings of others. In many circles he was notorious for this trait of self-centredness. Lady Angela Forbes claimed in her memoirs that she had 'never seen anyone so spoilt as Lord Rosebery at Dunrobin.* Everyone was kept waiting about until he made up his mind if he wanted to go stalking or not, and by that time it was generally too late for anyone else to go out.'[12] In a more specific way, his immediate elevation to the House of Lords damaged Rosebery by ruling out any apprenticeship in the Commons. As a result, he was ignorant of the conduct of Government business and isolated from the mainstream of his Parliamentary party, difficulties of which he was only too well aware and which he bitterly resented. The liberal journalist J.A. Spender, an admirer of Rosebery, argued that his entire career would have been different if he had spent some years in the Commons. 'No man can sit long in that assembly without discovering the unprofitableness of the lonely furrow.' And Spender added: 'Lord Rosebery has often told us that the greatest of his disabilities was to be a peer and on one occasion, he compared himself to the child outside the village fair, who, without a penny to gain himself admission, steals a furtive joy by peeping under the tent.'[13] Winston Churchill was even more sorry about Rosebery's ineligibility to serve as an MP: 'I feel that if I had his brain I would move mountains. Oh that he had

---

*The Scottish home of the Duke of Sutherland.

been in the House of Commons! There is the tragedy. Never to have come into contact with realities, never to have felt the pulse of things – that is what is wrong with Rosebery.'[14]

In the immediate aftermath of his grandfather's death, however, Rosebery was more determined to enjoy his new wealth than dwell on his political future. In particular, he relished the chance to become a race-horse owner for the first time. Soon after reaching his majority, in May 1868, he registered the Rosebery colours of primrose and rose hoops. Inspired by the dream of winning the Derby as an undergraduate, he bought his first horse – named Ladas after one of Alexander the Great's messengers – from a north country breeder, Mr Cowen. Though the horse had won three races at the time Rosebery bought him, Lord Randolph Churchill was scathing about the animal, calling him 'a brute of a beggar'. In addition to the excitement of ownership, Rosebery also started to bet heavily on the races, gambling what would have been astronomical sums to ordinary punters. In one meeting at Epsom he lost £165, at another in Northampton more than £1000. But he also had some significant winnings, such as the £5975 he made on the St Leger in 1869. Little wonder that Rosebery said rather flippantly later in life: 'Racing is the strangest of all amusements. It consists of an endless series of painful disappointments (agonising to those who are really absorbed in the sport) varied by a rare ecstasy.'[15] He also spent freely on breakfast and dinner parties, prompting his facetious aside that 'everything comes to an end, except an Irish grievance and an Oxford bill.'[16] Interestingly, despite the skills he had displayed as a debater at Eton, he refused to join the Oxford Union, traditionally the breeding ground for English statesmen. This decision reflected both the low priority he attached to politics, and his innate shyness; he found it far more intimidating to speak to a large gathering of competitive undergraduates than to a group of school friends. As a young man Rosebery was so chronically shy that he would sometimes hide his face in his handkerchief.[17]

Neither his mother nor his former tutor approved his frivolity and lack of direction. The Duchess of Cleveland wrote just after his twenty-first birthday: 'I hold that there is no perfect character without a grain of ambition and I cannot but regret its absence in you.'[18] Johnson, not yet embroiled in scandal, sent him in August 1868 another of his superbly intuitive analyses. 'Men with a character for prudence are very often men who shrink from responsibility and action. A man who takes the bat and works hard for a long innings gives many chances but he is more of a cricketer than one who stands somewhere in the field for an hour without having a ball to stop. What I am afraid of in your case is your being at 22 as cool and as critical as a sergeant-at-law or a retired East Indian.' He urged Rosebery to gain some hard, practical experience in industry or law so that he might be better fitted for public service. But he doubted that Rosebery was a 'good listener and I fear you have not that penetrative directness of statement which seems to me indispensable for men of influence.'[19]

For all his mother's disapproval, it was one of Rosebery's own family, his uncle and guardian Bouverie Primrose, who encouraged his equine interests. Primrose was anxious that his nephew should take up riding when he first went up to Christ Church, telling Earl Stanhope: 'If he wants to keep a horse it should in the first instance be given to him. I am almost disposed to compel him to keep a horse, so much importance do I attach to a man in his position in life being a "Plunger".'[20] This was the exact opposite of the opinion of the Christ Church authorities when news reached them of Rosebery's foray onto the turf. Ownership of a racehorse was technically a breach of college regulations, and Rosebery was urged to abandon his until after he graduated. More aware than ever of his own station, he absolutely refused to do so. He was thereupon given an ultimatum by Dean Liddell: he must give up either his horse, or his place in college. To the Dean's surprise, Rosebery chose the latter. At Easter 1869 he left Oxford University without taking his degree, and his name was struck from the college books. Once more he had refused to bow to the dictates of authority. Once more he had proved rigidly inflexible in the face of a personal challenge. As A.G. Gardiner wrote apropos this episode, 'It was said of Sir James Picton, that brilliant hero of Waterloo, that he would never have learned to command because he had never learned to obey. Lord Rosebery never learned to obey.'[21] There was, however, no taint of disgrace about Rosebery's premature exit from Christ Church. He had done nothing shameful or immoral and even Dean Liddell, more puzzled than outraged by the incident, did not hold his decision against him. Two years later, when Rosebery made his first important speech in the House of Lords, Liddell wrote to him. 'The commendations are well-deserved. You know how much I wished that you could have stayed here a little longer and really studied those subjects which would have been so useful to you in public life. However, for one who is resolute, this can done as well elsewhere as here.'[22] Rosebery's rehabilitation was soon complete. He was invited back to his old college to speak, while his name was restored to the record books. So untarnished was his reputation that more than thirty years later there were two concerted attempts to make him Chancellor of the university. Yet he never looked back on his time at

Oxford with anything like the same warm nostalgia he showed for Eton. The memories of university society, he told J.A. Spender, 'are not alluring to me. Those dinners of Heads of Houses and evening parties! They return to me in a cloud of gloom.'[23]

Rosebery came later to regret the rashness of his actions, but in the summer of 1869, still fired by the dream of a first Derby win, he was full of bravado. 'I have left Oxford. I have secured a house in Berkeley Square and I have bought a horse to win the Derby,' he told his appalled mother.[24] He was so confident of Ladas' chances that he encouraged his erstwhile colleagues at Christ Church to back the horse heavily, though the odds were 66 to 1. He also circulated some verses around the Oxford turf set, whipping up excitement over the race. One typical stanza ran:

There was wailing in the Common Room, the Censors tore their hair,
They turned away from port and punch and some began to swear,
They cursed the race of Lambton and wished Zenobia sterile,★
And wept that for so poor a colt their souls they should imperil.

Sadly, Rosebery's dream turned out to be a fantasy, as Ladas finished last in a field of 22 runners – or, as Rosebery put it to his friends, 'went a bummer'. The colt's weaknesses were summed up by *Baily's Monthly Magazine:* 'Ladas, who had been a fair public performer, did not train as had been expected and although he showed a good turn of speed at Epsom, he was lamentably deficient in staying power.' Nor did the horse perform much better in subsequent races, winning just one minor head-to-head contest all season and regularly coming nowhere. The rest of Rosebery's stable, nine in total, were equally unsuccessful, a single victory being achieved by the four-year-old Athena in a meeting at Doncaster. It was a dismal return on some heavy investment.

Initially Rosebery was not depressed by these failures and continued to be enthralled by the turf. 'A good day's racing but many upsets. Lost £725' was his diary entry for 15 September. The next day he wrote, 'A dull day. Lost £640.'[25] But then in November 1869 a row after a meeting at Stockton led to his sudden retirement from the racing world. He had entered one of his horses, Mavela, in a race there, and the attraction of his name meant that the locals backed it heavily. When Mavela ran poorly and was subsequently sold cheaply at auction, there were accusations of race fixing and even a suggestion, according to *The Sporting Life*, that 'the

★The stallion and mare which sired Ladas.

noble owner might be responsible for what had occurred.' Rosebery, who always found any direct public criticism intolerable, was 'incensed beyond measure'.[26] He immediately put his entire stable up for sale at Tattersalls. As *Baily's Monthly Magazine* said in a profile of Rosebery in December 1869, 'He imagined rightly, we think, that if he could not lose a paltry selling race without rendering himself liable to a suspicion of connivance in it, racing was not worth following as a pastime. This single incident will at once show of what an honourable and sensitive nature the mind of our subject is composed.' Twice in the space of six months he had shown a dangerously impulsive streak. But the magazine hoped that Rosebery's self-imposed exile would not last long. 'He may rest assured that his first retirement from the turf, far from diminishing him in the estimation of the racing world, has only served to increase the loss they feel they have sustained by the premature withdrawal of his horses.' This hope was soon fulfilled. A public apology to Rosebery was issued, the smear of corruption was repudiated and in November 1870 his return to the turf was marked by his election to the Jockey Club.

Rosebery's enjoyment of his role as a man of leisure was not confined to the race-course. He also travelled extensively in Europe, Russia and North America, using his gifts as a writer to enhance his vivid descriptions of his experiences. When he visited St Peter's in Rome in 1870, for instance, he was intrigued by the nature of the congregation, so different from one in Britain: 'Instead of our pews and glossy hats and chignons and neatly got-up lodge-keepers to represent an intelligent and prosperous peasantry, you are elbowed here by real want and poverty and squalor, to whom the Church is the only Home: and it is a home to them at all hours, however splendid it may be.'[27] In a lighter vein, on a visit to Paris in the spring of 1873 he was amused by a head-waiter at Bignon's restaurant who 'pronounced my name as if it was a play on Rosbif' and, at the circus, was impressed by an equestrian acrobat 'who jumped through a hoop the size of a virgin's wrist'. Extravagance was a theme of the remainder of the trip through France; in Avignon, he boasted that he had consumed an eight-course breakfast; in Nice, at the Casino, he lost badly at the tables.[28] He moved on to Italy, and there was an embarrassing moment in Turin when he and his travelling companion, Charles Stewart, were shown to a double-bedded room: 'I supposed they considered Stewart an odalisque in disguise,' wrote Rosebery. Fortunately, two separate rooms were available. In Venice, his note of a visit to the post office reveals his awareness of the peculiar satisfaction he derived from feeling disgruntled. Having sent off three letters, he found there was no post waiting for him. 'This was a double pleasure of 1) having performed one's duty; and 2) having a grievance.'[29]

Since he loved to travel, it was fortunate that Rosebery never suffered sea-sickness, even in a gale. Nor did he mind lengthy journeys. Late in 1873 he went on a trip to Canada and the United States, a country whose prosperity and optimism made a deep impact. Among the other passengers on the voyage across the Atlantic in the SS *Russia* was Beatrice Potter, travelling with her father. As the leading Fabian socialist Beatrice Webb, she later became one of Rosebery's most surprising political allies. Just over three decades after this first encounter, she wrote in her diary: 'Whenever I look on that distracted and distempered face, I think of that magnificent, self-complacent young man who swelled it on the *Russia* thirty years ago ("swelled it" is the appropriate expression, however vulgar it may sound) with health, power, intellect and charm.'[30]

The day after he arrived in New York, Rosebery felt almost overwhelmed. 'I never saw such a day – a day to dream of and to rave of: clear, bright, with a heavenly cheerfulness in the sky and a mad vivacity in the air. No one can wonder at the vitality and self-confidence of the Americans who has breathed their October air.'[31] He criss-crossed North America, visiting Congress in Washington and the Canadian parliament in Ottawa, a lunatic asylum in Brooklyn and a Mormon church in Salt Lake City. It is a reflection of the youthful peer's growing social stature that the doors of all the grandest homes were open to him, mayors called upon him, and he was even invited to a reception at the White House hosted by the Republican President Ulysses S. Grant. Throughout this memorable adventure, Rosebery's descriptive gifts never deserted him. His portrait of General Ben Butler, who had been the Republican Military Governor of New Orleans during the Civil War, was both hilarious and repulsive: 'His ugliness is startling. A head like the head of an enormous snake, two ferociously squinting eyes in bulbous caverns of corrugated skin, the end of his face passing directly into his neck without the hollow form of a chin: one could almost fancy seeing a rabbit projecting from it which he had gorged, as is said to be the case with a boa constrictor.' Rosebery also recounted a bizarre incident in the smoking room of his New York hotel, where late one night he fell into the company of a US judge named O'Sullivan and a Canadian MP named Thomson: 'Thomson announced that he had taken a great fancy to me at Ottawa from observing the shape of my head, upon which, without further ado, he laid on violent hands. It was a curious sight in a American smoking room at 2 a.m.: a young fellow in the hands of a muscular Canadian proclaiming revelations of his subject's character to O'Sullivan snoring and drunk.'[32]

The deepest friendship he made during this North American stay was with the lobbyist Samuel Ward, a man of epic generosity and fecklessness who dominated the Washington scene for decades and was as renowned for his epicurean dinners as for his dubious political methods. He had a eye for originality and a talent for publicity; having guided Rosebery through the salons of the USA in 1873, in 1882 he promoted Oscar Wilde's famous tour of the continent. One of his many eccentric quirks was to believe that he was the reincarnation of the Oriental poet Omar Khayyám, while he also collected pornography, and vintage wines. Though thirty-two years older than Rosebery, he shared his love of literature and a rich sense of humour, as well as a bent for extravagance – Ward had already managed to squander two fortunes by the time he met Rosebery, and a third financial disaster was not far away. The *New York World* newspaper called him 'the most elegant spendthrift that ever lived.' But he never let such mere pecuniary considerations inhibit his hospitable, open spirit, and Rosebery quickly became devoted to him. Sam Ward's niece later described Rosebery's attitude to her uncle as 'that of the adoring acolyte. During the long visit, he rarely took his eyes off him.'[33] This adoration was reflected on Rosebery's return to England in a letter that he sent Sam Ward, whom he had christened 'the universal uncle': 'When I am asked by the rising youth of this country to give an introduction to the principal poetical, theological and political celebrities of America, I invariably surprise them by giving them a simple note and superscription upon it. When I am asked the reason of my giving only one letter, I reply that under your sombrero may be found an epitome of all the poetry, theology and politics of America. Besides that, there are some sparks of geology, philosophy, facetiae, gastronomy and philoprogentiveness. You have studied in the native wilds that savage and ferocious animal, the mother-in-law. You have, moreover, moulded the millionaire, cauterised the courtesan and probed the prig. Hail! Representative of the highest culture!'[34] Sam Ward and Rosebery shared a fondness for the frivolous, and with the American journalist William H. Hulbert, an even bigger rogue than Ward, they formed a schoolboyish grouping they called 'The Mendacious Club'. Ward was 'The President', Rosebery 'The Sycophant', the title by which he always signed himself in correspondence with Sam, and Hulbert 'The Member'. In this climate of happy puerility, the lawyer and art connoisseur Sam Barlow was occasionally admitted to gatherings as 'The Perpetual Candidate', as was Rosebery's turf friend Lord Houghton, known as 'The

Observer'. According to Ward's biographer, it was at a dinner of the Mendacious Club that Rosebery made his famous boast that he had three ambitions: to marry an heiress, win the Derby, and become Prime Minister.[35]

Sam was thrilled by the success of Rosebery's American visit, writing to Frank Lawley, the *Daily Telegraph* journalist and a mutual friend, 'He has won diamond opinions everywhere – in Salt Lake, Canada, New York, Boston, Washington he awakened affection and left regrets.'[36] Lawley, however, was worried that Rosebery was enjoying himself too much, and might become romantically ensnared. 'Heaven grant that the affection with which he is regarded by the American girls may not be reciprocated, for most of them are the most heartless worldly b——s that can be imagined,' he told the turf enthusiast, gambler and ex-soldier Ousley Higgins.[37] Rosebery was certainly enchanted with many of the young women he came across in North America, and frequently commented on their good looks. He told Ward of his admiration for the 'quite unspoiled' Miss Minnie Stevens and the 'lovely' Miss Frances Beckwith. When he returned to England in February 1874 he asked Ward to 'tell me in your next letter how Miss Rogers, Belmont's* young niece whom I took to dinner at his house and who lives in Washington, is looking. She is a thing of beauty and I meditate over her, as over a sonnet.'[38]

It is impossible to look at Rosebery in this period and not recognise that, despite his past experiences in the febrile atmosphere of William Johnson's 'Mousetrap' at Eton, he had the same appetites as most other heterosexual young men. His writings at this time frequently refer to the physical allure of the opposite sex. In February 1872 he went to a theatrical ball given in the Freemasons' Tavern at Westminster: 'It was very well done with a sit-down supper for at least 200 people. But I found it dull, with very few good-looking women.'[39] Henry Labouchere, the Liberal journalist and politician, who was a friend of Rosebery's at this time but later became one of his most implacable opponents, had no doubts about the 5th Earl's inclinations, for in the early 1870s the two men were fond of spending evenings in the company of actresses at the Star and Garter hotel in Richmond.[40] Rosebery's delight in female company was so well known in society as to prompt an ill-judged approach from the Prince of Wales. In 1873 the Prince asked through his secretary Francis Knollys if he and his brother Alfred might use Rosebery's London home at 2 Berkeley Square

---

*August Belmont (1816–90), leading US banker and president of the American Jockey Club.

for assignations with 'their actress friends'. Rosebery treated the request with contempt, telling Knollys that 'he did not see how it could be managed' and that he 'did not know anything of these actresses'. He concluded: 'If the Prince of Wales mentions the matter again, then please tell him that the house is too small and unsuited for such entertainment.'[41] This reaction was driven not by prudery but by Rosebery's dislike of intrusive demands on his own private world. In fact there was always a vulgar streak in him, and he relished gossip and filthy jokes. The ever-perceptive Margot Asquith recorded that if Rosebery were in one of his icy moods he was 'impossible to interest unless of course you go recklessly into the private and rather compromising details of other people's loves and lives which never fail to interest him. He has infinite curiosity about small and I think rather nasty sides of life and Henry★ says that in the smoking room his wit often turns to coarseness.'[42] In this vein in the early 1870s Rosebery poked fun at the erotic impulses of the Prince of Wales, circulating among his friends a document entitled 'Copulation – Ancient and Modern' which pretended to be a report of a lecture delivered by Ferdinand Rothschild in the presence of the Prince. Using that tone of rich irony which was already his hallmark, Rosebery explained that the title 'had perhaps something to do with the intense interest that prevailed'. Rothschild's address 'betokened enormous erudition and a great practical acquaintance with the subject', while his description of the activities of the Roman Emperors 'caused tears to flow from many an eye'. In this parody Rothschild the lecturer was supported by Frank Lockwood (decades later the Solicitor-General in Rosebery's government), who 'presided at the blackboard with an ample supply of red and white chalk and by some happy and suggestive freehand sketches crossed every "t" and dotted every "i".'[43]

It was inevitable, since Rosebery was one of the most eligible young men in the country, that the question of marriage would soon arise. He was barely twenty when it first did so. In the late 1860s he was very close to Lady Holland, visiting her in Naples and staying frequently in her home in London. Lady Holland adored Rosebery, and early in 1868 harboured ambitions that he might marry her adopted daughter, the beautiful Mary Fox, who was the illegitimate child of a French maid. Mary herself, though only in her mid teens, was not averse to the idea. In her letters to Rosebery, whom she nicknamed Lord Dalmenus, she gave some signs of her emotions, referring to herself as an 'obedient little creature' in one letter and saying in another that 'I think even the birds who are singing to their

★ Her husband, the Liberal leader H.H. Asquith.

hearts' content would send you their love and say that they miss you.'[44] To one of her friends she revealed the depths of her infatuation, expressing the hope that she might soon be taken to the altar. 'I have a great consideration and friendship for my Lord Dalmenus and . . . enough! Your delicate feelings and tender heart will supply what my pen cannot write.'[45] It seems that Rosebery was strongly attracted to Miss Fox, and Lady Holland even claimed that he had possibly proposed to her, only to be refused by Mary because she was unwilling to abandon her Catholicism. This is unconvincing in view of Mary's love for 'my Lord Dalmenus' and Rosebery's own open-mindedness on questions of faith. In truth, at such an early age Rosebery was probably reluctant to consider marriage. Yet the strength of passion, especially on Mary's side, undoubtedly led to some kind of scene, which Lady Holland perhaps misinterpreted. This was Rosebery's explanation years later in 1914, having acquired his letters to Mary Fox, which he subsequently burnt: 'I certainly never proposed to Mary Fox but this seems to me the base of Lady Holland's letter to me and that Mary refused on the grounds of religion. After racking my brain, I seem to remember that Miss Fox took me aside into a room at St Anne's and declared spontaneously that she could not change her religion on marriage. I was only fond of her with a boy and girl affection. I was only 20 in June 1868 and Mary was only 16 but I cannot think that I contemplated marriage which Mary and Lady Holland certainly must have done. My recollection is that I was terribly embarrassed by Mary's declaration, which I saw could put an end to our friendship and to my delightful life under Lady Holland's roof.'[46] Mary Fox went on to marry Prince Aloysius Lichtenstein in 1872, a match that Lady Holland thought infinitely inferior to the putative union with Rosebery, as she told him: 'What a bitter disappointment. Where is her head? Even that might have remained where the heart was wanting but no – she makes herself ridiculous and disliked! You would have guided her better than that fool, but I am happier as it is, thinking that you are free.'[47]

Rosebery was indeed free, and in the early 1870s was determined to enjoy his bachelor status. He habitually escorted glamorous women to dinners, the theatre, suppers, the race-course and other society functions, leading to speculation in the gossip columns about his intentions, speculation that amused him. 'I entertain a pretty heiress with at least £100,000 to luncheon today, so you may soon see an announcement in the Court Journal,' he said to Ousley Higgins in 1873.[48] One of the women he saw regularly was Alma Egerton, whom he described in a later note in his diary as 'a perfectly good and virtuous girl who lived with her parents and had an unblemished character. She was also very pretty. She married and died young.' But he obviously became rather bored with her, writing after one evening in April 1874: 'Then to the Pall Mall where Francis Knollys was to have entertained two actresses but there only came Alma Egerton whom I had to drive home in my brougham.'[49]

Much more explosive was the affair he conducted with an unhappily married woman, Blanche Innes-Ker, daughter of a landowning MP, Colonel Thomas Peers-Williams, and wife of Lord Charles Innes-Ker, a dissolute son of the Duke of Roxburgh. Their relationship began in 1873 when she was 29, three years older than Rosebery, and soon became so intense that Rosebery was seeing her almost every day. Often his first action on returning from a trip was to call on her. His diary in the period up to 1876 is filled with references to the hours he spent with her. Alhough he reveals nothing about the nature of their relationship, it must have been emotionally if it was not physically intimate. 'Sat with Lady Charles Ker all afternoon' (28 January 1873); 'Sat for more than two hours with Lady Charles Ker (still in bed)' (1 March 1873). Of a visit to Windsor he commented: 'Alone with Lady Charles all morning until 12.30 when she drove me to the train. Went back by 5.20. Rowed with Lady Charles on the river. We dined alone' (19 July 1873). Four days later he was back with her: 'Went down to Old Windsor by the 10.30 train. Sat with Lady Charles all day' (23 July 1873). The same pattern continued the following year: 'All afternoon with Lady Charles Ker' (7 February 1874). On three successive days in June he went to the opera with her, dined alone with her, and then went to an exhibition with her. In July they were at Newmarket together: 'After the races, Lady Charles and I explored a churchyard, a poky little hole' (8 July 1874). The affair continued through 1875; they were still seeing each other most days when Rosebery was in London. 'Walked with Lady Charles Ker – a heavenly evening' (27 April 1875).[50] It was only in 1876, when Rosebery's romantic interests began to move elsewhere, that their relationship cooled. Occasionally Rosebery also met her husband, whose attachment to horse-racing was even deeper than his own. Indeed, Lord Charles was a wastrel who ruined his marriage with his irresponsible ways. He was regularly hauled before the courts for his debts, and in 1888 was declared bankrupt with arrears estimated at £27,900, an astonishing sum for the time. It is little wonder that Blanche sought comfort elsewhere. Even during the time of her relationship with Rosebery, she moved temporarily into the Clarendon Hotel to escape her husband. So desperate became her plight that in 1882 her sister Bronwen wrote to Rosebery, begging him to give Blanche £50 or £100 'as she is dreadfully hard-up and I am powerless to help her.'[51] Though she and Lord Charles separated, her position did not improve, and in 1905 she herself was taken to court for making a false declaration on a life assurance policy in order to secure a loan. It was a sad descent from her happier days with Rosebery.

With his enquiring mind, Rosebery was interested not just in the beauties of London and American society but in all aspects of the human condition. During another trip to America, in 1874 with Charles Stewart, he went to a brothel in Havana and was appalled by what he saw, 'women in evening dresses sitting in chains to be looked at. The client taps his merchandise on the shoulder and is conducted upstairs where the price demanded will be six paper dollars, equal to 11 shillings. I was never so sickened in my life at such a sight. One girl was pointed out to me, almost white and whom I should not have guessed to possess any black taint, whose name in bitter mockery was Lucretia and who was the slave of the proprietor.' He was just as shocked by other sordid aspects of Cuban society, including the local biological theory that 'negresses can always procure abortion by means of tea made from the leaves of holly at the root of the cotton plant.' He was also regularly confronted with the prevalence of what he called 'unnatural crimes'. On a plantation he came across 'a Chinese lad who was notoriously the "wife" of the Chinaman on the estate.' At one railway station a Chinaman came up to his companion Charles Stewart. 'I thought he was proffering his services as a porter but it turns out he was proposing them in a very different capacity. "Sir, I will do anything you like."'[52]

Rosebery may have been repelled by the blatant evidence of such proclivities, but in one very personal case the legacy of Eton continued to haunt him. The boy he had most admired at school was the cherubic Frederick Vyner, who like Rosebery went on to Christ Church. In 1870, a year after leaving Oxford, Vyner travelled to Greece with a group of friends headed by the Cumbrian peer and former soldier Lord Muncaster, but instead of enjoying the culturally-enriching holiday they had imagined, they were subjected to a terrifying ordeal. As they journeyed near Marathon they were captured by a group of ruthless brigands, who took them hostage and demanded a ransom of £25,000. The kidnappers released Muncaster, however, ordering him to go back to Athens to raise the money. The negotiations, conducted by an incompetent British diplomat who vacillated between surrender and defiance, were horribly bungled; after eleven days on the run the kidnappers grew impatient and bent on murder. Increasingly aware of his probable fate, Vyner wrote to Muncaster in a heart-breaking mixture of courage and innocence: 'We must trust to God that we may die bravely as Englishmen should die.'[53] In another letter he included some poignant instructions for his family: 'In case I am killed, I wish you would communicate to those at home that my horses, when they are done with, be shot and never sold. I give my little dog to my mother and want you if possible to get my body and have it buried in England as I hate this place too much to sleep in it in death.'[54] Shortly after writing this, Vyner was shot in the back by his captors during a skirmish with the Greek military. The bullet pierced his heart and he died instantly. Most of the brigands were killed in the battle. Those that survived were arrested and executed.

The incident created a storm in England, where the Palmerstonian concept of the rights of British citizens abroad still prevailed. The blundering diplomat, Edward Erskine, was sent into exile, while Muncaster lived the rest of his life consumed with guilt over his failure to save his friends. But Lord Rosebery felt the loss of Vyner, his 'pale, tall, beautiful English lad', perhaps more deeply than anyone. He never claimed to be psychic, yet he had felt an almost physical pain in the immediate aftermath of Vyner's death, though as he was travelling in France at the time he could have known nothing about the tragedy. A year later he wrote an account of the strange, paranormal grief he had experienced. He recalled that while he was in Nice, 'watching the play of light on the sea', he thought often about Vyner, 'laughing to myself at the fun we would have with him when he came home.' Yet only three days later, having journeyed north to Paris, he had a sudden feeling that Vyner was dead. 'I suppose I shall carry that sensation to my dying day, that tightness of the breast, the fullness of the heart, that indescribable sickness.' He immediately went to the British Embassy, where the truth was confirmed. That night he went back to England, and at home in London saw in *The Times* the report of Vyner's death. 'There it was, all categorical, all clear, all hopeless. I locked the door and looked on it with dry sobs. Why had he gone? His life was beautiful and pleasant. He lived in an atmosphere of love.' For months afterwards Rosebery was plagued by dreams that Vyner was still alive. 'The waking was very bitter,' he told Vyner's mother. Rosebery concluded his account with this tormented passage: 'As I sit and remember these things in the sunlight, with the birds singing in the scented air of spring, writing them as I think of them, there is a certain Voiceless Presence as if he were not altogether absent. How often have I seen him in my dreams since then, sometimes as I knew and loved him, sometimes with a pale absent look which is not of this world. I can believe in no future state where we can be divided. I hardly think that Death divides us now.'[55]

It would be hard to deny the homoerotic undercurrent of these words.

Indeed, his reference to not being 'divided' from Vyner finds an echo in the famous line of the lesbian novel *The Well of Loneliness*, in which Radclyffe Hall wrote, of the female lovers' consummation, 'that night, they were not divided' – a line that caused a sensation when the book was published in 1928 and eventually led to its being banned for obscenity. And the suspicion that Rosebery delighted in Vyner's youthful looks is reinforced by the obituary he produced for the *Morning Post* in which he wrote of Vyner's 'irresistible' and 'eminently lovable' attractions, 'his noble head and swinging stride', his 'languid grace', 'the pale brow fringed with black curls' and the 'sweet expression of his countenance'. Perhaps unsurprisingly, Rosebery insisted on anonymity. But in spite of his eulogising it can only be conjecture that Rosebery and Vyner enjoyed more than a boyish companionship, for there is no written evidence of any deeper relationship. Besides, just like Rosebery, by 1870 Vyner was responding to the appeal of women: at the time of his fatal trip to Greece he was in love with Muncaster's sister-in-law Mary L'Estrange and hoped to marry her.[56] What this episode does show, at the least, is that Rosebery's 'morbid sensitiveness' – to quote his daughter Sybil's phrase – was already part of him in his early twenties. In a letter to Gladstone's daughter Mary in 1881 he revealed how much he was still scarred by Vyner's death. 'The love of friends is to me the deepest of all love, for the same reason that one does not at all value what one inherits as what one acquires oneself. At first one believes that the absence, though painful, is only temporary. It is not for months afterwards that one realizes that it is forever as regards this world; never again to hear the voice or see the face that had become the fact of one's being through all the rest of the long pilgrimage on earth.'[57]

In that letter Rosebery rather disparaged the value he attached to his inheritance, but he did not hesitate to enjoy the fruits of it. Through the early 1870s he spent on an epic scale, particularly at the race-course. During one heavy week in February 1872 he noted in his diary that 'the fortune of a Rothschild would not stand another such day' – a wonderfully prescient comment. Such were his worries about his own profligacy that he occasionally withdrew from the turf to give his funds some respite, which led to good-natured teasing from his friends and self-deprecation on his own part. 'Circumstances (pecuniary) over which I need not dwell did not allow my going to Newmarket at my own expense. Thank heaven the Turf knows me no more till it covers me. I have had a bad year's racing and if it had not been for some evil-smelling paraffin* I *must* have left the

---

*This is a jocular reference to the brood mare Paraffin, purchased in 1870 to begin his stud.

country,' he wrote in 1871 to Ousley Higgins.[58] Lord Randolph Churchill wrote a joshing response to the news: 'I had in my folly and blindness believed that in spite of your many faults and imperfections you possessed to a great degree the virtue of liberality. I regret greatly to find that this one virtue has given place to the vice of extreme parsimony.'[59] In similar vein the Marquess of Huntly sent him a letter with a cartoon of Rosebery sitting beside an empty safe on which was emblazoned the slogan 'The squire's last shilling'. Huntly added below: 'Trusting that the beaks have not yet got possession of Dalmeny Park and House under the iron arm of the law and that your lordship will be spared to amuse the ladies of Edinburgh and the company in general. PS. For fear you have not got one, I enclose a postage stamp for your reply.'[60]

But Rosebery's indebtedness was something of a pose. Far from having imperilled Dalmeny, he was actually able to extend his possessions with the purchase of an eighteenth-century, ivy-clad house in Epsom, The Durdans, whose proximity to the race-course was one of its chief attractions. Having paid £25,000 for it in May 1874 he then greatly improved the property, adding paddocks and a magnificent library which Gladstone later described as one of the finest in the country. The combination of its racing associations, the charms of rural Epsom and the fact that he had bought rather than inherited it made The Durdans his favourite home, his 'beloved nest' as he used to call it. Later he gave an evocative account of how he had fallen under its spell on his very first visit. 'It was a beautiful day in summer and the bright sun lighted up the undulating grounds and ancient trees of The Durdans with its golden rays, setting off the sloping banks, the shrubbery and the grassy meadows to the utmost advantage. A wood pigeon flew across the glade and alighted upon a neighbouring tree. Presently the clear, soft notes of the cushat rang out from its leafy perch. "That will decide," I thought. "To hear the woodpigeons cooing within fifteen minutes of Hyde Park is itself a sufficient recommendation."'[61] Even as Prime Minister he would frequently travel from Downing Street to spend the night there. At The Durdans Rosebery established a breeding stable – another indicator of his real financial confidence – and after a string of humiliations in the wake of the 1869 Ladas Derby fiasco his fortunes on the turf finally began to improve. In 1873 he won his first important race, the Gimcrack Stakes, with Padarorshna, and then Aldrich proved triumphant in the City and Suburban, while his three-year-old Couronne de Fer finished second in the Derby.

Nor did Rosebery feel inhibited about leading a full life away from the race-course, as this entry from his diary shows: '*May 21 1873*: Remained in bed till 2, having gone to bed at 5 the previous day. Called on Lady Charles Ker. Presided at the Committee of the St James Club. Called on Mrs Vyner. Dined with Mr and Mrs Love. Afterwards to the Court Ball where I remained until 2.30.' Similarly, in August 1874 he went to two fancy-dress balls in one week in the same costume of Bluebeard the Pirate. This had embarrassing consequences, as he explained to Sam Ward. 'I had nothing on but a toque with a feather, a blue beard, blue powder, with a pink tunic and a maillot. I discovered how thin my costume was at another fancy ball given two days afterwards at Apsley House. I went with my partner into the garden and sitting down on a seat uttered a loud shriek. It turned out that there was a pool of water on the seat and as I had no breeches on, nothing indeed but my tights, I was drenched behind, so much so that the ballroom knew me no more.'[62]

Yet Rosebery was a far more complex figure than his extravagant habits at this period might suggest. In truth there was within him a perpetual conflict between a powerful, aristocratic sense of duty, and an attachment to sensual idleness. It was as if his stern, religious, moral, conscientious side was fighting for inner supremacy against his artistic, irresponsible, selfish, decadent side. In his writings he referred quite openly to this friction at the core of his personality, talking of the need for vigilance to ensure that 'my memory is strengthened and cultivated' and 'my immoral feelings and wicked passions thrown on the dung heap'.[63] At the end of his first trip to America in 1873 he wrote that as he drew nearer to England 'the struggle between duty and pleasure becomes more apparent . . . the hour is late, the times are evil, let us at any rate put our shoulders to the wheel.'[64] Indeed, one of the reasons he believed in keeping a diary was as an incentive to strengthening his own moral fibre: 'What an inducement to improvement, what a reproof to the stationary, what a lash to those who have retro-graded,' he claimed.[65] Even the most minor indulgences could bring out his Protestant guilt. 'Did a really selfish thing for dinner. Drank some '48 claret alone,' he recorded.[66]

Like writing, reading could act as a spur to service and sacrifice. 'A wise man should read and meditate on some part of a masterpiece each day to give himself the proper mental tone. Coleridge says that the language can never be vulgar of a man who studies his Bible.'[67] Biography, he argued, 'tells us what has been, what virtue, what courage, what patience, what unselfishness. We know the possible for we know what has been compassed through her and we burn to emulate or exceed.' Sometimes, he admitted, his conscience could be pricked by what he read. Of Flaubert's *L'Éducation sentimentale* he noted: 'There is one fine moral pervading every page: the emptiness of a life of pleasure.'[68] After completing a book titled *Lord Bantam*, about a young peer who is immersed in radical politics, exposed to the temptations of wealth and then succeeds to a title, he wrote that 'I may have been stung by what satire I found in it. It has often been a painful question to me – the contemplation of a possible and probable position in which principle would contend with selfishness in politics. I sometimes think the right would conquer, sometimes the wrong.' The only solution, he said, 'is to have laboured steadily and blindly in the cause of what belief one may be possessed of.'[69]

The discord within Rosebery was reflected as much in his actions as his words. Thus, in America he was one moment admiring Sam Ward's collection of lithographs from the Marquis de Sade's depraved *Justine,* the next arranging to pay for the college education of a black youth in New York. Back in London, he might attend a lavish dinner, take in the theatre, enjoy a supper at the Turf Club, then go home to read a book on Christian communism. In Edinburgh he might slaughter pheasants in the morning at Dalmeny, then in the afternoon deliver a lecture at an industrial school. But one of the most graphic illustrations of this dual existence occurs in his reflections on a weekend at the beginning of April 1873. On the Saturday evening he went with Alma Egerton to a 'tremendous supper' given at the home of his journalist friend Frank Lawley of the *Daily Telegraph.* Other guests included the Prince of Wales, his uncle the Duke of Edinburgh, and 'several actresses'. Rosebery's account continues: 'We had a great deal of romping and bear-fighting. The Duke of Edinburgh sat cross-legged on a pole and did something with a walking stick and four gloves. Then we had cock-fighting between the Duke and Christopher Sykes, then trying to light a candle in an odd position, then a can-can quadrille, then the Duke of Edinburgh on the hornpipe. Finally, having lasted from midnight to half-past four the supper broke up. I drove Alma Egerton home and did not get to bed until 5.30.'

The next day he was up at 8.45 in the morning to go to the City Tabernacle in Islington to hear a sermon by the celebrated nonconformist preacher Charles Spurgeon. He was deeply moved by the scene. 'With every seat crammed, every sound hushed, every eye eagerly fixed upon one central figure, the effect is sublime.' He was further struck by the composition of the audience, who were 'entirely middle-class without, so far as I could see, a single exception. Neither the upper nor the lower classes are represented. Spurgeon is the apostle of the grocers.' His experience at the Tabernacle compelled Rosebery to analyse the struggle in the British civic order, which mirrored that within his own psyche: 'Which would win the battle, "Society" flabby, flippant and enervated with no ostensible strength except that wealth which is in reality its greatest weakness – or this serious band of ironsides and round-heads, nerved by conviction and animated by genius? The battle has been fought before, and we know the certain result.'[70]

On another level too war was being waged within Rosebery: the war for his political soul.

3

'I shall be devoted to you, Archie'

❦

'T HE GREAT IMPORTANCE of establishing a fellow feeling between class and class cannot surely be over-estimated. You have on your side that feeling of fellowship, you are born to a leading position in the world and therefore on you sits the burden of taking the initiative,' Edward 'Blackie' Hope told his friend Lord Rosebery in 1871, urging him to take a leading role in politics.[1] Hope's words fell on already fertile ground, for Rosebery had long since decided that his duty lay in some form of public service. As early as 1868, when he was still at Christ Church, he had said to William Johnson that he intended to go into politics, prompting his former tutor to announce that he had 'revived the imaginative hopes that I formed years ago when you began Eton life'.[2] His intellect and oratorical skill, allied to his family's name, wealth and aristocratic connections, meant that even as a youth he was assiduously courted by both parties. He was, after all, not only the inheritor a great title, but also the son of a late Liberal Member of Parliament and the stepson of a Tory duke. Those two giants of the late Victorian age, Gladstone and Disraeli, were equally determined to recruit this prodigy to their own causes.

Disraeli was the first to make his acquaintance. In August 1865 he and his wife were guests at the Duke of Cleveland's northern home Raby Castle in Northumberland. Dalmeny, as he then was, had just finished his schooling at Eton, and immediately fell under the spell of the exotic couple, as his diary at the time reveals:

August 31   Mama came in from riding when they were all in the library; so she said, 'I was sorry to be so rude as not to be here to receive you, but the fact is that I had such a bad headache that I was obliged to go and take a ride.' To which Dizzy replied with an air, 'The pleasure of seeing Your Grace in your riding habit makes up for the loss of your society' – the kind of compliment in fact that one sees in *Coningsby*. I sat next to Mrs Disraeli at dinner . . . 'Do you care for politics, Mrs Disraeli?' 'No, I have no time, I have so many books and pamphlets to see if there is my name in any of them! And I have everything to manage and write his stupid letters. I am sorry when he is in office, because then I lose him altogether and though I have many people who call themselves my friends yet I have no friend like him. I have not been separated from him since we have been in the country except when I have been in the woods, and I cannot lose him' (here her voice trembled touchingly) . . . I think this half-crazy, warm-hearted woman's talk is worth setting down, for she is an uncommon specimen. Parts are very touching.

September 1   Mrs Disraeli greeted me at breakfast with, 'We have been talking about you.' 'I am indeed honoured, Mrs Disraeli.' 'Oh, but I did not say it was very good.' 'But to be talked about by you is enough honour.' I cannot help quizzing her by talking in this way though I really like her. She praised me in her own and her husband's name very warmly this evening.[3]

Dalmeny also enjoyed his verbal repartee with Disraeli. On the third morning of the visit, Disraeli came up to him and asked if he was going out shooting.

DALMENY: Partridges are scarce and today we intend to kill nothing but time.
DISRAELI: Then you have a certain bag.

The young aristocrat and the Tory leader took long walks together, during which Disraeli talked frankly about a vast range of subjects, including his difficult relationship with Sir Robert Peel, the orators of his time, the problems of Tory party finance, and the award of patronage. Of the Whig peer Lord Granville Disraeli made a remark which was to be of the greatest significance for Rosebery's future: 'He might have been Prime Minister once, and he ought to have accepted even with the certainty of failure, as it is a great thing to have one's name on the list of Prime Ministers.'[4] Like so many others, Disraeli was charmed by his new friend, describing him as 'very intelligent and formed for his time of life, and not a prig, which might be feared.'[5]

The friendship deepened over subsequent years, underpinned by shared humour, eighteenth-century cynicism, artistic sensibilities, and love of literature. The affection between them is revealed in several of Disraeli's letters, such as this one from September 1868 when Disraeli was in Rosebery's native land: 'This is my first visit to the highlands and I am quite delighted with all I see.' He then explained that his travelling companion Lord Bute reminded him of Tancred: 'I never venture to quote my own books but I can to you because I know you read them. Few things please me more than to hear from you.'[6] Mrs Disraeli, in telling her friends that the young Rosebery heir was rather 'smitten' with her, was perhaps only describing her own feelings, as Lord Randolph Churchill hinted in an invitation to his home, Blenheim Palace in Oxfordshire: 'Mrs Dizzy is here and is dreadfully disappointed not to meet you here. She is certain to have a fit if you do not come.'[7] Rosebery's journals are full of warm references to Disraeli. In December 1870 they met at a dinner at Stratfield Saye, the Duke of Wellington's house near Reading; 'Afterwards I walked for some time under Mr Disraeli's arm, up and down the gallery, he more I fear to avoid the general conversation than from any particular wish to talk to me. The Bishop compared us, I should have thought inappropriately, to Faust and Marguerite.'[8] Of a meeting at the Doncaster race-course in September 1875 he recorded: 'Saw Disraeli who told me it was his first St Leger. I regretted to him that Phorphorus did not run (vide *Sybil*). "Ah," he said, "you are my only literary friend so I may confess to you that I have never seen the Leger though I have described it. Had you any horses running today? I have not seen the papers today but I always look at the sporting column to watch your horses run."'[9] In December 1876 he met Disraeli at a dinner hosted by the Prince of Wales. 'He was very affectionate, calling me "dear child" and pressing my hand against his heart. He talked much about Mr Gladstone: "His character baffles me".'[10]

For all the puzzlement Gladstone caused Disraeli, it was his Liberal party that eventually proved more politically attractive to Rosebery. In the course of their first walks together in 1865 Disraeli had recognised that his companion had few Tory leanings, as a conversation with Mrs Disraeli confirmed: 'He is so delighted with his walk,' she told Dalmeny during the couple's visit to Raby, 'and so pleased with you. He is so sorry there is no chance of your being in the House of Commons. He would so like to have some young men like you to follow him. But then you are a Whig.' 'Who told you so?' 'He did.' Rosebery's tone of surprise was hardly credible; after all, both his father and his grandfather had served under the Whig and Liberal banner in Scotland. Furthermore, he had revealed Whig sympathies throughout his youth, encouraged by his tutor William Johnson, who told him that 'it would be much safer to be with prolific, originative intellects, with generous and enthusiastic temperaments' than with Tory thinking, 'which throws cold water on plans of improvement'.[11] As a student at Christ Church he once delivered a radical harangue to a mob of rioters in the city centre, hardly the conduct of an earnest young Tory. And in 1867, while he was at Oxford, his mother approached him with the idea of his standing at the next election as the Conservative candidate for Darlington, where the Cleveland influence could make itself felt. Rosebery's reply demonstrated that even if he was not yet politically committed, he had neither any time for the Tories nor any wish to oblige his mother: 'The first objection is that, though I have no politics and have never professed any, I am not at all prepared to come forward as a Conservative. Besides the Conservative party has practically ceased to exist and I think we shall see an entire transmutation of parties before 1869.'[12]

It was in 1869, more than four years after he had first met Disraeli, that Rosebery was contacted by the Gladstones, when the Prime Minister's wife invited him to a 'little dance' at Hawarden. 'Having known your mother so long I feel as though I ought to make an acquaintance,' she wrote.[13] In the same year Rosebery was introduced to Granville, the Liberal leader in the Lords, who was so impressed by the recently-elevated young peer's 'very friendly manner' that he invited him to second the Address in the Upper House at the opening of Parliament, if he felt he had 'sufficient confidence in Gladstone's Government'.[14] Rosebery's reply was a masterpiece of affected self-deprecation in the style for which he later became so well known in the political world. 'I cannot be insensible of the flattering nature of your offer, however incapable I feel of seconding the Address in a way either satisfactory to myself or anybody else,' he wrote. 'But you probably do not know that I am only a resident undergraduate of Oxford working for a pass degree and it might damage the Government if, with no counter-balancing quality, the Peer who seconded the Address was a lad In Statu Pupillari.' Despite these doubts, Rosebery confirmed his allegiance to Liberalism: 'My private sympathies and my reason have been wholly enlisted in the Liberal cause for some years: and as in June I must choose one side or the other, I see no use in postponing that choice for a few months, when I have so thoroughly made up my mind and so excellent an opportunity occurs of making that mind known to you. I can never be of the slightest use to the party, though I should be proud of any opportunity of showing my attachment to its principles. Still I sincerely feel that the fact I mentioned at the beginning of the letter must be a disadvantage to the Government, so I feel I must decline your kind offer.'[15] Even though his offer had been rejected, Granville was delighted at the news that he had won a glittering recruit to the Liberal benches in the Lords. He showed this letter to Gladstone, who, as Granville told Rosebery, 'was much gratified at the explanation you give in it of your political intention.'[16]

In future decades Rosebery's adherence to Liberalism was often regarded with cynicism, as if he had been bewitched by Gladstone and thus ended up in the wrong party. Lord Birkenhead, the Unionist Lord Chancellor of the 1920s, summed up this view: 'The truth is that he could never make up his mind completely on any subject. When the battle developed, Lord

Rosebery was not in the thick of it. His misfortune was that he was seduced by youthful credulity, by his own emotional and sometimes splendid rhetoric, and by the magnetism of Gladstone into membership of a party with which he never agreed and he was therefore one day bound to quarrel.'[17] To his critics, the words about political allegiance used by Rosebery in his 1906 biography of Lord Randolph Churchill seemed as applicable to the author as to the subject: 'Men are netted early into political clubs; or fall, when callow, under the influence of some statesman; or stand as a youth for some constituency before they have considered the problems of life. Many never consider them at all; but those who do must often find themselves in disagreement with the politics that they prematurely confessed.'[18] Yet in reality there was nothing eccentric or rebellious about Rosebery's decision. Before the great convulsion in British politics caused by the problem of Irish Home Rule there was little conflict between liberalism and landowning, since politics were not then divided vertically by class. Gladstone's cabinet of 1880, for example, contained two great landed magnates in the Duke of Argyll and the Earl of Derby. With his Whig heredity, Rosebery in his youth was certainly progressive, eager to question tradition and embrace reform, as he had shown in the debates of the Eton 'Pop'. Though he had squandered some of his expensive formal education, he had made up for it with the intensity of his subsequent private studies, which added to the originality of his political thinking. His reading, in which he was guided by the Principal of St Andrews University, Professor James Donaldson, was extraordinary in its breadth, ranging from French fourteenth-century history to the geography of the Sandwich Islands. In a contradiction of his dilettante reputation, he would often rise before six in the morning to work in his study either at Dalmeny or The Durdans. 'Remained in all day reading a voluminous Foreign Affairs bluebook,' he noted in his diary on 7 February 1871.[19] Rosebery was soon a figure well-known to the booksellers of Edinburgh and London, though some of his political material must have raised eyebrows. 'Went into Hackett's and ordered some communist books,' he recorded.[20] His sense of social concern was further deepened by his visits to the Clydeside ship-building works, where he became friendly with several of the engineers. There is a story that Rosebery, during a stay in Glasgow, called at the home of one of these engineers, with whom he corresponded frequently on political issues. Finding the youngest daughter busy with her mathematics homework, he said to her, 'I don't believe I could do those sums.' 'Well, ye wudna pass yer fifth grade,' the little girl told him. Similarly, in London his closeness to Canon William Rogers, the old Etonian radical campaigning Rector of

Bishopgate, encouraged in Rosebery a compassion for the sufferings of the unemployed of the East End, which eventually led to his emergence as the dominant force in London municipal politics. Just as influential were his early visits to America. The frustration he felt over the rigidities of English society was all too apparent in the last page of the journal recording his 1873 trip:

> I am back in England. Miserably smoky and narrow as ever. Is it a dream that I have been in a country where all are born equal before the law? Where every man has the means of obtaining the dearest object of the Anglo-Saxon's heart, a plot of land of his own on which to live and die? Where each son of the soil carries in his wallet not the staff of a field marshal, for field marshals are abhorrent to the spirit of the country, but a possible pass-port to the White House, to the Bench of the Supreme Court, to every emi-nent person without exception that the State can afford. Where none as in heaven is before or after another, where none can afford to shut himself up in the shallow exclusiveness of wealth, lest he be left fixed though not a star, where every citizen is a conductor of the electric spark of political power.[21]

In 1871, two years after Rosebery had declined Granville's invitation to speak at the opening of Parliament, the Liberal leader in the Lords tried again. This time he was more successful, and Rosebery agreed to second the Address. Wearing the striking green uniform of a member of The Queen's Bodyguard for Scotland, the Royal Company of Archers, com-plete with feathered bonnet, the 5th Earl of Rosebery made his maiden Parliamentary speech on 10 February 1871. He was just 23 years old. It was a typically precocious, flowing performance. The bulk of it was devoted to the current Franco-Prussian war, and Rosebery spoke in graphic terms of the heroism shown during the siege of Paris: 'For four months she held on, she fed her population of epicures on husks and rats, yet there was little repining and no crime.' He went on to express the hope that 'when this disastrous war is concluded' the German Empire 'may use her great power in the interests of peace and civilisation.'[22] At the end of his speech Rosebery was warmly congratulated from the benches opposite by the Duke of Richmond, who made reference to the seconder's 'conspicuous ability', while *The Times* commented that 'the Earl spoke with a graceful emotion which became his years.' It was not a flawless performance, how-ever, as Rosebery struggled to master the difficult acoustics of the Lords, something that he never quite achieved in all his long career. Three months later he spoke in support of the Bill to abolish clerical (religious) tests for university admissions, provoking the magisterial anger of Lord Salisbury, who complained that Rosebery's opinions were based on nothing more than the gossip of Oxford scouts. But on the Liberal side, the Earl of Kimberley was struck by Rosebery's maturity: 'He made a clever speech with a good deal of acid humour, unusual in a young man.'[23]

Another notable speech came later in the year when, in November, he spoke to the Edinburgh Philosophical Society about the union between England and Scotland. To an extent this address suffered from over-preparation. Crammed as it was with historical references, much of it read like an essay; one commentator described it as 'well put together but rather dull in parts'.[24] But it was the peroration that electrified his audience and displayed the vigour of his radicalism:

> A powerless monarchy, an isolated aristocracy, an intelligent and aspiring people do not altogether form the conditions of constitutional stability. We have to restore a common pulse, a healthy beat to the heart of the Commonwealth. It is a great work – the work of individuals as much as statesmen, alien from none of us, rather pertinent to us all. Each in his place can further it. Each one, merchant and clerk, master and servant, landlord and tenant, capitalist and artisan, minister and parishioner, we are all privileged to have a hand in this work, the most sublime of all, to restore and create harmony between man and man, to look, not for the differences which chance or necessity has placed between class and class, but for the common sympathies which underlie and connect all humanity.[25]

This was an eloquent summary of what was to remain, for all the mockery to which he was later subjected, Rosebery's political outlook for the rest of his political career. At the turn of the century he wrote to the journalist Charles Geake in very similar terms: 'Liberalism mainly consists in the determination that neither class nor creed nor privilege shall hinder the progress of our national development.'[26]

The Duchess, a High Tory, was aghast at this effusion. Taking particular objection to the phrase 'an isolated aristocracy', she told her son imperiously that 'men are not better esteemed in other classes for deprecating their own'. Rosebery's response showed no inclination to surrender to maternal fury. 'I maintain, and no Liberal can say otherwise, that the House of Lords is isolated in sympathies from the country. And I say that no Liberal can think otherwise because the House of Lords rejects those measures which the country, through its representatives, has ratified. On that ground therefore I had a perfect right to use the word isolated.'[27] Her assertion that he should not criticise his own class ran utterly counter to his views: 'Your argument strikes at the very root of political morality. I hope it will be long in England before people act or speak merely to please a class or classes.'

Outraging his mother, filling the newspaper columns, winning glowing tributes from his fellow peers, Rosebery was becoming firmly established as an important figure in society. Already a friend of the Prince of Wales, he was first invited by Queen Victoria to dine at Windsor Castle in May 1870. 'Lord Rosebery is pleasing and gentleman-like and wonderfully young-looking,' she recorded in her journal.[28] In the autumn Rosebery spent three nights at Balmoral, which he said had the ugliest drawing room in Britain. In his account of the visit he described the first evening: 'The conversation during dinner was sustained and almost gay. If one talks to one's neighbours the Queen, who has a very sharp ear, joins in the conversation. The dinner is served very rapidly & coffee after it. When coffee is finished, the Queen rises, we also rise and stand behind our chairs, and the Queen comes slowly round the circle, talking for five minutes or so with each. When this circuit is finished she retires with Princess Louise, and the rest with Prince Arthur adjourn to the billiard room and play at billiard bowls. We retire about 11.30.'[29] Rosebery was also winning glowing opinions from journalists. It was in April 1872 that he first met Frank Lawley of the *Daily Telegraph*, who could hardly have been more fulsome in his praise. 'I have seldom met one so young who had so well digested his reading or who gave more earnest of a wise and firm manhood. I have been thinking of him constantly today and yesterday. If I met many youngsters like Rosebery, I would live in the West End and dine out every other night,' he wrote to Ousley Higgins.[30]

Most important of all was the confidence in him shown by the senior Liberal politicians, especially Gladstone. 'I had a long talk with Mr Gladstone this morning who spoke most warmly and kindly of Rosebery, of his character and ability, adding, "I have often thought of proposing that noblemen should be permitted even when in full possession of their titles to sit in the House of Commons until they had reached the age of 25",' Lawley reported to Higgins in June of a conversation with the Prime Minister.[31] Considering that Gladstone was at the zenith of his powers and Rosebery had made just a handful of speeches, this was a vivid illustration of the impact he had already made in the political world. Rosebery himself heard indirectly of Gladstone's high opinion. Walking down Pall Mall after a breakfast with Gladstone and some artists on 6 May 1872, he ran into the painter J.G. Herbert, who said, 'I like to tell a young man what may cheer him in his pilgrimage. As you passed out this morning, Mr Gladstone nudged me and said, "Look at that young man – that will be a man of great mark some of these days."'[32]

In fact Gladstone was so impressed with Rosebery that already, in February 1872, he had offered him a job in Government combining both

Royal and political responsibilities, as a Lord-in-Waiting representing the
Poor Law Board in the Upper House. Rosebery turned it down, establishing a pattern that was to be endlessly repeated over the next twenty
years, pointing to his 'incompetency to perform satisfactorily either class
of the duties which would devolve upon me.'[33] A year later Gladstone met
the same response when he offered Rosebery the post of Lord Lieutenant
of Linlithgow. On this occasion Rosebery explained rather haughtily that
he was too rarely in Scotland to fulfil the obligations entailed, at the same
time admitting that the 'office of Lord Lieutenant has, I believe, in Scotland
at least, hardly any public duties.'[34] It was an early indication of the perplexing nature of his new political ally, but Gladstone was unwilling to
accept rejection. He asked Granville to speak to Rosebery, then on 22 May
summoned the young peer for an interview. In the detailed account
Rosebery kept of their meeting it is clear from Gladstone's arguments how
loyal he remained to the Monarchy, despite Queen Victoria's personal vindictiveness towards her Prime Minister. 'He spoke very kindly but dwelt
especially on the duty which I owed the Queen. During Her Majesty's present retirement powerful influences, even if they were negative, were daily
undermining the throne and that its future depended on those who stood
with the inner concentric circle around it.' Gladstone added – and a slight
note of blackmail is discernible – that if he had to tell the Queen, 'who
forgot nothing', then 'she would remember my refusal of the lordship-in-
waiting and associate the two matters.' Rosebery's account concluded: 'Mr
Gladstone said that there was no one he could appoint with so much satisfaction as myself and it was not a matter of selfish consideration but a
matter of duty. I sat mute but at last I said I could not see any duty
involved.'[35] Under such pressure Rosebery nevertheless capitulated, telling
Gladstone that 'if you still wish or think it proper to appoint me, I will
defer to you.'[36] At last, after so much persuasion, he had set a reluctant foot
on the ladder of political responsibility.

In his public utterances Rosebery continued to give full vent to his radicalism. During the Lords debate on the Scottish Education Bill in July
1872 he came out strongly in favour of nondenominational teaching in
schools, a cause dear to the Liberal nonconformists. Accepting the
Freedom of Queensferry in September he spoke in support of the claims
of agricultural workers, urging them to form their own trade union. In the
Lords, he argued for the secret ballot and the reform of Church patronage
in Scotland. But it was a speech he delivered in Glasgow in September 1874
that dramatically raised his profile as both an orator and an advanced democrat. He had been asked to preside at the annual meeting of the Social

Science Congress, another indicator of his growing stature. As President, Rosebery might have been expected to make some Whiggish, platitudinous remarks in his address to the congress. Instead, he used the platform to launch a passionate attack on the failure of Parliament to improve the living standards of the working class. In emotive words that could have come from any trade unionist, Rosebery said that 'Parliament can give a workman a vote, but it cannot give him a comfortable home . . . In this city we are surrounded by a great aggregate of humanity – seething, labouring, begrimed humanity; children of toil who have made Glasgow what she is and alone can raise and maintain her; not mere machines of production but vehicles of intelligence.' Warning that this section of British civilisation was 'little removed from barbarism', he dwelt in more detail on the hellish lives of the impoverished under-class, such as the 30,000 children working in the brickfields, 'looking like the moving masses of the clay they bore.' The most urgent task, Rosebery argued, was to introduce a system of universal, compulsory state education. Such a measure would reduce not only pauperism and crime, but also industrial conflict. Just as importantly, it would mean that Britain did not 'lag behind in the world of commerce'. In outlining his case for improved education, he took direct swipes at the aristocracy, and at his former school. 'The only class for which, so far as I know, technical education is never even proposed is the class for which it is most necessary – I mean our rulers. Is there any school or college in Great Britain which professes to educate men for Government or statesmanship? Eton, I believe, trains a very large proportion of our legislators yet I have grave doubts if Eton provides any special instruction for them in their future duties.' The House of Lords was also subjected to a verbal assault. 'We have no hereditary surgeons or priests or soldiers or lawyers. We have, however, a large body of hereditary legislators . . . For these technical education is not provided or even contemplated. We agree that an artisan cannot do his work properly without special instruction; but for those to whom we entrust our fates, our fortunes and our honour, no such training is requisite. It is expected that a peer should take to politics as a duck takes to swimming.'[37]

Rosebery's Glasgow address inevitably led to controversy. Francis Knollys, the Prince of Wales's secretary, wrote to Rosebery to warn him that his words had caused 'an uncomfortable impression in Royal circles'.[38] But no one could deny that, as an orator of the highest promise, he had arrived. His delivery was compelling, his content imaginative. His hours of private study, about which his turf friends knew little, were reflected in the evidence he used to support his arguments: statistics on Swiss productivity, wage inflation in the mining industry, Prussian schooling, trade unionism in America, and Belgian public housing were all quoted to effect. Fascinatingly, many of the themes in that speech, especially those dealing with the need for technical training, Lords reform and the irrelevance of so much Parliamentary business, were still at the heart of his political philosophy at the beginning of the next century.

In a rare moment of self-congratulation, Rosebery admitted in his diary that his Glasgow performance had been 'fairly successful'.[39] Yet the attractions of pleasure remained as powerful as ever, as this account of a day in March 1874 reveals. 'Lunched at the Gridiron; afterwards a walk in the park with Lady Charles Ker; dined with Knollys and Carrington; afterwards to Eldorado at the Strand theatre; then to the Turf; then Lady Cork's ball.'[40] Nor was his publicly vaunted esteem for the working class always translated into his private life, which was very often characterised by the luxury he condemned in others. '*September 19th 1875*   Arrived at York to find the 1 a.m. train did not run until 2.30 a.m. So had to wait. Obliging guard number one let my bag fall, breaking a pint of champagne provided to make me sleep and spoiling my bag. Obliging guard number two secured me the only empty compartment and then held it pompously open so another traveller bounced in and was not be dislodged. It was decidedly not my evening.'

Rosebery was as dedicated to racing as ever, not least because he was enjoying more success with his horses; 1876 was his best year to date, as Controversy won the Lincolnshire Handicap and six other races. But his link with the turf was frowned upon by those who wanted him to devote himself to politics. In fact, Gladstone was so concerned that his sporting pursuits were 'engrossing too much of his time' and distracting him 'from a sense of responsibility and studious habits' that the journalist Frank Lawley felt it necessary to mediate on Rosebery's behalf. After several talks with the Prime Minister, Lawley reported that he had 'obtained from Mr Gladstone a tacit acquiescence and a promise that your connection with the turf should not operate to your prejudice in his eyes. It was abundantly evident that he would rather you did not and he was eloquent about the absorption of time and thought of which race-horses are the occasion. But I told him that a discreet and prudent connection with the turf (such as yours was sure to be) would make you popular and extend your influence.'[41] Gladstone may have acquiesced, but others remained anxious that Rosebery was showing insufficient diligence, as indicated by this letter from the MP Edward Horsman: 'It is a very interesting and critical period for you and I should like very much to try to show you how much there is both to inspire and repay you in the future, if you really brace yourself to a life worthy of your opportunities and gifts. But time is very precious and great prizes are not won without consciousness of the necessity for great efforts.'[42] Moreover, Rosebery's image in some sections of the press still tended to be that of a frivolous young man. In an article in 1876 the *Daily Telegraph* issued a warning in rather hectoring tones. 'Lord Rosebery has hitherto had scanty opportunity of showing how much or how little of real practical ability there may be in his composition. But he who would rise to an eminent position among counsellors in whose hands are our national destinies must remember that long indulgence in what seem to many the natural and congenial pleasures of youth is certain to be purchased at too dear a price.'[43] A profile in *Vanity Fair*, written by the magazine's founder Thomas Gibson Bowles, adopted a tone of condescension: 'He is very fresh and pretty, very popular, well-dressed and known in the clubs and under thirty. He may, if he will, became a statesman and a personage.'[44]

All this was somewhat unfair, since by the mid 1870s Rosebery was increasingly active in politics. In 1875 he spoke out bravely and humorously against the Bill to give Queen Victoria the title 'Empress of India', which was not intended for use in Britain. Comparing the Bill to a medicine, Rosebery told the Lords that it 'might properly be labelled poisonous, for outward application only'. He chaired a Committee of Enquiry into the methods of electing Scottish representative peers,★ became President of the Glasgow Public School Union, and made a speech to the fledgling Working Men's Club and Institute Union in which he condemned the puritan obsession with the drinking habits of the working class. The high priest of Victorian free trade radicalism, the MP John Bright, was moved to comment in his diary after meeting Rosebery for the first time: 'Intelligent and liberal. My impression of him very favourable.'[45] More significantly, in late 1876 he joined in the ferocious attack made by Gladstone on the Eastern policy of the Conservative government. The Liberals had lost the 1874 General Election and Gladstone had announced his resignation from the Liberal leadership in 1875, after which he was nominally a backbencher. What galvanised him into a return to front-line politics was the news of the massacre of thousands of Bulgarian Christians by Turkish irregular troops. In September 1876 his pamphlet *The Bulgarian*

★ Since the Union of Scotland and England under Queen Anne a Scottish peerage had conferred no automatic right to sit in the House of Lords. Instead, Scottish peers elected from among themselves a set number of representatives. Rosebery's earldom was a Scottish peerage, but he sat in the Upper House as Baron Rosebery in the peerage of the United Kingdom, a title conferred on his grandfather in 1828.

Horrors and the Question of the East set Britain ablaze and marked the beginning of a moral crusade against Disraeli (now Earl of Beaconsfield), who was accused of indifference to the Turkish Empire's cruelty. Those who thought of Rosebery as a cynic must have been surprised by the passion of his denunciations of Tory foreign policy over the next two years, culminating in a slashing speech at Aberdeen in October 1878 in which he excoriated the Treaty of Berlin recently negotiated by Beaconsfield as a settlement of the Eastern question. 'What have the Government done? They have partitioned Turkey, they have secured a doubtful fragment of the spoil for themselves. They have abandoned Greece, they have incurred responsibilities of a vast and unknown kind, which no British Government has a right to incur without consulting the British Parliament and British people.'

Away from politics, Rosebery was ready for another, much more personal form of commitment. From the time he left Oxford his friends had been wondering when he might marry, and the gossip columns had linked his name with a string of English and American society beauties. The fevered speculation that surrounded his intentions was captured in a letter in May 1874 from his close friend Edward 'Blackie' Hope: 'I have been in awful tribulation since Saturday night. Then again yesterday I tried to muster up the courage to put to you the question, "Are you in love with Miss Grey?" I had my suspicions and if my suspicions are correct, for God's sake, my dear D., go in for the stake and win it if possible. It will be best for her, for me and I venture to think for you also. I told you that I long to see you happily married. I can now add that you have often been seen in my eye as the man. My proposal is not unselfish for, in the first place, I have no such claims to relinquish and, in the second, had I such claims I would be content to see her in the safe-keeping under the circumstances of my best friend.' The truth was, however, that Rosebery had no strong attachment to Miss Grey, the daughter of Lord Grey, whereas Blackie Hope was in love with her. Once this was revealed to Rosebery, he agreed to tell Miss Grey of his friend's love, and did so at a dinner hosted by the Prince of Wales. The result was a disaster because Hope, as he later admitted, had 'absurdly misjudged' the young woman's feelings. Ordered by the Grey family never to speak to their daughter again, Hope could only apologise to Rosebery for 'having dragged you into the matter and doubled the vexation and trouble on all sides.'[46]

Rosebery's character was always much less flippant than it was occasionally painted, and his grave side was demonstrated in the reverence with which he regarded the institution of marriage. When his elder sister Mary announced her engagement in July 1885 he wrote to his mother: 'I am one of the few who think that marriage is a serious matter, not in any case a matter for congratulation without much consideration. To me marriage, even of people I don't know, is the most solemn and awful of cere- monies.'[47] Furthermore, his solitary nature made him sometimes doubt whether he was equipped for such a union. In the course of his literary studies in 1872 he copied out this passage from an essay by the Scottish author Dr Robert Chambers: 'Solitude at home is my element and sup- plies a strong argument against matrimony. If the offensive peculiarities of others be so apt to distress me, why hazard my future tranquillity upon a wife?'[48]

But by 1877 Rosebery was certain he had finally found someone who would enhance rather than reduce his tranquillity. He had first met Hannah de Rothschild at a race meeting at Newmarket in 1868. It is often said that they were introduced by Mrs Disraeli, but in 1901 Rosebery gave the *Daily Mail* a probably embroidered description of their first encounter. 'His meeting with her was as romantic as anything ever conceived by any nov- elist. His carriage collided with hers and by extraordinary agility, combined with no less extraordinary presence of mind, he sprang out and caught her as she fell, having been thrown upward by the force of the impact. Then he carried her stunned to a neighbouring house.'[49] Revealingly, there is no reference to these exciting circumstances in either Hannah's or Rosebery's diaries.

Hannah, aged seventeen, happened to be at Newmarket because her father, Baron Meyer de Rothschild, was a devotee of the turf and owned a house there. He was the sixth of seven children born to the remarkable Nathan Meyer de Rothschild who arrived in Manchester in 1799 as a cloth merchant and, through diligence and acumen, extended the family bank- ing house into England, created a financial empire and established the Rothschilds' influence at the heart of British society. Baron Meyer – the title derived from an Austrian barony conferred on his father – used his inheritance to build Mentmore, one of the most imposing houses in England, on a 700-acre estate in Buckinghamshire. Work began in 1852 and the architect Baron Meyer hired was Joseph Paxton, whose revolu- tionary Crystal Palace had amazed Britain the year before and earned him the nickname of 'the new Christopher Wren'. For Mentmore Paxton chose a Jacobean style based on Wollaton Hall, the home of the Willoughby family outside Nottingham, and incorporated some of the innovations for which Crystal Palace had become so celebrated. Thus, tra- ditional mullioned windows were replaced by huge sheets of plate glass, providing spectacular views over the Vale of Aylesbury; the central hall was in effect an Elizabethan courtyard, covered with a forty-foot-high roof of glass.

Gigantic in size, Mentmore was designed to astound visitors rather than put them at ease. Indeed, Rosebery complained that he found the house inconvenient, as the Liberal politician Lewis 'Loulou' Harcourt recorded after a visit there. 'The house, especially the large hall, looks like the Louis XVI section of the Kensington Museum with the cases moved out and is about as comfortable (or the reverse). Rosebery says that when he came here before his marriage, he used to sit in his bath for comfort!'[50] This feeling of being in a museum can only have been increased by the unique collection of furniture and works of art which Baron Meyer had assembled in the course of his travels across Europe. 'I do not believe that the Medici were ever so lodged at the height of their glory,' wrote Lady Eastlake. The treasures included an enormous black-and-white marble fireplace bought from Rubens's house in Antwerp; three massive gilded lanterns taken from the barge of the Doges of Venice; a bureau belonging to Louis XV; crimson silk curtains and medieval tapestries; displays of Limoges enamels, Sèvres porcelain and eighteenth-century German and French silver; paintings by Turner and Murillo; and elaborately carved furniture from the ducal palace in Venice. The very guest bathrooms boasted Louis XVI marble-topped basins and commodes. Rosebery's daughter Peggy described the wonderment that Mentmore inspired in her as a small child:

> A riot of beauty and richness everywhere; carving, embroidery, marquetry and bronzes dazzled and bewildered senses accustomed to the sobrieties of the Scottish nursery. On either side of the great central hall were high doors of glass in narrow walnut frames. Through one door could be seen the broad marble staircase of shallow steps leading up to a landing on which stood scarlet chairs of state on either side of a pedestal surmounted by a marble head. Through the doors at the other end of this huge room more marble steps were visible; these led down to the south entrance and so on to the terrace. On the gilded tables in the south entrance were alabaster vases and also, for a time, stands on which perched red and blue macaws and a white cockatoo. The discordant cries of these birds and the brilliance of their plumage added to the strange sense of the exotic.[51]

Apart from housing his unrivalled art collection, Mentmore enabled Baron Meyer de Rothschild to pursue his other great interest, the ownership of horses. He established a successful stud farm nearby, and enjoyed a series of victories on the turf, winning the Thousand Guineas three times and the Goodwood Cup twice. Though he served as MP for Hythe for nearly fifteen years, he had few political ambitions. His marriage to his cousin Juliana Cohen proved happy, if not notably fertile, for Hannah, born in 1851, was their only child. Baroness de Rothschild was an accomplished woman and a brilliant talker, though rather overpowering in her conversation; as Peggy wickedly put it, 'she shared with Diderot every gift except that of dialogue'. She was also something of a hypochondriac, who could not stand the smell of flowers and was so obsessed with draughts that she usually wore a hat indoors, and had her room at Mentmore almost hermetically sealed.

It was inevitable that Rosebery, with his social status and his fondness for racing, should have been drawn into Baron Meyer's circle. He was particularly close to Ferdinand, known as 'Ferdy', one of Baron Meyer's cousins and a widower, his wife Evy having died tragically young. Gauche, sensitive and loyal, Ferdy was deeply attached to Rosebery, perhaps to an extreme degree. Some of his letters reveal not only sorrow in his loneliness but also an unstable neediness typical of the whirlwind of passion and frustration that Rosebery so often provoked in others: 'I am more devoted to you and fonder of you than I ever was . . . Pray don't, as you threatened, withhold your trust from me in the future – I assure you I am worthy of it – I have very few friends in my life, hardly any true ones, and it would grieve me beyond anything if I thought that when we meet there was no longer the free exchange of thought and feeling that has existed and on which I pride myself – I am lonely, suffering and occasionally a very miserable individual despite the gilded and marble rooms in which I live,' he wrote in September 1878. In another letter, three years later, he told Rosebery, 'You know I love you more than any man in the world', and in 1884 he wrote: 'That I am "yours" entirely you are aware of and if I am occasionally "peculiar" put it down to my nervous system and not to any other cause.'[52] As Ferdy's correspondence indicates, Rosebery appears to have found his anguished expressions of devotion more irritating than irresistible. In fact Ferdy sometimes protested against Rosebery's wounding treatment, especially his sarcastic tongue: 'I am the incessant butt of your chaff,' he wrote in 1888, 'which you no doubt think amusing but is not always equally gratifying to myself.'[53]

Rosebery did, however, reciprocate the feelings of another Rothschild. Like Ferdy, Hannah had known severe loneliness, first as an only child, then from the loss of both her parents by her mid twenties. She had been shy and awkward as a girl, traits not helped by her parents' tendency to indulge her whims. Her cousin Constance, Lady Battersea, who never liked her, wrote in her diary years later: 'I remember a little girl living in a large and beautiful house, an only child, petted and spoilt by her parents, with no serious bringing up, whose education was woefully neglected but who at a very early age was brought into contact with some of England's greatest men. She was never allowed to enter a cottage, to go where sickness and sorrow dwelt, she was never brought face to face with want or sickness. "The poor" was merely a phraseology for her. She had but few redeeming qualities as a child. That was Hannah de Rothschild.'[54] Constance also accused her of being 'most selfish', and a 'cold hostess' who took 'no interest in big subjects'.[55] This is too harsh. Despite the deficiencies of her schooling Hannah was clever, and musically accomplished; on his first visit to Mentmore in 1872, Rosebery was struck by the quality of her singing. Moreover, she showed far more poise than Constance Battersea recognised. When the Prince of Wales visited Mentmore in 1868, Ferdy was amazed by the calm way in which Hannah, just seventeen, handled the Royal guest, while the rest of the household was gripped by nervousness.

Never could Hannah have been described as ravishing. The Prince of Wales's mistress Daisy, Countess of Warwick thought she was 'without beauty'.[56] In similar vein, the Duchess of Manchester circulated a story about a trip to India made by the Roseberys in 1887, during which they attended a large dinner party hosted by a rajah. When Hannah was first discreetly pointed out to him, the rajah expressed surprise at her unglamorous appearance and said, 'Oh, that is Lady Rosebery. Then I presume that his Lordship has *other wives*.'[57] Even more devastating was the verdict of the American novelist Henry James, who after a visit to Mentmore wrote that she was 'large, coarse, Hebrew-looking, with hair of no particular colour and personally unattractive'.[58] In another reference, however, James described her as 'good-natured, sensible and kind', and this was the key to her attractiveness to Rosebery. Deprived of maternal affection throughout his young life, he needed a warm-hearted, emotionally generous woman who would give him unconditional love rather than disapproving lectures. Furthermore, it would be a mistake to exaggerate Hannah's plainness, for contemporary pictures reveal a quality of voluptuous serenity about her. Late in his life, one of Rosebery's grandchildren asked him 'Was Granny beautiful?' 'I thought she was,' he replied. And while it is easy enough to read sneering anti-Semitism into Henry James's comments about her looks, Rosebery himself found Jewesses physically appealing. In her candid private portrait of her father, Sybil noted that 'His sense of beauty was a salient characteristic and one he most appreciated in the Jewish race.'[59] After seeing Madame Heilbronn make her London debut in *La Traviata*,

Rosebery described her in his diary as 'a dear little Jewess with a pretty throat and voice'.[60]

By the mid 1870s Hannah and Rosebery were meeting frequently in society, and at Mentmore. Baron Meyer had died in 1874, and when her mother died suddenly in 1877 it was Rosebery who comforted the heiress. Their relationship now deepened. At the beginning of 1878 Hannah returned from a trip to Brighton, and on 3 January Rosebery travelled to Mentmore. At 4.20 p.m., sapphire locket in hand, he proposed to her. He later suggested that his courage had been fuelled by a little alcohol; in his account of a visit to Mentmore soon after the marriage, Lewis Harcourt wrote: 'Rosebery gave us some very good claret after dinner, the same he declares which Hannah brought out to inflame him up to the point of proposing.'[61] This was probably just a joke, if not a very gallant one. Hannah immediately accepted, overwhelmed with happiness, as her letters to her new fiancé demonstrated. 'My darling, good morning. You see, I cannot resist writing. My pen is new. I have heaps of things I want to talk over with you, your loving Hannah', she wrote on 5 January. In a letter of 21 January she asked, 'Do you know the feeling that intense loving gives one, as though one's heart must influence the mind of the person who occupies it? Every hour I see how much more and more I love you.' And she poured out her gratitude to Rosebery for saving her from a miserable life of solitude. 'I feel very happy this evening for I am realizing the immense change in my life and the delight of feeling someone of whom I am very, very fond is caring for me. I cannot be thankful enough for the absence of the terrible loneliness. My darling, you are so kind to me. I am very silent, you say, because I am afraid of boring you. I am still a little shy or I could tell you better how much I love you,' she wrote on 24 January.[62] To a relative, Annie Yorke, she wrote, 'My happiness is intense.'[63] Sadly, few of Rosebery's letters to Hannah appear to have survived, but his own exhilaration can be gauged from this letter to his sister Constance the day after he proposed: 'I was engaged to Hannah yesterday. I love her so much that I could never be happy if you do not love her too, your ever loving brother, Archie.'[64]

Nevertheless, amid all this ardour, Rosebery's intrinsic reserve sparked in Hannah a feeling of insecurity about being excluded from parts of his life. In a portentous letter which reveals both a penetrating insight into her future husband's character and her own exalted ambitions for him, she wrote on 7 January:

> Remember, darling, I have no one on earth but you. I don't think you know much about my ideas of happiness. I am afraid of seeing little of you in the future. I can be very quiet when you want and work only to help you. If

you are Prime Minster, let me imitate Montagu Corry.* Lady Beaconsfield used to say he was so useful because he was so devoted to his master; I shall be devoted to you, Archie. I am for you, but for God's sake don't leave me running behind after politics. I have a restless feeling you don't let me know much of what passes through your mind, because I said yesterday that people easily forced things out of me; the only thing ever discovered was my love for you which I could not hide, Archie. I would never say a word you told me not. Don't laugh at me, darling. I feel loving this evening. Your presence fills the atmosphere of the room. I seem to see you. Perhaps you are thinking of me.

A potentially more serious obstacle for the couple was religion. It was not an issue for Rosebery, who loathed sectarianism; a regular worshipper in the Presbyterian Church of Scotland, he was nevertheless happy to have an audience of the Pope during a visit to Rome in 1870, and kept a copy of Cardinal Newman's *Apologia* by his bed. But his mother, an ardent High Church Anglican and strong anti-Semite, disapproved of the match, and expressed her views in a typically forthright letter.

> You are right in believing that I should dislike this marriage on religious grounds: & to me the question is of grave importance. You can easily suppose how unhappy I must feel in finding that you have chosen as your wife and the mother of your children one who has not the faith & hope of Christ . . . I myself do honestly and from the bottom of my heart disapprove of such marriages & I could not say otherwise without acting against my conscientious convictions. You would not wish me to do that, or to approach my own child on the most important occasion of his life, with any words that were not the exact truth upon my lips. I can at least sincerely say that I am glad to hear of your great happiness; & in this feeling the Duke cordially joins. I will receive the future Lady Rosebery with all the kindness & consideration that are her due & I do not think she will ever have occasion to complain of me. But for the moment I would plead to be spared any agitating interviews on the score of my own health. I am not strong & rapidly feeling myself growing old; with a feeble heart (like my poor brother's): & any strong emotion makes me physically ill.

Such a plea of decrepitude – a ruse to which Rosebery himself often resorted during moments of political crisis – now seems hardly convincing since the Duchess outlived both Hannah and the nineteenth century. But in view of their past history of mutual antagonism, it was never likely that Rosebery would take much notice of his mother's objections.

The Rothschilds, if by no means as openly hostile as the Duchess, had

---

*Montagu Corry, later Lord Rowton, was Disraeli's private secretary.

their own concerns about a mixed marriage. The family's acceptance into English society had not lessened the strength or orthodoxy of their faith. In London, attendance at the synagogue was strictly observed; in the country, prayers were said at home. No pork was allowed on their tables, and fasting was observed on the Day of Atonement. Hannah, inspired by her devout father Baron Meyer, took her religion seriously. Hers was not, however, the first marriage between a Rothschild and a Gentile. In 1839 Meyer's sister, another Hannah, had married The Honourable Henry Fitzroy, second son of the 2nd Baron Southampton, a union which the family strongly opposed. On the death of the Fitzroys' son Arthur in 1858, aged just fifteen, Constance de Rothschild wrote this passage in her diary, reflecting the bad feeling the marriage had caused: 'I cannot help thinking that all the misfortunes and distress which have overwhelmed poor Aunt Hannah Meyer have been a punishment for having deserted the faith of her fathers and for having married without her mother's consent.'[65] Then in 1873 Constance's sister Annie married The Honourable Eliot Yorke, an event that again led to consternation in the family. 'Papa looked so sad. We all feel it dreadfully,' Constance wrote on Annie's wedding day. Ironically, four years later Constance herself found a husband outside the faith when she married the rather effeminate Cyril Flower, later an MP, a junior Lord of the Treasury, and Lord Battersea.

The flames of Rothschild resistance, exhausted by these traumas, were all but extinguished by the time of the Rosebery marriage. In fact, Constance's mother Louisa, Hannah's aunt, was only too pleased by the development, as she wrote in her journal. 'On Saturday, heard the great news of Hannah's engagement. Her delight was immense. Much seems combined to make the match a brilliant and happy one – position, wealth and talent; the future alone can say if any other ingredient is wanting but now all appears most bright.' As early as 1874 Louisa Rothschild had hinted that Rosebery would make an excellent husband for Hannah – 'He is very pleasant and quite apart and above the other young men of the day.'[66] But although the family were fond of Rosebery personally, the religious difference meant that no male Rothschild except loyal Ferdy attended the wedding ceremonies. Hannah herself was only too aware of the difficulty, as she explained in an uncomfortable letter to her fiancé. 'A great dread has come over me about religion. You remember my first words to you? I cannot become a Christian because though respecting Jesus I cannot believe in him. You said that you would not wish me to change and now I am frightened. If my religion is in your way, don't marry me. It would break my heart but I could not face to be a hindrance.'[67] Rosebery rejected any such idea and reassured her on this point, as her next letter demonstrated: 'Your letter has done me good. Do you know I seem to freeze occasionally. I have been so long without much affection that it takes a long time to break through the stiffness which you see'[68] – words as applicable to her beloved as to herself.

Outside the two families, there was much disquiet. It might not have been the first Jewish–Gentile marriage in England, but it was certainly the most significant. In her own right Hannah de Rothschild was one of the richest women in England, with a fortune of more than £2 million and an annual income of over £80,000;* Rosebery was the possessor of a great title and a reputation as the rising star of the Liberal cause. Outrage was expressed in the Jewish community over the desertion of one of its leading daughters, as indicated by an article that appeared in the *Jewish Chronicle* in October 1877, when rumours were spreading of a possible engagement. Referring to the 'most poignant grief' caused by the news, the paper continued: 'The intelligence has thrilled through the communal frame. It quivers under the impact. And shall we suppress the cry of pain heaved forth from the soul?' On the other side, anti-Semitism was a powerful force in late Victorian England, when Jews were regularly portrayed as grasping and unprincipled. This caricature was highlighted by an article in *Truth*, the magazine run by the radical Liberal Henry Labouchere, which took the opportunity of Rosebery's marriage to condemn Jews as 'essentially speculative; their fondness for making money is only equalled by their love of spending it and their mania to gamble with it. Left entirely to himself the Jew would succumb to the Anglo-Saxon. He holds his own and elbows the Anglo-Saxon out of the way by the support which he finds in the corporate cohesion that distinguishes his race.'[69]

In the face of all this narrow-minded disapproval, the marriage of the 5th Earl of Rosebery and Hannah de Rothschild went ahead on 20 March 1878. There were actually two ceremonies, a civil one at the Boardroom of the Guardians in Mayfair,† followed by a more elaborate event at Christ Church in Piccadilly. Lord Carrington, a cousin of the Primrose family and an enthusiastic Liberal, was Rosebery's best man, and the bride was given away by none other than the Prime Minister, Lord Beaconsfield, displaying a commendable lack of personal resentment at Rosebery's attacks on his party. It was a further sign of the social standing of Rosebery and his

---

*Contemporary figures.
†The Boardroom of the Guardians, in Mount Street, Piccadilly, was the headquarters of the local Poor Law Board. In his diary Rosebery wryly notes, 'Married at the workhouse in Mount Street.'

new wife that the Prince of Wales and the Duke of Cambridge, Commander-in-Chief of the British Army, were among the guests. In contrast to such high society splendour, the officiating minister was Rosebery's mentor, the radical cleric Canon William Rogers. 'How delighted Hannah must have been with all the show and such a troop of grandees to witness her espousals,' said her aunt Louisa.[70] A florid commentary in *The Times* described Hannah's appearance: 'The bride wore a princess dress of the richest pearl-white satin *duchesse*, with trimmings and deep flounces of exquisite *point d'Alençon*, divided by orange-blossom fringes. Over a wreath of orange blossoms descended a large veil of the very tiniest *point de l'aiguelle*, which descended to the flounces of the dress and corresponded in artistic design with the *Alençon* flounces. She wore no jewels beyond diamond and pearl earrings.' During the wedding breakfast held afterwards at Hannah's London home, 107 Piccadilly, the Prince of Wales proposed the toast to the couple before Rosebery and Hannah, now clad in a blue velvet dress with blue fox fur trimmings, left for their honeymoon at Petworth House in Sussex, home of Rosebery's sister Constance, now Lady Leconfield. After just a week of marriage, Hannah wrote to her sister-in-law: 'You will be surprised to hear Archie is not yet quite bored. We two old bachelors agree & are becoming accustomed to married life though I may own that he usually gets his own way; you see we are both (as he said if you remember) spoilt children & I, being the laziest, am the more amenable.'[71]

This set the tone for what became a generally happy and successful marriage. The adoring Hannah was only too eager to accommodate Rosebery's wishes. In turn, he had found in her a partner who could give him the drive he so often lacked and the affection he craved. He later described her as 'very simple, very unspoilt, very clever, very warmhearted. I never knew such a beautiful character.' Both were intrinsically shy people, but Hannah was far less moody and self-absorbed than her husband. It was she who often drew him out, and forced him to confront his political responsibilities. Lord Granville, noticing that she was perhaps the more ambitious of the pair, told her just before her marriage, 'He is charming and most agreeable, and one who, if you keep him up to the mark, is sure to have his page in history.'[72] Driving her husband to fulfil the promise of his talent was always Hannah's aim, as Rosebery's secretary Thomas Gilmour noted in 1885: 'She is thoroughly genuine and very tender and devoted to Lord Rosebery. It is easy enough to see that she is very, very proud of him and as she is a woman of considerable force of character and great energy, she may prove to be a very powerful ally in his political career.'[73] After her death Edward Hamilton, who was perhaps Rosebery's closest friend, praised her influence on him. 'Her judgement as a whole was singularly sound and calm; indeed, there was a sort of intuitive wisdom about the advice which she would recommend or the consequences of which she would foretell. Hers was a singularly well-balanced mind; her shrewdness and foresight were mostly certain to lead others as well as herself to form right conclusions. Having the power of seeing through people quickly, she gauged the characters of her fellow creatures with great perspicacity and she thus knew whom to trust and of whom to beware. She had a high sense of duty, and would never allow pleasure to interfere with the judgement of it.'[74] Her essential decency and modesty, despite the luxury of her upbringing, were important factors in her husband's growing popularity, as was reflected in an endearingly naïve letter she wrote to Hamilton after attending a football match in Glasgow on her husband's behalf. The crowd was dominated by '10,000 working men from Govan', which prompted her to remark that 'football seems an extraordinarily popular sport in Scotland'. After presenting the trophy, 'I walked round the ground; they did not receive me unkindly. In fact, the cheering was very great. They shouted three cheers for "England's crack nobleman" and then gave two cheers for the GOM.★'[75]

Yet for all Hannah's adoration, there lingered a suspicion that Rosebery had only married her for her money, and never loved her. There were those in society who saw him as an ambitious politician, bon viveur and race-horse owner cynically exploiting a lonely, unattractive heiress for his own ends. Lewis 'Loulou' Harcourt, who always relished gossip against Rosebery, recorded in his journal a conversation in 1882 with his Old Etonian friend Reginald Brett: 'Regy was talking about Rosebery today and said that he would never recover with his friends what he lost by his marriage with Hannah which disgusted so many.'[76] This sense of contempt can only have been heightened by the widespread circulation of Rosbery's notorious, but perhaps apocryphal, remark that his three aims in life were to win the Derby, become Prime Minister, and marry an heiress. Just as telling were the eagerly reported observations of his behaviour towards her when she occasionally appeared to be the butt of his cruel humour. On one occasion when they were travelling through India Rosebery allegedly instructed that he would journey ahead, and 'Hannah and the rest of the heavy baggage will follow the next day.'[77] Moreover, even after his marriage he maintained his secretive, private habits, insist-

★ An abbreviation of Gladstone's popular nickname, the 'Grand Old Man'.

ing for instance on opening his own mail, and often sleeping alone at the ancient castle of Barnbougle in the grounds of Dalmeny. Learning that he had accepted a commission to write a book on his hero, Pitt the Younger, without informing her, Hannah felt aggrieved enough to complain to Edward Hamilton. 'Now about the Pitt secret, I cannot fathom why I have not been told. I am sure he does not mistrust my discretion and I am convinced you would lose no opportunity of saying I am discreet. I have often found things he has not actually told me he has not been surprised at my knowing.'[78]

In support of the theory that Rosebery's marriage was founded on insincerity, it has even been suggested that he was mildly anti-Semitic, and revealed his scorn for Hannah's race in moments of humour or high drama. According to Loulou Harcourt, when Rosebery became Foreign Secretary in 1886 he was approached by the London MP Sir Julian Goldsmid, who was 'dying to have office' as Under-Secretary. 'Don't you think that if you were appointed people might think our office a little too Semitic?' Rosebery is alleged to have said to him. Lord Balcarres (later 27th Earl of Crawford) recorded in his diary a story which later became one of the best-known about Rosebery: 'One night at Mentmore, when Hannah Rothschild had had a house party in which her compatriots were unusually numerous, all the ladies had gathered at the foot of the great staircase and were about to go up with lighted candles. Rosebery, standing aloof from the bevy of beauty, raised his hand – they looked at him, rather puzzled, and then he said, in solemn tones, "To your tents, O Israel".' Warming to his theme, Balcarres also noted a conversation with Laurie Magnus, a Jewish publisher, who told him that 'within a week of Hannah's death, he (Rosebery) began to cut off subscriptions to Jewish charities and before long all had been cancelled.'[79] Further, it has been stated that Rosebery harboured a dislike of his son and heir Harry (later the 6th Earl) on the grounds that he looked Jewish. 'Le Jew est fait, rien ne va plus,' Rosebery is supposed to have said after Harry's birth.[80]

Instinctive antipathy towards an eldest son was of course something Rosebery might well have inherited from his mother, while a parade of his witticisms as evidence of his racial prejudice displays no more than a failure to understand his sense of humour. He had, as Constance Battersea pointed out, 'a strong sarcastic vein', and could 'strike alarm into the heart of some timid companion'.[81] Had Rosebery really been anti-Semitic, why on earth would he have married a Jewess? He was in reality unusually pro-Jewish for a man of his time and station. Thus in February 1882 he made an impassioned denunciation of the persecution of the Jews in Russia, although this was hardly a burning political issue of the day. 'The Jews have been a people of many sorrows; their sufferings have been protracted through the centuries; but the vitality of their race has been in no degree impaired. They still survive this persecution, as they have survived many others; but it is melancholy to think that in the nineteenth century a great Jewish population should again be destined to change its abode and to exchange the barbarity of the Old World for the large toleration of the New.'[82] Years later, moreover, Rosebery's hostility to France at the turn of the century was partly motivated by his contempt for French anti-Semitism as exemplified by the notorious imprisonment of Colonel Dreyfus on trumped-up charges of spying. 'Rosebery is vehemently anti-French – the Dreyfus case has made him more so than ever', wrote the senior Liberal R.B. Haldane to his mother in September 1899.[83]

The idea that Hannah's fortune was her primary attraction for Rosebery is similarly misguided. He was already a wealthy man, and though his racing habits were expensive, they represented no genuine threat to his position. He must of course have been well aware that his marriage would transform him into one of the country's greatest magnates, complete with palace and stud. Was he immoral if he could view the prospect with equanimity? It was after all an era when money and status were inevitable considerations in almost every aristocratic marriage. At least Rosebery could know with certainty that his bride was marrying him for love and not for his own fortune. Above all, despite his banter and occasional moments of intolerance, a tenderness for Hannah shines through much of his writing, as it does in these two letters to Gladstone's daughter Mary. The first was written in June 1880, when the Roseberys were travelling through Germany shortly after the birth of their daughter Sybil. 'Hannah is too good for this world or at least for Hamburg, which was once a hell. She has never complained for a moment about leaving her baby, though she devours the daily letter about it and thinks about it all day long.' In January 1881, with another birth looming, he was concerned about her health and wrote to explain his reluctance to be away from her: 'Hannah is in that nervous state which makes her unhappy if I leave the house so, if the House of Lords is doing nothing (which is much the best phase of its existence), I am hardly ever in London.'[84]

Beneath his cynical façade – which until her tragic death never allowed him to reveal the true love he felt for Hannah – Rosebery was far too serious, too principled a man to have allowed any base considerations to drive him into marriage. The solemnity he attached to the institution was demonstrated again in the advice he later gave when his young political ally

Ronald Munro-Ferguson told him of his own engagement in 1889: 'I shall never see you again as a bachelor. When I next meet you, you will have been through the great transformation. For though it need not change a man in essentials, it is the great gate of life's pilgrimage though which most of us must pass and on the further side of which is a different landscape to that we leave behind us, different in tone, in most cases finer and better, but still different.'[85]

Rosebery's marriage certainly transformed the landscape of his life. Before 1878 he was just one of a number of rich, able young aristocrats. Now, backed by vast wealth and an ambitious hostess, he could become one of the leading figures in British politics. And he was about to do so in the most famous political campaign in British history.

4

'A conceited little ass'

~~~

IN AUGUST 1878 the newly-married Roseberys made their first visit to
Scotland. The leap in the Earl's popularity and fame was immediately
demonstrated by the crowds which gathered around Waverley station in
Edinburgh to catch a glimpse of the couple. They then travelled to
Dalmeny, where three days of official celebrations included a banquet for
250 guests in a specially erected pavilion. In his vote of thanks Rosebery
won a loud cheer when he said, 'My wife, as you know, is a Jewess by race,
an Englishwoman by birth and today, by adoption, you have made her a
Scotswoman.'[1]

The acclamation Rosebery met in Scotland further quickened his growing political ambitions. He was already regarded as one of the rising hopes
of the Liberal cause and even hardline radicals like Sir Charles Dilke and
Joseph Chamberlain had made overtures to him. In January 1877
Chamberlain invited him to dinner to meet Dilke and 'see if it might be
possible to arrange some joint actions',[2] an invitation Rosebery courte-
ously declined because he was more interested in working with Gladstone
than with the left-wing fringe; later, in 1885, he told Queen Victoria that
the driving force of his Liberalism was the desire to be 'associated with the
best man in the best work'.[3] Rosebery's new-found political determination was further shown when he ran a tough, partisan campaign to become
the Lord Rector of Aberdeen University. This was a period when battles
for university rectorships, especially in Scotland, were rumbustious affairs,
as highly charged as Parliamentary elections. Rosebery had been invited to
stand by the students of Aberdeen but there was talk of a rival Liberal candidature from Lord Aberdeen, son of the Peelite Prime Minister of the
1850s. Drawn by the nostalgic link with his old chief,* Gladstone was keen
for Aberdeen to stand, but Rosebery, after consulting the Scottish Liberal
Chief Whip W.P. Adam, refused to back down. 'It is Lord Aberdeen who
has got himself into this difficulty and it is he who should withdraw. Why

---

*After Sir Robert Peel, the 4th Earl of Aberdeen was Gladstone's greatest political hero.

I am to expiate his political aberrations is a point that I do not clearly understand.'[4] Faced with this inflexibility, Aberdeen, who had few Liberal credentials, withdrew and Rosebery won the Rectorship by just three votes against the former Tory Home Secretary Richard Cross. For the first time, Rosebery had proved his mettle in a tightly-fought contest.

Soon it was to be tested again. Rosebery had been President of the East and North of Scotland Liberal Association since its foundation in 1877, and both he and Adam were keen to strengthen the Liberal party in the central Scottish lowlands. A high-profile campaign in a key Parliamentary seat at the next General Election seemed a good means of achieving this. The ideal constituency was Midlothian, a marginal seat close to Dalmeny currently held by Lord Dalkeith, solid but uncharismatic eldest son of the Duke of Buccleuch. The ideal candidate was William Gladstone, nominally in retirement after resigning the Liberal leadership, but in reality still the most dynamic politician in the country. The passions aroused by his crusade against the iniquities of the Turkish empire only served to make the idea of his candidature more appealing. Moreover, he was on the hunt for another constituency, having resolved never to stand for Greenwich again after its ungrateful voters almost threw him out in the 1874 General Election, and he had already proved his popularity in Scotland by winning the Lord Rectorship of Glasgow University against the Tory Sir Stafford Northcote in 1877. As the son of a Liverpool merchant he had been flirting with the idea of a northern industrial seat but then, on 16 May 1878, Rosebery and Adam called to ask him to stand for Midlothian. Gladstone's imagination was captured, but he recognised that the election would be tight; he therefore delayed making a decision until the local Liberal association had conducted some discreet canvassing to ascertain his chances of victory. Rosebery was now increasingly in command of the operation, and the two local Liberal officials, John James Reid (Secretary of the East of Scotland Association) and Ralph Richardson (the Midlothian agent) sent him a flow of optimistic reports on the political mood in the area. 'The returns keep coming in steadily and the results continue to be excellent,' Reid told Rosebery on 24 December 1878.[5] At the beginning of 1879 Reid felt the Liberals were still ahead: 'The Tories are working day and night at a regular canvass but our people are doing well too, I think.'[6] By the second week in January Adam was predicting a Liberal majority of 200, a substantial margin in an unreformed constituency of barely 3,000 voters, prompting Rosebery to tell Gladstone that 'there is, humanly speaking, no doubt whatever of your return.'[7]

Despite such confident speculation, some local Liberals were worried about the burden they were shouldering, since the forthcoming election would focus the eyes of the nation on Midlothian. 'All of our Executive Committee are enthusiastic supporters of Mr Gladstone,' Richardson told Rosebery, 'but many dread the responsibility of hazarding so great a man.'[8] To allay such anxieties Rosebery returned early from a trip to Paris to attend the Executive Committee on 8 January, at which it was formally agreed to invite Gladstone to become the Liberal candidate. 'Harmonious and enthusiastic show of hands for Gladstone. I was then asked to speak. Spoke with apparent success,' recorded Rosebery.[9] Buoyed by the Earl's favourable reports Gladstone was now ready for combat, and accepted the invitation. On 3 February his candidature was publicly announced. The role played by Rosebery in securing Gladstone had been crucial, as this letter from Lord Granville to W.P. Adam reveals: 'I was against Midlothian when Gladstone first mentioned it to me but was converted by you and Rosebery on the ground of the stimulus it would give the Scotch election and of its being a certainty.'[10]

Having helped to win round Gladstone, Rosebery then set about organising his campaign. Once more the radical, democratic Rosebery was to the fore, using revolutionary new techniques, many influenced by his experiences of American politics, to orchestrate the public mood. During his US tour of 1873 he had visited the Democratic Convention in New York before the Presidential elections, and had written this account:

> Last night I stood in Madison Square, and looking down Fifth Avenue there appeared a moving column of lights, clustering and silent . . . There was cavalry indeed, but it was unarmed, there were banners but they bore the names of peaceful citizens or the shibboleth of political principles, there were cannon but they were loaded only with ballot balls. All was silence, earnestness and decorum. It was a monster procession of American citizens on its way to salute a political chief . . . This was both a great moral spectacle and a great political lesson. No European potentate, not the Queen of Great Britain saluted by the thunders of her fleet, nor the Emperor of Russia reviewing his hundred thousand Guards before breakfast, not the Pope borne amid smoking incense and the blare of silver trumpets and the awful silence of kneeling multitudes can produce a sight so impressive as this.[11]

It was just such an atmosphere of moral fervour and visual drama that Rosebery wanted to create in Midlothian, woven round the real political chief of British democracy. What he planned for Gladstone was not in the usual style of Victorian electioneering, based on perhaps a couple of addresses in the constituency, but something more sustained and spectacular, something to capture the imagination of the British people far beyond the boundaries of Midlothian.

He succeeded brilliantly. In late November 1879, before Disraeli had officially called the General Election, the Gladstones made their first pilgrimage to the constituency. Travelling by the Midland Railway from Liverpool, near their Flintshire home of Hawarden, they were greeted at every stop on their route by cheering crowds, to whom Gladstone spoke from a platform at the back of an American-designed Pullman car. The journey reached its climax in Edinburgh, where Rosebery's handling of the press and of Liberal organisations ensured that excitement had reached fever pitch. No British politician has ever received a more enthusiastic public reception. The scenes in the centre of the city were something between a carnival and an evangelical revivalist meeting, an effect enhanced by Rosebery's sense of theatre. After arriving at Waverley station, the Gladstones and their party were led by Rosebery through the teeming mass to his waiting barouche, which was flanked by a group of uniformed outriders. Dalmeny was to be Gladstone's headquarters for the campaign, and all along the seven-mile route from Edinburgh there were more crowds, their eager faces illuminated by flashes from rockets exploding in the wintry night sky or by the glow of bonfires burning in the countryside. Gladstone's daughter Mary described the experience as 'overwhelming; not only was the station densely packed with roaring crowds, but right on through the streets till the town faded away and most exciting it was galloping in our open carriage, four horses and many outriders, the noise more than deafening, hundreds flying along by the side of the carriage and the whole way to Dalmeny more or less lined with people and torches and fireworks and bonfires.'[12] Once the party reached Dalmeny, there were more fireworks in the grounds of the majestic house. 'I have never gone through a more extraordinary day,' Gladstone wrote.[13] Rosebery sensed that Gladstone, despite his public deprecation of vanity, was 'secretly pleased at his wonderful reception'.[14]

The wild enthusiasm continued the next day, as the conquering hero and his lieutenant drove through the packed streets of Edinburgh to a meeting at the Music Hall in George Street. 'It looked like the road to Epsom on Derby Day,' commented Rosebery of the throng lining the route.[15] The thousands gathered in the Music Hall were joined by a phalanx of Liberal leaders on the platform and more than seventy reporters in the upper gallery. Encouraged by the rapid expansion of telegraph facilities, newspaper coverage of politics was undergoing a revolution at this time, with an increasing emphasis on extra-Parliamentary speeches;

Midlothian was one of the first campaigns to exploit this change. In an oration lasting two hours, Gladstone passionately denounced the Tory government for its extravagance, its arrogance, and its dishonouring of both Britain's constitution and her international reputation. On 27 November, as he drove out from Dalmeny to West Calder, Gladstone passed beneath a series of triumphal arches erected along the route, another theatrical Rosebery touch. Then, on 28 November at the Waverley Vegetable Market, he spoke to an audience estimated to number more than 20,000, so densely bunched together that people started collapsing. 'It was a strange sight,' noted Rosebery, 'Gladstone composedly perorating about Bulgaria while the fainting people were lifted up, pale and motionless, into the reporters' enclosure. He felt it, though he did not show it, and spoke for barely 20 minutes. A frightful business getting back into the carriage through the mob.'[16] The climax came on 5 December, when Gladstone delivered another powerful denunciation of Lord Beaconsfield at St Andrew's Hall in Glasgow. Altogether 70,000 people had applied for tickets to this meeting, though there was only room for 6,500.

In total, Gladstone estimated, he spoke to more than 86,000 people during the first Midlothian campaign. It was, in the words of Sir Philip Magnus, an 'astonishing and never-to-be-forgotten fortnight, during which Gladstone erupted with greater effect than at any other time in his life.'[17] Lord Rosebery, architect of this unprecedented campaign, had become a major national figure in Scotland. From Waverley station to the constituency's outlying villages, his name was now a popular political battle cry. As Gladstone put it to Lord Granville on 21 December, 'The exhibition of Liberal feeling would be hard to describe, impossible to exaggerate. Rosebery has made a great impression and is a hero not only in Edinburgh but in Glasgow.'[18] When Rosebery presided at a meeting in the Edinburgh Corn Exchange, his speech in praise of Gladstone met with prolonged, full-throated applause. At St Andrew's Hall in Glasgow, after Gladstone sat down the crowd chanted for Rosebery until he agreed to speak, which he did with his usual wit. 'Fellow Liberals of Glasgow, I did not think that in a free land like this so much tyranny could exist,' he opened. It was, in Mary Gladstone's words, 'a perfect little speech, which under its playful humour hid the most telling sarcasm.'[19] Reflecting on Rosebery's popularity, his wife Hannah wrote to her sister-in-law Constance Leconfield: 'I wish you could have seen the control Archie exercised over the dense masses of the people. I never heard Archie speak in public politically but after the first minute I felt I could never be nervous at his making a speech. The audience show him great affection at their political meetings; and they patted me on the back till my shoulders were sensitive.'[20]

The second Midlothian campaign, held in March 1880 just before the General Election, was almost as great a success, the crowds as large and fervent as four months earlier. As a girl of fifteen Margot Asquith, then still Margot Tennant, recorded of one Edinburgh rally: 'When Gladstone and Rosebery stepped onto the platform it seemed as if the thunder of cheers would only cease when the roof had fallen in. Men and women scrambled onto their seats waving hats and handkerchiefs and Laura [her sister] and I hardly dared to look at one another for fear of bursting into tears.'[21] But the first sign of that frostiness between the Roseberys and the Gladstones which later became such a feature of Liberal high politics now emerged, in the form of the resentment Mary Gladstone felt at the demands for her attendance during the campaign. 'What a mad world; the fight I have had about Midlothian with the Roseberys has quite exhausted me. It makes me rather cross, it's so silly the exaggeration of it. They talk as if the whole election depended on it. They have a ridiculous notion that I am the wire puller about everything in my family, such nonsense.' A compromise was reached by which Mary would travel to Edinburgh after Easter: 'To give up Holy Week entirely, all for the sake of fidgetting at Dalmeny between Hannah and Mama for four days was really beyond a joke.'[22]

By Easter 1880 there can have been little doubt about the outcome of the election. From their detailed canvass returns the Liberal organisers were predicting a healthy majority for Gladstone; in February 1880 Richardson had told Rosebery that it could be as high as 384.[23] In the end, this forecast proved optimistic: when the result was announced, on 5 April, Gladstone had won by 211 votes, gaining 1,579 to Dalkeith's 1,368. At the news of Gladstone's triumph an immense crowd gathered outside the Liberal headquarters in George Street, Edinburgh, where the Gladstones and the Roseberys were dining. The Chief Constable warned that the crowd, more than 15,000 strong, would not disperse until they had heard from Gladstone. So, flanked by his wife and daughter, both bearing candles, he spoke briefly from the balcony. Nor was Rosebery permitted to consume his dinner in peace. The now familiar cry of his name was chanted. To a roar which filled the streets, the upper windows opened again and he emerged to tell the cheering crowd: 'No Midlothian man will ever spend a prouder night than this. It is a great night for Midlothian, a great night for Scotland, a great night for your county member, a great night for Britain and – aye – a great night for the world. And a bad one for Dizzy.'[24] Afterwards, he helped Gladstone and the rest of the party avoid the multitude by guiding them along a secret passage to a nearby hotel and thence by carriage to Dalmeny.

The Midlothian result was mirrored across the rest of the country as the Liberal party was swept back to power. Though the increase in the Liberal vote was just 1.5 per cent, it was enough to inflict a heavy defeat on the Conservatives, who were left with just 239 seats compared to the Liberals' 351. Gladstone was the true begetter of this landslide. The force of his moral indignation, the magnificence of his rhetoric, and the volcanic energy of his campaigning had pulverised the opposition. In lamenting publicly during the Midlothian campaign that he was 'unable to compete with Mr Gladstone in that brilliant oratory which he had at his command',[25] his opponent Lord Dalkeith had symbolised the enfeebled Tory response to Gladstone's crushing authority. Aware of his debt to Rosebery, Gladstone was fulsome in his gratitude. 'It was almost like one of the occasions of old when the issue of battle was referred to single combat. The great merit, I apprehend, lay in the original conception, which I take to have been yours and to overshadow even your operations towards the direct production of the result. But one thing it cannot overshadow in my mind: the sense of the inexpressible aid and comfort derived day by day from your considerate, ever-watchful care and tact.' There was much truth in Gladstone's compliments, for everything had been felicitously stage-managed by Rosebery, from the press facilities to the Pullman car. Rosebery's great friend Edward Hamilton, who was also Gladstone's secretary, was subsequently made acutely aware of the Earl's importance in shepherding Gladstone through Scotland. In 1884, during the third Midlothian campaign, he wrote: 'There was nothing more remarkable than the extraordinary manner in which Rosebery was received at the meeting, though it had been assembled to listen to another and greater man. One realised for the first time the immensity of the position which he holds in Scotland. I doubt if there is any parallel for it. The audience insisted on his saying a few words which he did with much neatness and veiled humour. We got back here (Dalmeny) about 9.30 for a late dinner. The cooking here and also the wine are the very best and the arrangements are all perfection. Nothing seems forgotten. I expect R. does an immense deal himself.'[26]

To his political intimate Lord Granville, Gladstone was just as effusive about Rosebery. 'He is very decidedly a remarkable man, not a mere clever man and is to be evidently the leader of the Liberal party in Scotland and that in a sense beyond any, I should think, in which they have heretofore had a leader. From the first time I ever saw him I liked him and thought highly of him; but he has opened out to me marvellously. I could heap many epithets upon him and I must say upon her also but the subject must keep until we meet.'[27] These sentiments were shared at local party level, in the Midlothian Liberal Association. The day after the result was announced, the Midlothian agent Richardson wrote to Rosebery: 'The part borne by your Lordship in the struggle has been of the utmost importance to the Liberal cause. You gave us the approval of the greatest landowner in the country. You gave a friendly reception to our illustrious candidate. And the modesty displayed by your Lordship in withdrawing yourself as much as possible from direct contact with the contest has been remarked on by us all with pleasure.'[28]

The Midlothian campaign was riddled with delicious paradoxes. It heralded a new age in British democracy, when for the first time the power of mass public opinion was deliberately courted and wielded in a party political cause, yet its mastermind was an aristocrat who was never democratically elected to Parliament. It was the first truly modern political campaign, featuring all the weapons of press manipulation and party rallies, yet the constituency itself could have hardly been more old-fashioned, with barely 15 per cent of its male residents entitled to vote because of the property qualifications which still restricted the franchise. Indeed, in many ways Midlothian resembled a throwback to the corrupt political arrangements of the eighteenth century. Until the result was declared, Liberals were anxious lest the tenants of the Duke of Buccleuch, who possessed 430,000 acres in the Lowlands, should be persuaded to vote in their landlord's interest. And throughout the campaign there was a constant worry on both sides about their opponents' attempts to create 'faggot' votes by putting property in the name of party supporters in order to qualify them for the franchise. 'The Tories are making faggots like mad, but I doubt they will be able to do anything seriously to shake the position,' W.P. Adam warned Rosebery in January 1880.[29]

But the greatest paradox of all was that the entire thrust of the Midlothian campaign was a refutation of the principles by which Rosebery later governed Britain's destiny. All the strongest themes in his own foreign policy – continuity with his Tory predecessors, the maintenance of the strength of Empire, the primacy of British interests over moral abstractions – were those so loudly rejected by Gladstone in his attacks on Lord Beaconsfield. Whereas Rosebery, like many Victorian radicals, believed in the supremacy of the Anglo-Saxon race, Gladstone talked the Little Englander language of the world community. Rosebery specifically rejected the concept that Britain should act as a global policeman enforcing human rights, but Gladstone publicly warned that 'there is no duty so sacred and incumbent upon any Government in its foreign policy as that careful and strict regard to public law.'[30] Gladstone was an internationalist, Rosebery an imperialist. It is fascinating to look at Gladstone's most famous speech in Midlothian, in which, referring to Afghanistan, he said, 'Remember that the rights of those savages, as we call them, and the sanctity of life among the hill tribes and the happiness of their humble homes amid the winter snows . . . are as sacred in the eyes of Almighty God as are your own', and to compare this with Rosebery's pragmatic insouciance over the fate of the Siamese people at the hands of French imperialist aggression, as expressed to Queen Victoria in 1893: 'The behaviour of France to Siam has it appears been base, cruel and treacherous. Perhaps nothing so cynically vile is on record. But that is not our affair. We cannot afford to be the Knight Errant of the World, careering about to redress grievances and help the weak. If the French cut the throats of half Siam in cold blood we should not be justified in going to war with her.'[31]

Such differences were not apparent in 1880, when both men could bask in the glow of victory. Midlothian transformed the political landscape of Britain, restoring Gladstone to the first place in the Liberal party. Though he was nominally no more than a private member at the time of the campaign, the two official Parliamentary leaders, Lord Granville and Lord Hartington, recognised that he was the only man to form the new Government. Queen Victoria was appalled by this development, saying that 'she would sooner abdicate than send for or have anything to do with that half-mad firebrand who would soon ruin everything and be a dictator.' But once Granville and Hartington had refused the Premiership she was left with no alternative, and on 23 April 1880 Gladstone became Prime Minister for the second time.

There was widespread speculation that Rosebery would be offered a major post in Government, perhaps the Viceroyalty of Ireland, or even a place in Cabinet. But Gladstone always tried to cling to the dictum of Sir Robert Peel that no man should advance directly to the Cabinet without having previously held junior office; he was not about to make an exception for Rosebery, who was untested in administration and had limited Parliamentary experience. Yet Gladstone did want him in his Ministry, and on 24 April he offered him the position of Under-Secretary at the India Office, a department which, he told him, 'was of paramount importance and difficulty'.[32] What Gladstone had not reckoned with was Rosebery's near-paranoid sensitivity over accusations that his main purpose in organising the Midlothian campaign was to win political promotion. In particular, he was bitterly resentful of claims that he had used his personal fortune to gain influence over Gladstone by paying all his election expenses, a charge continually levelled by the Tories during the 1880 election. Certainly his expenditure on Midlothian was substantial; in his diary for 30 June 1882 Edward Hamilton recorded that Rosebery confessed to having spent £50,000 – perhaps an exaggeration, though it may have included the purchase of a local estate to boost the 'faggot' vote.[33]

In his mood of fastidiousness over Midlothian, Rosebery had long since decided that he would reject any offer from Gladstone. After a meeting with the new Prime Minister he noted: 'I in a troubled voice told him of my resolutions taken a year ago to accept no office. He argued vehemently against this, took my hand and said that there were things which we could never forget etc. I, much pressed, begged for a reprieve.'[34] This was followed by a letter to Gladstone that exuded a spirit of martyrdom.

> I have laid awake nearly all night thinking it over, for of course to me it is the most critical moment of my life. I cannot deny that for some time past it has seemed to me possible that this period of trial might come. Otherwise it would have been useless to take the resolution that I did. But the crisis has come, I must face it. If I take this appointment I lose the certainty that what I have done in this matter of the elections, however slight, has been disinterested. In losing that I lose more than political distinction could repay me. I would feel that where I only meant personal devotion and public spirit, others would see, and perhaps with reason, personal ambition and public office-seeking.'[35]

To some, Rosebery's pained response seemed out of all proportion to the offer Gladstone had made. Lord Granville wrote to him in tactful but admonitory tones: 'When Gladstone told me your answer I said to myself that at a moment when repudiation of office is not the general fault of the times, "Bravo Rosebery". But a moment's reflection proved to me you and I were wrong. If Gladstone had offered you high office, one to your merits, then your acceptance might have provoked some sneers. But Gladstone has done the contrary. As he himself says, he has only offered you the post of danger and difficulty . . . There was never such an opportunity for a man of your power of speaking, with all the ammunition of the Indian office at your disposal, a chief who has perfect confidence in you and on whom you can thoroughly rely.'[36] His appeal fell on deaf ears, as Granville told the Queen: 'Lord Rosebery would accept nothing, as he said it would look as if Mr Gladstone had paid him for what he had done.'[37]

Others were more supportive. Rosebery's devoted Hannah was keen to justify her husband's refusal, telling Constance Leconfield: 'You may feel disappointed but you will enter into and love the scruple which has caused

Archie to refuse. Of course wrong motives will be attributed but he has done right. You can scarcely have a conception of the extent of this sacrifice made of honour. I know every offer from Lord Chancellor to Lord-in-Waiting would be equally refused but the world will say he was not offered what he considers high enough. I know the harder the work, the greater the engagement for Archie. The world will say the contrary. No post could have been more congenial in every way.'[38] Edward Hamilton was equally understanding, writing that 'with the very prominent part he has taken about Mr Gladstone and Midlothian, it is probably most wise that he should clear himself in the eyes of the world from the charge of ambition and self-interestedness.'[39] Mary Gladstone even thought his sacrifice was heroic: 'No words of mine can possibly express what I think of your decision. However much one may regret it, I think it is quite *splendid*. I think it is quite grand.'[40] Embarrassed by such praise, Rosebery told her that 'there is nothing "grand" in what I have done, for I had literally no option in the matter. Nothing but the resolution I took could have enabled me to get through the election or to have lived with your father in terms of frankness and freedom. When you analyse my motive, it is little more than a half selfish sacrifice to peace of mind. Moreover my real motives are so well known that it would be a waste of time to dilate on them. They are: 1) Annoyance at not being asked to join the Cabinet. 2) Dislike of hard work. 3) Passion for the Turf.'[41] Beneath this veneer of humorous self-deprecation, there was some accuracy in what Rosebery said of himself. His talk of personal honour could not conceal that he had a streak of deep ambition and a high opinion of himself; Gladstone in 1890 described Rosebery as 'the most ambitious man he had ever come across (ambitious in the sense of being conscious that he had the power to lead and wishing to exercise it to the full).'[42] Combined with his prickliness, this was to lead him into an increasingly erratic and often contradictory pattern of behaviour during the second Gladstone administration.

After confirming his refusal, Rosebery concluded his diary account of the business on a note of self-pity: 'So ends my one chance of public life. I subside to obscurity and turnips.'[43] But Gladstone had not given up; in July, when the Indian Under-Secretaryship fell vacant once more, he offered him the post a second time. On this occasion Rosebery had a more convincing excuse for his refusal: ill-health. Earlier in the year he had contracted scarlet fever, from which he had not fully recovered, and in June 1880 his doctor ordered him to take the cure in Germany for three months. It appeared, too, that in the aftermath of Midlothian, the highly-strung Earl was suffering a mild nervous breakdown, as he admitted to the Prime

Minister in explaining his second refusal of office. 'The absolute, miserable and decisive reason that now compels me to hold aloof is my health. It is a disagreeable subject to dwell upon . . . I do not know what is the matter with me, medically speaking, but speaking as the patient, it is prostration physical and mental. I felt tired when I left London but not the annihilation of the present moment.' Rosebery added that he had seen a doctor in Frankfurt who, when told of Gladstone's offer, 'screamed at the idea, said it was out of the question and that three months' office now would do me more harm than ten years' hard work hereafter. I believe he is right but at the present I am good for nothing.'[44]

Teutonic medical techniques appeared to have little effect, however. 'Result of my cure: complete depression and exhaustion,' Rosebery noted in his diary towards the end of the first month.[45] His darkening mood revealed itself in a letter to Mary Gladstone in which, talking of his second rejection of office, he said: 'It is worse than the first time, as this hamlet is so quiet and lonely that one has nothing to do but brood and ever since this position has arisen I sleep as badly again . . . I was wonderfully well for two days the week before last and I should have accepted the command of the Channel Fleet or the See of Canterbury but I suppose I over-estimated myself and went down like a stone.'[46] In August it was the turn of the India Secretary Lord Hartington to try to interest him in the job: 'Were it not for the waste of time in everlasting attendance in the House, which makes all official work a burden, I cannot imagine anything more interesting than the work of the India Office.'[47] But Rosebery was still adamant that he was unfitted for such duties, and Hannah warned Constance Leconfield that 'Archie is very low spirited.'[48] Delicacy of this kind made Gladstone rather unsympathetic to Rosebery. 'He is physically rather too self-conscious, perhaps, for his health,' the Prime Minister told Granville.[49]

By the end of the summer Rosebery was fed up with German cures. He decided to return to England, vowing that he would live 'as a country gentleman who has no aspirations except to get *The Field* and *The Times* regularly and to produce a fatter ox than my neighbours.'[50] This was, of course, just a pose. Rosebery could not escape involvement in politics; nor, had he really wanted to, would his wife and friends have let him. 'You have scarcely an idea how strong the affection of the Scottish people for you is. In all political and many social gatherings you are the first they think of, and when you refuse, as in many cases you must, there is genuine vexation and grief,'[51] wrote his old St Andrews mentor Professor James Donaldson in October. His popularity is Scotland was illustrated at the beginning of November, when over the course of just one week he spoke at a banquet in Edinburgh for the Scottish Chief Whip W.P. Adam, was elected Rector of Edinburgh University, and travelled to deliver his Rectorial address at Aberdeen University, where the students were so excited by his presence that they not only dragged his carriage on foot from the railway station to his hotel, but also founded a Rosebery Club in his honour.

In his personal life Rosebery appeared, on the surface, to be content. Hannah was proving a fertile as well as a loving wife, providing him with two daughters in the first three years of their marriage: Sybil, born in September 1879, and Margaret, known as Peggy, born in January 1881. Two sons followed, Harry, who became the 6th Earl, born in January 1882, and Neil, born in December of the same year. If his marriage had turned Rosebery into a great magnate, there were drawbacks, as he joked in his diary: since his wedding, he wrote, 'I have divided mankind into three categories (with a few brilliant exceptions): 1. Those who abuse me because my wife has money; 2. Those who want some of that money; 3. Those who do both.'[52] He was now firmly established as one of the leading figures of society, which meant that all his activities were a source of interest to the press. In June 1880, for example, when he went on a driving tour of Scotland with a group of US millionaires led by the Iron King Andrew Carnegie, the *Pall Mall Gazette* covered their departure and referred to his high spirits: 'Lord Rosebery, who with his close-shaven face and spruce attire, his bell-shaped hat and humorous smile which plays about his mouth, is the very ideal of a prosperous comedian.' Backed by the Mentmore stud, he was more successful than ever on the racetrack, winning the Oaks in 1883 with Bonnie Jean. He was a fine shot and at Dalmeny during the 1880 season he often produced a daily bag of more than 400. He remained on good terms with Royalty. In June 1881 the Prince and Princess of Wales spent a day at The Durdans, an occasion that as it turned out was fraught with hazard. 'I went to meet them at the station and as they arrived five minutes too soon I was within an ace of being late. They looked at blood stock, played lawn tennis and amused themselves. I, attempting to hit a bad tennis ball over the house, as nearly as possible sent it through the open window where the Prince was endeavouring to enjoy a quiet Sunday – my second near escape today,' ran Rosebery's spirited account in his diary.[53] A wonderful picture of the rhythm of life at Dalmeny was left by Sam Ward, who had to flee America in 1882 because of money troubles and was given temporary sanctuary by Rosebery.

> Life here is as réglée as music paper. Breakfast is at 9.30, lunch at 2, tea at 5 and dinner at 8, this always a case of grande tenue. We join the ladies in the parlour at 10, they retire at 11 and we adjourn to the smoking room. The

eminent charm of this life, apart from its hospitality and sans-gêne, is that everything is so noiseless. The major domo never appears at the table for less than six persons but his directing hand is everywhere. I have a footman detailed to me who looks after me like two Jerrys. Every possible wish is anticipated and the only duty is that once a day you wear the uniform of a gentleman, the putting on of which is always refreshing.

A few months later, Sam was present in the occasion of a large servants' ball in the great dining hall of Dalmeny. 'There were 160 guests and more than a dozen footmen and valets who looked like finished gentlemen with graceful manners. Lord Rosebery opened the dance by taking out a splendid specimen of majestic womanhood, Mrs Mackay, who had been the chief nurse attendant on Lady Rosebery.'[54]

Further insights into the domestic circumstances of the Roseberys at this time are provided by the waspish Loulou Harcourt. After a visit to Mentmore he wrote that 'Rosebery is a large eater and drinker and very fat for his age and height. How he survives the good living of this place I don't know; truffles seem to be treated here much as potatoes elsewhere.'[55] And he saw the same plumpness in other Roseberys: 'Sybil Primrose is very nice but comparatively as fat as her mother [Sybil was 18 months old].'[56] Harcourt also went up to Dalmeny, and was impressed. 'The chief beauty is the size and numbers of the trees growing near the sea and walks by it through the pine woods.' He was less taken with Rosebery's project to restore the ruined castle of Barnbougle in the grounds of Dalmeny. This granite fort, which had looked out over the Firth of Forth since the twelfth century, had fallen into disrepair after the building of Dalmeny; it had always been liable to flooding, which only worsened its collapse. 'What good it will be when it is finished is more than anyone can make out but at present it gives him something on which to spend his money.'[57] Harcourt greatly underestimated the value Rosebery set on Barnbougle; once the work was completed in April 1882, he used it as a sacred retreat. After The Durdans it was probably his favourite home, one where he could find real solitude and peace, and he zealously guarded its privacy. 'No admittance is allowed except by him in person,' noted Mary Gladstone.[58] He had a library built there to house his collection of Scottish literature, and in the great vaulted banqueting hall he installed a minstrels' gallery, in which he would rehearse his major speeches. In seeking to overcome the insomnia that plagued him, Rosebery took to spending his nights there, finding the stillness of the waters conducive to sleep. 'I dined at Dalmeny but slept at Barnbougle for the first time. It was a strange feeling inhabiting the disused home of one's predecessors. But it was delightful sleeping . . . with the outlook entirely sea,' he wrote in his diary for 7 April 1882. Three days later he recorded of Barnbougle, 'I sleep here but live chiefly at Dalmeny.'[59] In future years guests at Dalmeny grew used to the sight of the 5th Earl trudging off into the darkness at the end of the evening, escaping to his craggy sanctum.

Another portrait of the Roseberys' early domestic life is provided by the novelist Henry James, who was a guest at Mentmore in the autumn of 1880. 'With youth, cleverness, a delightful face, a happy character, a Rothschild wife of numberless millions to distinguish and demoralize him, he wears them with such tact and bonhomie that you almost forgive him,' he told his mother. Of Mentmore he said: 'Everything is magnificent. The house is a huge modern palace, filled with wonderful objects accumulated by the late Baron Meyer de Rothschild, Lady Rosebery's father. All of them are precious and many exquisite and their general Rothschildish splendour is only equalled by their profusion . . . They are all at afternoon tea downstairs in a vast, gorgeous hall, where an upper gallery looks down like the colonnade in Paul Veronese's pictures and the chairs are all golden thrones, belonging to ancient Doges of Venice. I have retired from the glittering scene to meditate by my bedroom fire on the fleeting character of earthly possessions.' At one luncheon party, James was amused to listen to Rosebery arguing 'that "the ideal of a happy life was that of Cambridge, Mass., living like Longfellow." You may imagine that at this the company looked awfully vague and I thought of proposing to exchange Mentmore for 20 Quincy Street.'* Henry James preferred the more homely atmosphere of The Durdans in Surrey, which he visited in January 1881. 'This is a delightful house, full of books and entertaining sporting pictures (to say nothing of several charming Gainsboroughs and Watteaus) and worth to my mind a hundred times over all the grandeurs of Mentmore.'[60] But it was the lavish setting of Mentmore that served as the model for one of his later and less readable novels, *The Spoils of Poynton*, its plot based on a family struggle over the belongings in a large country house, Poynton Park. After his visit to Mentmore James told Rosebery that he was 'touched' by his friendship and wanted 'to do/write something striking and picturesque to prove to you that I am not on the whole unworthy of your confidence' – but in fact the novel was not written until 1897.

Usually so perceptive when it came to the human condition, Henry James was wrong about Rosebery's 'happy' character. In truth, despite all his wealth, popularity and fecundity, Rosebery still knew moments of blackest despair, made all the worse by the enervating illness from which

---

*James's family home in the USA.

he suffered during much of 1880. In the course of that year he penned these verses, which bear all the indications of a form of clinical depression:

> Oh baleful star, that parches up my days,
> Such as of old portended plague and death,
> Sinister sign of woe in bloody days,
> Casting a blight on the world beneath.
>
> Let there be darkness, thou hast said it Lord,
> Let there be darkness, lo, and I am dark,
> Nor hope, nor solace can my mind afford,
> No comfort, not a glimmer, not a spark.[61]

In this mournful state Rosebery had become increasingly dissatisfied with his political position, and by the beginning of 1881 two related grievances were looming large in his mind. The first was that Scotland was receiving little attention from the Liberal government because Gladstone was so concerned with Ireland. As his friend Charles Cooper, editor of the *Scotsman*, told him, 'Scotland is very much discontented with the manner in which she is being treated. After making allowances for the Irish trouble, there is much left to complain about. I am quite concerned that there will never be comprehensive treatment of Scotland until she has a political representative in Government capable of making her voice heard.'[62] This was exactly the conclusion Rosebery had reached. He complained to the Home Secretary Sir William Harcourt (father of Loulou, who served as his private secretary from 1882) about the inadequacy of the current arrangement whereby Scottish affairs were dealt with in the Commons by the Lord Advocate, and urged the appointment of a separate Minister for Scotland, perhaps by reviving the old post of President of the Privy Council of Scotland, abolished at the time of the Union in 1707. In a letter to Gladstone's secretary Arthur Godley, Rosebery warned: 'If things go on as they are, you will have Scotland as well as Ireland on your hands. I am sorry to say that a feeling is gaining ground that Scotland, having served her purpose at the General Election, is now completely neglected. I write strongly because I feel strongly and because blame is unjustly thrown on me.'[63]

The second, more personal, grievance was that Gladstone was ignoring his claims to office. This seems rather ludicrous of Rosebery since he had twice in the previous year declined an under-secretaryship. Yet his resentment festered for months until it finally burst open at Easter 1881, when the Cabinet post of Lord Privy Seal became vacant. Sir William Harcourt pressed Rosebery's case with the idea that he could take over Scottish business, but Gladstone, maintaining his conservative Peelite ideas about Cabinet advancement, refused to consider him and instead appointed the lightweight Ulster peer Lord Carlingford. Rosebery exploded with fury. Harcourt reported to Gladstone on Good Friday after a visit to The Durdans that he had found Rosebery in a 'very great state of disappointment and irritation at the recent appointment to the Privy Seal, which office he says he did not expect – though that I consider is not quite an accurate view of the matter – but because he seems to have expected confidences on the subject which he did not receive. However unreasonable this may appear I can assure you that the annoyance is very strong and the vexation very deep. One of the symptoms of the provocation is that he wholly declines to be consulted on Scotch business, on which I was in the habit of taking his opinion, as he says that he has "now no relations of any kind with the Government".'[64]

Some saw this as the irrationality and self-centredness of a spoilt child. Having discounted all thoughts of office one year, the next Rosebery demanded, if not a Cabinet place himself, then the right to advise the Prime Minister on the composition of the Cabinet. Gladstone found this stance ridiculous, and said as much in his reply to Harcourt: 'The notion of a title to be consulted on the succession to a Cabinet office is absurd . . . I believe Rosebery to have a very modest estimate of himself and trust he has not fallen into so gross an error.'[65] Granville was rather more scathing, telling Gladstone on 16 April that he 'always had doubts of the refusal [to take the job] of under-secretary being pure chivalry.'[66] Just as dismissive was Edward Hamilton, now working in Downing Street and usually loyal: 'I believed better things of him. Mr Gladstone is extremely concerned. What Rosebery evidently wants is to be lifted straight into Cabinet without subordinate office and that is not feasible, to be taken into consultation regarding the constitution of the Cabinet, on which Cabinet ministers themselves are not consulted except such as Lord Granville and Lord Hartington.'[67]

The problem was made worse by Hannah, who fed Rosebery's discontent and berated the Gladstones. The distance between the two families, which Mary Gladstone had remarked on during Midlothian, now widened, with Hannah complaining about the obtuseness of the Prime Minister. 'He may be a marvel of erudition, but he will never understand a man, still less a woman.'[68] News of the falling-out spread through the highest circles in the Liberal party, as Loulou Harcourt recorded. 'There has been a big row between Mrs Gladstone and Lady Rosebery over the way the latter's husband was treated on the Privy Seal question. Mrs

Gladstone has had hysterics.'[69] Rosebery was so worried about the quarrel that he sought the advice of Sir Charles Dilke. 'She has been silly but Mrs Gladstone is so silly also that rows were inevitable,' wrote Dilke privately.[70] In fact, Granville thought that Hannah was the real difficulty. 'I very much doubt communications with the Countess,' he told Gladstone at the end of April. 'Women are always more unreasonable than their husbands about the claims of these and this seems especially the case with Hannah. A little confidential talk with him, on the state of affairs, would more likely soothe him than anything else.'

As a result of this letter Gladstone had a meeting with Rosebery on 2 May at which, according to Dilke, 'the differences between the two were patched up and peace restored'.[71] As a mark of the reconciliation, Gladstone agreed to go down with his wife to The Durdans. 'I really think all is smooth here; certainly nothing can be more kind. The country is perfectly delicious,' he told Granville.[72] Yet such signs of warmth did not mean that Rosebery was ready to surrender to Gladstone. At the beginning of May he was yet again offered the despised post of Under-Secretary for India. Once more he declined, setting out his reasons 'with great plainness' in an interview with Gladstone. '1. Scotland, to which I am bound by gratitude and which I should have to give up if I took subordinate office; 2. India office no longer giving opportunities this year; 3. Myself – great age required as qualification for cabinet – did not want to be buried in an out-office till I was 60.'[73] Mary Gladstone was almost as perplexed as her father by Rosebery's obstinacy. In a letter of 12 May she urged Rosebery to 'see that it is entirely with a view of getting you into the Cabinet' that the offer was made. She added, 'I can't help feeling if only you would be content to leave your fate in his hands, you might trust him.'[74] But the personal relationship between the two men could never return to the intimacy which had existed at Midlothian, not least because of the friction between their wives. When Loulou Harcourt went down to The Durdans in June, shortly after the Gladstones' visit, he 'found Lady Rosebery in a perfect state of fury with Mrs and Miss Gladstone who, she said, had made themselves perfectly odious during their stay there.'[75]

Throughout this episode Rosebery behaved with a touchiness and an arrogance that hardly matched his political experience. He virtually stated that he would have Cabinet office – or nothing. But Gladstone cannot be absolved entirely from blame. Rugged and imperious, he could be curiously unappreciative of the sensitivities of other men, as he later showed during the Home Rule crisis of 1886 in his disastrous management of Joseph Chamberlain, a far tougher figure than Rosebery. The Colossus of

Victorian Liberalism, concentrating his energies on his great moral crusades and epochal legislation, had little time for the normal compromises of human existence. Gladstone's own daughter Mary admitted to Rosebery that her father was 'not exactly quick at understanding people's insides'.[76] Nor did Gladstone share Rosebery's ready wit. The Earl once told his secretary Thomas Gilmour that 'Mr Gladstone was absolutely without a sense of humour and the only jokes he could appreciate were of the schoolboy kind.'[77]

Even in the face of such differences, Rosebery's isolation from the Government could not last indefinitely. In July 1881 the Under-Secretaryship at the Home Office became vacant, and Gladstone offered it to Rosebery. Mundane in its way, the attraction of this post for Rosebery was its supposed connection to Scottish business. Moreover, Gladstone – in a letter that was to cause him untold trouble over the next two years – hinted that acceptance would lead swiftly to promotion to the Cabinet. 'The office is entirely at your disposal,' he wrote on 30 July, 'and such a disposal, I need hardly say, would give me great pleasure. For my hour glass is running out and I should be grieved not to see you brought into closer relation with the Government of your country and with your natural and destined career . . . I do not think the arrangement would last very long in its present form. There must be within the next six months further manipulation of political offices and with this there is the likelihood of development, uncertain as to time, but certain.'[78] Rosebery still paraded doubts, telling Gladstone that 'people may attribute personal motives to my having urged some change in the management of Scottish business', but finally accepted: 'You are always devising some friendly plan for me and I fear you must often have thought me crotchety with regard to them . . . I am pleased and proud to think that I shall at last serve under you.'[79]

There was widespread relief that, after more than a year of prevarication, Rosebery had finally accepted office. 'He deserves it thoroughly and I am sure it is the right thing for a politician to serve his apprenticeship in the ranks and not be lumped into the Cabinet,' wrote Edward Hamilton.[80] Sir Charles Dilke, President of the Board of Trade, spoke for many in the Liberal party when he told Rosebery, 'I congratulate ourselves on having you among us, pending the coming of a time when you may hold an office worthy of you.'[81] But a more cautionary note was sounded by Frank Lawley of the *Daily Telegraph*. In a clever line later borrowed by Rosebery – and wrongly thought to have originated with him – Lawley wrote that 'the two happiest days of a man's life are said to be those on which he first takes office and first quits office'. In an uncannily prophetic note he added,

'To go into office with Harcourt (whom I have never been able to regard as quite a gentleman) as your chief cannot be an ecstatic experience, especially when so much has to be given up and so little gained as in your case.'[82] With a journalist's insight, Lawley had highlighted a central problem Rosebery was to face in his tenure at the Home Office: the character of the Secretary of State Sir William Harcourt. A large man in both personality and physique, Harcourt was a superb Parliamentarian who relished the noise and smoke of a battle on the floor of the Commons. His mastery of detail and capacity for hard work also made him an excellent administrator. But he was a politician riddled with flaws, the worst of which was his ungovernable temper. Intolerably rude, he seemed as eager to pick fights with his colleagues as with the Opposition. 'I hope that among the many good works you may do at the Home Office you will do your best to mollify the somewhat rough manners of your Secretary of State which too frequently give offence,' Hamilton said to Rosebery.[83] In addition, like many lawyers Harcourt had a reputation for insincerity which rendered less effective the power of his rhetoric. He was said to lack any real political faith, preferring abuse to rational argument. More than a decade later the Earl of Kimberley, one of the Liberals' elder statesmen, summed up the view of Harcourt's enemies: 'Utterly without principle, an arrant coward and a blustering bully, he combines every quality which unfits a man for the conduct of the affairs of the nation.'[84]

Before the summer was out it was obvious that Rosebery's spell at the Home Office would not be harmonious. Harcourt, who had supported in principle Rosebery's elevation to the ranks of Government, now complained that this particular appointment left him with no minister in the Lower House to ease his burden. 'Already I find the Department in confusion and despair at the loss of a House of Commons Under-Secretary,' he wrote to Gladstone on 5 August.[85] Nor was Rosebery ideally suited to performing the routine duties of Home Office administration as a subordinate. He was capable of sustained industry, but only if a subject or a role interested him, as his old tutor William Johnson had so often complained. Foreign affairs and the Empire might stir his soul, but for all his conviction that Scotland was neglected at Westminster, the minor intricacies of Scottish bureaucracy were hardly likely to do so. Among the issues he handled for Harcourt in the autumn of 1881 were the appointment of the Inspector of Salmon Fisheries, police estimates for Scotland, the composition of the Edinburgh Board of Works, conditions in Ayr prison, a vacancy on the Lunacy Commission, and the work of Greenock Magistrates' Court. Little wonder that he wrote to Sam Ward in November 1881: 'I am driving, with a quill behind my ear, on a high stool, with a coroner on my right and a policeman on my left, earning £500-a-year by confinement in a gaseous, chilly, blue-booking, dusty, musty imitation of a sub-editor's office.'[86] An intriguing note in the Rosebery papers of a conversation with Gladstone at this time shows Rosebery's sense of ennui. The Prime Minister opened by asking Rosebery how he liked his work at the Home Office:

ROSEBERY: 'Pretty well, though there is a great deal of detail which is not enticing.'

GLADSTONE: 'There is no harm in that. It is a good thing to become acquainted with the various offices.' He then said he was planning 'a con-siderable re-constitution of the present Cabinet'. But he warned that this re-constitution 'may only happen when I go, and if I go so will Bright.'

ROSEBERY: 'So will others. I should certainly resign for one.'

At this, according to Rosebery, Gladstone looked much surprised and said, 'Oh, I hope not. Surely Granville is an excellent fellow to get on with, an excellent specimen of a Liberal peer.'[87]

Added to Rosebery's boredom with his work was his deepening frus-tration over the conduct of Scottish business, which was still handled in the Commons by the Lord Advocate, an arrangement widely condemned in Scotland. The difficulty was that Gladstone was too immersed in Ireland to contemplate change; in December 1881, for instance, he told Rosebery that 'it would be very difficult for me under the pressure of necessary busi-ness'[88] to receive a deputation on the question of Scottish courts.

Gladstone's declared mission to pacify Ireland was failing. His land legis-lation of 1881, intended to quell Irish agrarian grievances, had done noth-ing to halt the country's slide into anarchy, as the nationalist movement led by the cold, implacable figure of Charles Stewart Parnell – paradoxically, a Cambridge-educated, cricket-loving, Protestant landowner – prevented its operation. The boycott of landlords was reinforced; Fenian terrorism worsened. What the Irish wanted was not merely land reform, but a mea-sure of real self-government. Gladstone was not yet ready for such a radi-cal step, and instead moved in the opposite direction, locking up Parnell and the other leading nationalists in Kilmainham gaol in the autumn of 1881. The dilemma for Gladstone now was how far to balance the repres-sion of extreme nationalism with further attempts at the amelioration of perceived injustices. Like most Liberals, Rosebery believed that a policy of pure coercion would never work. Even in the face of Parnellite agitation, he told a meeting in Hull in December 1881, the Government had to continue the attempt to make Ireland more prosperous, and reconciled to

British rule. 'We can but sow the seed hoping that if we ourselves are not spared, others may reap the harvest.'[89] And just as he despised anti-Semitism, so he harboured none of the virulent anti-Irish prejudice that characterised some other late Victorian politicians: 'We are dealing with an exceptional race,' he told his Hull audience.

Early in 1882 the policy of reconciliation was tried again. Through the rather incongruous channels of Joseph Chamberlain and W.H.O'Shea, husband of Parnell's mistress, an agreement was negotiated whereby Parnell was released from Kilmainham in return for a promise of co-operation over land reform. The Irish Chief Secretary W.E. Forster was so disgusted that he resigned from the Cabinet. Rosebery took the opportunity to indulge in one of his favourite pastimes: considering his position. 'I had a talk with Rosebery at the office and found him in very low spirits,' wrote Loulou Harcourt in his diary for 5 May, 'as he is a little bit of a "Forsterian" and thinks everything will go to the deuce now that Chamberlain has got his own way in Irish affairs.' The next day at The Durdans Rosebery wrote a long memorandum on Ireland which is interesting for its revelation of his near-obsession with his own reputation and independence.

What then is my personal relation to these events? This is not egotism, but honour. Nicety of honour can hardly be carried to too great a length. This is emphatically a new departure. There was no question of alliance with, or reliance upon, Mr Parnell when I joined the Government. I suddenly find myself embarked on an enterprise which I cannot justify or defend. If I remain in the Government I am for life connected, however humbly, with this policy, just as every lord-in-waiting has to bear his share: and yet this policy I believe to be a fatal mistake. What then am I to do? Should I not resign? This it would seem is the obvious course. But it is not so obvious. In the first place, my position in the Government is so humble and one that no one could believe that, if I remain in, I remain from regard to my place. It was no doubt higher than my merits deserved but nevertheless to me personally the acceptance of it was a great sacrifice: nay, my retention of it is a sacrifice and irksome to a degree which many may not understand. So if I remain in office I cannot suspect my own motives whatever others may do. In the second place there is my connection with Mr Gladstone. By that I mean my personal devotion to him and my sense that he deserves all support at this moment.[90]

Fortunately for Rosebery's standing among his Liberal colleagues, this self-regarding memorandum was neither completed nor circulated. Instead, on the same day, 6 May, he asked Gladstone for an interview to discuss his doubts about the so-called Kilmainham treaty, 'a matter which puzzles me greatly and which is of first importance to me as a member of your Government.'[91]

This request was immediately overtaken by what was probably the worst tragedy to afflict Gladstone in his long public life. On 7 May Forster's replacement as Irish Chief Secretary, Lord Frederick Cavendish, who was also Gladstone's nephew, and the Dublin Castle official T.H. Burke were brutally stabbed to death in Phoenix Park by a gang of Fenian terrorists. Cavendish and Rosebery had been close, indeed they had been together in London just days before the murder, discussing the problems of working with Harcourt. Now Rosebery, whose melodramatic streak was often displayed in times of crisis, rushed up to London to the Gladstones: 'I can only say, "God sustain you all." It is past all words.'[92] In his diary he noted with a flourish that all his doubts about Gladstone's Irish policy had been swept away by the tragedy: 'Of course this event has cleared my course completely. All hands to the pumps.'[93]

The Government, which only two years earlier had come to power on a tide of optimism over the righteousness of its external policies, was lurching from one disaster to another. In the Transvaal in South Africa, a revolt by the Dutch Boers in 1881 had resulted in an embarrassing defeat for the British at Majuba Hill. The subsequent Pretoria Convention, by which the Boers effectively regained their independence, only reinforced the humiliation. In Egypt, a Muslim revolt led by Arabi Pasha against the ruling Khedive resulted in a massacre of foreigners in Alexandria in July 1882. As anarchy developed and British financial interests came under threat, Gladstone ordered the bombardment of Alexandria and the invasion of Egypt; a military expedition under Sir Garnet Wolseley destroyed Arabi's forces at the battle of Tel-el-Kebir in September. The victory somewhat restored Gladstone's – and Britain's – prestige, though many radicals were infuriated by the contrast between the Prime Minister's Midlothian rhetoric about the 'rights of savages' and the harsh reality of his aggressive Egyptian policy. Gladstone's closest radical ally, John Bright, resigned from the Cabinet after the attack on Alexandria, expostulating to Rosebery that the Government's policy was 'simply damnable – worse than anything ever perpetrated by Dizzy'.[94] Rosebery fully supported Gladstone over Egypt – party because, cynics suggested, he wanted to protect his finances: at the time, due to his Rothschild links, he held some £10,000 in Egyptian bonds.* Unfortunately, Rosebery's innate flippancy served only to confirm

---

* A charge that could also be made against Gladstone, who in December 1881 held £40,500 in Egyptian bonds (Roy Jenkins, *Gladstone*, 1995).

this impression. In a grotesque misjudgement during the course of a visit to Downing Street in June 1882 he told the poet and Arabist Wilfrid Scawen Blunt that his 'only interest in Egypt was that of a bondholder'. Blunt, who despised British imperialism in general and Rosebery in particular, reported this remark across London society. Rosebery later explained to his confidant Ronald Munro-Ferguson exactly how how his humour had landed him in trouble: he had called to see Edward Hamilton, Gladstone's secretary, and Blunt happened to be in the room. When Blunt asked Rosebery if he was interested in Egypt, 'I, with a view to turn away the conversation on which it was generally understood that Mr Blunt was something of a bore, laughingly replied that my interest in Egypt was solely that of a bond-holder. Mr Blunt at once replied that in that case I might be assured that the only chance of my bonds being worth the paper they were written on lay in the British Government supporting Arabi. I at once discontinued the conversation, feeling at the time, I remember, that I had made a mistake in joking with a fanatic.'[95]

On top of all these political problems, there was the dark side of Gladstone's life to be dealt with. Now in his seventies, Gladstone had displayed renewed enthusiasm for his work in trying to 'rescue' prostitutes from the streets of London. While his Christian motivation was sincere, his diaries and correspondence suggest that he also derived a sexual frisson from bringing fallen women back to Downing Street. As in Rosebery there was a perpetual conflict between pleasure and duty, so in Gladstone there was always a tension between high morality and carnal desire. That erotic urge was comically highlighted in a comment he made to Regy Brett at a dinner in 1890. 'I often walk in Regent Street,' said Gladstone, 'and I observe the heels of ladies' boots with great and marked interest.' To which another guest, David Plunkett, made the riposte, 'I thought, Mr Gladstone, that it was their souls rather than their heels that you were specially interested in.'[96] Rosebery, still devoted to Gladstone, feared the destruction of the Prime Minister's reputation if these nocturnal interludes were made public, as did Edward Hamilton. 'Rosebery came to see me today much exercised in his mind as to further proof of Mr Gladstone's walking in the streets at night. It is a terribly unfortunate craze of his and the only wonder is that his enemies have not made more capital out of it,' recorded Hamilton on 9 February 1882. Hamilton thought Rosebery, in view of his closeness to Gladstone, should speak to him directly, but instead Rosebery called on Lord Granville, who was 'horrified to hear of the recurrence of the night walks and quite agreed that something ought to be said. He and Rosebery tossed up as to which of them should undertake the disagreeable and delicate task. R., having lost, came this morning and having made an excuse for an interview, courageously broached the subject. Mr Gladstone took it in good grace and was apparently impressed by Rosebery's words.'[97] He refused to give up his rescue work, however, ever if it left him open to blackmail. More than a quarter of a century later, Rosebery was made aware of the real danger Gladstone had been in. Noting a conversation in March 1908 with Sir Robert Anderson, the former head of Scotland Yard's detective department, Rosebery wrote that Anderson did not doubt Gladstone's double life was 'very immoral'. Anderson told Rosebery that in 1886 one of his constables had seen Gladstone going into 'a house of ill-fame' at noon one day, a sight also witnessed 'by plenty of workmen at their dinner'. According to Anderson, the incident came to the attention of the leading nonconformist ministers, who learnt that 'Gladstone was a constant visitor to the street . . . That's why they changed their voting intention and why Spurgeon called Gladstone mad.'* Anderson further informed Rosebery that he 'knew a former prostitute who had a letter from Gladstone written in terms of endearment. He had visited her and had a connection.' And there was another incident that showed how vulnerable Gladstone had made himself: a prostitute wrote to Gladstone, asking him to go to her home, as she sought to repent. Thinking this suspicious, Gladstone took along his wife. 'When they arrived, the door was opened by a woman stark naked,' said Anderson. In the teeth of Anderson's evidence Rosebery nevertheless concluded: 'I remain rooted in the conviction that all this, though injudicious, was apostolic. Not one word or innuendo to the contrary do I believe.'[98] Perhaps he was right; Anderson was an Irish Presbyterian obsessed with Biblical prophecies and the coming of the Anti-Christ. But Rosebery's reverence for Gladstone's street work should not be exaggerated; he joked that it was not as if Gladstone had achieved much, since he only 'saved' ten women in all his years of trying.[99]

By mid 1882 the intimacy that allowed Rosebery to talk frankly to Gladstone was coming under threat, as the Under-Secretary at the Home Office grew ever more disgruntled. Neither his accession to the Privy Council in August 1881 nor Gladstone's vague promises of some future promotion could assuage his indignation, and his foul mood was compounded by his long-standing grievance over the alleged unfair treatment of Scotland. In May, less than a fortnight after the Phoenix Park murders,

*Charles Spurgeon, the 'Prince of Preachers', was one of the great nonconformist leaders of the nineteenth century. In the mid 1880s part of the nonconformist movement broke away from Liberalism, ostensibly over Ireland, though Anderson here hints at a more personal cause for disillusion.

he urged Gladstone to appoint a Scotsman to the vacant Lordship of the Treasury, warning that without such a step as this Scotland's discontent could 'become consistent and general'.[100] In June he even hinted at resignation over Government indifference to the Scottish Endowments Bill: 'Not one minute of Government time has been allotted to Scotland or Scottish affairs. Can you be surprised that the people of Scotland complain?' Inevitably, Rosebery painted himself as the real victim of this neglect, moaning that 'the view taken in Scotland is that I have a considerable share in the responsibility and certainly wherever the Scottish halfpence may go, I shall get the Scottish kicks. That is not an eventuality I am prepared to face, when I am of the opinion that the aggressive boot contains a toe of justice.'[101]

The issues of Scotland and promotion to the Cabinet became conflated in Rosebery's mind by the revival of the idea, first floated by Harcourt in early 1881, that the Lord Privy Seal might take over Scottish business. Charles Cooper of the *Scotsman*, always eager to stoke Rosebery's Caledonian sensibilities, suggested that he would be ideal for such an appointment: 'the point is to have a Scotsman who shall be Scottish Minister in the Cabinet.'[102] Gladstone was having none of this, in part because there was no immediate vacancy, and in part because other more senior politicians had prior claims to Rosebery's, as he explained in conversation with the Earl after dinner on 2 August. 'Gladstone spoke of the difficulties (which I acknowledged) in reconstruction – the different shades of party, interests and nationalities that had to be thought of.' But Rosebery, while disavowing any personal feelings in the matter, was clearly annoyed at the way Gladstone had conveyed the impression that there were no ministers outside the Cabinet fit for promotion.[103]

When the 'reconstruction' finally occurred, in December 1882, Rosebery's worst fears were confirmed: he learnt from Gladstone that only the Earl of Derby and Sir Charles Dilke were to be admitted to the Cabinet. On 6 December he penned a letter to Gladstone in which he quoted accusingly from their previous correspondence at the time of his Home Office appointment, claiming that Gladstone had promised a reconstruction of offices within six months: 'I should never have connected myself with what I must regard as a very imperfect system of managing Scottish affairs or indeed have surrendered my liberty at all', said Rosebery, had it not been for that assurance. 'I am compelled to view the situation in a new light,' he concluded.[104] During the next week Rosebery sent the Prime Minister a series of angry letters, one of which, written on 10 December, summed up his outrage over both Scotland and his own position. 'I have never considered that the responsibility for Scottish administration should rest with the Under-Secretary for the Home Department. On two occasions last summer I ventured to point out to you that the arrangement could not last and I understood you assented. Now it seems that we are going into the next Parliament with the system unaltered.' Turning to his own case, Rosebery complained bitterly that 'if a somewhat Chinese principle of seniority is to prevail in promotion, it will be many years before I cease, except by my own act, to be an Under-Secretary. I am almost, if not quite, the junior member of the Government. In merit, I have no doubt that my inferiority would be equally undoubted. If I could ever hope to rise higher, it could only be by the favour and support of my fellow-countrymen. But if seniority is to be reckoned against me, that, and the probable succession of one, as well as the probable elevation of other ministers in the House of Lords, would keep me for ever in a subordinate position.' Finally came the usual threats of resignation: 'I do not value office at all. It is a sacrifice of much that renders life pleasant to me, leisure and independence and the life of the country. But, unattractive as it is, your remarks appear to open a gloomier vista still: and if the result of all this should be my retirement into private life, I should have nothing personal to regret, while I should feel that I could be of more use both to Scotland and yourself as an independent member than in my present position.'[105] In thus whipping up his own discontent Rosebery may have been unduly influenced by the example of his political hero William Pitt, who in 1781 had declared that he would not serve in a subordinate position in Rockingham's government. 'That he was wise, there can be no doubt. He retained his freedom and used that freedom well,' wrote Rosebery in his 1891 biography of Pitt.

Further peevish letters followed as Charles Cooper encouraged Rosebery to see himself as engaged in a battle of wills with the Prime Minister: 'I foresee unending complications and difficulties if you have to resign. But I do not see how it is to be avoided except on surrender by the Chief.'[106] On 15 December Rosebery grumbled to Gladstone that the business was 'absolutely nauseous to me from every point of view. As regards politics and office, I don't think I shall ever get the taste of it out of my mouth.' A day later he was attacking Gladstone's priorities: 'That you have been too busy to attend to Scottish business arrangements I readily believe. But that is exactly where the mischief lies. No minister of importance has the time to look after Scottish matters and so they have to be dealt with by subordinates who are not of importance, an arrangement which I know to be, as I have already said, derogatory and injurious.'

Few British prime ministers can ever have received such a fusillade of sullen criticism from a junior minister. Yet Gladstone, despite his draining workload, was initially conciliatory, gently reminding Rosebery on 12 December that 'Your prospects are brilliant as well as wide, but even you cannot dispense with much faith and patience.'[107] But gradually, as Rosebery's epistles accumulated, Gladstone's exasperation deepened. As he saw it, one of the main difficulties was that Rosebery had not set out any definite proposal for reforming the administration of Scotland. 'If you will lay before me your views of existing wants and the proper mode of supplying them, so that they may be considered by me and by the Cabinet, this shall not be neglected. At present I hardly know that I have any materials before me,' Gladstone wrote on 20 December. This merely sent Rosebery into another paroxysm, for in his view he had been making explicit demands regarding Scottish administration throughout the past eighteen months, and as long ago as April 1881 had sent Sir William Harcourt a detailed memorandum on the subject. Rosebery warned Gladstone that he had only taken office 'on the express terms that it would form the nucleus of a new office for the conduct of Scottish business which would soon be developed'; now he realised he had misunderstood the situation. 'An acute crisis' had therefore developed, which could only be resolved either by his own resignation or by the promise that a new arrangement would immediately be made.

Gladstone was shaken by this ultimatum. If he had understood Rosebery correctly, he replied on the 21st, 'I own I should hardly know how to deal with you or any man upon such terms.' To Granville Gladstone explained: 'I am sorry to say that Rosebery has inflicted on me a set of letters which appear to me astonishingly foolish, about the neglect of his country, the necessities of his position and the like: a tempest in a tea-kettle. It is marvellous how a man of such character and such gifts can be so silly. Nor does it mend yet.' Indeed it did not. On the 22nd Rosebery sent perhaps his most aggrieved letter yet, denying that any of his actions were motivated by feelings of pique. 'I am now running the risk of blighting my whole career, in the official sense, by leaving your Government and losing the intimacy with yourself that has been my happiness for three years and which made the drudgery of politics and office a grateful task. My personal devotion to you can never change . . . But my personal relations to politics can never be the same again. I can only wish to leave them and forget them. Whereas formerly it might have been a pleasure to serve you in any higher office you might have called me to, I never could willingly do so now. I entered upon office to secure attention and a definite department for my country. I shall leave it because I have failed.'[108]

At the highest levels of Government, patience with Rosebery's egotism was wearing thin. Gladstone had experienced nothing like it before, and even contemplated postponing a visit to Midlothian, planned for January 1883, while Rosebery 'continues in his tempestuous state of mind'.[109] He sent the entire correspondence to Lord Granville and Harcourt with a question: 'Is he beside himself or am I?' Harcourt, whose robust nature was such a contrast to Rosebery's, thought his Under-Secretary was being absurd, as his son Loulou recorded: 'Rosebery has been pressing what he chooses to call his claims very strongly and has used most immeasured and objectionable language to Gladstone. If he does resign, no doubt we should lose one or two seats in Scotland but apart from that the only mischief he would do would be to make himself rather disagreeable to Lord Granville in the House of Lords. The Home Secretary's only comment was that Rosebery was a conceited little ass and he should like it if he got the chance to kick his bottom. So would a good many other people.'[110]

Even Edward Hamilton, though he expressed no desire for such violent retribution, was disappointed. At first he had been sympathetic to Rosebery, who he believed had some justification for feeling that he had been misled by Gladstone. But by early December he had changed his view, and come to the conclusion that Rosebery was being irresponsible. 'He should confine himself to demanding improved arrangements for the conduct of Scotch business. I fear, however, he is inclined to be pig-headed.'[111] And he repeated this in a frank letter to Rosebery of 11 December: 'I have long looked upon you as the one among my immediate contemporaries designed to take a great and most leading part in the future political affairs of the country and anything that may damage that prospect and upset my calculations I deplore from the bottom of my heart.' He warned Rosebery that in resigning, he would look 'unreasonable'. He admitted that Scotland might be disappointed over its treatment, 'but they would surely say, if you went off, that you had retired in a huff and for a want of self-control had wrecked a career which had such great promise.' Rosebery's reply, the next day, showed that he could be just as testy with his confidants as with the Prime Minister. 'I only claim liberty of action. When I became an official I did not lose the rights of an intelligent being. I accepted a certain office on what I believed to be a definite understanding. I find I was mistaken. I depart. I firmly believe that without such an understanding I should not have been serving the interests of my country but the reverse.'[112]

By Christmas Rosebery was complaining of exhaustion over the whole sorry affair. 'This business ought not to hang on much longer. It has now lasted a fortnight and the nervous tension is too much for me,' he told Hamilton on 23 December, though he added that it was up to Gladstone to abandon his 'non-possmus attitude'. Other parties tried to bridge the divide. Granville, while admitting that Rosebery was 'morbidly suspicious', urged Gladstone to show more sensitivity:

> I do not see in your letters much trace of that warm affection and that remarkable appreciation of his character and abilities, just, but which would have even been considered excessive by some which you have so constantly and in so many different circumstances expressed to me . . . Rosebery has a brilliant career before him and he once told me that it was the only thing he really cared about. But brilliant as his career may be, there will be no brighter episode than his connection with you and the work you achieved together . . . I cannot help thinking that, if you gave him some more definite assurance of considering the Scotch question while reserving perfect freedom of action and were to say only one tenth of what you have said to others, as to the standard by which you judge him, this affair so annoying to you and so likely to be damaging to him might be satisfactorily settled.[113]

Coincidentally, at the same time Mary Gladstone urged Rosebery to be more sympathetic towards her father. 'His character is so extraordinarily simple I don't think he knows how to understand these ins and outs. But don't think he would ever for a moment dream of you as in any way a self-seeker. To him in a way, political life is very simple; "follow the man you trust and wait till that man sees a proper moment to re-arrange." Scotch business has never flourished before as it has done lately & that for the moment has satisfied him. I see the huge sacrifice you make in now wishing to resign; there is one greater still to which you are called – & that is not resign.'[114] And Mrs Gladstone also tried her doubtful powers of persuasion on Rosebery: 'Have you not considered him more as a father? Have you not surely taken in his affection and deep interest? Do not throw away your future but take counsel.'[115]

But there was no thaw in the iciness that now gripped the relationship. Gladstone had come to the conclusion that Rosebery was slightly unhinged. 'It is a most singular case of strong self-delusion: a vein of foreign matter which runs straight across a clear and vigorous intellect and a high-toned character,' he told Harcourt.[116] In the same month he told his son Herbert that 'the people who bother him at this moment more than all England are the Queen and Lord Rosebery.'[117] When Rosebery travelled to Hawarden in the New Year, he found the Gladstones far less friendly than usual. The Prime Minister even refused to discuss the recent Scottish business, so Rosebery left, 'not a syllable having been said about the subject of our previous correspondence and the object of my visit.'[118] In fact the affair had so depressed Gladstone, who as a rule had the constitution of an ox, that he suffered a psychosomatic illness himself and was ordered abroad by his doctor. This enforced cure, taken at Cannes, proved convenient in necessitating the abandonment of another proposed Midlothian campaign, which could have only imposed further stresses on the relationship between the two men. At it was, their wives were exchanging insults on their behalf. When Mrs Gladstone made a trip to Edinburgh on 12 January, she took the chance to lecture Hannah about the misery Rosebery had caused her husband. Not content with chastising him for his impatience, Mrs Gladstone also criticised his love of the turf, warning that he should not be leading 'a wasted life'. The meeting ended when Mrs Gladstone swept out of the room with such suddenness that, as Hannah noted, 'I had no need, thank God, to kiss and shake hands.'[119]

Rosebery and Gladstone were on a collision course, the former bent on resignation if Scotland did not receive her own Minister, the latter refusing to consider any major Scottish reforms. To those around them, the impending crash seemed unavoidable. 'The Rosebery wrath cannot be said at all to have subsided and I fear the hearts of the Pharaohs of Mentmore are hardened against the Grand Old Man,' thought Loulou Harcourt.[120] 'Rosebery is not an easy fellow to stop when he has got the bit between his teeth. A rupture with the Government would indeed be deplorable,' wrote Hamilton in his diary. 'The impression produced upon Mr Gladstone was that in all his administrative experience he never remembered to have seen a big question more irrationally handled by a clever man.' Gladstone wanted to put the question of Scottish business to a Parliamentary Committee, 'but how Rosebery is to be provided for and retained is not easy to say.'[121]

It is a reflection of the strength of Rosebery's personality that in the first half of 1883, amidst all the Government's problems with Ireland, Egypt and Parliamentary reform, his threats of resignation ensured that the comparatively minor question of Scottish administration stood high on the Liberals' agenda. Desperate to retain their mercurial star, ministers were compelled to devote time to the study of a problem which had previously been of little concern. But Rosebery was by now almost past caring. When Granville approached him about Scotland in March, he replied, 'I have now no personal interest in the matter except the desire to be released from an equivocal position.'[122] The Scottish grievance had been only part of a deeper sense of anger at his treatment by Gladstone. In April his embitterment plumbed new depths when he discovered that Sir Charles Dilke, the

President of the Local Government Board, was to assist Harcourt in the House of Commons on certain Home Office questions, a move which Rosebery regarded as an infringement of his prerogative. 'Rosebery is very angry at my taking Home Office work and refuses to do anything,' noted Dilke.[123] The Earl sent Dilke a furious letter in which he complained of the way 'a number of subjects have been removed from this office to the Local Government Board.'[124] Dilke then wrote to Harcourt, 'Can you set matters straight? It is very unpleasant for me as it stands. I'm sorry to bother you but you know my acting is not of my making.'[125] On the instructions of Harcourt, who despaired of his volatile Under-Secretary, Dilke gave Rosebery this reassuring message: 'No subject whatsoever had moved from the Home Office to the Local Government Board. What has happened is that Harcourt has asked me to help him and that he has drawn up a list of subjects in which he wishes me to work for him.'[126]

Rosebery may have been temporarily appeased on this point but his irascibility remained, and even another reassurance from Gladstone about the likelihood of his imminent promotion did little to lessen it. On 7 April Gladstone wrote to Rosebery, 'I do not hesitate to say that, as matters now stand, among those Peers who do not hold high office, your claim for consideration would in my estimation stand as the first, upon the occurrence of a suitable opportunity.'[127] Though Rosebery told Gladstone the next day that he would not 'take any hasty action', within less than a week he was yet again threatening resignation, explaining, on 13 April, that his personal sacrifice was being 'carried to a degree inconsistent with self-respect and thus involving the loss of legitimate influence.' Trying to stave off this eventuality, the Cabinet on 5 May discussed proposals for Scottish reform. So keen was the wish to keep Rosebery that a rearrangement was accepted, despite the lack of any strong support for such a move. The Earl of Derby left a summary of this meeting. 'The Premier raised the question of Scotch administration, which led to a long debate. The Scotch, instigated by Rosebery, are asking for a Secretary of State or a Minister on the same footing as the Irish Secretary: there is no work for him to do and in the judgement of most English persons the proposal is a mistake but it seems that a certain amount of Scotch feeling, real or fictitious, has been got up on the subject.' Derby's account continued: 'Chamberlain and Dilke both spoke freely as to the bad effect produced if we lose Rosebery. I said it seemed very much a personal question affecting Rosebery: if we gave him promotion and promised a bill next year, would that not be enough? Granville took the same line. The Premier disliked the notion of a bill and should not like to argue for it. But he gave way.'[128]

That evening Harcourt ran into Rosebery at a Royal Academy dinner and congratulated him, somewhat sarcastically, on his influence. 'He said to me, "Well you ought to be greatly flattered: the Cabinet agreed today to do a thing they do not care about doing, simply to please you." '[129] Hamilton was concerned about the element of blackmail in the Cabinet's decision. 'It is a compliment to Rosebery that the Cabinet should have sacrificed their principles in order to save him, but it is not a pleasant business at all. That pistol-holding at the Cabinet's head is not nice. Moreover, though Rosebery triumphs for the moment, it is most probable that he has damaged himself seriously in the estimation of his colleagues.' Hamilton was also concerned about Gladstone: 'He has a horror of anything which savours of a political job, especially when the man concerned in it is a close personal friend of his like Rosebery. I trust with all my heart that this may be the end of the business. Rosebery must now remain on.'[130]

Hamilton could not have been more wrong. Rosebery was not to be dissuaded from his course, especially when Gladstone appeared reluctant to implement the Cabinet's agreement. False speculation in the press about Rosebery's forthcoming elevation to the post of Lord Privy Seal only increased his irritation, as Hamilton noted on 10 May: 'These rumours embarrass Mr Gladstone and do incalculable harm to Rosebery by unsettling him and bringing upon him purposeless congratulations.' And his impatience was further heightened by his Scottish friends, especially Charles Cooper, who enquired anxiously, 'Are you Lord Privy Seal?', adding that, if the answer was negative, then Rosebery would have 'been left in the dock'[131] by Gladstone. The depth of Rosebery's anger was felt by Dilke when they met at the Queen's State Ball on 28 May. 'Rosebery broke out to me against Mr Gladstone. He swears he will resign, giving his health as the reason. He is not a gentleman for he reproaches Mr Gladstone with the benefits he has conferred upon him, but he has been ill-used,'[132] wrote Dilke, not unsympathetically.

The last straw for Rosebery came on 31 May. During a debate on the Civil Service Estimates in the House of Commons several members, including the former Tory Cabinet Minister Sir Richard Cross, complained about the position of Home Under-Secretary being held by a peer. Rather than defending Rosebery, Sir William Harcourt, in bantering vein, joined in the attacks, arguing that in view of the increase in the work-load of the Home Office, the department was 'inadequately represented, not only in the House of Lords but also in the House of Commons'. The only reason, he told the House, that a peer was his Under-Secretary was to please the Scots. Not surprisingly, Rosebery took all this as a personal censure, and he resigned, explaining to Gladstone on 4 June that the Commons discussion 'on the Under-Secretaryship in the Home Department being held by a peer makes it impossible for me to hold that office'.[133] He added, in a swipe at Harcourt, that the Government had even supported the demand that his job should be held by an MP. Gladstone was by now only too glad to be rid of his troublesome junior minister, and made little attempt to keep him. His only concerns were, first, that the separation should be as amicable as possible, and second, that Rosebery should not rule out a swift return to the Government. As Rosebery proved willing to fall in with the Prime Minister's wishes, he left on good terms. '*June 5th*: Mr Gladstone wished to see me, so I saw him for two minutes (Mrs G. in the room). Nothing of importance passed but his manner was very cordial and he said, "God bless you" with great warmth when we parted,' he recorded in his diary. In his usual convoluted style, Gladstone told Rosebery's friend Professor James Donaldson of his satisfaction over the way the departure had been handled. 'The resignation has been effected in the best manner. It is placed on defined and insulated ground, from which references cannot readily be drawn; & it is accompanied with a clear understanding which goes as far as possible towards placing any resumption of office a short time hence on a footing nearly approaching that of continuance.'[134]

Gladstone must take some of the blame for Rosebery's action. Undoubtedly he had, wittingly or not, misled Rosebery over the terms of his appointment and his immediate prospects of advancement to the Cabinet. Furthermore, he had been less than frank with Rosebery throughout, preferring to use vague language which was open to misinterpretation. And despite the warmth between the two men during the Midlothian campaign, Gladstone often appeared cold, even dismissive, in his dealings with Rosebery after the election, refusing to appreciate the position which Rosebery had made for himself. This may partly have been a consequence of the exceptional demands on Gladstone's time, not only those posed by the Irish and Egyptian crises, but because of his unwise decision in 1880 to take on the post of Chancellor of the Exchequer in addition to the premiership. There may also have been an element of envy in the ageing Prime Minister's attitude to his aristocratic young lieutenant, for, as Rosebery had noted at the time of Midlothian, Gladstone was not without vanity. Just after Gladstone's retirement in 1894, Regy Brett wrote in his journal: 'Mr Gladstone certainly liked Rosebery the *least* of his possible successors. He was always jealous of him, much as some men are jealous of their eldest sons.'[135] This is what Rosebery himself thought, as his closest political intimate Ronald Munro-Ferguson recalled. 'I remember observing to him that Mr Gladstone was of a jealous disposition, which he did not dispute. They never really liked or trusted one another.'[136]

But Rosebery's conduct was worse, veering from self-pitying petulance to offensive arrogance. In parading his grievances, he showed a troubling inconsistency; thus, he threatened resignation unless Scotland was given her own Minister, yet when the Cabinet agreed to his demand, he immediately found another issue on which to depart. Hamilton felt that the resignation had exposed several disturbing aspects of Rosebery's character. 'One cannot help making great allowances for him. He is so horribly oversensitive and this constant reappearance in the papers of his probable promotion goads him to desperation. He feels as if everyone pointed their finger of scorn at him and said that he has been tried and found wanting. He won't be persuaded that the real difficulty is the already too great preponderance of Peers in the Cabinet and that but for this Mr Gladstone would be certain to put him in the Cabinet. I am afraid whatever happens Rosebery cannot . . . come out of this business without some damage to himself. It has been the most troublesome personal question with which I have ever been connected.'[137]

Rosebery's action did not end the embarrassment for the Government. In the week after his departure several newspapers, led by the *Standard*, hinted that his resignation had been caused not by political motives such as Scotland or the representation of the Home Office in the Commons but by Rosebery's loathing for his master, Sir William Harcourt, because of his language and temper. So powerful were these rumours that the Home Secretary was forced to make a statement in the House of Commons, in which he quoted from a letter Rosebery had sent him. 'As to the relations between Lord Rosebery and myself, they have been for many years and I am happy to say are still those of the closest political friendship and personal affection which has never been disturbed for a single moment . . . Lord Rosebery wrote to me this morning: "I know what you must be feeling under so undeserved an innuendo, but I am quite as indignant as you are."' The Home Secretary's wife Lily insinuated that Rosebery was insincere in his protestations of friendliness: 'Rosebery's letter is, of course, affectionate but I wish I felt a little more security for real feeling.'[138] It was a view largely shared by Derby: 'The official explanation is that the House of Commons wished to have an under-secretary who was not a peer. I imagine this was little more than an excuse as he got on badly with Harcourt and thought he should improve his chances of promotion by cutting himself clear from subordinate office. He wants the direction of Scotch business and the ostensible as well as the real control of it. He is very clever, very rich and I fancy quite unscrupulous so that he must be kept in good humour at whatever cost.'[139]

The intuition of Lady Harcourt and Lord Derby was accurate, as were the rumours in the press: the public harmony between the two men was just a sham, and Rosebery had only sent that note in response to five anxious messages from Harcourt, who was desperate not to be blamed for the loss of his junior minister. The truth, never revealed until now, was that Rosebery did indeed find Harcourt unbearable, and it was the complete breakdown in their relationship that finally drove him from his first ministerial job. Among Rosebery's papers is this memorandum about his 1883 resignation, written in November 1910:

> All things considered I had been ill-used . . . But the prime cause of irritation was Harcourt. He made servitude intolerable. At first he was all milk and honey. Then he changed. I got on better with the Treasury than he did, for I was reasonable and he was not. Then afterwards I found out that he was annoyed by something someone (not I) was supposed, rightly or wrongly, to have said. For the last six months he sent me to Coventry and my only communications from him were minutes on the papers of an irritating kind and one of which was so offensive that I took it to his room and made him cancel it there and then. All this time I had no idea of what had caused the rupture. When I did resign I wrote at his urgent instance a kindly note which, though marked private, he read to the House. Harcourt was not a bad-hearted man but his temper was intolerable and he led me a cruel life. Even if I were not promoted, as I had some claim to be, I would not remain where I was.[140]

The explanation of what had caused Harcourt such offence seems embarrassingly childish. During the early 1880s Barnum's Circus was at the peak of its fame in London, and one of its most popular attractions was Jumbo the elephant. In parts of London society it was joked that the Home Secretary bore a striking resemblance to this lumbering creature, hence his less than reverential nickname 'Jumbo'. Working in Rosebery's office was a young civil servant with a gift for caricature, who drew a cartoon of Harcourt as an elephant with the caption 'The Right Honourable Sir William Jumbo', and left it on Rosebery's desk. Unfortunately it was seen first by Harcourt, who understandably took out his anger on Rosebery and proceeded to treat him with calculated hostility. This may seem a little unfair, since Rosebery was the innocent party, but Harcourt was not to know the identity of the culprit. Even if he had, he must have been outraged by the fact that Rosebery appeared to tolerate an atmosphere of such disloyalty and ridicule towards himself. And he can only have felt that whoever was responsible reflected, in his malicious draughtsmanship, Rosebery's own low opinion of his political master.[141]

Sadly for the Liberal party, the rupture caused by this cartoon never healed. On such a trivial event did the course of Victorian Liberal politics turn.

5

'A dark horse'

⌒⌒

THERE WAS A widespread belief at Westminster that Rosebery would soon be back in the government. Many saw his resignation as nothing more than a cynical ploy to strengthen his position, the view held by his erstwhile master Sir William Harcourt. 'The Home Secretary thinks that it will not be long before Rosebery gets into the Cabinet,' wrote his son Loulou. 'He is strong in Scotland and can rouse a good deal of feeling, I suppose. Besides, on general principles, Hannah has always appeared to me through life to get everything she really wanted. She has the best temperament of the two for public life. Politically, for the good of the whole, I have always thought they were better in than out.'[1] Granville, who always doubted Rosebery's protestations about his personal honour, saw naked ambition behind the move, as Lord Derby confirmed in his diary: 'Talk with Granville about the Rosebery affair; he confirms my impression that the resignation is simply a strike for promotion, the state of Scotch business being an excuse.'[2] Cooper of the *Scotsman*, whose rash correspondence had hastened Rosebery's exit, inevitably painted him in a favourable light: 'I do not remember a case of the kind in which the Minister going out has so much general approval as you have received.'

But Cooper's mood was soon to change. Like many others, he had expected that Rosebery would immediately become Scottish Minister once the legislation establishing the new Local Government Board for Scotland had been passed by the House of Lords. What he had not counted on was Rosebery's combination of self-effacement and ruthless ambition. On the one hand, Rosebery was extremely wary of anything that smacked of self-interest. Having argued for a Scottish Ministry, he thought it might look undignified if he were to take it himself. On the other, in direct contradiction of this high-mindedness, he was aggrieved that the proposed Scottish office did not carry a seat in the Cabinet. It was an exact repeat of the post-Midlothian saga of three years earlier, when refined scruples and resentment of a lowly offer had prevented his acceptance of a job at the India Office. Now, when Gladstone asked him to lead the new Scottish

Ministry in the event of the Bill becoming law, he again refused. In a letter of 30 July he explained to Gladstone that 'I have been so much the advocate for the office being formed that if I should accept it, I am open to the accusation, which has been freely urged in the candid press, of having pressed for it in order that I might fill it myself.' Then Rosebery, with the insolence that increasingly annoyed Gladstone, explained his other reason for rejection. 'I have made up my mind never to re-enter the Government except as a member of the Cabinet. I am convinced that for me there is no middle term of usefulness between that of absolute independence and Cabinet office. As absolutely independent I hold a position in Scotland, of which I do not think so highly as some others may but one which I greatly cherish. As a Cabinet minister I should hold a position in Great Britain which it is an honour to covet. But by accepting office outside the Cabinet I lose both positions. On that point I have some experience to guide me.'[3]

As Edward Hamilton told Rosebery on 31 July, this decision was 'a special source of disappointment to Mr Gladstone after he had acquiesced in a proposal to which I did not think he would have agreed had he not had a fair expectation that by means of it you would again find a place in Government.'[4] Cooper was just as dismayed. For the first time his eyes were opened to the erratic nature of Scotland's political hero. 'It is beyond all question', he wrote in despair to Rosebery on 12 August, 'that Scotland has expected you to complete the work you have begun. There is no one, friend or enemy, who does not attribute the Local Government Board Bill to you.' Pleading that Rosebery reconsider his decision, he continued: 'I believe your deferral to take the office will, if preserved, wreck it. Scotland has claims upon you; your future is as important to her as it is to yourself and you do her an injury when you put yourself back.'[5]

On 15 August, at a dinner at Rosebery's London home, Gladstone again pressed him on the Scottish post but met with the same response. That night, Hamilton noted, 'There is no concealing the fact, I fear, that Mr Gladstone is disappointed with Rosebery in two ways – disappointed in his official aptitude and his qualifications for a statesman's career and disappointed with his conduct in first declining everything and disclaiming all selfish interests and now trying to dictate his own terms into the Cabinet.'

Towards the end of August, however, the debate over Rosebery and the Scottish Ministry was rendered academic by two circumstances. First, on 21 August the House of Lords threw out the Scottish Local Government Bill by a majority of 15, 'rather a relief,' thought Hamilton, 'considering Rosebery would probably not have allowed himself to be named as President of the new Board and without him Scotland would have cared nothing for the Bill.'[6] Second, Rosebery decided to embark with Hannah on a tour to America and Australia, a voyage that he predicted would take him away from Britain for at least eight months. While the Roseberys were abroad, their four children were to be looked after by his sister, Lady Leconfield. Having no pressing responsibilities, Rosebery felt this was an ideal moment to travel: 'I am still young, my children are still younger and each year will diminish my opportunities,' he told Gladstone.[7]

They left at the beginning of September and enjoyed a gentle crossing of the Atlantic, reaching America on the 12th. *The New York Herald* gave a compelling portrait of their arrival: 'Lord Rosebery, a middle-sized gentleman wearing a high hat, whose somewhat corpulent form was concealed beneath a Scottish plaid Ulster with a hood of ample proportions, looked on at the busy scene [in New York harbour] with an interest half-serious, and half amusing. Anyone to note his cheery, smooth face, would have mistaken him for a well-to-do British farmer.' This comparison to a rustic yeoman can have hardly pleased Britain's most dazzling young aristocrat. The *Herald* was slightly more flattering about Hannah: 'Lady Rosebery is of full figure and erect carriage. She is rather above than below the medium height. Her complexion, though somewhat dark, is singularly clear. Her features are of Hebraic type, eyes large and dark, with long drooping lashes that fail to conceal their brightness when engaged in conversation. In repose, Lady Rosebery's face is firmly set and almost expressionless but when animated is singularly sweet in its every varying changes. It is one of those faces to which a photograph never does justice. Her mouth is somewhat large, but full and well-shaped setting off a fine and even set of teeth that a dentist might envy. Her movements are easy and graceful and possess a peculiar dignity of their own.' In contrast to the self-importance displayed by Rosebery in his recent dealings with Gladstone, the *Herald*'s reporter announced that he 'never saw any passengers so considerate for the feelings of others, which consideration was extended to everybody from captain to cabin boy.'

It was a tribute to Rosebery's charisma – and his wife's wealth – that the couple's visit should have attracted such comment in the American press. Hannah's fortune included significant financial interests in the United States, such as ranches in Texas and mines in Montana. Their investments were looked after by a young American of extraordinary charm, Ferdinand Van Zandt, whose classical good looks were so striking that he was nicknamed 'Apollo' or 'Adonis'. When Sir William Harcourt's wife Lily first met him at Mentmore in February 1883 she was moved to call him 'beautiful', and told her son Loulou that he was 'the most delightful new being who has been produced for a long while'.[8] Sadly, Van Zandt's business acumen did not match his gracefulness, and over the next decade his flawed decisions not only caused Rosebery deep anxiety but also brought about his own tragic demise. But at this time he was one of the Roseberys' closest friends and helped show them the continent in the course of a visit that took in Chicago, Utah, Omaha and San Francisco. 'The inhabitants of California are far more entertaining than I can possibly give you any idea. The women are very handsome, think nothing of dresses costing £80, "fix up" their faces very frequently and are generally divorced,' wrote Hannah to her sister-in-law.[9] From San Francisco they went on to Honolulu, 'a warm, lazy paradise' in Rosebery's view, and then to Australia. Just as Rosebery had been thrilled when he first set foot in the United States in 1873, so he was captivated by his first sight of Australia ten years later. Sydney, he thought, was 'next to Naples, the finest thing I have seen', while Melbourne he described as 'a noble city – great wide streets like Edinburgh New Town or St Petersburg.' He also travelled to the outback in Queensland, but Hannah stayed behind in Sydney because, as he explained to Mary Gladstone, 'I do not think bush hotels are possible for ladies.'[10]

Australia had an impact on Lord Rosebery far beyond mere pleasure at its sights. As 1870s America had quickened his liberal instincts, so 1880s Australia confirmed him as an imperialist. Since his youth, the romantic historian in Rosebery had always been attracted to the idea of Empire, not least because the two Pitts, his heroes, had played such a vital role in the extension and protection of Britain's overseas territories. In the address to the Social Science Congress in Glasgow in 1874 at which he first made his name as an orator, he had described the Empire as 'the greatest secular agency for good that the world has seen'. Now, in Australia, he was confronted with the vibrant reality of the British Empire, rather than a mere abstract theory or historical saga. And he was moved by the vision of a dynamic new open society being built from British stock on the other side of the globe. What particularly appealed to him was that this Australian colony involved a new concept of Empire, one based not on the conquest and subjugation of an alien people but on bonds of kinship with the Mother Country.

This was the Imperial theme that Rosebery continually repeated in his speeches during the Australian visit. At a dinner in the New South Wales Parliament on 10 December 1883 Rosebery described Britain's relations with her colonies as those of 'a complicated and . . . intricate nature. They are connected by a golden thread of affection and descent. They are cemented more closely than anything by the fact that there are few of us in England who have not got relations or kinsfolk among you here.' In a speech at Melbourne in January 1884 he graphically enlarged on the image of a fibre uniting the Empire: 'There is an old tradition that in the British Royal dockyards every rope that is manufactured, from the largest cable to the smallest twine, has a single red thread through it, which pervades the whole strand and which, if unpicked, destroys the whole rope. That was the sign of the Royal production of those ropes. Though I distrust metaphors, I believe that that metaphor holds good to some extent of the British Empire. It is held together by a single red line and that red line is the communion of races. I have always hoped that that communion of races might exist as long as my life lasted but since my visit to Australia it will become a passion with me to preserve that union.' His audience, according to the *Melbourne Argus*, responded warmly. 'Lord Rosebery earned rapturous applause by his declaration that as a result of his tour it will become a passion with him to lend whatever aid he can to the preservation of the union of the Empire. When he had finished, his audience could understand why, apart from his friendship for Mr Gladstone, the Earl of Rosebery holds a high position in Imperial politics and is regarded with hope as a coming man.'[11]

The term 'the coming man' was frequently used of Rosebery over the next decade, but it was another phrase, uttered by Rosebery himself in his final speech at Adelaide, that immediately gripped the public imagination and soon entered the lexicon of politics. In referring to Australia's drive from colonial status towards that of a federated nation, Rosebery pronounced: 'I claim that this country has established the right to be a nation and that its nationality is now and will be henceforward recognised by the world . . . Does this fact of your being a nation, and I think feeling yourselves to be a nation, imply separation from the Empire? God forbid! There is no need for any nation, however great, leaving the Empire, because the Empire is *a Commonwealth of Nations*.'[12] Rosebery was not the first politician to utter the word 'Commonwealth' in reference to the British Empire. The Tory politician A.J. Balfour, in an article in *The Nineteenth Century* in January 1882, had written that 'the sentiments with which an Englishman regards the English Empire are neither a small nor an ignoble part of the feelings which belong to him as a member of the Commonwealth.'[13] And Rosebery's fellow Liberal W.E. Forster, a passionate believer in Imperial unity, had used it in a speech in the House of Commons in 1876, when he claimed that white colonists were not adventurers but 'founders of a Commonwealth'.[14] But Rosebery was the first to give it popular currency, an indication of both his star quality and his gift for capturing the mood of the times. He may not have been an original thinker, but he had an instinctive grasp of the currents of public opinion. As one of his previous biographers E.T. Raymond put it, 'if he had been born poor he would have been worth a good ten thousand a year to any enterprising newspaper proprietor. For there is no more valuable gift in journalism than the art of first divining what people would like to say and then of saying it for them as they would like best to say it. This art Lord Rosebery carried to such perfection as to earn, not only the fame of brilliance which was justly his, but a reputation for clear and deep thinking which he did not always deserve.'[15]

By 1884, as Rosebery intuitively understood, there was a growing interest in Britain in the future of the Empire. The exploration of Africa, the scramble for new colonies, the acquisition of Egypt, the growth of trade, the development of the telegraph and the establishment of sporting links – Test cricket between England and Australia began in 1877 – all helped to foster this mood, as did various books propounding the new Imperial gospel, none of them more influential than *The Expansion of England* by the Cambridge historian J.R. Seeley. Published in 1883, it profoundly affected Rosebery's outlook, persuading him to make the Empire one of his primary concerns. Seeley argued that traditional British history placed too much emphasis on progress towards constitutional liberty and on narrow party politics, thereby ignoring the far more important tale of colonial development. Pointing out that the population of the British Empire was greater than that of Europe, he wrote: 'There is no topic so pregnant as this of the mutual influence of the branches of the English races. The whole future of the planet depends upon it.'

Throughout his work Seeley was explicit about the benefits of racial homogeneity. 'Ethnological unity is of great importance,' he argued, adding that 'Greater Britain is united by blood and religion.' An exception to this was India, which Seeley described as a 'millstone round our neck' because 'everything, which Europe and still more the New World has outlived, is still flourishing in full vigour: superstition, fatalism, polygamy, the most primitive priest craft, the most primitive despotism.' In Australia, though, the aborigines hardly mattered: 'The native Australian race is so low in the ethnological scale that it can never give the least trouble.' In expressing such views Seeley was reflecting perhaps the most pivotal element in the new enthusiasm for imperialism: a belief in the innate superiority of the Anglo-Saxon race. This stemmed largely from Charles Darwin's ground-breaking work on biological evolution, which had encouraged the theory that the different human races were engaged in a battle for survival, and that Britain's emergence as the greatest imperial power proved that its civilisation was the most advanced. Such ideas were common among the later Victorians. Disraeli himself had said, 'All is race; there is no other truth', while the radical politician Sir Charles Dilke regarded the extermination of the 'lower races' as a fact of nature.[16]

Though racialism today is associated with the far right, in late nineteenth-century Britain it was just as likely to be found on the left, as Dilke's comment shows. Joseph Chamberlain, the Fabians, and socialist academics like Karl Pearson were all virulent racists. Rosebery himself certainly believed in social Darwinism and the need to maintain the vitality of the British race. Under Seeley's influence he argued that race was the glue that held the self-governing colonies together, since 'empires founded on trade alone must inevitably crumble'. 'What is Empire but the predominance of race,' he once asked. It was Britain's imperial mission, he claimed in 1893, 'to make it part of our responsibility and our heritage to take care that the world, as far as it can be moulded, shall receive an English-speaking complexion and not that of other nations.'[17] In his Rectorial Address at Glasgow University in 1900, which so brilliantly captured the imperial mood of late Victorian Britain, he was even more explicit about his Darwinian beliefs: 'An empire such as ours requires as its first condition an imperial race, a race vigorous and industrious and intrepid. Health of mind and body exalt a nation in the competition of the universe. The survival of the fittest is an absolute truth in the modern world.'

It was precisely this belief in the Anglo-Saxon imperial destiny that encouraged Liberals like Rosebery to take up the cause of social reform. To them, the Empire represented both an opportunity and a challenge. The vast open spaces of Canada, Australia and South Africa could be the answer to Britain's problems of poverty and overcrowding. As Rosebery put it to his fellow Scot Sir William Mackay in December 1884, just months after his return from Australia, 'Half the distress in Ireland and the Hebrides has been caused by the swarming superabundance of population in certain localities. Meanwhile the inhabitants of Great Britain keep increasing at a rate which must make the thoughtless think.' The solution, said Rosebery, lay in utilising the colonies whose 'vast importance' had hitherto been overlooked. 'This is the real working-men's question – to preserve these great realms of plenty and content in which our superabundant populations may find their future and their homes without ceasing to be Britons.'[18] Yet the Empire also imposed on Britain a duty to raise the quality of the British stock. In another letter to Mackay he warned that the 'over and reckless production of children is debasing our race'.[19] To halt this degeneration, imperially-inclined Liberals argued not only for colonial emigration, but also for better housing, education and sanitation for the working class. As Rosebery put it in his Glasgow speech of 1900, 'In the rookeries and slums which still survive, an imperial race cannot be reared.'[20] These ideas had long been debated in progressive circles, particularly at Oxford, where a generation of students – among them Alfred Milner, later the most ideological of pro-consuls – was inspired by Arnold Toynbee's active concern with urban destitution and John Ruskin's altruistic imperial zeal, epitomised by his famous Slade lecture of 1870 in which he said that 'England must found colonies as fast and far as she is able'. But it was Rosebery who was their most famous advocate. Through his eloquence and magnetism the new doctrine of Liberal Imperialism, embracing state action at home and colonial strength abroad, became one of the dominant forces in British politics by the turn of the century. In a speech in 1885 he summed up what Liberal Imperialism meant to him: 'If a Liberal Imperialist means that I am a Liberal who is passionately attached to the Empire – if it means, as I believe it does, that I am a Liberal who believes that the Empire is best maintained upon the basis of the widest democracy and that the voice is most powerful when it represents the greatest number of persons and subjects – if those are accurate descriptions of what a Liberal Imperialist is, then I am a Liberal Imperialist.'[21]

The concept of Liberal Imperialism was anathema to Gladstone's brand of laissez-faire, Little Englander Liberalism. As early as 1838 Gladstone had warned that 'whenever settlers from a people in an advanced stage of civilisation come into contact with the aborigines of a barbarous country, the result is always prejudicial to both countries and most dishonourable to the superior.'[22] Though he had dumped some of the baggage of his past, he retained to his deathbed his hostility to imperialism. And this proved another source of friction in his difficult relationship with Rosebery. Indeed, soon after Rosebery returned from Australia in March 1884 he met Gladstone in London, and found him in choleric form. 'He seemed changed. Talked to him about Lord Aberdeen's correspondence. He replied, "No one cares a damn for Lord Aberdeen."' The Prime Minister was hardly more relaxed when he went to The Durdans for an Easter visit in April. 'Talked to him about reform. I argued with him about the Irish. He suddenly broke off: "I am sick of contention. I cannot at my age spend the rest of my life in contention."'[23] The next month, Rosebery added to Gladstone's woes by embroiling him in yet another dreary row over office. Having risen to the heights of noble rhetoric in Australia, he was now back to his peevish worst. The position Gladstone offered him was only a minor one, the Lord-Lieutenancy of Midlothian, which had fallen vacant through the death of the Duke of Buccleuch, but it needed someone of social weight and Gladstone rightly thought Rosebery would be ideal. As was his wont, Rosebery immediately refused, with the patronising aside that lord-lieutenancies 'seem to be positions of mere ornament and expense'.[24] Gladstone did not give up, and Rosebery eventually gave way. 'I have been so bullied by you and others', he wrote to Hamilton on 6 May, 'that I have swallowed my pill and send herewith my letter of contingent surrender to Mr Gladstone as to the Lieutenancy. But it must be understood that I only do it as a final sacrifice to the party and to Mr Gladstone: and that I am not to be called upon until the resources of civilisation are exhausted.* I close my 37th year with an act of mortification which I trust may not have to be repeated in any other year.'[25] As so often before, Hamilton felt let down by his friend. 'One can't help feeling much distressed at his frame of mind. Even granting (which I cannot grant) that Mr Gladstone has done every-thing to thwart Rosebery and has treated him badly, such a frame of mind is suicidal to his political prospects and makes one despair of his future.' Another of Gladstone's secretaries, Horace Seymour, added that 'there is something very small in all Rosebery's behaviour until he succeeds in get-ting into the Cabinet. An ill-natured person might say that his Midlothian outlay was directed to this one object. His future career will show what stuff there is in him.'[26]

Having been so tiresome over the Lord-Lieutenancy, Rosebery was sur-prisingly constructive during the following months. On 20 June 1884 he returned to one of his favourite themes, the reform of the House of Lords, urging that a Select Committee be appointed 'to consider the best means of promoting the efficiency of this House'. Among his suggestions were the introduction of life peerages, and wider representation from science and the arts. Rosebery's speech may have enhanced his radical credentials but it did little to raise his popularity in the Lords. Much to his anger, even the Government front bench, led by Granville, refused to support his pro-posal, which was heavily defeated. In his diary Rosebery complained that 'the front bench got into hopeless and ridiculous confusion', a view shared by Regy Brett, who felt that 'Rosebery was very badly treated by Granville'.[27]

For once, Rosebery did not sulk. Rather, in July 1884 he came to the aid of the Government in dramatic fashion, making a brilliant speech

---

*A parody of Gladstone's warning to Parnell in 1881, during the Irish Land League's cam-paign of outrages, that 'the resources of civilisation are not yet exhausted'.

during the Lords' debate on the Parliamentary Reform Bill which aimed to extend the franchise to householders in the counties, thereby adding two million voters to the electorate. As well as supporting the democratic principles of the Bill, Rosebery argued that the House of Lords had no moral justification in rejecting a measure to reform the Commons. He spoke of the 'perilous consequences' in the country if the Bill were thrown out, and declared that the tide of democracy could not be resisted. 'What is the feeling of this host of two millions of men who you are trying to keep out? You cannot substantially retard the enfranchisement which they desire. They will have the vote in 1886, whether you pass the resolution or not. They consider it a birthright born of the general election and the decision of the House of Commons.' This was by far Rosebery's most successful Parliamentary speech to date. 'Rosebery was excellent. He is the inevitable leader of the Lords if he sticks to politics,' wrote the Earl of Derby in his diary.[28] Even the Prince of Wales was moved to tell Rosebery 'how much I admired your speech. It was simply splendid and so much to the point in every sense of the word. You spoke for upwards of an hour – and it seemed to me like ten minutes.'[29] Though the Liberals did not win the vote in the Lords, the cogency of Rosebery's arguments strengthened the Government's position and helped to pave the way for the negotiations between Gladstone and Salisbury in the autumn which ensured the passage of the reform legislation.

Rosebery was also active on other fronts. On 29 July he attended the inaugural conference of the Imperial Federation League, which aimed to promote the idea of a closer union between Britain and her self-governing colonies, based on the unity of the Anglo-Saxon race. The League argued that, both economically and constitutionally, the Empire should evolve into a more cohesive unit. After his Australian visit and his reading of Seeley Rosebery was strongly committed to this goal. Within two years of the League's creation he had become its Chairman, succeeding W.E. Forster, who died in April 1886. His belief in Imperial federation was further demonstrated when he made an impassioned address to the 1884 Trades Union Congress, praising the Empire and pointing out that the advances made by the working classes in Australia and Canada should be an inspiration to their counterparts in Britain.

In August Rosebery hosted a visit by the Prince and Princess of Wales to Scotland and the event again emphasised his enthusiastic local following, as the Scotsman reported: 'One other gratification that the Prince and Princess must have experienced; it was to hear and see the demonstration of the popularity of Lord Rosebery, their host. Everywhere he was received with the warmest welcome. Hearty cheers told how strong is the hold he has on the affections of his countrymen and how ready they are to recognise worthy service in their and the imperial cause.' There were similar manifestations when Gladstone made his much-deferred third Midlothian campaign visit at the end of August. At every meeting there were loud cries of 'Rozbury, Rozbury' and demands for a speech from the Earl. At one gathering, when Rosebery playfully asked why he was shown such kindness, a voice from the back of the hall yelled 'It's because we like ye', a remark greeted by thunderous applause. On the final day of the visit, 2 September, Mary Gladstone recorded: 'This was as to enthusiasm and excitement and numbers the climax of the campaign and the entry into Waverley Market is still overwhelming to think of; it looked like millions of faces and millions of voices and they kept up the ringing wonderful cheers as we walked half round the meeting. Archie Rosebery holds them in his hands, he can do anything with them; the passionate devotion to him was perhaps the most striking feature of the week.'[30]

Outside politics and official duties, he was as busy as ever. He continued to read voraciously: 'today spent £150 on books' he recorded on 26 March 1884. He went yachting in Holland and shooting with the Prince of Wales at Sandringham: '473 head today, including 60 pheasants and 380 partridges', he noted in November. He also entertained on a lavish scale, having decided in 1881 to rent Lord Lansdowne's magnificent house in Berkeley Square for £3,000 a year while its owner was in Canada as Governor-General; according to Edward Hamilton, the move to Berkeley Square was made because 'the Roseberys dislike and have outgrown their house in Piccadilly.' Lord Lansdowne was angered by news of the great ball the Roseberys held in the house in March 1882; 'considering Rosebery's rent, this seems childish,' thought John Morley, the rising Liberal politician.[31] The watchful eye Hannah kept on the expenses for this party surprised Loulou Harcourt – but he was always on the alert for any new gripe against the Roseberys. 'She talked about the arrangements and decorations for her ball and showed the parsimonious way in which it has been done by saying, "I got all my flowers from Cannes and they cost £25. I don't think that was much, do you?" Lady Rosebery then explained that the Princess' bouquet had not arrived, "I thought of sending out for one but they are so expensive in London." When it turned up late, Lady Rosebery sent it back to the shop and would not pay for it. If that is not a mean and stingy transaction I do not know what is.'[32]

Despite his active life Rosebery continued to be dogged by insomnia, especially when he was away from the soporific haven of Barnbougle

Castle. 'Went to bed at 2.30 but not sleeping so rose at 4 and walked to Covent Garden market and back by the silent parks. No one about but all the birds in cages singing like mad,' he wrote in his diary on 8 July 1884. The next night he tried what was now his favoured remedy for sleeplessness: 'Rode after dinner by moonlight till 10.30.' During this period Rosebery suffered two serious accidents, the first of which nearly killed him. In September 1881 he was travelling through Ayr when his carriage crashed into another. Immediately his horses took fright and bolted. Pulling the broken carriage at breakneck speed, they were heading down a steep road towards an open quay when a local bystander, William Young, heroically intervened. He managed to grab hold of the horses and, though he was dragged some distance, eventually brought them under control. As a reward for saving his life, the Earl gave Young a marble clock. Three years later, on 23 September 1884, Rosebery was out riding at Dalmeny when he had a bad fall and broke his collarbone. In agony he staggered back to the house, and went straight to bed. The next day the pain was even worse, partly because there had been internal bleeding in his stomach, and his doctor injected morphine to send him to sleep. Gladstone and another Liberal politician, Lord Reay, happened to be visiting Dalmeny when this incident occured. 'Lord Rosebery suffers a good deal and is I grieve to say, though not alarmingly, seriously ill,' wrote Gladstone to Sir William Harcourt.[33] Rosebery had not, however, lost his sense of humour. 'Reay came in at intervals in a black dressing gown looking like the Angel of Death himself,' he noted in his diary for 24 September. From his sickbed he told Gladstone that he could visit Barnbougle whenever he liked, 'a privilege never before conferred on mortal man'.[34]

Rosebery was by this time back in favour with Gladstone, thanks to his Lords speech and the third Midlothian campaign, and Gladstone was determined, at last, to bring him into the Cabinet. There was a difficulty, however: at present no vacancy existed, and the weakest member of the Cabinet, Lord Carlingford, Lord President of the Council, adamantly refused to move. Gladstone, the most reluctant of butchers, dropped heavy hints to Carlingford that he should make way for Rosebery: 'There is no doubt that we should improve our position here in Scotland', he told the Lord President on 7 September, 'without worsening it elsewhere by bringing in some Scotchman, whom Scotchmen know and love, into the Cabinet.'[35] But Carlingford remained oblivious to such pressure, and declined to be tempted by an offer of the Embassy at Constantinople. 'Carlingford has put himself entirely in the wrong and has behaved very badly,' wrote Loulou Harcourt in his diary. 'If he would have resigned,

Rosebery would have been made Lord President of the Council. The Government had been quite convinced from what they have seen of Rosebery in office that though he ought to be taken into the Cabinet as a political force, he is quite incompetent as an administrator.'[36] A conference of leading ministers held on 7 October confirmed that, despite a unanimous wish to bring in Rosebery, little could be done while Carlingford remained so obstinate.

Today, of course, Carlingford would simply have been sacked, but such a recourse was almost unknown in Victorian politics and would certainly not have been resorted to by Gladstone, always a stickler for constitutional niceties.★ Gladstone was therefore constrained to write to Rosebery on 10 October to tell him that 'the time, eminently suitable for your introduction, is not favourable to an ejectment.'[37] Rosebery, still recovering from his injury, was good-natured about the problem, telling Gladstone that he would have found it 'distasteful' to take an office compulsorily vacated by another. In fact, when Lord Spencer ran into Rosebery at Balmoral a week later he discovered that 'Rosebery was in very good spirits and took a comical view of the Carlingford incident which had been fully told to him.'[38] Edward Hamilton confirmed this opinion when he saw the Roseberys on 19 October. 'His appearance was an agreeable surprise. Though looking pulled down, he maintained he was all right. I don't think he feels any real mortification about not being admitted to the Cabinet. The fact is that by standing outside, he loses nothing personally. The loss is the loss of Mr Gladstone. I am afraid she [Lady Rosebery], in her heart of hearts, is disappointed.'

At the beginning of November Gladstone thought he saw a way out of the Cabinet impasse without removing Carlingford: if he were to extend the size of the Cabinet by two places, he could bring in Rosebery without upsetting the delicate balance of peers and commoners. On 8 November he therefore offered the Post Office to the colourless Bradford MP George Shaw-Lefevre, and the Commissionership of Works to the glamorous Earl. But Rosebery rarely made life simple for Gladstone. He first hesitated and then, on 11 November, turned down the offer. Part of the justification for this latest refusal was, much to Gladstone's surprise, Egyptian policy. There were two strands to this. First of all, Rosebery argued that the Government had displayed a singular lack of vigour in maintaining British control of Egypt. The Sudan, on Egypt's southern

★ The only precedent at the time was Disraeli's eviction of Lord Chelmsford from the post of Lord Chancellor in 1868 in favour of Lord Cairns.

border, had been effectively abandoned after the defeat of British forces by the Mahdi rebels in 1883. Following this disaster, the Government in January 1884 had ordered General Charles Gordon to rescue the beleaguered British garrisons in the Sudanese desert – a bizarre decision, for Gordon was a mystical, half-mad adventurer who had no intention of evacuating the Sudan. Having ignored his instructions, he was soon isolated in Khartoum. After months of dithering the Government finally agreed to send an expeditionary force under Sir Garnet Wolseley to save him. Rosebery felt, with some reason, that this shambles was indicative of the Government's enfeebled approach to Egypt, a preference for retreat over resolution; Sir William Harcourt, reflecting the view of most Liberals, had said in March 1884 that 'we must get out of Egypt, as soon as possible at any price'.[39] Rosebery's stance was the exact opposite, as he told Gladstone in his letter of refusal: 'We cannot leave Egypt until we have established strong and stable government.'

The second strand was more personal, related to his wife's fortune. Rosebery was concerned lest he be accused of a conflict of interest, in view of the fact that the House of Rothschild had recently loaned the Government £1 million to meet Egypt's debts. His awareness of this difficulty was doubtless heightened by the anti-Semitic rhetoric of his Tory friend Lord Randolph Churchill, who railed about 'Jewish usurers in London and Paris seducing Ismail Pasha* into their net' and Gladstone delivering the Egyptians 'back into the toils of their Jewish taskmasters'[40], but his involvement in Egypt's finances was real enough. 'If you have a few spare thousands (from £9 to £10) you might invest them in the new . . . Egyptian loan which the House brings out this week,' Ferdy had told him in 1878, soon after his marriage to Hannah, while in August 1885, just months after the fall of the second Gladstone government, he was allotted £50,000 of a new Egyptian loan issued by the Rothschilds. Indeed, Rosebery's close relationship with Hannah's family prompted Natty Rothschild† to say, in January 1886, that it was 'out of the question' for him to become Foreign Secretary.[41] Rosebery was frank enough to admit the awkwardness of the Rothschild connection in his letter to Gladstone of 11 November: 'It would put me in a delicate and disagreeable position if I were to enter the Cabinet just as the Egyptian financial scheme were being decided.'

*The Khedive of Egypt.
†The son of Lionel de Rothschild and great-grandson of Meyer Amschel, the founder of the dynasty, Nathan de Rothschild was Liberal MP for Aylesbury before becoming the first Jewish peer, as Baron Rothschild of Tring, in 1885.

These explanations of Rosebery's refusal were understandable, even honourable. But his other reason was far less so. In his disdainful way, he felt that the Office of Works did not match the grandeur of his station, as he told Lord Granville on 12 November: 'It is not indeed an attractive post, having neither dignity nor importance, and is I think the least of all the offices, being only a sort of political football for contending connoisseurs.'[42] Such an argument was hardly likely to win much credit with Gladstone, who, in Hamilton's words, feared 'that this sort of hesitancy of mind and angularity of disposition betray weaknesses of character and show an inability to pull with others and subordinate his individual views to those of the men with whom he is in general political harmony.'[43] Loulou Harcourt was even more dismissive of Rosebery than usual: 'He intimates what is offered him is not good enough. What a fool and what a contemptible politician!' he wrote on 10 November.

Gladstone might have been forgiven had he now decided to give up on Rosebery as a serious politician, but Loulou Harcourt, displaying more perception than bile, hit on the strange nature of their relationship: 'They are like a husband and wife who love one another very much but are always quarrelling.'[44] Ever tolerant, Gladstone decided he could leave the Office of Works vacant for a few months, hoping once more that time would win Rosebery round. But others were far less patient. Cooper of the *Scotsman*, for instance, was reduced to near apoplexy. On 11 November he warned Rosebery that he was in danger of 'acquiring the character of an impracticable man whose place in a Ministry could never be certain because of his resolution to press his view on particular points against the general opinion. I feel much of your future depends on your action now.' A day later Cooper was descending into hysteria: 'I was never more anxious about anything in my life. You have literally everything to gain and nothing to lose by acceptance.' Two days later, he was just as emotional: 'I am positively ill with anxiety about you. I am depressed almost beyond endurance.' On 16 November Cooper asked, 'Can you recall a case where any man who has made his mark in the Government of the country has refused to take office because he did not agree absolutely and in every detail of every point with the Government of the day?'[45]

Another less highly-charged analysis of Rosebery at this time was provided by one of his new secretaries, Thomas Gilmour, a young journalist introduced to him by Charles Cooper. Gilmour took up his post in January 1885, and kept a diary of the first few weeks after his arrival at Mentmore. 'On entering the outer hall my first sensation was one of astonishment at the gorgeousness of the place. It quite overwhelmed me for a time and it was some days before I could get over the sensation of living in a museum.' Initially, wrote Gilmour, 'my duties were light. I went to Lord Rosebery at 10, took down shorthand letters at his dictation, wrote them out and then took them to him for signature. Politeness is one of Lord Rosebery's strong points. He thanks a man for his "interesting paper" and then hands it to me and probably never sees it again.' But, continued Gilmour, 'the easy times did not last long. Lady Rosebery is a woman of energy. She always has something in hand.' So Gilmour was asked to catalogue and file all Rosebery's press cuttings, putting them in a series of albums. 'I have not been troubled by spare time,' he wryly commented. On the first Saturday after his arrival Gilmour attended a large dinner party, where he saw his new master in action.

> Lord Rosebery is brimful of that fine species of humour which is bred of deep sympathy and which is probably at the bottom of his wonderful hold on the public mind. I am getting to know him better but the process is a very gradual one. He is not a man who gives his confidence readily. I never met a more delicately sensitive man and yet in a public meeting when thousands of sober-minded Scotsmen are cheering as if they were mad, he, the object of their enthusiasm, is to all outward seeming the only perfectly collected and unaffected person present. Great self-command united to extreme sensitiveness is a rare combination but they produce a very high type of character.

Even when he moved on to politics, writing out drafts of speeches, Gilmour found it hard to penetrate Rosebery's exterior. 'The political work is much more congenial to me than re-arranging the library. We are gradually getting to talk about politics but Lord Rosebery is the reverse of communicative.' It was through Lady Rosebery that Gilmour learnt an intriguing fact about Rosebery's health, one which may account for some of his notorious aloofness: 'Rosebery's pulse is abnormally low, frequently under 50. Even when he had a fever, it was still lower than the normal register. Lady Rosebery drew the conclusion that he should drink wine in the transaction of business. Is there any connection between this abnormally low pulse-beat and his wonderful insensibility to emotion in the face of the most overwhelming popular demonstrations?'[46]

While Gilmour toiled at Mentmore, further attempts were being made in Downing Street to entice Rosebery into the Cabinet. The Office of Works could not be left vacant indefinitely, and on 25 January 1885 Gladstone wrote to Rosebery again, arguing that the Egyptian difficulties should not be an insurmountable obstacle. Rosebery felt otherwise. 'The present situation does not differ materially from the state of affairs which existed when I wrote my letter of November 12. I bitterly regret that it should be so, as I cannot disguise from myself that I may probably now be shut out from what was once a fond hope of mine, that of sitting in a Cabinet presided over by one I so much love,' he replied on 1 February.[47] Nor could Rosebery be persuaded by Mrs Gladstone's sentimental appeal: 'The door is not shut; if upon reading my husband's letter you stop things – surely. Poor old husband! What you could be by his side.'[48] Hamilton also weighed in, in the role of candid friend. When Rosebery told him that it would be 'acting a lie' to enter the Government, Hamilton replied: 'If absolute agreement on all points of political detail were a necessary condition of entrance into Cabinet, no Cabinet would ever be formed at all.'[49] In a series of long talks at Mentmore, Rosebery revealed to Hamilton his more selfish motives in refusing.

> He does not like the risk of being saddled with a share of the responsibility of the past blunders of the Government . . . He believes that to enter the Cabinet now would prejudice his political position and career and he apparently does not think his personal obligations to Mr Gladstone are sufficient to warrant his taking a step which would, or at any rate might, be suicidal to himself . . . I can well understand his unwillingness to surrender the remarkable position he has made for himself as an independent politician. But however attractive independence may be, a man can never be a real power in the state or a real use to his country unless he is prepared to put his neck through the official collar.'[50]

Within days, however, the political situation was transformed by the news from the Sudan that Wolseley's expeditionary force had reached Khartoum, only to find that General Gordon and the rest of the garrison had been massacred. The Queen was furious, sending Gladstone a scornful telegram which, because it was not ciphered, amounted to a public rebuke: 'To think that all this might have been prevented and many precious lives saved by earlier action is too fearful.' Yet Rosebery, instead of distancing himself further from the discredited Government, chose instead to indulge in one of his grand heroic gestures. He immediately wrote to Gladstone on 8 February to say that he was willing to accept Cabinet office. 'The question now is one less of policy than of patriotism. We have to face a crisis such as rarely occurs in a nation's history, which the nation should face with a united front. The Government at such a juncture has a right to appeal to the public spirit and place under requisition the energies of everybody.'[51] With a sense of relief rather than gratitude Gladstone welcomed Rosebery's change of mind, and at Granville's suggestion added to the Office of Works the post of Lord Privy Seal because, as Granville put it, Rosebery was 'silly enough to care.'

More than five years after the first Midlothian campaign, Rosebery had finally entered Gladstone's Cabinet. But he did not do so in any spirit of exhilaration. 'You will see that I have sacrificed myself to a sense of duty at this juncture. I could not force myself to write to anybody about it even if I had been free to do so because my heart has been too heavy,' he told his sister.[52] He was showered with praise for his noble act. Hamilton wrote of his 'truly unselfish and patriotic step', while the *Pall Mall Gazette* told its readers that 'Lord Rosebery brings into the Cabinet a new and fresh force of intellect and character, a keen perception of the facts and forces of political life and an independence of judgement which is very essentially needed in public men.' But others were more cynical, among them, of course, Sir William Harcourt. 'The Home Secretary told me that Rosebery has accepted office though he makes rather a favour of it to us instead of taking it as one to him,' noted his son Loulou.[53] 'Rosebery is undoubtedly a great gain, being one of the best speakers in the Lords and lately having shown signs of an inclination to make himself unpleasant if his claims were overlooked: so that we neutralize a probable enemy as well as secure an ally,' thought Lord Derby. More disgruntled was his secretary Thomas Gilmour, whose account of the acceptance of office reveals how Rosebery, so sensitive about his own feelings, could be cavalier about the sensibilities of others. On the morning of 11 February Gilmour was at Mentmore, where a champagne breakfast was being held at the start of a hunt. Hundreds had turned up for the meet, including Ferdy Rothschild, 'smileless and troubled with liver', and Cyril Flower, 'forty and with a touching belief in his powers of fascination'. During the breakfast it was whispered that Rosebery had accepted office.

> Rosebery himself did not say a word to me on the subject. He had time enough to tell me if he had chosen to do so and I think he ought to have done so. I naturally felt annoyed that it was left to another to carry to me news which he knew would greatly interest me and which would considerably affect my relations with himself. It was entirely owing to Lady Rosebery's courtesy that I was saved from an exposure which would have carried with it something of a humiliation. I don't think for a moment Rosebery deliberately intended to wound me. He is naturally a very reticent man and the heavy demands on his thoughts which the decision entailed would naturally exclude from his view other interests.[54]

Sir Charles Dilke, who had always been suspicious of Rosebery and thought he had 'a taste for deceit', feared that his promotion might weaken the Radical influence on the Government. But Joseph Chamberlain believed that Rosebery shared much of the Radicals' outlook, and was therefore keen to cultivate him. 'I fancy we agree about most important things in politics and we can be content to differ about the details if necessary. I have always looked forward hopefully to the prospect of more active co-operation with you,' Chamberlain told him.[55] Rosebery was unresponsive, largely from his personal dislike of Chamberlain, whom he found hard and unsophisticated. 'One must draw the line somewhere with one's political friends and I draw mine at the screw-making fraternity, the brothers Chamberlain,' he once said.[56] On another occasion he told his secretary Thomas Gilmour that Chamberlain was 'a very strange man. The Italians would certain say that he has the evil eye.'[57]

There was in any case little time left for co-operation in the second Gladstone Government, which had been fatally undermined by the Gordon fiasco, Ireland, and a growing split between the Radicals and the moderate Whigs. As Lord Northbrook warned Rosebery, 'I think you have joined a very short-lived Cabinet.'[58] During Rosebery's first Cabinet meeting, on 16 February, Granville passed him a note asking 'I wonder what you thought of us all?' With characteristic wit Rosebery replied, 'More numerous than the House of Lords and not quite so united.'[59] The lack of harmony was further emphasised at a meeting on 28 February, when there was a stormy four-hour debate over whether the Government should resign following a motion of censure in the Commons which saw the Ministerial majority drop to just 14. Eventually, amid much acrimony, a vote was held and the two sides emerged with the same total; Gladstone therefore used his casting vote in favour of staying in office. Rosebery was the only Cabinet member who abstained, something which astonished Lord Carlingford: 'Rosebery would not vote!' he noted.[60]

It is one of the many paradoxes of Rosebery's career that, though he was renowned as an Imperialist and an expert on foreign policy, his first two Ministerial jobs could hardly have been more insular – or more prosaic. As Under-Secretary at the Home Office he had handled the minutiae of Scottish administration; now, at the Office of Works, he was in charge of government buildings, hardly the most inspiring of tasks. 'Dealt with precautions for workmen and the cricket ground at Greenwich Naval College . . . Visit to Aldershot to choose the site for Wellington's statue' ran two of his diary entries. He was also involved in frequent arguments with the Treasury over departmental accommodation in Whitehall, at one stage joining in the mania for threatening resignation by warning the Treasury that they might soon have to 'find another First Commissioner of Works to execute their behests'. He still found time to be engaged in foreign policy, however, urging the Government to take a resolute stance when Afghan troops were attacked by Russia at Penjdeh in March. Like other imperialists, Rosebery feared that Russian aggression in the area might undermine the security of India. Some, such as W.T. Stead, the maverick editor of the *Pall Mall Gazette*, accused him of war-mongering, a charge Rosebery dismissed. 'I am not for war. I am anxious for a durable understanding on this central Asia question. But to be durable it must involve a real frontier, fairness between the contracting parties and no humiliation which would leave a rankling memory.'[61] Rosebery's view prevailed; the Government voted the army an emergency £11 million to prove its seriousness, and the Russians agreed to arbitration on the Afghan border. In another useful intervention, Rosebery deepened a close friendship – which had begun in 1882 – with Count Herbert Bismarck, the son of Prince Bismarck, the 'Iron Chancellor' of Germany. The two men exchanged unofficial visits during these months which helped to improve Anglo-German relations, though Rosebery, who met the Prince during his trip to Berlin, later said he was one of only two people who truly frightened him; the other was Queen Victoria. Both Gladstone and Granville were impressed by the diplomatic skill Rosebery displayed on his German trip, one result of which was that Prince Bismarck promised to be 'more conciliatory in his language' towards England.[62] The Germans appeared to have been equally favourably impressed by Rosebery. 'All the German press, Liberal as well as Conservative, express high satisfaction with your visit; there is not a single exception,' Count Bismarck told him.[63]

Amid all this success Rosebery experienced a personal tragedy when his younger brother Everard died of fever in April 1885 while serving with the British forces in Sudan. Rosebery and Everard had never been close, partly because their mother had been so obvious in her favouritism. There may also have been some resentment over the disparity in their wealth, as indicated by Rosebery's impatient reference in his diary to their last meeting on 28 September 1884: 'Saw my brother twice. Gave him £500.'[64] Everard's death occurred in the heat of the African desert, in pitiful circumstances. Where he was camped with his battalion near Abu Fatmeh there were two buckets, one used as a latrine, the other for drinking water. Everard and two other soldiers drank from the wrong bucket, and contracted typhoid. His commanding officer, General Sir Garnet Wolseley, kept Rosebery fully informed by telegraph regarding his brother's fluctuating health; 'the last telegram gives me hopes that in two or three weeks he may be well enough to move,' wrote Rosebery to Wolseley on 10 March.[65] But his optimism was misplaced, and Everard died on 8 April. 'And so I strike the word brother from my dictionary,' wrote Rosebery in his diary. 'How hard it is to have been so hopelessly separated from him in this long illness, to have realized him sinking slowly, hopelessly, in the hard, hot glare of the desert sun, caring so much for all the people and all the things from which he was cut off.' Rosebery did not feel so fraternally devoted when he learnt the contents of Everard's will: 'I find my poor brother has left me his executor. Everything he possesses – a house full of furniture and papers – is in Vienna and nothing is to be parted with. What I am to do I cannot remotely conceive but it makes me feel quite dizzy,' he told Herbert Gladstone.[66]

Herbert's father knew that his second Government was entering its last phase. There were almost daily threats of resignation and rows over foreign policy. In May, Edward Hamilton estimated that ten out of sixteen ministers had threatened to go in the last month alone, though Rosebery joked that 'many members of the Cabinet were restrained from resigning by the knowledge that such a proceeding would entail upon them the necessity of having an interview of three hours with the Home Secretary.'[67] In addition, H.C.E. Childers, the Chancellor of the Exchequer, made a hash of presenting his Budget to the Cabinet; 'Childers stated his case wretchedly', wrote Rosebery, 'and got unmercifully handled. It was Childers Bait (as we would have said at Eton) for two hours.'[68] Above all, the perennial problem of Ireland continued to cause disunity. Lord Spencer, the Lord-Lieutenant of Ireland, sought to introduce another coercion measure to quell the nationalists' agitation, while Dilke and Chamberlain wanted to assuage Irish grievances by granting a large measure of self-government based on a central board in Ireland. Rosebery was sympathetic to the idea of Irish devolution, partly because it matched his democratic beliefs about the development of self-governing colonies, and partly because he was now increasingly drawn to the concept of Scottish devolution. As he told Chamberlain, 'I am Scottish home-ruler as well as Irish.' Chamberlain saw another opportunity to win over Rosebery, and on 17 May sent him his scheme for a central board in Ireland. 'My object is to get rid of everything which is not absolutely essential to the security and integrity of the Empire. It is only in this way that we can relieve an overburdened Parliament of work which prevents it from giving attention to Imperial affairs.'[69] At the same time, Gladstone began to take Rosebery into his confidence about his Irish plans, because, he said to Rosebery, 'Ireland has so important a bearing on Scottish affairs' and because 'I was the member of the Cabinet with the most interest in the future'.[70] Though Rosebery had held senior office for little more than three months, Gladstone seems to have recognised that he could one day emerge as the leader of the Liberal party. Moreover, he was so struck by Rosebery's conciliatory attitude on Ireland that he half thought of swapping him with Spencer in their respective posts.[71]

But the Cabinet was too hopelessly divided to do anything concrete about Ireland. On 5 June there was yet another discussion of Spencer's call for coercion, a step to which Dilke and Chamberlain violently objected. Chamberlain passed Rosebery a note: 'Can't you give us a lift in this matter? I fancy you are with us though I have not liked to ask you your opinions.' According to his diary, Rosebery replied that he 'was in favour of a strong local government measure but could not throw over everything which Spencer declared to be the least possible legislation with which Ireland could be governed.'[72] All this was an irrelevance. Three days later, on 8 June, the Government was defeated in a Commons vote on beer duties; after another long internal debate Gladstone and his ministers agreed on 24 June to resign. The Tories now took office and the 3rd Marquess of Salisbury became Prime Minister for the first time. Rosebery was less than impressed by his first experience of Cabinet: 'It cannot properly conduct the affairs of the country. It is too large and not homogenous enough.'[73] But some of his colleagues were not especially taken with Rosebery: 'During the short time he was with us he scarcely opened his mouth and remains quite a dark horse. The impression is that he will run very cunning,' wrote Lord Kimberley.[74]

That was not the view of Gladstone, now closer to Rosebery than he had been at any time since the first Midlothian campaign. He admired Rosebery's brief performance as a Cabinet Minister. It was, he told Hamilton shortly before the Government fell, 'impossible to get anything out of Rosebery but a clever and brilliant reply, no matter how uninteresting the subject.'[75] Out of office and with more time to ruminate, Gladstone decided that there was no alternative for Ireland but Home Rule. Land reform and coercion had failed; Chamberlain's municipal scheme was too limited to satisfy Irish nationalism. During that autumn Gladstone came to regard Rosebery as one of his most trusted advisers, and at Hawarden and Dalmeny they discussed Irish policy at length. But Gladstone was reluctant to make public his conversion to Home Rule, especially before a General Election. He recognised that any such measure would lead to an upheaval in British politics, and had the potential to tear the Liberal party asunder; he therefore felt it would be much better if it could be implemented by the Tory Government, which was presently in an informal, anti-Liberal alliance with Parnell's Irish party. In a long paper to Rosebery, written at Dalmeny in November 1885, Gladstone explained his reasoning. 'The production at this time of a plan by me would not only be injurious but would destroy all reasonable hope of its adoption. Such a plan, proposed by the heads of the Liberal party, is so certain to have the opposition of the Tories *en bloc* that every computation must be founded on this anticipation . . . The idea of constituting a Legislature for Ireland, whenever seriously or responsibly proposed, will cause a mighty heave in the body politic.'[76] Rosebery shared Gladstone's caution, though he did not believe that the Salisbury–Parnell alliance would last long. With hindsight, the idea that the Tories might introduce Home Rule appears preposterously naïve, but to Gladstone at the time it did not. Apart from the link with the Parnellites, Salisbury's Government contained a fervent Home Ruler, Lord Carnarvon, as Lord-Lieutenant of Ireland, and had passed a considerable measure of land purchase reform. Furthermore, Lord Salisbury had pronounced that he was not opposed to some form of Irish devolution, though as it turned out this was nothing more than an opportunistic – and successful – attempt to win the Irish vote at the forthcoming General Election.

The charge of opportunism over Home Rule was often levelled at Rosebery; it was said he never had any real faith in the cause, and only supported Gladstone in 1885–6 in order to win higher Cabinet rank. This is unfair, on a number of grounds. First of all, the idea that Rosebery was fixated on holding high office is absurd: throughout his career, it was something he continually tried to avoid. In fact, by backing an elderly leader in a dangerous policy, he was at risk of undermining his political future. Secondly, even in 1885 Rosebery was seen as the coming man of the Liberal party: he did not need to adopt any particular policy to enhance his following. A note Rosebery made in his diary for 27 October 1885 after seeing the Liberal Chief Whip Lord Richard Grosvenor is revealing: 'We talked about the future Prime Minister – Hartington, Chamberlain, Granville and Spencer. R.G. then said, but for my age, he would consider me best! I burst out laughing in his face.' Similarly, at a banquet held by Scottish Liberals in November 1885, the Earl of Aberdeen, to resounding cheers, described Rosebery as 'a man who is marked out not only by his own striking qualities but by the perceptive instincts of this country as a future leader of Liberal party.' Thirdly, Rosebery genuinely believed in Home Rule, as long as it did not involve the break-up of the Empire. Not only would it 'cut off forever the poisonous spring of discontent', to use one of his own phrases, but it could also be a precursor to the achievement of Scottish self-government and Imperial Federation. In December 1885 he set out his position in a letter to Regy Brett, a fellow Old Etonian who after a brief, unhappy spell as a Liberal MP had embarked on a career as a political intriguer and courtier: 'I detest separation and I feel that nothing could make me agree to it. Home Rule, however, is a necessity for both us and the Irish. They will have it in two years at the latest. Scotland will follow and then England. When that is accomplished, imperial federation will cease to be a dream. To many of us it is not a dream now, but to no one will it be a dream then.'[77] He was just as forceful with his Liberal ally Ronald Munro-Ferguson: 'Those who oppose Home Rule confuse union with centralisation. If union were centralisation, then where would the Empire be with its countless colonies? The true spirit of that Empire lies in this, that every part of it should be contented and ruled so far as may be by its own representatives. Irish self-government is inevitable. No human power can resist the march of events.'[78]

In the 1880s Rosebery had nothing but contempt for Ulster Unionism, the cause the Conservatives tried to use as a weapon against Home Rule. After a walk into Edinburgh in September 1886 with Rosebery, in the course of which he 'spoke with a freedom which is quite unusual', Gilmour recorded that 'He called the outcry of the Orangemen simply contemptible. They have ruled Ireland with our help for two centuries and half and the result is what we see. They are the wealthy and prosperous section of the community and they ought to be able to take care of themselves. I am convinced that if Irishmen – all the inhabitants of Ireland – do really get control of their affairs, the outcry will be that the men of the North get far more than their fair share of power and influence. At any rate, we have a demand on the part of the great majority of the nation for the management of their own affairs. We are entitled to say to Ulstermen, "Throw in your lot with your fellow countrymen and do the best you can for your common country."'[79] Rosebery's over-riding concern was whether Parnell could be trusted by the Liberals, especially after the construction of his cynical alliance with the Tories. Years later, when he was reading a biography of Parnell by his mistress Kitty O'Shea, Rosebery described to J.A. Spender his personal loathing for the Irish leader: 'It is an extraordinary book – quite unlike any other. Are not Parnell's gross superstition, gross ignorance and devilish cantankerousness remarkable features in his complicated character?'[80]

Rosebery's radical politics shone through in other ways apart from Ireland. In Reigate in September 1885 he made a stinging attack on the excessive hours endured by workers who were not protected by trade unions, likening them to those suffered by the blacks under slavery. He even told his audience, to some jeering, that though he was not keen on socialism, he would 'not disdain to borrow from that science' if it would lessen the brutality of such working conditions. This remark led Lord Hartington to dub Rosebery sarcastically 'the Coroneted Socialist'. A month later, at Sheffield, he called railwaymen's hours 'a scandal' and urged the introduction of an eight-hour day. Despite being a great landowner, he could be just as progressive about property, demanding the abolition of the law of primogeniture and the creation of more allotments for the working class. To the consternation of the Prince of Wales, he gave £50 to an election fund to help the farm workers' leader Joseph Arch stand for Parliament. Forced to explain himself, he wrote to the Prince's secretary Francis Knollys: 'It seemed to me a farce to give the agricultural labourer the franchise and then not admit their chief representative to Parliament. Without extraneous assistance he could not enter Parliament and without him the new House of Commons would be glaringly incomplete.'[81] Amid such seriousness, Rosebery retained his gift for phrase-making. In June 1885, when the debate was raging in the Liberal party over its future direction, Rosebery came up with a verbal formula which seemed to embrace all wings of the movement, saying, 'When I ask myself, what is a Liberal, I remember that the name "Liberal" is good enough for Mr Gladstone and good enough for Mr Bright. I am quite willing to walk under an umbrella with these two gentelemen.'[82] The phrase 'Gladstonian umbrella', a direct contrast to Joseph Chamberlain's hard-nosed demand for a specific Liberal programme, became so popular with the electorate and the press that Rosebery soon admitted that he was 'extremely sick of it'.

The General Election was to take place at the end of the year, on the franchise enlarged by the recent Reform Act, and Rosebery entertained Gladstone for his fourth Midlothian campaign. The Earl's popularity was greater than ever, according to Edward Hamilton's account of Gladstone's departure from Waverley: 'The enthusiasm of the crowd outside the station knew no bounds. They mobbed him and shouted for him. "Rozbury, Rozbury" was the universal cry, the crowd running with the carriage till we were fairly out of town. There was never a man who had the Scotchmen so completely at his feet.'[83] Away from the public gaze, Hamilton warmed to Rosebery as never before. 'There is so much sympathy and tenderness under the stolid and placid exterior which so greatly adds to his charm. It is certainly wonderfully fortunate and interesting to be so intimately associated with the great man of the political future.'[84] Mary Gladstone, soon to become engaged to the penniless curate Harry Drew and on her final campaign, also saw that the public fervour for her father and Rosebery was as strong as ever. 'At Edinburgh just the same as other years, the most passionate welcome as we emerged from the station and drove through the streets.'[85] Though Rosebery sent her a warm letter of congratulation on her forthcoming marriage, telling her that 'the important thing is she is to be with the man *she* loves',[86] he was rude behind her back, as Loulou Harcourt recorded. 'Rosebery was very funny about Mary Gladstone's engagement. He said he thought she had no desire to preserve her virginity and that perhaps a long, continued intercourse with hordes of muscular Lytteltons★ had made marriage a necessity. Poor Mary!'[87]

Staying at Dalmeny during the Midlothian campaign, Gladstone learnt that his hopes of a crushing Liberal victory had evaporated. The Conservatives won 249 seats, the Liberals 335, and Parnell, who had urged Irishmen in England to back the Tories, held the balance of power with 86. It was a trying time for the Rosebery household, with the usual tension surfacing between Hannah and Mrs Gladstone, as Lady Spencer noted. 'Poor Mrs Gladstone is in such an awful fret of anxiety over the elections that it is almost painful and she jumps down Hannah's throat if she ventures to say she has heard the majority may only be 10 or 20.'[88] Deprived of a commanding position, Gladstone now clung to the hope that the Salisbury–Parnell alliance might still implement Home Rule without his having to announce his own plans. On 8 December he summoned his two confidants, Rosebery and Spencer, to Hawarden to discuss the way forward. Gladstone wanted to maintain his silence until Parliament met in the New Year on 12 January; if the Tories were able to reach a deal with Parnell regarding Ireland's governance, he argued, then they should be supported. If they could not, then they should face an immediate vote of confidence in the House. The important point, he believed, was to proceed with the utmost caution, as he told Granville on 9 December: 'I think my conversations with Rosebery and Spencer have been satisfactory. What I expect is a healthful, slow fermentation in many minds, working towards the final product.'[89]

Only a year earlier Rosebery had been the disaffected outsider, refusing a Cabinet place. Now he was a key Liberal player, conducting delicate negotiations behind the scenes on Gladstone's behalf. In this task he briefly formed a double act with the ultra radical, Republican-inclined MP for Northampton and editor of *Truth*, Henry Labouchere, who was simultaneously holding private talks with the leading Irish nationalist Tim Healey. Though Labouchere was an unprincipled left-winger, his humour and generosity made him good company, and Rosebery had been on friendly terms

---

★William Gladstone's in-laws.

with him since the 1870s. But he did not share Rosebery's wariness about taking action on Home Rule or going for the Irish party's votes. From November, egged on by Healey, Labouchere was privately urging Gladstone to produce a detailed scheme so he 'could see Parnell at once and show him something in black and white'.[90] Gladstone was not against Rosebery giving Labouchere a vague outline of his Home Rule scheme, as long as he did not reveal too much. 'My father thinks you might use your discretion as to greater explicitness with Labouchere, only that if you touch in general terms on the plan itself you would speak as expressions of your own opinion of what might be expected from my father,' wrote Herbert Gladstone to Rosebery on 10 December.[91] But Rosebery maintained that it would be disastrous to become involved in an auction for Parnell's support. Two days later, he called on Labouchere and 'told him I was averse to negotiations with Parnell'.[92] That night he sent Gladstone a memorandum which summarised his meeting with Labouchere and his own thinking on Ireland. Rosebery explained that he was against direct talks with Parnell because there were 'irresistible natural forces which will compel Parnell to act with us.' Parnell, he said, would win nothing from the Tories and would soon have to turn to the only party who would give him anything. Rosebery added that there was a 'wide difference' between an Opposition leader talking to the Irish leader with the apparent aim of turning out the Tory Government, and the Prime Minister conferring with the recognised leader of Irish opinion. Gladstone, of course, could go much further in setting out his views but, Rosebery concluded presciently, 'I have the strongest opinion that any step of the kind on your part at this moment might be fatal to our cause and party.'[93]

Within four days exactly the step that Rosebery dreaded had been taken by Gladstone's own son Herbert. Acting on his own initiative, he decided to brief several reporters from the National Press Agency on his father's plans for Home Rule. When the story was published the next day in *The Standard* it caused a sensation in the country, and outrage in many sections of the Liberal party. Sir William Harcourt fulminated against Gladstone's 'insane folly', while Spencer told Rosebery he was in despair over what had become known as 'The Hawarden Kite', fearing that the overwhelming opinion of the Liberal party was now hostile. 'I feel you and I will be looked upon by ex-colleagues as conspirators in aiding and abetting the Grand Old Man in his wickedness. As far as I can judge, we – and I know not whether you still hold the views you did at Hawarden; you might well have gone back from them – will stand alone among Mr Gladstone's colleagues. Possibly Lord Granville will follow Mr Gladstone but I know of no one else inclined to do so. We three peers and John Morley could not form a

Gladstone government and I see no prospect of Mr Gladstone getting a following enough to justify his going on.'[94] In reply, Rosebery expressed both his annoyance with Herbert and his realistic view of the immediate future: 'Infinite harm has been done by these disclosures. Like war-elephants, they have trampled down our own ranks before attacking those of the enemy. However, it cannot be helped. We must face the situation as it is.' Rosebery then spelt out again his belief that there was no alternative to Gladstone's policy: 'Home Rule is now inevitable. Even if the abstract principle were wrong, the practical necessity is certain: because once a man of Mr Gladstone's position declares in favour of it, Ireland will never be quiet until it has been tried.'[95]

There is no doubt that Herbert had been reckless, but it is doubtful whether he really caused as much damage as has often been claimed. After all, Gladstone was going to have to reveal his hand at some time, and whenever he did so there would have been an outcry against him. The Liberals who favoured the Union were never going to accept Home Rule, no matter how gingerly Gladstone moved. Furthermore, though Gladstone may not have approved of his son's actions, there was a part of him that was desperate to have his views on Home Rule publicly known. As Labouchere put it to Rosebery on the very day of Herbert's interview, 'Between you and me, the Grand Old Man's mind is so large a one that he absorbs two ideas – one to tackle Parnell at once, the other to wait.' In the same letter Labouchere revealed Herbert's impatience to act. 'Saw Herbert yesterday. When I said it was well not to appear in a hurry with Parnell, he said, yes, but it was essential not to lose time.'[96] Rosebery himself recognised that Gladstone had helped to lead his son down this controversial path, as he told Hamilton: 'I fully share your regret as to Herbert's indiscretions . . . But I greatly fear that he has been encouraged to this by an illustrious relative who is or has been most anxious that his opinions on the subject should be known in various quarters. That is why, I suspect, Herbert has not heeded your remonstrances. I am not at all sure that the country and the Liberal party will refuse to follow Mr Gladstone on this question. Disregard the London Clubbites who are sure to be wrong.'[97]

Whatever else it achieved, the Hawarden Kite made inevitable the return of Gladstone to Downing Street. With the prospect of Home Rule beckoning, Parnell's Irish Party abandoned its Tory alliance and, in a vote of confidence on 27 January 1886, helped the Liberals to defeat the Conservative Government. Salisbury resigned immediately. In the most unpropitious of circumstances, Gladstone now had the task of trying to form his third administration.

6

'You have a great political future'

~~~

'I DO NOT like the look of political affairs just now. Nothing but a miracle can save us from the breaking up of the party and a great disaster,' wrote Joseph Chamberlain to Rosebery at the beginning of 1886.[1]

Gladstone's burden in taking the Premiership for the third time was indeed a formidable one. Not only did he have to draft one of the largest, most important pieces of legislation of the nineteenth century, the Government of Ireland Bill; he also had to cope with a gaping fissure in the ranks of the Liberal Party. Lord Hartington, the leader of the Whigs in the Upper House, had told Gladstone that because of his opposition to Home Rule he could not accept office, while Chamberlain proved a reluctant minister despite his advocacy of Irish devolution the previous year.

As he struggled to form his government, the Foreign Secretaryship posed Gladstone almost as great a problem as the Irish question. It had been obvious for most of his second administration that Lord Granville's powers were failing badly. Never on top of his work, he committed error after error, the fiasco of the Sudan being but the most serious, and his mixture of indolence and rudeness alienated foreign embassies. His two nicknames 'Pussy' and 'Granny' reflected the widespread contempt in which he was held. Almost every minister of the last Government had raged against his ineptitude. Sir William Harcourt complained that Granville was always 'coming into the Cabinet and throwing his papers down with a request that he should be told what to do'.[2] By 1886 he was over seventy, and suffering badly from gout. He also had, unfortunately, a weak bladder, which meant that during Cabinet meetings he regularly had to use the chamber pot; years later, Rosebery recalled with horror his memory of Granville 'constantly pump-shipping in a cupboard in the corner'.[3] In addition, his severe money problems, caused by the failure of the family ironworks business in Shropshire, left him distracted and almost bankrupt.

Showing her habitual lack of respect for the constitutional limits of her role, Queen Victoria warned Gladstone that Granville's return to the Foreign Office was unacceptable. 'I have been forced to confide the formation of the

Government to that crazy old man Merrypebble,'★ she wrote to her daughter Vicky, later briefly Empress of Germany, 'and I have made it a condition that Pussy should not go to the Foreign Office, which he had to own he was not surprised at.'[4] For all his devotion to Granville, Gladstone had come to the same conclusion. But he now faced two related difficulties: how was Granville to be prised away from a post he cherished and, more importantly, who would replace him?

Granville was dismayed at the idea of giving up the Foreign Office. Gladstone's friend Lord Rendel recalled that he 'was totally unprepared for being thrown over. The blow staggered him. For a day or two he retired to his tents.'[5] Granville threatened that if he could not have foreign affairs then he would refuse to serve at all rather than come back in some 'degraded official capacity'.[6] But eventually, after an anguished correspondence with Gladstone, he caved in and accepted the Colonies.

A number of people were touted as his possible successor. The Queen initially favoured George Goschen, the Liberal moderate, until she was told that his anti-Home Rule views made his service under Gladstone impossible. Gladstone himself thought that 'Kimberley will do', but this plan found favour with neither the Queen nor Kimberley himself, a solid but second-rank performer who, with a self-awareness rare in a politician, said that 'it would be a great mistake to appoint an unpopular man like myself'.[7] Gladstone must have been secretly relieved, for he thought that Kimberley was 'the most long-winded man he had ever known in Cabinet'.[8] This left Rosebery as the only realistic alternative. Even his enemy Sir William Harcourt was willing to put up with him if that was the price to pay for the removal of Granville; similarly, Joseph Chamberlain 'did not think Rosebery fit for the place but would willingly accept him or anyone else to get rid of Granny'.[9] For the first time in his political career, it looked as if Rosebery were to be offered a job he might actually want. Though in the run-up to the formation of the 1886 Government he told friends that the Colonial Office was his highest ambition, Edward Hamilton shrewdly suspected otherwise. During a visit to Mentmore in September 1885 he and the Earl had indulged in fanciful Cabinet making, Hamilton putting Rosebery in the Foreign Office. 'I have given him the place which in his heart of hearts he would prefer, though he will not admit it.'[10]

By the end of January it was clear that he was the choice of the Court as well of most of his political colleagues. Indeed, as early as October 1885 the Queen had 'jumped' at the idea of Rosebery one day becoming

★ The Queen's name for Gladstone

Foreign Secretary.[11] Her affection for him was shown after a dinner at Windsor in 1884, of which Lady Spencer left this account: 'The Queen talked for a long time to Lord Rosebery. She sat down and whether it was that Her Majesty found her chair so comfortable or Lord Rosebery so amusing or both, she remained there such a time that we all began to stand on one leg, and thought she would never move.'[12] It was on this occasion that the Queen told Rosebery she wished he would buy a highland estate near Balmoral, because 'we would like to have you as a neighbour'.[13] When the Queen's secretary Sir Henry Ponsonby visited Mentmore on 27 January 1886 he told Rosebery that the Queen 'would like Salisbury to be Foreign Minister under Hartington but failing that has fixed upon you'.[14] But Gladstone had not yet resolved the painful Granville question, and had besides developed a feeling – as he told the Queen – that Rosebery might be too young for the job.[15] Briefly, his choice veered towards Lord Spencer. But this idea quickly passed, helped on its way by some discreet lobbying by the Prince of Wales and Edward Hamilton, who were both determined to see Rosebery at the Foreign Office, though Hannah warned Hamilton not to push too hard on her husband's behalf: 'I am not sure if you yet thoroughly understand Archie. Anything right and to prevent an incompetent to hold a particular office he will endeavour, but I doubt his even saying a syllable which would make an idea possible of his having entertained the notion of taking a high post.'[16] On 30 January 1886, after learning that Granville was willing to accept the Colonies, Gladstone summoned Rosebery to his London home at Carlton House Terrace and offered him the post of Foreign Secretary. 'I said it was too big a thing for me and that, at any rate, I must have an hour or two to consider. He admitted that was fair but asked me to be as quick as possible. At 5 I sent in my acceptance. It is an awful scrape,' Rosebery wrote in his diary.[17] His letter to Gladstone, which reflects some genuine trepidation, read: 'I have absolutely no experience of the Foreign Office, which I have never entered except to attend a dinner. My French is I fear rusty.★ I have never had to face anything like what you would call hard work. I have no knowledge of diplomatic practice or forms and little of diplomatic men. And I am sensible of many deficiencies of temper and manner. Moreover the Foreign Office is usually considered, and justly I think, to be the chief of all offices. I should gladly have climbed into it in ten or twenty years, had I been fit for it then. But I know very well that I am not fit for it now . . . Nevertheless, if you wish

---

★ This carries self-deprecation too far. He was in fact one of the most accomplished French speakers in the Government, and frequently read French literature for pleasure.

me to try my hand and if you have that confidence in me which I have not in myself, I am willing to put my shoulder to the wheel and do my best.' That evening, by way of celebration, Rosebery dined at Brooks's with the new Liberal whip Arnold Morley and Ronald Munro-Ferguson. All three went on to the circus at Covent Garden – a form of entertainment in which Rosebery always took a childish delight – and then at eleven, in response to a Royal summons, he called on the Prince of Wales to discuss his appointment, before taking the train to The Durdans at 11.55. Over the next few days he overcame any potential conflict of interest in respect of his Rothschild connection by selling his extensive Egyptian investments and all other foreign securities 'at a considerable loss'.[18]

It was the first occasion on which Rosebery accepted a position without the preliminary of a lengthy, letter-strewn saga. But even his brief hesitation was too much for Loulou Harcourt. 'He pretended to be much taken aback and said he never had any idea that he would be offered the FO and asked time to consider his decision. Beastly humbug. He knew perfectly well all the time.' Harcourt also revealed the continuing emotional chasm between the Gladstones and the Roseberys. According to his account, when Gladstone was with Spencer discussing the Foreign Secretaryship, 'Spencer said, "I'm sure Hannah is quite prepared to take it" at which Mr Gladstone broke out, "Hannah! Why she would think herself capable of being Queen of the Realm and think the place only just good enough for her."'[19] Others had a less jaundiced view of the appointment; Matthew Arnold wrote in *The Nineteenth Century* magazine, 'Lord Rosebery, with his freshness, spirit and intelligence, one cannot but with pleasure see at the Foreign Office.' After dining with the Roseberys on 11 February, Edward Hamilton wrote: 'She is naturally delighted and proud. I hear the Foreign Office are very pleased at having got him and they are already struck with his cleverness mingled with deference and they feel sure of his success as Foreign Minister.' For all his understandable anxiety over his lack of experience, Rosebery was elated at his promotion. To his sister Constance he said, 'I feel as if I had agreed to become Pope.'[20] Writing to his mother, he struck a wistful note: 'It is a gigantic responsibility but one I cannot in honour avoid. But my mind is constantly dwelling on a telegram I had from Everard on a similar occasion last year, a voice which can never again wish me well.'[21]

Another and more politically important letter sent by Rosebery on his appointment was to Sir Charles Dilke, the leading Radical. 'One of my chief thoughts in this business has been of you. Had you not felt compelled to stand aside, this office would have been yours by universal consent. You have all the knowledge and ability that I so sadly lack. You must feel this strongly but you cannot feel it half so strongly as I do.'[22] Dilke replied generously, declaring that he 'could have never taken the Foreign Office without the heaviest misgivings' and expressing the hope 'that whenever the Liberals are in, up to the close of my life, you may hold it'.[23] But the reason for Dilke standing aside was far less edifying than all this high-minded sentiment might suggest. At the time of the formation of Gladstone's third administration he was caught up in one of the Victorian era's most gripping sex scandals, in which the Scottish Liberal politician Donald Crawford sued his wife for divorce on the grounds of her adultery, citing Dilke as the co-respondent. Though the evidence against Dilke was dismissed when the case came to court on 17 February 1886, Crawford was nevertheless granted his divorce, a contradictory verdict which did nothing for Dilke's reputation. Further attempts by Dilke to clear his name in the courts only worsened his position, especially as the details of Mrs Crawford's confession had been made public. According to her account Dilke had a sexual appetite of unbridled exuberance, and enjoyed affairs not only with Mrs Crawford but also with her mother and a servant-girl, Fanny Gray, who was alleged to have been enticed into sharing a bed with Mrs Crawford and Dilke. 'He taught me every French vice. He used to say that I knew more than most women of thirty,' claimed Mrs Crawford, to the delight of a Victorian public wallowing in excited disapproval.

Dilke, the great radical hope of the Liberal cause, was finished as a senior politician. He lost his Chelsea seat in 1886, and though he returned to Parliament in 1892 as the Liberal member for the Forest of Dean he was never again received in society and died an embittered, isolated, tragic figure. He always claimed to have been the victim of an elaborate political conspiracy, but this is unconvincing since in the context of Victorian morality he was a notorious libertine, said to have conducted as many as six affairs at once. Smitten by Randolph Churchill's beautiful American wife Jennie, he had fallen to his knees and begged her to be his mistress. Jennie related this incident to Rosebery, much to his amusement. Lord Randolph was less amused when he heard of it, however, and physically attacked Dilke.[24] The widely held view of the political world was reflected by Hannah in a letter to Edward Hamilton. 'Sir Charles Dilke's behaviour is very astonishing in some reports, though it is not an actual surprise to me.'[25]

Rosebery himself was convinced of Dilke's guilt, believing that he revelled in keeping a part of his life in the shadows. In a conversation with Gilmour in September 1886, after Dilke's downfall, Rosebery said:

'Undoubtedly he is a very able man but he was passionately fond of intrigue and I believe that half the pleasure of his double life was the way in which they were absolutely separate. He would find pleasure in thinking no one in one life knew anything of the other and I fancy him timing his visits from the office to Tottenham Court Road and saying, "Done in three-quarters of an hour – they can't prove anything in that time."'[26] When Dilke announced in October 1885, shortly before the Crawford divorce trial, that he was engaged to one of his many mistresses, Emilia Pattison, widow of Mark Pattison, the late Rector of Lincoln College, Oxford, Rosebery wrote cynically to his friend Herbert Bismarck: 'When a single man in England is charged with violating the sanctity of marriage, he almost invariably marries himself to show his supposed unimpaired faith in the institution.'[27]

Rosebery had first learnt of the impending scandal on 20 July 1885 as the news was spreading like wildfire through London society, recording in his diary, 'It is rumoured that Dilke has been found in an intrigue with Mrs Crawford.' Rosebery was close to his fellow Liberal Scot Donald Crawford, who regularly stayed at Dalmeny and Mentmore, and a week later the two men discussed the case in depth. 'Met Crawford in the lobby and had a long talk with him in a committee room about his tragedy.'[28] In the 1885 General Election Crawford won the seat of North-East Lanarkshire; shortly afterwards he stayed at Dalmeny, just when the scandal was reaching its height. Rosebery was also kept up to date with the latest inside gossip by his American journalist friend George Smalley of the *New York Tribune*. 'Crawford has not yet succeeded in getting the evidence without which it would be useless for him to file a petition,' Smalley wrote in August. 'The wife's testimony uncorroborated would go for nothing in court . . . When it is asked why Mrs Crawford should on this occasion have confessed, the answer becomes difficult to explain except on the theory that she wishes to be divorced.'[29]

Dilke, however, suspected that the answer to this question might lie with Rosebery himself. Through a number of anonymous letters and whispered accusations, Dilke was led to think it possible that Rosebery had plotted to bring about his disgrace, his motivation said to be his desire to remove his most serious rival for the Foreign Office and, eventually, the leadership of the Liberal party. His method, allegedly, was to bribe Mrs Crawford to make a false confession. Dilke found such insinuations all too plausible, since he thought Hannah 'odd' and her husband both devious and fiercely ambitious; indeed, he once described Rosebery as 'the most ambitious man I have ever met'. He took the claims seriously enough to write to Rosebery on 12 December 1885:

Some time ago friends of mine who are also friends of Mr Crawford and of yourself expressed surprise that he was staying with you. I replied that it was not unnatural, there being nothing I know of against him. Today I have however heard a statement so incredible that I hesitate to repeat it to you even in a secret letter. It is that Mr Crawford states that Lady Rosebery had promised him help in this case. Now, no doubt he believes the wicked and monstrous lies that have been told him, but no one else who has any acquaintance with the matter believed them and I make no doubt that the nature and authorship of the plot against me will be fully exposed. Still it is not pleasant to have a colleague's name used in this way and I think it best to write to you rather than to write to relations of Lady Rosebery's or to colleagues of ours or common friends.[30]

Rosebery was understandably insulted by this letter, and replied the next day: 'I should have thought that even in this age of lies no human being could have invented so silly a lie as you mention. But, if you wish me to contradict it, I will only say that there is not a vestige of truth or even possibility about it. Under no circumstances could I, much less my wife, connect myself with anything of the sort.'[31] Dilke professed himself satisfied by this: 'Your letter is all I could expect and wish. He (Crawford) thinks he has received the greatest of injuries at my hands. I have received none at his because I have never for an instant doubted his belief in what he was told.'

Dilke's willingness to attach any credence to such a bizarre tale of intrigue only shows how desperate he had become in the run-up to the Crawford trial. Not a shred of evidence has ever been uncovered of any payment by the Roseberys to Mrs Crawford, while Dilke, like many others, greatly exaggerated Rosebery's eagerness for office. In later life Dilke said that he 'never believed' the story, though his determination to confront Rosebery with it seems to suggest otherwise. Furthermore, he continued to repeat the allegation privately for years afterwards; in 1894 he went so far as to claim that it was a member of Rosebery's own household, a certain Irishwoman, Mrs Bridgemount, who had circulated the report of the Earl's bribery of Mrs Crawford. There is no evidence in the Rosebery papers of any Mrs Bridgemount working for the Roseberys, however, and Dilke appears to have relied on hearsay information about her from a solicitor based in County Mayo in the west of Ireland. Dilke's own loyal secretary, J.E.C. Bodley, always thought the tale of a Rosebery vendetta implausible, telling his employer in 1887 that he had 'never heard a word as to Rosebery's hostility to you except the very frequent and obvious observations that your being out of the way was worth a good deal to him'.

And he added, with a vulgar note of anti-Semitism, that there was no sign that Hannah's family was out to destroy him: 'As you know I never had any intimacy with the Jew gang. I never heard they had shown any great hostility to you excepting of course the national line the tribe would take of kicking a man when he was down.'[32] Rosebery's own family thought the idea ridiculous. In the Crewe papers there is an interesting exchange of letters between Lord Crewe, Rosebery's son-in-law, and the historian J.L. Hammond.* Having been examining Dilke's memoirs in the British Library, Hammond wrote to Crewe in 1936 to report that 'Dilke appears – or professes – to think that Lady Rosebery supplied Mrs Crawford with the funds for the case', a charge that Hammond regarded as 'disgraceful'. Crewe swiftly replied: 'As a matter of fact, the Roseberys' sympathies were entirely with Donald Crawford, whom I remember meeting at their house not long after the divorce. I can only account for this passage by concluding that Dilke was suffering from a persecution mania and the conviction that everyone was more or less against him, which was more or less true, owing to his conduct of the case, though a few people tried to stand up for him. My wife,† to whom I have shown the letter, agrees there could be no question of her parents helping Crawford.'[33]

In truth, there was no need for a complex plot – masterminded by Rosebery or anyone else – against Dilke. The most promiscuous politician of his age, he was the author of his own downfall, as he revealed all too clearly in the first Crawford trial when he refused to go into the witness box. That was hardly the behaviour of an innocent man fighting a potential injustice. Yet stories of conspiracies, no matter how absurdly based, swirled around Rosebery throughout his life. The Oscar Wilde trial of 1895 and the row over the Jameson Raid in 1896 were two later examples in this pattern. The reason for this probably lay in the air of mystery and reserve with which Rosebery tended to shroud himself, provoking others to think he was permanently engaged in dubious activities. When he was in Downing Street as Prime Minister, for example, Rosebery insisted on great privacy, as Loulou Harcourt reported. 'He says that the pillar room must be kept available for his visitors and has given special instructions that a man coming in to see him shall not meet the man going out – so like his love of secrecy.'[34] After a dinner in Lansdowne House in July 1886, Joseph Chamberlain admitted to Hamilton that he found Rosebery 'a little too

---

*Author of the definitive book on Gladstone and Ireland, *Gladstone and the Irish Nation* (1938).
†Peggy, née Primrose.

scheming and calculating',[35] while John Morley famously described him as a 'dark horse'; Morley once in a conversation with the Liberal peer Lord Rendel argued that Rosebery had a 'secret cupboard' in his life, and Rendel asked, 'Is the dark place in Rosebery not, in fact, a void?'[36] Even those most sympathetic to him could feel this; Regy Brett, having tended to hero-worship in his youth, later complained of Rosebery's 'silly mystery' when talking to friends, and said he was 'too lacking in frankness for perfect intimacy'.[37]

Most of Dilke's erstwhile colleagues took a malicious delight in his ruin. 'The only career open to him is to start lectures on French fancy bedwork, with illustrations by Lady Dilke, Fanny and himself,' Labouchere told Rosebery after the first disastrous trial.[38] But Rosebery never forgave Dilke for making the charges against Hannah, and beyond a couple of formal letters never had anything to do with him again. In a private note written after Dilke's death he explained his feelings about the man and the case.

> Dilke's difficulty and that of his biographers was to find any motive which should induce Mrs Crawford to make a false confession. But at last, some six years I think after the trial, Dilke revealed to the chosen that the whole business had been engineered by a noble lady, then safely dead, to get Dilke out of the way of her husband's devouring ambition. Now a man who could invent so foul and infamous a falsehood must have had a moral taint like a cancer pervading his whole being; a hundred adulteries would not demonstrate so conclusively a complete depravity. Up to the time of his outrage, I knew him fairly well; after it, I cut him dead and knew him no more. Adulterers are not uncommon in society but this particular case had features which are abhorrent even to those who did not know the particular crime of which I was cogniscent.

As to other aspects of Dilke's character, Rosebery described him as 'hard working' and 'a good administrator', but someone who in company was 'cold and dictatorial'. After his fall, wrote Rosebery, 'he became a failure and bore', who was hated by the Liberals for his 'pathetic attempt to rehabilitate himself'.[39]

While Dilke was being dragged through the courts in early 1886, Rosebery was emerging as a commanding figure at the Foreign Office. Though Gladstone had expressed to the Queen some anxiety about his age, Rosebery was at 38 not especially young for the post of Foreign Secretary; Derby, Liverpool and Canning had all been younger at the time of their respective appointments. In many ways the Foreign Office was the ideal position for him. Diplomacy came easily to a man of his intellect, aristocratic self-confidence and charm. He spoke French and German fluently. His long hours of private study had given him an unparalleled grasp of international history and politics. Winston Churchill rightly said of him that 'His life was set in an atmosphere of tradition. The Past stood ever at his elbow and was the counsellor upon whom he most relied. He seemed to be attended by Learning and History, and to carry into current events an air of ancient majesty.'[40] As his love of travel indicated, he was the least insular of men, and the Foreign Office gave him an outlet for his romantic fascination with distant climes. In a speech at the Royal Academy in 1893 he reflected on the joys of the post: 'I have only to open a red box to be possessed of that magic carpet which took its possessor wherever he would go. Perhaps sometimes it carries me a little farther than that. I open it and find myself at once in those regions where a travelled monarch and an intellectual Minister are endeavouring to reconcile the realms of Xerxes and Darius with the needs of nineteenth-century civilisation. I smell the scent of the roses and hear the song of the bulbul. I open another box, which enables me to share the sports of the fur-seal, his island loves, his boundless swims in the Pacific; I can even follow him to Paris and see him – the *corpus delecti* – laid on the table of the Court of Arbitration.'[41]

When he took office, Rosebery had two over-riding concerns. The first – in contrast to Granville in his incompetent tenure – was to avoid Cabinet discussions as much as possible. Rosebery never had much faith in that body as an instrument of governance, and certainly not when it came to conducting foreign policy. In adopting this approach he was strongly encouraged by Queen Victoria, who wrote in her journal: 'I urged Lord Rosebery not to bring too many matters before the Cabinet as nothing was decided there and it would be better to discuss everything with me and Mr Gladstone.'[42] The second was to maintain the continuity of Lord Salisbury's foreign policy. This marked a decisive break with the previous Liberal Government, which had prided itself on its rejection of 'Beaconsfieldism'. Rosebery strongly believed that Britain's national interests were far more important than party politics, and argued in a speech at Leeds in 1888 that 'the more the Secretary of State for Foreign Affairs is considered as a non-political officer, the better for the country'.[43] Salisbury himself was reported to be relieved that Rosebery had succeeded him, as Herbert Bismarck told Rosebery on 31 January 1886: 'Salisbury has called on Hatzfeldt★ (quite confidentially) and has said he hoped you would take the Foreign Office for in that case he could resign without anxiety. He has spoken in very flattering terms about you and has added that he was sure

★Count Hatzfeldt, the German ambassador to Britain.

you would do great things and that the foreign policy would be in the best hands if you took charge of it.'[44]

Living up to Salisbury's expectations, Rosebery immediately demonstrated a confident grip on foreign affairs. His central objective, like that of all the most effective British foreign secretaries of the late nineteenth century, was to use Britain's influence to maintain the balance of power in Europe, thereby protecting British imperial interests and avoiding a conflagration on the Continent. In practice, this meant restoring Britain's relations – so badly damaged by Granville – with the Triple Alliance of Germany, Italy and Austria-Hungary, which he saw as a vital barrier to French and Russian ambitions. His biggest problem occurred in the Balkans, that bloody peninsula which has been such a blight on the history of Europe for at least the last two hundred years. As so often before, the Balkan crisis of 1886 was the outcome of emergent nationalism exploiting the weakness of the gangrenous Ottoman Empire. In September 1885 the people of Eastern Rumelia, that artificial state created by the 1878 Congress of Berlin, had risen up in revolt against Turkish rule and demanded unification with their neighbour Bulgaria, whose population was of the same ethnicity. Lord Salisbury might have been expected to oppose the creation of this new nation of 'Big Bulgaria', given that traditional Tory policy in the Near East was to uphold the Turkish Empire as a means of protecting the vital route to India. Yet, contrary to such forecasts, he supported the idea of unification under the Bulgarian sovereign, Prince Alexander of Battenberg. This was partly because Prince Alexander, despite being a nephew of the Tsar, had proved himself a strong Bulgarian nationalist since coming to the throne, blighting hopes in St Petersburg that he would turn his country into a Russian vassal state. By 1885 Salisbury had come to regard him as a bulwark against Russian expansion in the Balkans.

Acting on the principle of continuity with Salisbury, Rosebery pursued the concept of Bulgarian unity. The great difficulty was that support for Prince Alexander also served to embolden other Balkan states to rise against Constantinople. Greece in particular mobilised on the Turkish border, seeking to gain from Turkey the territory she felt she had been unjustly denied by the Congress of Berlin. British Liberalism had always embodied a powerful Philhellenic strain, inspired by Lord Byron and upheld by Gladstone, but Rosebery, while sympathising with it to some extent, regarded any war between Greece and Turkey as disastrous because if Russia were to enter the fray on the side of Greece, there was a risk that the whole of the Balkans might be set ablaze. He feared moreover that the

Greeks would be instantly obliterated by Turkey; about the only part of the rotting Ottoman Empire that still functioned efficiently was its barbarous army. If war occurred, he warned, 'the Turks would be at Athens in four days, the King would be at Claridge's hotel in a fortnight, and it would not be altogether a simple matter to get the Turks out of Athens again.'[45]

The situation was fraught with danger, as Rosebery admitted to the Queen, 'because although neither the Sultan nor the Czar desire war, it is very easy to drift into war without wishing it, and this is just one of those occasions when involuntary hostilities might commence.'[46] Rosebery now had to perform an extremely delicate balancing act, pursuing the aim of Bulgarian union while persuading the Greeks to abandon their belliger-ence. It was a task he performed with consummate skill. Working in con-cert with the other leading European Powers, he employed a combination of diplomacy and threats of naval action as a means of persuading Greece to disarm, without raising the stakes too violently. At the same time, he presided over awkward negotiations regarding the future of Eastern Rumelia. Eventually, in April, a Turco-Bulgar convention was agreed by which Prince Alexander was to become Governor-General of the state for a term of five years – less than the Prince and the Bulgarian nationalists wanted, but the best that could be realistically achieved. As Rosebery wisely commented, 'If the Prince can keep on the throne five years he will be safe for an unlimited period. If he cannot, what is the use of a longer term?'[47] With the Bulgarian question temporarily resolved,* Rosebery could focus with more vigour on Greece, which had still refused to aban-don its bellicosity towards Turkey. As Rosebery had explained to Queen Victoria on 28 March, he was unable to act before the signing of the agree-ment: 'Unfortunately we cannot put pressure on Greece while Prince Alexander resists, as Greece can always point to his attitude as a justifica-tion for hers.'[48]

Rosebery now took the lead in organising a naval blockade of Greece, again using the Concert of European Powers. He was, however, disap-pointed by the duplicitous behaviour of France, who quibbled over the final ultimatum and sent a secret communication to the Greeks warning that the Powers were about to act. 'It is the proceeding of a little boy who runs to tell the pilfering comrade that the policeman is round the corner,' he wrote.[49] In implementing the blockade from 16 April Rosebery proved himself a spirited adversary, telling the First Lord of the Admiralty, the Earl

---

*Though not for long. In August 1886, after Rosebery's departure from the Foreign Office, Prince Alexander was kidnapped by the Russians and forced to abdicate.

of Ripon, that the term 'Greek ships is to mean all ships including merchant ones'.[50] Thanks to Rosebery's diplomatic skill, the Powers remained united through the crisis and, remarkably, all of them contributed to the Allied fleet: Russian ships joined a British squadron, while both the Austrians and the Italians provided torpedo-boats. The Greeks went through a charade of resistance, but since they were without any external backing, capitulation was inevitable. They gave way at the beginning of June, and the blockade was lifted.

It had been tough going for Rosebery. At one stage of the crisis he wrote to Gladstone, 'I have had a bad time of it – five ambassadors a day gnawing at my vitals and Bismarck's with the sharpest teeth.'[51] But he had proved his mettle in the most compelling fashion. When his appointment was first mooted Loulou Harcourt had written: 'From my knowledge of Rosebery's extreme timidity and his dislike of coming to any decision when he was at the Home Office, I should think he would make a bad Foreign Secretary.'[52] He could not have been more mistaken. Rosebery had been firm, patient, cool, and resolute – all qualities his critics so often claimed he lacked. Just after the beginning of the united Greek blockade, Gladstone wrote to him effusively: 'I do not remember an instance of such an achievement carried through in the first quarter of a Foreign Secretaryship. And it is one to which your personal action has beyond doubt largely contributed. It is a great act and a good omen.'[53] The next day, 17 April, he told Lady Rosebery that 'if the Government had done nothing but bring out Rosebery's great talents as a Foreign Minister, it would not have been formed in vain.'[54] Hamilton was delighted that his friend was at last realising his true potential as a statesman. 'He is engrossed in his work and never was a Foreign Secretary more widely appreciated. He is grata persona to Her Majesty; he is respected by the diplomatic world; he has the complete confidence of his colleagues and the country. His short tenure of office has certainly placed the political ball absolutely at his feet and he has got the nous to kick it the right way.'[55]

Rosebery showed his steel in other areas beyond the Balkans. The British pro-consul of Egypt, Sir Evelyn Baring, later Lord Cromer, was assured that there would be no early attempt to evacuate the country, despite the Liberal party's antagonism in general to its occupation. Similarly, when the Russians violated the Treaty of Berlin by ending the status of Batoum as a free port, Rosebery sent a stinging rebuke to St Petersburg. He knew the issue to be one of little practical importance, but felt it necessary to register Britain's objection to this 'act of insolent perfidy'.[56] So stern was his language that the Russian Foreign Minister N.K.

Giers moaned, with laughable self-pity, that it was 'the most wounding communication that has ever been addressed by one power to another. It has gone straight to my heart and remains there till I die.'[57] Kitchener, the roving military imperialist, was impressed by Rosebery's willingness to stand up to Germany in disputes over territory in Zanzibar: 'I must say Lord Rosebery has done me very well,' he wrote to his sister on 6 June 1886. 'He sticks up to the Germans like fun. I admire him. I gave him a hint of the dirty trick the Germans were playing and he positively almost frightened me by the persistence with which he rubbed it in at Berlin.'[58] In private, though, Rosebery was not much enamoured of the scramble for Africa, which was well under way in the 1880s and would reach its vexatious peak in the 1890s, for he was always more of a consolidator of Empire than an aggressive expansionist. He put it with some irony to Herbert Bismarck. 'You will soon receive a circular from me to say that we have annexed the rest of the universe. There is but little that remains and that little is composed chiefly of swamps inhabited by cannibals. But having done that and refused permission to the consuls of any nation whatever to establish themselves there, I shall either be at universal peace or universal war and either would be better than these interminable lessons of geography − hunting for the last bog or reef on which the representatives of France or Germany are exchanging with the representatives of England billions and distorted views of international law.'[59]

Rosebery's immersion in the Balkans left him little time to assist Gladstone on the Home Rule debate which dominated his third government. In 1885 Rosebery had been the linchpin of internal party discussions on the subject, and Gladstone relied more on him than on any other Liberal politician. Yet in 1886 his involvement was only limited, as Loulou Harcourt noted: 'Rosebery takes no interest in the Irish policy of the Grand Old Man and wraps himself in the Foreign Office to the exclusion of all else.'[60] Flushed with his diplomatic triumphs, Rosebery joked at one stage, 'Ireland is not yet a foreign country: when it is I shall look after it.'[61] This was something of an exaggeration, for Gladstone still occasionally consulted him, as Rosebery's diary for 24 February shows: 'Gladstone beginning to expound his Irish plan, with which he said he did not trouble me as he knew how busy I was, then said he was acting within the scope of what he knew to be my ideas. I implored him to spare me but when he sketched the vast skeleton I could not resist saying, "Is it six or seven years since you told me you had lost all power of constructive legislation?" He could not help chuckling.' And Rosebery remained a strong supporter of the proposal, telling George Buckle of *The Times* − much to his astonishment – that 'the old methods of procedure in governing Ireland were past and something new must be tried'.[62]

Gladstone's heroic attempt to resolve the Irish question was doomed. The Home Rule Bill was defeated on its Second Reading in the House of Commons on 8 June, when 93 Liberals, led by Hartington and Chamberlain, voted with the Conservatives. Parliament was immediately dissolved, and in the subsequent General Election – for which campaign Rosebery donated £5000 to the Liberal cause – the Gladstonians performed disastrously, holding just 191 seats against 316 for the Conservatives. Salisbury became Prime Minister for the second time. From the noble wreckage of Gladstone's third Government Rosebery emerged as one of the few ministers with an enhanced reputation, attracting tributes from all sides. 'I hear nothing but praises,' wrote Regy Brett. 'It is a charming relief to hear that the Foreign Office is worked off its legs.'[63] From the Conservative side, Lord Randolph Churchill told him: 'After your success as Foreign Minister you should never enter the Cabinet again except as Prime Minister.'[64] Queen Victoria took the same admiring line when Rosebery saw her on 7 July at Windsor. 'It has been a great pleasure to have you where you are. All has gone so well and our communications have been so pleasant. You have a great political future ahead of you,' she told him.[65] The Queen felt so relaxed with her handsome young minister that despite her age and long widowhood she could be mildly flirtatious with him. When he requested her in March to open the Colonial Exhibition with 'all conceivable pomp' she replied, 'With all the pomp you like, as long as I don't have to wear a low-cut dress.'[66]

Rosebery's own staff at the Foreign Office had been won over by his brilliance and humour. The diplomat Rennell Rodd later recalled 'the perfectly charming attitude Rosebery adopted at the Foreign Office towards his younger officers – unlike some others who had little personal contact with them.'[67] Surrounded by these devotees Rosebery often gave full rein to his wit and gift for mimicry, as Cecil Spring-Rice, one of his Foreign Office clerks, recorded in June 1886: 'Rosebery was on the best form at The Durdans, especially with Lady Dalhousie, whom he chaffed in his most amusing way . . . He also made a most beautiful sketch he would have delivered on the occasion of the Queen's Jubilee – how she was born in happy innocence, etc. etc., and wooed and wed the husband of her choice. We all screamed with laughter, especially Sanderson,* whose spectacles

---

* Sir Thomas Sanderson, Permanent Head of the Foreign Office; created Lord Sanderson in 1905.

came off in his soup.'[68] Spring-Rice also felt the force of Rosebery's sarcasm. Turning up a day late for work, after a weekend spent sailing, he found a notice left on his desk by Rosebery: 'Situation of précis-writer vacant: No yachtsman need apply.'[69]

But the most memorable accolade came from Gladstone. In a speech at Manchester on 25 June he referred to 'the youngest member of the Cabinet, of whom I will say to the Liberal Party of this country and I say it not without reflection for if I said it lightly I should be doing an injustice no less to him than to them – in whom I say to the Liberal party that they see the man of the future.' Rosebery, although moved by such words, was genuinely equivocal about his political future. As he explained to Gladstone soon after the Manchester speech, 'I feel from my heart you are mistaken through partiality and kindness. I have attained much more than the highest summit of my ambition and the further reach of my capacity . . . I doubt if a peer can ever lead the Liberal party again. He has the gain of comparative ease, against which must be set the disadvantage that he must not wrestle for the prize. I indeed count that no disadvantage for I am more than satisfied and have won a greater prize than I could have dreamed of.'[70]

Gladstone's view that Rosebery was now his likely successor was shared by others in the Liberal establishment. At the beginning of July Rosebery's secretary Thomas Gilmour lunched with Francis Schnadhorst, the powerful secretary of the National Liberal Federation. Inevitably, in the wake of Gladstone's speech, the discussion shifted to the future leadership. Schnadhorst said that Chamberlain was 'impossible' because the feeling in the Liberal party against him was 'very bitter'. John Morley, the sensitive and literary Chief Secretary for Ireland, was thought to lack 'dogged persistence'. Schnadhorst therefore concluded, 'As far as I can see, Rosebery is the man. He is tremendously handicapped by being in the Lords. But he has been marked out by Mr Gladstone, is popular, a clever speaker and an able man. He ought to be as well-known in England as he is in Scotland. In these times, to appeal to an electorate numbering millions, a man must constantly appear before the electors. We are going into opposition. Well, reputations are made in opposition.' Gilmour subsequently reported this conversation to Rosebery, who commented: 'The only thing is that if I were certain that speaking in England would make me Prime Minister, I would certainly not speak in England.'[71]

Such diffidence was not a front. According to a diary entry by Gilmour for 5 November 1885, 'I am treated as one of the few. I am a Roseberyite. I am bound to say that the Chief himself is the least eager of the band who glory in the name. "I am", he once said, "by preference a hermit" and I fully believe it.' In the same way, on an occasion when the Queen referred to his glittering prospects, Rosebery told her that 'a great political future has no attractions for me'.[72] That conflict between political duty and private pleasure, always pulling him in the opposite directions of service and solitude, never left Rosebery, even after his success as Foreign Secretary. To Herbert Bismarck he wrote in October 1886: 'When I look up at the windows of the Foreign Office in London, I execute a *pas seul* such as William Tell and his friends might have danced.'[73]

Rosebery's desire to escape politics led him to make a lengthy trip to India in the autumn of 1886, accompanied by Hannah and Ronald Munro-Ferguson, a former soldier turned Liberal who had served as one of his private secretaries at the Foreign Office. The voyage out was enlivened one night by a fancy-dress ball, of which Rosebery left this hilarious account. 'As each such lady or gentleman – each more gorgeous than the last – entered the room, a long sigh was distinctly audible. And as the agony of admiration increased, the sounds expressed rather the tumultuous emotions of the Salvation Army on the warpath than the moderate sensibility of the dyspeptic and impassive Anglo-Saxon. Soft divans invited the Northern races to forget their austerity in Persian luxury. The deck was converted into a boudoir where the delights of seclusion might be obtained. All went merrily. A dexterous female musician produced appropriate tunes with super-human vigour and vulgarity.'[74] Of greater dignity was their stop at Malta, which Rosebery told Gladstone had 'more places of worship in proportion to the population than any place on earth except Rome', making the whole place seem like 'a Church inside a castle'.[75] Once in India they travelled by train all over the sub-continent, even up to the Afghan frontier. Rosebery was moved by the sight of the Taj Mahal to describe it as 'a gate of heaven could we find the key'. In Calcutta they were followed 'by a swarm of dirty, good-humoured pedlars, from whom we made many purchases, Ferguson standing by like Judas with a great bag of silver'.[76] But the racial and religious differences meant that he never felt at ease in India, as he later told the historian Herbert Fisher. 'My feeling when I was there was the discomfort of living among hundreds of millions of people of whom no one seemed to know anything, but who, one suspected, silently knew all about us – and I cannot rid myself of that intuition.'[77] Rosebery departed having acquired little affection for the country; he was confirmed in his belief that imperial unity should only embrace the white, self-governing colonies. Eventually, like his mentor Seeley, he came to believe that the British Empire would have been much stronger without India.

In March 1887 the Roseberys returned to Britain to find the political world in turmoil. On the Liberal side, a round-table conference held to end the split caused by Home Rule had broken down because of ideological differences over Ireland and Gladstone's hatred of Chamberlain – 'the greatest blackguard I ever knew', he told Rosebery. On the Tory side, the alliance with the Liberal Unionists looked dangerously fragile, and the Government was still recovering from the extraordinary resignation in December 1886 of the Chancellor Lord Randolph Churchill, one of Rosebery's closest friends in politics. His departure, as he later admitted to Rosebery, was a disastrous error. He had not meant his letter of resignation – on the question of the army and navy estimates – to be taken seriously by Lord Salisbury, but rather that it should be seen 'as the beginning of a correspondence'.[78] Salisbury, however, had eagerly seized the opportunity it afforded him to be rid of his most troublesome minister, whose volatile temper at Cabinet he had found intolerable. The antagonism was mutual. Lord Randolph told Rosebery that Salisbury's family was 'uncouth . . . One day at Hatfield Lady Salisbury kept me in the recess of the dining room after breakfast from 10.30 till 1.45 talking nonsense on every subject and all the time I was thinking what millions I would give for a cigarette.'

Now in the wilderness, Churchill and Chamberlain dreamt of forming a centrist national party – that chimera which was to beguile so many politicians right up to the First World War. A reaction to Home Rule and the rise of socialism, this concept of a moderate, patriotic alliance usually included the figure of Rosebery, who because of his Imperialism was widely regarded as a statesman above the usual party strife. In July 1887 Churchill met Rosebery to spell out his vision of a centre party government, with Rosebery as Foreign Minister under a Hartington premiership. Rosebery was unpersuaded: 'I told him I was not especially anxious to be the Foreign Minister and that there were too many jarring principles and personalities.' In addition, Rosebery said he was delighted with the position of the Liberal party following its adoption of Home Rule: 'We were not as we had been – a flatly disconnected majority – but a compact minority united by a principle.'[79]

Rosebery's dismissal of Churchill's vision was founded not only in his own continuing adherence to Liberalism, but also in his deep ambivalence about politics generally. In 1917, having been looking back through his papers, he wrote: 'I am mainly struck by one feature of my life: the repulsion I almost always felt for political and public life. Almost always when the compulsion of office was absent, I used to swear to myself that when the next speech had been delivered I would never make another one for speech-making was odious and intolerable to me.'[80] This was penned, admittedly, when he was at his most gloomy in the First World War, but thirty years earlier he had resented almost as forcefully the way politics intruded on his time and privacy. So it was in the spring of 1887, when Ronald Munro-Ferguson was urging him to be more active on his return from India; Rosebery would have none of it. 'Do not send me invitations to speak in the month of April,' he wrote in one letter; 'you might as well send me proposals of marriage.' Turning to the accusation that he had not 'done enough', Rosebery warned: 'I propose to remain the judge of what I am to do as far as may be. If I were indeed entirely the judge, I should never be heard braying again, but should retire to the The Durdans where the wicked are at rest. As it is, no power that I know of will compel me to bound from the jungle into the arena, like a heathen tiger brought to devour the Christian martyrs.'[81] To Ferguson's assertion that Scottish Liberals 'rage after you' because they had 'made up their minds who is to be the next leader' and feared that 'the leadership was going a-begging', Rosebery replied: 'As for the leadership going a-begging, let it beg; you know that I would not entertain any ideas of that sort.'[82]

Rosebery's equivocal attitude to politics continually perplexed his followers, who thought he was betraying his talents. An example of such dismay was to be found in ranks of the Imperial Federation League, of which Rosebery had become chairman in 1886 on the death of W.E. Forster. As one of the most outspoken advocates of imperial unity, Rosebery was expected to take the organisation to new heights of influence and popularity. Instead, he left only a trail of disappointment. As well as refusing to take part in a deputation in August 1886 to Lord Salisbury to discuss a possible colonial conference on imperial defence, Rosebery failed to attend either of the Annual General Meetings in 1886 and 1887. When he discovered the possibility of Rosebery's second absence, Munro-Fergson warned him that there would be 'a great commotion among the Federation people', to which came the lofty response, 'Why do not the League postpone their annual meeting if they are in such despair?'[83] In truth, Rosebery's enthusiasm for the grand project of a united Empire had begun to wane soon after he became chairman, and he found the League rather a 'tiresome burden'.[84] Unlike the zealots of Federation who clung to the goal of a single political entity of a Greater Britain, Rosebery came to believe in a much looser, informal 'union of sympathy' under the Crown. By the middle of the 1890s he had specifically ruled out the idea of federalism. 'I for my part should not strive to bring the unity of the Empire very much nearer because it seems to me to rest on a liberal and affectionate comprehension and what surer basis of an Empire is there than that,' he told a dinner for South Australians in March 1896. This move away from his early imperial creed provoked fury from the *Fortnightly Review*. 'Here was a menace of a breach of promise. Imperial Federationists had looked to him to lead them to the consummation of their ambition and after years of striving and promise and encouragement, he presented them with the alternatives of a purely platonic union or none at all.' The magazine concluded that Rosebery's abandonment of federation was 'one of the most pitiable spectacles in public life for the last ten years. Sheer funk dominates Rosebery's conception of Empire. Either he has a craven fear of being great or, in his attempt to combine Radicalism and Imperialism, he has landed himself in hopeless mental chaos and instability.'[85]

Rosebery's behaviour also puzzled his supporters inside the Liberal party. In 1888 he deigned to attend an important party gathering in Birmingham but then, to the astonishment of activists, left early without making any speech. Ishbel Coutts, Lady Aberdeen, a leading Liberal hostess who was infatuated with Rosebery, wrote him a long letter of chastisement and pleading:

> You ran away without even an explanation, leaving people to shout for you, to wonder what in the world was the matter . . . It is not just because we want you to be our leader and Prime Minister for your own sake – of course we do that – but that is not the main reason. You are the one man who can take up the work that Mr Gladstone lays down; you are the one man that can be in touch with all classes of the people and understand their wants and we know that all you undertake will be undertaken from the highest motive with the purest aim . . . On these occasions you must take your place and show it is your rightful place – as Heir Apparent. You must not make people doubt and hesitate by making them feel a blank.

Lady Aberdeen went on to say that after the meeting, all the gossip was about Rosebery's refusal to speak and his premature exit. She told him that he had given the impression he was 'piqued' and 'thin-skinned', causing many Liberals to mutter that 'This will never do for a leader.' She further reported that 'people in England have strange notions about you' and that some doubted his sincerity, especially with regard to social reform. One party member had said to her, 'Believe me, Rosebery only works for his own ends.' She concluded: 'Of course such things must be said of all public men. But I do think that you leave yourself unwarrantably open to these doubts by being so reserved. Just now, when the question of leadership is all important, you have no right to hide your real self, that your character and powers must be seen as they are.'[86]

Rosebery's position in the late 1880s as the likely 'Heir Apparent' to Gladstone was remarkable, in view of his limited political experience. He had served in Cabinet for less than a year. He had no great legislative achievement behind him. He had never contested an election. His status as a peer meant his Parliamentary record was thin. What he did have, however, was star quality – or 'music-hall popularity', as Sir Charles Dilke called it. Part of this was based, of course, on the fascination of his enormous wealth, which would have attracted interest had he never been involved in public life. Like some great tycoon or actor, he created a buzz wherever he went, especially when surrounded by an entourage of servants and officials. The Liberal politician Sir Edward Grey once described to his wife how Rosebery nearly brought Waterloo to a halt by his arrival. 'The obsequiousness of the station officials to Rosebery was wonderful; his neat little man in black had gone ahead, bought a ticket, engaged a compartment and put the whole station on the alert . . . It seemed as if the train would hardly be able to start, so great was the occasion.'[87] Rosebery's association with horse-racing further enhanced his appeal, especially when he became successful with the Mentmore stud he acquired on his marriage. In his politics he managed to embody the two most 'popular' themes of late Victorian England, democracy and Empire, while still retaining the grandeur and glamour that went with being an aristocrat and grandee. Although never a journalist himself, he was adept at cultivating newspapermen, who appreciated his flair and mystery. And the press, like society in general, adored his witty *bons mots*. About Lord Derby, he said that 'Demosthenes put stones into his mouth to teach him to speak. Derby had the advantage of finding them there already'; to the Queen, in 1893, 'If Members of Parliament are to be paid by results, it does not appear likely there will be a heavy charge'; or in this attack in 1905 on one of Balfour's speeches, that 'it was expected to be a trumpet blast but it was only a fog horn, an instrument that betrays in its melancholy tone the confusion and perplexity of the surrounding atmosphere.' At times he was almost Wildean; this aside to Herbert Bismarck in 1894 could easily have been uttered by Lord Henry Wotton, the cynic in *The Picture of Dorian Gray*: 'All the brilliant marriages this season have been made by plain girls. This is as it should be. It is compensation enough to be pretty without anything further.'[88] Even his own son-in-law, the Marquess of Crewe, a reliable politician but a poor speaker, could be the butt of his humour. When his daughter Peggy was about to give birth, Rosebery said, 'I hope her delivery will not be as slow as Crewe's.'

But perhaps the most important source of Rosebery's popularity was his gift for oratory. As a peer, he was fortunate to live in an age when platform speaking was replacing Commons debate as the dominant means of political communication; indeed Rosebery, through his organisation of the Midlothian campaigns, had played a vital role in bringing about this change. Political meetings had become hugely popular events, generating the kind of excitement and press coverage that today is only achieved by pop concerts or football matches. In our own age of political apathy it is hard to believe that some rallies of a century ago led to such a demand for tickets that touts operated outside the venues. When Rosebery spoke at the Empire Theatre in Edinburgh in 1896, tickets were unofficially changing hands for up to £10 each.[89] In this context of a political speech as a form of public entertainment, Rosebery was a tremendous box office success. Packed with epigrams and humour, his performances rarely disappointed. Eschewing the thunderous moral earnestness of Gladstone, the cold, remorseless logic of Chamberlain and the vicious invective of Lloyd George, he relied instead on irony, romance, urbane mockery and rich imagery to cast a spell over his audience.

In 1906 the author John Buchan called Rosebery 'without doubt, the greatest living orator', adding that 'there are few better masters of the English tongue'. Buchan thought the secrets of his oratorical brilliance were his 'intellectual vitality' and his wit, 'bubbling up spontaneously'.[90] In addition to his eloquence, Rosebery had the right physical equipment to command an audience, including a strong, melodious voice and a striking presence. 'His voice is not loud, yet it fills easily the largest halls. Every note rings clear, full and musical', ran a contemporary account.[91] Though below medium height he nevertheless exuded a potency to which the gravity of his face and demeanour contributed, while his highly-strung personality added to the physical tension of his performances, as his Liberal colleague Augustine Birrell recalled. 'A certain nervousness of manner, that suggested at times the possibility of a breakdown, kept his audience in a flutter of nervousness and excitement. He was certainly the most interesting speaker I ever heard.'[92] An excellent description of Rosebery in action is to be found in the *Sunday Sun* newspaper, written in 1901 just after his famous speech at Chesterfield. 'The first thing that strikes one in connection with him is the almost overwhelming force of his personality. It is dominating, overpowering. To see him upon the platform is to be convinced more than ever that personality and individuality are the sole factors that make for success in all walks of professional life.' Then, in a well-drawn analysis of Rosebery's methods, the *Sunday Sun* continued:

Lord Rosebery steps up to the platform, places his hands upon the table or rail in front of him, and surveys the audience before he commences to speak. It is during that survey that his audience receives the impression of his superiority. It is as if he said, 'I am master here. You must listen to every word I have to say!' And they listen and accept his mastery. He is a lord and he acts in a lordly manner. He knows that it is one of the peculiarities of a crowd, no matter how democratic it may be, to delight in being mastered and he masters it! He is never emotional but can of course become heated with a theme upon occasion. He has a habit of raising his deep, well-cultured voice to almost shouting pitch, and dropping it again immediately to what is almost a stage whisper. It is immensely effective, not to say impressive. Sometimes, when he has aroused a storm of enthusiasm, he will lean an arm upon the rail to watch the effect of his words. This action, more than ever, gives one the impression that he is engineering the thought of his hearers, that he has them, in fact, in the palm of his hand.

Another of Rosebery's methods, reported the paper, was to address a passage directly to one man in the audience. 'It requires will-power to encounter the concentrated gaze of a real genius. There is something weird about it; and the writer noticed many eyes drop when they became in direct line with those of Lord Rosebery.'

Other contemporaries testified to the almost hypnotic hold that Rosebery could achieve. Thomas Robartes, a young Liberal candidate who accompanied the Earl on a campaigning trip to Cornwall in 1905, wrote to his son Neil Primrose after a meeting in Falmouth. 'He was magnificent. He absolutely mesmerized everybody in the hall. He stood there and seemed to be talking miles away from everybody and everything just as if he were thinking aloud, quite like a dream. It had a wonderful effect. I have never seen anything like it. What a bishop he would have made.'[93] Watching Rosebery at a Liberal party rally in 1892, Lady Monkswell recorded in her diary: 'His very size and squareness and massive head impress at once. Then directly he opens his mouth; his deep, rich voice, which for a good part of his speech he hardly raised, and his beautiful, clear pronunciation is delightful to listen to. He is an orator; without any effort he makes one's blood run faster.'[94] In the same vein, Sir Ian Malcolm recalled: 'I can see him now, in one or other of the great halls in Edinburgh, thrilling vast audiences with his matchless voice, as in measured tones he declared a policy or denounced a sham; his hands clasping the lapels of his coat, his wide-open, expressionless eyes gazing over the heads of his hearers; or leaning upon the balustrade of a platform and staring into the faces, almost into the hearts, of a breathless multitude.'[95]

Unlike Gladstone, who would happily speak for hours without either note or preparation, Rosebery usually went through several long-hand drafts of his speeches. He found that the best way to work out the structure was in the course of a long walk in the gardens of one of his great houses. For his literary addresses he often had a detailed manuscript with him; for his political orations, he would write down headings on quarto paper. But he never went to the extremes of Lord Randolph Churchill, who learnt his speeches by heart, or Sir William Harcourt, who relied on a verbatim text. Rosebery once claimed that 'slipshod boldness is the prevailing characteristic of my speeches'[96] and he was willing to take the risk of speaking extempore, something about which his ultra-critical friend George Smalley of the *New York Tribune* regularly complained. 'You still have never done on given occasions quite as well as you might have done, simply because of a want of absolute completeness of preparation. You trust, as you have a right to, to your gift of thinking on your legs but except in debate I consider this improvisation ought to be mainly confined to diction,' he wrote to Rosebery in 1885. Three years later Smalley remained unsatisfied. 'I perceive you are still stubborn against writing. To put down on paper and commit to memory certain passages is good and very many of the best passages of oratory have been written out.'[97] But Rosebery disliked such rigidity, preferring to allow himself the opportunity to be caught up in the excitement of the occasion. In his biography of the Earl of Chatham he explained, reflecting his own experience: 'The orator is probably unconscious or at the most half-conscious of what seems dramatic; he is moved by an irresistible blast of passion which carries him as well as his audience away. The passion may have been stirred beforehand but at the moment of outpouring it is genuine enough.'[98] His daughter Sybil thought that this was one of the essential ingredients of her father's success on the platform. 'He had the sense of the dramatic which is the natural accompaniment of imagination but it remained always obvious that he was carried away right out of himself and away from the morbid ghost at his elbow – when in the act of making a speech. That is why he carried audiences off their feet. That is also why he roused so much jealousy amongst eminent colleagues whose ability lacked that quality of enchantment.'[99]

Perhaps the most sensational example of this particular alchemy occurred in Rosebery's speech at Bradford in October 1894 on one of his favourite subjects, House of Lords reform. As he came to what seemed to be the beginning of his peroration, he suddenly picked up one of his gloves from the table in front of him and hurled it to the ground with the defi-

ant words, 'We fling down this gauntlet. It is for you to take it up.'* This
action must have been entirely impromptu, for Rosebery sat down leaving
untouched a pile of notes covering the remainder of his planned speech.
Occasionally such improvisations were forced upon him, as in the case of
a nightmarish incident on the way to deliver an address in Birmingham,
Joseph Chamberlain's heartland, in 1883. Rosebery recorded a vivid
account in his diary: 'To Birmingham by the 1.30 train. Meant to put my
speech together in train and found en voyage that I had left all my notes
materially behind. I was never in such a cold sweat. Arrived at
Chamberlain's at 5. Large dinner to be at 5.30. In despair I knocked some
notes together and recalled some of my meditations. Notes arrived from
the station 10 minutes before the meeting – too late. Spoke very
indifferently, but not an utter breakdown.'[100]

The greatest criticism levelled at Rosebery's oratory was that his gestures were too theatrical and did not always match his flowing rhetoric –
especially 'that pump handle action' as Algy West, Gladstone's secretary,[†]
described it. 'Gesture with Lord Rosebery,' thought Morley, 'though often
emphatic, was divorced from the message of the orator and was purely personal.'[101] This was particularly true when he was older, and his performances had grown increasingly histrionic. Margot Asquith, at one time in
love with Rosebery but disillusioned by the turn of the century, left this
description of an occasion at Edinburgh in 1905: 'Rosebery's speech was
most tiresome, I thought. After quite facile and rather inventive chaff, he
pulled himself together like an actor for a little righteous indignation. He
waved his little, short arms à la Gladstone, resting a very round waist across
the desk and came down with an almighty crashing fist on the words
"Chinese Labour". Some people like this sort of thing but Pamela
Tennant[‡] called it "an ebullition of paste-board wrath".'[102] Sir Ian Malcolm
also bore witness to this trait: 'although his matter was of equal quality and
his skill in debate was formidable, he seemed in later years to be straining
for effect and at times to become almost melodramatic – pitching his voice
to a loud, gloomy note, thumping the table, raising his hands above his

---

*Not 'back me up', as was reported in the press at the time.
[†]Algernon West (1832–1921) was Chairman of the Board of the Inland Revenue before
becoming head of Gladstone's secretariat. Rosebery was outraged at the posthumous publication of West's private diaries in 1922. 'It was a terrible breach of confidence for a man
in his position to keep that diary and leave it for publication; it would have been more cour-
ageous if he had done it in his lifetime.' Rosebery to Mary Drew, 4th November 1922 (Mary
Gladstone papers, Add Ms 46,237).
[‡]Margot Asquith's sister-in-law.

head and finding great difficulty in bringing them down again with intent and grace.'[103] So explosive could Rosebery's gestures be that once, speaking in London, he smashed his hand into the railing in front of him with enough violence to force the jewel from his ring.

What was particularly sad about Rosebery's oratorical talent was that he took absolutely no pleasure in it. Just the opposite: for him, speeches were a chore, one of the most tiresome aspects of a political life. His eagerness to avoid the platform in part explains his continuing reluctance to be involved too deeply in politics. In contrast to Gladstone, who derived some of his titanic energy from the response of a crowd, Rosebery, in his innate shyness, felt nothing but repulsion – one reason why he was able to maintain his composure so easily in the face of public acclamation. At a private dinner at Mentmore in 1885 he confessed that 'I never stand before an enthusiastic audience, cheering wildly, without feeling the most profound unworthiness. Physically, the effect great cheering has on me is to send a shiver down my back.'[104] The build-up to important performances made him sleepless; their aftermath left him exhausted. 'No one knows the physical distress which these long speeches to large audiences impose on me, the wakefulness before and after,' he wrote in 1902 to Wemyss Reid of the *Leeds Mercury*. [105] Again, Sybil recalled from first-hand experience that he suffered 'the agony of spirit' before an appearance. 'Then indeed was he at his gloomiest, most morbid, most irascible. He honestly dreaded and hated the prospect of speaking and life became nearly impossible for everyone in the house. And then – once the moment arrived – there occurred that transformation – the triumph that everyone believed had cost him nothing.'[106]

His antipathy to speaking extended to the smallest or most insignificant gathering. The Countess of Warwick, in one of her several autobiographies, recalled an occasion when she and her husband took Rosebery to a luncheon at an Essex agricultural show. It was naturally expected that he should speak, but he proved anxious not to. 'Lord Rosebery did all he could to support his contention that his host would be the better person to address the farmers; failing to produce any real reason, he said hesitantly, "I think you ought to do it; after all, you are an Essex man." My husband replied that the farmers would be disappointed if the speech did not come from Rosebery himself. I noticed that he ate scarcely anything and looked thoroughly miserable; I encouraged him laughingly, but I began to fear a miserable fiasco. But the moment his name was called, a change took place in the man. He rose, amid cheers, and speaking confidently, as though it was the one thing he had been most eager to do, made the best speech I have heard, before or since, at an agricultural meeting.'[107] Similarly, in 1909 Rosebery tried to wriggle out of a commitment to speak at the main banquet of the first Imperial Press Conference at Shepherd's Bush, claiming at the last moment that he had to travel to Italy on urgent business. The organisers refused to accept this, and in the end Rosebery was virtually bundled into a cab at The Durdans and driven up to London. But once on his feet he instantly warmed to his imperial theme, delivering what Lord Northcliffe called 'the best speech I have ever heard'.[108].

Rosebery was never at his finest in the House of Lords, in whose surroundings his style could seem 'painfully mannered'.[109] His expansive, theatrical platform method and the resonant voice that so electrified mass rallies were out of place in the more intimate, less volatile atmosphere of the Upper House. There was also, as Lord Kimberley put it, 'general want of sympathy between him and the Peers'[110] because of Rosebery's known hostility to the unrepresentative nature of the House, and it had been made all the worse by the Home Rule crisis; after 1886, the Liberal peers numbered only about forty. Rosebery regarded the innate Conservative bias of the Lords as both an affront to democracy and a danger to the House itself, something which could only widen class divisions in the long term. In 1888 he again moved that the Lords establish a committee to look into reform of the House, making a daring, slashing attack on the right of his fellow peers to be legislators. In the longest of all his Parliamentary efforts, lasting more than two hours, he warned that 'a House based solely, or even mainly, on the hereditary principle is a House built on sand. What you require in a hereditary chamber, by the mere fact and principle of its existence, is an unblemished succession of hereditary virtue, hereditary wisdom and hereditary distinction. When you create a hereditary peer, you are attempting far more than is possible.' He elegantly attacked the partiality of the Lords towards Conservatism: 'This House, which strains at a Liberal gnat, will swallow a Conservative camel.' And in seeking a change in its membership, he called for life peerages and for representation from the colonies and the judicial system. Once more the Lords showed no inclination to accept reform, and his motion was thrown out by 97 votes to 50. After this second failure Rosebery grew so disillusioned that he seriously considered making an attempt to overturn the legal bar on peers sitting in the House of Commons – almost eighty years before Tony Benn, 2nd Viscount Stansgate, succeeded in changing the law. In October 1890 he went so far as to see Lord Herschell, the Lord Chancellor in Gladstone's last government, to ask about standing at the next General Election in order to test the disqualification of peers from the Lower House. The result, according to Edward Hamilton, was 'rather to quash the idea. I gather that in Herschell's opinion everybody – political and legal – would be so against Rosebery. Moreover there might be no small difficulty in getting voters to support him with such a risk of their votes being declared invalid.'[111]

But by then Rosebery had found another outlet for his determination to achieve democratic legitimacy – through the unlikely vehicle of local government. In the 1880s Britain's municipalities were in as urgent need of reform as the House of Lords; it was calculated in 1883 that there were no fewer than 27,000 different local authorities in England and Wales, imposing 18 different kinds of rates on the public.[112] London was perhaps in the greatest mess of all, governed by local vestries and the Metropolitan Board of Works, a body notorious for its incompetence and irresponsibility. Since 1876 there had been several attempts to set up a proper city-wide authority; one made in 1884 by Sir William Harcourt foundered through lack of Parliamentary time and the limited nature of his measure, which Chamberlain complained would establish 'a mere jobbing committee' in charge of the capital. It fell to the Tories to implement an effective overhaul of local government by creating in 1888 a network of 62 county councils, 60 boroughs, and the new London County Council.

To strengthen the impact of the LCC, which some feared might prove to be no better than the defunct and discredited Board of Works, there was a cross-party movement to urge Rosebery to stand for election as a councillor, led by his old radical friend Canon Willam Rogers who had presided at his marriage a decade earlier. As part of this appeal, a petition containing more than 1,100 signatures was forwarded to him. Rosebery proved receptive to the call, encouraged by Gladstone, who said his candidature was 'a great patriotic undertaking'.[113] Although a Scot by ancestry he was a Londoner by birth, and had always loved the city. He was a familiar figure in the West End and had just bought a large town house at 38 Berkeley Square (so he no longer had to rent from Lord Lansdowne), and was renowned for his philanthropy in the East End; in May 1888 he donated £2,500 for the construction of new public swimming baths on the Mile End Road. Moreover, he had long been a powerful advocate of the need for a democratic authority for the capital. In October 1885 he said in a speech in Paisley, 'If you had one great municipality for London, you would have some chance of developing the public spirit of that great city. At present we have to search through a perfect haystack of municipalities in order to reach the needle of central government in London.'[114] Rosebery initially thought of standing in Whitechapel, but Canon Rogers told him he would be better off as an independent candidate for the City of London: 'You must represent the highest interests. At Whitechapel you would have to go through no end of dirt at the election. Cheesemongers, etc., would be constantly asking favours. I know these fellows well.'[115]

Those who regarded Rosebery as nothing more than an aristocratic dilettante posing as a radical were surprised at the ease with which he took to electioneering. On the municipal stump in January 1889 his deep-seated inhibitions appeared for once to fall away in the heat of the battle. 'Here at length was his chance of representing a popular constituency; and those who watched him moving about those dark streets in the wintry weeks of January can still recall how he enjoyed the struggle,' said a contemporary report.[116] He spoke effectively at Farringdon, Houndsditch, and Bishops-gate, where he told electors, 'I owe some very important things to Mr Rogers; he married me and I hope that, without any dissolution of the former union, he will marry me again to the City of London.' Rosebery's hopes were easily fulfilled. He was returned for the City by a landslide, alongside Sir John Lubbock, soon to be his closest ally on the LCC and whose daughter Amy was married to Rosebery's ill-starred American business associate Ferdinand Van Zandt.

Rosebery, weighed down by so many other political and personal commitments, had intended to be nothing more than a backbencher on the LCC. But it soon became obvious that this would be impossible. The Council, though it had a large 'Progressive' or left-wing majority, wanted a prestigious figure as its first chairman, and Rosebery was the obvious candidate. His friend Regy Brett told him that he had no alternative: 'If you refuse to accept the Chairmanship of the LCC and if the council accept anyone else, they will stultify themselves and damn the whole thing. Having assumed the lesser responsibility by becoming a member of the council, you cannot properly or rightly shirk the latter.'[117] Rosebery agreed with this view; only a rump of hard-left extremists objected, and on 12 February 1889 he was elected the first chairman of the London County Council by 104 votes to 17. He showed a nice touch of self-deprecation in his response to this decision: 'Of course my thanks are due to the majority but my sympathies are entirely with the minority.'[118] One of the many who congratulated him on his new role was John Morley. 'Well done, my dear Rosebery. I am truly delighted. It may prove to be an event of the utmost importance: a) to London; b) to yourself; c) to the Liberal party. Since Dick Whittington turned again, it is the happiest thing to have befallen London.'[119] Interestingly, three women had been elected at the polls, but they were not allowed to take their seats; not until 1907 was gender discrimination in local government legally removed. Rosebery himself was never sympathetic to the cause of women's political rights. Over dinner in 1889 he and Morley 'admitted that logic and argument were against them but female suffrage would at least make this country look ridiculous'.[120] One of the less orthodox arguments Rosebery advanced against women's suffrage was that it would create 'a very bad impression in India', because Hindus and Muslims found the concept of female rule so repulsive.

His first meeting as chairman was a difficult one. Rosebery's aim was to keep party politics out of municipal business as far as possible, and he told members, 'My view is that you ought to put the County Council first and politics second because, after all, we are and must be mainly an administrative body.'[121] But the Progressives, led by the burly figure of J.F.B. Firth, the council's deputy chairman, thought otherwise, and through the power of their caucus ensured that all but one of the LCC's nineteen aldermen – those councillors with the most authority – were from this party. Though the Progressives did not constitute a united group with a clear programme, most were Radical Liberals who believed that the LCC should help tackle the poverty and squalor of the capital. The urgency of their demand for social reform was captured in the radical London paper *The Star* of August 1889: 'Think of London's poor, of the over-worked bus and tram driver, of the dweller in the Whitechapel municipal slums, of the sweated tailoress in her den, of the unskilled labourer watching for his turn at the docks, of the rent-crushed toiler for daily bread, which he can scarce snatch out of the landlord's maw, of the multitudinous oppressions of this great wealth-ridden city.'[122] To this end they sought municipal intervention in housing, public sanitation, the utilities and transport, as well as pressing for the LCC to act as a model employer in the matter of wages and working conditions. Their agenda, incoherent as it was, marked the first attempt to bring any sort of political ideology into London local government. In this respect they were pioneers for such later socialist administrations at County Hall as Herbert Morrison's partisan rule in the 1930s, when he promised to 'build the Tories out of London', or Ken Livingstone's dogmatic and chaotic leadership of the GLC (as the LCC had become) in the 1980s.

Rosebery was not unsympathetic to the Radicals' plans; in fact, the concept of municipal activism was to form an important part of his call for 'national efficiency' in the following decade. But he felt that the LCC should first prove its competence before taking on sweeping new powers. 'Do not break the back of the Council. The back of the Council has quite enough to bear already,' he warned the more impatient Progressives.[123] It is a tribute to Rosebery's authority and personal charm that he was able to act as a restraining influence without provoking bitter divisions in the Council chamber. The democratic tone of his management was immediately set when he supported a Progressive demand that no personal titles be used in the chamber. As the unadorned 'Mr Chairman' he presided with a masterly touch, ensuring the efficient conduct of business while upholding the freedom of members to speak. Rosebery's reluctance to make heavy-handed interventions from the Chair was demonstrated at his first meeting, when a Progressive councillor, F.N. Charrington, made an emotional plea for temperance reform, illustrating his argument by reference to the gruesome case of a drunken young man who had literally kicked his mother to death: so savage were his blows that both her eyes were driven from their sockets. As Charrington went into the shocking details of the case, another councillor, Mr Carr-Gomm, cried out, 'Lord Rosebery – I mean – Mr Chairman, please, will you stop him.' Rosebery replied magisterially: 'I am sorry, Mr Carr-Gomm, that you should be upset by Mr Carrington. He has a perfect right to use any illustrations he chooses in making a speech and I must ask you to sit down.'[124] Rosebery could still be prickly, however. After a minor argument with a councillor over a point of procedure, he warned, 'I must remind the honourable member that it is not in order to patronise the Chair.'[125] And he could never completely hide his sarcasm: 'I knew he was reading the epitaph of his own motion,' he said of another member's speech.[126]

In accepting this chairmanship Rosebery had taken on a phenomenal work-load, for he had to preside over the establishment of more than twenty committees as well as most of the senior appointments. The LCC took up almost all his time, obliterating much of his social life. 'County Council meeting lasted until nearly nine. Rosebery and I were both to have dined with the Coupers but of course we could not go,' reads a typical diary entry made by his fellow councillor Sir John Lubbock.[127] Spring Gardens, former headquarters of the Metropolitan Board of Works and the cramped, ramshackle base for the Council before the opening of County Hall in 1928, became almost another home. On one occasion Rosebery had to be in Edinburgh to fulfil a long-standing speaking engagement. Travelling up from London on Tuesday, he spoke in the evening, then returned by the night train and was back in committee on Wednesday morning. To Herbert Bismarck he wrote: 'London leaves me hardly a moment, except a Sunday at The Durdans. I have become a sort of beadle and never write a line except on drainage and street crossings.'[128] In another letter he expressed his regret to Bismarck for being on poor form during the latter's visit to London in April 1889: 'The fact is that a post horse worked in an omnibus like myself is a different creature to the imperious animal with his neck clothed in thunder, as Job says, that prances in high political chariots. I hope you will make allowances for this jaded animal, jaded not so much by labour as by the kind of labour.'[129] It is estimated that in his first sixteen months as Chairman he presided over 44 full meetings of the Council and 280 regular meetings of committees. By the autumn of 1889 Hannah was growing anxious about her husband's hectic schedule. 'From a personal and selfish point of view,' she wrote to Edward Hamilton, 'I hope that pressure will be brought to bear to enforce Archie into taking a less prominent part in the daily work of the LCC. I do not see how mind and body can stand the present work coupled with two public speeches in November.'[130] Her pleadings went unheeded. In November 1889 he was unanimously re-elected Chairman 'amidst a prolonged volley of cheers'.[131]

'In a brief space of time,' wrote William Saunders in a contemporary account of the LCC's first years, 'Lord Rosebery made himself acquainted with the offices from attic to cellar; he soon knew every officer and every councillor, ruling all with an iron hand in a velvet glove.' Rosebery's almost Stakhanovite enthusiasm for LCC business might seem inexplicable in a man so manifestly bored during his spells at the Home Office and the Board of Works. But at the LCC he felt he was in charge of a great experiment which might prove more far-reaching than the creation of a Dublin Parliament. 'He is greatly immersed in his LCC work, which interests him enormously,' wrote Edward Hamilton in his diary for April 1890, after dining with Rosebery. 'He thinks the importance of it cannot be overrated. The LCC is no doubt the most democratic body ever assembled in this country and he believes it will remain so.'[132] The significance Rosebery attached to the LCC is reflected in this story recounted by Lord Monkswell, another peer-councillor. 'Once I had to leave a debate early because of work in the House of Lords. Rosebery reacted with surprise and indignation when I told him. "What on earth can you possibly have to do in the Lords that is one tenth as important as your work on the LCC?"'[133] Moreover, he revelled in the novel experience of being a genuine participant in democracy. For the first time he could say that he owed his position to his own talent rather than an accident of birth, as he explained in 1895 when describing the wrench of having to retire from the LCC because of his other political duties: 'I had hoped to continue a councillor as long as I remained in public life. It was a pride to me to be a popularly elected member of a representative assembly and so have a relation to my fellow countrymen which circumstances otherwise denied me.'[134] One of the other great advantages of the LCC for Rosebery was that there he was the undoubted master of his own house. By far the biggest personality on the Council, he had to deal with no demands from a powerful leader like Gladstone, no challenges from a rival like Harcourt. Unlike the House of Lords, where the monumental figure of Salisbury faced him from the benches opposite, he reigned supreme in the Council Chamber. Uniquely in his career, he was in control of his own destiny. In his later years Rosebery often complained that he had never enjoyed real power. That might have been true in the case of the national government, but it was certainly not true of the LCC, where as Chairman his writ ran large.

Rosebery might urge the Progressives to be more realistic in their ambitions, but he was certainly no closet Tory, the charge so often made against him. Indeed the dockers' trade union leader Ben Tillett, who served on the LCC in the 1890s, wrote in his memoirs in 1931 that 'Lord Rosebery was one of our great men, despite being an aristocrat . . . He entered deeply into the life of the poor. He certainly studied poverty and he came into contact with the worst and most offensive side of slumdom: the fetid atmosphere, the tuberculosis-laden air of wretched hovels into which the poor were crushed as in a lethal chamber.' Under his chairmanship the LCC began a programme to expand the number of parks in London, providing them with facilities for sport, bathing and boating. The chronic deficiencies of the fire service were addressed by the recruitment of 113 more men and the building of three new stations. New public housing was erected at Deptford, and the Strand was widened. The operation of London's sewers was improved to such an extent that in April 1890 Rosebery was able to boast, with a whiff of municipal pride, that 70,000 tons of slurry were being removed every month. He also showed his sympathy for London's bus drivers by attending a midnight meeting organised to discuss their pay, and won them over by stating that it was 'proof of the hardness of the busmen's lot that we can only meet to consider your grievances at this unholy hour.' And in a decisive move, Rosebery used his influence as Chairman in favour of building the Blackwall tunnel, still today one of the capital's main thoroughfares.

It was one of the last decisions he made. In July 1890 he announced that he would not be seeking a third term once his period of office expired in November. Most of the other members were despondent at this news and sent him a petition begging him to reconsider because, they said, the Council still needed his 'wise and skilful guidance'. But Rosebery told Sir John Lubbock, who eventually succeeded him, 'I am clear that no appearance or example of permanence should be afforded as to the presidency of so essentially popular and municipal a body . . . I do not leave the Chair at a moment of weakness or danger. Were it otherwise, at any cost, I would stay where I am. On the contrary, the Council has passed through its teething and rickets, through the ailments and doubts of childhood. It is strong, it is braced for its work, its path should be upward and onward. I stand aside and wish it God speed.'

He had not entirely abandoned his devotion to the LCC. He stood again in the elections of 1892, this time giving up his political independence and his seat in the City by campaigning as a fully fledged Progressive in the working-class constituency of East Finsbury. His Radical platform included municipal control of the police and water, the removal of central controls on spending, and the takeover of the City of London Corporation by the LCC. Much of the Liberal establishment was disturbed by his flirtation with the left; the Liberal peer Lord Sandhurst wished 'Lord Rosebery would lead a real, good, London Liberal Party. He would then command great confidence and I think would have a much more moderating influence than if he started with a hole in the corner party. He is too big a man for the LCC.'[135] Sandhurst need not have worried. Although Rosebery had another brief spell as Chairman in 1892, the mounting success of his political career in the Liberal government meant he was not able to devote the same time to LCC business as in the past.

But the legacy of his early work remained. Ben Tillett argued that Rosebery 'brought to the chairmanship of the London County Council an almost regal demeanour. He raised the Council, as he did the Chair, to a position of great authority. His was pioneer work in the great revolutionary effort in municipal life, and it stands as a model today. He really made London government a living thing.'* The philosopher and London councillor Frederic Harrison, often a stern critic of Rosebery, proclaimed in 1890 that 'the Chairman's example of the model organisation of a difficult task will not be forgotten by the people'.[136] Another unlikely source of praise was the Irish nationalist Justin McCarthy, who wrote that 'Lord Rosebery undoubtedly has done more than any other Englishman to raise the municipal government of London to that position which it ought to have in the life of the state.'[137] Yet perhaps Rosebery's very success as Chairman highlighted his potential weakness as a national politician, for his influence as a unifying force in the council chamber betokened

---

*This and the quotation on page 177 are taken from Ben Tillett's *Memories and Reflections* (1931).

qualities the opposite of those required in a Prime Minister. In this context the words of Sir Henry Harber, a Conservative LCC Councillor during Rosebery's time, served as a worrying portent for the future of the Liberal party: 'I have watched Lord Rosebery closely and I am convinced he can never be a political leader. Political leaders are always men who see their side of the question much more strongly than the other. Lord Rosebery has a rare capacity for seeing both sides of the question. It makes him a first-rate chairman but it is bound to paralyse him as a leader.'[138]

7

'Our happy home is a wreck'

◆━◆

ROSEBERY'S COMMITMENT TO the London County Council did nothing to alter his frequently stated aversion to politics. In 1887, little more than a year before he agreed to stand for the Council, he told Cooper of the *Scotsman* that it would be 'glad tidings of great joy if I knew that I should never have to fill a post or make a speech again. I am too happy among children, books and houses to make public life anything but a sacrifice for me. Indeed, if it were not for a feeling of what I am pleased to believe are duty and patriotism, I should be taking measures now to realize my dream.'[1] At the same time, writing to inform Munro-Ferguson of the purchase of 38 Berkeley Square, he said, 'I left the matter absolutely to Hannah's decision for, as I hate London, it cannot matter much where I live in it'[2] – a bizarre remark from someone who was soon to give most of his waking hours to the running of the capital.

This changeability was at the heart of Rosebery's character. Aldous Huxley said that 'the only completely consistent people are the dead', but even so, Rosebery elevated inconsistency to an art form. In every aspect of his life he could be contradictory and unpredictable. 'Very able, shy, sensitive, ambitious, the last two qualities rather at war with one another' was the verdict of Benjamin Jowett, the Master of Balliol.[3] Some of this was a consequence of his pronounced moodiness, which meant that his attitude to people and events could alter violently and suddenly. As John Buchan wrote, 'He could be caustic and destructive, a master in the art of denigration; he could be punctiliously judicial; in certain matters he refused to be other than freakish, making brilliant fun out of bogus solemnities; he had also deep and sober loves.'[4] His chronic insomnia and his restlessness contributed to his instability; John Morley joked that Rosebery's 'favourite pastime is catching the next train',[5] while his daughter Sybil wrote that 'he seldom appears to have spent more than a few hours in any place during the week'.[6] Another factor was his acute shyness, which caused his manner to alternate between the intimidating and the charming. Lord Spencer, who called him 'The Great Sphinx', wrote of him: 'I do not attribute the coldness, the want of cordiality or even the apparent rudeness to malice but to the extraordinary self-consciousness, shyness and awkwardness which possess him.'[7] After a day spent at Barnbougle Margot Asquith, who often mused on his 'contradictoriness of character', wrote a perceptive description of the contrasting layers of his personality. 'I have never seen him in such sunny spirits. His brain goes quicker into phrases of old-fashioned, rather elaborate, drollery than almost any other humorous talker I have ever known. He rather paralyses and at no time fortifies other jokers but this Sunday he laughed easily at his own jests and we were all happy. I delight in Rosebery when he is alone with Henry [her husband H.H. Asquith] and perhaps one other. He seems to thaw and lose the life-size imitation of a great man – that icy abruptness and almost forced, though I believe perfectly sincere, social stare by which he often greets the remarks of a less timid guest.'[8] It was Lord Randolph Churchill who said of Rosebery's cold look, 'Don't think you're going to terrify *me* with that poached-egg eye of yours.' Beatrice Webb, herself a woman of raging internal conflict between Puritanism and passion, wrote this about Rosebery in March 1900 after meeting him at a dinner hosted by Richard Haldane: 'He is a strange being, self-conscious and sensitive to a more extreme degree than any mortal I have ever come across. Notwithstanding this absurd self-consciousness, he has a peculiar personal charm, the secret I imagine of his hold on a section of the Liberal party and of the public. He might be a great statesman, a Royal Prince, a beautiful woman and an artistic star all rolled into one.'[9] Rosebery's propensity for striking poses, combined with his responsiveness to his environment, also made him appear a different man in different settings, as Sir Ian Malcolm noted.

> One could almost feel the various features of Lord Rosebery's character were reproduced in the houses he inhabited and in their surroundings: at Mentmore the English squire and his broad acres of agricultural land; at Dalmeny and Barnbougle the library man among his books, breathing the air of Scottish romance which permeated him through and through; on the moors the true sportsman and lover of nature, keener about the quality than the quantity of game that he kills; in Berkeley Square we find the man of public affairs, the Prime Minister at the centre of the political and social life of the Empire; at The Durdans, the patron of the Turf, breeding, training and racing his horses in the grand manner of the eighteenth century and entertaining friends of every nationality at lavish board.[10]

None of Rosebery's private pursuits were free of contradictions. He was one of the most prolific collectors of his age, yet he had little real understanding of painting or music. Possessed of the temperament of an artist, he struggled to appreciate the visual arts and had the most conventional, philistine views. Visiting the Paris Salon in 1875, he described the work of the Impressionists as 'a hideous collection of wretched daubs'.[11] At the opera, he was likely to lapse into yawning indifference. He once admitted privately, 'A person like myself who knows nothing of music and drawing experiences a deprivation of expression.'[12] His purchases of fine art and furniture were usually driven not by joy at their aesthetic beauty but rather by pleasure in their historical associations. Margot Asquith, in a diary entry for 1905 recording a conversation with Balfour, claimed that she 'never saw a man with less taste or feeling for art, colour or arrangement than Lord Rosebery', though she 'admired' his interest. In response, Balfour said he 'had no sympathy for collectors of the kind that Rosebery was. He hated people who collected the hair or toothbrushes of great men.'[13]

The same paradox could be seen in Rosebery the man of the turf. With the Duke of Westminster and the Duke of Portland he was one of the three dominant figures of British horse-racing during his lifetime, winning no fewer than 11 classics, including, in a golden spell between 1894 and 1895, the Two Thousand Guineas, the Derby and the St Leger. The Durdans, purchased because of its proximity to Epsom race-course, was filled with paraphernalia from the racing world: magnificent oils by Britain's finest painter of horses, George Stubbs, rare prints, and an excellent book collection. In a speech at York in 1897 he admitted that one of the drawbacks of the turf was that 'the pursuit is too engrossing for anyone who had anything else to do in this life'.[14] He once told a Downing Street official, only half in jest, that he thought 'politics and racing are inconsistent – which seems a good reason for giving up politics'.[15] Yet Rosebery had no real understanding of horses, disliked hunting, and was a poor rider. His success as an owner owed everything to his wealth and nothing to his judgement. The racing historian George Plumptre went so far as to describe him as 'a lamentable horseman', a fact that made him 'one of the most enigmatic figures on the Turf'.[16] He often seemed bored with the whole process of breeding horses, and took only a distant interest in the management of his studs. His letter of complaint to one of his Newmarket trainers, Percy Peck, in September 1913 is revealing: 'I am kept in total darkness about my horses and am told nothing about them. I never go to see them as they are not worth the journey and therefore it is all the more important that I should be kept fully informed with regard to them.'[17] A true lover of horses would surely be only too keen to visit his Newmarket stables, rather than rely on correspondence. For all his success and the strength of many of his friendships in racing – such as those with Lord Houghton and Lord Durham – the sincerity of his attachment to the sport was often questioned. Typical was this barbed comment by St Loe Strachey in *The Nineteenth Century* a few months after Rosebery won his first Derby in 1894: 'The Newmarket Lord Rosebery is an artificial creation. Lord Rosebery, it is whispered by those who know both him and the Turf, has none of the genuine love for racing that distinguished the great Earl of Derby. He wanted to win the Derby and did win it, but only as a man wants to possess and does ultimately acquire a first folio Shakespeare. Lord Rosebery, in a word, wanted to create a racing and horsey atmosphere round himself and so to obtain that mixture of the sportsman and the politician which has always been so warmly appreciated by the English people.'[18]

Rosebery never played golf and was bored by cricket, despite the fact that his son was a distinguished Captain of Surrey. Rare in an aristocrat but typical of him was his fondness for soccer; he played regularly with his servants in the yard at The Durdans and usually attended the FA Cup Final at Crystal Palace, the top football venue before the building of Wembley in 1923, as well as Scottish and English internationals. 'Went with the boys to the FA Cup final. A wonderful sight. 66,000 people banked around, their faces moving like waves, the trees full of people like huge rooks, the whole scene something between a bullfight and the Derby,' he wrote in his diary for 10 April 1897. He also served as Honorary President of both the Scottish Football Association and Heart of Midlothian FC. At a match at Celtic Park in Glasgow, Rosebery was seen to 'wave his hat at every Scottish success, with all the abandon of an Aberdeen tripper in the shilling enclosure.' In a tribute to his patronage, until 1951 the Scottish national team often turned out in his racing colours of primrose and pink hoops. He enjoyed sailing, largely because of the sense of freedom it gave him. 'There is nothing like yachting,' he told Herbert Bismarck while sailing in the Mediterranean in 1904; 'the health of it: no hotels, no trains to watch. You travel like a tempestuous snail with your home on your back.'[19] But by far his favourite sport after horse-racing was shooting, and here he was an expert practitioner – though he did once manage accidentally to shoot Sir Charles Tennant in the testicles. His slaughter was sometimes on a near industrial scale, as his diary for 4 January 1888 suggests: 'Sandringham. Shot with the Prince of Wales. A bag of 1,916, including 1,252 rabbits. We shot 1,075 rabbits in an hour.' It was not until he was in his mid fifties that he began to lose some of his enthusiasm for the sport, largely because of deteriorating eyesight. As he explained to his friend Ronald Munro-Ferguson in November 1903 when declining a shooting invitation, 'Since I took to wearing glasses, my shooting has gone off so much that I am determined to confine my performance to the confidential recesses of my own woods and the partial judgement of my own keeper.' Yet here again, even in this mass culling of game the usual Roseberian paradox lurked, for he had a sentimental affection for birds. One of the sounds he loved best was the song of the nightingale. As his daughter Sybil recalled, he once brought a nightingale from Spain, 'to the bird's extreme annoyance, for not only is a captive nightingale an anachronism, but it proved to have a fiendish temper.'[20] Undeterred, in the final decade of his life he acquired from Edward Grey a number of rare mandarin ducks.

Rosebery could veer between ascetic restraint and eager self-indulgence. He was sometimes gripped by an urge for physical fitness, when he would import an expensive exercise machine from Germany, or take long walks lasting three hours or more through Edinburgh or London. Inheriting some of his father's faddist views on health, he once lived for a whole week on nothing but a jug of water a day. But he was also famous for the abundance of his table; 'I retain vivid recollections of tête-à-tête dinners, consisting of grilled herrings, roast grouse and wonderful claret,' wrote Sir Ian Malcolm. In fact nothing was allowed to interfere with Rosebery's love of grouse, not even his ministerial duties. In his diary he records an embarrassing occurrence just after his appointment as Under-Secretary at the Home Office: '*12 August 1881*: Land Bill in the Lords. Ordered a grouse punctually at eight at Brooks's. Went to eat it, returned in about half-an-hour and found I had missed two divisions. A nice beginning for a subordinate of the Government.' This epicurean tendency meant that in his middle years Rosebery was inclined to portliness, as highlighted when Gladstone had to borrow a formal suit from him after his luggage was mislaid on a trip to Dalmeny. In a collar three sizes too large, the Grand Old Man looked a clownishly uncomfortable figure at dinner.

Rosebery was not physically a vain man, despite his clean-shaven good looks; the distinguished journalist Sir John Robinson said the Earl reminded him of Lord Byron, 'with his round full neck and smooth face'. He intensely disliked being photographed or having his portrait painted; the latter feeling was confirmed by his experience with the renowned artist G.F. Watts. As Rosebery noted in 1915, 'the sittings spread over some years and I dreaded them unspeakably. He was deaf and went droning on. When I made some reply, he would leave the easel and ask me to repeat my worthless remark. I mentally resolved that I would never sit for my picture again and I never have.'[21] During his lifetime he refused to hang the famous portrait of himself by Millais, preferring to keep it in a lumber room at

Mentmore. 'I do not think one's own effigy is an agreeable piece of furniture, even if one is at one's best,' he told Mary [Gladstone] Drew.[22] Nor did he have any of the sartorial quirks which so often mark out the egocentric. Except on ceremonial occasions when he wore a frock coat, he generally dressed in a conventional short black jacket or morning suit of dark serge. His ties were invariably black, though he had a partiality for brown boots. His own minor contribution to fashion was the 'Rosebery collar'; this had rounded points rather than the usual sharply angled ones, and was devised by him to stop the silk facings of his coats being torn. Despite its practicality, it never caught on.

His shyness was accompanied by a genuine streak of modesty, and he lacked the snobbery of some of his class – one reason why he was such a success as Chairman of the LCC. Another radical London cleric, the Reverend Henry Solly, quoted in his memoirs a story about a political meeting in the Strand at which a republican saddler was denigrating Rosebery. The saddler persistently referred to him as 'Mr Rosebery', prompting Mr Solly to make profuse apologies. 'Oh, if these men only knew how little we care for our titles they wouldn't make such a fuss about them,' said Rosebery.[23] His social sensitivity could be both graceful and endearing. During a crowded reception at 38 Berkeley Square a gauche Scottish farmer invited by Rosebery proceeded to devour all before him until he came to the ice cream, something he had never previously tasted. After one anguished mouthful he went up to Rosebery and said, 'I don't suppose you know, my Lord, but there's been a mistake somewhere. The pudding's froze.' Rosebery took a spoonful himself, then replied, 'So it is. That's strange. I'll find out what the problem is.' He disappeared into the kitchens, then returned to the farmer: 'It's all right. Apparently this is a new kind of Italian pudding. They freeze it on purpose.'[24]

As always with Rosebery, however, the picture was complex. For all his lack of physical vanity, he could be touchy if he felt his dignity was being offered an affront. At a dinner hosted by Alfred Rothschild,* for instance, he had an explosive falling out with Sir Henry Drummond-Woolf, whom he felt was 'wanting in deference'. When Drummond-Woolf tried to apologise by explaining that an apparently offensive remark had been meant only as a joke, Rosebery icily responded: 'I cannot admit what you said was a joke or in any way resembling one . . . If you consider your behaviour to a former chief in the presence of a large company as a joke there is no more to be said about the matter.'[25] On two occasions Lord Hartington

---

*Hannah's cousin.

offended him. On a visit to Chatsworth, Rosebery's name was accidently omitted from the list for a shooting party; he left the house in a monumental huff. Then in 1887 Hartington dared to support a Unionist candidate in the Glasgow Rectorial election. 'That was not the act of a friend. And as a friend I ceased to regard you,' wrote Rosebery some time later, explaining why he had not spoken to Hartington for three years.[26] He could be blighting to anyone who failed to accord his witticisms due reverence. One evening, at a party given by Lord Tweedmouth, Rosebery delivered – apparently off-the-cuff – a wonderful classical epigram, at which a youth of seventeen piped up from the other end of the table, 'Did I not see you studying Marcus Aurelius in the library just before dinner?' Rosebery looked down at him with his coldest of fish-like stares and said, 'All my life I have loved a womanly woman, admired a manly man, but I never could stand a boily boy.'[27] And for all his dismissiveness of the importance of titles and honours, he seemed curiously keen to possess them. In 1885 he was bitter because Gladstone did not offer him one of three vacant Garters – not, he claimed, because he wanted it for himself, but because it would have enhanced Hannah's social standing. In a dairy note of a dinner conversation four years later, in April 1889, Edward Hamilton recorded Rosebery's bitterness: 'He did not care for decorations himself but at that time the Garter would have been a great service to him. It would have made all the difference to Lady Rosebery's position abroad. At a place like Vienna, for instance, the possession of the Garter by the husband would have alone ensured a proper reception for his Jewish wife. His acceptance of the dignity would have been one of the few means by which he could make some repayment to Lady Rosebery.'[28] Rosebery was even said to have vowed, in a fit of temper, never to serve under Gladstone again. 'What a mind a man must have to care so much for a Ribbon and Star,' wrote Loulou Harcourt in 1885.[29] In his talk with Hamilton in 1889 Rosebery further asserted that 'nothing would induce' him now to accept the Garter. Yet three years later he did so. And in June 1911, when he was granted the additional title of Earl of Midlothian by George V, he confessed boyishly: 'The fact is that I love the name (though I think I shall continue to bear my present one) and greatly wished to possess it. I am very pleased.'[30]

This complexity was reflected in his attitude to his servants, of whom he employed a considerable retinue to look after his family, his guests and his many homes. When in the right mood, he could be appreciative and understanding. There is a touching entry in his diary for Christmas Day at The Durdans in 1880: 'Bitterly cold because my fire would not burn and I did not like to disturb the Christmas festivities downstairs by employing the bell.' Similarly, towards the end of his life, in December 1925, he sent this heart-breaking letter to his staff: 'I wish to thank my household, both inside and outside, for all their kindness and attention to me in my long and tedious illness. Their attentions have been almost tender in their nature and I am truly grateful to them, for nothing can be so wearisome as long waiting on a solitary and sick man.'[31] But in darker moments he could be a domestic tyrant, as Regy Brett noted during the crisis of his premiership: 'Rosebery got very irritable and angry with the servants and said to me, "I am unfit for human society."'[32] Again, some of that spirit comes through his diary notes. On a trip to the Continent with Hannah in June 1880, Rosebery was shocked by the ignorance of one of the hired maids: 'Hannah was called Mrs by the maid at Calais which suggests unsuspected improprieties in her demeanour.' One night in July 1885 he went back to The Durdans and found, to his horror, 'my footman smoking a cigar bare-headed outside my door'. And he was quick to criticise his staff for their errors. Once, having missed an appointment at Berkeley Square with the journalist W.T. Stead, he wrote to him: 'I cannot for the life of me under-stand how the mistake arose except that I have a footman of phenomenal perversity of intellect.'[33] Another time, in 1918, he told Margot Asquith: 'I cannot use the telephone and the servant who does perpetrates the most astounding gaffes.'[34] He could be equally difficult with his secretaries, from whom he demanded total personal loyalty. The very idea of them marry-ing while they were in his employ was almost out of the question. When Harry Graham, a dashing former Guards officer, told Rosebery in 1905 that he was engaged to Ethel Barrymore,★ the internationally acclaimed American actress, he was immediately told to find alternative work. When he left, Harry Graham pointedly expressed to Rosebery the hope that he would 'find a satisfactory successor to me before long, one who will suc-cessfully avoid the shoals of matrimony.'[35] He also told Arthur Guise, who took over from him, that Rosebery was 'awfully difficult to please'. Even George Murray, most calm and efficient of civil servants, who was Rosebery's Downing Street secretary during his premiership, experienced the characteristic wrath, according to an account left by Loulou Harcourt in February 1895. 'Rosebery was in a towering rage on Friday at missing his train to Osborne by going to Victoria instead of Waterloo. Whilst wait-ing for the next, he returned to Downing Street, came into Murray's room in a passion and swore at him.'[36]

★ He never managed to get Ethel Barrymore to the altar. She married Russell Griswold Colt in 1909.

At the Foreign Office, there was the same contrast in views. When Rosebery had to give up the Foreign Secretaryship, the diplomat Charles Villiers wrote to Hamilton, 'The loss of such a chief is a great blow to the Office on private as well as public grounds, for Lord Rosebery has shown such a personal interest in us which has in an exceptional degree gained our affection. For myself I cannot but feel deeply the severance of a connection which has been so interesting and so pleasant.'[37] But a far less favourable opinion has been left by another diplomat, Esme Howard. He was working late one night at the Foreign Office when Rosebery, at the time Prime Minister, burst in, demanding to see the Foreign Secretary, Lord Kimberley. On being told that Kimberley was out, Rosebery said he would wait. 'He began pacing up and down the room with his hands behind his back, looking like Napoleon on board the *Bellerophon* on his way to St Helena. He was not lacking in a certain histrionic power on these occasions and I could not help wondering if he did not feel that he was on his way to his own St Helena and was playing up to the situation . . . He told me I might sit down and go on with my work, which I tried to do but I found myself too fascinated by that pacing figure to think of anything else. He never spoke and the silence could have been cut with a knife. I prayed almost audibly for Lord Kimberley's return.' In another picturesque but even crueller description, Howard compared Rosebery to a 'highly-polished eighteenth-century snuff-box of onyx and lapis lazuli, set with cunningly wrought gold and diamonds, filled with perfumed snuff, which would be opened on special occasions . . . He had certainly the highly-polished light-reflecting surface which the eighteenth century loved but which Sir Edwin Lutyens rightly warns us against as a form of decoration, "Vanity of vanities, all is vanity."'[38]

Part of this polished grandeur derived from his aristocratic temperament, but it was naturally magnified by his stupendous wealth. It has been estimated that his total gross income from his estates and from a trust fund of £700,000 set up on his marriage to Hannah was approximately £140,000 a year. In addition to Mentmore, Berkeley Square, The Durdans and Dalmeny he also owned a large shooting lodge near Carrington in Midlothian and a substantial Georgian house in Postwick, Norfolk, while in 1897 he bought a fabulous villa overlooking the Bay of Naples. His money enabled him to live and travel in the grandest style. When he did not use a special train for his own convenience, rail companies were persuaded to stop their expresses at his own stations of Dalmeny, or Cheddington for Mentmore. A glimpse of the scale of operations when Rosebery was on the move is provided by a letter to his sister Constance

Leconfield regarding a proposed visit from Mentmore to Sussex just after Christmas, 1891: 'I go by 9.36 train to Willesden, then by special engine to Victoria, where I catch a train to Petworth which should arrive at 1.45. Our party is: I and my valet, four children, two maids, and a footman.' Rosebery also wanted to bring his secretary, but said deprecatingly to Constance, 'I hardly like to propose a tenth guest. I cannot come down like a plague of locusts.'[39]

Although he sometimes railed hypocritically against the luxury and excess of the late Victorian age, there was at least no meanness about Rosebery. As a rich and well-known figure, he was constantly assailed by letters from the improvident and the impudent. W.T. Stead's mistress Valentina Glover, the journalist T.H.S. Escott and the once-successful novelist Marie Louise de la Ramée – Ouida – were among the army of those who openly begged him for money. Other public figures did not hesitate to seek financial support for their causes. Mary Drew was a wearisome offender in this regard, especially in her requests for help in expanding her late father's memorial library of St Deiniol's at Hawarden. As Rosebery explained to his sister, 'At one time Mary Drew's handwriting gave one the pip. One knew it was a request for something. I am sure it was all for a good motive but I told her I would rather the money went to buy books for herself than for St Deiniol's, in which I have no interest.'[40] Little wonder that Rosebery felt the burden of being seen as a sort of national lottery fund. When in a speech in 1886 his old Eton friend Lord Randolph Churchill sneered about Rosebery's 'enormous wealth', he was rebuked with this semi-serious fusillade from the Foreign Secretary:

> Never in the annals of civilised warfare has so inhuman an outrage been perpetrated as you committed last night . . . in consequence of what you said, thousands of mendicant pens are now being sharpened. The parson's widow, the bedridden Scot born at Dalmeny, the author who has long watched my career, the industrious grocer who has been ruined by backing my horses, the poet who has composed a sonnet to the GOM, the family that wishes to emigrate – all these and myriad others are preparing for action. Not to speak of the hospital that wants a wing, the roofless church, the club of hearty liberals in an impoverished district, the football club that wants a patron, the village band that wants instruments, all of which are now preparing for the warpath.[41]

Nevertheless, Rosebery was generally both patient and generous when it came to requests for donations. He gave substantial backing to a wide range of institutions, such as the Bodleian Library in Oxford, as well as to tenants on his estates and a host of other individuals. But for all his wealth he could lose his sense of proportion in certain minor matters, becoming strangely neurotic about them. During the First World War, for example, he was involved in a ridiculous correspondence with Margot Asquith over the disappearance of a kettle-holder which had belonged to a maiden aunt. Rosebery repeatedly accused her of petty larceny, and instructed her to 'Search diligently for the relic and if you have a church near you do some public form of penance.' When Margot eventually sent him a kettle-holder, Rosebery first claimed it was not the right one, then proceeded to lose it, an event he described as 'a great calamity'. He searched for it for months, and finally gave up in May 1919. 'What has become of it I cannot guess, unless the house-maids have been unable to keep their hands off it.'[42] In 1903 he developed a fixation with a finger bowl from Chevening that he had used as a child. Appalled to hear that it had been 'smashed to atoms', he drove over to Chevening and, according to his cousin the 6th Earl Stanhope, 'he carried off two blue finger bowls to replace the breakage.'[43]

Equally surprising was Rosebery's sense of insecurity about his fortune, based on three events of the early 1890s. 'I have been troubled by money nearly all my life,' he once wrote. 'The only exception, perhaps, was when I first married and then both my wife and I thought we had boundless resources.' The first problem arose out of a disastrous series of investments in America overseen by Ferdinand Van Zandt, whom Rosebery called an 'honest and noble friend but a bad man of business'. Rosebery had bought £200,000-worth of shares in a Texas ranch but the deal turned to catastrophe 'after a rogue stripped the cattle off the land and sold them'. In an attempt to recover his money Rosebery was persuaded by Van Zandt to invest heavily in a silver mine in Montana, a project that was soon drowning in a flood of litigation. In January 1891 Rosebery confessed, 'I am for the present moment overwhelmed with an enormous debt caused by an American speculation, a liability which not only weighs me down but has for five or six years past been drawing from me every sixpence.'[44] Just over a year later, in March 1892, Van Zandt, realising the scale of the mess and seeing no solution, shot himself in Brown's Hotel in London. Just hours before he put the gun to his head he had called on Rosebery at Berkeley Square, but found he was out. When Rosebery heard the news the next morning he noted in his diary: 'What an end to a splendid glowing life. Thank God I never said or wrote an unkind word to him.' Van Zandt's family disagreed with the verdict of suicide, prompted, according to the Coroner, by 'temporary insanity'. Sir John Lubbock, Van Zandt's father-in-law and a colleague of Rosebery on the LCC, recorded in his diary: 'Of course, it *may* have been an accident . . . I almost fancy there may have been a tumour or some disease of the brain. Ferdinand did not say a word to us of any pecuniary troubles and they do not seem to have been insuperable.'[45] Rosebery's second crisis, following swiftly on the death of Van Zandt, resulted from a crash in his Australian investments. 'Misfortunes never come single,' he told Edward Hamilton. 'I had a smashing telegram from Australia yesterday announcing utter loss and swindling there. I shall not merely lose all I had invested there but be compelled to take legal proceedings which I hate. I shall soon be like Diogenes in his tent and am becoming a stock philosopher.'[46] The third disaster had its roots in corruption inside the Bank of England, when the stock-broking son of the chief cashier, Mr May, who conducted much of Rosebery's domestic business, was caught fiddling securities, with the connivance of his father. The son, like Van Zandt, committed suicide, May was dismissed, and the Bank of England was forced to refund Rosebery £20,000 to make up for his losses. 'I had a terrible shock and ever since I have lost my financial nerve,' wrote Rosebery in November 1910. As Loulou Harcourt pointed out,* Rosebery's worries may have been responsible for some of his strange behaviour during his premiership.

Rosebery's attitude to religion was as enigmatic as any other aspect of his character. He could be categorised as that rarest of individuals, the devout agnostic. A regular worshipper and reader of the Bible, he found comfort in church sacraments and brought up his children in the Christian rather than the Jewish faith. In his room in Barnbougle he kept a small crucifix above his bed, and prayers were said daily in whichever of his houses he happened to be staying. Although John Buchan once described him as a seventeenth-century Calvinist at heart, Rosebery had not a shred of bigotry. As in other parts of his life, religiously he was sensitive to his environment; in Scotland, he would attend Presbyterian services, in Malta, Catholic. He was an admirer of Cardinal Newman, and one of the most moving descriptions in his diary is of seeing Newman's body laid out on the high altar just after his death in 1890. 'This was the end of the young Calvinist, the Oxford don, the austere vicar of St Mary's. It seemed as if a whole cycle of human thought and life were concentrated in that august repose. That was my overwhelming thought. Kindly light had led and guided Newman to this strange, brilliant end. Seeing him on his right side in outline one saw only an enormous nose and chin almost meeting – a St

---

*Loulou Harcourt knew about the May scandal through the City connections of his own father Sir William, who was Chancellor at the time. Loulou's diary for 14 May 1895 records a meeting in the City at which he was told that Rosebery had been 'gambling tremendously in stocks, including mines, and lost a great deal of money'.

Dominic face. The left side was inconceivably sweet and soft, with that gentle corner of the mouth so greatly missed in the other view, the body, so frail and slight that it ceased to be a body terrestrial.'[47] In fact, Regy Brett once said that Rosebery's 'inner mind works oddly. It would never surprise me if he became a Catholic.'[48] Rosebery cared deeply for the symbols of Christianity, and hated to see their neglect. 'Does progress really require such sacrifices? Is it necessary to purge these old temples of the voice of faith and the worship of God?' he wrote to Munro-Ferguson after visiting an old Italian monastry which was filled with pigs.[49]

But for all that, Rosebery struggled continually with his faith. He respected the moral precepts of Christianity but, unlike Gladstone, he lacked the certainty of the true believer. In the privacy of his study he often pondered the concept of divinity, and in 1913 he wrote this frank summary of his outlook. 'Christianity is an impenetrable mystery before which we incline ourselves in adoration, but which we cannot profess to understand. We do not comprehend, we worship.' He noted that there were several different kinds of faith: 'brutal, unthinking, superstitious devotion'; the unaffected belief, 'a high privilege and divine endowment'; then the fierce determination of faith, like that of Cardinal Manning, 'with teeth clenched and eyes closed'. And, finally, his own: 'If one is warmly sensible of the necessity, for our own comfort, elevation and guidance, of religious devotion, if in a word is religious without the complete consistion of faith, one becomes a religious agnostic, a phrase I invented for myself. Every thoughtful and devout mind must be agnostic, though the word has an ugly sound. Failing the divine inspiration of faith and necessarily failing knowledge, we can strive for faith, strive for light and strive for conviction.'[50] In another, separate note written amid the carnage of the First World War, he tried to take solace from the Christian injunction to virtue: 'Suppose all that the sceptics say is true, that Christianity is a fable, that there is no future life, yet still the practising Christian would be infinitely superior to all others by his character and life and infinitely happier for his faith.'[51] There was one typically eccentric feature of these religious doubts: in spite of his regular church attendance, Rosebery loathed sermons, and would often walk out of a service before the minister had reached the pulpit. When rebuked for this habit by the Canon of Christ Church, Oxford he dismissed the notion that sermons represented God's message: 'They are at best human, fallible productions and should be judged accordingly.'[52]

Often melancholic and introspective, Rosebery continually talked of his love of solitude, once telling Mary Gladstone that 'There ought to be solitary intervals in one's existence and I have thought of committing some petty larceny lately which would give me a month in a cell.'[53] Even when he had guests at Dalmeny he would sometimes scarcely appear, preferring to hide among his books and thoughts in his eyrie on the top floor of Barnbougle. Yet he was also known to complain when his friends deprived him of their company. 'You have become an unknown quantity: absent, absorbed and transient. Nothing short of a bomb brings you out of your shell,' he complained to Regy Brett on 29 November 1894[*] – exactly the sort of words so often used about Rosebery.[54] He could be the most flattering of Royal courtiers, rivalling even Disraeli, as he demonstrated in a toe-curling letter he wrote the Queen after her Golden Jubilee celebrations in 1887, referring to that 'touching and magnetic moment in the Abbey when Your Majesty appeared alone and aloft – symbolising so truly Your Majesty's real position – to bear silent testimony to the blessings and the sorrows which it had pleased God to bestow on Your Majesty and Your people during two generations.'[55] But he also had tremendous rows with Edward VII, whom he had known well since the 1870s. During one house-party at Ascot he sulked the whole time, and as good as refused to speak to the King. On another occasion he shocked the Tory leader Bonar Law by his mockery of stolid George V at a Buckingham Palace luncheon.

These contradictions were just as apparent in his role as a father. Those who knew the moody and imperious statesman were surprised by how relaxed he became in the company of children. The mask of inscrutability would be dropped, replaced by a spirit of playfulness and good humour. It was not uncommon for Rosebery to be found lying on the floor of the nursery at Dalmeny with two or three of his children piled on top of him, shrieking gleefully. A colonial Premier, visiting Dalmeny in 1887, was surprised to be greeted by the sight of the great imperialist carrying one of his girls on his shoulders. As a girl growing up in Scotland Margot Asquith (then Tennant) saw this side of Rosebery when he visited her family home Glen in Peebles-shire: 'There was no after dinner game he did not play with us, and I can see him now in my mind's eye draping himself with the carriage rug to act in "Beauty and the Beast", a small play which we improvised together to amuse the family.'[†] Lord Ronald Gower recorded after meeting Rosebery at Dunrobin in 1894: 'Rosebery is seen to greatest advantage when playing with my little great-nephews. He is very fond of children and they are attracted to him by the fuss he makes over them.'[56]

---

[*] His last remark proved to be an embarrassing if inadvertent gaffe, for that day, by a grisly coincidence, Regy's wife had almost been killed by a bomb planted by anarchists who were probably trying to kill the Bretts' neighbour, Justice Hawkins.
[†] Margot Asquith, *More Memories*.

In 1915 Constance Battersea visited Mentmore and was impressed by Rosebery's benevolence towards both his little grandson Robin and a troop of 36 scouts who were staying nearby on a disused farm. 'His adoration of Robin is quite touching,' Constance noted. 'The diary of that strange child amused us both very much. On Monday, he had written "Grandpapa gave me some cyder at luncheon which exhilarated me unduly and I made a fool of myself." The scouts were a revelation to Rosebery and he and I had an amusing time with them between the rain showers. I must say Rosebery was delightful with the boys.'[57] Rosebery's tolerance of poor behaviour by children was demonstrated in an incident in 1921 recalled much later by Sir John Colville* in his memoirs. Staying in Epsom as a six-year-old, he sneaked over to The Durdans one morning with a friend. 'We prowled inquisitively about the stables, where Lord Rosebery's huge bay carriage horses had recently returned from the nightly expedition with their own, unhappy victim of almost constant insomnia, who had driven himself along the country lanes while others slept.' In one loose box they found a lamb, which was lying prostrate on the straw and appeared to be ill. Little John Colville had heard that brandy could revive a sickly animal, so he crept into the house, found a bottle in the dining room, ran back to the stables and gave it to the lamb. The creature dropped dead instantly. 'That evening Lord Rosebery sent for us. He stood in the library, a frightening figure in dark green glasses. He spoke to us in sorrow rather than in anger. "My children," he said, "you little know what you have done to me." What we had done was to pour his last bottle of Napoleon brandy down the throat of a lamb of such quality that it had been segregated from the herd. It had been confidently expected to win a Championship at the Royal Show.'[58] Rosebery had little affection for the world of infants, however, as he revealed during a trip to Madrid in 1895. 'I had dinner in close proximity to a Portugese wet-nurse in the active exercise of her useful and succulent functions. Fortunately I was able to interpose a screen otherwise I must have fasted.'[59]

Unlike many Victorian parents who were only too anxious to maintain a distance between themselves and their offspring, Rosebery made his own children a central part of his domestic life, partly because it helped to draw him out of his morbid introspection. John Morley, whose long relationship with Rosebery was always ambivalent, recorded after a dinner at Dalmeny in 1892: 'Dined at seven with the children at the table. They were delightfully merry. To see Rosebery with them is to blot out his singular

*Private Secretary to Winston Churchill during the Second World War.

flaws and leave him wholly lovable.'[60] Rosebery's own diary is full of affectionate notes about his children, especially Sybil, the imaginative one, such as this from 3 January 1885: 'Sybil, when I left this morning, cried bitterly, but I had to leave her. Her maid could not find her to come down to breakfast and at last came upon her kneeling by her little bed and praying to God out loud to preserve her dear papa and bring him safe back to her, with tears running down her cheeks.' Or this, from 5 February 1890: 'Took the children to the pantomime, *Jack and the Beanstalk*. Sybil and Harry enjoyed it most demonstratively, Peggy and Neil more disciplined.' Their mutual warmth was also demonstrated after Rosebery returned home in 1891 from a long trip overseas, having grown some facial hair. In mock outrage his children sent their aunt Constance Leconfield a letter, its wording clearly inspired by their father: 'We, the undersigned nephews and nieces, beg to address you on a subject of great importance. You may have observed that our parent has returned from foreign parts with an odious pair of whiskers. What do you think of them? If you agree with us in thinking them terrible, will you exert your influence to have them removed. We thought we saw an expression of pain pass over your countenance as your eye rested on them, so we build great hopes on you, signed Peggy, Harry, Neil and Sybil.'[61]

But it would be wrong to pretend that this was the whole picture, for Rosebery could be just as difficult with his sons and daughters as with colleagues and footmen. Following his mother's example, he was hard on his eldest son and heir Harry, who was often the object of his derision. Just after Harry's birth he told Mary Gladstone, 'I cannot pretend to be much excited about an event which occurs to almost every human being and which may cause me a good deal of annoyance.'[62] Years later, Harry bitterly recalled the occasion on which Rosebery ordered the butler not to offer him any cigars after luncheon: 'I give you a big enough allowance to buy your own.' He could be equally rude about his second son Neil. 'However great an ass a man may be he can always produce a son who is greater. I look at Neil and meditate this great truth,' he once wrote to Munro-Ferguson.[63] He also frequently attacked his sons for their youthful academic idleness and their involvement in a fast set centred on the turf – both areas where he was on shaky ground. But Neil, whose family nickname was Puff, enjoyed the intellectual gifts and political astuteness Harry lacked, eventually becoming a member of Lloyd George's government. Though Rosebery always denied it, there is no doubt that Neil was very much his favourite son, and in later life they were so close as to be more like brothers. 'I personally think that Neil is the image of his father.

Rosebery is about as ambitious for Neil as he is for himself,' thought Regy Brett.[64]

Nor was his relationship with his two daughters free of clashes and distress, particularly when he took charge of their education and sacked a beloved governess. There is a fascinating passage in Margot Asquith's diary, written in November 1897 after a lengthy conversation with Sybil about her father.

> The two girls have not yet forgiven their father for sending away Miss Vibert, the Governess that was with them. I think Rosebery was probably right in getting rid of her but his manner of doing it seems to have been wrong – one of the violences of the Napoleonic order of which his family has a little too much. Sybil said it was entirely jealousy of any influence but his own with them, that in his anxiety to bring them up well all friendships were absolutely forbidden and in consequence they were both shy and gauche. She spoke with a great deal of feeling about the impossibility of being intimate with her father. I thought it advisable to say that he had been so hardly brought up by the old Duchess and had been so thrown in upon himself by her injustice that it made it difficult for him to be unreserved and easy . . . Sybil told how her father had 'made her sink into the earth' when they were out in a shooting party – she was standing with a good-natured lady and her swain when Rosebery said, 'Come with me, Sybil. Two is company and three none.' Poor girls. I feel profoundly sorry for them. They have no freedom, no friends and no pocket money worth speaking of.[65]

Rosebery's apparently excessive concern for the upbringing of his daughters stemmed from the emotionally shattering event of November 1890 which left him a broken man and his children bereft. Throughout much of 1890 Hannah Rosebery was in poor health; Edward Hamilton had noted in April, 'I don't think she is at all well and is a very bad patient. She is quite conscious of being by no means strong.'[66] Later in the year Hamilton's fears were realised. On 7 October Rosebery returned home to Dalmeny to find Hannah ill in bed. Two days later she was diagnosed as suffering from typhoid fever, in the Victorian age an often fatal illness and that which had killed his brother Everard Primrose in the Sudanese desert. Over the next few weeks Hannah's health and Rosebery's spirits oscillated wildly. Sometimes it appeared that she would pull through, and he was elated. 'So far as I can gather from the doctors, all is going well here: sleep, strength and pulse all good,' he wrote to Gladstone on 16 October.[67] Then she would decline again, and Rosebery was sunk in despondency. One of the darkest days came towards the end of October, when her physician Dr Broadbent declared that all hope was lost, and she would probably die in the night. That afternoon Rosebery had the following note sent by hand to Mrs Gladstone, who happened to be staying with her husband in Edinburgh: 'I want to know if you or Balfour could cause the prayers of the congregation to be asked on behalf of Hannah at the Cathedral tomorrow. I do not know whom to ask at the Cathedral – or whether they will pray for a Jewess. She took a turn for the worse in the night and Broadbent told me this morning early that now humanly and practically he entertains no hope. Pray for me and the bairns.'[68] But by the next morning, 26 October, Hannah had temporarily recovered, partly through the strength of her willpower. To his cousin Earl Stanhope, Rosebery admitted his emotional exhaustion: 'The fluctuations of this fever of which this is a specimen are almost as terrible to the watchers as to the patient.'[69] Rosebery later penned a record of that painful day, 25 October, which reveals not only his heartache but how he and Hannah, in their devotion to each other, could not bear the thought of being torn apart. In his account, Rosebery was at her bedside when Hannah, aware that she might be facing death, said, 'Archie, lean your head close to me. Do you think I shall ever pull through?' Rosebery could not bring himself to utter a lie, and it was only after a pause that he said, 'I hope so.' Hannah then continued, 'How short everything is in life, when I think of how you came to Mentmore and brought me the sapphire locket. No one could have made me so happy as you. I sometimes have felt it was wrong that I thought of the children so little in comparison to you. I will try to live for you. Some years hence you may care for someone else – you may forget me. It seems so strange that I should think so much of this: what she may be like. How dreadful it would be were it the other way.' Rosebery demurred at this: 'I have prayed that God would take me instead of you.' To which Hannah responded, 'That would never do. I could never live a day after you. Poor Peggy, I think it will break her heart. Sybil is more Jewish, more shallow; she requires great care. Archie, you will never leave the children.'[70]

At the beginning of November Hannah seemed to be past the worst. She and Rosebery talked of convalescent trips to Torquay and Corfu when she had sufficiently recovered. Her generous spirit is revealed in her last letter to their closest friend, Edward Hamilton: 'I am never too ill to glance at one of your nice, chatty letters. Please write as I have not seen a newspaper for a week and a little gossip is rather amusing. I feel very ill and I am sure you feel sorry. Typhoid is a very exhausting illness. I have four excellent nurses. Dr Broadbent is staying here and is increasing in his kindness and attention. I have the greatest confidence in him for this disease.'[71] But she then suffered a relapse, and from 13 November was delirious. What

Rosebery had not been told was that she was also suffering from Bright's disease, a kidney complaint that meant it was almost impossible she should survive a prolonged bout of typhoid. By 17 November it was obvious that the end could not be far away, some soothing words from the doctors notwithstanding. 'My invalid progresses very slowly, if indeed at all,' Rosebery told Gladstone. 'It cannot be far from the 50th day of fever and how the human frame resists such strain is more than I can understand.'[72] Hannah's frame could not resist much longer. On the morning of November 18 she breathed her last. In his diary Rosebery described her final, agonising hours.

> Hannah had a sort of collapse and after that hope ceased, though I did not know this until 11 p.m. when I asked for the doctor. She had been delirious for fully a week, only waking up when I came in the room, 'Archie, this is nice', in her old, sweet, childish way. About 10 she spoke to me very clearly, 'Archie, Archie, I am going home', but she probably still thought she was in Paris where she fancied herself last week. But those were the last words I heard her say. She was always trying to say my name and her eyes would rest on me or Connie★ with a ghastly smile. All the night, her loud, groaning, breathing went on. We could hear it all over the house. About 5 she became quiet and at 5.50 her last breath came quite quietly – a gentle sigh of rest, almost pleasant to hear. I went down to the Castle and watched a beautiful dawn of melting fog until it was time to see the children. I first told the boys when I heard chattering. Neil cried bitterly but Harry was quiet. With the girls, Peggy sobbed painfully, Sybil whispered into my ear at once, 'I must be a mother to them'.

Hannah's body was taken from Edinburgh to the Roseberys' London residence, followed by a Jewish funeral at Willesden on 25 November. In a demonstration of the affection in which she was held, most houses in the streets around Berkeley Square had their blinds drawn down on the morning of the funeral as a mark of respect. Constance Battersea, Hannah's cousin, described the scene at 38 Berkeley Square. 'Crowds were already collecting in the street. I went upstairs and in the large front room, on a bier, stood a large oak coffin, which enclosed two other coffins, the inner one containing the mortal remains of dear Hannah. Flowers abounded everywhere; they lined and carpeted the floor, covered the coffin and stood like sentinels at its head. There was true, sincere and heartfelt regret at poor Hannah's decease.'[73] From Berkeley Square the coffin was taken in a simple hearse to Willesden Cemetery, where children carrying black banners rep-

---

★Constance Leconfield, Rosebery's sister.

resenting various Jewish charities lined the route to the grave. An air of tragic solemnity hung over the day, reinforced by the arrival of a heavy black wreath from the Queen, carried by her secretary Sir Henry Ponsonby. The *Jewish Chronicle* gave this description of the moment before the coffin was lowered into the earth: 'For some minutes Lord Rosebery, holding by the hand his young sons, stood before the coffin which held all that was left of the loving wife and mother, and the haggard look on his Lordship's face and the unmistakable evidence of a great mental struggle to suppress his emotion, increased the sympathy which was already abundantly felt for him.' As her coffin was lowered, the Rabbi uttered the prayer 'May she come to her appointed place in peace'. In accordance with orthodox Jewish custom, only men attended the ceremony. Most of Rosebery's political colleagues were present among the mourners, including William Gladstone, who confessed that though the service was 'dignified and touching', he felt the absence 'of our Lord's name'.[74] This was precisely the emotion Rosebery experienced, as he explained in a letter to the Queen of 28 November:

> There is one incident of the tragedy only less painful than the actual loss; which is that at the moment of death the difference of creed makes itself felt and another religion steps in to claim the corpse. It was inevitable and I do not complain: and my wife's family have been more than kind. But none the less is it exquisitely painful. Your Majesty has passed but too often through the Valley of the Shadow of Death, and will understand me when I say that there seem only two consolations. The one that the Almighty and All Good has certainly ordained all for the best. And the other that love, such as my wife's, cannot perish, that is with me as much as my skin or the air I breathe; and that so it must be to the end. Great love I firmly believe never dies or runs dry, but is part of the poor heritage of mankind.[75]

Rosebery managed to maintain a front of grim composure during the day of the funeral, mainly by dint of staring at the ground, but in private he was distraught, his grief all the deeper because, always so suspicious of intimacy, he had no one in whom he could confide. All his traits of solitude, isolation, reserve and shyness increased dramatically in the wake of Hannah's death, as he grieved alone in Barnbougle Castle, unable to face the world. His wretchedness was a graphic refutation of the whispered gossip that he had married Hannah for her money. No widower could have been more miserable. As he wrote to Ferdy Rothschild just days after her death, 'Our happy home is a wreck, her children are motherless and I have lost the best wife ever man had. I do not see the elements of consolation, except in the memory of her beautiful, unselfish life.'[76]

The first indications of the seriousness of Hannah's illness had caused loyal Edward Hamilton to worry about the effect on Rosebery should the worst happen. On 12 October he had written that in this event 'He would lose the best and most devoted of wives; and those who know her as I do would lose the staunchest and most sterling of friends. Indeed, if anything happened to her, there is no saying whether Rosebery might not throw up his political career and devote himself entirely to his children and his books, which constitute the first mortgage on his affections.'[77] Hannah had been far more than just a wife to Rosebery and a mother to his children. With her devotion and ambition she had been his guiding light, his counsellor, the woman who gave his life a purpose and a focus. As Hamilton wrote of her on the day he received the news of her death, 'There was no woman whose confidence I ever possessed so completely. She withheld nothing from me, always consulted me and always turned to me. I shall always regard it as a great privilege to have had the confidence of so good and remarkable a woman, and so unswervingly.'[78]

Exactly what Hamilton feared now took place, with Rosebery descending into a pit of despair, unable to contemplate his future. As often happened in times of personal crisis he suffered a psychosomatic ailment, telling his sister on 8 December that he had 'a violent cold with which I have been engaged in single combat for some 40 hours, at present without conspicuous success. It takes place of all plans in addling a perplexed head.'[79] Just after Christmas 1890 he confessed his troubled, listless state to Sir William Harcourt, who had abandoned his customary hostility to send a letter of sympathy. 'At first, one was dazed with the hundreds of letters one received and perhaps stunned as well by the freshness of the blow. Now the sympathy of one's friends comes with a double healing power, for the senses are clear and the loneliness infinitely greater. I am here with nobody and nothing but the children. Even the perceptions have fled. But it is best so. It is like lying on the grass and blinking up at the sun in the semi-consciousness of an afternoon in the open air.'[80] To Regy Brett he wrote, 'I should greatly like to see you, if anybody. But the fact is that I am anti-gregarious just now and perhaps morose.'[81]

In the New Year Rosebery's seedy inertia gave way to another characteristic condition, restlessness. Overcome by the feeling that he had to escape his mournful home, he embarked on a long tour of the Continent, travelling under the rather transparent alias of 'Mr Rose' to prevent well-wishers disturbing him. Herbert Bismarck was one of those anxious to comfort Rosebery, and suggested they should meet in Italy. But Rosebery was reluctant. 'I have sustained a great shock to my nerves. I creep like a wounded animal into a hole. You should make plans without me for I am a broken reed. I am more fit to wander among the tombs like the unclean spirits.' When Bismarck protested against this attitude, Rosebery became stubborn: 'I wish to lose myself for a while and be out of the way of letters, ministers, consuls and obliging friends.'[82] Alone he travelled to Milan and then to Greece, visiting the spot at Marathon where his beloved Frederick Vyner had been assassinated twenty years earlier. In March he returned to Italy, house-hunting – unsuccessfully – in Naples and reading Gibbon in Rome. A trip to the old Jewish ghetto in Venice exposed some ambivalent feelings about Judaism in the aftermath of Hannah's death; in his diary, Rosebery referred to the 'piteous little synagogue with a sense of dreary Jews droning their dreary devotions'.[83] He returned to England briefly in the middle of the month, mainly to attend the funeral of Lord Granville, whose estate was in financial chaos when he died. Thanks to the generosity of Hartington and Rosebery, who each donated more than £2,000, the family were saved from bankruptcy. But Rosebery could not escape the torment of bereavement. He went to Granville's funeral with John Morley, who according to Hamilton 'thought Rosebery was in a most unnatural state – restless, morbid, hypersensitive, e.g., pulling down the blinds of the carriage whenever they stopped for fear of being recognised.'[84] Staying at The Durdans one troubled night, he dreamt that he was back in the room in which Hannah had died. 'She asked me, "Have I been good while you have been away." I said "Yes". "Then I am quite happy."'[85] The next day, 14 March, the anniversary of his marriage, he went with his two daughters to Hannah's grave at Willesden. 'There was a bright glint of sunshine and solitude. It seemed to me that peace and rest were there. There was nothing gloomy. From the grave, there seemed to smile a placid contempt for the frets and worries of this petty stage. Sybil much moved and in tears, Peggy in a different way.' A few days later when he was dining with Sybil the conversation drifted to widowhood. Rosebery said, 'I wonder what mourning your mother would have worn for me if I had died.' Sybil replied, 'She would not have worn any. She would have died at once.'[86]

Rosebery's restlessness was as strong as ever. Towards the end of April he went to Spain, yet everything he did there only seemed to reinforce his sense of desolation. After looking over an art collection in one of Madrid's palaces, he felt that 'Velasquez had a morbid delight in what was painful and hideous.' At his first bullfight, he was horrified to see 'a young debutant attacked from behind by a bull and fall on his sword, which stabbed him three inches deep into the hip.' A series of wretched, wakeful nights in Spain led him to journey across the Continent to take the waters at Marienbad and Gastein, but these cures did little to improve his temper. 'It is hardly conceivable to spend a drearier day,' he wrote on 20 June. In August he was forced to return home by another death in the family, that of his step-father, the Duke of Cleveland. For once, joined in grief at the loss of their respective spouses, he and his mother had something in common, as Rosebery admitted in a letter to the Duchess: 'I cannot recollect that we have ever been two days alone together in our lives and I have enjoyed them greatly: the more, as, widowed mother and widowed son, the hand of God has brought us near to each other.'[87]

Towards the end of 1891 Rosebery's political colleagues grew worried about his distress, and his reluctance to re-enter public life. Some of those who lacked any appreciation of his highly sensitive nature thought he was too wrapped in self-pity. When Rosebery – only after the strongest persuasion – attended a Liberal conclave at Lord Spencer's home at Althorp in December 1891, John Morley noted in his diary,★ 'Rosebery struck everybody as very low and depressed. It was his first visit and his first interview with Lord Spencer. Still, it is a year since his wife died and one ought not to carry the mourner's flag forever. I found it hard to understand the callous silence with which he has watched Mr Gladstone battling in deep waters since November 1890 without seeming to take the least interest in it all, or even be conscious of it.'[88] Rosebery's political inactivity was particularly disturbing to those who regarded him as Gladstone's natural successor. Just before the Althorp meeting Edward Hamilton wrote to him in explicit, reproving terms: 'Whatever may be your inclinations, I am afraid that you have no real choice. There are many Liberals – probably the best and most intelligent portion – who look to you as the only man who can save and lead them, ultimately, if not immediately. Your retirement would be a terrible blow to them; and sooner or later they would make a distinct and direct call upon you. I am convinced you cannot escape and that being so, I think you ought to make an effort to re-enter the political arena before long. It is hardly fair on others that you should not in a difficult time give them the full advantage of your counsel.'[89] But Rosebery continued to dismiss any idea of his reappearance on the national stage. His arguments were summed up in a letter to Ronald Munro-Ferguson of April 1891: 'For me, there are no "political opportunities" at present – nor can there be. I must devour my great disaster alone. Of this I alone can be the judge. Were it not for this, I should not be abroad. I should be much happier and better in the country with my children. But in England, it seems, I cannot be left

★ After remaining hidden for decades, Morley's private diary was recently donated to the Bodleian Library. It provides a much franker account of Rosebery than Morley's published *Recollections*.

quiet. I only ask to be ignored and forgotten, for a time at any rate. There ought to be no difficulty in this.'[90] If anything, he became more disconsolate towards the end of 1891. In December he admitted to his sister, 'I feel the most lamentable and discreditable shrinking from strangers. I am really ashamed of myself. I am afraid my seclusion grows on me.'[91]

There is no doubt that Rosebery never fully recovered from the loss of Hannah. In the years immediately before her death he had seemed to have everything an ambitious man could want: a healthy young family, a burgeoning career, a wide circle of friends, wealth, property, fame, and a powerful intellect. But all this had been rendered meaningless by the untimely end of a loving wife who mattered to him far more than anyone or anything else. He was perhaps not always the most chivalrous or patient husband while she was alive, but her demise left a gaping hole that could not be filled. It might be suspected that the role of the lonely widower, staring bleakly out from his castle at the grey waters of the Firth of Forth, appealed to the melodramatic, martyred streak in Rosebery. Like many Victorians, he took a morbid interest in death; one of his less attractive habits was rushing off to see the remains of friends before they were buried. Yet Rosebery's lifelong grief over Hannah was certainly genuine. For years afterwards, everybody who knew him was struck by the way he had been changed by her death. Much of the wit and sparkle which had made him such a popular figure disappeared. The valleys of depression grew deeper, the uplands of happiness much rarer. His solitary, moody ways were so magnified that some feared his mind was unbalanced, even suicidal; at one stage in August 1892, during the complex negotiations over the formation of Gladstone's last government, John Morley found Rosebery's behaviour so odd that 'it was to me as if he was going to drown himself in the Firth that night'.[92] His innate dislike of politics, which Hannah had always fought against, grew more intense, leading to a long series of perplexing misjudgements and ill-timed retirements. In 1912, when Ronald Munro-Ferguson was looking back on Rosebery's career, he said regretfully, 'many things would have gone otherwise had Lady Rosebery lived. Her loss is today as great a calamity from every point of view as it was at the time of her death.'[93]

Rosebery was even physically altered by the tragedy: he aged prematurely and grew inclined to speak of himself as an old man, though he was still only in his forties. Flecks of grey appeared in his glossy dark hair; his eyes were often ringed and dark from sleeplessness. 'He is not handsome now, he looks so sad and ill,' wrote Lady Monkswell in March 1892.[94] He withdrew from Society, and after 1890 he hardly ever dined out in the evening, preferring to eat alone with just a book for company. Throughout the rest of his life he only used writing paper with a heavy black border, while Hannah's room at Dalmeny was kept as a shrine, untouched from the day she died. During the First World War, when Dalmeny was turned into a military hospital, Rosebery was appalled to discover that the room had been repainted for use as an operating theatre. 'They wanted lighter walls. It is an outrage and a pang. Indeed, the cup of bitterness at Dalmeny must be nearly full.'[95]

Apart from his children, Rosebery's only true solace was his love of books. Delving into history, biography and fantasy transported him out of his paralysing self-absorption. In his libraries at The Durdans and Barnbougle he achieved the peace that travel, company and politics could never provide. 'No man was ever more devoted to his books than Rosebery. I have actually seen him go plump down on his knees and unpack a parcel of them and take them to their appointed places,' recalled the Liberal politician Augustine Birrell.[96] He had been a voracious reader since childhood, inspired at first by Macaulay, and he began collecting books and manuscripts while he was still at Eton. 'He told me that when he was a boy of 12 or 13 people used to ask what he would have as birthday presents and he always asked for letters from Cromwell, Napoleon, Wellington, Pitt, etc.,' recorded Margot Asquith.[97] Once, when Hannah took the children into a bookshop, she told them, 'To your father this is a toy shop.' By 1890 he had one of the most magnificent private collections in the country, full of rare treasures such as a perfect First Edition of the 1611 Authorized Version of the Bible, a Shakespeare First Folio, Napoleon's travelling library, manuscripts by Dr Johnson and Disraeli, and King Charles I's 1637 copy of *The Book of Common Prayer*. But he was no literary snob. Though historical biography gave him the greatest pleasure, the range of his reading was surprisingly diverse, from French novels to obscure geography. Nor was he above the occasional thriller; as he told John Buchan in 1926, 'I have not long ago read *The 39 Steps* over again with keen relish. It is one of the most absurd and extravagant of works and therefore very pleasant to an invalid.'[98] The only subjects he rarely touched were science, and military history. He was a keen critic, and enjoyed passing on to friends his views on his latest reading. Here he is in 1907 writing to the civil servant Arthur Godley about a new Life of William Morris: 'Surely the test of a biography is that it should make you interested in its subject, whatever your previous disposition may be. I did not feel the smallest interest in Morris, except as a man who sold hideous sage green wallpapers and who postured as a socialist. I have read the book and feel, if anything and if possible, less interest.'[99] As a bibliophile he was also fortunate in possessing, in the words of his daughter Sybil, 'the almost unfair gift of reading and remembering the contents of a book by merely cutting its leaves, the super mastery of the art and craft of "skipping".'[100] Such was his love of reading that he could never bear to be without a book, even in the most adverse circumstances; in 1907, when his car crashed in a snowstorm on the road to Edinburgh and he and his chauffeur had to make a hazardous escape through the nocturnal drifts, the only item he carried with him from the wreckage was a two-volume Life of Lord Durham.

What Rosebery hated in writing was pretension. He thought Jane Austen's work almost flawless, but of others less accomplished he wrote, 'The curse of great novelists as a rule is that after their first success or successes they become inebriated with their triumph and attempt a higher flight in which they are lost in the clouds and become diffuse, or philosophical or what. In this foolish ambition, they drop their own gift, that of telling a story.'[101] Though he professed to be 'a devoted admirer of Trollope at his best', Rosebery felt that he was often 'little more than a bookmaker. He wrote like a journalist though he was not one.'[102] His dislike of artifice was especially strong when it came to poetry, an area of literature with which he often struggled. 'It always seems to me to express either too little or too much,' he told Lord Crewe. He had a strong aversion to William Wordsworth, as he told John Morley after reading a volume: 'What strikes me so forcibly is that the old fellow never seems to know when he is writing poetry and when he is not, when he hits and when he misses. Suddenly, after weltering through a mass of didactic prose, he stumbles into the sublime and, when one has realized that, one hears him, plosh, plosh, wading again into a bog of heavy didactics. Who but Wordsworth could begin a sonnet, "Jones"? That shows what I consider his insensitivity to the poetic instinct.'[103] It should be added, however, that Rosebery's attempts to display his own poetic instincts usually resulted in embarrassing verse. The lightness, imagination and vibrancy that were such a feature of his oratory and conversation were entirely absent from his leaden poetry. Here are some lines written to mark his 28th birthday in 1875, which do not even boast the virtue of rhyming properly:

> The cup of pleasure has not lost its savour,
> Shall we not quaff where we have quaffed?
> Winking and smiling with its palled sweet flavour,
> Shall we not laugh where we have laughed.

Equally infelicitous was his Jubilee Hymn to Queen Victoria in 1887:

Bless her subjects, bless our land.
Church and Senate, home and mart;
Bind her people hand to hand.
Closer and closer, heart to heart.

Fortunately for Rosebery's reputation, little of his poetry reached a wide public audience. He was much more successful in prose, and his elegant style, knowledge of history and understanding of human foibles were perfectly suited to the art of biography. Unlike many politicians, including Morley and Salisbury in his own era, Rosebery never worked as a journalist, having neither the need nor the inclination. But in 1889 he accepted a commission to produce a brief Life of his hero William Pitt the Younger as part of Macmillan's 'Twelve English Statesmen' series, which was being edited by John Morley. The result was a brilliant success. The lack of original research was more than balanced by Rosebery's dry wit and polish, his ability to produce memorable character portraits and vivid summaries of complex historical events. Here is Rosebery on Charles James Fox, Pitt's great rival: 'It has been said that his private life was conspicuously disordered. And yet even when it was blameworthy it was lovable and it mellowed into an exquisite evening. Whether we see him plunged into Theocritus after a bout at faro which has left him penniless; or cheerfully watching the bailiffs remove his last stick of furniture; or drinking with the Jockey of Norfolk; or choosing wild waistcoats at Paris . . . or speechless with generous tears in the House of Commons when quivering under the harsh severance of Burke – he still exercises over us something of the unbounded fascination which he wielded over his contemporaries.' Just as powerful is his description of Addington: 'the son of a respected family physician, who had prescribed colchicum to the elder and port to the younger Pitt, he carried into politics the indefinable air of a village apothecary inspecting the tongue of the state.' Perhaps as interesting is the way Rosebery's insights into Pitt reflected on his own personality. In one passage he referred to Pitt's notoriously cold demeanour: 'As a constant weapon, too often used, he had an endless command of freezing, bitter scornful sarcasm' – similar to the words later used by Winston Churchill about Rosebery: 'He could cast a chill over all, and did not hesitate to freeze and snub.'[104] There is also a reflection of Rosebery's own obsession with solitude in this sentence on Pitt's later years: 'Always secluded, he had become almost inaccessible.' Above all, when Rosebery wrote of Pitt as a mass of contradictions, it was almost as though he was admitting that he himself could be regarded in the same light. It was a mistake, he argued, to look on 'human nature as consistent and coherent. The fact is that congruity is the exception, and that time and circumstance and opportunity paint with heedless hands and garish colours on the canvas of human life.'

Pitt was published in November 1891, after a number of disputes over the final text between Morley and Rosebery who, like many authors, was aggrieved by his editor's demands for changes. 'Some of Morley's criticisms strike me as petulant . . . The condemned passages represent my honest and deliberate opinion and I cannot, I fear, suppress them,' he complained to Hamilton.[105] But once it appeared, both the book's reception and its sales were excellent. Gladstone called it 'the ablest monograph of the kind I have ever read', while Benjamin Jowett told Rosebery, 'I know of no life of an English statesman which is equal to it in justice of appreciation or in pathetic interest. It will greatly raise your reputation, not merely as a literary man, but as a politician. The sadness, the courage, the greatness, the tragedy of Pitt's life are given as they have never been before.'[106] There were only a few who were hesitant in their praise. Lord Kimberley felt that 'the style has too much straining for picturesque sayings',[107] while John Morley regarded the book as little more than 'a brilliant prize essay'. In his diary he confessed to his relief, because of Rosebery's touchiness, that his role as editor precluded him from reviewing the book himself: 'I could never have praised it up to the level of his expectations and every word of real criticism would have been treated as personal.'[108]

Three other biographies followed. The next, published in 1900, was *Napoleon: The Last Phase*, which examined Napoleon's fateful six-year-long exile on St Helena. Napoleon had always intrigued Rosebery, and he had built up an unparalleled collection of his memorabilia. But it was typical that he should have been drawn to write about the darkest, most tragic part of Napoleon's life. Like *Pitt*, the book abounded with powerful descriptions such as this, on the fallen dictator: 'One is irresistibly reminded of a caged animal, walking restlessly and aimlessly down his confined den and watching the outside world with the fierce despair of his wild eye.' Yet it enjoyed nothing like the success of *Pitt*, and was criticised for its limited scope; the *Times Literary Supplement*, for example, said that 'the fault we find with it is that it is tantalisingly short'. Equally slim was his next book, a Life of his friend Lord Randolph Churchill, which came out in 1906 and is widely regarded as the most readable of the quartet. Churchill had died in 1895 after a prolonged mental and physical decline caused by either syphilis or a brain tumour. Rosebery's best line, his reference to Churchill as 'the chief mourner at his own protracted funeral', has become part of the fabric of British political history. Again, what is interesting today is the way this biography illuminates the author's personality as much as that of his subject.

Many of the most compelling passages could apply to Rosebery just as much as to Churchill, such as this: 'he was often petulant, had something of the spoilt child about him'; or this, on Randolph's moodiness: 'His nervous system was always tense and highly strung; a condition which largely contributed to his oratorical success but which was the principal cause of his political undoing.' Of Churchill's love of racing, he wrote: 'strangely enough, for one who spent his best years on the Turf, he seems to have had no knowledge of men, no consideration for their feelings, no power of give and take' – precisely the way many of his Liberal colleagues would have described Rosebery's own failings. Similarly, there is a great deal of Rosebery in this description of Churchill's charm: 'When he felt himself completely at ease, in congenial society, his conversation was wholly delightful. He would then display his mastery of pleasant irony and banter; for with those playthings he was at his best.' Rosebery's last book, *Chatham: His Early Life and Connections*, published in 1910, was his strongest in terms of historical scholarship, for he had new research to present to the public, having been given unique access to the Pitt family papers at Dropmore and Holland House. But the originality of his material could not save Rosebery from producing by far his dullest book. This was not entirely his fault, since Chatham's early life and writings were, it turned out, almost entirely devoid of interest. Moreover it was a mistake – as Rosebery himself later conceded – to bring the book to a close just as the real drama of Chatham's political career was beginning. Nevertheless, though it lacked the glitter of the other three, it was still a well-crafted work, one described by Robertson Nicholl, influential editor of *The British Weekly*, as 'in some respects his very best production. The narrative is clear and orderly. The biographer stands over his materials, moulds them into form and guides them to their end.'[109]

Even his most severe detractors had to admit that Rosebery could be a lyrical writer. Philip Guedalla, who despised Rosebery as a politician, felt that he 'brought to the forms of historical writing an unusual talent . . . He wrote with a speaker's aptitude for compression; flitting notions were caught and pinned to the page by the sharp turn of his wit; richly allusive, vividly phrased, more than a trifle Asiatic, his prose was a full and honourable employment of ideas and language.'[110] In 1906 the *Times Literary Supplement* argued, on the publication of *Lord Randolph Churchill*, of which 'every page attracts, instructs, inspires', that if Rosebery were not involved in politics, 'we might well be tempted to think that his true vocation is in the pursuit of letters.' Yet beyond praise for his style, exactly the same criticism was levelled against Rosebery as a writer that was made of him as a politician: that he failed to make enough of his ability, that he preferred style over substance and rhetorical flourishes to hard labour, that he was a flippant aristocratic amateur rather than a serious professional. 'He could only begin Chatham and end Napoleon. He could not see it through,' wrote Lord Birkenhead. The aristocratic Scottish nationalist and writer Ruaraidh Erskine of Marr said of Rosebery in 1936: 'He wrote, as he spoke, uncommonly well: his principal fault was that in neither one field nor the other could he ever rise much above "slightness", or appear to any greater advantage than to be occasionally "suggestive" in a superficial and fleeting sort of fashion. In fine, it seems to me that even at this distance of time his whole career and performance in life, when submitted to the pressure of an impartial examination, give forth a strong aroma – exotic and, to say truth, a trifle sickly at times – of shame and dilettantism.'* In fact, when turning down the Presidency of the Royal Historical Society in 1890, Rosebery admitted that the post needed a working historian and 'anything but an amateur'.[111] His writing was also attacked for its lack of any guiding philosophy, another charge made against his politics. In an interesting essay on Rosebery as both author and statesman written in 1897 Norman Hapgood argued that

> Some of his passages reach nobility, none reaches grandeur; many are persuasive, none is compelling. What is lacking is as necessary to a philosopher or a poet as it is to a man of action. It is easiest, perhaps, to see it as a moral weakness, although it is of equal importance from the aesthetic and practical sides. It is a want of unity, of strong single feeling, of purpose. His perceptions, like his efforts, are unsustained and unrelated, lacking in concentration and therefore force. There is no single unifying conviction or conception, no faith or passion or need of accomplishment. So it is that the more serious the subject, the farther removed from the spectacular intellectual world, the nearer to reality demanding action, the less adequate is Lord Rosebery in speaking and writing.[112]

Despite being an admirer, John Buchan, that prince of Caledonian diligence, admitted that Rosebery's output amounted to 'a slender literary baggage'. There was some regret that Rosebery never brought his skill to bear on a full-length biography, especially since he was offered the opportunity to do so. At the height of his career he had the unique experience of being urged by publishers to write the official lives of both Gladstone and Disraeli. He turned the projects down because he claimed his political commitments did not leave him time. When he was approached again in the 1920s about writing a shorter Life of Disraeli, he said that he was

*Ruaraidh Erskine of Marr, *King Edward VII and Some Other Figures* (1936).

'physically incapable of anything of the kind'.[113] The reality was that although Rosebery often claimed to prefer a literary life to a political one, he did not enjoy the actual task of writing a book. Just like his oratory, he found authorship a burden rather than a pleasure. 'When one has delivered a book to the printer, does not one indeed wish to forget the incubus and nightmare?' he asked the historian Herbert Fisher just after the publication of *Chatham*.[114] This book, he told Regy Brett, had required 'many weeks of unremitting drudgery'.[115] Furthermore, he disliked the publicity and the invasion of privacy that went with being a literary figure. He refused ever to contemplate producing his memoirs, and strongly objected to publishers bringing out collections of his speeches. When the journalist Charles Geake put together a compilation of his *Appreciations and Addresses* in 1899, he refused to co-operate in any way, saying the whole project left him 'perfectly sick'.[116] Twenty years later he was a little more friendly towards John Buchan, who was editing an anthology of his non-political essays and speeches, and allowed him some access to his private records. But he still refused any involvement in the production of *Miscellanies Literary and Historical*, or indeed any royalties from the substantial sales, and even claimed never to have read the book.

As Buchan's *Miscellanies* demonstrates, Rosebery was probably at his best in the lively essay rather than the full-length book. In the shorter form, his power of concision and gift for the striking phrase were more apparent. The writer Edmund Gosse, reviewing *Miscellanies* in the *Sunday Times*, declared that 'the general impression which Lord Rosebery's style gives the reader is of a conversational charm. It never fails to be various and vivid. Not like Macaulay, who deafens the ear at last by the persistent clatter of his tongue, holding the table bored and bound by the monotonous emphasis of his method, Lord Rosebery understands every art of retaining attention by variety . . . The man who can write in this way must be a great talker. He must have no inclination to dazzle or deafen his auditors, but to hold them thrilled and charmed, to send them away with the conviction that they have been listening to the magic flute.'[117] This is exactly what so many contemporaries said of Rosebery's conversation. When in the right mood, he never failed to entertain with a scintillating flow of anecdote and epigram, all imbued with the depth of his learning and the magic of his voice. His daughter said his talk was 'like a fountain playing in sunlight'.[118] But he could also be cruel. Sir John Colville, who knew Lady Leconfield's family well, recalled that sometimes at Petworth Rosebery would 'carefully survey the assembled company with the aim of choosing the most vulnerable on whom to display his wit and exercise his powers of sarcasm.'[119] Of

'The most fascinating of our public men.' Archibald Primrose,
5th Earl of Rosebery

Rosebery caricatured as Napoleon, one of his political heroes. Drawn to men of 'strong mind and iron will', he did not always reflect those qualities in his own career

'A statesman full of possibilities' was how *Vanity Fair* described Rosebery in a profile of him in 1901

Published in *Punch* in 1904, this cartoon of Rosebery by Sir Bernard Partridge was adapted from William Hogarth's famous engraving 'Industry and Idleness'. It captures the struggle between diligence and diffidence which lay at the heart of Rosebery's political character

PRACTICE   AND   PRECEPT.

Rosebery as a child. 'He is so sensitive that a harsh word throws him into a flood of tears,' wrote his mother

The young swell as an undergraduate at Christ Church, Oxford, shortly before he was sent down. 'Lord Rosebery never learnt to obey,' argued the historian A.G. Gardiner

Rosebery's mother, Lady Wilhelmina, a great beauty in her youth. Her relationship with her eldest son was marked by coldness and indifference

Rosebery in the USA in 1873, where he won 'diamond opinions everywhere'. He is pictured with his two fellow members of the 'Mendacious Club', the political lobbyist Sam Ward and the journalist William H. Hulbert

Above left: Peggy, whose wedding to the Marquess of Crewe in 1899 brought central London to a standstill, such was her father's popularity

Above right: Sybil. Even more eccentric than her father, she spent much of her time living in a caravan

Left: Rosebery with his sons Harry and Neil, who was very much his favourite. 'They were more like brothers in their easy and affectionate intimacy than like father and son,' wrote Lord Birkenhead

Dalmeny, built by Rosebery's grandfather the 4th Earl, and the Rosebery family home to this day

The ancient castle of Barnbougle in the grounds of Dalmeny had almost collapsed into the sea by the time Rosebery inherited the estate. After restoration, it became his private sanctuary

Opposite page, above: Mentmore in Buckinghamshire, designed by Joseph Paxton, architect of the Crystal Palace. 'A riot of beauty and richness,' said Rosebery's daughter Peggy

Left: Rosebery's wife Hannah, the only child of Baron Meyer de Rothschild and one of the wealthiest women in England. 'Large, coarse, Hebrew-looking, with hair of no particular colour and personally unattractive,' thought the American novelist Henry James. But Rosebery was devoted to her

Below: Rosebery and Hannah, with William and a rather pained Mrs Gladstone, during the first Midlothian campaign of 1879. Rosebery, still in his early thirties, was the architect of this remarkable triumph

Right: Ladas II, Rosebery's horse which won the Derby in 1894. Rosebery was one of the dominant figures on the turf for almost forty years

Below: The Durdans, Rosebery's Epsom home, purchased in 1874. Full of horse-racing associations, it was his 'beloved nest'

Left: Rosebery entering the chamber of the London County Council. He surprised many of his critics with his dedication to municipal government

Below: The new Prime Minister at the first meeting of his Cabinet in March 1894, casting a rather anxious glance at the overbearing Sir William Harcourt, his Chancellor of the Exchequer

his gift for dishing out verbal humiliations Margot Asquith wrote in the second volume of her memoirs: 'His enjoyment at making butts of his family and his guests – an enjoyment not always shared by the latter – made one uncomfortable and though I always found Lord Rosebery a fascinating, stimulating and flattering companion, I observed that oftener than not, other people found him an embarrassing one. It was not only his brilliant chaff, and ready rapier-play, but in certain humours he appeared purposely to make his hearers ill at ease.'

Besides his books, essays and conversation, Rosebery left his mark on the literary world in another way. As well-known figures in society, he and his wife may have been the inspiration for certain fictional characters; Mrs Humphrey Ward's *Marcella*, for instance, was said to be based on Hannah, while Rosebery appeared as Lord Appin in Buchan's *A Lodge in the Wilderness*. Recently a not implausible case has also been made that Rosebery was the model for the 'clean-shaven, dark-haired' Sir Robert Chiltern in Oscar Wilde's *An Ideal Husband*. But perhaps the most intriguing fictional link is between Rosebery and *The Hound of the Baskervilles* by Sir Arthur Conan Doyle, who was a friend and occasional travelling companion of Rosebery. There was an old legend in the Primrose family that if any tragedy was coming to the laird, an unseen hound would be heard baying from the shoreline near Barnbougle. It was said locally that on the night Hannah died, a mournful bark echoed through the November night. Knowing Conan Doyle's fascination with the supernatural, Rosebery probably told him the myth of the Barnbougle hound, thereby providing the original inspiration for the most famous of all Sherlock Holmes's stories, though the details and the background to the tale – such as the chilling Dartmoor setting – were the work of Doyle's friend Fletcher Robinson. In support of this thesis there is a letter from Conan Doyle to Rosebery, dated 22nd March 1902, which reads: 'I am so glad the hound amused you. It is its best justification.'[120]

Rosebery himself makes the most fleeting of appearances in H. G. Wells's *The Time Machine*. One of the first questions put by the sceptical newspaper editor to the Time Traveller is 'These chaps here say you have been travelling into the middle of next week! Tell us all about little Rosebery, will you?'

It was a question that many real editors – and Wells himself – would be asking a lot over the coming decades.

8

'It is pretty Fanny's way'

———

$\mathbf{A}$T THE BEGINNING of the 1890s Rosebery's political position appeared to be stronger than ever. Right across the Liberal party and in progressive circles he was seen as the Prime Minister of the future. In her diary for December 1890 Beatrice Potter, soon to marry the Fabian activist Sidney Webb, assessed the leading Liberal politicians, calling Gladstone 'senile', Morley 'a moral preacher' and Harcourt 'a windbag and weathercock' before concluding that 'Rosebery is the best of the lot'. She felt, however, that there might be an element of cynicism about his radical stance. 'He looks at political opinions with the shrewd suspicions of a Scotch trader: which set of views will find the best market or prove ultimately the most sought after.'[1] In the same year John Morley, Gladstone's most devoted disciple, told Rosebery that he was the only possible successor to the Grand Old Man. In a confidential letter he explained that his 'ideal' would be Rosebery as Prime Minister, with himself as Leader of the Commons. 'Things being as they are, the latter half of the programme is quite impossible and the former now only attainable by irresistible acclamation' which, Morley hoped, would ensure that 'Lord Rosebery will take the post that genius, ambition, service and the fitness of things entitle him to.'[2] Rosebery was particularly influential among a group of young, intellectual and ambitious Liberal MPs led by H.H. Asquith, a tough, Yorkshire-born, Oxford-educated lawyer, Richard Haldane, a brilliant Scottish philosopher and barrister, and Sir Edward Grey, a Northumberland aristocrat who lacked the distinguished academic record of the other two but was renowned for his personal integrity. Ronald Munro-Ferguson was another member of this group, and from 1887 onwards he organised a series of dinners at Westminster so Rosebery could meet these rising Liberal politicians. In 1889 Ferguson's dinners were formalised under the auspices of the Articles Club, whose 39 members met weekly at the National Liberal Club. Though other experienced figures such as Morley and Spencer were involved in this new organisation, it was Rosebery who was the undoubted star, the man whom the young Liberals regarded as their leader. What attracted them was not just his glamorous persona but his political outlook, that enticing blend of support for imperialism abroad and progressivism at home. Like Rosebery himself, the new breed of Liberal Imperialists felt that the internationalist, libertarian shibboleths of Gladstonianism were irrelevant for the complexities of governing the British Empire or combating problems like unemployment.

The most realistic alternative to Rosebery as Gladstone's likely successor was Sir William Harcourt, who had more experience but less charm. With his blustering manner and hectoring insensitivity, he continually alienated his colleagues. A classic example of his disastrous approach was demonstrated over the Anglo-German treaty concluded in June 1890 by which the Salisbury Government agreed to hand over to Germany the small North Sea island of Heligoland in return for the recognition of British territorial interests in central Africa, including a protectorate in Zanzibar. On grounds of both continuity and imperialism Rosebery was strongly in favour of this agreement, but in his usual bull-headed way Harcourt had developed a misconception that the Earl wished to make trouble over Salisbury's policy. Demanding an urgent meeting of the shadow Cabinet to settle the Liberal line, he raged to Gladstone, 'I cannot admit the right of a single member of the Party to appear to commit us at this critical moment to an opposite opinion.'[3] Rosebery, who had not uttered a single disapproving public word against the cession of Heligoland, was infuriated by Harcourt's arrogance and quite prepared to have a row with him in shadow Cabinet. At the meeting Harcourt meekly backed down, however, having realised how mistaken his assumptions had been. All he had achieved was to reinforce his reputation for impetuosity and insincerity. As Edward Hamilton put it in his diary for 27 June, 'This incident seems to show how impossible a man Harcourt is. He is jealous of R. and thought he saw a favourable opportunity of giving R. a slap in the face; and without the smallest justification, for R. had expressed no opinion on the Anglo-German agreement. Harcourt's rage was founded on what he thought R. might be going to say. Having related the facts, R. said he did not see how he was ever going to serve in a Cabinet with Harcourt without some very explicit understanding.' The absurdity of Harcourt's stance was further demonstrated in July when the agreement was debated in the House of Lords, and Rosebery expressed his full support for Salisbury: 'For my part, I shall offer no opposition. I for one will never be party to dragging the foreign policy of this country into the arena of party warfare.'[4]

By this time Salisbury's second premiership had already lasted four years, a remarkable achievement in view of the fragility of the Unionist alliance, the refusal of Chamberlain and Hartington to serve, and the explosive departure of Lord Randolph Churchill, an event which many, including Rosebery, predicted would lead to Salisbury's downfall. But the Tory Prime Minister was also helped by the serious problems bedevilling the Liberal party, which was, in Professor John Vincent's phrase, little more than 'a miscellany of vaguely humanitarian enthusiasms'. Like the Labour party in the 1980s, the Liberals towards the end of the Victorian age were riddled with pressure groups and competing factions, leading to perpetual conflict. Perhaps the most obvious ideological clash was between Liberal capitalist employers, who strongly opposed state intervention, and the growing number of trade union representatives. Divisions could also be seen between Liberal Imperialists and 'Little Englanders', between Anglicans and nonconformists, between radical extremists and moderate realists. In addition, a host of single-issue fanatics – temperance campaigners, municipal socialists, Welsh devolutionists, proponents of Scottish Church disestablishment, House of Lords abolitionists, and education reformers – demanded that their own causes be given the first priority on the Liberal agenda. 'There is something unnatural, uncanny and unwholesome in the condition of our party,' Rosebery told Regy Brett at this period.[5] The spirit of sectionalism led to the National Liberal Federation, at its conference in Newcastle in October 1891, adopting a large rag-bag of radical proposals which became known as 'the Newcastle Programme' and was cynically designed to appeal to as many different groups as possible. Like most senior Liberal politicians, Rosebery disliked the idea of comprehensive programmes because they gave too much influence to the activists and fettered any future government. 'It is a programme which begins by offering everything to everybody and it will end by giving nothing to nobody,' he said.[6]

It is one of the paradoxes of late nineteenth-century Liberalism that the only two issues that united the party, Irish Home Rule and reverence for Gladstone's leadership, were also the source of its greatest weaknesses. Gladstone's name could still inspire supporters throughout the country, yet by the end of 1890 he was 81, an increasingly decrepit figure, plagued by deafness and failing eyesight. The flames of his great oratory were burning to a low flicker; his ability to manage his fractious colleagues had all but disappeared. The fact that he was willing to give his blessing to the gallimaufry of the Newcastle Programme showed how weary he had become. The Liberal party was, in effect, led by a totem. As the evening descended on his career, his one obsession, compelling him to clutch ever more feebly at the reins of power, remained his mission to give Ireland self-government. And though Home Rule may have been a noble quest it was politically disastrous for the Liberals, since it not only led to the breakaway of the Unionists but was also profoundly unpopular with the British electorate, who saw it as a threat to the Empire and to security. In the two decades after the Liberals' adoption of the policy they were in office for only three years. To his fellow Liberals, Rosebery initially argued that Home Rule was 'a great cause to arouse us and unite us',[7] but he later came to see that a terrible price had been paid for this unity. The Irish difficulty was made all the worse in 1890 by the destruction of Parnell, when the husband of his long-standing mistress Kitty O'Shea sued for divorce on the grounds of adultery. The scandal finished Parnell, who died an isolated and exhausted man in October 1891. Just as damagingly, it split the Nationalist party, severely tainted the Irish–Liberal alliance, and undermined nonconformist support for Home Rule.

According to Hamilton, Gladstone took Parnell's disgrace 'much to heart. He feels that he has been betrayed by a man for whom he always had a liking and indeed too fond a regard.'[8] Rosebery himself was indifferent to the Irish leader's fate, Hannah having died in the very week that the O'Shea divorce trial began. Indeed, as he went into his self-imposed exile from public life in the wake of his personal tragedy, he appeared entirely indifferent to the Liberal party. 'I am so constituted that I must chew my bitter cud in solitude,' ran one letter to Harcourt in March 1891. 'I am completely withdrawn from all politics and must necessarily remain so for the present at least,' he said in another two months later.[9] But this retirement far outlasted the conventional period of mourning, and Liberal chiefs, including Gladstone and Morley, were worried by his protracted grief. Gladstone's view was that Rosebery had 'great qualifications for the future but he was oversensitive and his over-sensitiveness might seriously interfere with his usefulness', while Morley considered that 'his shutting himself up so completely and thus avoiding all political duties rather lowered Rosebery in his estimation'.[10] In October 1891 Rosebery set out in a private paper his reasons for remaining in privacy:

1   The sole object of my ambition that I am conscious of has disappeared with the death of my wife;
2   My children and my property require most constant and careful supervision;
3   I have lost all interest in politics. Can they be sufficiently cooked up artificially to enable a man to work at them with the reserve of impetus and nerve power that they require? I doubt it;

4 I have long been conscious that as a platform speaker I am a failure. With
   no heart in the business I should get even worse;
5 Each year I hate the atmosphere of the Lords more and more.[11]

By the spring of the following year Rosebery was showing no more
sign of wanting to be involved, much to the despair of friends and party
organisers. 'The more I think of it,' wrote Hamilton on 1 March 1892,
'the more I am convinced that what you want now, more than ever, is a
distraction from private cares and worries. Occupation of your mind with
public affairs can alone afford this distraction. It won't do for you now to
look to retirement which would only aggravate your present distressed
condition of mind as well as cause the bitterest disappointment to your
friends as well as the country at large.'[12] Knowing how essential was
Rosbery's prestige to the success of the Liberal party, Arnold Morley, the
Chief Whip, told him in March that it was his personal duty to return: 'I
do not think you have the right to stand aside when the final struggle
comes. Those who have been your colleagues and who have borne the
burden of the contest have the right to expect you to stand by them. You
occupy an exceptional position and, if you will allow me to say so, your
friends are better judges than you can be of your fitness for various duties
which public life imposes upon you. As a party we owe you much but the
debt is not all on one side.'[13]

As usual, however, there was no consistency in Rosebery's attitude.
Despite his avowed determination to withdraw from public life, he was as
active as ever on the London County Council, winning the seat of East
Finsbury as a Progressive party candidate in the elections of March 1892.★
The contrast between his attitude towards local politics and national baffled
those who thought he should be aiming for the highest office rather than
joining a caucus of municipal left-wingers. Regy Brett sent several letters
begging him not to stand. 'Your success on the LCC was absolute and
unquestioned. Why jeopardize it by putting yourself in a position of
extreme difficulty?' he asked in one.[14] Rosebery took no notice of this
advice and won the seat easily in the teeth of forebodings that he would
face a struggle. Yet even as he resumed his duties in Spring Gardens – and
agreed to take the LCC chairmanship again for a month – he was telling
Liberal colleagues that he had 'made up his mind to give up public life'.
He went so far as to inform Arnold Morley that, whatever the outcome of
the next General Election, likely to be held in the summer of 1892, the

★The main thoroughfare in Finsbury, Rosebery Avenue, the home of Sadler's Wells
Theatre, bears the name of the old borough's most distinguished municipal representative.

Liberal party 'must not reckon on me any longer. I can stand aside or retire without remark or without the reproach of desertion.'[15]

These reiterated threats of retirement were not taken too seriously, particularly because in the late spring Rosebery made a number of barnstorming political speeches across the country, in Edinburgh, Birmingham and London. His central theme was the justice of the case for Home Rule, and his fiercely partisan attacks on the Unionists thrilled Liberal supporters. The Queen, however, was appalled. After his Birmingham address she said to her secretary Sir Henry Ponsonby that 'she was dreadfully disappointed and shocked at Lord Rosebery's speech, which is radical to such a degree as to be almost communistic. Hitherto he always said he had nothing whatever to do with Home Rule and only with Foreign Affairs and *now* he is as violent as anyone. Poor Lady Rosebery is not there to keep him back. Sir Henry must try and get at him through someone, so that he may know how grieved and shocked The Queen is at what he said.' The Queen then revealed that, before these radical outbursts, she had been contemplating sending for Rosebery, rather than Gladstone, if the Liberals returned to office. 'In the case of the Government's defeat, the Queen meant to send for him first, but after the violent attack on Lord Salisbury and this attempt to stir up Ireland, it will be IMPOSSIBLE; and the GOM at 82 is a very alarming lookout.'[16]

For all its fiery brilliance, Rosebery's platform oratory only reinforced the exasperation he provoked with his vacillations over his role. 'How tiresome all this sort of thing is,' Morley told Harcourt, who swiftly replied, 'It is pretty Fanny's way and we have survived a good deal of it for many years.'[17] Edward Hamilton was certain that Rosebery, for all his protestations, would eventually accept a full return to office. 'He is rather like the proverbial coy maiden who "first she would, and then she wouldn't." I have come to the conclusion that it is best not to urge him to do this and that, but to leave him alone. In the long run, he does the right thing, though he loves to do it mysteriously.'[18] This was not the way Rosebery saw it. By May he had worked out in his mind a logically coherent position whereby, out of a spirit of loyalty, he would assist Gladstone and the Liberal party up to the General Election. Once the contest was over he would retire from politics to be with his books and his children, his bereavement having left him, he considered, unfit to be a cabinet minister. But others viewed Rosebery as irresponsible and incomprehensible. He was either in public life, or he was not. To go on the stump while privately refusing to serve amounted to a deception of the public, they argued, especially of those Liberal voters who might be drawn to the party precisely because of

Rosebery's charisma. And it would be unfair to desert his followers who looked to him as their future leader, as well as a betrayal of Gladstone. On 24 June Gladstone himself described Rosebery's doubts as 'ludicrous', adding that 'he had committed himself too far; he could not now draw back'.[19] But Gladstone did not want it thought that Rosebery was the only possible Foreign Secretary, and argued that in the event of his refusal Morley could fill the post perfectly well. When Gladstone put this to Morley, 'I observed with a hearty laugh that if Rosebery heard this, it would be sure to help him make up his mind.'[20]

At the end of June 1892 Parliament was prorogued and Gladstone, with his wife, went up to Dalmeny for his last Midlothian crusade. Both politically and personally, it was by far the most disappointing of his campaigns. Liberal hopes of a large majority in the country, possibly in excess of 100, soon began to evaporate as the hustings demonstrated little public enthusiasm for the party. In Midlothian itself there was an obvious decline in Gladstone's popularity. All the excitement of the past, the torchlight parades and teeming crowds, had disappeared, while Gladstone was a shadow of his former self, his voice and energy fading badly on the platform. The permanent heavy drizzle hanging over Scotland throughout his visit was an appropriate symbol of the darkness that enveloped the campaign. His poor eyesight – exacerbated by a serious injury he had received in Chester, when a protestor threw a rock-hard gingerbread biscuit at him – meant that in private at Dalmeny he had to wear a pair of thick, black goggles, giving him the appearance of a pantomime grotesque. In his diary entry for 6 July Rosebery revealed the sad state of the Grand Old Man: 'Mr Gladstone was very much upset this morning. His large majority has disappeared, his eye troubles him and his last familiar tooth has come out.'

Rosebery's morose political isolation only compounded Gladstone's electoral, ocular and dental problems. Throughout the visit he was in his most forbidding mood, insisting he would not take a place in the next Liberal Government. 'Mr Gladstone was depressed and feeble, saying he supposed I had no comforting consideration to offer him, which indeed I had not,' Rosebery recorded on 8 July.[21] The social awkwardness which had long existed between Rosebery and the Gladstones once more intensified. Rosebery wrote to Edward Hamilton on 10 July, 'I cannot tell you what a week I have had since last Saturday and I have three more days of it',[22] prompting Hamilton to note: 'It is evident that Mr and Mrs Gladstone have got on his nerves, which are not in the best of conditions, and they have been apparently more than tactless.' In another diary entry Hamilton observed that 'it was extraordinary the want of nous which Mr G. showed about R.' Gladstone, in his turn, believed that Rosebery was deliberately snubbing him. As so often in times of stress, Rosebery retreated to his bed at one point, complaining of a heavy cold. And he was his usual contradictory self in his attitude to negotiating with Gladstone. On the one hand he tried to avoid discussions with the GOM for fear he might compromise himself with regard to his future, yet on the other he simmered with resentment at being ignored. 'I am never consulted in these matters but always expected to pay the bill,' he told Loulou Harcourt.[23] When Morley visited Dalmeny for the campaign at the beginning of July he was greeted by Gladstone's friend the historian Lord Acton, who 'described the state of things as electric between my host and his illustrious guest. Mr Gladstone had been there for a week and they had not exchanged a word on politics.'[24] Morley's diary provides a wonderful glimpse into the faintly surreal atmosphere of Dalmeny at this time, as the following selections show:

> Mr Gladstone and I were having another talk in the library when who should enter but Rosebery; he retired with something as much like confusion as is possible. (It is only his manner that is confused. His interior is always boiling and fermenting, I am sure.) . . .
>
> I came upon Rosebery and I took him by the arm and said, 'I came here expecting to have pleasant talks *a trios*. I find you holding icily aloof. I wish I had never come.' . . .
>
> After dinner, Rosebery and I went to the sitting room and had a long talk as to his going to the Foreign Office. He was very obstinate on the grounds of his children, his affairs, etc. I did not feel that I had made much impression any more than I had fathomed the true reasons for his obstinacy. But he won't be able to stand out. I feel that a big majority would make the difference. Yet he is not all calculation for he has gallantry in him. He is a riddle, as if the riddle were rare in human nature.[25]

As the election results came in the atmosphere at Dalmeny only worsened, as Gladstone's secretary Algernon West – another visitor to the house – noted on 5 July: 'There was an indescribable cloud over the whole thing . . . in the evening the election telegrams kept pouring in, not so satisfactory as we had hoped – Rosebery always laying a strong emphasis on "your" victory or "your defeat", and said he meant it, as it did not interest or affect him in the slightest degree.'[26] Morley, who bravely returned for a second visit from 12 July, was even more disturbed by what he then found, 'a black pall of physical decline hanging over all, slowly immersing the scene and its great actor'. Morley's diary continued, 'My host could not contain his weariness. They had passed a horrid week of rejection and dismay, the telegrams of the polls coming to the house all day long and smashing the illusions of many months; Mr Gladstone, in his dark goggle glasses, slightly mad, rambling about the Scotch church. I laugh at it today, but at the moment, like Rosebery, I felt something horrible and gruesome about it.'[27]

Less than two years after Hannah's death, Rosebery's non-cooperation was certainly motivated by genuine anxiety about returning to office. But in the maelstrom of his emotions there were also more Machiavellian forces at work. Despite all his hesitations he remained a singularly ambitious man, preoccupied by his own reputation and dignity. Believing that Gladstone's next administration was doomed to embarrassing failure, part of him felt that he could only be damaged by association with it. Such thinking was apparent in a conversation he had with Algernon West at Dalmeny. 'Rosebery proposed a drive, taking me to his castle of Barnbougle, a very sacred spot where nobody went. He for the first time talked politics, and declared his determination to leave them. Mr Gladstone's age made the whole prospect a terrible tragedy and he did not want to take any part of it.' This was also the impression gained by Gladstone's confidant, Lord Rendel, as he recorded in his memoirs: 'Rosebery's whole attitude and conduct at that time had been most mysterious and painfully embarrassing. He seemed torn between personal loyalty and political disaffection. I presume he was embarrassed to the last degree between his desire to retain his supposed place in Mr Gladstone's political will and his dread of committing himself more deeply to Mr Gladstone's political creed.'[28]

Another consideration may have been that, by forcing the party to plead so earnestly with him, he was seeking to prove his indispensability not only as Foreign Secretary but as a future leader. In the papers of George Murray, another of Gladstone's officials, there is an interesting letter from Lord Acton which hints that Rosebery was more calculating than he often pretended. One of Acton's stratagems for trying to entice Rosebery was to combine the Foreign Office with the Liberal Leadership of the House of Lords, currently held by Lord Kimberley, with the implication that leadership of the party would follow. Gladstone acted on this suggestion, but did so in such a convoluted fashion that Rosebery was unclear whether he had actually been offered the Lords' leadership or not. In one of their few talks at Dalmeny, Gladstone merely declared that Rosebery would be 'the fittest person' to lead the party in the Lords. Already in turmoil about holding any public office, Rosebery was reluctant to seek clarification, and the question was dropped. But while Kimberley remained in post the issue obviously preyed on Rosebery's mind. In December 1892 Acton gave

Murray this account of a meeting in July at Dalmeny and a subsequent one at The Durdans a month later.

> At Dalmeny, it was my end to secure Rosebery at any price. So I advised that the Leadership should be offered in addition to the Foreign Office. I said that it involved the *jus successionis*. I could not tell Mr Gladstone that Rosebery *was playing to supplant, not to succeed him.*★ . . . In the very awkward negotiations that followed early in August, the offer was not withdrawn but not definitely accepted. When all was settled (i.e., Gladstone's Cabinet-making), Rosebery contrived rather ostensibly to be alone with me and asked what I thought about the leadership. I replied that he was supposed to have difficulty in speaking without preparation (long words for saying he was not a good debater). He answered most eagerly and strenuously, as one offended, Not at all! That is quite a mistake, etc! Ho! Ho! I said to this, then the thing is settled, meaning that his sensitiveness implied that the question is settled in his own mind. He did not commit himself further.[29]

Rosebery always denied that Gladstone had made any clear offer of the Lords' leadership with a view to the ultimate succession. In 22 July 1892 he informed Acton that he had avoided talking to Gladstone too exclusively about his own future: 'In my own house, I could not discuss a topic that I fear would only be painful to him.'[30]

Rosebery had become so pessimistic about the General Election that he actually feared Gladstone might lose his Midlothian seat. With the local Liberal party in disarray, no canvassing was carried out – a far cry from the meticulous party polling of 1879. Rosebery's forecast was not realised, but Gladstone's majority did fall dramatically from 4631 to 690. Overall, the Liberals' hopes of an outright majority were crushed. Having gained 273 seats to the Unionists' 315, they had to rely on the votes of 81 Irish nationalists to come back into power. Nevertheless, after Salisbury's resignation the Queen accepted that she would have to send for Gladstone, though she said she would have preferred Rosebery to having 'that dangerous old fanatic thrust down her throat'.[31] The one hope she clung to was that Rosebery would be her Foreign Secretary, to maintain continuity in foreign affairs and safeguard the Empire. On 19 July Ponsonby told Edward Hamilton that the Queen 'counted confidently on R. giving her his services as Foreign Secretary and indeed that She would make his acceptance of office a condition with Mr G. as she practically did in 1886. R. could hardly decline such a command and if there be vanity at the bottom of it, his vanity would be flattered.'[32]

★My italics: LM.

The Queen even thought of sending directly for Rosebery to urge him to take the post, a dangerously unconstitutional course from which she was dissuaded by Ponsonby, though she reserved the right to communicate her wishes to him by letter. Hamilton relayed to Rosebery the substance of his talk with Ponsonby: 'The Queen is prepared to submit to her fate but it will be, I feel pretty sure, that the submission will be accompanied with one special stipulation – and that is not difficult to guess – a stipulation that you should be Foreign Secretary . . . I am sure she will take steps to communicate. It is clear that you are the man on whom she proposes to lean and to whom she wishes to turn, notwithstanding that two of your speeches come a little extreme for her.'[33] In a later conversation with Hamilton, Morley declared it would be an outrage if Rosebery only took office at the request of the Queen: 'R. would be able to figure as a sort of special nominee of the sovereign and that he would not only feel himself indispensable but his indispensability would be proclaimed in the most singular manner. I blazed forth at these ridiculous pretensions, "What R. won't do from duty he will do from vanity. Loyalty to his friends and party chief count for nothing; loyalty to the Crown for everything." '[34]

After the chaotic Midlothian campaign, while Gladstone was locked into pivotal negotiations about his Government, Rosebery had sulkily headed off from Dalmeny to go yachting around Scotland, ignoring all pleas to go to London to assist the Liberal leader in his task. He admitted to Hamilton that he was trying to escape the crisis he had long dreaded: 'Yachting is the most immoral life in the world. One divests oneself as far as possible in this world of all human responsibility. And neither post nor press can reach you except at your leisure.'[35] As Rosebery sailed around the coast, the frustration of his colleagues mounted. 'Pray think of us and come and help us,' begged Spencer, that emollient Northamptonshire peer known as the 'Red Earl' because of the colour of his beard rather than his politics. Harcourt sent two letters and a telegram urging Rosebery to join their consultations: 'I greatly mistake your character if you should be unwilling to give us your aid and counsel and support in this critical juncture,' read his letter of 1 August.[36] Ronald Munro-Ferguson told Rosebery in the starkest terms that he had no alternative to acceptance: 'I honestly believe in the Liberal Party going, as a whole, to the devil before very long if you leave it. Mr Gladstone's government cannot stand without you. You would be the only man who could give confidence abroad . . . the thing is impossible. You can't live to be out of affairs. If you are in affairs, you must control them.'[37] Kimberley was just as disconcerted at the thought of trying to proceed without Rosebery. 'We should be terribly weakened by losing Rosebery, not only because he is by far the most acceptable man for the Foreign Office but because next to Gladstone he is much the most influential man in the country of our party,' he confessed in his journal.[38]

Rosebery returned to Dalmeny on 2 August but still refused to go to London. By now the Gladstones were furious with him, Mrs Gladstone saying she would 'like to give him a piece of my mind'. Her husband was equally indignant. When Morley visited him on 29 July, Gladstone described Rosebery's conduct at Dalmeny as 'most condemnable. When I approached him about politics he took up a position which was not intelligible and was assuredly not justifiable.' Three days later, Gladstone's temper was just as hot: 'I have never before been treated as I am being treated now. It has been reserved for my 83rd year to suffer such conduct.' Morley fully shared Gladstone's anger: 'Whether from the point of view of private friendship or public duty, I cannot conceive of anything shabbier, meaner or more grossly selfish than this abandonment of the heroic old man in the midst of all his sore difficulties. If Rosebery ever rises to be a historic character, history ought to punish him sharply for this petty conduct. It stamps him.'

The bombardment of letters from London failed to shift Rosebery from his Edinburgh redoubt. To Lord Spencer he said on 3 August that 'I have never wavered in the resolve that so far as my own will can avail, my political career should end with the General Election.'[39] Harcourt received a similar message: 'The eighteen months I have spent in seclusion have convinced me that I was not intended or fitted for a political life; all my interest is now divorced from it.'[40] To Morley he telegraphed baldly 'Am much better away', at which Morley muttered, 'Yes, better for himself. Was ever conduct so odious?' But by far the most important missive was the one he sent to Gladstone, written on board his yacht on 31 July but not delivered until 3 August. It read:

> For more than a year past – during the whole period that I have spent in retirement – my constant preoccupation has been to extricate myself forever from politics. For public life I have ceased to feel either taste or aptitude and my passionate wish is to retire into private life and the most private. To this I am urged indeed by considerations connected with my family and fortune with which it is needless to trouble you. Twice during this period I have left my seclusion. Once was to assist the Liberals on the County Council of London who seemed to need all assistance at their General Election; and once, more recently, to take part in the Parliamentary General Election so that it should not be said that I held aloof from differences of opinion. With these elections I look and have long looked to close my account. Indeed,

were it otherwise I should be re-entering a bondage I detest with little hope of escape. Now there is a substantial Liberal majority and at such a moment one can disappear without being missed.

He added that Kimberley would make 'an admirable Foreign Secretary'.[41]

The *Spectator* once argued that 'Lord Rosebery should be described as a great political melodrama rather than as a statesman'. The truth of that comment was never more apparent than in the summer of 1892 when Rosebery managed to build a turbulent crisis around himself, even when he was off-stage, dragging in the Royal family and most of his own party. It is an indication of his importance to the Liberal cause that no one, not even Sir William Harcourt, could contemplate forming a government without him at its centre. His absence would put the entire project in jeopardy. That is why his letter to Gladstone caused such consternation, arriving like a death notice in a squabbling family. Gladstone himself, according to Morley, was 'broken', for 'this bombshell was almost as much a catastrophe as the Parnell affair'.[42] The reaction of Edward Hamilton was typical: 'I never felt more utterly concerned and dismayed. It is a death-blow to Mr G's Government before it is formed; it will cut Mr G. to the quick; it will produce a scare not only in this country but (it is not too much to say) in Europe at large; it is the absolute wrecking of a brilliant career; it is an act of suicide that will baffle all explanation; electors may justly complain that they have been deluded and befooled – they voted under the conviction that Foreign Affairs would be safe in R's hands.'[43]

Yet even in this darkest hour the leading Liberals would not accept Rosebery's refusal as absolute and final. A series of urgent meetings was held on the evening of 4 August at Spencer House, the House of Commons and the United Services Club during which it was decided that Gladstone should write a personal appeal to Rosebery, the letter to be delivered by hand by one of their number travelling overnight to Scotland. Loulou Harcourt, caught up in the excitement of the event, offered himself, but it was thought he was not senior enough, so it was agreed that Morley should make the trip. Fatigued and rheumy-eyed, Gladstone did not realise the personal sacrifice Morley was making, for he thought Rosebery was only at The Durdans. Hamilton, who had played a vital role in bringing together the key players on that difficult evening, thought that the right man had been chosen, partly because, if the operation reached the press, it would at least crush speculation that Morley and Sir William Harcourt were intriguing to keep Rosebery out of the Government. More importantly, he believed that Morley was the most persuasive of the group. 'He understands R. and I have great faith in his diplomatic powers,' he wrote.[44] Morley was indeed well suited for the mission because although his Liberal politics were the opposite of Rosebery's and he was from a completely different background, he was close to him temperamentally. Born in Blackburn, the son of an Anglican surgeon, he had intended to go into the Church but suffered a crisis of conscience and, having been cut off by his disappointed father without a penny, had made his living in journalism before entering politics, where he pursued a brand of radicalism that comprised suspicion of Empire and worship of Ireland. But like Rosebery he was both exceptionally bright and extremely thin-skinned. His sensitivity led the Irish nationalist T.M. Healey to nickname him 'The Grand Old Maid', while Harold Laski later described him as having 'basically a feminine mind with the difficult vanity of a brilliant woman.' Like Rosebery, he could be hopelessly contradictory; having spent a lifetime campaigning against the Empire, he took the post of Secretary of State for India in the Liberal Government of 1905; nor did his opposition to the House of Lords stop him accepting a peerage. And like Rosebery, he experienced a constant tension between his literary and his political lives; rare was the year that passed without him threatening to leave office to return to his books. These similarities gave Morley a unique psychological insight into Rosebery's personality. Some of his writing, in which he addressed the problems of a solitary, literary life, was directly applicable to Rosebery. In his book about Rousseau of 1873, for example, he had written of 'the egoistic character that loves to brood and hates to act'.[45]

Morley was in the heart of the action now, attempting to save Gladstone's government. Just after he had finished dinner on the night of 4 August, a messenger arrived from Carlton Gardens with the vital letter from Gladstone and another from Gladstone's wife. Morley then sent a telegram to Dalmeny to warn Rosebery that he would be arriving the following morning. At 10 o'clock he set off for King's Cross to catch the 10.40 train to Edinburgh. Just as he was settling into his compartment for the long journey Loulou Harcourt appeared, flustered and breathless, carrying some notes from his father for arguments to be used on Rosebery. Eager to heighten the clandestine drama of the mission, Loulou also gave Morley a simple cypher telegram code by which he could secretly transmit news from Dalmeny, with the names Tom, Dick and Harry substituted for Gladstone, Rosebery and Harcourt. 'J.M. is very sick at the prospect of his mission and does not expect to be successful but I don't see how Rosebery can refuse to come up and *see* Mr Gladstone at any rate and if he does come half the battle is won,' wrote Loulou optimistically on his return from King's Cross that night. Morley's opinion of Rosebery was equivocal.

Always drawn to charismatic figures, he admired Rosebery's popular touch and dashing platform skill, two qualities he himself lacked. But Morley could be deceitful. Having told Rosebery in 1890 that he would be his 'ideal' as Prime Minister, he had simultaneously reached a secret agreement with Loulou Harcourt, an incorrigible conspirator on behalf of his father, that he would support Sir William for the Liberal leadership when Gladstone retired. This informal deal, known as 'the Malwood Compact' – named after Sir William's mock-Tudor country residence in the New Forest – was to bring in its train untold bitterness and accusations of betrayal over the coming years. Now, as he travelled through the night towards Scotland, Morley was preparing to ignore the implications of Malwood as he thought about his negotiating strategy to win over Rosebery.

It was a glorious morning when Morley arrived at Dalmeny station, to be met by one of Rosebery's drivers. As the carriage took him along through the wooded parkland he could see the imposing turrets of Dalmeny in the distance; Morley later confessed in his diary, 'My thoughts were collected and firm but I was full of anxiety, hoping but little from my mission and knowing well the disastrous consequences of failure, alike to Mr G., to our party and government and to R. himself.' In the hallway he was greeted by Rosebery. 'His hair was ruffled and he had a flushed confusion in his look, as if he had been up all night, but his eye turned upon me with that bright and kind flash which always wins me.' Morley gave him the Gladstones' letters, which Rosebery left unopened on a table in the hall. The pair then went out for a stroll in the gardens overlooking the Firth of Forth. Morley's account of their conversation is probably the most candid description ever recorded of Rosebery's tortured mind:

> We lost little time before, as he said, we fetched the skeleton out of the cupboard. I let him begin. With profound weariness on his brow, he said he was ashamed to tread the old ground again. Ambition was dead with him. He had sought to play his part in life because that was the only way in which he could repay his wife for all she had done for him. Now she was dead. With her, his ambition too lay buried. All this was too sacred for me to meddle with, so I listened to his grave, quiet tones in silence. Next he dwelt on the conviction which had been growing and strengthening in his mind: that he was wholly unfitted for English public life; that he should undoubtedly prove himself inefficient and disappointing. This also I left unanswered. Any response must have been banal and silly and he is not a man with whom to try a banality. It was not until he took up his third line of defence that I found anything to say. This was that his enjoyment of privacy became daily

more keen; that his life during the last year and a half had given him a perfect passion for solitude. On this I warned, 'A man must be very sure of himself before he seeks the existence of a solitary. It is well enough in the hour of fatigue and depression to find solace in drawing pictures of tranquil isolation from the common herd. But it is all delusion and dream. I have, like plenty of other people, had hours of misery which I soothed with semi-voluptuous thoughts of suicide. Your plan is one of slow suicide. Solitude is a slow poison. You would no sooner have definitely committed yourself to it than you would awake with a ruinous shock to the ghastly thing you had done. The poison would work. You are in a morbid state now. But resolute solitude would make you more and more morbid, up to the point of downright mental danger.'

After this admonition Morley passed to other objections to Rosebery's 'extraordinary course'. He accused Rosebery of 'deserting his chief in his hour of extremity', and pointed out that the press would say that Harcourt had succeeded in ousting him. Once Morley had finished the pair went inside, Morley to take a nap, Rosebery to read the Gladstones' letters. The longer one, from the Liberal leader, dismissed Rosebery's claims about his unfitness for office, which ran 'against the clear, unhesitating, unanimous judgement of friends and the no less unequivocal judgement of the world'. Gladstone further wrote that Rosebery had given him no indication during the Dalmeny visit that he would not accept the Foreign Office or the Leadership of the Lords: 'When I left in your hands provisional statements connecting your name with the Foreign Office, when I discussed with you and leant to its association with the Leadership of the Lords, without receiving any adverse sign (any more than one favourable), my impressions were such that I am now taken by surprise.' He concluded, 'I am sure I may rely upon your kindness not to send an unfavourable decision in this important matter without seeing me.'[46] Mrs Gladstone was, predictably, more emotional: 'I who know your love for my Husband, I must seek your sympathy . . . though I cannot say enough for his friends' kindness and desire to help, without flattering you, I know you're the one who would do him most good.'[47] Just as Rosebery finished reading these two letters the afternoon post brought another, from Sir Philip Currie, the Foreign Office Under-Secretary, pointing out 'how dangerous it would be to Europe if our foreign relations went to untried hands'. This letter, which could not have been written without the approval of Lord Salisbury, who remained Prime Minister until the new Parliament met, made 'a powerful impression' on Rosebery, according to Morley.

Later the two men took another walk in the park, 'for he is unable to hold important conversations sitting still in a room', wrote Morley. Rosebery then dramatically announced a change of heart: he had decided to go to Paris for two days 'to clear the cobwebs out of my brain', then he would see Gladstone. Rosebery, as Morley recorded, explained his reasons for this volte-face: 'Two things seem to me to be almost irresistible. One is the desertion of Mr G. as you call it. The other is the effect on our foreign relations and on the state of Europe. I confess I don't see how to answer two such points as these.' Morley admitted that, inwardly, 'seldom have I felt a livelier elation of spirit than when I heard this strange alteration of purpose'. As they walked further, Rosebery raised the delicate subject of the Lords' leadership, which Gladstone had so mishandled at Dalmeny. 'Such obfuscation is the curse of my illustrious chief. So twisted and veiled was the alleged offer that to all intents and purposes it might as well have never been made,' recorded Morley. Again, like Acton, Morley suggested that leadership of the Lords could open the way to a higher position, as Rosebery noted in his own diary: 'Morley said that Mr G., before talking to me about the leadership of the Lords – and as he fancies offering it to me and my accepting it – told him that he considered it carried with it the *jus successionis*, as he did not consider Harcourt could ever lead the Liberal party.'[48] That evening at dinner they drank champagne. 'We hardly had a serious word and politics ceased to exist. All was mirth and lively humour. Who could have thought how near we had been to a hurried catastrophe? I wish I could have known what thoughts were passing through his strange brain and whether he realized the narrow escape he had made. I wonder if he intended all along to come in and was acting purely out of petulance and pique rather than real resolve. Does he feel a sting of remorse at all the pain into which he has plunged us for all these days? He never said so.'

That night, 5 August, Rosebery and Morley took the train south to London. Just before they left Waverley Morley sent a telegram to Sir William Harcourt: 'a great step gained and things may turn out right'. On their arrival at King's Cross they parted with 'a long, firm clasp of the hand',[49] then Rosebery went off to Victoria to catch the morning mail to Paris while Morley travelled to the Harcourts' London home to give a full report of his visit. 'I have brought the bird with me and Rosebery in all probability will now join,' he declared.[50] When Loulou saw Lord Spencer the Red Earl expressed both his relief at the news and his annoyance with Rosebery for 'having given us so many bad quarters of an hour'. Spencer had also just seen Ponsonby, who said that the Queen, though she was 'most anxious' that Rosebery should be in the government, had decided she could do nothing 'as it might seem like an interference with Gladstone's discretion over his choice of colleagues'.[51] Gladstone later suggested to Rosebery that the Queen's reluctance to intervene might have been driven by less honourable motives: 'She thought this affair seemed loosely hung together and hoped it might fall through.'[52]

But the Liberal High Command should have known better than to place too much confidence in Rosebery's apparent acquiescence. The most volatile temperament in British politics was never going to make their lives that easy. Rosebery returned on 10 August from Paris, where all his old doubts had returned. That evening he saw Lord Spencer, who described him 'as rather agitated, walking incessantly up and down the room, with a flushed face and eye. He did not seem like joining.'[53] Rosebery was due to see Gladstone on the afternoon of the 11th, a meeting he approached with a mounting sense of dread. Hamilton called at 38 Berkeley Square early on the morning of the 11th, and found Rosebery 'more and more convinced that he was unsuited for public life'. They talked about the Queen's wish to have him in government, at which Rosebery said he was pleased she had not communicated with him, for 'had she done so, she could not have more effectually done me a bad turn in the event of my wishing to resume public life as I should have been considered the Queen's minion, which would have been fatal to me.' But Hamilton was not completely down-hearted. 'Being accustomed to the liking he has of leading even his most intimate friends off the scent, I parted with him under the belief that when he saw Mr G. he would consent to take the plunge.'[54] Hamilton was mis-taken. Rosebery saw Gladstone at two o'clock at Carlton Gardens and during an awkward, brief conversation explained that 'his loathing of pol-itics' was greater than ever. According to his own account, Rosebery told Gladstone: 'Perhaps it was my nervous system that had sustained a greater shock in 1890 than I was then conscious of but there it was and he could not understand it. He said with great vehemence that he did, that for years past he had abhorred and loathed the contentious side of politics.' Rosebery then referred to his 'orphan children', but again Gladstone countered this and 'implored me for the sake of my children and my pos-terity not to take such a course'. Finally, 'after about a quarter of an hour I rose to go. I stood in front of him as he sat on the sofa. He clasped my hand in his and said, with the most pathetic violence, "God Almighty in his infinite mercy and goodness guide you to the right decision", repeat-ing this two or three times with the greatest solemnity.'[55] Afterwards, Gladstone confessed that he had found the interview 'very trying and rather sad'.[56]

The saga was now heading towards its climax. Rather than resign immediately after the election, Salisbury had decided to wait for the return of Parliament. Although the Tories were in a minority, he felt that the cohesion of the Liberal–Irish coalition should be put to an immediate test at Westminster. On the very day of Gladstone's painful talk with Rosebery, a vote of confidence in the Government was held in the House of Commons. In the biggest division to date in the history of the House – all but three MPs voted – the Unionists were defeated by 40 votes. On 13 August, after accepting Salisbury's resignation 'with much regret', the Queen asked Gladstone to form his fourth Government, though she admitted to the Marquess of Lansdowne that she 'hated to entrust the Empire to the shaking hand of an old, wild, incomprehensible man of 82'.[57]

But Rosebery remained the stumbling-block on the path back to office, so the pressure on him was now turned up inexorably. Both Lord Kimberley and Edward Hamilton called at 38 Berkeley Square to make yet further appeals. Hamilton also sent another letter of entreaty: 'I implore you for your own sake and for those who love you not to close the door finally yet. I am convinced that on this decision depends the whole of your future peace of mind; and if a false move is made you will regret it as will countless others. I must therefore, as your oldest friend, protest in order that at any rate I may have a free conscience as to having done my best to prevent the most direful act of political suicide in history.'[58] Rosebery's American-born friend Jessie Phipps, later a stalwart of the London County Council, also did all she could to persuade Rosebery to accept, but was 'in despair and broken-hearted at the prospect of his not doing so".[59] The strain on Rosebery was beginning to show, in his ever more restless and eccentric behaviour. On the morning of Saturday the 13th he sent Morley a note asking to see him at Berkeley Square at 2.30 that afternoon. Yet when Morley turned up, he found that 'the bird had flown'; Gilmour, Rosebery's secretary, explained that his master 'had been obliged to go out of town, to which I answered not one syllable but turned my back and walked silently out of the house.'[60] Rosebery had in fact fled to Mentmore, from where he sent a telegram of apology that Saturday night, but it did not entirely appease Morley. 'His conduct cannot be pardoned if he is in right mind,' he wrote. Not everyone was sure that Rosebery *was* 'in right mind'. Herbert Gladstone expressed the fear that 'Rosebery will go mad', while Ferdy Rothschild, Hannah's cousin, said that 'if he does not join, I can't think what will become of him. It will kill him or drive him into an asylum.'[61]

Ensconced in his Buckinghamshire palace, Rosebery still could not escape. The Queen had decided she could not intervene, but this did not stop her son, the Prince of Wales, sending a long letter in which he said that 'I, for one, who have my country's interest so deeply at heart, would deeply deplore if you were unwilling to accept the post of Secretary of State for Foreign Affairs, a post which you have filled before with such great ability and which has not only been appreciated at home – but by all foreign countries.'[62] The same day, Sunday 14 August, Regy Brett raised the argument that 'moderate men, who would have abstained from voting, voted because they felt confident you would be Foreign Secretary. This to my mind is the most serious criticism of your present action. The future, under your leadership, seemed bright for the Liberal party. Without you, the party repels me.'[63] More influential were two other personal interventions. The first was by his cousin Henry Primrose, who spent hours over the weekend wrangling with Rosebery about the right course. One of his key arguments was 'that it showed cowardice to retire before responsibility'.[64] The second was a visit from George Buckle, editor of *The Times*, with whom Rosebery had 'a long and earnest talk'. Buckle's visit was followed by a 16-page letter containing arguments that Rosebery privately admitted were 'powerful and affecting'. Brilliantly exploiting Rosebery's love of history, he invented a hypothetical situation in which a historian of the future, looking back on the crisis, tried to work out why Rosebery had refused office. Was it because of disagreement on Irish Home Rule? No. Was it because of an attempt to fetter the Foreign Secretary? No. So the historian would 'have to fall back on the theory that either you feared the troubles ahead or were too prudent to mix up your name, as that of a rising statesman, with what you foresaw as the fiasco of Mr Gladstone's fourth government'. Buckle dismissed Rosebery's claims that his pre-election campaigning did not imply acceptance of office: 'Speeches constitute an obligation – to your party, to the rank and file.' He also bravely invoked the memory of Hannah: 'There can be no doubt what she would have wished you to do.' Finally, he appealed to Rosebery's sense of duty: 'It may be a blow to your pride but it is better than wrecking your life. Don't suppose that I don't sympathise with your feelings but I urge you to conquer them and do your duty. No one appreciates more than you do the men like Pitt, Wellington and Nelson who have set their duty to the country before everything. Now is your chance to emulate them. Don't miss it.'[65]

In the face of this barrage, Rosebery's obduracy began to weaken. Returning to London on the morning of Monday 15 August – the day Gladstone was due to kiss hands with the Queen at Osborne – he told Hamilton that 'he did not see how he was to resist any longer'. Hamilton in the meantime had come up with a cunning strategy to force Rosebery's hand: he proposed that Gladstone, instead of seeking a final 'yes' or 'no' from Rosebery, should write informing him that he planned to put his name to the Queen as Foreign Secretary. Crucially, Gladstone should send this note just before leaving for Osborne, so it would be received 'too late to give Rosebery the chance of having his name taken out'.[66] In this way, his membership of the Government would in effect be a fait accompli, though of course he could still make objections if he were determined on refusal. Seeing no realistic alternative Gladstone, after much consultation but with little enthusiasm, accepted Hamilton's plan. On Monday morning he wrote to Rosebery: 'Viewing the flight of time and all the circumstances, I propose to submit your name to the Queen today in conformity with her wish and I trust you will allow the matter to terminate in this way for the advantage and happiness of all parties as well as for the public good.'[67] Hamilton was with Rosebery at Berkeley Square when Gladstone's letter arrived, brought by the Liberal Chief Whip Arnold Morley. Rosebery, though he now recognised that surrender was almost inevitable, had not entirely given up the fight. 'He was rather agitated and it was some little time before I could persuade him to send Mr G. a telegram putting an end to the uncertainty. At last he wrote down on a telegraph form "So be it" signing it "Mentmore". I carried off the form in triumph and despatched the telegram from St James's Street for Mr G. to find on his arrival at Osborne.'[68]

Rosebery was finally Foreign Secretary. 'This tragic-comedy has at last come to an end,' wrote Morley with relief.[69] Loulou Harcourt, looking back on the episode, wrote, 'I now see how much Hannah, poor lady, had to fight with his character.'[70] Hamilton's reaction was far more euphoric:

A national calamity has been averted; the formation of a Government by Mr G. has been made possible; the minds of the commercial classes will be made easy; foreign and home securities will stand steady; our interests and honour abroad will be in safe hands; a great political career has been saved from wreckage; a man of real genius born to lead others and to serve his country will be saved from a life of misery and remorse. R. has often been a puzzle to me, though probably I know him almost better than anyone else; but I believe I at last understand him and he has gone up in my estimation. My belief is – and Henry Primrose shares it – that R. has a genuine dislike, or imagines he has, of public life; that he loves seclusion; that he is not really ambitious – whatever ambition he had was buried with his poor wife; that he has been unable to realize the importance of his own position; and that he thought his only chance of escaping from public life was to cut himself adrift now, or else it would (or might) be never.[71]

The crisis over Rosebery's Foreign Secretaryship is unique in modern British political history. Never before nor since have such efforts been made to bring a reluctant public figure into office. The fact reflects not only the qualities of Rosebery, but also the weakness of the Liberal party. Its majority was so small, its leader so exhausted, its ranks so divided, its policies so discredited, that Rosebery's presence was essential to reassure the press, the public and the Sovereign. As Sir William Harcourt later told Rosebery, 'If you had not joined, the Government would have been ridiculous – now that you have, it is only impossible.'[72] There is no doubt that, for all the anguish he was suffering in the wake of his bereavement, he behaved selfishly and irresponsibly during the summer of 1892, particularly in his peevish attitude to Gladstone at Dalmeny and in unintentionally deceiving his colleagues by his activism on the platform and in the LCC. But the pressure exerted on him was almost brutal; in the end, his own wishes were treated with contempt. The senior Liberals had decided they needed him, and he was to be given no choice in the matter. The behaviour of Loulou Harcourt was especially duplicitous – rushing hysterically round London to secure Rosebery's services and even offering to go up to Edinburgh, while all the time believing that Kimberley would make a better Foreign Secretary. He only wanted Rosebery in the post because it would ensure the return of the Liberals to power and the chancellorship for his father. John Morley was another who was expert at pleading with Rosebery to his face while raging against him behind his back.

At least Loulou had a good feeling for politics. He wrote in his diary on 15 August: 'I suppose Rosebery will take a high hand in Foreign Affairs.'

9

'The ideal master to serve'

⌒

O N 18 AUGUST 1892 the members of the new Cabinet travelled to Osborne to receive their seals of office. The Queen was not impressed with her ministers. 'These horrid new people came and there was a terrible thunderstorm when they left,' she told her daughter Vicky.[1] The only one for whom she had any fondness was Rosebery, whose diary records their audience. 'She held out her hand warmly. I kissed it. "It is so long since I have seen you and you have gone through so much." I said I wished she could have left me where I was. "Oh no, I hope the work will be good for you and then think of the reception of your name." "It is nothing but a name." "Oh no, much more than that. You know I have always given you good advice" – or words to that effect, quite maternally.'[2]

The Queen found Rosebery 'very low and thinks he can do very little'.[3] His mood was not improved by Lord Salisbury's refusal to see him personally to discuss the handover of the Foreign Office, on the grounds that he was going abroad. 'But', came the rather lofty message from Salisbury, 'Sir Philip Currie could tell him what he needed to know.'[4] Rosebery was offended, especially since he had given such strong public support to Salisbury's foreign policy. According to Loulou Harcourt, he regarded Salisbury's behaviour as 'a piece of gross discourtesy'. At the same time, he was dragged into yet another attempt to make him Leader of the House of Lords, in place of Kimberley. Earlier in the summer, the ambitious side of his nature had been slightly tempted by this post, insofar as it would tend to strengthen his position as Gladstone's likely successor. Now Gladstone referred to the issue again, telling Rosebery on 18 August that he had 'consulted your peer colleagues and they're all of the opinion that the Leadership of the Lords would be best in your hands.'[5] Rosebery told him he was 'indifferent' to the position – which Gladstone argued was 'no answer at all' – and then said that any definite decision should be postponed for a period. But it is clear once again that Rosebery did not want to rule himself out, as the conversation he had on 29 August with Edward Hamilton demonstrates. 'On Mr G's retirement, R., I believe, must lead;

and the assumption of the lead of the party will be made easier when he is installed as Leader of the House of Lords – a position which he is very coy about accepting. He went far, however, to contemplate it when he alluded to his having the determination of the choice of men to represent departments in the Upper House, which is the prerequisite of the Leader of the House of Lords.' As Rosebery became more heavily involved in the Foreign Office, however, he soon lost any lingering trace of enthusiasm. At the beginning of December 1892 he told Kimberley that, because of the amount of work he had to do as Foreign Secretary, he must absolutely decline the Leadership. 'I did all I could to persuade him,' wrote Kimberley. 'It is silly to make me lead. Rosebery has weight with the nation, wit and eloquence. I have none of these requisites.'[6] Despite further attempts by Gladstone and Hamilton, Rosebery would not be moved. 'I fear that night work may bring me back to insomnia and I can just get along without night work or discreditable arrears under the present circumstances. But if I were leader, I could not,' he told Gladstone.[7] On 12 January 1893 Kimberley was confirmed as Leader of the House of Lords on a permanent basis.

Yet this diffidence was not a sign that Rosebery remained trapped in the anxious, introverted desperation that had caused him such misery earlier in the summer. This time, he was acting on far more reasonable grounds: his work as Foreign Secretary was indeed demanding. When Hamilton went to see him at Berkeley Square on 29 August he found Rosebery's study 'almost blocked by Foreign Office boxes', while Rosebery himself estimated that the duties of the office had at least quadrupled since the days of Lord Palmerston. This was partly due to the growth of the Empire, partly to the arrival of the telegraph, which meant that overseas officials increasingly sought instructions from London rather than acting on their own initiative. The result was that responsibility for decision-making was ever more centralised. To the journalist Sir Edward Cook Rosebery admitted that the flow of work was 'very incessant' and by his side 'there is always a pile of those boxes'.[8] But he refused to be overwhelmed. One of the many fascinating aspects of his character was the way he could suddenly switch from one role to another: so now he was transformed from the irresolute, brooding widower who had lost his interest in politics and his grip on reality into the strong, decisive, industrious Foreign Minister in command of a great Empire. It was almost as if some elixir in those despatch boxes was invigorating him. Having spent six months bewailing his unfitness for high office, he now openly relished the responsibilities of his job. The change was noticed by those around him almost immediately after he had seen the

Queen. 'Rosebery seems to have been quite in his old form at the Cabinet and cracking jokes with his neighbours all the time,' wrote Loulou Harcourt after the first meeting of the new Cabinet on 19 August.[9] Three days later Hamilton lunched with Rosebery at the Foreign Office and thought he was 'in good spirits; and I believe he has already begun to feel the benefit of regular employment.'[10]

Rosebery soon demonstrated his toughness in his handling of the potentially explosive issue of the British minister in Washington. The left-wing MP Henry Labouchere had developed an ambition to be Her Majesty's representative in the United States. The Queen found the proposition outrageous: not only was Labouchere an avowed republican, but he had lived with his ex-actress wife before they were married, conduct unacceptable to the morality of the Victorian Establishment. Labby, as he was known, was supremely indifferent to what the world thought of him, which was fortunate since the world regarded him as a liar, a fraudster and a hypocrite. His record included dubious share dealings in the City and physical violence against the editor of the *Daily Telegraph*. It is hard to imagine anyone less suitable for a senior diplomatic post, especially as he made no effort to conceal his contempt for the foreign service: 'What the weather is to Englishmen the Eastern Question is to diplomatists. For their sake, let us hope that it will never be satisfactorily settled. Diplomatists, like many other apparently useless beings, must live,' he once said.[11] Many of his enemies, including Gladstone's confidant Lord Acton and the new Liberal Chief Whip, Edward Marjoribanks, actually wanted Labby posted to Washington so that the House of Commons would be free of his troublesome presence. But Rosebery thought this would be a disastrous move, one that would turn the British legation into a laughing-stock. He and Labby had once been friends, but he had since wearied of the frequency with which he was lampooned in *Truth*.

Labouchere claimed to have 'no personal feeling' against Rosebery, though he disliked his imperialist policies and saw him 'as far too clever a peer to have as Prime Minister'. Now, with breathtaking cynicism, Labby told Wemyss Reid, editor of the *Leeds Mercury*, that if Rosebery supported his bid for Washington, then he was 'prepared to bury the hatchet and come to a concordat about the succession to Mr G.' If he were refused, however, he would show 'triple venom' and become a 'dangerous nuisance' to Rosebery. 'I am quite prepared to use the arms put into my hands for my own advantage, for I am not of a modest or retiring habit of mind.'[12] Rosebery refused to give into this explicit blackmail. Labouchere's wife then tried the effect of feminine charm. To create a vacancy for Labby at

Washington she had worked out an elaborate reshuffle of the foreign ambassadorships which included shifting the current American representative, Sir Julian Pauncefote, to Madrid. In an interview at the Foreign Office on 24 November Rosebery told her frankly that her scheme was 'absurd'. He pointed out that 'Labby has gone out of his way to attack me . . . how could Labby accept a post from a Foreign Minister in whom he said he had no confidence?' And he also referred to Labby's hypocrisy: 'What would be the position if this proposal were made, not on behalf of a Radical leader, but of a destitute duke? Would not the columns of *Truth* teem with just and violent diatribes against so colossal a job?'[13] Downhearted, Mrs Labouchere reported her failure to her husband. In response, on 27 November he drew up a memorandom setting out his position: 'As regards my attacks on Rosebery in *Truth*, the Liberal Party are divided as to what our principles of foreign policy ought to be in Europe and Africa. He takes one side. I take the other. Of course I fight for my side. There is nothing personal in this. I did not adopt my opinions to attack Rosebery, but I have always held them.'[14] Henrietta Labouchere passed this statement to Rosebery, who now tried to draw a line under the affair. On the 30th he wrote explaining – not entirely truthfully – that there was 'no ill-will on my side' but that he simply could not appoint Labby to Washington because of the serious political differences between them. 'You announced your entire distrust of me as Foreign Minister before even I received the seals and have constantly reiterated that feeling since. I would be inevitably accused of having bribed into silence a formidable opponent.' Though Marjoribanks entertained the hope that Rosebery might back down so that Labby would be 'aloft, abroad or below, out of the House of Commons for the next session', Gladstone agreed with his Foreign Secretary's decision.

The actress in Henrietta Labouchere now descended to hysteria. 'I cannot tell you what a disappointment your decision has been to me. When I die – if my body is opened – you will find, like Queen Mary, *Washington* and *Rosebery* engraved on my heart,' she wrote to him on 9 December. In January, showing remarkable patience, Rosebery agreed to one more interview with her, at which she put forward a new plan, whereby Labby would resign his Parliamentary seat on the grounds of ill-health, go abroad for a while, and *then* apply for a diplomatic appointment. Rosebery laughingly told her that the project was 'insane'. Abandoning all sentimentality, Henrietta warned that her husband would fight Rosebery over foreign policy, to which he responded laconically, as he noted later, that 'if Labby did succeed in turning me out, I would consider an estimable service would have been rendered to myself and begged her to say so to her husband.' Recognising that Rosebery would not be moved, Henrietta then burst into tears and expressed her regret at *Truth's* hostile attitude. 'Mrs Labouchere said she thought *Truth* so dull she was never able to read it. I was too polite to express my cordial concurrence.' Nothing was achieved by further correspondence from the Laboucheres, such as this pointed letter from Henrietta on 17 February 1893: 'I see from the papers that another ambassador is dead.' Rosebery could only keep reiterating that their request was 'impossible'.

At the end of January 1893 Labouchere told Rosebery, 'I hope you will understand that in opposing your foreign policy in the House of Commons, I am not activated by any cussedness about Washington but I am merely doing what I always did.'[15] This was just another example of Labby's hypocrisy. In fact he became one of Rosebery's most virulent critics, continually scheming against him in the smoking-rooms of the Commons and satirising him in the pages of *Truth*. The very week in which he wrote that conciliatory letter he went up to Marjoribanks and 'declared war to the knife against Rosebery'.[16] Even Loulou Harcourt felt that Labby's enmity was excessive. In January 1893, for instance, Labby gave an interview to the French paper *Le Temps* which Loulou described as 'very insulting towards Rosebery'. A flavour of Labouchere's negative, menacing attitude is reflected in this mock advertisement which he sent to Rosebery in early 1894: 'If any of the Noble Lords in the House of Peers makes a special ass of himself, either in manner or matter and you should feel it your duty to inform the world of his antics, information would be thankfully received up to Tuesday morning. Also if anyone who had not the honour to be a peer should, either in the sporting or social world, do anything at once foolish or ridiculous or, in fact, anything out of which a paragraph might be manufactured – information is requested.'[17] Not surprisingly Rosebery, who usually refrained from extreme moral judgements, came to regard Labouchere as little short of an evil force in British politics. In a private note he described him as a 'man without a soul. Having lost every shred of self-respect, he became a scoffer at all that was decent and reputable, trying to degrade all mankind to his own level. He himself was vile and he determined everyone else was vile.'[18]

Rosebery showed greater courage than many of his appeasing Liberal colleagues in standing firm against Labby. He soon had the opportunity to display the same fortitude on a much bigger scale, as he took on the unenviable role of protecting Britain's imperial interests while working with a Cabinet that did not believe in Empire. More than almost any other late Victorian politician except Joseph Chamberlain, Rosebery had sensed the passion for Empire which had been aroused in the British public. The exploits of Livingstone and Stanley, the redcoat heroism of Rorke's Drift and Kabul, the expansion of the populist press, the growth of history teaching in schools, the spectacular success of the 1897 Jubilee, and the stirring words of Kipling had all contributed to this mood, as had the triumphant capitalism of Cecil Rhodes in the Cape and the growth of democracy in Canada, Australia and New Zealand. Although Rosebery was a fervent evangelist for Empire he always tried to distinguish between his own brand of Liberal Imperialism, with its emphasis on self-government and closer union with the colonies, and what he called 'wild-cat Imperialism', based on exploitation and conquest. But his instinct for consolidation and racial homogeneity did not prevent him supporting imperial expansion where it suited Britain's needs. In a speech at the Colonial Institute in 1893 he declared:

> It is said that our Empire is already large enough and does not need extension. That would be true enough if the world were elastic, but unfortunately it is not elastic, and we are engaged at the present moment, in the language of mining, 'in pegging out claims for the future'. We have to consider not what we want now, but what we shall want for the future . . . We have to look forward beyond the chatter of platforms and the passions of party to the future of the race of which we are at present the trustees and we should, in my opinion, grossly fail in the task that has been laid upon us did we shrink from responsibilities and decline to take our share in a partition of the world which we have not forced on but which has been forced upon us.[19]

Following the doctrines of J.R. Seeley, who argued that the development of empire was the most important theme of modern British history, Rosebery urged that the central thrust of British foreign policy, so long dominated by Europe, had to change to meet the requirements of the new imperial era. Speaking to the City Liberal Club during his Foreign Secretaryship he said: 'Our great Empire has pulled us by the coat-tails out of the European system and though, with our great preponderance, our great moral influence and our great fleet, with our traditions in Europe and with our aspirations to preserve the peace of Europe, we can never remove ourselves altogether from the European system, we must recognise that our Foreign policy has become a colonial policy and is in reality at this moment much more dictated from the extremities of the Empire than it is from London itself. That is a very remarkable fact. Is it a fact we should deplore? I think not.'[20]

Within weeks of Gladstone taking office, the clash between Rosebery's imperialism and the more limited vision of his Cabinet colleagues made itself felt over the vexed problem of Uganda. By the Anglo-German agreement of 1890, this central African territory bordering the great lakes had been recognised as part of Britain's sphere of influence. The Imperial British East Africa Company, one of those chartered enterprises so often used by Britain to build her Empire without incurring too great a burden on the state, sent a full-scale expedition under Captain Frederick Lugard to occupy the country. Lugard was a soldier of great skill, intense devotion to the British flag, and suicidal temperament. As a young man of 28 he had fallen in love with a divorcee but his heart had been broken when he found her in bed with another man. Emotionally crushed by this experience, he first joined the London Fire Brigade and then set off on the rampage through Africa, hoping to die nobly in the imperial cause, battling against the slave trade.[21] When Lugard arrived in Uganda in 1890 he found a country in chaos, nominally governed by the tyrant-king Mwanga but torn apart by tribal conflict and un-Christian feuding between French Catholic and English Protestant missionaries. Through his own military acumen he managed to establish a degree of order. The problem was that he had to spend so much time achieving a settlement that he had none to spare for expanding trade, which was after all the central purpose of the Company. Losing money at the rate of £40,000 a year in Uganda, they decided in December 1891 to evacuate the country. Both the Christian missionaries and Lugard were shocked by this decision, warning that in the vacuum left there would be wholesale massacres. 'Hundreds – nay thousands – of lives will be sacrificed and the blood must lie at someone's door,' said Lugard.[22] The Church Missionary Society raised enough money to postpone the evacuation for a year, but it seemed certain that Uganda must be abandoned by December 1892 – unless the British Government intervened.

As Foreign Secretary Salisbury had inclined towards withdrawal, but had been reluctant to take any action beyond commissioning a study of the feasibility of building a railway from the eastern harbour of Mombasa to Uganda, which would in the long term improve trade and communications. In the short term, the decision as to evacuation now rested with Rosebery. On the face of it, there was nothing to be gained by staying in an inhospitable, backward, strife-torn country which offered little in terms of wealth, unlike South Africa with its vast diamond and gold mines. Sir William Harcourt, in a letter to Gladstone of 20 September, summed up the argument against staying: 'I see nothing but endless expense, trouble and disaster in prospect if we allow ourselves to drift into any sort of responsibility for this business, and devoutly hope that we shall have nothing to do with it. The Company has made this terrible mess and they must bear the responsibility . . . I have no doubt the Company are raising all sorts of alarms in order to blackmail the Government, and to compel us to entreat them to remain, in which case they would demand a subsidy.'[23] Harcourt was not necessarily opposed to empire, just to its expense. Of Cecil Rhodes he once said, 'Rhodes is a great jingo but then he is a cheap jingo.' And he felt that Africa, unlike India, would never be profitable for Britain, because of the calibre of the natives; English settlers, he told Rosebery, could 'never get these savages to work for them. These savages are not like the mild Hindoo with whom you can do as you please.'[24] Most of the Liberal Cabinet, including the Prime Minister, were inclined to evacuation. Gladstone argued that the decision to withdraw had effectively been taken by Salisbury, and he could not see 'any new facts to warrant or recommend the re-opening of the question decided by the late Government'. In addition, he was contemptuous of the Christian missionaries: 'It is rather a sad spectacle on the whole – there are few things to my mind more hazardous and objectionable than missionary operations dependent on military support from the Government,' he wrote to Rosebery.[25] Even Lord Spencer, by no means a 'Little Englander', thought the case for remaining weak. 'Are we justified, for the upholding of imperial interests,' he asked Rosebery on 23 September, 'to incur more responsibilities which will increase year after year? Ought we not, for the putting down of the slave trade, to be satisfied with our naval means of checking it? They may be imperfect but they know the limit of their responsibility.'[26]

Rosebery thought all his colleagues were missing the much bigger, strategic picture. If Britain pulled out of Uganda, the country might well be taken over by the French who, once in possession of the headwaters of the Nile, could threaten Britain's position in Egypt. In fact, less than a week after Rosebery's appointment Sir Reginald Wingate, Director of Military Intelligence in Cairo, sent the Foreign Office a memorandum warning that if the Company left, France might move in and then advance through neighbouring Sudan. Offering a different but just as disturbing prospect, Herbert Kitchener, Sirdar of the Egyptian army, said that in the event of Britain's withdrawal Uganda might fall into the hands of the Sudanese Dervishes. In Rosebery's view, anything that undermined the security of Egypt would be disastrous, for Egypt was the guardian of the route to India. Since the building of the Suez canal and with the accelerating decline of the Ottoman Empire during the nineteenth century, Napoleon's dictum that 'the master of Egypt is the master of India' seemed more telling than ever. There were two additional considerations. First, Rosebery wanted to prove to the other chancelleries of Europe that, under his influence, a Liberal government would not mean weakness in foreign affairs. He therefore had to provide an emphatic demonstration of his personal ascendancy over the Gladstonian Cabinet. Uganda was to be a test question for him. As he put it to Regy Brett, 'If we were to pull away, every government all over the world would begin to "try it on" with the Government, to see how much we could stand.'[27] Secondly, he was haunted by the fiasco of the Sudan evacuation exactly a decade before, so woefully mishandled by his Liberal predecessor Lord Granville. His Sovereign was quick to remind him of this point: 'The Queen could never support anything which lowers the dignity and power of Empire and she trusts Lord Rosebery *especially* to uphold this. The fate of Gordon is not and will not be forgotten in Europe and we must take great care what we do.'[28] To Gladstone's secretary Algernon West Rosebery confessed on 28 September that 'he was sleeping badly as it was, but he could not sleep at all if, after all our warnings, we allowed the story of Khartoum to be repeated.'[29]

Gladstone, Harcourt, Morley and the rest of the anti-Imperialists attached no weight to arguments involving Egypt, for the simple reason that they wished to evacuate that country as well. Yet it is one of the ironies of Gladstone's career that he was responsible for the creation of Britain's Egyptian and central African empire. By his decision to occupy Egypt in 1882 in the name of quelling disorder, he ensured that Britain would be committed to protecting the Nile right up to the lakes. The resulting wars in the Sudan and struggle for Uganda were the direct consequences of his decision. When attacking Disraeli's jingoism in 1876 he had predicted with uncanny accuracy what would happen once Britain became involved in Egypt: 'Our first site in Egypt, be it by larceny or eruption, will be the almost certain egg of a North African empire, that will grow and grow until Victoria and another Albert, titles of the Lake sources of the White Nile, come within our borders.'[30] But it was Gladstone, not Disraeli, who presided over just this eventuality.

Initially Rosebery's battle to retain Uganda looked hopeless. When on 13 September he circulated to the Cabinet a paper nominally from Sir Percy Anderson, the head of the Foreign Office's Slave Trade Department, arguing for annexation, his colleagues exploded with a mixture of fury and derision. Harcourt called it 'jingoism with a vengeance', while Gladstone told Rosebery the document was nothing more than 'a pleading from a missionary society or from the Company'.[31] Rosebery had carefully refrained from commenting on the Anderson paper, but in reality he had written much of it. The reaction of the Cabinet told him it would be useless to fight this battle on the grounds of protecting Britain's imperial or strategic interests; another, more politically effective weapon was needed, one that would touch the humanitarian consciences of his Liberal colleagues. He would therefore stress the dangers of the murderous anarchy that was likely to prevail in the event of evacuation. On 15 September he circulated a telegram he had received from Sir Gerald Portal, the Consul-General in Zanzibar, which warned that withdrawal 'must inevitably result in a massacre of Christians such as the history of this century cannot show', adding on 19 September his own Cabinet memorandum which stated that 'the evacuation of Uganda, according to every authority, involves not merely the restoration of the Slave Trade but the massacre of those native Christians who do not fly and the missionaries who will not fly.'[32]

Unconvinced by these dire forecasts, Gladstone and Harcourt refused to change their opinion. The issue became something of a fixation with Gladstone, who bombarded Rosebery with increasingly agitated correspondence. After his previous experience of working with the malleable, ineffectual figure of Lord Granville, Gladstone was outraged at the presumption of his young Foreign Secretary; he later condemned Rosebery for his 'total gross misconception of the relative position of the two offices we respectively held'.[33] On 20 September he asked 'why the British government should go into a hornets' nest, the scene of anarchy for six years past, to make war on all and sundry?'[34] On the 23rd he sent Rosebery no fewer than three letters on the subject, one of them arguing, rather coldly, that he had just as much responsibility for foreign policy as Rosebery. Elsewhere he dismissed the claims of Lugard – 'I hardly attach much value to his authority' – and also repeated his view that Salisbury's government had agreed upon evacuation. Rosebery thought this last assertion absurd. If the Tories were really bent on leaving, why had they commissioned a survey into the building of the Mombasa railway? 'It cannot be doubted that they would have held on to Uganda had they held on to office. But they left the question to us,' he wrote to Gladstone on the 20th.[35]

The crisis was fast developing into a battle of wills between the Prime Minister and his Foreign Secretary. On 24 September Gladstone told Rosebery that he had spoken to most of his Cabinet colleagues, and 'they are all against any move to occupy'. In a letter to Rosebery of the 23rd, John Morley spoke for the great majority: 'The mess in which occupation will land us will be near and certain. We had better face the temporary difficulty than leave the country in really infernal embarrassments. Our Government is not likely to be long-lived but I should be sorry that it should leave behind such a damnable legacy as this would be.'[36] But Rosebery was not to be browbeaten. Showing a sense of determination which must have surprised even his admirers, he demanded a meeting of the Cabinet at which to set out his case. Gladstone was reluctant to agree to this, hoping that before such a step 'I might exhaust every chance of inducing Rosebery to recede from his untenable and most dangerous position.'[37] Rosebery insisted, and a Cabinet was fixed for Thursday 29 September. In the run-up to this meeting Gladstone betrayed signs of exhaustion and anger. 'It is the first time, during a Cabinet experience of 22 or 23 years, that I have known the Foreign Minister and the Prime Minister to go before a Cabinet on a present question with diverging views. It is the union of these two authorities by which foreign policy is ordinarily working in Cabinet,' he wrote to Rosebery on the 25th.[38] The next day he moaned to Harcourt that 'the last ten days have been simply horrible', while he told Lord Spencer, 'I have of late had a really terrible time. Rosebery has I think been carried off his legs by the Jingoes of the Foreign Office and its agents and correspondents and wants us to interfere with the coming evacuation which even the late Government had accepted, though they had not abandoned ulterior views about a railway. His tone has been excellent throughout and this is the only consolation in what otherwise I reckon as one of the very strangest occurrences of my life of 60 years in the Commons.'[39]

With the opinion of his Cabinet colleagues so heavily weighted against him, Rosebery seemed certain to lose on the direct question of withdrawal. 'Rosebery must be beaten – and may resign,' predicted Loulou Harcourt on 23 September. The danger of his resignation was very real, but it was precisely that possibility which strengthened his position. Always a reluctant minister, Rosebery was quite willing to indulge in brinkmanship, knowing that the mere idea of his departure terrified his colleagues. Fearing that the Government would collapse without him, they were desperate for a compromise; the grim predictions of anarchy provided one. A week before the Cabinet meeting the Home Secretary, H.H. Asquith, had written to Rosebery saying that 'the only ground upon which it seems we can assume responsibility for postponing the evacuation is to present the emergency of a massacre for those whose safety, directly or indirectly, England can be said to be answerable.'[40]

Now, as political disaster loomed, ministers seized eagerly on this concept of a delay. At last sensing his first opening in the crisis, Rosebery wrote to Gladstone on the morning of the meeting to emphasise his support for a compromise based on postponement: 'The real question is whether we are content to face the consequences of leaving the territory, the inhabitants and the missionaries to a fate which we cannot doubt . . . Portal asserts that there is bound to be a massacre. All therefore that I ask is that, as Foreign Secretary and holding a very strong view, I shall not be placed in the position of simply acquiescing, without enquiry, in an evacuation which, under circumstances of such precipitation, must in my opinion be inevitably disastrous.'[41] The meeting itself was far less turbulent than had been forecast, as the Cabinet agreed to postpone any evacuation for a period of three months beyond the original planned date of December 1892. In the same spirit of reconciliation, it was also decided to pay the British East Africa Company a subsidy to cover the costs of their continued operations there. The detailed wording, finalised by an incongruous alliance of Rosebery and Harcourt, was accepted at another Cabinet meeting the following morning, 30 September. But if Harcourt thought he had simply delayed the inevitable, Lord Kimberley gave him this warning: 'I am afraid that we shall find it extremely difficult to get out of Uganda when the three months expire. The British public is easily stirred by the cry of the extension of the gospel of peace.'[42]

Rosebery had handled the crisis with masterly skill, displaying an instinctive understanding of his colleagues' political sensitivities. By gaining a delay, he won the first round of the fight to stay in Uganda. Just two members of the Cabinet – A.J. Mundella and Henry Fowler – supported his policy, and all the biggest figures were against him, yet still he had triumphed. Writing to the Queen, he could not conceal his pride in his achievement: 'Lord Rosebery believes that on the whole he has done the best thing that could be done under circumstances, personal and political, that were complicated to an unusual degree.'[43] The Foreign Office was thrilled by its chief; Munro-Ferguson told Rosebery on 7 October that 'you will be backed in your office after this as no one was ever backed before. The delight there is as unbounded as the hope to see you win.'[44] He now moved ruthlessly on two fronts to ensure that the temporary extension of British rule became permanent. At home, he sought to galvanise public opinion, especially the Liberal nonconformist masses, in favour of retention by emphasising the horrors that awaited the Christian missionaries if they were deserted. In this campaign he was greatly helped by the arrival in England of Captain Lugard, who had been dismissed as a 'mischievous lunatic' by Harcourt but proved to be a superb public performer. Throughout the autumn Lugard spoke to packed meetings across the country, and the explorer Henry Stanley also spoke out publicly against evacuation. Rosebery himself addressed a deputation of the British and Foreign Anti-Slavery Society on 20 October, telling them that history would judge Britain, not by its military or commercial prowess but 'by the heroic self-denying exertions which she had made to put down this iniquitous traffic'.

By mid November, 174 public petitions had been sent to the Foreign Office demanding that Britain stay in Uganda, the majority of them laying particular emphasis on the need to suppress the African slave trade. It seemed that, as regards Uganda, the British public were only too keen for their Government to take up the white man's burden. 'The majority of the nation is suffering from violent jingo fever. In such circumstances, argument is useless,' wrote Kimberley in his journal.[45]

In Africa itself, Rosebery moved to forestall any possibility of Uganda slipping from Britain's grasp. At the beginning of November he had another fierce tussle over Uganda in Cabinet, during which he again hinted at resignation – 'well, if it is all settled against me by the Triumvirate,★ let me go at once,' he announced at one stage[46] – but in the end he managed to persuade the Government to send out a Special Commissioner, ostensibly to report on the situation but in reality to uphold British rule. After talking with Harcourt and Morley, Asquith explained to Rosebery why they were willing, despite all their reservations, to go along with the plan: 'They are not prepared to break up the Cabinet, split the party, encounter defeat in the House of Commons, face another dissolution and indefinitely postpone Home Rule and the Newcastle programme rather than send a Commission to Uganda.' Asquith now felt indeed that evacuation was impossible, and saw the job of the Commisioner as being to devise a way 'to retain Uganda at minimum cost and interference'.[47] Initially, Rosebery favoured an experienced diplomat, West Ridgeway, for the role; Munro-Ferguson, reflecting the more vicious side of Victorian imperialism, said to Rosebery, 'If Stanley had not killed all those niggers, he would be our man.'[48] Eventually, however, it was agreed to send Sir Gerald Portal, whose blood-curdling telegrams from Uganda had so influenced the wavering Cabinet in September. On the surface Portal, a protégé of Lord Salisbury, appears an odd choice for a Liberal government, given that he was personally opposed to evacuation. On the other hand, he had argued that the Sultan of Zanzibar – whose own lands were under a loose British protectorate – could administer Uganda for half the sum charged by the Chartered Company, something that inevitably had its appeal for Gladstone and his Chancellor Sir William Harcourt, not just because it saved money but because it would avoid direct British intervention. Algy West commented wryly that if the Zanzibar idea had been put forward a month earlier, Gladstone and Harcourt 'would have gone out of their senses with rage. What a healer Time is!'[49] Now, Harcourt was positively

★ Gladstone, Morley and Harcourt.

enthusistic about the proposal: 'If that amiable black man would only render us this service, I would everlastingly bless him.'[50] With a mixture of deviousness and contempt for his colleagues, Rosebery gave Portal two sets of instructions. One, for Cabinet consumption, stated that Portal should assess the state of Uganda and find 'the best method of dealing with that country'. To Gladstone's annoyance the Zanzibar plan was not included. When Morley saw the Prime Minister at Hawarden on 9 December, he found him 'a strange wild figure, eyes ablaze, hair flying, face pale, pen in hand and every sign of haste and hurry,' re-writing Rosebery's draft instructions to Portal. 'His agitation of manner was indescribably painful, almost King Lear,' Morley noted in his diary.

The GOM would have risen to even greater heights of tragedy had he known of Rosebery's more secret set of orders to Portal, telling him that the only plan he should consider was one involving British rule in some form. Evacuation was not to be countenanced. 'There may, of course, be indicated to you the possibility that should the difficulty of retention be found insuperable, or at any rate too vast, you should so report. But as a rather one-horse Company has been able to administer I suppose the Empire will be equal to it, and therefore the saving clause is mainly one of form.' In another private letter to Portal he wrote, 'I may say this as my confident though not my official opinion, that the public sentiment here will expect and support the maintenance of the British sphere of influence.'[51]

The true imperialist nature of Portal's mission became obvious early the following year, as the Tories and Radicals in the House of Commons sought an explanation of his role. Rosebery, in response to worried questions from Gladstone, explained blandly on 4 February 1893 that Portal 'has a staff with him expressly to make provision for the administration of the Uganda pending the consideration of his report. It was certainly not in the contemplation of the Cabinet that he should go as a mere reporter, to take down something in writing and hurry away bag and baggage to the coast, leaving the population to its fate. But I am afraid some such impression has been produced.'[52] The Cabinet now realised for the first time how comprehensively it had been outmanoeuvred by the artful Foreign Secretary. 'R. has completely jockeyed us,' wrote Morley on 6 February. 'If he had told the Cabinet what Portal's mission means, we would never have agreed to it upon that footing. The way in which Rosebery has left us in the lurch is hard to forgive and impossible to reconcile with decent loyalty to colleagues. I feel extremely bitter about it.' Morley told Gladstone that he would have resigned in protest but couldn't, because he was too committed to Ireland.

'I feel just as you do,' replied Gladstone. Three days later, Asquith complained to Morley that 'Rosebery has used us.' Rosebery then tried to soothe Morley by inviting him to lunch, but the sensitive Irish Chief Secretary refused: 'I certainly do not feel in Christian charity with my noble friend.' Morley then happened to run into him on 8 February, and 'there were a few sparks flying. I let fall some sentences to intimate that it was not likely I should sit with him in a Cabinet after this.'[53] It was almost a fortnight before they were on friendly terms again, after meeting at a levee. 'He gave me his most friendly look and hearty grip of the hand. It is a pity he's so egotistic and intensely self-conscious,' wrote Morley.[54]

Most members of the Cabinet, despite their anger at Rosebery's deception, lacked the stomach for yet another drawn-out battle about Uganda. With their energies focused on the great struggle over the second Irish Home Rule Bill, they were too distracted to take on the daunting combination of public opinion and Rosebery's imperialist tenacity. They therefore issued no new instructions to Portal, made no new demands for evacuation. Rosebery's invincibility was underlined in a Commons debate on 20 March 1893, when a motion by Labouchere to reduce Portal's mission was heavily defeated by 368 votes to 46. But there was a melancholy twist in the tale. In October 1892 Sir Gerald Portal had privately declared that he was 'fighting like a wildcat to prevent the Government giving up on Uganda'.[55] When he arrived he was appalled by what he saw of the Company's mismanagement, describing it as 'a miserable fraud' and a 'disgrace to the English name'.[56] In the provisional report he sent to the Foreign Office on 25 June 1893 he expressed himself as still strongly opposed to withdrawal, yet Rosebery was concerned lest Portal's evidence of British misdeeds in Uganda might be used to undermine his goal of annexation. Disillusioned, he began to question the reliability of Portal, complaining that 'he makes up his mind in five minutes on every subject and abuses all those whom he follows and works with'.[57] So there followed a long hiatus during which Portal, having returned to England, had to subject his document to endless refinement and re-writing. There is little doubt that Rosebery, though he professed to Gladstone in November that he had 'not touched the report with tongs', was at the heart of this process, seeking to make the case for retention as powerful as possible.* It further seems likely that Rosebery wanted to ensure there was no positive refer-

---

*In her authoritative biography of Captain Lugard written in 1956, Margery Perham says of Portal's report, 'Who else but Rosebery could have instructed him, either directly or indirectly, how to revise it?'

ence to the involvement of the Zanzibar sultanate, a proposal he had only pretended to support the previous autumn as a means of softening up Gladstone and Harcourt. Sadly, Portal did not live to see his long-delayed report published: in January 1894 he died of fever contracted in Uganda.

After yet more polishing, the document was finally presented to Parliament on 6 April 1894. It argued that Britain must stay in Uganda, not for commercial reasons, 'since no hope could be entertained of Uganda being able to defray the cost of its occupation', but for strategic ones. In words that betray Rosebery's influence, Portal warned that 'it is hardly possible that Uganda, the natural key to the whole of the Nile valley, should be left unprotected and unnoticed by other powers because an English company has been unable to hold it and because Her Majesty's Government has been unwilling to interfere.'[58] Moreover, Portal now rejected the notion of handing Uganda over to the Sultan of Zanzibar, on the grounds that he was a Muslim and should not therefore have authority over Christian missions. Two days later, in keeping with Portal's conclusion, the Government announced that Uganda was to be a British Protectorate. By the time it had been established Rosebery had ceased to be Foreign Secretary, but he was its real architect.

'If Rosebery gets his way about Uganda, he will be very difficult to manage,' Lord Ripon wrote to Lord Kimberley in November 1892. Yet Rosebery was no arrant bully, unlike Harcourt, who had become more intolerable than ever. He was assured, cool, resourceful, the true master of his domain. He achieved his ends not by petulance or bluster but with daring tactics, a firm grasp of political realities, and a clear vision of Britain's imperial needs. At times, and especially in the case of Portal's mission, he may have been duplicitous, but he rated the demands of patriotism more highly than the anxieties of his colleagues. Above all, he had shown his unchallengeable status within the Cabinet. As Hamilton noted in October 1892, 'That his colleagues should have acquiesced even in temporarily assisting the Company is strong evidence of R's own power. They know too well they can't get on without him.'[59]

Rosebery's abilities were similarly demonstrated in another imperial crisis, closely related to the Ugandan struggle. When Gladstone entered office for the last time, it was still the dream of the 'Little Englander' Liberals to pull out of Egypt, a prospect that appalled the British Consul in Cairo, Sir Evelyn Baring, created Lord Cromer in March 1892. A member of the famous City banking family and known to his critics as 'Over-Baring' because of his authoritarian manner, he was described by one British engineer in Egypt as 'a rough, rude sort of fellow but a strong able man'.[60] Cromer was no aggressive jingo, for he believed in the liberal traditions of free trade, sound finance and religious freedom. It was precisely because it brought with it the benefits of civilisation that Cromer felt British influence was essential, since the natives were in his view incapable of self-government and prone to Muslim fanaticism. If the British were to abandon Egypt he believed it would be taken over by another European power, which would be disastrous for Britain's position in the Mediterranean and for the route to India. Despite Rosebery's reputation as an imperialist, Cromer was understandably concerned by the succession of a Liberal government. 'I regarded the change of ministry with some apprehension,' he later recalled. 'I had the fullest confidence in Lord Rosebery's energy and political insight but it was different acting under a Minister, like Lord Salisbury, who truly represented the whole of his Cabinet and one who, like Lord Rosebery, notoriously represented views in connection to foreign affairs to which many of his principal colleagues were strongly opposed. I had the apprehension that a policy of immediate evacuation would be adopted.'[61] Cromer need not have worried. Rosebery shared his opinions and was determined to uphold them, even in the face of Cabinet opposition. He was particularly anxious to avoid any deal over the future of Egypt with the French, whose intentions he always regarded with suspicion. One of the negative side-effects of any such agreement with France, he privately argued, was that it would invoke the hostility of the Triple Alliance of Germany, Italy and Austria-Hungary, thereby upsetting the balance of power in Europe. For Rosebery, the twin advantages of the Triple Alliance were, first, that it pinned down German and Austro-Hungarian resources in Europe and, second, that it served as an impediment to French and Russian imperial ambitions.[62] Unlike Cromer, the anti-Imperialist radicals sensed that Rosebery would be able to ensure the maintenance of British rule. 'It is announced that Rosebery has taken office after all,' wrote the poet W.S. Blunt, who had personally criticised Rosebery a decade earlier over his Egypthian investments, on 15 August 1892. 'This will neutralize any good that might have come from a change of Government to Egypt. Rosebery will continue to represent the bondholders.'[63] Rosebery himself never treated Blunt with much respect, as he explained to the Queen: 'This invaluable subject of Your Majesty spends his time in masquerading like an Oriental in a circus, under a tabernacle outside Cairo, and intriguing against the British occupation of Egypt. Fortunately he is not looked on as a serious personage.'[64] But Harcourt, in another sign of his distance from Rosebery, was willing to entertain Blunt, though he urged him, only partly in jest, to be careful about their assignations: 'Rosebery has doubtless got his touts on the look-out for you,' he wrote after one visit by Blunt to the Chancellor's office in 11 Downing Street, 'so I must beg you, when you come again, to put on a false nose and I will let you through the garden gate.'[65]

In the course of Henry Labouchere's campaign for the Washington legation John Morley had observed that 'Rosebery has a curious dread of not appearing absolute in his own house, the Foreign Office'.[66] In his handling of Egypt Rosebery appeared equally determined to bow to no one, not Gladstone, not the Cabinet, not even Cromer. The first sign of trouble arose in late October, when Rosebery learnt that the French ambassador, W.H.Waddington, had approached Gladstone directly to discuss the possibility of opening negotiations over the future of Egypt. In a naively optimistic spirit, Gladstone reported the thrust of this meeting to Rosebery on 1 November: 'He inquires whether we are prepared for a friendly conversation or whether such a conversation is barred. If we are so prepared, he thinks that his Government would be prepared to indicate a possible basis of settlement.'[67] Rosebery personally disliked Waddington, a twice-married diplomat of English descent whom he regarded as unctuous and unreliable – Lord Salisbury had said of him, 'He is apt to misapprehend the exact meaning of what you say to him.' On this occasion he was incensed at the way Waddington had deliberately bypassed normal diplomatic channels in an attempt to exploit the political differences between the Prime Minister and his Foreign Secretary over Egypt. 'Waddington's proceedings are unprecedented, I should think, in the annals of diplomacy,' he told Gladstone, adding that his action 'had made the transaction of business almost impossible.'[68] At the same time, Rosebery asked the British ambassador in Paris, Lord Dufferin, to lodge a formal complaint. 'Tell Ribot★ that if he thinks to expedite matters by sending Waddington to Mr Gladstone to deal over my head he is gravely mistaken. Under that system I can assure him that Austrian or Chinese procedure will seem electrical [sic] to mine. I do not think any diplomatist ever made a much greater blunder.'[69] Dufferin did as he was told, warning Ribot that he 'must refuse to conduct the business of the two countries on such a footing as was implied by Waddington's démarche.'[70] Persona non grata at the Foreign Office, Waddington was effectively finished as French ambassador, and in December 1892 he announced that he would be returning to Paris the following spring. Rosebery told Dufferin wryly that he had managed to receive the news 'with composure'.

★ The French Foreign Minister.

Many in the Government's ranks, including Gladstone, thought Rosebery had over-reacted in the vehemence of his complaints about an intrigue behind his back. Mrs Gladstone told Loulou Harcourt that in her opinion 'Rosebery wants a great deal of discipline but it is unfortunate that he should have to undergo it while he has the Foreign Office in his hands.'[71] Gladstone's friend Lord Rendel spoke for many when he said, 'Rosebery might in form have been right but to allow wounded *amour propre* or diplomatic etiquette to carry him so far as to subordinate the very interests at stake was a grievous error.'[72] But the truth is that Rosebery was acting not out of pique but from a real concern about the machinations of France. He was surely right in suspecting that the French were stealthily trying to undermine his own resolute policy on Egypt by opening up a second channel of communication with the Prime Minister, an established Francophile. After his talk with Ribot, Dufferin wrote to Rosebery: 'My impression is that Ribot did tell Waddington in a general way to gain Mr Gladstone's ear on Egypt.' This is confirmed by Lord Rendel's memoirs, in which he states 'Mr Gladstone told me that actually Waddington came to him at Ribot's insistence.'[73] What so angered Rosebery was that in all his own previous talks with Waddington, the ambassador had ostentatiously refused to touch on the subject. 'He prides himself on never mentioning Egypt,' Rosebery told Dufferin. Furthermore, Waddington had approached several other ministers for an interview, among them the Indian Secretary Lord Kimberley. All this undermines the plausibility of Waddington's own explanation for his conduct. In an abject letter of apology to Rosebery, he claimed that he had called on Gladstone mainly to talk about Uganda; it was only at the end of the visit that 'I mentioned Egypt, touching very lightly on the subject and merely asking whether the English government would be inclined to "reprendre la conversation" in a friendly way, without entering upon any sort of detail. Further, I went to the Foreign Office fully intending to tell you that Egypt had been mentioned in my conversation with Mr Gladstone. But you appeared to me to be worried and out of sorts and as there was no sort of hurry in the matter I deferred speaking to you about it until my next visit. Nothing could be further from my thoughts than the wish to conceal anything from you.'[74] Even Gladstone admitted that he could 'neither defend nor explain' Waddington's treatment of Rosebery.[75]

Rosebery had no intention of opening discussions of any sort with France about Egypt. His sole aim was to maintain Cromer's status quo. As he put it to Gladstone, 'negotiating now the evacuation of Egypt would be a pernicious waste of time and energy'.[76] At the same time, he was to prove himself no pawn of Cromer, whose role as British agent in Egypt was unorthodox. Although the country was neither colony nor protectorate and remained under the suzerainty of the Turkish Sultan, Britain, as the occupying power, exerted a decisive influence over its government, especially in finance, military affairs, and political appointments. She could not, however, throw her weight about too violently, for fear of awakening nationalist and Muslim sentiment. Constant sniping from the Radicals at home and Blunt in his Cairo tent notwithstanding, Cromer had in general proved an excellent administrator. One of his many achievements, in which he was ably assisted by a young Oxford graduate, Alfred Milner, had been to sort out the chaotic finances of the Khedive, the nominal sovereign of Egypt. But from November 1892 he began to sense a growing anti-British atmosphere, inspired by the new young Khedive Abbas Hilmi, who had proved less malleable than expected. 'The Khedive is an extremely foolish youth. It is difficult to know how to deal with him. I think he will have to receive a sharp lesson. If the youth gets his head in the air and thinks he can do as he pleases, things in general will go wrong,' Cromer wrote to Rosebery on 13 January 1893, his tone that of an aggrieved father. The crisis broke three days later, on the 16th, when the Khedive dismissed his Prime Minister Mustafa Fahmy, regarded in many Arab quarters as a British puppet, and sought to replace him with the more independently-minded Tigrane Pasha. He also demanded the removal of the ministers for Finance and Justice, who were known Anglophiles. Cromer, who had not been consulted about these changes, treated the Khedive's action as both a political *coup d'état* and a personal affront. He again telegraphed Rosebery, this time in even more vexed terms: 'The whole situation, not only of the English officials here, but also of the English government, will be changed if the Khedive is permitted to act as he has done in this matter and much trouble will be the result. A struggle with the Khedive is, as I have for some while foreseen, inevitable, and it is not advisable to delay it.' He then stated that the Liberals were partly to blame for the crisis: 'The Khedive has adopted his present attitude, I have excellent reasons for believing, to a great extent on the erroneous belief that HM Government will not support us so fully as the late one did.'[77] Rosebery immediately telegraphed to ask Cromer what action he planned to take in the event of the Khedive's refusal to back down. The answer was an inflammatory one, even for a committed imperialist like Rosebery: Cromer proposed that a British military force should seize possession of the ministries of Finance, Justice and the Interior, as well as the telegraph office. British officials would then take charge of the three departments and 'act generally under my instructions until such time as the Khedive had submitted to me the names of Ministers whom Her Majesty's Government could accept'.[78]

The crisis was discussed at a hastily summoned Cabinet meeting on 17 January, at which there was general agreement that Cromer's course was far too precipitous. For once on an imperial question Rosebery fully concurred with his colleagues, believing that military action should be the last, not the first, resort. He feared that if Cromer were to proceed with his alarming plan, the European powers would have an excuse to intervene in Egypt and Britain's role there would be threatened. With the support of the Cabinet, Rosebery telegraphed Cromer: 'We consider the means proposed by you too violent and such as might constitute a breach of International Law. It would be better to inform the Khedive, in case of his refusal, that he must be prepared to take the consequences of his act and that you must refer to HMG for instructions. That would give you breathing time to concert something less violent.'[79]

Cromer, furious at what he saw as Rosebery's betrayal and privately comparing him to Lord 'Pussy' Granville, fired back: 'I can suggest nothing less violent than the measures which I have already proposed.'[80] He then complained to the Queen who, predictably, took up his case, writing to Rosebery on 18 January: 'I am much surprised that such an important decision was not submitted to me before being telegraphed to Lord Cromer. The Khedive has been warned already of the grave consequences but he evidently sees that this means nothing, as the action of the British Government now proves.'[81] In response, Rosebery argued that 'Lord Cromer is in error in supposing that Lord Rosebery would not have given him his rigorous support. He did not think, however, at this stage a military occupation of public offices would be justified.'[82] Cromer realised that without the backing of his government, he would have to compromise. Much to his reluctance, he therefore agreed not to press for the reinstatement of Mustafa Fahmy, and instead accepted the Khedive's new choice as Prime Minister, Riaz Pasha. In his turn, the Khedive agreed to take Cromer's advice on important appointments in future. During this brief but potentially disastrous storm Rosebery had shown a surer touch than Cromer, who had over-reacted. Personal pique at being challenged by a young man of eighteen may have been part of the problem; in a letter to the Queen Rosebery suggested another possibility: 'Lord Cromer is gouty; but gout, though a disease by no means incompatible with statesmanship, is an element in the situation which requires vigilance on the part of the sufferer. That is to say that he must watch himself to see that it does not affect his manner or style.'[83]

The crisis was far from over. According to Cromer, still smarting over the affair, the perception in Egypt was that the Khedive had triumphed, for he had not been forced to reinstate the despised puppet Mustafa Fahmy. In his view, anti-British feeling had now reached a dangerous level, as he warned Rosebery: 'It would take very little to place the Khedive in the position of an Egyptian patriot opposing foreigners and Christians. The ultra-Muslim masses are very violent and mischievous.'[84] To suppress such potential discontent, he asked Rosebery to strengthen the British garrison in Egypt. This time Rosebery was ready to support him, believing that in the wake of the ministerial crisis Britain had to prove she was serious about maintaining her paramountcy in Egypt. 'We have had a significant warning and if we do not take it, we are at a new and alarming phase of the Egyptian question,' he wrote to Gladstone on 19 January. Gladstone could scarcely conceal his anger, telling Hamilton, 'It is appalling, this demand, as well as preposterous. With such pistols as are presented at my head, my life is a perfect burden to me. I would as soon put a torch to Westminster Abbey as send additional troops to Egypt. It can't be. Such proposals make me fearful for the future. I can see nothing for it but for Rosebery to resign.'[85] Hamilton managed to calm Gladstone before the Cabinet meeting later that day, at which Rosebery – 'very firm and at times almost vehement', according to Morley[86] – argued for more troops but initially received the support of just one other minister. Once more, however, the fear of losing him deterred the Cabinet from an outright rejection. Harcourt in particular was worried that Rosebery would be driven out of office, so he used his influence to broker a temporary deal by which a 'holding' telegram was to be sent to Cromer: 'We shall be prepared if necessary to increase the British garrison in Egypt but do not think the time propitious for an announcement; request authority before making it.'[87]

Rosebery, who had achieved far more than he had deemed possible at the start of the Cabinet meeting, was astonished by Harcourt's emollience. As Foreign Secretary and Chancellor checked the final wording of the telegram, Loulou recorded that his father 'has been in his most conciliatory mood today, most helpful and useful. I promptly asked if he was ill, which amused Rosebery very much.'[88] But Cromer was not at all satisfied, detecting the same climate of delay and compromise that had led to the nightmare of Khartoum. In the same condescending tone he had adopted with the Khedive, on 21 January he launched into Rosebery and the Liberal Ministry: 'The system under which Egypt has been governed for the last ten years has broken down. It was always very artificial and unsatisfactory and the wonder is that it has lasted so long. I cannot carry it on successfully any longer. You will have to choose between going backwards or forwards, i.e., either asserting yourself more strongly or retiring from the country.' Usually Rosebery would have been stung by such criticism, but on this occasion he concentrated on the central issue of military reinforcements. 'There is a Cabinet on Monday,' he telegraphed Cromer on the 21st, 'and if you do not receive the powers you ask by Monday evening the Foreign Office will have passed into other hands.'[89] With this stark message he succeeded for the first time in impressing Cromer, who replied on Sunday 22nd: 'I am very grateful for the confidence shown me in your private telegram. I have little doubt of the result but I need hardly say that if you unfortunately leave the FO I shall follow your example in my smaller sphere. The result will almost certainly be that many of the high English officials here will resign or be dismissed. In fact, the whole machine will collapse.'[90]

At the Cabinet meeting on 23 January Rosebery did not have to threaten resignation openly to bring his colleagues into line: they were all too aware of the possibility, without anything being said. As a way out of their predicament they lit upon an ingenious solution. A troopship on its way to India happened to be passing through the Suez Canal; Sir Henry Campbell-Bannerman, the bluff War Secretary, suggested that the infantry battalion it carried, the Black Watch, might be temporarily disembarked at Port Said to strengthen the garrison. In that way Cromer's demands would be met without overtly upsetting Gladstone's delicate sensibilities about direct military intervention. Ever the cynic, Loulou Harcourt noted that 'the troops could do no harm as they were mainly invalids and had no arms'.[91]

Intriguingly, Rosebery had no need to rely solely on official reports about Egyptian affairs; he had another, more private, source of intelligence about Egypt, one which would certainly have caused the hair of Labby, Blunt and the Radicals to stand on end had they known of it, confirming all their worst suspicions about the influence of bond-holders. Information was an essential element of the Rothschild family's widespread banking interests, and they regularly supplied Rosebery with diplomatic and financial news. In January 1893 he asked Regy Brett to tell them about the strengthening of the Egyptian garrison, and Regy reported after a visit to New Court, the Rothschilds' headquarters: 'I saw Natty and Alfred and told them that you were much obliged to them for having given you all the information at their disposal and therefore wished them to know of the reinforcement before reading it in the papers. Of course they were delighted and most grateful. Natty wished me to tell you that all the information and any assistance which he can give you is always at your disposal.'[92] The anti-Semites might have believed otherwise, but there is no evidence that, beyond the exchange of information, the Rothschilds brought any influence to bear on Rosebery's foreign policy decisions.

Cromer himself was relieved by the news of the battalion's arrival. The effect of their presence, he claimed, was 'instantaneous. The Europeans were reassured and the mood in the provinces checked.' Years later, in the course of a talk with Rosebery in 1915, Cromer learnt the full story of the Cabinet battle and was amused by Gladstone's sophistry: 'It is extraordinarily characteristic of Mr Gladstone's mentality that he should have seen any substantial difference between sending reinforcements from Malta or elsewhere and stopping a battalion on its way through the Suez Canal.'[93] Understandably in view of these events, Cromer regarded Rosebery much more favourably than Gladstone. 'Eastern politics were, in fact, distasteful to Gladstone,' he wrote. 'He naturally had no local knowledge, neither was he gifted with that rapid intuition which is often more valuable than local knowledge and which enabled statesmen such as Lord Salisbury and Lord Rosebery to grasp the main factors of any oriental problem presented to them for solution . . . Lord Rosebery had placed Egyptian affairs on as sound a footing as was possible under a difficult situation. He had scattered to the winds the idea that a speedy evacuation, regardless of the consequences, was contemplated. He let all concerned know that a great nation cannot lightly throw off its responsibilities which it has solemnly assumed in the face of the world.'[94]

Exactly a year later, during another Egyptian military crisis, Rosebery again displayed his toughness. In January 1894 the Khedive made another attempt to reassert his authority against Cromer by criticising the Egyptian army's British officers, led by the Sirdar, Herbert Kitchener. Amid claims of inefficiency, one of the Khedive's more frivolous complaints was that a British officer, passing him in the middle of the night, was too drunk to salute him properly. Prompted by Kitchener, Cromer demanded a public commendation for the army, and the sacking of the Khedive's War Minister, Maher Pasha, who was thought to be behind this mischief. He also telegraphed Rosebery, who was by now so confident in his role that he did not bother to consult his colleagues but wrote straight back, 'I regard this as very serious and so you may tell the Khedive. It has become a deliberate practice of his to insult British officers. This we cannot allow and if we could the nation would not.' He fully endorsed Cromer's proposed measures, adding that if the Khedive refused to remove Maher Pasha, then the entire Egyptian army should be placed under British command. Such a dramatic threat forced the Khedive to back down completely and agree to all Cromer wanted. 'He learnt it was useless to resist British policy in Egypt,' wrote Cromer.

The Liberal Cabinet had learnt it was useless to resist their magisterial Foreign Secretary. Through the force of his personality and against all the instincts of his party, he had proved victorious in the two most difficult crises of the administration. After initial suspicions, the other governments of Europe had learnt the greatest respect for Rosebery. 'His victory in the Cabinet', reported the German ambassador Count von Hatzfeldt on 5 February, 'and the undivided support which his energetic action in Egypt won for himself throughout the country have increased the confidence in himself and today he has no doubt that if the Cabinet holds together at all, his position in it is almost unshakeable.'[95] That was a view shared in Constantinople, as the British representative there, Sir Vincent Corbett, reported in March 1893. He said that when Rosebery first took office the Sublime Porte had regarded him patronisingly as 'a young man without experience, out of sympathy with his party, who need not trouble us too much as he is sure before long to quarrel with Mr Gladstone and come to grief.' But over the last seven months, opinion had completely altered. 'To put it frankly, the idea is that you are a wolf in sheep's clothing, out of sympathy with the Radicals, but supported by the Queen. The Austrians and Italians are inclined to think you are even better than Lord Salisbury, the French and Russians that you are, if possible, worse.'[96] Rosebery's successes had also completely won over the permanent officers in the diplomatic service; after dining with Charles Hardinge, Head of Chancery at the British embassy in Paris,* Edward Hamilton informed Rosebery: 'He tells me that he and the service at large are better pleased with their present Foreign Secretary than they have ever been before. Indeed, you seem to be a sort of fetish amongst them.'[97] Sir Rennell Rodd, who enjoyed a long diplomatic career, wrote in his memoirs that Rosebery 'has always remained to me the ideal master to serve'.[98]

Rosebery also had a strong supporter in the Queen, who basked in his courtly charm. 'Lord Rosebery is my support and is very open towards me and much devoted to me,' she wrote to her daughter in November 1892.[99] In August 1893 Rosebery recorded that he had a 'long and curious talk' with the Queen at Osborne, in which she said that it was ridiculous for a man of 83 to be Prime Minister: 'You ought to be there, Lord Rosebery, I wished you to be there and I hope you will be there. You are the only

---

*Later Baron Hardinge of Penshurst, Permanent Head of the Foreign Office.

one of the Ministry with whom I can talk freely.'[100] The one aspect of his relationship with the Queen which he found tiresome was her insistence that every document submitted to her must be in handwritten form. Through Ponsonby, Rosebery bravely tried to persuade her to change this arcane practice, passing on some samples of typefaces which he thought might be acceptable. 'We swarm with typewriters here at the Foreign Office and in every embassy, legation and consulate – or most of them,' he wrote to Ponsonby. 'These ingenious machines are paralysed by the Queen's displeasure. We have consequently set ourselves to mend our ways and I now send for your submission to Her Majesty a specimen which, to my admiring eyes, is rather the print of a family Bible than the faint scratch of a typewriter. Will she deign to smile on it and so liberate a fettered industry?'[101] Her Majesty would not, and right up to her death, the use of typewriters for any of her personal communications was banned.

Part of Rosebery's success lay in his heroic diligence. Unlike his floundering predecessor Lord Granville, he remained on top of the correspondence and the telegrams that flooded into his office, even when the despatch boxes built into a six-foot wall in front of his desk. He admitted to his sister, however, that the stress of his work was considerable, though balanced perhaps by his domestic responsibilities. In the very week of the Egyptian crisis in January 1893 he saw off his two sons Harry and Neil to Eton for the first time, an event he described in his diary for the 21st: 'We spent a miserable makeshift morning but the boys were very brave. I made all the children write their names in my bible and read John XIV. Then I went and bought the boys bibles and frames to hold their parents' portraits. Before the Cabinet yesterday, I sent the boys in to see Mr Gladstone to ask for his blessing before going to school. It was a very touching and beautiful sight. They and I were deeply moved. Alas, five minutes afterwards, Mr Gladstone and I were hammer and tongs over Egypt. At last, at 3.25, the boys went off, though poor Sybil sobbed over them. I shall never forget the cab with the precise initialled luggage on top.' Soon after their departure, he told Constance, 'I received more distracting telegrams. The strain on public grounds would have been very severe all this week and I think the private strain has so to speak tugged me straight. When I am anxious abroad I think of my trouble at home and vice-versa and like a whipping top am kept going by constant stripes.'[102] Regy Brett also left a memorable description of Rosebery working at home at The Durdans during that crisis: 'Rosebery reads everything. He did his boxes in the billiard room. He was humming a tune, which he suddenly discovered as "Rule Britannia". He said it was desirable that the Foreign Secretary should hum "Rule Britannia" so that the Foreign Secretary did not lose heart.'[103]

But Rosebery did not think those boxes provided a full enough picture of the mood abroad, so he instituted a new system by which every embassy was required to send him a weekly newsletter recording the social and intellectual news from its own country. Taking office in August 1892, he explained the reasoning behind this move: 'The Secretary of State is not to my mind sufficiently informed of the gossip of the various capitals. I was greatly struck by the different method pursued at Berlin. There they know *everything* – no detail is below their attention and in this I think they are right.'[104] Dufferin in Paris brought a perhaps excessive degree of prurient excitement to his interpretation of this new duty. Informing Rosebery of the 'collapse of morals' in the French capital, he wrote that 'men and women fly in the face of nature, arresting the propagation of the race by artificial means. The most abominably immoral literature is rampant. Lady models have appeared at a ball in their professional costume.'[105] Though he might seek gossip from overseas, Rosebery took little interest in London society. He invariably dined at home, and turned down most social invitations on the grounds of both Hannah's memory and his own workload. Edward Hamilton felt that this habit was tantamount to political negligence, as he wrote on 4 July 1893: 'R. refused to dine at the Russian Embassy and with the Fifes this week – both entertainments given for all foreign and home Royalties in connection with Prince George's wedding;* which I am sure was a mistake on his part and a step open to be misunderstood . . . It is all very well for him to say that he cannot get through his work unless he remains at home in the evening. But it is quite as important in his position that he should discharge his social duties as get through his "boxes". This anti-dining out craze is one of his peculiarities or eccentricities which it is impossible to fathom.'[106] More solitary than ever, Rosebery often confessed that he disliked entertaining. When Sir William Harcourt went down to The Durdans on 20 February 1893 he noticed from the visitors' book that he was the first to stay there since John Morley in November 1892. 'There was little food to be had and no drink. It was only with great difficulty that a thimbleful of brandy was obtained,'[107] complained Harcourt, though possibly that had more to do with Rosebery's low opinion of his colleague than his inadequacy as a host.

---

*The Duke of Fife was married to the Prince of Wales's daughter Louise; Prince George, the Prince of Wales's son, later King George V, was to marry Princess Mary of Teck on 6 July.

The most common error made about Rosebery as Foreign Secretary – and made as much by the political left in his own time as by historians since – has been to see him as an imperialist hawk, continually plunging Britain into danger by his 'forward' policies and only restrained by his less belligerent colleagues. Like so many pictures of Rosebery, this one is far from the truth. In fact, caution was one of the hallmarks of his spell in office. He preferred pragmatism to ideology, negotiation to war-mongering, consolidation to expansion. He was not one of those politicians, he once wrote, who were 'ready to risk embroiling the whole world for the possession of a worthless morass'.[108] It is telling that in the twin crises of Egypt and Uganda his aim was to uphold the status quo of British rule, rather than the more radical plan of evacuation. In Europe, his idea was always to preserve the balance of power by maintaining relations with the Triple Alliance without becoming a formal partner. With Russia, he avoided diplomatic and military trouble by carefully negotiating the settlement of potential disputes in Persia and in the Pamirs on the Afghan border. He was often accused of being anti-French, but he only was so where he felt British interests were being directly threatened; thus in Morocco, in which Britain had no stake, he was willing to let the French assert their supremacy.

This moderation was most clearly illustrated in Rosebery's handling of the problem of Siam. The French had long been involved in a dispute with the Siamese government over territory on the left bank of the Mekong River. As the row escalated in April 1893, the French despatched gunboats to Bangkok to enforce their demands. Despite the urgings of the British Minister in Bangkok to respond by sending in the Royal Navy, Rosebery refused to retaliate. 'The quarrel is not one in which Lord Rosebery desires to be mixed up,' the Foreign Office announced.[109] Rosebery had only two interests. The first was to protect British commerce, since Britain had three-quarters of all European trade with Siam; more importantly, he sought to ensure that the whole of Siam did not fall under French domination, for the result would have been a shared border between the British province of Burma and France's Far East empire – a sure recipe for continual antagonism and the costly deployment of increased numbers of British troops in the region. All Rosebery wanted was a Siamese buffer state to guard the Indian Empire from French incursion. Since France's current territorial demands did not affect the Burmese border, he was quite willing to urge the Siamese government to concede them. 'An attitude of defiance and unyielding opposition was only too likely to lead to an increase in French demands,' he warned.[110] In a letter to the Queen he set out the central goal of his policy:

261

It is to keep a buffer between the French frontier and that of India, in order that a vast expenditure and danger may not be incurred by the immediate proximity of a great military power on our south-eastern flank. If we can secure such an intermediate zone, state or territory, we shall have obtained all that Great Britain really requires . . . Lord Rosebery fears that Your Majesty will think all this very cold-blooded. He at any rate is not so. It makes his blood boil to read of the French proceedings. They invade and butcher the Siamese, and demand two-fifths of Siam for doing so. The Siamese indeed are not a very truthful or respectable race, but that is no excuse for treating them like vermin and for behaving to them not with common honesty, but with uncommon dishonesty. We cannot however keep the police of the world: the Empire is sufficient responsibility without that.[111]

The problem of Siam suddenly took a new turn when on 26 July the French announced that they were imposing a blockade on Bangkok to force the Siamese government to yield; friendly vessels, including those of the Royal Navy, were given three days to leave the area. Rosebery now felt he could no longer maintain his conciliatory stance; he had to confront the French. He therefore summoned the ambassador and warned him that this action could lead to war – if not a direct clash in Siam, 'then "une guerre sourde" ★ in every part of the world'.[112] In the face of such decisiveness, the French government in Paris proved reluctant to push Britain too far. After an interview with the French foreign minister Jules Develle on 27 July, Lord Dufferin reported to Rosebery that France was willing to accept 'a buffer state between our two empires'.[113] His suspicions of Gallic deviousness meant that Rosebery was never able to take statements from Paris at their face value. As he told Dufferin on the 28th, 'There seems to be no more connection between the French Government and French officials than there is between Mr Gladstone and Mr Chamberlain and the one seems just as likely to obey the other . . . I will take nothing verbally. If the whole French nation were to swear verbally to anything on the Old and New Testaments and the Apocrypha I should require strong corroborative evidence.'

Rosebery's scepticism proved well-founded. Despite the submission of the Siamese government and a promise by Develle to put 'in writing that they will accept a buffer state', the blockade was not lifted but in fact seemed to be intensified. On Sunday 30 July a British ship stationed off Bangkok, HMS *Linnet*, reported that she had been given an order by the

★ 'a silent war'.

French to withdraw, news that was immediately communicated to the Foreign Office. Rosebery knew his response could mean war between Britain and France, but in the heat of this crisis he did not flinch. He ordered HMS *Linnet* to remain where she was, then wrote to Gladstone demanding that an urgent Cabinet meeting be summoned: 'The French persist in the blockade, in spite of the unconditional surrender of the Siamese, and they order our gunboats to leave Bangkok which would leave our subjects and commerce absolutely unprotected.'[114]

Rosebery had effectively called the French government's bluff. The next day Develle announced that the blockade had been lifted, committed himself again to a buffer state, and promised that the French would pull out of the two Siamese provinces of Angkor and Battambang – something Rosebery had neither expected nor demanded. It was further explained that the matter of the so-called ultimatum sent to HMS *Linnet* had been no more than a terrible misunderstanding arising from a British naval officer's misinterpretation of the instructions he had received from the French. The crisis passed; no Cabinet meeting was needed; no war was declared; and peaceful negotiations began as to the precise boundary of the buffer state, though they were not concluded until 1896, after Rosebery had left his post. Rosebery was full of praise for the diplomatic section and its display of 'energy, persistence and the iron hand, sometimes with the velvet glove, sometimes without'. But in truth, this was Rosebery's shining hour. He had protected Britain's interests by means of a judicious mixture of tact, realism and toughness. In the end, he had won the peace by not quailing at the risk of war. On 2 August Dufferin told him it was his resolution that had shaken the French: 'When Develle found that the pretty strong language I held to him was reverberated in London and vice versa, he understood we were in earnest. It is half the battle when you feel you can count on your chief.'[115] Even Loulou Harcourt was forced to comment, as through gritted teeth, 'Rosebery has done very well in this business and will gain credit from it.'[116]

But one man refused to recognise Rosebery's accomplishments in office: the Prime Minister. Apart from a brief spell in 1885, Gladstone and Rosebery had never recovered the warmth that had grown between them during the first Midlothian campaign. Their relationship now was at freezing-point. Rosebery found Gladstone condescending and interfering. He claimed that the GOM never accepted a draft without making some pettifogging change, nor did he treat him properly in Cabinet; he told Algy West how when he tried to speak in the discussions on the Home Rule Bill on 16 February 1893, Gladstone put up his hand and said, 'Do hold your tongue.' After this meeting, Rosebery had sworn impetuously that he would never attend the Cabinet again.[117] Gladstone in his turn viewed Rosebery as aloof in manner and aggressive in policy, complaining frequently of his lack of judgement and telling Lord Rendel that he was 'disappointed in him as Foreign Minister from the very beginning'.[118] In October 1892 he was annoyed by Rosebery's high-handed attitude over his offer of the Order of the Garter, which – characteristically – Rosebery was at first inclined to refuse. When he finally accepted it, he did so without much grace. 'It seems to me that the time for Garters and the like has long gone for me, and there is no one now to be pleased,' he wrote to Gladstone on 6 October. 'If you prefer to press your present proposal I shall not be so ungracious as to resist. Only I would ask that whatever you decide I may not hear any more on the subject.'[119] By 1893 Gladstone's attitude towards Rosebery verged on the contemptuous. In a note written in his retirement, he expressed regret at ever having made him Foreign Secretary. 'My bringing him to the Foreign Office was indeed an immense advancement, but was done with the belief, not sustained by subsequent experience, in his competency and wisdom.'[120] When Morley talked to him in December 1893 about the possibility of Rosebery becoming his successor as Prime Minister, he found that 'the idea stings [Gladstone] and makes him thoroughly angry'.[121] There was undoubtedly a tinge of insecurity in Gladstone's annoyance. Earlier in the year, during the Siam crisis, Morley called at Downing Street to find Gladstone attacking Rosebery 'with his usual sharpness. "Rosebery has no confidence in me," he repeated several times, "none, none whatsoever. Was he thinking of the succession?" I said I had no doubt that it was in his mind. That it was in fact not possible that it should not be; that his victory over us all as to Uganda had given him a new view of his position in public confidence and esteem. Mr Gladstone replied, "Uganda has precious little to do with it." His anger against Rosebery led him to attack Harcourt. "But for those two, the Cabinet would be admirable."'[122] Indeed, Gladstone once told Henry Asquith that 'of all the men he had presided over in his many Cabinets, Rosebery was the most difficult.'*

The greatest issue of Gladstone's last premiership, Irish Home Rule, did nothing to improve relations. As Gladstone waged the final battle of his career he perceived, with some justification, that Rosebery was providing only lukewarm support. Rosebery's enthusiasm for the measure was indeed starting to wane, largely because of the damage it was causing to

*Margot Asquith, *More memories*.

Liberalism, and he told the Queen in June that he did not regard Home Rule as 'a panacea for the secular ills of Ireland'. But there was, he said, no realistic alternative, for 'were the hope of Home Rule to be removed, the latent forces of anarchy and revolution would break out with renewed horror. He considers therefore that the Government has no choice but to go on with their measure.'[123] Having passed the House of Commons on 2 September 1893, the Home Rule Bill then reached the Lords, where the Unionist majority was overwhelming. Rosebery was due to speak on behalf of the Government; shortly before the debate he received a poignant, rambling letter from his old friend Lord Randolph Churchill, who was in the grip of terminal illness. Churchill's pitiful decline had already been demonstrated in a speech of embarrassing incoherence he had made in the Commons on the Bill's second reading. He now summoned the energy to urge Rosebery to oppose the Bill: 'I have never known or read of anyone in modern English history', he wrote on 2 September, 'who occupies so high an official position, possesses so large an amount of popular confidence and who, at the same time, was so free from anything approaching political animosity from any quarter.' Because of this unique position, he said with some exaggeration, Rosebery had 'the power to decide between repeal and union'. And again he raised the chimera of some new centre party alliance: 'It is my dream that someday I may have the satisfaction of finding myself in the same party and holding the same opinions as you will hold.'[124] Within little more than a year of that letter, Churchill was dead.

Rosebery had no intention of breaking party ranks in the debate on Home Rule. But his speech on behalf of the Government only confirmed Gladstone's disappointment in him. Rather than addressing the case for Home Rule he made a light-hearted, bantering address which, as Lord Kimberley noted, 'most ingeniously evaded saying much in the support of the bill'.[125] John Morley, the Irish Secretary, felt almost as let down as his chief: 'It was an ill-judged, ill-balanced performance,' he wrote.[126] Interestingly, Rosebery privately agreed with this assessment, but noted in his diary that the cause was not political, but rather the inadequacy of his preparation – the failing for which his friend George Smalley of the *New York Tribune* had regularly chastised him in the 1880s: 'Ill prepared and by an unlucky muddle thought I had been speaking two hours instead of one. This made me omit some important arguments and disturbed the balance of my speech. Went home profoundly disgusted with myself.'[127] Even the oratory of Cicero would not have made any difference to the outcome, however; the Lords defeated the Bill by the resounding margin of 419 votes to 41. Ireland was to go through another thirty years and two bloody wars before finally achieving self-government.

In November Rosebery appeared to recover his Midas touch, this time on the domestic rather than the foreign front when he confirmed his reputation as a constructive Radical. During much of Gladstone's last government Britain was in the grip of an economic recession, caused by a downturn in international trade and growing industrial competition. The result was a tide of industrial unrest; in 1893, 30,440,000 working days were lost to strikes and lock-outs.[128] Traditional Gladstonian Liberalism, with its emphasis on individual freedom and minimal state interference, seemed to have no answer to the growing problems of labour at the end of the nineteenth century, though there was a younger breed of Liberals, among them Rosebery and Asquith, who were prepared to contemplate a more interventionist economic approach. In his leadership of the LCC Rosebery had shown he was willing to adopt such innovative measures as limits on working hours and the extension of municipal trading; like local government, the coal industry was another area where new thinking was desperately needed. Prices had fallen by 40 per cent since 1890, with a consequent cut in wages of up to 25 per cent.[129] In this depression a fierce struggle had developed between the miners and the coal-owners. The Miners' Federation rejected a demand for wage cuts, and at the end of July a strike began. In keeping with high Victorian Liberal principles, the response of the Government was to do nothing. But as the stoppage dragged on and the miners faced the prospect of hardship and even starvation, Liberal backbenchers grew restive. On 1 November, a meeting held at the National Liberal Club declared its full backing for the miners. Under this pressure, on 10 November Gladstone discussed the strike with Asquith and Arthur Acland, the Education Minister, and, as the latter informed Rosebery: 'Your name has been mentioned as a possible moderator, after all the skill you showed on the LCC. I believe that if you were to offer to sit as Chairman only, without a casting vote, without proposing to offer any opinion, at the next meeting of masters and men for one day, they would not separate without coming to an agreement.'[130]

Rosebery accepted although, as he confessed to the Queen, he was 'very ignorant of the questions involved'.[131] On the morning of 17 November the two sides met at the Foreign Office, with Rosebery in the chair, assisted by Llewellyn Smith, a Labour Department official, acting as secretary. For several hours the negotiations appeared to be going nowhere, until Rosebery put forward the idea of creating a Board of Conciliation, with 14 representatives on each side, to meet in a month's time. The employers then disappeared for two hours to discuss the proposal over a cold luncheon that Rosebery had provided in another room at the Foreign Office; the miners were much more businesslike, spending only twenty minutes over their meal. By late afternoon both sides were ready to accept Rosebery's proposition, and at 5.20 agreement was formally reached. After sixteen weeks, the strike was over. Rosebery's tact and shrewdness had enabled him to pull off a magnificent coup. In a mood of exultant celebration the Trade Secretary A.J. Mundella wrote to him immediately after receiving the news: 'Thank God! This should be one of the happiest moments of your life. Everywhere in London men are cheering for Lord Rosebery. In every town and hamlet, in every home in England the people will bless you. The House of Commons is delighted. I am personally grateful to you, while rejoicing in what this will bring to you. It means more than you can realize at this moment. Llewellyn Smith describes your management in rapturous terms.'[132] Rosebery dined alone that night, tired but contented. 'It would have been a good day to die on,' he wrote in his diary.

Rosebery had not only gained a personal triumph; he had also set a far-reaching political precedent. His intervention marked the first time that a Cabinet Minister acted as mediator in a serious industrial dispute. Within only a few months of his settlement, Asquith was arbitrating in a strike by London cabmen. Within two years, a Conciliation Act was passed giving the Board of Trade the power to oversee industrial relations. Rosebery's action paved the way for Butskellism,* tripartite talks, and 'beer and sandwiches at Number Ten', those interminable meetings of the 1960s and 1970s that encapsulated the trade union domination of the British economy.

In late 1893, however, Rosebery was by far the most popular politician in the country, a man who apparently could do no wrong. *The Times* marvelled at his industriousness, versatility and political skill, describing him as 'an over-worked Atlas'. In comic vein, the newspaper wrote that 'if Foreign Secretaries were properly organised on trade union principles, some apprehension might reasonably be felt that Lord Rosebery should be boycotted as a black-leg for the flagrant violation of recognised precedents tending to undermine a cherished tradition of his craft.' But in mitigation, *The Times* said he did not appear to suffer by his work. 'His speeches are so bright and easy that, even when most suggestive, they appear to be the

---

*A term used in the 1960s and 1970s to describe the consensus between Labour and Conservatives in favour of an interventionist economic policy and permanent engagement with the trade union movement. It was named after the Tory Chancellor Rab Butler and Labour leader Hugh Gaitskell.

spontaneous outcome of his thoughts at the moment when they are uttered. The air of genial good humour which they breathe is one of the chief secrets of Lord Rosebery's popularity with his countrymen.'[133] A distinguished French author, Augustin Filon, later cited Rosebery's handling of the coal negotiations as one of the reasons why he was regarded with such bafflement and admiration in both Britain and Europe:

> Surprises, contradictions and contrasts have combined to produce this remarkable statesman who is, by turns, the spoilt child of both parties, the hope of Imperialism, the man of the County Council, the victor of the turf, acceptable at Court and in sympathy with advanced democracy – a man whose very advent puts an end to the most formidable strike, and who sets gaily to work to demolish the aristocracy to which he himself belongs, without probably losing the friendship or good opinion of any of his fellows. How can the same individual please so many people, advance so many causes, play so many parts, and play them with frank good humour and a genial bearing which preclude the idea of doubtful cleverness or insincerity? Amongst all these successive or simultaneous Roseberys, where is the real Rosebery, the authentic and final Rosebery?[134]

In one of his incarnations, as patriotic Foreign Secretary, Rosebery was concerned that the Royal Navy was becoming increasingly weak and old-fashioned in comparison with the navies of other European powers. He saw the navy as the key to upholding Britain's Empire, especially in a volatile world where clashes with France and Russia seemed inevitable. As he explained to the Queen when writing about the need for a strong navy, 'Lord Rosebery is more interested in this question than any of Your Majesty's Ministers, for the authority and weight of the Foreign Office suffers obvious diminution when the Navy is suspected of weakness.'[135] In this he had been heavily influenced by the seminal work *The Influence of Sea Power Upon History*, published in 1890 by the American naval historian Captain Alfred Mahan, who asserted that no power could be imperially or commercially great without a powerful battle fleet. Rosebery's fears about the Royal Navy were not based just on literary scare-mongering. Britain faced a genuine problem in the early 1890s, since for all the vast size of the Royal Navy, rapid advances in ship design, armour and gunnery meant that it was in danger of becoming obsolete unless it kept pace with the developing forces of France, Japan and Germany. When Rosebery was born in 1847, British naval supremacy was based on wooden ships that lasted sixty years. Now, at the end of the century, changing technology meant that the useful life of British vessels was inevitably far shorter. Rosebery was keenly aware of the need for Britain to embark on an extensive building programme to provide new classes of battleship. During 1893 he constantly badgered Earl Spencer, the First Lord of the Admiralty, and his views were echoed by the campaigning journalist W.T. Stead, who worked up the cry of 'two keels to one', by the Queen, and by the Sea Lords, who warned Spencer in December 1893 that France and Russia would achieve numerical superiority to the Royal Navy within three years unless drastic action were taken. Despite his closeness to Gladstone Lord Spencer supported naval expansion, but not vigorously enough for Rosebery. When on 20 December 1893 the Tory MP Lord George Hamilton, a former First Lord of the Admiralty, put down a Commons motion demanding a 'consideration addition' to the Royal Navy estimates, he was defeated by 240 votes to 204, for the Liberal Whips treated the division purely as a question of confidence in the Government. Rosebery, who always despised any suggestion that party loyalty should come before the needs of Empire, wrote to Spencer in harsh terms: 'What I deplore is that at the moment when a clear and decisive note should have been sounded in Europe, which would have anticipated many evils and guaranteed peace, we had something, abominable from the point of view of House of Commons tactics, but ambiguous, obscure and therefore disastrous. You do not seem to take in that what was wanted, quite as much as much as new naval strength, was the moral effect of a timely if general declaration.'[136]

At the same time Lord Spencer was being assailed from the other side, as Gladstone and Harcourt, the twin pillars of Liberal economy and antimilitarism, dismissed the calls for a bigger navy as 'alarmist'. When Spencer warned that he might resign and spend his time hunting in Northamptonshire, Harcourt responded by saying that *he* might retire to look after cabbages at Malwood. But Gladstone was even more determined than Harcourt in his opposition, calling the higher naval estimates 'mad, mad, mad'. And in this opposition on the part of the Prime Minister lay the origins of the leadership crisis which was about to convulse the Liberal party.

10

'I must be a real Prime Minister'

ON 14 DECEMBER 1893 Gladstone's secretary Algy West called on Rosebery. 'He was full of Mr Gladstone's ageing, in which I am very inclined to agree. Discussed how his retirement could be brought about; he wished it had been in 1880, or that it had taken place when the Lords threw out the Home Rule Bill.'[1]

Even Gladstone's keenest admirers could not deny that by the end of 1893 he was rapidly losing his fitness for office. On 29 December he celebrated his 84th birthday. His failing eyesight meant that he lived in a permanent fog, barely able to read. His physical decline was almost palpable. John Morley was shaken to sit beside him one evening in the House of Commons and find him 'looking like a witch'.[2] His sense of proportion was dwindling. When the Queen made a mild enquiry about Britain's defences in time of war, a fit of vomiting and diarrhoea forced him to take to his bed. He repeatedly condemned the increased naval estimates as insane, yet there was an air of madness in his ravings about supposed militarism. 'The admirals have got their knife into me,' he shrieked at Algy West. With his Cabinet colleagues, whom he tried to see as little as possible, he was either angry and argumentative or quiet and pathetic.

There was nothing noble about Gladstone's senile isolation. In its wilfulness it was, as Morley wrote, more like 'the resistance of a child or an animal to an uncomprehensible & (incredible) torment.' His stance on the navy was regarded by the rest of the Cabinet as irresponsible and unrealistic, especially since the increase in expenditure demanded by the First Lord of the Admiralty was hardly exorbitant, amounting to just £3 million. While Spencer and Rosebery hinted at resignation if the increase was refused, Gladstone's two most likely allies, Harcourt and Morley, abandoned him. After subjecting Spencer to much 'brutality and insolence',[3] on 6 January 1894 Harcourt finally accepted that he would just have to 'make the best of a bad job'. Similarly Morley, the arch economist, was willing to swallow Rosebery's argument that 'for us to strengthen the navy is the surest guarantee of European peace'.[4]

But Gladstone remained adamant. At a meeting of the Cabinet on 9 January he subjected his colleagues to a harangue lasting 50 minutes, which Edward Hamilton claimed was 'the longest speech probably ever made in Cabinet.'★ When Harcourt, responding as Chancellor of the Exchequer, said that Spencer's plan was inevitable and could be paid for, Gladstone wheeled theatrically on his chair and turned his back on him. Rosebery then pressed for a decision on the naval estimates, pointing out that further delay was impossible and would only undermine the Government. The Cabinet provisionally agreed to Spencer's proposal, though Gladstone again loudly voiced his objections and warned that he was on the verge of retirement: 'I can go at once if you wish it,' he said roughly to Harcourt. But rather than carrying out this threat, at the end of the meeting he announced that he would be disappearing for a month to the resort of Biarritz on the French west coast. The Cabinet was left on tenterhooks as to what his next move would be.

Whatever Gladstone decided, it was clear that the end of his illustrious career was rapidly approaching. The questions now were the manner of his departure, and the choice of his successor. There was a remote possibility that without its figurehead the Government would fall apart completely. Now that Home Rule had been defeated, Gladstone's leadership, no matter how enfeebled, was the only distinct and unifying force in the Liberal party. Alternatively, to remain in office the Government could opt for a less controversial leader who might be able to promote consensus and avoid divisions – an 1890s Liberal equivalent of Lord Liverpool, the modest Tory who became the nineteenth century's longest-serving Prime Minister. The two obvious names in this regard were Lord Kimberley, the Indian Secretary and present Leader of the House of Lords, and Earl Spencer, first Lord of the Admiralty. Little known by the public, lacking in authority, self-confidence and oratorical talent, neither was a political heavyweight. But both were reliable and solid, respected in the Liberal party for their long record of service – Kimberley had been an under-secretary at the Foreign Office as long ago as 1852. Interestingly, both had followed Rosebery's example of aristocratic municipal leadership by becoming chairman of their respective county councils, Spencer at Northamptonshire and Kimberley at Norfolk.

Yet speculation about a Kimberley or Spencer leadership, though common enough in early 1894, was an irrelevance. Everyone in the Liberal party knew that the real decision lay between the two biggest stars of the

---

★ This was in fact far from true; in 1853 Gladstone had spoken to the Cabinet for three hours in explaining his budget.

Cabinet, Rosebery and Harcourt. Despite the personal tragedy of his wife's death, Rosebery had enjoyed five years of almost unbroken political success. His rare combination of imperialism and radicalism made him the darling of the Liberal press and public. 'We have not forgotten,' thundered an editorial in the left-wing *Daily Chronicle* at the height of the succession battle, 'and the miners of Lancashire and Yorkshire have not forgotten that Lord Rosebery saved the country from industrial war and guaranteed to thousands of workmen a living wage.'[5] In London and Scotland, two of Liberalism's key bases, he had achieved heroic stature. Through his personal charm he had the priceless political gift of making every interest and class feel that he was on their side, as he had so spectacularly demonstrated in settling the coal strike. Though many Liberals disliked his foreign policy, they were impressed by his decisiveness. Above all, as Foreign Secretary his unrelenting concentration on his own portfolio had prevented him from interfering in the departmental work of other ministers, with the result that he had made few enemies in the Cabinet.

The same could not be said of Sir William Harcourt, who was notorious for his bullying interventions against almost every other minister. Length of service and breadth of experience gave him some right to think he should have been the natural successor to Gladstone, especially as he was by twenty years Rosebery's senior. He had been the Liberal MP for Oxford when Rosebery was at Christ Church. Where Rosebery might display rhetorical brilliance on the platform, he wielded real debating power in the Commons. Where Rosebery had chaired a county council, he had controlled the nation's finances. Besides, he was more in tune with the traditional Liberal mainstream of his Parliamentary party than the enigmatic Earl. Had the vote been decided by a ballot of MPs, then according to John Morley's estimate, Harcourt would probably have won by a margin of three to one. But the decision was effectively in the hands of the Cabinet and the Sovereign, and therein lay Harcourt's biggest problem: he was loathed in both quarters. 'He is a person I particularly dislike and cannot respect,' wrote the Queen to her daughter Empress Vicky, after granting the Chancellor an audience in October 1892. 'He is terrible-looking now, but it was said that I had better see him as he was very amenable to any attention paid to him. But I hate it.'[6] To Rosebery she complained in 1899 that she 'could never bear Sir William',[7] a feeling shared by almost every member of the Cabinet, no matter what their political views. Complaints about his rudeness and his lack of principle were incessant during this era. 'He is brutal, no doubt. It is a strong word but there is no other word for this extraordinary man,' said Gladstone.[8] The Liberal Cabinet Minister

George Shaw-Lefevre wrote: 'It seemed to me that a demon possessed Harcourt during this period and brought him into antagonism with nearly every one of his colleagues. I was a subject of it myself and found it almost impossible to do business with him.'[9] The journal of Lord Kimberley, in general a mild-mannered man, crackles with irritation at Harcourt, as these two entries show:

11 August 1888 Harcourt changes his opinions as fast as the chameleon its colours. I have often known him within 24 hours to argue with equal vehemence on opposite sides of important questions and this not in orations but private discussions. How can he ever lead the party?

19 September 1893 Found Harcourt in a ridiculous fuss about the Indian budget. He fumed and raged for an hour, after which we went quietly together to luncheon. He really is quite intolerable as well as absurd.[10]

Nearly all ministers found Harcourt bad enough as Chancellor; the thought of him as Premier was abhorrent. This was certainly the feeling that was conveyed to Algy West after a meeting in July 1893 with the Home Secretary H.H. Asquith, a good barometer of Cabinet opinion: 'In the Commons, nobody could lead with Harcourt there; he appears an impossibility, as his colleagues would neither serve under him nor with him.'[11] Rosebery himself once described Harcourt as a 'man of many qualities, all marred by a violent, uncontrollable temper.'[12] Yet Harcourt was not malicious, and most of his brusqueness was on the surface. Unlike so many politicians, there was nothing sly or scheming about him; had there been, he would not have been so aggressive in his dealings with his colleagues. Sir Evelyn Ruggles-Brise, as a young man his secretary at the Home Office, gave this description of him: 'His anger had much of the quality of summer lightning. It was fierce, but it did not last or do much damage. It was my first business in the morning to call on him at 7 Grafton Street to take letters and receive instructions. He used to come down to me in his dressing-gown, very large, very red and generally very angry with some intolerable person or some impossible demand. But having exploded his anger, the sun came out and his natural gaiety and temper would revive.'[13] This may have been true, but Ministers of the Crown resented being treated in such a manner.

None resented it more strongly than John Morley, the Chief Secretary for Ireland, who should have been Harcourt's closest ally during the succession crisis. After all, Morley and Harcourt's son Loulou had concluded the secret 'Malwood compact' in 1890 by which Morley promised to back Sir William for the leadership when Gladstone retired, in return for one of the great offices of state, probably the Treasury. After 1892 Morley found Sir William's behaviour so offensive that he privately decided he was no longer bound by the terms of the agreement, but even before Gladstone's last government had been formed he had been complaining that Harcourt was 'an awfully tiresome creature'.[14] He was aggrieved to discover that Harcourt, without telling him, had at that time held a number of informal meetings with colleagues – known in the press as the 'Brook Street Conferences' – to discuss the composition of the Gladstone Ministry. The importance of these consultations was probably exaggerated but Morley, vain and sensitive, felt snubbed and never forgave Harcourt. The following year, 1893, his trust and dissatisfaction turned to fury when Harcourt, whose backing for Home Rule was even more tepid than Rosebery's, refused to give him any help with the financial clauses of the Irish Bill. 'What you do', he told Harcourt, 'is ostentatiously to hold aloof from the business, and then when others do the best they can, you descend on them with storm and menace.'[15] Feeling more insecure than ever, Morley severed all relations with Harcourt and made himself 'unapproachable'. In July 1893, when Asquith determined that he would not serve under Harcourt and told Morley 'no more would you', Morley replied, 'That at least is fixed and certain.'[16] Six months later, shortly before the fateful Cabinet meeting of 9 January 1894, he met Campbell-Bannerman, a granite-like Scot of sound judgement. 'To my surprise he took much the same view of Harcourt as the rest of us, i.e., we all agreed that Harcourt was no good to us, he constantly muffed things and that if he were gone we should be much better off without him. This is extraordinary, yet there he is and there he shall have to rest.'[17] Morley's desertion was to prove disastrous for Harcourt's hopes of Downing Street. He was never leadership material himself, being too querulous, inconstant and insubstantial – a man who, in Rosebery's words, 'was constantly threatening to talk big and sound the big drum but, when it came to the point, said nothing or else made the smallest audible sound only.'[18] But Morley was a pivotal figure in Liberalism. Because of his closeness to the GOM and his role in the development of the Home Rule policy, he was seen as the keeper of the Gladstonian flame. Denied the chance to seek power himself, he could now exert decisive influence as a power-broker inside the party.

It might seem strange that Morley should want to use this influence not just negatively against Harcourt but positively in favour of Rosebery, who had clashed so bitterly with Gladstone and was no evangelist for Home Rule. Yet as he had demonstrated in his logistically exhausting attempts to persuade Rosebery to accept the Foreign Office in 1892, Morley had a deep appreciation of the Earl's qualities as a statesman. Since the late 1880s he had been close to the group of bright young Liberal MPs headed by Asquith, Grey and Haldane who looked to Rosebery as their future leader. He regularly attended their Articles Club dinners and, according to Asquith's biographers, he was 'uncritically accepted and whole-heartedly admired' by these young Liberals as 'a mentor, sponsor, in matters political a guide, philosopher and friend'.[19] For all his democratic credentials, there was a Whiggish element in Morley's character that favoured political elitism and was drawn to aristocrats 'trained by the habits and tradition of public affairs and great duties'.[20] And no one fitted this archetype better than the 5th Earl of Rosebery, whom he described, late in life, as 'the most natural-born leader I have ever met'.[21] From an undistinguished, provincial, middle-class background himself, Morley was attracted by Rosebery's patrician glamour and authority. He stated as much during the leadership crisis, when he praised the way Rosebery 'does excite interest and curiosity; he is a Peer, with great wealth, an air of mystery, an affectation for literature and is probably going to win the Derby.'[22] Possibly there was also a more Machiavellian reason why Morley wanted Rosebery to be Prime Minister: as a Little Englander he was implacably opposed to Rosebery's imperialist policies, and therefore decided that the most convenient way to end his control of foreign affairs lay in helping promote him to the higher post. According to the journal of Loulou Harcourt, who saw Morley almost every day throughout the crisis, Rosebery himself said to Morley on 3 March, 'I believe one of the principal reasons you desire me to be Prime Minister is in order to get me out of the Foreign Office.' In Loulou's account, 'Morley admitted that this was a fact.'

Unlike some later British chancellors, Sir William Harcourt was not consumed by an ambition to become party leader. While he would have liked the post, he had never done much to promote himself, cultivating neither the press nor colleagues. He admitted, with laughing insouciance, that he was 'a fool not to control his temper'. But one figure was obsessed with his reaching Downing Street: his own son Loulou. Sophisticated, adroit and feline, Lewis Harcourt had worked as his father's secretary for a decade, putting all his political skill into furthering Sir William's career. So great was his filial devotion that he rejected offers of safe Liberal seats and prominent public positions in order to remain by his father's side. As the leadership crisis unfolded, Loulou was determined to use all his talents for intrigue and manipulation to secure his father's triumph. 'He says he did not work for ten years at wire-pulling if he is not to reap the fruit,' recorded Regy Brett after a talk with Loulou on 14 January.[23] But Loulou was not just a cunning young man: he was also a singularly unpleasant one. His most notable characteristic, apart from his passion for his father's work, was his sexual craving for adolescents. It was an urge that had first gripped him when he was at Eton,[24] and had led to his expulsion. In spite of this disgrace, as an adult he could not keep away, and he and Regy Brett, who shared his tastes, made regular trips there to drool over the pupils. Instead of having the two perverts arrested, Eton merely warned its boys not to go for walks with them. In the privacy of Loulou's library he and Regy also pored over child pornography, and it was alleged that during his lifetime Loulou amassed the largest collection in Britain of such material. But there was this difference between the two men: whereas Regy Brett was essentially a romantic in his feelings towards boys, Loulou was much more inclined to physical aggression. This tendency to pounce brought about his end, long after his father had died and he himself had reached Cabinet rank. Though his proclivities had long been whispered about in society, because of his standing as a Liberal elder statesman no action had ever been taken against him. In the autumn of 1921, however, he tried to assault a boy, Edward James, who was visiting the Harcourts' Oxfordshire home with his family. In his memoirs James recalled fighting off the advances of this 'hideous and horrible old man'.[25] Loulou had gone too far: James's mother was outraged, and threatened to expose him. In the face of imminent scandal, Loulou retreated to the study in his London home and took a drugs overdose. The cause of his death was hushed up.

The sinister ruthlessness and lack of chivalry displayed by Loulou in his personal life were brought to bear in his fight on his father's behalf. Plotting came naturally to this tall, emaciated figure, 'as lean as Cassius', in A.G. Gardiner's memorable description of him. Loulou had never been particularly fond of Rosebery, but now, in the heat of the contest, he grew openly hostile. As he planned the battle, his first goal was to persuade his father to fight. On the night of 10 January, over dinner, inevitably the question of the leadership came up. When Loulou asked his father what he would do if Rosebery, having accepted the Queen's commission, asked him to serve, Sir William replied, 'What can I do but say yes? How can I allow it to be thought and said by our own people that I allowed what I considered my personal claims and interests to stand in the way of the continuance of the Liberal Party in power?' Loulou's journal continues: 'I argued against this feebly but I knew he was right. It will be a splendid sacrifice if it has to be made but it will be easier for him than it will be for me. He has hardly any ambition and I have a double dose – his and my own share – but all directed to his advancement. I have given up the ten best years of my life to make him Prime Minister and I will not see it fade away without a struggle.'[26] In addition to bolstering his father, Loulou next had the difficult task of trying to persuade Morley to stick to the Malwood compact. With his instinctive grasp of the political situation Loulou knew that Morley could make or break his father's leadership bid. On 11 January, the day after his talk with his father, he ran into Morley at the House of Commons. 'The future is very dark. It is a great pity that the Malwood compact has been broken up – and broken up not by my act or my desire,' said Morley.[27] Disturbed by this remark, Loulou sought a full interview with him, which took place the next day. According to Morley's diary, 'Loulou asked, "Do you mean you no longer hold your old Malwood opinion about my father not serving under R?" I replied that it held no longer, that I was as convinced as ever of the immense difficulty of a Liberal Prime Minister being in the House of Lords where he would only have about 30 followers, where he would never be able to guide or control the House of Commons, but that his father's unhappy conduct on the Irish Bill and Irish policy generally had made it out of the question for me to retain my old political relation to him. Loulou's face fell very low at this announcement.'[28] In Loulou's account, he recovered his composure enough to warn of the dire consequences if his father was not supported, telling Morley that Sir William 'ought to say at once that under no circumstances will he serve under Rosebery. I said Rosebery had no right to ask it, that Chex* had done the larger part of the fighting for the party with J.M. for the last six years, that he had been 20 years longer in active politics and was 20 years older. J.M. pointed out that it would be impossible to form a government without Chex, that then the responsibility for the break-up of the Government would lie with him.' The conversation then turned to the Foreign Secretaryship, which Morley secretly coveted as an escape from the drudgery of the Irish Office. Loulou dismissed any idea of his father taking the post: 'The place would not suit him and any subordinate place is out of the question.'[29] Morley replied that a Harcourt premiership 'would mean the Home Rule flag flying at half-mast'. 'Not much lower than it would fly under Rosebery,' said Loulou, and ended the conversation on a note of menace: 'All I can say is that other people can have bad eyes as well as Mr Gladstone. If I have any influence that will be my advice.'[30]

---

*Chex, short for Chancellor of the Exchequer, was Loulou's nickname for his father throughout this period. When Sir William was out of office, Loulou simply referred to him in his journal as 'papa'.

Loulou's machinations were predicated on the belief that Rosebery actually wanted to be Prime Minister, but this was far from clear. The Earl was too complex a man to harbour such a straightforward ambition. His dislike of politics was real enough. His pride left him apprehensive that he might not be fitted to the post. He was enjoying his work at the Foreign Office, where he had real power – 'he is absolute master at the Foreign Office. He informs his colleagues very little and does as he pleases,' wrote Regy Brett.[31] Local government aside, he had little experience of domestic issues. In the new age of democracy, a peer Premier, especially a Liberal one, seemed to him an anomaly. From what he had seen of Gladstone's leadership, the premiership could well be the least rewarding of all political offices. In April 1887 Edward Hamilton, who had already decided Rosebery was the only possible successor to Gladstone, recorded this conversation at The Durdans: 'The duties of Prime Minister would with him go much against the grain. He had amused Bismarck by his definition of the Prime Minister of this country. He had likened it to a "dunghill", on which the other ministers threw everything that was disagreeable – a simile in which there is much truth.'[32] In April 1891 Regy Brett saw Rosebery at Berkeley Square and had a 'very satisfactory' talk about the future. 'He will not be Prime Minister,' wrote Brett, 'or lead the House of Lords. As Prime Minister in that House, a Liberal Minister is a mere cockshy for his colleagues in the House of Commons. R. said, "Place Harcourt in a position where it becomes his great endeavour to keep the Ministry together." This means Harcourt to be Prime Minister. Then as Foreign Secretary, R. would be unfettered as Harcourt would leave him alone for fear of breaking up the Ministry. It is a well-planned scheme, carefully thought out, but will he stick to it?'[33]

Late in 1893, just months before the leadership crisis, Rosebery was influenced by a conversation he had with Dr Robert Spence-Watson, a leading figure in the National Liberal Federation. 'Can you tell me, Dr Watson, why should I not make an admirable Prime Minister?' asked Rosebery. Watson replied, 'Yes, Lord Rosebery, I will give you three reasons. In the first place, you were born with a silver – or rather a golden – spoon in your mouth and to your misfortune had your slightest wants extravagantly anticipated. That was a very bad beginning. Secondly, you never fought a Parliamentary election in your life and therefore never came into intimate touch with the requirements of democracy. Thirdly, as you keep racehorses, you will always offend the Nonconformist Conscience.' With a rueful laugh Rosebery replied, 'Yes, I believe you are right, Dr Watson.'[34]

The irony of the situation was that Rosebery was one of the few ministers who claimed he would have been willing to serve under Harcourt's leadership, provided that he remained in complete charge of foreign policy. 'If Mr G. does go,' wrote Hamilton after seeing Rosebery on 15 January, 'R. believes that on the whole, if the difficulties with other colleagues can be surmounted, the best arrangement would be for Harcourt to be head. Under it, R. would himself be left with a perfectly free hand, and would be really more powerful (for good) than if he were Prime Minister, while Harcourt would be forced to be on his good behaviour towards everyone. For R. to be Prime Minister there would be two very grave difficulties – an irreconcilable Harcourt and no one to conduct Foreign Affairs.' Nothing had changed by the end of the month, as Hamilton noted after dining privately at The Durdans: 'R. would hate to exchange the Foreign Office for the Premiership; and he could not combine both offices. The change would be taking him entirely out of his element. He is, he feels, now in his proper place; in the post of Prime Minister he would be a fish out of water. It would be like taking a good ploughman and promoting him to the post of head gardener.'[35] Throughout January, Rosebery professed that his main concern was not for his own position as a future leader but to ensure that the Government continued if Gladstone retired. On 9 January, at a meeting with Sir William Harcourt just after Cabinet, Rosebery had told the Chancellor: 'I never could dismiss from my mind the deplorable figure cut by Mr Pitt's Government on Mr Pitt's death: that our breaking up would be so much the worse, that it would be proved that the Liberal Party would have to declare itself unable even for a moment to carry on the Government after the resignation of a statesman in his eighty-fifth year; and that sooner than stomach such a humiliation I would serve in a government headed by Sir Ughtred Kay-Shuttleworth* (the first name of a subordinate Minister that came into my head) or anyone else. I admitted that we could not in any case go on for long, but insisted that we should not commit political suicide.'[36]

Sir Ughtred Kay-Shuttleworth's no doubt estimable claims aside, the remorseless logic of Rosebery's statement was that only he could be Prime Minister, since Spencer and Kimberley were not serious contenders and Harcourt was unacceptable to his colleagues, particularly to Morley. As Hamilton rightly put it, 'However grave the difficulties may be, they will have to be got over, for R. is really the only man who has the capacity for forming and carrying a Government.'[37] This was the hard truth that lent

*Liberal MP for Clitheroe.

an air of unreality to the endless leadership negotiations of the following weeks. As long as the Cabinet did not alter in its *non possumus* attitude towards Harcourt and as long as Rosebery maintained that the Queen's government must be carried on, there could only ever be one outcome, a Rosebery premiership. Rosebery himself later spelt out this reality in his personal history of the crisis, written some time in 1894: 'I was prepared to serve under him [Sir William Harcourt] or indeed anybody who would prevent the Government from falling to pieces under Mr Gladstone's retirement. But I can say this of no other Minister. I now think it quite possible that had my colleagues been placed between the devil and the deep blue sea, that is, had they been placed in the position of choosing between Harcourt as Prime Minister and their extinction, they would have submitted to Harcourt. But I did not think so then, for their language to me was violent in a contrary sense, as used or reported to me.'[38]

Rosebery has, understandably, been accused of being disingenuous about his ambition to reach the highest office. It is undoubtedly true that, in recording his own version of events, he pretended to be more innocent than he really had been of the machinations within the Cabinet. In his memorandum he proclaimed, 'I myself was passive, for I was engrossed in the business of a great department. I had indeed during this Government become purely a departmental Minister – content to hold aloof provided I were left alone in my special work.'[39] This was patently untrue, for Rosebery was frequently to be found giving his advice to allies such as Asquith and Acland. Even at the time Morley thought Rosebery was trying to mislead, as this diary entry shows: '*14 January*: Exchanged letters with R. who claimed to know nothing of recent developments. Yet I was aware that he had taken a walk with Asquith every morning and was in possession of every detail. It is curious that so clever a man should stoop to an affectation of this sort.' But even Rosebery's worst dissembling could not alter the fact that Sir William Harcourt was doomed because no one was prepared to serve under him.

Morley was the one man who could have changed the situation, but in his dudgeon against Harcourt there was no likelihood that he would do so. His opposition to a Harcourt premiership was the one fixed point of a nervous, changeable spirit that oscillated between support for Rosebery and personal resignation. He was often said to be guilty of over-rating himself, but his diary shows that as the leadership crisis started to come to the boil he was filled with anguish rather than ambition. On 14 January, as he contemplated a government with Rosebery as Prime Minister and Harcourt as Leader in the Commons, he wrote: 'To me this is wholly impossible, I think, though it is the plan which would seem most natural and which Parliament would expect in a general way. Loulou implies that his father will not fall in with this but my impression is that the compulsion of things will drive him to fall in. Will it not drive me also? On what grounds can I object if I am promised a free hand in Ireland?' And he concluded that, as far as the electoral fortunes of the Liberal party were concerned, 'Harcourt is not the best, but the worst man to impress the country.' Towards the end of the month Loulou received further confirmation that Morley was the block to his ambitions for his father when Regy Brett visited Malwood on 22 January: 'Regy reports that R. is "quite willing *personally*" to serve under Chex but there are differences with "other people", which of course means John Morley. R. knows he has to fight me and is prepared for it. The Devil take the hindmost.'[40]

The surreal atmosphere at the top of the Liberal party was only enhanced by the bizarre conduct of Gladstone, who now appeared to be driven by a cocktail of megalomania and paranoia. On 13 January, just before setting off for Biarritz, he declared through his son Herbert that the solution to the problem of the navy estimates would be the resignation of Spencer and Rosebery, those two militarist villains of the Cabinet. When Lord Acton called on him at Biarritz he found him 'wild, violent, inaccurate, sophistical, and governed by resentment.' Indicative of this mood was Gladstone's sudden decision that he could overcome the difficulty with the naval estimates by calling for the dissolution of Parliament on the grounds of the House of Lords' obstruction of Liberal legislation. It was a ludicrous idea, for there had been no popular agitation whatsoever against the Lords since the rejection of the Home Rule Bill. In a rare moment of unity the Cabinet telegraphed back to France that Gladstone's proposed new crusade was 'impossible'. Sir William Harcourt called the plan 'the act of a selfish lunatic'. Rosebery added that it looked as though Palmerston's prophecy about Gladstone would be fulfilled – that he would ruin the Liberal party and die in a madhouse.

While Gladstone was in Biarritz the London press was filled with rumours about his forthcoming retirement. But to the mounting irritation of the Cabinet he still gave no indication of when he might go, not even to Algy West, who heroically went out twice to see him. On his return, West painted this picture of the declining Prime Minister, as recorded by Edward Hamilton: 'Nobody knew, Algy West said, what he had been through at Biarritz; he never got a civil word out of Mr G., who either fulminated against everybody as if they were all criminals or treated everything with the greatest levity. It is the old, very old man. Mr G. was (Algy

West was sure) absolutely immovable. "You might as well try and move the rock of Gibraltar as move me."[41] Gladstone continued to play this game after his return to London on 10 February, prompting even Morley to complain of his 'childish duplicity' and his 'horribly aged and anxious' appearance. At a Cabinet meeting on 12 February Gladstone said nothing about his future, or about the navy estimates. There was another fatuous scene on 17 February, when Gladstone called a special Cabinet dinner at Downing Street, the first to be held for 43 years. Naturally, given the rarity of the event, ministers expected some formal announcement from him, perhaps a few words of farewell 'to put an end to this cruel delay', in Morley's phrase. Morley's diary gives a wonderful description of the scene that evening.

> Mr G. sat with Rosbery on his left and Herschell★ on his right. We ate dinner gaily. Mr G. chatted cheerfully with his neighbours about indifferent things. At last the meats came to an end. Would he address us at once? Would he wait until the coffee had been served? We sipped claret and port and kept up a feeble pretence of interested talk. No address. Then came coffee and cigarettes. Nobody touched the latter for Mr G. cannot bear tobacco. If we had only known all, we could every one have smoked like chimneys, for revenge is sweet. We toyed with spoons; the talk was more of a pretence than ever. At last his lips moved and we caught the words, 'Shall we go into the drawing room?' Into the drawing room we all went, as crestfallen a flock as I have ever seen. We stood about with tigerish hearts and sheepish looks. Mr G. fell into conversation with Kimberley. After some ten minutes, we brought the farce impatiently to an end.[42]

There was one additional element to the anti-climax, which Rosebery covers in his own less colourful diary entry. As the coffee was being served, Rosebery tried to drop a hint to Gladstone that an opportune moment had arrived for an announcement. 'I said, "If any secret matters are going to be discussed, we ought to look to the doors." "Certainly," replied Mr G. airily. "If anybody has a topic to raise it might be done now." This was all that passed. Back to The Durdans.'[43] Rosebery saw the humour of the incident but, he wrote later, 'it had also its tragic side, as the Cabinet were left in absolute ignorance of what was going to happen – whether they were to live or whether their thin-spun life was to be slit by the resignation of the Prime Minister. Never since Lord Chatham's premiership was a Government so absurdly or unpleasantly situated in relation to its head.'[44]

As Gladstone prolonged the agony of his retirement, Loulou worked

★ The Lord Chancellor.

tirelessly for his father's premiership. One of his tactics was to continue to threaten that Sir William would have the first place, or nothing. When he saw the Liberal Chief Whip Edward Marjoribanks on 11 February, he told him bluntly, according to his diary, that 'I would be damned if I see Chex serving under Rosebery.' Marjoribanks responded that Sir William's retirement was impossible. 'Not at all. It is the most simple thing in the world. We've already got a messengership for the butler.' Trying to conciliate Loulou, Marjoribanks mentioned that Rosebery might be reluctant to leave the Foreign Office. 'I said that of course this was a pose on R's part as he would be a fool if he did not take his chance when it came.' Another of Loulou's manoeuvres was to try to win over Morley, mainly through promises of either the Exchequer or the Foreign Office, the latter a portfolio that certainly appealed to Morley's vanity. Moreover, Loulou knew that Rosebery would never be willing to make the same offer, because he distrusted Morley's Francophilia and anti-imperialism. But Morley gave little sign that he might be tempted into backing Harcourt. On the afternoon of 11 February the two men had another vital meeting, at which Loulou repeated that to ask his father to serve under anyone would be 'an insult'. The subject of the Foreign Office was then raised. Morley did not deny that he hankered after the post, but pointed out that the Queen would never accept him. When Loulou suggested the Exchequer, Morley replied that he 'wasn't up to it'.[45] At the conclusion of the conversation Morley again stressed his opposition to a Harcourt premiership: 'I cannot serve under your father from my experience of our work together on the Finance clauses of the Home Rule Bill. If he is to be Prime Minister, I must stand aside and slip into obscurity.'[46]

With Morley proving unco-operative, Loulou began to sense the prize slipping away. But now he faced an even greater difficulty, one that could destroy the very basis of his campaign. For almost a month Loulou – acting on his own initiative – had been trying to intimidate the party with threats of his father's retirement in the event of a Rosebery ministry. Yet when he returned home on the evening of 12 February, he found to his disgust that his father was considering serving under Rosebery. What Loulou had failed to recognise in all his plotting was that his father did not share his neurotic fixation with reaching Downing Street. Despite a long talk, 'I failed to shake his conviction that if Rosebery asks him to lead the House of Commons, he cannot refuse.' Trying to make the best of this disastrous situation, Loulou persuaded his father to draw up a list of his terms for accepting the Commons leadership in a Rosebery government. The conditions were so onerous that they would have rendered the premiership itself little more than a cypher: Sir William would only take office 'if he were left to act and speak on all questions as they arise with perfect independence and without the necessity of any previous consultation with the PM. In fact, his position would be in this respect precisely that of a Prime Minister in the House of Commons; further that in all questions of Foreign Dispatches and policy he should be consulted before action is taken, as is the case with the Prime Minister, and no important appointments to posts inside or outside the Government shall be made without previous consultation with him; also that the power of recommendations to Honours shall rest equally with him as with the Prime Minister.'[47]

Loulou knew any self-respecting potential Prime Minister would have found these demands intolerable. But that was exactly the point: if Rosebery accepted this document, he would be left without any real power; if he refused, then Harcourt would stay out and Rosebery's attempt to form a government would become almost impossible. Superficially, therefore, this was a clever move. But on another level it was a conspicuous error, for it revealed the weakness of his father's position. For the first time, Loulou was admitting the possibility of defeat in the battle against Rosebery. In effect, he had opened the negotiations for surrender – but his previous strategy had left him nothing with which to bargain. Having spent weeks proclaiming that Sir William would never serve under Rosebery – which now proved to be untrue – Loulou looked rather foolish attempting to dictate the terms of that service. Privately, he faced this truth; arranging to see Lord Ripon on 16 February, he wrote, 'I will tell him that I won't have Chex serving under R. – though in my heart it is inevitable but that is no reason I should not continue to fight till the end.'

After 20 February, the crisis reached new levels of intensity. On that day, Lord Kimberley received a characteristically enigmatic letter from Gladstone, full of veiled remarks about the imminence of his resignation. He then saw Rosebery and told him that, if asked, he would advise the Queen to send for her Foreign Secretary. That evening Morley and Sir William Harcourt met alone in the Chancellor's office at the House of Commons, without the malignant presence of Loulou. The conversation quickly reached the essence of Harcourt's problem. Morley's account in his diary reads:

> Harcourt sat by the fire with a cigar. He said that it was the duty of all the Cabinet to acquiesce in the reconstruction. I said I agreed. Then I told him, 'Neither Spencer nor Rosebery have any desire for the first place. Rosebery likes his office; does it well, as he thinks and as the country thinks, regards his presence as a sort of guarantee of European peace. Therefore neither of

those two is other than willing to make room for you or anybody else. If it were thought for the good of the party that you should be the head of Government, they would not resist. The only resistance – and I will be frank with you – comes from one person and that is MYSELF.'* Harcourt said he had heard with pain and regret and surprise from Loulou what was my view. If anything had been wrong, I must set it down to temperament and inadvertence and that he hoped I would believe he was profoundly sorry. Harcourt cried out with much contrition, 'You must not blame me, you must blame nature.'

The conversation then switched back to Rosebery, with Harcourt warning that Rosebery wanted to be both Prime Minister and Foreign Secretary. 'I assured him I had told Rosebery a hundred times that this was utterly impossible and that Rosebery did not for a moment dream of such a construction.' Morley wrote that their conversation ended with a handshake. 'Oddly enough, so curiously mixed a being is man, we were both perfectly sincere in this effusion. Effusion, however, did not prevent a slight feeling of satisfaction at the strange collapse of this grand game of bluff and intrigue which has been going on since 1892.'[48]

In Loulou's version of the meeting, Harcourt spelt out his demands for acceptance of the Commons leadership under Rosebery, stressing to Morley that 'it was impossible for the Leader of the House of Commons to act in emergencies except on his own responsibility and as if he was actually Prime Minister.' But this apart, the interview was a catastrophe from Loulou's point of view. Amid all that frank cordiality Harcourt had apparently conceded that he would serve in a Rosebery government, giving 'his qualified assent to second place'. In fact, according to Loulou, he told Morley 'he did not care about being Prime Minister but his chief interest was that I [Loulou] should not be disappointed after devoting so much of my life to that object.'[49] Desperate to salvage his father's position, Loulou rushed round to see Morley at Elm Park Gardens on the morning of 21 February. He again repeated his own offer of the Chancellorship, which Morley rightly, since Sir William had failed to make it the night before, did not take very seriously. And he became rather irritated when Loulou again raised the spectre of his father's retirement: 'Don't let's have any heroics,' he said. 'Your view is wrong and impossible and if under the circumstances

---

*Morley's account contradicts the version given in Peter Stansky's *Ambitions and Strategies*, in which he wrote that 'Morley, apparently, had completely come round to supporting Harcourt. Loulou had accomplished his task.' Stansky seems to have based this on Loulou's journal. But Loulou was, of course, not at the meeting, so had to rely what his father told him, and Sir William was likely to have painted the interview in the most favourable light.

your father were to retire from public life, people would say and believe, not without cause, that he got out because he saw the party was going to pieces.'[50] Morley further said that, for all Harcourt's skill in the Commons, Rosebery was far more popular in the country, and 'the majority of Liberal caucuses would be rather in favour' of him. Loulou came away downhearted: 'I can't help thinking that J.M. has entrapped Chex into being complacent towards a Rosebery government.'

The 'grand game of bluff' was now approaching its close. One outcome, a Harcourt premiership, had been unlikely from the start and was now effectively ruled out. As Asquith wrote later, 'Morley, in the general course that he took, was really acting as the exponent of the general will of those immediately concerned. He had his own special reasons for soreness but he knew his colleagues well enough to be fully aware that (even if he had desired it) a Harcourt Government was out of the range of practical politics.'[51] The real issue now was whether Rosebery, backed by the majority of the Cabinet, would consent to become Prime Minister with Harcourt as leader in the Commons. In his *Pitt* Rosebery had written, 'Between a Prime Minister in the House of Lords and the leader of the House of Commons such an implicit confidence is indispensable.' Rosebery was concerned that if he accepted the premiership, Harcourt would make his life miserable; news of Harcourt's demands only reinforced these anxieties. The three main conditions – an independent role in the Commons, the right to see all Foreign Office despatches, and a share of patronage – were reported to Rosebery at a lunch with Morley and Asquith on 21 February. The scene is captured in Morley's diary: 'Rosebery listened with hardly suppressed excitement. He flamed out at the three conditions. He said, "It is easy enough to see what all that means. It means that Harcourt is like the real PM without its responsibilities. His demand for the Foreign Office despatches means that he is to checkmate me in foreign policy. The Prime Minister is to be a dummy. Well, all I can say is that I'd much rather serve under Harcourt than over him."'[52] Rosebery then marched off in one of his dark moods, leaving Asquith and Morley to talk on their own: 'We agreed that Rosebery would have to take the job, nauseous as he would undoubtedly find it.' While they talked, Rosebery saw Edward Hamilton at the Foreign Office. 'Rosebery would decline point blank to accept the Premiership on such terms,' recorded Hamilton, 'however much he might be pressed by his colleagues to form a Government. Indeed, he could not be Prime Minister with Harcourt as Leader in the House of Commons on any terms: he had the profoundest distrust of Harcourt and they had absolutely nothing in common with one another.'[53]

Just when the Liberal party needed the two men to come together, the gap between them was widening. Stung by his son's anger over the casual way he had handled the interview with Morley, Harcourt went into Hamilton's office on 22 February and, knowing his words would go straight back to Rosebery, said, 'I understand that you are under the impression that I think a Rosebery Government is possible. I wish to tell you frankly that I do not take that view.'[54] A few days later, Harcourt went into a volcanic rage when he learnt of Rosebery's comment that he would rather 'serve under Harcourt than over him'. In the light of Sir William's bombast and Loulou's slipperiness, so neatly captured in their self-important language about the Commons leadership, Rosebery's response appears mild. But it was too much for Sir William. He stormed off to see Marjoribanks, the Chief Whip, and told him: 'There are things no man has a right to say of another. I have never said or thought such a thing of Rosebery. It makes all personal and friendly relations between us absolutely impossible for the future. I will do anything for the advantage of the party but I will have nothing but official relations with Rosebery after this.'[55] When Morley confronted Loulou and told him he should go to see Rosebery directly to try to heal the rift, Loulou's reply was limp: 'I have known Rosebery for a long time but I have never been intimate with him. He always makes me shy and I don't think he has very friendly feelings for me.'

On 23 February Gladstone gave the Cabinet the news they had been awaiting for more than a month: he was at last ready to announce his imminent retirement, on the grounds of ill-health rather than of opposition to the navy estimates. 'The words fell like ice on our hearts. There was an instant hush. Then we broke up in funereal silence,' recorded Morley.[56] Rosebery was one of the first to write to Gladstone. After almost two years of dispute with his leader, he managed a genuinely touching note in his letter: 'We have seen, if I may say so, glorious days together – the recollection of which still stirs my blood, you as Chief and I as esquire. And now all is passing or past and it is a moment of anguish – to all your colleagues I believe – most particularly to me . . . Goodbye is a hard saying – hard at all times, but scarcely tolerable when I think of what you are and have always been to me, of the Old Midlothian days, of the times of storm and sunshine in which I have stood by your side and, above all, of the time to come, when that may not be.'[57]

Gladstone, increasingly eccentric in his last days as Prime Minister, had not yet communicated his decision formally to the Queen, but Rosebery presumed he had, and the misunderstanding gave rise to a comical series of incidents on 24 February, as Rosebery described in his diary:

A day of disasters. I was to go to Sandringham so arranged to take in Newmarket, going by 11 o'clock train with my boxes. Arrived at 11.1 with train gone, boxes with it, messenger wringing his hands. Started in special in pursuit. Arrived Newmarket. Pressing personal telegram from the Queen to ask me to Windsor tonight. Telegraphed Sandringham for luggage to return, to FO to stop messenger, and retreated to London. Telegraphed to Windsor that I was coming naked but not ashamed by 7.15. Ultimately rigged myself out. Arrived Windsor. Telegram from the Prince of Wales to beg me to come tomorrow for the night. This is the last straw. Refused point blank. After all this, the Queen had nothing to say.[58]

Loulou, who had something of an *idée fixe* about Rosebery's weight, wrote cattily when he heard this story: 'Rosebery managed to hunt out in a cupboard at Berkeley Square some very old shorts worn 20 years ago, which must have been a very tight fit for him.'[59]

Although he had mistaken the Queen's social invitation for a political summons, Rosebery knew he was about to be confronted with the most important decision of his career, now that Gladstone had announced his resignation to the Cabinet. On 27 February he wrote a memorandum on his position, with the purpose of clarifying his thoughts. He began by arguing that Sir William Harcourt was 'clearly marked out for the post' of Prime Minster, but noting sadly that his 'idiosyncrasies render him almost intolerable to his colleagues'. In this situation, 'some of them at least, have God knows why, fixed on me.' With his characteristic emphasis on the negative, Rosebery then set out a host of reasons why he would rather not accept: 'I do not care about office at all and would far rather be without it' was one; 'Of the work of the Prime Minister, nay of current domestic politics I am as ignorant as any man can be' was another. He thought that 'a Liberal Peer as Prime Minister heading a score of dubious peers would be a ridiculous spectacle', and that it was the wrong time to have a change at the Foreign Office because of 'the present delicate situation in Europe'. Turning to Harcourt's terms, which had by now been circulated in the Cabinet, he said that 'they would not be entertained by any man of self-respect'. Rosebery therefore maintained that the matter 'resolves itself into a choice of evils: either the irksome yoke of Harcourt or a ministry headed by a reluctant peer in face of strenuous opposition in the House of Commons, headed by Harcourt.' Given this reality, he had 'always urged a Harcourt Ministry on the simple common-sense ground that he would try to make his own government a success, and any other a failure'. But then he threw a new factor into the equation: his own position as Foreign Secretary. Referring to the events of the last two months, the differences over policy, the intrigues of Loulou and, above all, the nature of Harcourt's terms, Rosebery contended that it would be 'impossible for me to serve under him without a loss of self-respect and even character'.

This led him to pose two further questions: Would his resignation from the Foreign Office break up the Liberal government? And if Harcourt failed, would he have to attempt to form a new Government? On the first point Rosebery, with a marked degree of self-deception, told himself there would be no problem because 'I should simply retire abroad or into the country and disappear.' Equally unrealistic was his answer to the second: 'I have no responsibility. I have studiously refrained in view of this eventuality from saying a word in public or attracting attention in any way ever since I took the seals. I have lived in my office in absolute obscurity.' This was, of course, a bare-faced exaggeration in view of his LCC work, his speeches, and his settlement of the coal strike. But it led Rosebery to this conclusion: 'The case is clear. Harcourt may not be personally palatable to all of us. But he deserves the premiership by inheritance, he will do his best to make his ministry agreeable and successful and his ability to do so is unquestionable. Moreover, if he does not obtain it, he will place himself at the head of an extreme party and will exercise his undoubted powers as a belligerent. For me, it is also clear I could not hold the Foreign Office under him and my retirement from the Foreign Office is (though I tried another solution) equivalent to my retirement from the Government.'

For all Rosebery's hesitations, the pressure on him was to accept. As Kimberley put it, 'I think he can hardly shrink when it really comes to the point whatever he may say now but he is rather a sphinx.'[60] In the Cabinet, Sir William's arrogance had only served to alienate his colleagues still further, while Loulou's feverish plots now belonged in the realm of fantasy.[61] On 23 February Lady Fanny Marjoribanks, the Chief Whip's attractive wife, spelt out some home truths to Loulou. 'She deplored Chex's roughness and rudeness of manner to his colleagues, which had frightened and offended them. If it had not been for these defects, she says that Chex would have been chosen PM by the unanimous consent and desire of his colleagues.'[62] In the wider Parliamentary party there was little active support for Harcourt, now his Cabinet colleagues had made their preference so clear. An attempt by Labouchere to drum up a Radical movement against Rosebery was a dismal flop, and its failure only tainted Harcourt by association. Labby had been in constant touch with Loulou throughout this period, feeding him a stream of anti-Rosebery gossip and exaggerating the extent of support for Sir William on the left. Having assured Loulou that 'the feeling among Radicals was growing in strength', Labby only managed to find 18 MPs willing to join him in a deputation to Marjoribanks to protest against having a Prime Minister in the Lords. Sir Charles Dilke had been eager to join the group but when he saw how small it was he found some convenient business elsewhere. Knowing Labby to be driven by feelings of personal vindictiveness, Majoribanks did not attach any importance to this action; he told Acland that 'he had seen the same kind of threatened revolt before more than once and it ultimately comes to very little.'[63] Morley, who had always despised 'the pranks of Labouchere and the men below the gangway', regarded it as another example of the Harcourts' opportunism.

Nor did the antics of Labby and Loulou reflect opinion in the Radical press. The *Daily Chronicle*, an advocate of Rosebery's leadership, condemned the deputation as a 'cowardly and malicious attack made under the guise of democratic sentiment by men who do not understand the ABC of democracy'. The paper also argued that having Rosebery as Prime Minister would help rather than hinder the cause of Lords reform: 'The idea that a Peer could not be Prime Minister would be sound enough if he was going to support the House of Lords. But as there is not the smallest chance of his doing anything of the kind it strikes us as something of an advantage that the moral dynamite is to come from within rather than without the Chamber. No statesman in the Liberal Party has more absolutely detached himself from the atmosphere in the House of Lords than Lord Rosebery.'[64] Loulou Harcourt was so shaken by the fervour of the *Chronicle*'s backing for Rosebery that he concluded the paper's leading journalist, Henry Massingham, must have been bribed by the Rothschilds. This view was shared, predictably, by his fellow intriguer Labouchere, who claimed that Massingham 'was seen at 38 Berkeley Square just before the crisis' and had also dined at the home of Marjoribanks, 'where he was made to swear allegiance to Rosebery before he was allowed to leave the table'.[65] But these allegations reflected only the feverishly suspicious minds of Loulou and Labby. The Rothschilds were no political allies of Rosebery; in fact, Edward Hamilton records Natty talking in disparaging terms about Rosebery, saying he 'was no platform speaker, his speeches were watery and he was over-rated as a Foreign Secretary'.[66] Nor was Massingham a Rosebery loyalist; by the end of 1894 he was writing harsh articles against Rosebery – hardly the behaviour of a man labouring under the burden of a bribe. According to Regy Brett, who heard the rumour a few months later and thought it 'quite unjust', Rosebery did not even know Massingham.[67] The rest of the national and provincial press were almost universally in favour of Rosebery rather than

Harcourt. 'Sir William Harcourt would understandably be hurt to be told he has to yield to one 20 years his junior but there is unexpected unanimity amongst Liberals in favour of Lord Rosebery's succession. Lord Rosebery's strength, which has steadily increased as the country has come to appreciate his abilities and convictions, is mainly drawn from his conspicuous and determined adhesion to Imperialism,' said *The Times* on 1 March, stressing another aspect of Rosebery's unique appeal.

After much pointless mystery, Gladstone finally wrote to the Queen on 27 February to tell her of his impending resignation. The next day he had an official audience at Buckingham Palace. Predictably, the Queen refused to express the slightest regret at his departure, preferring to talk about fogs and rain. His colleagues were more emotional when he held his last Cabinet meeting on 1 March, the 556th such meeting at which he had presided.[68] Lord Kimberley broke down as he tried to speak a few words of farewell; 'his simple and unaffected emotion was as manly as could be and touched every one of us to the core,' wrote Morley. More embarrassingly, Harcourt then pulled out of his pocket a copy of a letter he had written Gladstone days earlier and began to read from it. 'His performance was grotesque, nauseous and almost obscene,' thought Morley, describing how Harcourt ploughed through his eulogy, 'with tears in his eyes and sobs in his voice, keeping us all on tenterhooks of shame and anguish until he had got his four quarto pages fairly out. Never, never was such an exhibition of bad taste and want of tact and decency and the sense of the fitness of things.' Rosebery, in his account, said that Gladstone 'was obviously disgusted' by this 'somewhat pompous valedictory address'.

By now Rosebery was feeling much more bullish about taking the premiership, having grown thoroughly weary of the Harcourts' condescension and presumption. Sir William's conditions, noted Morley, 'set Rosebery's back up in fine style and were the very thing calculated to make him quite ready to undertake this perilous job, whether Harcourt joined or refused to join. Rosebery asked me, "Why should we fear Harcourt standing aloof? His memorial would cover him with ridicule. Why should I not lead? Why should Campbell-Bannerman not lead? Who's afraid?"'[69] His increasing bitterness against Sir William was reflected when he turned on Hamilton for trying to defend him: 'It is all very well for you but you have not been his colleague. We cannot easily forget how we have suffered from him in Cabinet.'[70]

Immediately after Gladstone's last Cabinet meeting, Rosebery had Morley, Acland and Asquith to lunch at 38 Berkeley Square. There he read out a paper which demonstrated a much greater willingness to accept the premiership. It said:

My position seems to be this: I share all the views held against a Peer being head of a Liberal Ministry. My wish is to remain at the Foreign Office. I know nothing of the other post and should be in every way unsuited for it. But if it be absolutely necessary for party purposes that I should exchange the one place for the other, it is clear – to make the arrangement barely possible –

1. That it must be in obedience to a clear and decisive call.
2. That there must be mutual harmony and confidence between me and the Leader of the House of Commons.
3. That as I cannot remain in the Foreign Office I must be unfettered in my selection of the Foreign Minister.

Summed up, it comes to this – that there must be cordiality and confidence between the Prime Minister on one hand and the Party, the leader of the Commons and the Foreign Minister on the other. Without these conditions it must be clear that an experiment, sufficiently difficult in itself, must break down, and another combination must be sought.[71]

According to Rosebery's account, there was a murmuring of assent around the table. But privately, Morley was apprehensive about Rosebery's demand for an 'unfettered' choice of Foreign Secretary. The obvious candidate was Lord Kimberley, widely experienced and universally trusted, if not admired. But the appointment of Kimberley would mean that the two most senior positions were in the Lords, something that would deny the Commons any real say in foreign policy. Such an outcome was odious to Morley, much of whose strategy had been partly based on his determination to wrest control of foreign affairs from Rosebery. Now it seemed that he, like the Harcourts, had misread the game.

The next day, 2 March, Morley called on Sir William to report on his conference with Rosebery, Asquith and Acland. He found him 'self-controlled and not at all boisterous'. Resigned to defeat, Harcourt said that he would do his best for the party and denied, untruthfully, that he had ever said he would not serve under Rosebery, though still he harped on about his conditions for accepting office. He also complained self-pityingly of the way Rosebery's allies had intrigued against him, a laughably hypocritical accusation in the context of Loulou's behaviour. When he moaned about a 'cabal' in the Cabinet against him, Morley blew up: 'There has been no Cabinet cabal. Some of us thought that Rosebery would be a better leader than you for the country and I think so strongly.' There was greater unanimity about the Foreign Office, which both men agreed must be held in the Commons under a peer Premier. As the key Liberal negotiator, Morley wanted to achieve a settlement of the crisis before Rosebery was summoned by the Queen, so finally he suggested that Harcourt should see Rosebery to come to an understanding about his conditions and the Foreign Office. Harcourt agreed to do so, and Morley set off to arrange a meeting with Rosebery.

But Rosebery was in no mood to open negotiations with Harcourt, having more important and immediate concerns than attempting to soothe his rival. The previous evening, 1 March, he had received a note from the Prince of Wales stating that the Queen would send for him imminently. This news was confirmed the next morning in an audience of the Prince at Marlborough House and by a letter from the Queen's physician, Sir James Reid, stressing 'how important for Her Majesty's health it is that the present political crisis should be over in time to allow her to start for Italy on 13 March'. Reid added, 'She tells me that you are the *only* man of your party she likes and trusts and that if you do not help in the present crisis, she does not know what she can do, as it would worry her beyond measure to have to fall back on anyone else.'[72] In replying to these messages Rosebery wrote to the Queen's secretary, Sir Henry Ponsonby, making the usual noises about his unfitness for office, the problems of a Liberal Prime Minister in the Lords and his love of the Foreign Office. 'Why should I be taken out of a round hole and put into a square one?' he asked rhetorically. 'These are the objections that I see and which I express without reserve, for I think it is my duty to make the Queen aware of them.'[73]

Gladstone happened to be at Windsor Castle when these communications were being made, but the Queen never formally requested his advice about his successor. Had he been asked, he would have suggested Spencer, whom he thought had 'more of the very important quality termed weight' than either Rosebery or Harcourt.[74] Ponsonby tried to elicit his opinion on an informal basis but, Gladstone told him, 'my lips are sealed'. In a letter to Rosebery written on 4 March,★ Gladstone explained his reasons for not wanting to be drawn into the debate over the succession. The first paragraph of the letter deserves to be quoted in full as an example of Gladstonese at its most gloriously obtuse: 'I think that, speaking generally, in the peculiar circumstances of the case, and with feelings I am both bound to entertain and happy in entertaining, towards all parties concerned, it may be as well for me to avoid the formation, unless of special cause, of opinions upon facts current variable and more or less fugitive.'

On the late afternoon of the 2nd Rosebery was about to take the train to The Durdans to ponder the Queen's messages when Morley turned up

★ The letter was never sent.

in an excitable mood at Berkeley Square, eager to give the latest bulletin on Harcourt's disposition and his own views on the Foreign Office. Rosebery warned that he was in hurry, but Morley would not be put off, and insisted on going with him in his brougham to Waterloo. Rosebery's resentment at this intrusion shines through his record of their brief conversation. When Morley suggested an urgent meeting with Harcourt, Rosebery said impatiently that 'it was best to tell Harcourt that they should defer any interview until the Queen had sent for either of them'.[75] When Morley made his protest about having a peer as Foreign Secretary, his retort was angry: 'You people put me up on a pinnacle and then tell me I am to have no voice in any decisions. I am not to nominate the Leader of the House of Commons, whom you have chosen for me. I am not to select my successor at the FO; in fact, I am to settle nothing and be a mere cypher. If that is the case I had better remain at the FO and you can make Harcourt Prime Minister.'[76] In his diary that evening, Morley said that he was taken 'considerably aback' by Rosebery's harshness. He also wrote sheepishly to Harcourt, explaining: 'I am sorry my intervention has come to little. I don't intend to meddle more, if I can possible help it. The angers of celestial minds are too much for me.'[77] Loulou Harcourt, knowing that his father's position was hopeless, wrote, 'I shall always look back to this as a very black day.'[78]

On Saturday 3 March Rosebery was in a better temper, and wrote to Harcourt saying he would be happy to have an interview that day. Unfortunately, by the time this letter had been delivered, Harcourt was on his way from Paddington to Windsor for a meeting of the Privy Council. By an even greater stroke of misfortune for him, before the Council met he was led into the Queen's presence for a private audience. Harcourt thought that, contrary to every expectation, he was about to be requested to form a government. But it was all a misunderstanding on the part of the Lord-in-Waiting, Lord Acton, who had wrongly ushered in Harcourt instead of Lord Kimberley, the Lord President of the Council. Rather to his embarrassment, according to the account Harcourt gave Morley, 'she talked about the difficulty of knowing who to send for when nobody seemed to be obviously distinguished for the post'. For the rest of her life, the Queen took a malicious delight in recalling the incident.

Once the Council was finished, the Queen wrote to Rosebery asking him to become her Prime Minister: 'She is fully aware of all the difficulties but he is the only one of the Liberal Government in whom she has any real confidence and she earnestly presses him to undertake this task for a time, at least for her sake and for the good of the country.'[79] Sir Henry

Ponsonby delivered the letter to Rosebery by hand at 3.30 p.m. The reply was immediate: 'Lord Rosebery . . . cannot resist Your Majesty's appeal and will endeavour to carry out Your Majesty's wishes.' But he warned that he might still face difficulties over his choice of successor at the Foreign Office: 'As to that, he is quite determined: he will renounce the undertaking rather than yield the right of submitting to Your Majesty the person he deems best qualified for this office.' The Queen, Ponsonby later reported, was 'immensely delighted' with this news.[80]

Rosebery was in command of the situation. He had accepted the commission from the Queen. The Harcourts' campaign was in tatters, their Radical supporters exposed as an irrelevant rump. 'Harcourt is now prepared to take the second place with as little talk as possible,' wrote Morley.[81] When Harcourt met Rosebery on the afternoon of the 3rd, after his humiliating visit to Windsor, he was in more mellow form than usual, assuring Rosebery that he was 'perfectly prepared' to act in a co-operative spirit. Harcourt did not mention the memorandum setting out his conditions, rightly presuming Rosebery to be aware of its contents. But, fatefully for the future of the Liberal Government, he took the lack of discussion as acquiescence on Rosebery's part, which was hardly the case. The one point they discussed at length was Rosebery's insistence that Kimberley should be his Foreign Secretary, because he was the person most fitted for the role. Harcourt objected strongly, saying that the Foreign Secretary had to be in the Commons 'so that he might speak with the authority of his office'. No agreement was reached on this point and Harcourt left the interview warning that 'the matter was of such grave importance that I must reserve my opinion on it'.[82] The follow morning Harcourt asked for another meeting to discuss 'the relation and communication between the FO and the H. of C.' Rosebery agreed to a further conversation, but warned, 'One thing must be clear. I cannot have any conditions imposed upon me which have not been accepted by previous Ministers. I must either be a real Prime Minister or I will not be Prime Minister at all.'[83]

Never the most stable of men, John Morley was dismayed by Rosebery's inflexibility about the Foreign Office. He wailed to Loulou that, with Kimberley in place, Rosebery planned to 'make the FO a secret bureau controlled by himself'. Rosebery's refusal to consider Morley for the Foreign Office, or indeed for any other post except the 'back kitchen' of Ireland, only heightened his sense of betrayal. Such was his anger that he started to play Harcourt's game of threatening not to serve under Rosebery. At a dinner given by Lord Kimberley on the night of the 3rd, which both he and the Harcourts attended, Morley was in a 'great rage', attacking

Rosebery for not consulting any of his colleagues over the Foreign Secretaryship. Claiming he had been 'tricked', he even had the gall to tell Sir William Harcourt that 'It was a great pity our combination was broken up.' In response, Harcourt said that now Morley had ceased to be useful to Rosebery, his advice would be ignored. After this row Loulou gloated in his journal: 'The situation is delightful to me as J.M. is *the* man who has deprived Chex of the Prime Ministership and now finds himself discarded and of no importance.' Briefly he scented an opportunity for yet another anti-Rosebery plot, with Morley and his father standing out together. But he quickly recognised the futility of such a course: 'I consider things have gone too far to alter now. There would be an outcry if Rosebery was displaced and Chex substituted and we should never make the public understand the point on which it was done. So I think the thing must go on and we must make the best of it.'[84]

His father now took this line as well, warning Morley on Sunday morning, 4 March, that he should not go too far in his threats against Rosebery, 'as it was no use taking up a position that they could not maintain'. The positions of Morley and Harcourt had exactly reversed from those of a month earlier, yet another bizarre twist in this draining saga. Harcourt remained conciliatory when he saw Rosebery later on the 4th for their second interview. Crucially, he dropped his objections to Kimberley as Foreign Secretary, admitting that he was the best candidate, and that he himeself 'could not designate any special person in the House of Commons to occupy the post'.[85] His only request was that 'the Foreign Secretary should communicate as fully and freely with the Leader of the House of Commons as he did with the Prime Minister'. Rosebery agreed to this, and suggested that Harcourt talk directly to Kimberley about the best way to implement this arrangement. It seemed a small concession at the time, though in the long run it had serious consequences for the harmony of the Government.

With Harcourt having accepted office, Morley felt he had no choice but to do the same. He was still after a promotion, perhaps to the India Office, but Rosebery warned that if he left Dublin it would unsettle the Irish and give an apparent signal that the new Government was abandoning Home Rule. Morley swallowed these arguments, but only in the most peevish manner. 'It must be understood that I am not to be asked or expected to take part in debate on non-Irish subjects, nor to address meetings outside of Parliament,' he wrote to Rosebery on 5 March. Rosebery replied angrily: 'I have no choice but to accept your "conditions". I won't disguise from you that I am deeply pained by them. You would not have imposed them on Mr Gladstone or, I believe, on anybody else. It is because your perhaps most intimate political friend undertakes the Government largely because of your action that you insist on a pound of flesh bond which sets forth absolute want of confidence and a cold denial of all assistance and cooperation. Had I known that this would be your definite attitude, I certainly would not have undertaken the Government and if I could honourably now I would give it up.'[86] Morley's sulks over his position also infuriated Loulou, who recorded this confrontation in Morley's office in the Commons: 'I told him I thought he was behaving extremely badly to Chex, who depended on him as deputy leader in the H. of C. I said, "It is you who are responsible for my Father's present position and it is you who desert him when he wants your help in the House of Commons." Morley was surprised – tried explanation – that his action was directed against R., not Chex, but I stumped out of the room with simulated anger and concealed amusement.'[87] Asquith, who remained Home Secretary, was just as disgusted with Morley, saying he had 'all the hysterical characteristics of the eternal feminine'.[88]

In this Government of exquisite sensitivities, Rosebery also offended the *amour propre* of James Bryce, the Chancellor of the Duchy of Lancaster, by asking him to take over the Board of Works. 'I declined the office when Mr Gladstone gave me the choice between it and the Duchy in August 1892 and it is a post for which I have no turn or taste. I should consider it a step downwards,' he responded huffily.[89] Thus Bryce remained at the Duchy. 'It is quite extraordinary what exalted ideas politicians have of their own claims,' wrote Edward Hamilton. 'Bryce has gone quite high enough for he is little use in Cabinet or in the House. He is too donnish in appearance and priggish in manner.'[90] The rest of the Cabinet-making was more straightforward, with most ministers keeping the portfolios they had held under Gladstone. The only important changes were at the India Office, where Henry Fowler, much to Morley's jealousy, became Secretary, and in the Whips' Office, from which Edward Marjoribanks had to retire because of his sudden elevation to the House of Lords as Lord Tweedmouth on the death of his father on 4 March. His place as Chief Whip was taken by the Welshman Tom Ellis. Rosebery himself assumed the Lord Presidency of the Council, an office which carried precedence over that of Prime Minister.* In fact, the Lord President officially took precedence over every

---

*The office of Prime Minister did not formally exist until December 1905, when it was recognised by Royal Warrant. Sir Henry Campbell-Bannerman was therefore technically the first holder.

subject except the Royal Princes, the Lord Chancellor and the Archbishops of Canterbury and York. On the afternoon of 5 March, with most of the arrangements in place, Rosebery went to Buckingham Palace to kiss hands. The ceremony took place at 3 p.m. in the late Prince Consort's room, which remained unchanged since his death. The Queen recorded in her journal, 'He said the task I had entrusted to him was very difficult and not what he would have wished to undertake but I repeated that he was the only person in the Government I considered fitted to the post and in whom I had absolute confidence, for which he thanked me.'[91]

Rosebery was undoubtedly sad to leave the Foreign Office for this daunting new challenge. According to Regy Brett, on his last day at the FO 'He did not say good-bye to anyone but crept down the back staircase. He is certainly very grieved to go. He would have been content to remain there for a while under anybody – even Harcourt.'[92] The first night after he accepted the Queen's commission, on 3 March, he had dined alone with Hamilton, who told him he had no choice but to accept what the Queen, the party and the country expected him to do. 'Perhaps so,' replied Rosebery, 'but I call you to witness that I undertake the duty of forming an Administration with the greatest reluctance. The Foreign Office was an ambition of mine, I admit. I consider it by far the finest post to occupy. But the Prime Ministership I have never coveted. In doing what I have done today, I consider that it is the most daring act of my life, unless I except what I did just 32 years ago, which was steering the "Defiance" at Eton without ever having been on the river.'[93] To Herbert Bismarck he complained, 'It is very awkward not to have the leader in the House of Commons. I hate leaving the Foreign Office and I do not love my new post which has more oratory and publicity connected with it than I like.'[94] There is no doubt that these sentiments were genuine, prompting the question – one Rosebery often asked himself in later life – why he accepted an office which had 'always been abhorrent to me'? Apart from his duty to the Queen, the most convincing answer is that because of his colleagues' repugnance for Harcourt, only he could have formed a Liberal government. Had he refused the premiership, he would have been personally responsible for its smash. With his keen sense of history, he would have hated to be judged in this way. As he had explained to Munro-Ferguson, 'It would be a disgrace if the Government were to break up simply because of Mr Gladstone's retirement, whenever that event takes place. It would probably very soon be beaten. But any defeat would be far better than a confession of futility and helplessness.'[95] In a letter to George Buckle, editor of *The Times*, in December 1895 he explained his reasoning in more depth: 'I never had the slightest ambition to be Prime Minister. I knew something of the drawbacks if not the misery of that position and I knew that a Prime Minister in the House of Lords, unless he has an alter-ego in the House of Commons, is liable to find himself in a position of impotence and possibly of indignity. But if the Liberal party had to confess that it could not continue in office without a leader who had passed his 84th birthday, it would practically have admitted that it had ceased to exist. I rightly or wrongly believed my duty to be clear, so very unwillingly and under pressure severer than I had undergone in 1892 I consented to the nominal headship of Government.'[96]

In accepting, Rosebery must have known that the judgement of history would be equally harsh if he failed in office. On Rosebery's accession to the premiership Mary Gladstone wrote in her diary, 'Difficulty is his great opportunity. And he will (as I fully believe) rise to it.'

II

'You have chosen Barabbas'

—◦—

'I DON'T SUPPOSE any public man had a more difficult task before him,' wrote the Prince of Wales's secretary Sir Francis Knollys on Rosebery's accession to the premiership.[1] His inheritance appeared indeed a grim one. His party was divided, his personnel fractious. With Gladstone's retirement, the central pillar of Victorian Liberalism had gone. *The Times* predicted on the day he saw the Queen that he would have only a short spell in office: 'Lord Rosebery finds himself with a chaotic party on his hands fettered in all sorts of informal ways by all sorts of incompatible engagements and destitute of any coherent body of conviction or any intelligible principle of action. Sooner or later the party must go into retreat in order to prepare for a new career of usefulness.'

The long-drawn-out leadership battle, perhaps the strangest in modern politics apart from the Tory succession to Harold Macmillan in 1963, had left the Cabinet exhausted and several of the protagonists bitterly opposed to Rosebery. Relationships between Prime Ministers and their Chancellors have often been awkward, but they have rarely plunged the depths of open inimicality that existed at the start of the 1894 government. Nursing his bruised ego, Harcourt was all too keen to parade his grievances. 'I have been trampled and spat on and obviously used,' he complained to Arnold Morley, the Postmaster-General.[2] 'Whenever I go into the Cabinet, I know that I meet 16 men who hate me,' he said on another occasion.[3] When Edward Hamilton called on Lady Harcourt, Sir William's wife, on 8 March, 'She quite broke down with me. She said she could not talk of recent events but she hinted that Rosebery had not shown her or her husband the consideration he might have done.'[4] In a reference to Rosebery's neighbours in Downing Street, Regy Brett wrote to him, 'You will be bound to have a stormy time with Harcourt presently but I suppose you will continue to make the almost impossible work smoothly.' His wife added a postscript: 'I think you have iron nerves to be able to face the thought of the agonised sniffing of the lady at Number 11.'

Morley, the architect of Rosebery's triumph, was simmering with

resentment over what he perceived to be the Earl's treachery regarding the
Foreign Office. 'The man who thinks of himself first and second and third
will hardly suffice to rally all elements of the party,' he wrote of what he
considered Rosebery's selfishness.[5] Shortly after Rosebery accepted the
Queen's commission, Morley had talked to Loulou. 'He asked me anxiously if I thought there had been trickery on Rosebery's part. I said,
"Plenty, but what did you expect?" If it was not pitiable it would be amusing to see the poor ladder lying kicked in the gutter after it had ceased to
be useful.'[6]

Yet it would be wrong to exaggerate the problems Rosebery faced.
Despite the discord promoted by Harcourt and Morley, he had the backing of the overwhelming majority of the Cabinet. Moreover, he enjoyed
a working majority in the House of Commons of around forty votes, and
it was impossible to conceive of any circumstances in which the Irish
would suddenly join the Unionist ranks. Interestingly, for all his coldness
towards Rosebery, Gladstone thought he would make a better Prime
Minister than Harcourt, as he told his son Herbert: 'Rosebery might fall
short but he would hold on more tenaciously than Harcourt.'[7] In the wider
party and electorate, he had the kind of popularity of which other Liberal
politicians could only dream. The *Westminster Gazette* was awestruck by the
breadth of his following: 'A strong radical who nevertheless is not
unfavourably regarded by the stern unbending Tories; a Home Ruler who
is half trusted by the Unionists; a socialist politician who is related to the
Rothschilds; a political reformer who commands in equal measure the
confidence of the extremists and the moderates; a man of the world in
the widest sense, whose personal friendships include the Heir Apparent to
the Throne and the leaders of the new democracy – did ever a Prime
Minister at the outset of his career stand in so remarkable a position?' Even
Sir Charles Dilke recognised the political strengths of his enemy: 'The new
Prime Minister undoubtedly increases the popularity of the Liberal Party
in Scotland, as compared with that it can have attained under Sir William
Harcourt,' he wrote in the *North American Review*. 'And there can be little
doubt that . . . Lord Rosebery is a stronger electoral leader in London than
would have been Mr Gladstone.' Dilke further stated that Rosebery was
more liked than Harcourt among 'the trade unions and the working-classes
generally in the industrial counties'. Above all, Rosebery had 'considerable
music-hall popularity, as it is contemptuously called, the popularity with
the apolitical crowd or the mob itself, as the owner of a Derby favourite.'

Although Rosebery's fight against Harcourt had been driven by a clash
of personalities, in another respect the leadership contest was about two

different visions of Liberalism: the narrow, traditional, isolationist, anti-interventionist outlook represented by Harcourt, who was fond of referring to himself as an eighteenth-century Whig, and the dynamic, modern approach of Rosebery, which concentrated more on the needs of Empire and the working class than on the internal debates of Parliament. Far from seeing the arrival of Rosebery as a sign of Liberal weakness, the Unionists feared his leadership might give fresh impetus to the Liberal cause. Soon after his victory Austen Chamberlain wrote to the journalist Leo Maxse, reflecting this concern. 'The gain to the Gladstonian party and to the country lies in Rosebery's Imperialism. We shall henceforth be able to make no party capital out of Uganda, South Africa etc., nor will there be any cause to fear for the efficiency of the naval programme. We shall therefore not get some votes that Mr Gladstone's weakness on these points would have driven to us. That the country will be the gainer even if we lose by having our views and policy adopted by the party in power. I am content to lose on such terms.' But on a personal rather than a political level, Chamberlain thought Rosebery's emergence as leader reflected badly on the Liberal party: 'What an awful sell-out it must be for Harcourt. Rosebery has been preferred partly because he is a Lord but mainly because he never committed himself on any subject and is therefore considered safe. His selfishness has succeeded wonderfully well, but it is not an edifying spectacle, nor a very moral one.'[8]

As he took office Rosebery was showered with so many messages of goodwill that he joked to Hamilton, 'It is worse than being engaged to be married.' In a rare moment of maternal affection, his mother the Duchess of Cleveland – a widow since the death of the Duke in 1891 – called personally to congratulate him, something she had never previously done, even when he was appointed Foreign Secretary; she later suggested, though, that her son 'should have never taken the premiership under such unfavourable circumstances'.[9] It is one of the minor quirks of history that Rosebery was the first Prime Minister to have a mother still alive, a tribute to both the Duchess's longevity and his own youthfulness. At 46 years and 10 months he was the fourth-youngest Prime Minister of the nineteenth century, after Lord Liverpool (42), Lord Goderich (44 years and 10 months), and Lord Grenville (46 years and 4 months). No younger Prime Minister occupied 10 Downing Street until the arrival of John Major in 1990. In terms of experience, he was the first Prime Minister since the Earl of Aberdeen in the 1850s who had never sat in the House of Commons, and the first Liberal peer to hold the highest office since Earl Russell in 1865; he was also the last to do so.

As the possessor of his own elegant house at 38 Berkeley Square, Rosebery had no need to move immediately into Downing Street, which was fortunate because it was undergoing extensive redecoration; he further expanded the works programme by ordering the installation of electric lighting, something of which his socially conservative predecessor Gladstone had disapproved. For himself Rosebery initially took just one room on the first floor, allowing the rest of the building to be used as somewhat chaotic accommodation for various other officials and politicians. In the downstairs Cabinet Room, however, he insisted on the removal of the chamberpot which Lord Granville had used to such noisy excess in the 1880s. It was not until March 1895 that Rosebery finally decided to take up residence in Downing Street, and then it was only because of his own renovation of his Berkeley Square house. As he explained to Gladstone, 'You will be interested to hear that I am going to take up my abode in Downing Street. Ever since this Government was formed, my right hand neighbour [in Berkeley Square] has hammered away at incessant repairs. My left hand neighbour is now engaged in demolition and reconstruction. So, like a true Scot, I wish to give as good as I get and show that there are two, or even three, who can play at this game. So I am doing my repairs. My vengeance necessitates a retirement to Downing Street, none too soon, as it was beginning to resemble the Winter Palace in the vast and varied population squatting within its walls, from the Lord Privy Seal downwards.'[10] Like Sir Henry Campbell-Bannerman, who later described Number 10 as 'this rotten old barrack of a house', Rosebery said he 'detested' Downing Street, finding it 'terribly cold'.[11] Apart from the electrics and the Cabinet Room's toilet facilities, his one other innovation there was to require the doorkeepers to wear a special uniform, comprising a blue frock coat with gold-edged lapels, to distinguish them from ordinary visitors.[12]

Rosebery had his own private secretaries, Thomas Gilmour and an Oxford graduate, Neville Waterfield, but he needed a more senior figure to oversee his prime ministerial business. He therefore chose George Murray, a Scot who had already displayed calmness, humour and efficiency in working for Gladstone at Downing Street, and later rose to the top of the civil service. Gladstone's confidant Lord Acton told Murray he would find Rosebery a very different master. In a revealing letter, he warned that there were 'certain peculiarities observable' in Rosebery. 'Of course you have discovered under the excessively agreeable surface the undisciplined temper and the strong self-consciousness. What one can hardly exaggerate is the exceeding sensitiveness, combined with secretiveness, that easily makes him suspicious. For he does not easily think very well of people and his likings are not predominant. One has to be careful not to be duped by the cordiality for he can be both very obstinate and very hard. I say to myself that caution is one of your merits and extreme trustfulness not one of your defects.'[13] After a brief experience of working for Rosebery, Murray wrote Acton this frank reply from 10 Downing Street: 'He is the most unfathomable man I have ever come across and I have almost given up the idea of understanding him. However, we manage to keep in step somehow, though I don't think he really likes me. His secretiveness (coupled at times with a frankness that verges on indiscretion) and his extremely erratic ways are the general difficulties which I have to contend with and of course they do not become less by contrast with the late regime. I think I should like him very well if I saw more of him, but I am *obliged* to be very much here and he *will* spend so much of his time in his own mansion.'[14] At the end of Rosebery's first month George Murray saw Loulou Harcourt, who noted happily, 'Murray is most amusing about Rosebery's methods of secrecy and concealment in all he does and writes and in the people he sees. Murray evidently finds a great change in his position for the worse since he exchanged Mr Gladstone for Rosebery.'[15]

One of the other odd habits which made life difficult for Murray was Rosebery's insistence on opening all his post himself, even in Downing Street. Hinting at some dark secret at the centre of Rosebery's life, Loulou claimed not to be surprised by this practice, 'from my knowledge of what his letters must – some of them – contain'.[16] Murray was more concerned about the logistics of the operation than any possible scandal, but his attempts to deal efficiently with the mail only roused his master's ire. 'I am a little uneasy about my letters,' Rosebery said to him. 'The process at present is this. When I tear them open, I throw them – often unread – into the large box. This goes to you and I never see them or hear of them again. But all letters that require an answer not of a routine character should be brought to me and some of them answered myself. I am afraid, half afraid, that we are each under the impression that the other is answering the letters.'[17] Rosebery's attitude to his letters is scarcely incriminating, for, as Acton said, he was an extremely reserved, suspicious person; for instance, he urged Mary Gladstone, with whom he had the most innocent relationship, to take elaborate precautions when writing to him: the envelope of every letter was to be marked 'strictly private' and placed within a second, larger envelope, thereby ensuring that the inner contents would be seen only by his own eyes.

Having chosen his ministers, his secretary, and his accommodation,

Rosebery held his first Cabinet meeting on 8 March. The main item was the forthcoming Queen's Speech at the start of the new Parliamentary session, and after all the rows over the previous two months Rosebery appeared to make a good start, despite Harcourt being 'sulky'. According to Hamilton, the Colonial Secretary Lord Ripon, who had no fewer than 33 years' ministerial experience, told him 'The Cabinet was more businesslike and better presided over than any other Cabinet he had attended.'[18] Sadly, this happy state of affairs was not to last. Queen Victoria, who liked Rosebery but profoundly distrusted his politics, was appalled by the proposed bills for the Disestablishment of the Scottish and Welsh churches. Trumpeting her role as Defender of the established Anglican Church, she urged that they be taken out of the Government's programme, pronouncing herself 'horrified' and telling Ponsonby, 'I could not sanction this being put into my speech.'[19] Once more her physician Sir James Reid added some medical blackmail: 'I have never seen Her Majesty more upset than she is tonight. I have just left her very much agitated indeed and I feel sorry for her as I am concerned about her,' he told Rosebery.[20]

Rosebery could not possibly abandon one of the Liberals' fundamental policies simply to avert Royal displeasure, and warned Ponsonby that he would have to resign rather than submit. In a heroically frank letter to the Queen of 9 March, he explained to her that 'the Government came in, if I may use the expression, on Welsh and Scottish disestablishment; fair notice was given in the last Queen's Speech, where the usual preliminary measures were announced. We could not exist for a moment without dealing with these questions.'[21] Impressed by Rosebery's firmness, Harcourt promised to 'stick by him to the last since this was a stand or fall matter'.[22] The Queen could not afford to lose her new Prime Minister after less than a week, so she agreed to a meaningless compromise by which the words 'Measures for dealing with ecclesiastical disestablishment' were substituted for 'Bills for disestablishment'.

Many, including Loulou Harcourt, were surprised that Rosebery should have been so quickly forced into a dispute with the Queen, for his courtly gallantry might almost have been modelled on Disraeli's. But from the Queen's point of view there was one significant difference between Disraeli and Rosebery: Rosebery belonged to the wrong party. Though the Queen affected to call herself a traditional Liberal, she was guilty in her old age of the most flagrant bias against the Liberals; nor did she show much understanding of her restricted constitutional role in an age of democracy. More than any incompatibility of temperament, it was her reactionary Toryism that really lay behind her insulting hostility to

Gladstone. 'The Queen is enough to kill any man,' Gladstone said in 1882 to Rosebery, who soon discovered the truth of those words. In fact, Rosebery had some awareness of the conflict that must inevitably arise once he became Prime Minister, simply because he would be responsible for policies she found abhorrent. On 4 March he wrote to the Queen explaining that 'it would be better for him to abandon the task than incur a risk which would inflict a sharper wound than is usually involved in the relations of a Sovereign and a subject.' In her reply, which again revealed her contempt for reform, she said, 'The Queen . . . does not object to Liberal measures which are not revolutionary and she does not think it possible that Lord Rosebery will destroy well-tried, valued and necessary institutions for the sole purpose of flattering useless Radicals or pandering to the pride of those whose only desire is their own self-gratification.'[23] Prescience was one of Rosebery's strengths, and he knew that the determination of his party to reform – or even abolish – the House of Lords was certain to herald a more serious rift with the Queen than that caused by Disestablishment. Towards the end of March, in response to the Queen's assertion that the House of Lords was 'part and parcel of the much vaunted and admired British constitution', Rosebery candidly told her that 'the Lords as present constituted is a danger to the state'. To reinforce this point, he then sent her a long memorandum, running through the history of the House of Lords and his own record of campaigning for reform. In showing how unrepresentative the Lords had become since the Home Rule split, he wrote, 'The moment a Liberal government is formed, this harmless body assumes an active life and its activity is entirely exercised in opposition to the Government. The House of Lords is in fact a permanent barrier raised against the Liberal party.' He could have written the same of the Queen, without changing a word. In her reply of 9 April, she managed to confirm all he had said about the partisan, anti-democratic methods of the Lords. Absurdly, she denied that the House of Lords was unrepresentative, since 'it represents the opinion of those who have the *greatest* stake in the country.' Condemning Liberal policies on Ireland, parish councils and employers' liability – three of the bills the Lords had rejected – she asked, 'What is the use of a second chamber which Lord Rosebery approves of if it is only to say "yes" to all (what the Queen *must* call) revolutionary legislation and democratic fancies which a small majority may force through the Lower House? The Queen cannot but think that some day even Lord Rosebery may be thankful for the power and independence of the peers . . . The Queen, in conclusion, would most earnestly and solemnly adjure her Prime Minister not to let her Ministers join in any attempt to excite the passions of the people on this important subject but rather to strive restrain them.' After firing another accurate shot in this skirmish, pointing out that 'the country has chosen a Liberal House of Commons to represent it, while nine-tenths of the House of Lords are opposed to that party',[24] Rosebery let the matter drop. But he knew it could not be long before trouble flared up again.

The early disagreement with the Queen was a minor problem, however, compared to Rosebery's self-inflicted wounds. At the Foreign Office on 12 March he addressed a meeting of the Liberal Parliamentary Party, telling the gathering, 'There is no change in measures – there is only the most disastrous change in men. We recede from none of our pledges, none of our proposals.' The *Daily Chronicle* wrote of this performance: 'He looked and doubtless was nervous but nothing could have been more composed than his entry into the room, his quiet bow to the assembly and the clear methodical speech in which he announced that the Liberal Party remained as they were before Mr Gladstone's retirement.' Yet it was noticeable that Sir William Harcourt, who followed Rosebery, received a louder cheer from the assembly. Afterwards, Loulou talked to Henry Labouchere, and left this note of their conversation in his diary:

LOULOU: There were no dissident voices of any kind.
LABBY: Rosebery did not go far enough for the men in the room. I could see it on their faces.
LOULOU: I think you're wrong, but, if so, we can screw him up to a higher pitch.
LABBY: We'll screw him *out*.

That afternoon there was great excitement in Parliament in anticipation of Rosebery's first appearance as Prime Minister. Large cheering crowds gathered outside Westminster, while the House of Lords had not been so packed since the death of Lord Beaconsfield in 1881. When he rose to reply to Salisbury in the debate on the Queen's Speech, a hush of expectation fell on the assembly. He started with a eulogy to the 'transcendent personality' of Gladstone, then moved on to foreign and domestic affairs. But, when he referred to Ireland, Rosebery made what was perhaps the greatest blunder of his premiership. He was speaking impromptu, and for him, with his love of humour and epigram, that meant he was walking an oratorical tightrope. On this occasion, he dramatically lost his footing, and crashed to earth. The words that caused his plunge were these: 'The noble Marquess made one remark on Irish Home Rule with which I confess myself in entire accord. He said that before Irish Home Rule is concluded by the Imperial

Parliament, England as *the predominant member*★ of the partnership of the Three Kingdoms will have to be convinced of its justice and equity. That may seem to be a considerable admission to make, because your Lordships well know that the majority of Members of Parliament elected from England proper are hostile to Home Rule.' The moment he uttered those sentences, politicians on all sides recognised their significance.

It might appear that Rosebery had stated nothing more than a political reality: that Home Rule could never be achieved until a majority of the English electorate were willing to accept it; indeed, the left-wing *Daily Chronicle* described the remark as 'a good, straight cold douche of hard fact'. But in a delicate political situation, when the Irish were looking for reassurance and the Liberals for a lead, Rosebery's throw-away line was disastrous. The Gladstonian Liberal party had endured years of strife, division and unpopularity because of its principled adherence to Home Rule; now Rosebery appeared to be telling his members that the struggle had been an irrelevance. Furthermore, the three Celtic nations, always touchy about their treatment by England, had been in effect dismissed as inferior – a strange line for Rosebery to adopt in view of his resignation in 1883 over the Government's supposed indifference to Scotland. Liberal and Irish MPs were in uproar, while the Tories looked on with glee. Gladstone, the high priest of the Home Rule cause, described Rosebery's declaration as 'an outrageous mischief' and 'very imprudent'. The only group who took a more positive view were Joseph Chamberlain's band of Liberal Unionists.

Rosebery himself was mortified by his error. He confessed to Morley that he had 'blurted it out'. To Asquith, he said his 'brain was suffering from paralysis'.[25] It was his old fault, a lack of thorough preparation. Years later, as he reflected ruefully on the distress that the 'predominant partner' speech had brought him, he explained that he had not spoken publicly for five months previously, and had delivered it without any premeditation. But, as Morley put it, 'Governments cannot be conducted by blurting'. The following day, the Liberals and the Irish took their revenge in the House of Commons. In the debate on the Royal Address John Redmond, the Irish nationalist leader, was savage in his denunciation of Rosebery. Then, in a vote that was understandably interpreted as one of confidence in Rosebery's leadership, the House passed by a majority of two an amendment to the Address moved by Labouchere, attacking the powers of the House of Lords. After two years, Labby had finally made Rosebery pay for his exclusion from Washington.

★My emphasis: LM.

Within days of taking office Rosebery had thrown his government into a crisis that could easily have made his spell as Prime Minister the shortest in British history. Even weeping Lord Goderich, the 'transient phantom' of 1828, had lasted longer. Rosebery, who admitted that 'a four-day government is not a very magnificent one', was full of contrition in Cabinet the morning after the vote, on 14 March, and its shaken members were in no mood to punish him further. It was agreed to ask the House of Commons to withdraw the entire Address, now wrecked by Labouchere's amendment, and accept a new one, which was duly passed without further embarrassment. But the damage had been done to Rosebery's reputation. He could take little comfort from the view of Edward Hamilton, who thought the entire fiasco was the fault of the new Chief Whip Thomas Ellis, who not only carried little weight but, even worse, 'speaks with a Welsh accent'.[26] In an angry letter to Rosebery the Queen too reprimanded the Whips for being 'very neglectful' but, typically, also attacked the Government's supposed extremism: 'The Queen is bound to say that if the Ministers themselves hold language like Mr Gladstone, Sir William Harcourt and (though in a much less strong degree) even Lord Rosebery did, one cannot be surprised when a regular Revolutionist like Mr Labouchere becomes very bold.'[27]

Rosebery was already engaged to make two important speeches, and in them he tried to rectify the situation. The first was delivered on the night of the 14th at St James's Hall, in his capacity as a London County Councillor. He needed a good performance and he gave one in brilliant style, making what he later described as the greatest speech of his life. It is a telling point, for those who regard Rosebery as a natural Tory, that his favourite speech should have been one of his most radical. Taking as his subject the work of the LCC, he outlined a vision for the future of the Liberal party which came close to socialism. He spoke in favour of public enterprise, limits on working hours, and fair wages. The extension of the suffrage was welcomed for the way it 'lit up the conscience of the community', carrying into politics 'the principles of higher morality'. He delighted in the new spirit in politics 'which aims more at the improvement of the lot of the worker and the toiler than at those great constitutional effects in which past Parliaments have taken their pride.' And he predicted the rise of the Labour movement: 'I am certain there is a party in the country, not named as yet, that is disconnected with any existing political organisation, a party which is inclined to say, "A plague on both your Houses, a plague on all your parties, a plague on all your politics, a plague on your unending discussions which yield so little fruit. Have done with this unending talk and come down and do something for the people.'''

The second key address was given three nights later at the Corn Exchange in Edinburgh, and its aim was to settle the anxious supporters of Home Rule. Morley had warned him beforehand that the situation was 'of no small gravity and danger', since a section of the Irish camp wanted to overthrow the Government. 'They are a minority but if your deliverance should be chilling or ambiguous, they will be reinforced by men enough to make them a majority,' wrote Morley on 16 March.[28] Confirming that he was still pledged to Home Rule, Rosebery explained that by his 'predominant partner' remark he had only meant that a popular demand in England for Irish self-government could not be resisted by the Lords. Although it lacked the power and conviction of his LCC appearance, this Edinburgh speech did enough to satisfy both the Irish, and the Liberal rank-and-file. 'The whole atmosphere of the House is different tonight. The tension is off and Edinburgh has cleared the air,' wrote Ellis,[29] though Rosebery's diary shows how difficult he found the experience:

> *16 March*   Tried to do something towards tomorrow's speech and failed.
> *17 March*   To Edinburgh. Mind a complete blank the whole journey. Entered the Corn Exchange in despair. Things went better than might have been expected.

One man dissatisfied with Edinburgh was Joseph Chamberlain, who had felt that Rosebery's declaration on Home Rule might open the way to a rapprochement between the divided forces of Liberalism. But after Rosebery's explanation at the Corn Exchange Chamberlain realised there was no hope that Home Rule would be abandoned. 'Rosebery had the ball at his feet after the "predominant partner" speech,' he said later. 'If he had stuck to that, his future would have been certain. We leaders were far too committed but he would have captured our followers. I was asked to speak soon afterwards. I waited to give my decision. If he had stuck, I would not have spoken; I should have had nothing to say. As he explained away, I said, "Yes, I will speak".'[30] And Chamberlain did so, in his most sarcastic vein, making a rollicking attack on Rosebery at Liverpool: 'Mr Gladstone was one of those of whom it was sometimes said that his earnestness ran away with his judgement, but Lord Rosebery allows his judgement to be run away by the earnestness of other people.'

Yet it was purest fantasy on Chamberlain's part to believe that Rosebery could have achieved a reconciliation with the Liberal Unionists by simply ditching Home Rule. Savagely anti-Irish, cold and authoritarian, he never understood that the mainstream of the Liberal party actually believed in the policy. If Rosebery had taken Chamberlain's line, he would soon have found himself in the wilderness. As Edward Hamilton wrote later, 'Had R. ever dreamt of this, he would have been practically admitting that he had held office under false pretences for a year and a half; and the Irishmen would have turned out the Government the moment it was formed.'[31] That was why Rosebery was so anxious to make amends at Edinburgh. But there is no doubt that the 'predominant partner' bungle had shaken his nerve. Always tense, ultra-sensitive to criticism, terrified of failure, he found his judgement questioned, his pride hurt. To his shame, he had been humiliated by his most venomous opponent, Labouchere, and forced to rely for help on his most implacable rival, Harcourt. His colleagues could immediately sense his confidence draining away in Cabinet, despite his relative successes in London and Edinburgh. On 2 April Morley recorded in his diary: 'R. overtook me in Pall Mall and we walked to Cabinet together. I thought him flurried and uneasy. In truth, he is absolutely not at ease with his new position. At Cabinet, just the same; no grasp, no aptitude for wrestling and all that order of process. An extraordinary phenomenon. The danger now is lest he should precipitate dissolution. I'm sure he regards the whole affair with absolute loathing. As Asquith says, "He is like a rider who has had a bad throw."' To Herbert Bismarck Rosebery admitted his unease: 'I have scarcely any boxes but an enormous responsibility of sayings and doings. One is watched. One cannot put on one's slippers. One is (or should be) always in uniform – buckled very tight. I have always preferred the FO and always shall.'[32]

Rosebery's aversion to the premiership was soon heightened by a damaging row with Harcourt over the Budget. The legacy of the battle for the leadership was already making itself felt in the 'gulf of ice' between the two men as they sat on opposite sides of the Cabinet table. Now, in his work as Chancellor, Harcourt showed a bumptious contempt for the authority of his Prime Minister. The Treasury was facing a deficit of £5 million, caused chiefly by the increased naval estimates of £3 million for which Rosebery had been the loudest advocate. Having initially toyed with the idea of a graduated income tax, as proposed by Loulou, Harcourt then decided to make up the required sum by means of three other measures. Two of them, a penny increase in income tax and a rise in spirit and beer duties, were straightforward, but the third, the introduction of graduated death duties, was highly controversial. This idea had been inspired by Alfred Milner, Chairman of the Inland Revenue Board who had previously worked for Cromer in Egypt, and it involved a momentous change in the way property was taxed on the death of its owner. Previously there had been only a limited form of inheritance tax, based on notional rental values; under Harcourt's proposed new regime, duty would be levied on the full, capital value of all estates. This measure, said Harcourt, would soon bring in £4 million a year; more importantly, it would 'place all property of whatever kind upon an equal footing in respect of liability to taxation'.[33]

With his artistic, literary temperament, Rosebery had never taken a keen interest in economics. He confessed 'an ignorance of finance' to Hamilton,[34] and he had shown, for a Scot, an odd lack of shrewdness in his own faltering overseas investments. Though well aware of his own weaknesses, Rosebery felt it important to question some features of Harcourt's proposed death duties, which he feared would tend to undermine property, further alienate the landed classes from the Liberal party, and exacerbate class divisions in politics. 'Tweedmouth came in and gave me a gloomy account of R's frame of mind, pacing up and down his room over the Budget. If R. had shown strength and grip, instead of slipping and sliding, Harcourt would have been different. He can never resist strength and capacity,' wrote Morley unsympathetically on 3 April. The next day Rosebery tried to assert himself by sending Harcourt a memorandum setting out many of his concerns. A primary one was that Harcourt, in his attack on landed property, was doing nothing for the working class. 'If we wish to counterbalance property, it must be by the help of the masses. The masses do not appear to support the Liberal Party as much as we have a right to expect . . . Will this scheme bring them back? It gives them nothing, if they be tee-totallers; if they drink spirits, those spirits are further taxed. So we can hardly hope for much enthusiasm or active support from the masses.' And he stressed his fear of class-based politics, 'in which the Liberal Party would rest on nothing but a working-class support, without the variety and richness and intellectual forces which used to make up the party.' Significantly, he did not urge that the death duties scheme be dropped, but only that the graduation of duties be mitigated, with a lower top rate. 'Proposals of this kind should be introduced with gentleness and high graduation appears to be essentially a war tax.'[35]

Since Rosebery was clearly open to the charge that he was activated by self-interest in making such criticisms, this intervention could be seen as brave. But Harcourt was completely dismissive, telling Loulou he was 'much amused by the high Tory line taken by Rosebery'.[36] He returned a scathing reply that night, 4 April, rebutting Rosebery's points in the most arrogant fashion. In a scathing reference to Rosebery's comparative youth, he wrote: 'You are not, as I am, old enough to remember the great battle fought by Mr Gladstone on the succession duties. That contest secured for him the lasting hatred of the landed proprietors and the enthusiastic support of the Liberal Party. The fears which your memorandum express are a faint echo of the panic and terrorism of that time.' Another reproach ran: 'Your argument seems to involve that it is necessary to maintain an unequal incidence of taxation in order to avert the breaking up of large properties irrespective of the character of their possessors. This is a very fine old Tory doctrine – it is one which the Liberal Party are not likely to accept.' Responding to the point about landed proprietors refusing to back the Liberal party, he took a swipe at Rosebery's premiership: 'The fate of the present Government and the issue of the next election are temporary incidents which I view with philosophic indifference.' He admitted that there might be room for manoeuvre on the scale of graduation of death duties, but his final barb was a warning that he planned to take Rosebery's memorandum to the next meeting of Cabinet: he well knew that Rosebery would be embarrassed to have his views given wide circulation. 'Harcourt's increased bitterness towards R. is very marked. He sneered at R's memorandum and prided himself at having in his reply torn R's arguments to pieces,' wrote Hamilton.[37] 'There is nothing to do with rubbish of this sort other than treat it with the contempt it deserves,' Harcourt told Lord Spencer.[38]

Most other Cabinet ministers had put up with this sort of abuse from Harcourt for years, but it was Rosebery's first direct experience. 'Insolence is not argument,' he noted privately. Morley wrote that on receiving Harcourt's memorandum, 'Rosebery came into my room with that well-known look of suppressed anger and worry in his eye. He flung himself on the sofa, full of strong language about our modern Brougham,* the indispensable and the intolerable. The antipathy is very sharp.'[39] But weakened by both his economic naivety and his woeful debut in the House of Lords, Rosebery was in no position to challenge his Chancellor. Having won a minor concession about the top rate of death duty, a reduction from 10 to 8 per cent, Rosebery told Harcourt that it was unnecessary to have their memoranda discussed in Cabinet; his arguments would not be pursued. In effect, he had run away from the fight. As Loulou recorded jubilantly, 'I thought the coon would come down, but I did not expect him to do it so quickly or completely.' Officially, accepting the principle of Cabinet responsibility, Rosebery defended Harcourt. When Queen Victoria

---

*Lord Brougham, Whig Lord Chancellor of the 1830s, another radical lawyer renowned for his eloquence but criticised for his arrogance and insincerity.

uttered her inevitable parrot-squawk of disapproval, he wrote, 'Lord Rosebery . . . cannot deny that there is much to be said for the Budget in the sense of its being logically just and he believes that the landowning class must avert its severer effects by two courses which in themselves are good: that is by handing over property in their lifetime to their children and by greater simplicity of living.'[40] In private, he was full of foreboding. 'R. was in too pessimist a humour about the Budget, declaring it would be the ruin of the country, by breaking up big properties and driving away capital; and he had to be a party to it! He is too timid,' wrote Hamilton on 16 April.

The 1894 Budget was to prove the greatest triumph of Harcourt's long career in Parliament. He masterminded the passage of this complex legislation through the Commons without once having to resort to the guillotine, a feat of which perhaps only Gladstone in his prime would have been capable. Far from damaging the Liberal party, as Rosebery had predicted, the introduction of estate duty proved popular with voters – in the short term. But in the long term, Rosebery was absolutely right. The 1894 Budget was the harbinger of a new era of class-based politics, in which the right sought to protect property and the left to expand state expenditure. In this brave new world of economic envy and anxiety, there was no room for the Liberal party. After the 1894 Budget, the Liberals were to win outright just one more election in their history. Within little more than a generation, the party had all but disappeared. Harcourt could not, perhaps, have halted this trend, but he certainly helped to accelerate it, for his death duties established the principle of confiscatory state taxation. Gladstone himself, the arch economist and no Rosebery supporter, feared the Budget was 'too violent' because 'it involves a great departure from the methods of political caution established in this country'. Rosebery's dislike of the Budget has often been taken as an illustration of his innate Toryism, kept hidden beneath progressive rhetoric until his own financial interests were threatened. Morley himself, when shown Rosebery's memorandum, thought that 'it contains very sound Tory principles'. But this was to oversimplify. Throughout his later political life Rosebery groped for an alternative between high-taxing socialism and laissez-faire Toryism, looking for a creed that embraced both Empire and government intervention without descending into the expensive paternalism of the welfare state.*

---

*On a personal level, Rosebery's forebodings about Harcourt's budget were justified. In 1977, faced with death duties of £4.5 million, the 7th Earl of Rosebery was forced to sell Mentmore.

Harcourt's triumph only worsened his relationship with the Prime Minister. 'The present position is intolerable,' wrote Morley on 16 April. 'The very success of the Budget has only added fuel to the flame, for Harcourt's success goes to swell the heart of a rival whom he hates and despises.' When Rosebery called a Cabinet meeting three days later over a routine piece of legislation, Harcourt exploded with anger at what he regarded as the Prime Minister's interference with the House of Commons. 'He has apparently got Rosebery on the brain, quite as much as Rosebery has Harcourt on his brain,' noted Hamilton on the 19th. A week later, Hamilton recorded Rosebery telling him that 'he considers it hopeless to get on better terms with Harcourt. He fully believes that Harcourt means retiring as soon as the Budget is through.'[41] The Under-Secretary at the Foreign Office, Sir Edward Grey, one of his strongest allies, sympathised with Rosebery but felt he should show more spirit. 'He will have a rough time of it and he seems to be facing it but I wish he was a little more buoyant and would ride over all but the biggest waves instead of ploughing through them and getting the brine in his eyes,' he wrote to his wife.[42]

It was in the field of foreign affairs that Rosebery had his next clash with Harcourt. Once more, the British Empire in Africa was the cause of the friction. In line with the approach he had taken over Uganda, Rosebery was determined to protect Britain's position on the Upper Nile from any French military incursion which might tend to threaten Egypt from the south. The French in Africa were a constant source of anxiety to him, as he explained over luncheon that May to the rising star of the navy, Jacky Fisher: 'Lord Rosebery said he thought our relations with France were about as bad as they could possibly be. He said that the French seemed to imagine that the whole of Africa had been made over to them, and they were so aggressive, it was difficult to say when trouble might not arise.'[43] But having so recently established a protectorate in Uganda, he was reluctant to burden Britain with further direct responsibilities. It is another common error to regard Rosebery as an imperial aggressor, constantly seeking to bring more of the globe under the British flag. In reality, he was more cautious. As he put it once to J.A. Spender, 'Imperialism should have as its main object the maintenance and consolidation of Empire; extension should be avoided where possible.'[44] Similarly, he rejected the notion floated by some imperialists that Britain should embark on a comprehensive reconquest of southern Sudan* to protect Egypt, recognising that any

---

* The Sudan of the late 19th century covered a much larger area than today, including Chad, Niger, Mali, and Mauritania.

such action would be prohibitively expensive and, for the Liberal party, politically untenable. Instead, he turned to complex diplomacy to strengthen Britain's role in the area, where there were constant territorial disputes between the European powers. In March he and Lord Kimberley, his new Foreign Secretary, opened negotiations for a far-reaching agreement with Leopold II, King of the Belgians. The ingenious plan was that Belgium would recognise the Upper Nile as a British sphere of influence and lease to Britain a strip of territory between the Belgian Congo and German East Africa; the importance of this corridor was that it left open the possibility of fulfilling Cecil Rhodes's dream of a British route from the Cape to Cairo. In return, Britain promised to lease to Belgium the Sudanese provinces of Equatoria and Bahr al-Ghazal, with the aim of creating a barrier against French Equatorial Africa in the west.

As Foreign Secretary under Gladstone, Rosebery had taken the line that diplomacy was too important to be left to the Cabinet. As Prime Minister, with an elderly, garrulous Foreign Secretary at his side, he was no longer completely in charge and could not be so secretive, especially since he had conceded during the leadership battle that Harcourt, as leader of the Commons, should be in regular communication with Kimberley. 'Must we not let Harcourt know of this negotiation?' wrote Kimberley to Rosebery on 27 March. 'He ought not to kick at it as it really tends to narrow our responsibilities. If we leave him in ignorance, we shall have trouble I fear worse than by letting him know early.'[45] Rosebery accepted this, and the next day Kimberley wrote to Harcourt: 'I think you ought to know that we are engaged in secret negotiations with the King of the Belgians with a view to transfer to him under a long lease our "sphere of influence" on the Upper Nile. The object is to prevent the French, who are about to send an expedition across Africa to that region, from establishing themselves there and to settle with the Belgians, who are there already, the questions arising out of our claims to a sphere of influence in that quarter.'[46]

Immersed in work on the Budget, Harcourt appeared to take little notice of this letter. A week later, however, he went into another of his volcanic rages when he learnt that the Government was about to announce formally the retention of Uganda, a step that had been a foregone conclusion since Portal had first been sent there more than a year earlier. But Harcourt could not bear to miss another chance to browbeat Rosebery, as Kimberley recorded: '6 April: Cabinet. Uganda. Harcourt on the rampage. How can we possibly go on with such a man for leader in the House of Commons? He does not possess a single quality which fits him to conduct the business of a Government except smart speech. He said to me, "Thank

God this can't go on much longer. The ship has got a hole knocked through its bottom." I replied laughingly, "You are no better than a wrecker" – which is true. I cannot say how low an opinion I and I believe every one of his colleagues have of him as a minister.' By a twist which must have amused Rosebery, it was Harcourt, in his role as Commons Leader, who had to announce the Uganda protectorate in Parliament, on 12 April 1894.

That same day, the Anglo-Congolese agreement was signed. On the 21st a copy of its terms was sent to Harcourt, who again suddenly exploded with fury, complaining loudly of a 'breach of that promise' to keep him informed of 'all important transactions in the Commons'. He then demanded a Cabinet, 'and on their decision will depend whether I con-tinue in my present position in the House of Commons'.[47] Rosebery called the meeting for the 23rd. On the basis of Loulou's jaundiced account, the meeting has often been presented as a triumph for Harcourt and a humil-iation for Rosebery. 'The members almost unanimously sided with Chex. He described Rosebery as looking like "a whipped hound" when he found the whole Cabinet against him,' wrote Loulou. In fact, this is simply false: just the opposite happened. After listening to Sir William's tirade about lack of consultation, Kimberley calmly produced a copy of the letter he had written him on 28 March, which had gone into some detail about the negotiations. Harcourt's bluster was completely deflated and he was left badly 'undermined', as Morley put it.

What the Cabinet did find objectionable, however, was not the sub-stance of the convention, or the treatment of Harcourt, but the intention to keep the agreement secret.[48] King Leopold had insisted on this condi-tion precisely because he feared the French would be angered by the Treaty, sensing the potential threat to their own African interests. But Liberal min-isters found clandestine diplomacy intolerable, and they demanded more openness. Rosebery hated such interference in the conduct of foreign policy, but as Kimberley told him, in referring to the Cabinet, 'If anything serious were to happen, we should be in a very awkward position if we keep them in ignorance and I do not think we could justify ourselves.'[49] King Leopold was therefore approached and asked whether he would agree to the formal presentation of the Anglo-Congolese Treaty to Parliament. Reluctantly, he acquiesced.

The Foreign Office was now alarmed about the likely reaction of France once the Treaty was published. 'Sanderson★ thinks the French will be

★ Thomas Henry Sanderson, Permanent Under-Secretary for Foreign Affairs.

furious and that the King may then ask us on account of the danger to relations between France and Belgium to withdraw or modify the agreement,' wrote Kimberley to Rosebery on 6 May.[50] This, not the invective of Harcourt, was the real problem facing the Prime Minister and his Foreign Secretary. Kimberley's lack of concern about Harcourt was reflected in this note to Ripon of 6 May: 'Harcourt wrote me an absurd letter full of blood and thunder which I hardly need tell you had not the slightest effect on us: I mean the violent language. His opinions I of course pay due regard to: only if they were expressed in rational terms, they would be more likely to carry weight with me.'[51]

After some further minor alterations, the agreement was published when the Commons met on 21 May. As predicted, the French protested in the strongest terms, warning that the Treaty would 'ruin relations' between Britain and France.[52] There was an additional complication: the Germans, who resented what they saw as British encroachment on their own sphere of influence in East Africa, were just as vehement in their denunciations, and threatened to make trouble over Egypt. The whole elaborate scheme began to unravel. Rosebery was willing to give up the British corridor between Uganda and Lake Tanganyika to which the Germans took such violent exception, but the French, who wanted the province of Bahr al-Ghazal for themselves, sought to have the entire agreement overturned. King Leopold appealed to Britain to stand by him; Rosebery however was disinclined to risk war for the sake of a deal from which Britain gained so little. In this mess, and faced by the formidable alliance of France and Germany, Rosebery felt Britain had no alternative but to abandon the Treaty.

After a long series of triumphs, it was the first setback for his diplomacy. Not without justification, he put some of the blame on Kimberley, who had handled the affair with incompetent complacency. 'R. fears that Kimberley is too old for the crushing work of the Foreign Office. I wonder whether it is really crushing or whether this is part of R's impatience,' wrote Morley after a visit to The Durdans.[53] An admirably modest and self-aware politician, Kimberley admitted in his journal that he was at fault: 'Naturally I got more "kicks than half pence" which I must say I deserve,' he wrote of the Cabinet discussions on the Congo agreement. 'The fact is I found the matter in progress: I trusted to Rosebery and Anderson★ and I thought I had done a pretty stroke of business. Imperfect knowledge and blind trust in other people, these are the reasons for the fiasco, but they are

★Henry Percy Anderson, Head of the Africa Desk at the Foreign Office.

no valid excuse for my blunder and my reputation will suffer accordingly, besides – what signifies much more – the damage to the public interest. I have eaten the German leek and have now got the French onion in prospect. Pleasant.'[54] But it was Rosebery himself who had insisted that Kimberley was the only man for the Foreign Office; it was Rosebery who had made a fetish of diplomatic secrecy; and it was Rosebery whose suspicion of the French had driven him to the lengths of the impracticable Anglo-Belgian agreement, of which A.J.P. Taylor once wrote, 'it is difficult to imagine a stranger transaction'.[55] Lord Spencer summed up the view of many in the Cabinet when he said he 'did not like Rosebery's administration of foreign affairs generally. He was too hostile to France.'[56]

The role of Harcourt in overturning the Anglo-Congolese Treaty has often been exaggerated, but the wider opposition of the Cabinet certainly weakened Rosebery's ability to stand up to France and Germany when the agreement was in danger. It was unfortunate for him that, just at the peak of the Belgian negotiations, ministers learnt of another set of secret instructions he had given Gerald Portal, the British Special Commissioner in Uganda, in August 1893. These orders had authorised him to send emissaries up the Nile to 'negotiate any treaties that may be necessary for its [Uganda's] protection'.[57] Nor were these powers just theoretical. In May 1894 it emerged that a British force had established a chain of forts as far north as Lake Albert Nyanza and planted the Union Jack at Wadelai. Harcourt was not the only one to be disturbed by this evidence that the Uganda protectorate was being expanded by stealth. Others voiced their concerns, and in Cabinet on 31 May, Rosebery's methods of private diplomacy were accorded little support. Morley left this account of the meeting and its aftermath:

> Rosebery, without any sort of heat or petulance, said he made no complaint. The issue was a clear one. If nobody would defend him or Kimberley, then they had only one thing to do. The tension slacked and a line was agreed for the House of Commons debate on Uganda. After Cabinet I saw R. in his room. He said, 'I knew that, in sending those instructions, I was carrying my life in my hands. I knew that the Cabinet would have a perfect right to slice off my head if they liked.' Of course the answer to all this was perfectly simple. 'You had a right to carry your life in your hands if you pleased. You had no right to commit the Cabinet behind their backs to a course of which you knew they would disapprove.' R's action was a breach of personal loyalty and honour to his colleagues. It is fundamental that the Foreign Secretary tells the Prime Minister everything and the PM decides what is to be submitted to Cabinet. Look at it one way, it is impossible to justify R's

conduct or his maxims and, much more than that, it is impossible to trust either the judgement or the character of any man in his place who is capable of such conduct and such maxims. The whole thing almost warrants Harcourt's violent language about him. Nothing more painful could have happened.

To Hamilton, Rosebery confessed that 'throughout his time at the FO he acted off his own bat but he felt that was the only way of avoiding the disastrous precedent of 1880–1885,* though such action was no doubt unconstitutional.'[58]

After this episode Harcourt's hatred of Rosebery intensified. 'He is a rogue and liar and he knows that I know him to be such,' he said to Morley in the Commons. 'You put in R. in order to pay me out for your grievance about Home Rule. You have chosen Barabbas.' Still smarting from the leadership contest, he turned on Morley again a few days later: 'Harcourt said he would never forgive me for the cruel blow that I had dealt to the mind and heart of Loulou; that I had gone against him [Sir William] in order to pay him out for his line about the Home Rule Bill; that my conduct had been a mere wreaking of personal spite; that the whole transaction had been a base thing, basely done, a filthy, degrading and degraded business. All this tirade was slowly and deliberately uttered, without any vehemence or anger. Then the strange fellow said that our political connection was over.'[59] By September, Sir William's attitude had hardly changed: 'He considers Rosebery an impostor and the least weighty man in the cabinet. He asserts that Rosebery never carries any of his colleagues with him on foreign questions,' noted Regy Brett after a visit to Malwood.[60] Harcourt's son maintained exactly the same attitude. When Rosebery went to Eton to give away the prizes in June, Loulou, on one of his ogling jaunts, jeered at him across the schoolyard.

Locked in a feud with his Chancellor, ignored over the Budget, distrusted by many in his Cabinet, his foreign policy in a shambles, Rosebery appeared to be failing on every front. 'We are tossed on an ocean of discouragement just now,' he told his friend Sir Edward Russell.[61] On 7 May the Queen rather acidly remarked, referring to his past work at the Foreign Office, '*there indeed he was a great support to her*'. Rosebery sent her a plaintive reply: 'He would ask Your Majesty to realize his position before withdrawing confidence from him. He is as Prime Minister more unfortunately situated than any man who ever held that high office. He has inherited from his prede-

---

*Lord Granville's inept handling of foreign policy which culminated in the humiliating death of Gordon.

cessor a policy, a cabinet and a Parliament; besides a party of groups – one of which is aimed against himself . . . Lord Rosebery in the meantime is shut up in a House almost unanimously opposed to his ministry, and, for all political purposes, might as well be in the Tower of London . . . What then does Your Majesty expect of him? He cannot now honourably withdraw from the post of hazard, however irksome it may be.'[62]

Edward Hamilton thought there was a 'want of discipline' in Rosebery's political life, a consequence of his having 'never practically served in the ranks'.[63] The most industrious of Foreign Secretaries, he seemed curiously idle as Premier. At a time when his father was slaving over the Budget, Loulou was both shocked and secretly gratified one mid-week afternoon to find Rosebery in an art gallery, browsing over some engravings. 'The House of Lords rises so early,' he said, by way of embarrassed explanation.[64] Yet the mental burden of responsibility often left Rosebery irascible. 'The PM has been in such a damned bad temper for the last three days that it has been impossible to do any ticklish business with him,' said George Murray at the end of July.[65] His alluring magic on the platform deserted him and he made feeble speeches in Manchester and at the City of London Liberal Club. George Buckle, editor of *The Times*, told Regy Brett: 'A sense of disappointment is very keenly felt by many of Rosebery's old admirers. I feel it very strongly myself. I thought he would show more tenacity. It is difficult to maintain that – in regard to domestic affairs –his speeches since he became Prime Minister have been satisfactory. They do not suggest either definite principles or conviction.'[66] Ignorant of Parliamentary procedure and lacking wide Cabinet experience, Rosebery appeared unable to cope with the administrative side of his job. Loulou noted this exchange between his father and John Morley in July:

MORLEY: Rosebery sees nothing of any of his colleagues except perhaps Asquith and knows nothing of what is going on or his duties as Prime Minister.

HARCOURT: That is your fault. He is your choice. You can't expect me to educate him in the duties of his position, and if you want me to go in every morning to talk to him, well, I won't.[67]

In his own diary at this time Morley wrote: 'Talked with Asquith and Spencer. We could not conceal from ourselves that Harcourt has gone up and Rosebery has gone down. The latter has gone down absolutely by his own defects. Spencer says that Harcourt has beaten him on his own ground, foreign affairs. Melancholy but true.'[68] Soon after this Morley complained to Hamilton that 'R. had not made the most of his opportunities as Prime

Minister. In the first place he would never come to the House of Commons . . . He had not taken enough interest in the work of the different Departments. He was nominally head of the Education office as Lord President but never had once concerned himself about Education matters.' So unsure of himself was Rosebery that he made simple logistical errors: when the Cabinet held a Whitebait Dinner at Greenwich, he contrived to miss the official ministerial steamer from Westminster pier and had to go out to the boat by police launch.

Even Rosebery's greatest asset, his humour, was turned against him. A speech at the Royal Academy dinner at the beginning of May was regarded by Hamilton as 'a little too flippant. He is rather apt to fly from excessive gravity to excessive levity.'[69] Nor were his own Cabinet colleagues amused when he issued a mock Cabinet circular containing a veiled reference to his predecessor's fondness for a specific kind of rescue work:

> A rumour has reached me (to which of course I attach no credence) that four of the confidential Ministers of the Crown have arranged to spend this evening in the contemplation of a courtesan at a minor theatre. It is however difficult to put a stop to a report which has obtained circulation; and I would implore all members of the Cabinet to so spend this evening as to be able to establish a satisfactory alibi. A public visit to inspect their own effigies at Madame Tussaud's would be both pleasing and popular: while for those to whom this would be too great a strain, it might be useful to bear in mind that Mr Haldane QC, MP, lectures on 'Schopenhauer and the Ideal London' at the George Odger Coffee Tavern, 3 Cowslip Terrace, Clerkenwell Green at 8 precisely (there will be a collection).[70]

More disgruntled than ever, the Queen wrote to him on 8 June: 'In his speeches out of Parliament he should take a more serious tone and be, if she may say so, less jocular, which is hardly befitting a Prime Minister. Lord Rosebery is so clever that he may be carried away by a sense of humour, which is a little dangerous.' It was not a danger that greatly threatened Her Majesty.

Amidst all this gloom there was one moment of glory for Rosebery. A quarter of a century earlier he had effectively been sent down from Oxford for keeping race-horses, one of which he had hoped would win the Derby; to his shame, the horse had come in last. Although he had enjoyed much success since then, Rosebery had only won a single Classic, the 1883 Oaks with Bonnie Jean. The great prize of the Derby had continued to elude him. But in 1893 he had a beautiful brown two-year-old colt that showed signs of special talent, winning four important races. Audaciously – in view of his earlier humiliation – Rosebery named this horse Ladas II. Soon his daring was justified. In the early season of the following year, 1894, Ladas II lived up to his promise by winning the Newmarket Stakes and, more importantly, the Two Thousand Guineas. The racing world now saw Ladas II as the favourite for the Derby, to be run on 6 June.

With the scent of victory in his nostrils Rosebery found it difficult to contain his excitement, and made regular if somewhat secretive trips to Newmarket to inspect the horse. On the eve of the race Ladas II was taken from Newmarket to Epsom in the style befitting a Rosebery treasure and the favourite, travelling by his own special train with a team of attendants. Like most men of the turf, Rosebery was inclined to superstition. On the morning of the 1869 Derby he had found a dead hedgehog and taken it as a bad omen; 25 years later, having risen nervously at six o'clock, he saw a hedgehog scurry across his path at The Durdans. He sensed his luck was changing. In the afternoon, as the horses went to the start, with Ladas II running at 9 to 2, Rosebery, glass of champagne in hand, took his place in his box beside Regy Brett. The result was never in doubt from the first moment: Ladas II won at a canter. 'After the race,' wrote Regy, 'he was genuinely moved. All he could say was, "At last." Such a reception never was seen or could be seen again at Epsom.'[71] In his own diary Rosebery noted, 'The scene was one of delirious enthusiasm, I scarcely know why.'

The answer was that Rosebery, the glamorous aristocratic Radical, was the first Prime Minister to win the Derby. The Prince of Wales gave a celebration dinner in his honour that evening at Marlborough House, and proposed his health. Thousands of congratulatory telegrams poured in, among them one from the American wit Chancey Dephew which read, 'Nothing left but heaven.' Tailors in the West End of London reported a sudden surge in demand for the round-edged 'Rosebery collar'. In the House of Commons there was loud cheering and frivolous talk of a motion to adjourn the sitting, which the Whips soon quashed. The wave of public euphoria seemed temporarily to crack even Rosebery's innate reserve. On 7 June Regy Brett saw him at The Durdans: 'He was in tearing spirits, at one moment standing on his head on a rug, a queer attitude for a Prime Minister.'

Not everyone was overjoyed. John Morley, still angry about Uganda, wrote, 'I cannot bring myself to be in a congratulatory mood.' A section of the dour, nonconformist wing of the Liberal party voiced a puritan disapproval of its Leader indulging in the Turf, drawing the withering response from Rosebery that it appeared to be acceptable for him to own race-horses as long as they never won. When the National Anti-Gambling League wrote to him expressing the hope that 'the growing evils which accompany horse-racing are not escaping your consideration', he replied: 'My position was and is a simple one. Like Oliver Cromwell, whose official position was far higher than mine and strictures of whose principles can scarcely be questioned, I possess a few race-horses and am glad when one of them happens to be a good one.'[72] Rosebery also poked fun at the hypocrisy of the nonconformist lobby, which had apparently worked itself into a frenzy of condemnation only because he was Prime Minister: 'I made the discovery, which came to me late in life, that what was venial and innocent in a Secretary of State or President of the Council was criminal in the First Lord of the Treasury.'[73] To W.T. Stead, who warned him of the influence of the nonconformist conscience, Rosebery replied, 'I cannot agree with you in wishing that Ladas had never been foaled. He has afforded the few gleams of sunshine in my life during the last 16 months.'[74]

Yet the Derby triumph, though it led to an outpouring of elation, did nothing to restore his longer-term political fortunes. In one respect, it only reinforced the impression that Rosebery was a lightweight party leader, without a serious or coherent approach to governance. Even his support-ers were frustrated. 'I have no confidence in Lord Rosebery. He is so anx-ious to please everybody that he ends up doing things which please nobody. We none of us have the least idea of what he is at just now,' the Edinburgh MP Richard Haldane wrote to his mother in August.[75] Foreign affairs failed to improve over the summer and autumn, as drawn-out negotiations with France, aimed at achieving a settlement in Africa, stalled badly in the atmosphere of mutual suspicion arising from the Congolese shambles. Rosebery's impotence was all too plainly demonstrated when he refused to intervene in the dispute between China and Japan which blew up in July, eventually resulting in war and a resounding military victory for Japan. Britain's long-term goal was to protect the territorial integrity of the Chinese Empire, but Rosebery declared he could take no concrete action because Britain lacked sufficient naval power in the Far East, and could not risk being dragged into a conflict on Russia's side against Japan. This stance was a further illustration of Rosebery's pragmatism; in a memorandum to Kimberley of 30 July he explained his position. 'I distrust all armed demon-strations unless you are prepared to go to all lengths. It is of course neces-sary to have recourse to them sometimes, but there is always a fear of their leading you further than you wish or of their becoming ridiculous. If we thus interfere, we must be prepared to engage in naval action, and to jus-tify that proceeding to Parliament. I think it very doubtful if we could so justify it.' And he warned that action taken against Japan could 'weaken and alienate a Power of great magnitude in those seas and which is a bulwark against Russia'.[76] This was a perfectly rational line, one that contradicted the Little Englander myth that Rosebery was by instinct a belligerent, but it stood in contrast to his confident management of the Greek crisis of 1886. Lord Rendel, who was strongly disposed to support China in the interests of commerce, was disappointed by the Prime Minister's inaction. He visited Downing Street several times to argue China's case, but failed to penetrate Rosebery's façade of charm. Later he learnt from John Morley that he might have caused offence by putting the case for China to George Murray, a personal friend, as well as to the Prime Minister. In his memoirs Rendel wrote, 'I admitted [to Morley] that I had found in Sir George Murray so much grit and go that I had been led to deal with him more freely than with Lord Rosebery. John Morley's comment was singular. He told me that Lord Rosebery was so super-sensitive that I had blundered in going so much to Murray and that I ought to have made myself more attentive to Lord Rosebery.'[77]

Rosebery's sensitivity also led him to remain distant from his Cabinet, and unreconciled to Harcourt; neither man would make any advance to the other. In July, Sir William Harcourt and his wife travelled to Dollis Hill to see Gladstone, and found Rosebery there. According to Loulou's account, 'the moment Rosebery saw them, he turned on his heel and walked away, without speaking, into the garden and escaped to his carriage. Such pretty manners.'[78] When Lord Spencer tried to effect a concord, Harcourt told him, 'I agree with you that the prospects of the Government are gloomy but that is not my affair. You have made your own beds and you ought not to complain if you find them hard to lie upon.'[79] In the middle of the same month John Morley visited Dalmeny; he left this picture of the troubled Prime Minister: 'It is but fair that he should take the rough of fortune, he who has had so much of the smooth. At the same time, I am sorry for him. He reads a hundred leading articles a day and tries to shape a course out of them. Too much scheming; all is scheming; little acts of management; no master's survey of the whole horizon, no real knowledge of the ground. The personal aspect of every incident comes first. There was painfully much talk about Harcourt and his "disloyalty". Mr Gladstone could complain, if he liked, about the disloyalty of a certain Foreign Secretary – and so could the whole cabinet.'[80] Sir Edward Russell, his candid friend from Liverpool, warned him of the sense of failure that was enveloping his office. 'Something is necessary to give you that hold as chief real as well as titular, which I most earnestly desire you should have for the best interests of the party and the country. What I mean is that people of more sorts than I expected have talked of you as of doubtful strength. This impression it is of vital necessity for you to efface.'[81] Most of the press were just as critical. 'There is no reason why Lord Rosebery should not continue in office for ever and ever. After all, 20 years of irresolute Government is what the country really needs,' sneered the *Daily Chronicle*, which had abandoned its previous support. 'Whenever Lord Rosebery is brought face to face with anything big, anything requiring nerve and high courage, he seems to flinch. He is incomparable when a movement is in the epigram stage, but when the time has come for action, he fails,' wrote the *Spectator* at the beginning of October. Citing a speech at Birmingham in which Rosebery had appealed for 'guidance and inspiration' from the public in the fight against the Lords, the *Spectator* asked, 'Did ever the head of a great party speak in more hopeless or helpless strain? Could a man have shown a greater want of nerve and fibre than Lord Rosebery did here? . . . Lord Rosebery has for democracy neither the sympathy of comprehension nor of approbation. He is very anxious to catch its tone and obey it, but he is not of it. It is to him something foreign and external, like the flood or the whirlwind.'

The Education Minister Arthur Acland later gave a perceptive description of Rosebery's eccentric, self-destructive behaviour in office, the more convincing because Acland, a solid, hard-working Rosebery loyalist, lacked the prickliness of many of his higher-placed colleagues. In 1903 he called on Beatrice Webb, who made the following entry in her diary:

We got on to Rosebery. Acland was not cordial to his leadership; intimated that he had been intolerable as Head of Cabinet in 1894–95; shy, huffy and giving himself the airs of a little German king towards his Ministers. He had neither the equality of public school Englishmen nor the courteous and punctilious formality of the well-trained grand seigneur, which is the best substitute for it. Acland said, 'He complained that his colleagues never came to see him but when we did go he had hurried off to The Durdans or Dalmeny. Then after a Cabinet he might ask one of us to come to lunch but of course we had, as busy ministers, already mapped out our day with deputations and Parliamentary work. If we pleaded a previous engagement he would seem offended.' Then Acland gave us a vision of the strange, weird ways which Rosebery indulged in at home – delighting in surrounding himself with some low fellows and being comrades with them, then suddenly requesting that one of his free-thinking colleagues go to church with him or insisting that some elderly, conventional guest should drive out at ten o'clock at night for a couple of hours in an open Victoria with a postilion galloping at high speed through the night air. 'Always posing,' was Acland's summary, 'imagining himself to be an extraordinary being with special privileges towards the world.'[82]

Stung by the growing chorus of negativity, Rosebery felt he had to take some action to regain the initiative. At the end of September he had talked at Dalmeny with Richard Haldane, who had long tried to convince him to use his position to shape public opinion. 'What the people look for from their leader is words which will move them, which will give outlet and expression to the ideal which they feel they cannot frame,' he wrote in June.[83] Haldane now urged Rosebery to focus on the reform of the Upper House, which, he argued, was the key to other important Liberal legislation currently blocked by the Tory peers, including Home Rule and employment protection. A highly original thinker, Haldane told Rosebery that the only practical measure would be to extend the restriction on the Lords' right of veto, which currently existed only on financial legislation. The way to proceed, he added, was through a Resolution passed by the Commons; if the Lords kept rejecting this, they would be openly flouting the will of the electorate. Haldane's lecture had a powerful impact on Rosebery, who had already been planning a verbal assault on the Lords. Hamilton, who was at Dalmeny at the same time, found Rosebery 'quite ready to speak out clearly and intended to do so at Bradford a few weeks hence. He had purposely laid low since he became Prime Minister. He wanted first to feel his seat in his saddle, and also to wait and see the result of the Session and what it brought forth . . . He had pretty well made up his mind what to say.'[84] As he prepared for Bradford, Rosebery struck an unconvincing note of defiance: 'My political motto is, "I don't give a damn",' he told Regy Brett. 'That is to say, I am determined to speak out (as far as any Minister can) and take the consequences. Many think I am riding for a fall. That is not so. But it does not suit my temperament to escape danger, as some reptiles do, by assuming the colour of the trunk or foliage on which I find myself placed.'[85]

Before Rosebery began his agitation against the Lords it was his duty to inform the Queen, who had began to turn against him from the moment he set foot in office. 'Lord Rosebery has pleased nobody,' she wrote to her daughter Vicky, Empress Frederick, 'and has gone as far as Mr Gladstone with the further disadvantage that he has not any conviction in what he says. It is a great pity and I regret he should be Prime Minister, for as Foreign Minister he could restrain the others which he cannot and will not do now.'[86] The Queen was even less pleased by his next foray onto the platform.

On 24 October, two days before he was due to speak at Bradford, Rosebery wrote to warn the Queen that he was about to 'lay before the country' his policy on the future of the House of Lords; the main point would be a call for a 'declaratory resolution' in the Commons, with the aim of making it impossible for 'their measures to be summarily mutilated and rejected by the House of Lords'. He added that this was 'the least that could be done', since a large swathe of the Liberal party favoured abolition of the House of Lords. That sort of pragmatism cut no ice with his splenetic Sovereign. 'The Queen has been much put out and perturbed by Lord Rosebery's letter,' she replied the next day. 'The action proposed she thinks mischievous in the highest degree and she must add disloyal. Is party to go before the interests of the country?'

But if anyone's actions were mischievous and disloyal, it was the Queen's. Before Rosebery had even spoken at Bradford, she had appealed for advice to the Leader of the Opposition, Lord Salisbury, asking 'is it safe to let this agitation go on' and, more divisively, 'is the Unionist party fit for a dissolution?' In contemplating a dissolution of Parliament with the connivance of the Unionists, the Queen was on dangerous ground. It was bad enough to harangue her Prime Minister; to conspire with the Leader of the Opposition represented a serious breach of her duty of political impartiality. She openly stated to the Prince of Wales, in a letter of the 25th, that she would try to thwart Rosebery: 'I am inclined to favour dissolution sooner than consent to any step which implies tampering with the Constitution.'

The Prince of Wales, keen not to be involved in this shabby episode, gave his mother a noncommittal reply: '[I] cannot advise' on dissolution, he said. 'I fear anything I write or say would avail nothing. Lord Rosebery is in the hands of his followers who do not consider him extreme enough.' But Salisbury took a very different, much more aggressive line. Betraying a ruthless eye for party advantage, the old Tory warrior gave the Queen some outrageously partisan advice, aimed at worsening the split between Sovereign and Prime Minister. 'If Lord Rosebery makes today the declaration of policy which he indicates in his letter,' he wrote on the 27th, 'his conduct will be open to very grave exception. On a matter of this vital importance he has no constitutional right to announce a totally new policy without first ascertaining Your Majesty's pleasure on the subject and if he is unable to convince Your Majesty, *it is his duty to tender his resignation.*★ Once he is out of office he may make what proposals he pleases but he has no right to make them as a Minister of the Crown if they are unacceptable to Your Majesty.'[87] This was, to say the least, a novel interpretation of the Prime Minister's powers in a constitutional monarchy, though one of which George III would undoubtedly have approved.

★My emphasis: LM.

Undeterred by the Queen's opposition, Rosebery went ahead with his speech at Bradford on 27 October. Far from breaking new ground with this campaign against the Lords, he was only following his own and the Liberals' long-standing policy. In April he had warned the Queen that he would soon have to tackle the question, while in June the National Liberal Federation had held a special one-day conference in Leeds to denounce the Lords. The speech itself, delivered in front of an audience of 5000 at St George's Hall, showed Rosebery at his most eloquently passionate as he called the Lords question 'the greatest issue that has been put in this country since your fathers resisted the tyranny of Charles I and James II.' He asked, 'When the dissolution comes, what will the election be fought on? Will it be fought upon Disestablishment or Home Rule or the liquor question? The next election will be fought on none of these things, but upon one which includes and represents them all – I mean the House of Lords.' Having set out the case for a Commons resolution against the Lords, he challenged the British people to demand reform. He concluded with that famously dramatic impromptu gesture, throwing a glove to the floor with the words, 'We fling down this gauntlet. It is for you to take it up.' A local Liberal, J.S. Fletcher, later spoke of the excitement Rosebery inspired. 'We all came out of St George's Hall that night feeling certain that here was a bold, a valiant, a resolved leader who was going to sweep away the ancient privileges of his fellow peers once and for ever.'[88]

This was precisely what rendered the Queen incandescent. Guided by Salisbury's words she wrote, on 30 October, that she was 'pained to think that without consulting her, not to speak of not obtaining her sanction, Lord Rosebery should have announced the Government's intended plan of dealing with "the greatest constitutional question which has arisen in England for two centuries".' And she added, with absurd egotism, 'the fact of such an important declaration of policy being made by the Prime Minister implies that he has the sanction of the Sovereign and doubtless the country will so consider it.'[89] To her daughter the Empress, she was more explicit. 'You will hardly believe it when I tell you that I was never told of this till 48 hours before he made that violent speech! That the House of Lords should perhaps be reformed all sides admit but to hold such language, to wish to rouse the country against the House and to agitate when there is no excitement in the country is wrong in the extreme. The sense of the country should be taken first. I am disappointed and shocked at Lord Rosebery but he is pushed on by others, I mean his followers.' Rosebery adopted a measured tone in his reply of 1 November, explaining that he had been compelled to act because a system whereby the Lords obstructed a Liberal but not a Tory government was 'obnoxious to the conscience of the country as well as to its best interests'. On the Queen's complaints about his intemperate language, he reminded her that 'he was speaking to a tumultuous audience of 5000; that under such circumstances it is necessary to use broad popular language; and that it is impossible to argue points under such circumstances in the style appropriate to a drawing room or library.' Above all, he denied that she had a right of sanction over his public speeches: 'He would humbly deprecate the view that it is necessary for a minister before laying a question of policy before a popular audience to receive the approval of the Crown. Such a principle would tend to make the Sovereign a party in all the controversies of the hour and would hazardously compromise the neutrality of the Sovereign.'

If only Rosebery had known how little the Queen cared for her neutrality. While she lectured him she continued to plot with the Unionists, asking Salisbury to find out from his colleagues if they would 'all agree to her insisting upon a dissolution'. Salisbury promised to do so but, in an indirect admission of the dubious nature of the task, he told the Queen he needed 'to see them orally, for there is a risk of too much communication by letter'. Most of the leading Unionists thought the course Salisbury was advocating unwise, likely to compromise the Queen and play into the hands of the Liberals. 'If Lord Rosebery were to refuse to acquiesce in a dissolution, he would be constitutionally within his right to do so,' warned Sir Henry James.[90] On 6 November Salisbury abandoned his earlier incendiary advice and told the Queen that dissolution 'would do more harm than good now'. The Queen knew all too well that she had been playing with fire, as is revealed in the following note she sent the Prince of Wales about the affair, in which she explained that 'in strict confidence she had ascertained the opinions of the "principals on the Opposition side" but they all agreed that such a step would be dangerous. H.M. is most anxious this should not become known.' She added that she had spoken to Campbell-Bannerman on the subject, 'but of course he was *not* told about the idea of forcing a dissolution.'[91] The episode fully justified Edward Hamilton's later verdict that the Queen was 'thoroughly second-class. She was a bully and had by no means a first-class intelligence. She was in fact greatly over-rated.'[92]

If Rosebery had been able to initiate a genuine agitation against the House of Lords, there might have been a serious constitutional crisis. Fortunately for the Queen, his Bradford speech, despite its rhetorical exuberance, awoke no response in the electorate. His error had been to concentrate too much on the theatricalities of his performance, and not enough on the politics underpinning it. Betraying his lack of experience, he had failed to consult any leading members of the Cabinet, or to set up any systematic campaign with Liberal organisers. Most of the country was apathetic about the Lords; the decision by the peers to block Irish Home Rule – not the most broadly popular cause in English constituencies – had aroused little outrage. A demonstration in Hyde Park in August against the House of Lords had attracted only 1,500 protestors. Rosebery had therefore no mood of public anger to exploit, and he scarcely bothered to try to create one before speaking at Bradford. His strength as a leader – his oratorical brilliance – was more than outweighed by his defects: his distance from his colleagues, his inadequate grasp of political realities, his ignorance of party organisation, his lack of strategic thinking, his want of fighting spirit, and his equivocal feelings about his own role. Joseph Chamberlain, the great political organiser, made a cruel comparison between Rosebery and his predecessor: 'I never remember anything as ridiculous in the history of political agitation and it is evident that the Gladstonian organisation has fallen to pieces. In the old time, we should have at least managed to follow up such a declaration by the leaders of the party with public meetings and resolutions. There would have been the appearance of energy, even if there was no popular enthusiasm.'[93]

The bewilderment caused by the sudden pronouncement at Bradford was reflected in the press. 'Lord Rosebery has no plan. He does not even have a resolution,' said *The Times*. 'We are sorry that Lord Rosebery, who does not seem to believe in this wild policy, has been driven to staking his future upon it. It is, however, only another indication that he is "a reed painted to look like iron".' Even in his native Scotland the verdict was negative: 'Like all men poorly endowed with enthusiasm,' argued the *Edinburgh Evening News*, 'the Premier strikes an unreal note when in the political sphere he tries to be eulogistic. His Bradford speech lacked any proportion. And yet, Lord Rosebery is a man of humour, a quality which usually saves a speaker from a descent into bombast. How then are Lord Rosebery's lapses to be explained? They are due to his political isolation. The Premier is not in touch with the people. Lord Rosebery's lack of popular feeling may at critical moments prove harmful. He may vacillate when he should be firm. His danger lies in mistaking the babble of the clubs for the calm and settled opinion of the constituencies.'

Rosebery had thrown down the gauntlet, both literally and figuratively. It seemed that no one was willing to pick it up. Aggrieved at having been kept in the dark, the other members of the Cabinet were disinclined to follow Rosebery's wayward lead. In terms of policy several ministers, including moderate figures like Lord Ripon and Asquith, disagreed with Rosebery, preferring abolition of the Upper House to its reform, while Harcourt proved as unco-operative as ever. So there was no agreement as to how to proceed on the resolution. On 1 November John Morley reflected: 'The difficulties of dealing with the House of Lords are immense and Rosebery has aggravated them with his gratuitous declaration in favour of a second chamber. I hear he is much annoyed at the want of response in London to his advances. This intense self-concentration is surely fatal to vision and fatal to real leadership. But it is no use dwelling any more on what is too painfully evident; not yet evident to the world but to us who know.' At a series of Cabinet meetings in November there were futile discussions about the next step, while the Chief Whip Tom Ellis reported that there was now complete apathy in the Liberal party on the subject of the Lords. Sensing that he had lost the argument, Rosebery came up with a plan for a joint conference between the two Houses, but this idea was rejected.

In Cabinet on 26 November it was agreed to drop the idea of an anti-Lords resolution altogether. 'I hope it is clearly understood that nothing is settled,' Harcourt said to the Cabinet. According to Loulou's account, everyone replied, 'Oh yes, nothing is settled.' Within less than a month of Bradford, the death-knell of Rosebery's campaign had been sounded. Shortly afterwards he informed the Queen that there could probably be no successful move against the Lords. According to an account he left of an audience on 7 December, he said: 'Ma'am, what I wanted to say to you is this – and I cannot say this as your Minister. I say it as an individual but it may relieve your mind. The Government must bring a resolution sooner or later to assert the predominance of the elected over the hereditary body. Then there will be a dissolution. If Mr Gladstone were at the head of the Government, with his eloquence, there might be a great majority for us. But as it is, I think we may be beaten or at any rate have only a small major-ity.' So, he predicted, the 'attempt at reform is bound to end in failure. My private belief is that it must be accomplished by a Tory government.' He begged her to keep his words 'an inviolable secret'.[94] Instead of being pleased with her apparent victory, the Queen was only further irritated by Rosebery's fatalistic tone, as she explained two years later to the Unionist Sir Henry James: 'He never seemed really to know his own mind. I scolded him for taking so strong a position against the House of Lords. I telegraphed to him twice and wrote to him. I did not like his talking about revolutions. He came and saw me and all he said was I need not trouble, as his views had fallen very flat and made no progress in the country. I did not think that was a right position for my Prime Minister to take up, and I was not sorry when he was turned out.'[95]

The Bradford speech, intended to reinvigorate his premiership, had only succeeded in further weakening it. As Loulou Harcourt put it, 'The battle against the Lords has been declared at the wrong time and in the wrong way. The party is thoroughly demoralized, disheartened and disorganized.'[96] Disillusioned, Rosebery felt his own supporters in Cabinet were beginning to desert him. 'He thought it a great pity that men like Asquith and Acland did not assert themselves more in Cabinet deliberations and that he had a right to expect more from them,' noted Hamilton.[97] Kimberley was in such a sulk, complaining about 'the prodigious fuss' Rosebery had made over policy in the Far East, that he refused to leave his Norfolk home for part of the autumn. 'Kimberley, it appears, has rigidly barred his door against all colleagues and even poor Spencer, who is somewhere in the neighbourhood, has not been able to get inside the gates,' George Murray told Rosebery on 1 October. Rosebery's laconic comment was that Kimberley took 'a rather old-fashioned view of Ministerial responsibility'.

As well as the problem of dealing with his colleagues, another aspect of his position Rosebery found vexing was patronage. Here again, he managed to alienate the Queen and certain of his followers without kindling any faith in the quality of his leadership. He freely confessed in private that making appointments gave him 'infinite anxiety',[98] especially those involving the Church. Within two weeks of taking office he wrote to Arthur Godley, Gladstone's former secretary, 'I am very homesick for the Foreign Office and I do not think I shall like any of the duties of my new position. Patronage is odious, ecclesiastical patronage distressing.' During his time as Prime Minister two episcopal vacancies arose, and both his choices to fill them attracted criticism. The first was his appointment of his Etonian friend George Kennion to the see of Bath and Wells. Kennion had previously been Bishop of Adelaide, which Rosebery, meeting him there during his 1883 tour, had pretended to find disconcerting: 'Fancy one's contemporaries being so shabby as to take a bishopric and make one feel a hundred.'[99] But both Kennion's colonial experience and his school connections provoked some disapproval; there were, said the *Church Times*, 'at least a score of Colonial bishops whom we could name with a record which would justify translation to England far better than that of Lord Arthur Hervey's★ designated successor.' As to the Eton link, the paper

---

★ The previous Bishop of Bath and Wells.

regretted that 'there is still some truth in the old saying that either private means or social influence are among the primary qualifications for high preferment. It must clearly be understood in these democratic days that such considerations are of comparatively small account.'

Rosebery's other promotion, that of John Perceval, former Headmaster of Rugby, to the see of Hereford, appeared more straightforward. But the Queen was strongly opposed, because Perceval was in favour of Welsh Disestablishment. 'On no account will the Queen appoint a Disestablisher,' she said. As with the Lords question, Rosebery ignored her opinion. Perceval was offered the position, and proved a highly successful Bishop of Hereford. What really upset the Queen, however, was the political bias her neurotically Tory outlook detected in Rosebery's other Church appointments, which included four deaneries and several canonries. Her secretary Sir Arthur Bigge was therefore instructed to write to Rosebery attacking his supposed Liberal partisanship. Rosebery had put up with a lot from the Queen over the last year, but this was too much. Not only did the allegation reek of hypocrisy, in light of the Queen's own reactionary prejudice, it was also unfair; more than most politicians, Rosebery deplored the influence of party in such matters. Through his secretary George Murray he delivered a thundering riposte to Bigge: 'Lord Rosebery doubts if any Minister of recent years has administered patronage with so little regard to political support. He is therefore really at a loss to conceive on what is based the allegation that his Church appointments are too political. He cannot deny that he is hurt by an imputation which he considers ill-founded. With regard to the general question, he would say that there is nothing he dislikes so much as having to consider politics in such matters.'[100] After that fusillade, the Queen did not pursue her charge.

As a historical biographer, Rosebery should perhaps have relished the fact that the chairs of History at Oxford and Cambridge fell vacant during his premiership, yet both professorships caused him trouble. For Oxford he wanted S.R. Gardiner, who refused the post, so he had to fall back on a far less impressive nominee, Frederick York Powell. At Cambridge the vacancy was caused by the death of J.R. Seeley, whom Rosebery had put forward for a knighthood in one of his first acts as Prime Minister. The University's chief goal was to keep out Oscar Browning, the tricycle-riding King's College don who had been dismissed from Eton for his paedophile proclivities and whose self-importance far outweighed his scholarship. Browning was not shy in pressing his case: 'I can only say that my confidence not only in your wisdom and judgement but also in your friendship is such that I am sure you will do everything you can for me,' he wrote to Rosebery.[101] Fortunately there were other, saner voices, like that of Gladstone's daughter Helen, then at Newnham College, to inform Rosebery of the 'horror' that would greet Browning's appointment: 'I do not believe that any single resident member of the University would approve. He would be a hopeless failure as Professor.'[102] The prayers of Cambridge were granted. Browning lost out to Lord Acton, who proved a brilliant appointment, confirming his own place in history with his immortal line 'power corrupts, and absolute power corrupts absolutely', and by the fact that he was the first Roman Catholic since the Reformation to hold a Cambridge professorship, another tribute to Rosebery's lack of sectarianism.

Rosebery's political appointments caused him more anguish, torn as he was between the competing claims of his supporters and fears of being accused of favouritism. His cousin Henry Primrose, for instance, felt offended when Rosebery refused to make him a CB (Companion of the Order of the Bath) in 1894 on the grounds of their family ties; his wife roundly abused Rosebery, accusing him of 'self-consciousness about nepotism' and calling him 'a great failure as Prime Minister'.[103] Similarly, John Morley was angered when Rosebery refused to put forward one of his Irish allies for a baronetcy: 'Rosebery treats his friends thoroughly ill in both form and substance. What a simpleton I was to hold on to this office after Mr Gladstone left,' he wrote.[104] Perhaps Rosebery's most difficult decision arose in October 1894 over the appointment of a new Solicitor-General, since the two leading candidates, Frank Lockwood and Richard Haldane, were both friends. Eventually he chose Lockwood, on the grounds of his legal experience and party popularity, but the young Liberal Imperialist group was disappointed. 'A very wrong decision come to upon inadequate grounds,' Asquith told Haldane. The tiresome difficulties Rosebery faced were highlighted by the Queen's doctor, James Reid, who revealed a ludicrous streak of snobbery when offered a knighthood. 'A simple knighthood [Knight Bachelor] is, as you know, rather looked down on here and no one holds one; the fact of its being offered me shows that I am not on the same platform as the rest of the people here,' he moaned; he was eventually persuaded to make do with appointment as a Knight Commander of the Order of the Bath.[105]

After taking office amid such high expectations, Rosebery was only too aware of the climate of doom that pervaded his premiership. By-elections, in which the Liberal vote had previously held up, now ran against the Government. A Liberal seat at Forfar was lost in November; in December, the Tory majority at Brigg in Lincolnshire was increased. Further speeches by Rosebery at the Guildhall in London and at Devonport failed to reverse the slide. 'I think the poor fellow knows what a terrible mess he has made of it and what a mess we are all in,' wrote Morley after lunching with Rosebery on 21 November. Margot Asquith, who married Henry in 1894, was equally unimpressed: 'To my mind he lacks imagination and in consequence does not foresee where what he says will lead him. His speeches lack a certain intellectual texture – his big orations strike me as thin, his little ones indiscreet. He has not *learnt* to say nothing, nor is it natural to him when he lets himself go to say anything good.'[106] Edward Hamilton's diary towards the end of the year became a catalogue of woe about Rosebery. Almost every day he met someone who declared the Prime Minister to be a failure, as this selection shows:

> *Saturday 8 December* Fife maintained that Rosebery had been a disappointment as Prime Minister and is losing his hold over Scotland, principally because he has not spoken out distinctly enough. And that he does not seem to have his heart in the policy he advocates.

> *Monday 10 December* Found Haldane at Brooks's this evening. On looking back, Haldane thought that Rosebery would perhaps have done better had he declined to take the head of affairs without having *carte blanche* to start afresh – with a reconstructed government and a fresh programme. Had he failed, he would still have been the 'mystery man' to whom unlimited powers of statesmanship might have been attributed. Had he succeeded his boldness would have justified the risk.

> *Tuesday 11 December* Went to see Lady Gosford. She takes the ordinary line of Society about Rosebery. They all regard him as a disappointment and profess to take it quite to heart. They look upon him as a trimmer.

'What a pricked bubble Rosebery is,' said Chamberlain to Balfour in early December.[107] This was the widespread view of the Unionists. When Loulou saw Sir Henry James he was told that, after the Budget, the Liberals' popularity had soared and the Unionists feared they were in trouble, but 'since Rosebery began his speaking tour, the Liberal organisation has gone to pieces all over the country, partly from disgust at Rosebery's shilly-shally attitude.' James thought that Rosebery 'as he reads his newspapers, must now be one of the unhappiest men alive.' Certainly he could not have been overjoyed to read his end-of-year report in *The Times*:

> The Ministry has lasted longer than expected. But the reputation of its chief has suffered. Lord Rosebery, whose Premiership began amid a chorus of hopes and praises, has disappointed the most demonstrative of his friends.

No one indeed can blame him for want of activity, for he has worked incessantly and has spoken very often on public platforms. But his speeches, models as many of them have been of cultured form, have neither satisfied his party nor pleased that vast body of middle opinion which in England does so much to assure or shake the position of the Prime Minister. Sometimes, as at Bradford, he has made damaging admissions. Sometimes, as at Edinburgh, he has tried without much success to explain away former speeches. Sometimes, as at the Royal Academy, he has made quiet people ask whether flippancy was the best qualification for the head of Government.

'The brilliant apple turned to bitter ashes in his mouth,' wrote Morley of Rosebery's crisis-ridden premiership. After failing so dismally towards the end of 1894, Rosebery was about to make one desperate and startling move to restore his authority.

12

'A damned cur and coward of the Rosebery type'

~~~

THE DAWNING OF 1895 brought little improvement in Rosebery's standing. He continued to be derided on all sides for the ineffectiveness of his leadership, the irrelevance of his speeches, the divisions in his Cabinet. After seeing Richard Haldane, the Fabian socialist Beatrice Webb noted in her diary on 20 January 1895:

> Haldane is utterly discouraged with the condition of the Liberal party. He says there is no hope that the Cabinet will pull themselves through. With the exception of Acland, none of the Ministers are doing any work. Rosebery sees no one but Eddy Hamilton, a flashy Treasury clerk, his stud-groom and various non-political fashionables. Sir William Harcourt amuses himself at his country place and abroad, determined to do nothing to help Rosebery; even Asquith, under the domination of his brilliant and silly wife, has given up attending to his department and occupies his time by visiting rich country houses and learning to ride! 'Rot has set in,' says Haldane, 'there is no hope now but to be beaten and then reconstruct a new party.'[1]

There was briefly a glimmer of hope that the relationship between Harcourt and Rosebery might improve, a consequence of troubles that befell their respective families. In the middle of January Rosebery's sister Constance Leconfield lost her eldest son George, an event which Rosebery confessed left him 'stunned and stupefied'.[2] At the time of George Wyndham's death Harcourt's own second son, Loulou's younger brother, was suffering from typhoid, and expressions of sympathy were exchanged. The frost melted enough for a civil meeting on 24 January, at which they agreed to oppose John Morley's demand that the Home Rule Bill be re-introduced into Parliament. But precious little else was achieved, for Rosebery spent most of the time complaining about the Liberals' decline. 'He seems to have chucked up the sponge, admitting that it is all over with the Government. I have no pity, only amusement and contempt at his situation,' wrote Loulou bitterly.

Rosebery's sense of disillusion, compounded by the loss of his nephew, led him to try to wriggle out of a vital speech he was due to give at the conference of the National Liberal Federation in Cardiff on 18 January. George Murray was horrified by such a possibility, for he feared it would only confirm party activists' suspicions about Rosebery's dilettantism. He therefore took a strict line, writing a letter which reversed the usual relationship between Prime Minister and private secretary: 'Your going to Cardiff is a public duty with which neither your own feelings nor your sister's ought to be to be allowed to interfere. This is not an ordinary meeting but a gathering of working-people from all over the country.'[3] Rosebery did his duty, and in the event made a fine speech, to a crowd of more than ten thousand.

This strong performance failed turn the tide. Occasional fine words were not enough to alter the harsh political landscape of a divided Cabinet, a disloyal Commons leader, an increasingly precarious majority, a hostile press, an implacable Upper House, an incoherent programme, and, above all, a Prime Minister who appeared to have lost all confidence. 'In several quarters there is an obvious desire to drive me from politics and the Liberal party,' Rosebery moaned to the Chief Whip Tom Ellis. As Haldane later wrote of Rosebery, 'In some ways, he was magnificent as the foremost figure. He had a most powerful personality and a great platform eloquence. He was so formidable that he was beyond the reach of London Society on one hand and the opposition of colleagues on the other. But he could not keep a Cabinet together. He was lacking in distinct plans and even in definite purposes. He got discouraged and turned away from his task by the fear of sleeplessness and minor disappointments. Although Asquith, Grey and I stuck by him tightly we did so at the peril of our own political lives because we never knew when he would retire altogether and leave us in the lurch. He would make no sacrifices himself.'[4]

From February 1895 Rosebery's premiership began to spiral towards disaster as the relentless political pressure and physical exhaustion took its toll. Regy Brett, according to Loulou, thought that Rosebery had 'lost all cast and authority, shown himself without principle or courage and . . . lost all wit and go in his speeches.'[5] On 11 February the government narrowly survived a Commons motion put by the Unionists demanding an immediate dissolution. A week later, in another Commons debate, Dilke and Labouchere made personal attacks on Rosebery without any government colleague rising to defend the Prime Minister.

Rosebery found this lack of loyalty unforgivable, and now took a step that shook his Ministry to its core. Seething with resentment, he summoned a Cabinet meeting at Downing Street on 19 February. When the fifteen other members had gathered round the table, he read a four-page statement.

'I am sorry to inform my colleagues,' he began, 'that in my judgement my position has become untenable. It is an inseparable incident of the position which I hold that I should be fiercely and unscrupulously attacked and I am no exception. But I am an exception in this, that there has always been some sort of defence. In my case this has been conspicuously absent. The position of a Prime Minister who is a peer – more especially if he be a Liberal peer – is difficult and delicate. He is kept secluded in the House of Lords, while his policy, his character and his speeches are the subject of criticism in the House of Commons. He relies therefore for defence entirely on his party and on his colleagues.' He then turned to his specific complaints: that he could not 'call to mind a single instance in which any individual in the party or the Ministry have spoken even casually in my defence within the walls of Parliament'; and that 'so far from there being any such defence, the most venomous and violent attacks upon me have proceeded from members of our own party which would seem to make the task of repudiation all the more necessary.' Rosebery continued:

> I have waited patiently and I hope uncomplainingly for a year in order to see whether there will be any change. There has been none. On the contrary, the last two nights have been taken up with a debate on a vote of confidence directed obviously and especially against the Head of Government. The discussion has been marked with more than the usual violence against the Prime Minister, and there has been no defence and only one word even of association with him. There was not even an indication that the government and the Liberal party did not share the hostility expressed towards the Prime Minister. It seems strange that on the lowest grounds neither the party nor my colleagues view the position of the head of government as one of the smallest importance or relevance to themselves . . . I have come to the conclusion that no man with a vestige of self-respect could under the circumstances continue to hold the office I occupy . . . God knows I never sought my present office and would have done anything consistent with honour to avoid it (or even joining the Government of 1892) and I renounce it to say the least without regret.

Rosebery begged 'no one of his colleagues to blame himself for I blame nobody but myself. All the prophecies with which I combated those who wished me to take the Government have been fulfilled to the letter and I rightly pay the price of having allowed myself to be overruled on that question.'[6]

This was Rosebery at his self-centred, thin-skinned, defeatist worst. Such a statement might have come from Morley, but certainly not from Asquith, Campbell-Bannerman or Harcourt. According to Rosebery's account, 'many warm and angry protestations followed from the Cabinet, who unanimously declared that the Cabinet could not go on without me', so he agreed to defer any final decision until the next meeting. But away from his presence, most ministers were shocked and annoyed by the Prime Minister's precipitate declaration. Morley said, 'This is done in a fit of irritability'; Asquith thought 'Rosebery's conduct could only be excused on the ground that he was mad', and told Sir William Harcourt that *he* would have to carry on the Government if Rosebery carried out his threat. That night, Loulou and his father discussed various potential outcomes if Rosebery were to go, including the possibility that the Queen might send for Salisbury rather than Sir William. Loulou took little pleasure in thinking that his father might at last achieve the premiership; he wished such an event had happened a year earlier: 'We should have had a run for our money and gone down fighting like a hell cat. Now we shall go down like a cat with a brick tied round its neck.'[7] Loulou did not, however, think Rosebery would actually resign: 'The whole affair is a fit of bad temper which he will get over.'

Others in Cabinet were terrified of the threat becoming a reality. The Lord Privy Seal, Lord Tweedmouth – a man Rosebery never much cared for – implored him 'not to persist in the intention you announced this morning. Such a course would be fatal to the Government, to the party and most of all to yourself and your own reputation. I can well understand and keenly sympathise with your feelings about the attacks made upon you but I do assure you that there is no depth in them and they only serve to disgust the rank and file of the party.'[8] In his journal Kimberley was less sympathetic: 'The whole thing came on us like a thunderbolt, no one having the slightest idea that he would contemplate such an amazing *coup de tête* . . . Making every allowance for Rosebery's natural irritation, the folly of this sudden resignation is inconceivable. It would make him and his colleagues and his party look simply ridiculous. As for his vituperators, he would give them a triumph. They would justly boast that they had driven him out of office. All that they have said against a "Peer Premier" would be amply justified. I can't believe on reflection he can commit such an insane act.'[9]

The next morning, as the crisis engulfed Downing Street, George Murray went into Loulou's room and told him that 'Rosebery is in no better mood today than he was yesterday morning. This outburst has been brewing for a long time.' Murray felt that Rosebery meant to go, but might stay if he were to secure some declaration of support from his colleagues. 'He will get nothing of the sort from me,' exploded Sir William. A series of other ministers trooped in to see the Prime Minister through the day, a spectacle that prompted Sir William to comment, 'if you stroke the frog gently and assure it you love it, it may yet live!' Finally, in the late afternoon, Harcourt was persuaded by his colleagues to call on Rosebery. He did so at 5.15, and stayed one hour. His account of the meeting was recorded by Loulou: 'Rosebery was in a very excitable state, walking up and down the room, resting his elbow and head on the window frames and then gesticulating. Rosebery began with various grievances and complaints but Chex said he had not come to enter into any controversy or recrimination. Chex told Rosebery that he should have been struck by the unanimity of his colleagues. Rosebery was having none of this. "I am no use or importance in my Government. No one wants me. Everyone will be glad if I were gone. I shall tell the Queen you will all do very well without me." Chex allowed him to run on like this for some time and described it to me as being like a big salmon – you had to let him have plenty of line when he made his rushes and then reel up slowly afterwards.'[10] At the close Harcourt tried to strike a conciliatory note: 'All I can say is that if there is anything that I can do to make your position easier, or more satisfactory to yourself, I am willing and anxious to do it, for your sake, for my sake and for the sake of the Party. I don't see how it is possible for me to say more than that.'[11] By his own account, predictably, Rosebery was more bullish, attacking Harcourt for his treatment of his colleagues and his failure to consult them: 'I said I had never received a single communication from him on the business of the House of Commons since I had been Prime Minister, that this was the first time he had been in my room during that year, and that I was resolved to put an end to a state of things which under the peculiar circumstances of the Budget it had been possible to endure but which would be intolerable for another session.' Though Harcourt claimed they parted with 'warm handshakes', the interview, according to Rosebery, had been 'cold and stiff'.[12]

That night Loulou concluded the entry in his journal, 'I do not and never did believe that Rosebery means to go but he is behaving like a spoilt child and wants slapping. He will probably have a sleepless night and if he does not commit suicide (which I always think is possible) I believe he will take back tomorrow everything he has said today.' Loulou was quite right. The next morning in Cabinet Rosebery said that he had received 'satisfactory assurances' from his colleagues, and therefore did not propose to resign. His relieved ministers received the news in silence.

In a private memorandum Rosebery later claimed he had never intended to depart at all, that the threat was merely a device to bring his ministers into line: 'It would not of course have been possible for me to resign. But it was the only way in which I could restore any discipline or deal with the open and insulting disloyalty of one member of the Cabinet at least. This had come to a head the previous evening which had been entirely devoted to attacks on me while the Government sat silent.'[13] This is not convincing, however, since Rosebery was never a hard, calculating politician. It is far more probable that he acted emotionally, in a fit of pique. Lonely, insecure, dragged down by endless criticism, he indulged in a spectacular gesture to prove to himself that he was still cherished by his colleagues. Like a star actor threatening to storm off the stage set, he sought affirmation of his indispensability from the rest of the cast and crew. Having achieved that, he decided to stay with the production. Yet in the process, he had made himself look absurd. Great leaders thrive in adversity; Rosebery slid into wounded narcissism. 'I am crucified to my place and it is damnable,' he wailed to W.T. Stead at the time of the resignation farce. Pursuing the analogy, he compared the speeches of Dilke and Labby to 'nails in his hands'. Stead was not able to take this too seriously; 'very spongy nails', he replied.[14]

Rosebery's political decline was mirrored by a collapse in his health. All his life he had been prone to psychosomatic ailments, but not on a scale to seriously threaten mind and body. Now he suffered such a disturbing malaise that his doctor worried he might not survive. The first sign of trouble occurred on 22 February, the day after the Cabinet meeting at which he withdrew his resignation. He woke at three in the morning 'unspeakably sure that I was suffering from influenza'.[15] His physician Sir William Broadbent hurried to The Durdans and confirmed the diagnosis, but pronounced the fever more severe than Rosebery had thought: his temperature was over 101 degrees Fahrenheit and his pulse was 'scarcely perceptible'. The patient was immediately sent back to bed and 'soon was in the full flush of the illness'. Unfortunately, the influenza aggravated Rosebery's chronic insomnia, leaving him hopelessly weak and exhausted. On the first two nights Sir William gave him only bromide to help him sleep, but when it failed to work injected morphine. To his surprise, this too proved ineffectual. On 27 February Broadbent reported to Reid, the Queen's physician, that 'His Lordship slept, though only in a fragmentary way, after a single injection of morphia last night but tonight I have been compelled to repeat it.'[16] That day, George Murray visited Rosebery for the first time and reported to Loulou that he was 'a little better but will see no papers and do no work. If letters are sent to him he throws them on the floor. He keeps up a temperature of about 101 degrees and is very restless; slept a little last night for the first time; opiates have had no effect for the last three days.' Murray saw him again the next day, the 28th, but found him even worse. 'He had no sleep last night in spite of large doses of morphia. Rosebery says that he begins to discover the importance of a Prime Minister from the fact of his being cut off from business for more than a week and no one being or fearing the worse.'

The lassitude that seemed to overwhelm Rosebery dragged on through March, forcing him to stay at The Durdans, where he was attended by two nurses and Broadbent, who was increasingly perplexed. On 3 March Broadbent confessed to Reid that injecting morphine hypodermically had 'not had much effect at any time and finally had failed altogether'.[17] On the 11th, despite his continuing illness, Rosebery felt strong enough to visit Windsor for an audience of the Queen, who, he recorded, 'was very kind and insisted on my sitting down. I kissed her hand on entering and leaving. Nearly toppled over from weakness on rising the second time from my knees.'[18] The visit left Rosebery more tired than ever. For three weeks now he had barely slept, and was a source of genuine worry to Broadbent. In his journal for 13 March Regy Brett recorded Broadbent telling him that in all his experience 'he has never known so bad a case of insomnia; nor could he have believed that any man would struggle so gamely. If it goes on, of course, there must be a fatal termination.'[19] Regy was visiting The Durdans at this time, and his writings paint an evocative picture of a Prime Minister in torment, a 'lonely, sleepless man' hobbling about on a stick, despite being in the 'prime of life' and having 'everything that men toil for: wealth, power, position'. The two men went for a long drive in a phaeton through the Surrey countryside, Rosebery 'not cheerful' but willing to talk over 'every imaginable thing'. Politically, Rosebery felt he had made a mistake in not allowing Harcourt to form the Government, for he thought that other ministers would have followed 'like lambs'. The account continues: 'He admits his extreme sensitiveness to newspaper criticism. It is sad, but so human. He complains of loneliness. His intimacies are intermittent. He ought to marry again. He requires companionship. He denies that he was always grown up from early youth.' Regy then reflected on Rosebery's character: 'His rapid and early growth into manhood with the aloofness entailed by it and that necessary element of what is called "pose" in everyone, who is a man at an age when others are boys, fitted him for oligarchic rule but not to be Chief of a Democracy. He is curiously inexperienced in the subtler forms of happiness which come from giving more than one gets. He has been satiated with the sweets of life and the long process has left him longing for affection, universal approval and omnipotent authority. He said to me, "You think me a spoilt child" and I could not deny it.'[20]

With no sign of improvement in his patient's condition, Broadbent confessed that he was 'at his wit's end'. But at least he thought he had discovered the cause of the crippling insomnia: it was, he said, a distended stomach, which put pressure on the heart and failed to expel gas from the body. Broadbent believed that this 'stomachic derangement' was caused by Rosebery's habit of reading while eating his meals alone, 'with the result that the nervous power had gone from the stomach to the brain'.[21] This unusual analysis, even if correct, did not bring with it any immediate remedy, as Broadbent admitted that 'the most powerful medicines' had no effect in stimulating the stomach to function properly. Rarely enjoying more than two hours' sleep a night, Rosebery continued to deteriorate. On the 18th, when Edward Hamilton visited The Durdans, he found Rosebery depressed. 'It could not go on,' he said: 'if he did not break down in body, he would certainly break down in mind. Moreover, how long was he properly justified in retaining the head of affairs without being able to attend properly to his duties?'[22] Murray thought he had better warn the Queen of the dangerous situation, and wrote to Bigge on the 19th. 'I am sorry to say that I can give only a poor account of Lord Rosebery . . . His appetite, his spirits and his temper are all pretty good but if the sleeplessness goes on much longer one cannot but fear that he must break down.'[23]

Since Rosebery's time one Prime Minister, Sir Henry Campbell-Bannerman, has died in Downing Street, and others have suffered serious illness, whether terminal (Andrew Bonar Law's throat cancer) or poignant (Sir Winston Churchill's stroke). But only one other leader, Sir Anthony Eden after Suez, has been driven by crisis into physical and mental prostration similar to that endured by Rosebery in early 1895. By 20 March the news of his illness had leaked out to the press; *The Times* reported that he was unfit for his work and would probably soon resign. Regy Brett made another visit to The Durdans and found Rosebery in 'a pitiable state, jumpy, very irritable, swearing at the servants, undecided in action and thought, apparently incapable of reasoning and generally a moral and physical wreck.'[24] Turkish baths, massages, glasses of porter during the night, political business during the day – nothing seemed to make any difference. 'His Lordship has not made the progress I hoped to see,' reported Broadbent to Reid on the 21st. 'From time to time he has a terribly bad night and is thrown back and discouraged. This is particularly the case after any attempt to undertake serious work. On Tuesday, he went up to London, held a Cabinet Council and returned here in the afternoon. That night he was absolutely helpless and on Wednesday he was weak and depressed.'[25] Loulou Harcourt was almost beyond himself with excitement: 'Rosebery told

Murray that he lies awake all night thinking of all his worries and mistakes in the last ten years. What a purgatory he is suffering! I would like to be one of his nurses watching him pass through it.'[26]

Throughout April Rosebery's health continued to fluctuate wildly. Bursts of energy would be followed by the onset of enervating sleeplessness. 'Still bad nights,' he wrote in his diary for 3 April, though on the 9th he was able to record 'a slight improvement in my sleep'. But then, visiting him three days later, Hamilton found that 'Rosebery seems to have made little or no progress; the last three nights have been very bad again, and meanwhile Broadbent does nothing and tries nothing. He promised me more than a week ago that he would try douching; but as yet nothing has been done. R. is beginning to think himself that Broadbent's periodical visits are becoming a farce.' More disturbingly, noted Hamilton, 'Rosebery is certainly more depressed about himself than he was – and no wonder. He says that he can quite appreciate the feelings which prompt suicide, when night after night he lies awake.'[27] Rosebery admitted to W.T. Stead that his illness had not only made him lose his political grip, but also forced him into excessive use of drugs. 'One of the drawbacks of my indisposition', he wrote on 17 April, 'is a chronic chaos of papers. They lie like a miser's treasure in old stockings, beds, chimneys and so forth. I am strong enough if only I could get regularly half a night's sleep. I have tried every opiate but the House of Lords and that experiment must soon be undertaken.'[28] Rather than take the drastic step of venturing into the Upper House, however, Rosebery turned to a hypnotic, Sulfonel, hoping its soporific qualities would be as strong as the debates of his fellow peers. At last, after two months, he began slowly to improve, though he suffered from disastrous lapses in concentration. Speaking to the National Liberal Club on 9 May, there was a hiatus during his speech when he completely lost his train of thought. Loulou Harcourt was present at the reception and felt, with some cruel pride, that he might have been responsible.

> I went down the Reading Room [of the Club] where Rosebery was speaking. Towards the end of his speech he completely broke down in the middle of a sentence which he was unable to complete. There was a long pause and he turned round to Spencer and Sir H.G. Reade to ask them what he had been saying. They apparently could not help him and he attempted to begin again but was still unable to utter a word. He then turned to Lord Spencer who was now able to supply what he wanted and he made a fresh start, in a much altered voice. I rather fancy his breakdown had something to do with seeing *me* in the crowd listening to him! At all events it took place at the exact moment he caught my eye. I was standing by F.C. Gould, the carica-

turist, whilst he was sketching and we thought it the most painful incident we had ever witnessed. It seemed for a moment his brain had gone.

After this incident, Rosebery was encouraged by both Sir William Broadbent and the Queen to take up Lord Spencer's invitation to go on a brief cruise aboard the Admiralty yacht, *The Enchantress*, around the Scilly Isles and the south coast. He agreed to do so, and with the approval of the Cabinet travelled with Spencer from 13 to 20 May. 'Rosebery is in very good spirits, but is rather feeble,' Spencer wrote to his wife after their first day at sea.[29] It was the classic Rosebery pattern: illness and inertia followed by restlessness and travel. The voyage appeared finally to have put an end to his malady. 'Murray reports Rosebery being very much better and very cheerful,' wrote Loulou on the 20th. Although he was still frail, during the remainder of his premiership Rosebery suffered no return of the harrowing insomnia which had dragged him to the brink of insanity. Yet the months of despair and weariness left him permanently scarred: for the rest of his life he was haunted by the memories of that dark period. 'I can never forget 1895,' he wrote later. 'To lie night after night, staring wide awake, hopeless of sleep, tormented in nerves, like a disembodied spirit, to watch one's own corpse as it were, day after day, is an experience which no sane man with a conscience would wish to repeat.'[30] This was one reason why his public actions became so inhibited, why he became ever more reluctant to engage in politics. There was perhaps another, more insidious, legacy. Rosebery had taken unwonted quantities of drugs to pull him through his waking nightmare, and there were suspicions in political circles that he continued to use opiates, including cocaine, when he was under pressure. Beatrice Webb wrote that, as Premier, he had a 'drugged look', while as late as 1903 Lord George Hamilton reported to Curzon, 'Rosebery made rather a curious speech the other day in the House of Lords. I am informed, by those who watch him, that the impression is he takes some drug before speaking, which makes him brilliant for a moment but exceptionally flabby and invertebrate for the remainder of the day. He has got very big and looks like the fat boy in *Pickwick*.'[31] It should be noted that his daughter Sybil denied that he 'was addicted to drugs, whether for insomnia or anything else',[32] although the very fact that she mentions it at all is an indication of how rife the rumours were in society. Perhaps even more doubtful was the allegation circulated by Bob Reid, a Scottish Liberal MP and Attorney-General in the 1894–5 government,* who claimed Rosebery suffered from a drink problem. When Rosebery heard

*Later Lord Loreburn, Lord Chancellor 1905–12.

this gossip, he refused ever to speak to Reid again. He unquestionably enjoyed wine and champagne – and Hannah had thought wine good for his freakishly low pulse – but to suggest he was teetering on the verge of alcoholism was a wild accusation. The Unionist politician Lord Balcarres, no admirer of Rosebery, thought such talk nonsense. 'Rosebery, like many in the habit of making long and important speeches, imbibed copiously; but this kind of person holds his liquor well and I never heard anybody say they had ever seen Rosebery the worse for drink,' he wrote in 1924.[33] Sir Edmund Gosse, on the other hand, found Rosebery's consumption rather disconcerting and wrote of him in April 1905 that 'He eats extravagantly, and though he is never the "worse for liquor", he drinks heavily and continuously.'[34]

Early in March Rosebery had told Hamilton that political pressures were the cause of the collapse in his health. 'He attributed his illness, or at any rate his predisposition to becoming ill, to the harassing time he had had in seeing all his colleagues individually and hinting to them that he must be better supported.'[35] Later in life, he made the confession – a remarkable one for such a proud man – that he was simply unsuited to the premiership: 'I realized long ago, in 1895, my unfitness for office. I am not sufficiently pliant, patient or accommodating.'[36] But was there a more sinister reason for Rosebery's breakdown, beyond his feelings of inadequacy and his sense of political harassment? Was there a scandalous, even criminal, secret at the core of his life which made him terrified of exposure and led him to suffer those 'endless nights unblessed by sleep, ravaged by thoughts unutterably forlorn'?[37]

In an arresting passage dating from 1872, when he was just embarking on his public life, Rosebery wrote: 'A man may pass before the world in the splendour of a statesman; within himself he may be living as an imposter or a hypocrite, dreading discovery yet suffering in concealment, but all the time he is drifting – although the progress be unknown to himself and the world – into arrogance, sloth, selfishness and retributive catastrophe.'[38] It is very tempting to conclude that Rosebery was writing about himself. Throughout his life, Rosebery's air of mystery and his avoidance of intimacy led many to believe that he had something to hide. Beatrice Webb thought he was 'a strange, capricious creature, always posing to himself and others',[39] while Sir William Harcourt once said he 'had always disliked' Rosebery because 'he is artificial'.[40]

The mask that Rosebery wore was used, it has been claimed, to cover his true nature, a nature obnoxious to the morality of Victorian England. If the hidden part of his life were to be revealed to the public, he would be destroyed immediately. This was said to be the key to the enigma of Rosebery, the real explanation for all his hesitations and equivocations. The question was constantly asked throughout his career: who was the real Lord Rosebery? Some whispered that the answer was not the hearty follower of the turf, the magnificent statesman, the dazzling orator – but the effete, secretive homosexual. He might pose, they mocked, as the lonely widower, heartbroken at the loss of his only true love, but in reality he was a deviant who indulged in a series of clandestine relationships with young men in the secluded recesses of his Scottish castle or, later, his Italian villa. Just as his Liberalism was a sham to disguise his Tory sympathies, so his domestic family life was a cover for his Uranian proclivities.

During his lifetime Rosebery's supposed homosexuality was referred to only in the most confidential tones and in underground gossip. Since his death, the subject has been dragged, as it were, out of the closet. Indeed, such has been the force and prevalence of the allegations that it has almost become part of conventional historical wisdom that Rosebery was secretly homosexal. In a wide range of books, articles, films and websites his homosexuality is treated as an undisputed fact. It is true that a number of curious features in Rosebery's story might plausibly be cited in support of the thesis. There was his character – melodramatic, sensitive, artistic, moody and egotistical – matching the classic, old-fashioned stereotype of the homosexual. In 1950s New York the American psychologist Edmund Bergler analysed the lives of 1000 homosexual men and concluded that the following traits were common: 'masochistic provocation and injustice collecting'; 'flippancy covering depression and guilt'; 'hyper narcissism and hyper superciliousness'.[41] All could be attributed to Rosebery, to a greater or lesser extent. Berger would have enjoyed an entry Margot Asquith made in her diary in 1899: 'Rosebery is not really brave but he is highly dramatic by nature and by art. He is extremely sensitive and observant but he gives the impression of aloofness and powerful indifference. His nature is independent and lonely but being rather sentimental and self-centred he needs praise and friends and a certain amount of obedient bustle and interest around him. He is a difficult man to know because his love is not quite of the right quality, his intellect is not quite of the right quality and, like some fortunes, is larger on paper than in reality. At the same time he is not all pose and he has exceptional wit and even fascination. Selfish is too small a word for him. His selfishness is colossal. It dominates him and makes him superstitious. He cannot get away from himself.'[42]

Although the rugged Australian journalist George Morrison described him as 'very grey, with a weak, ill-formed mouth and somewhat prominent upper teeth – the same kind of mouth as Oscar Wilde's',[43] it would be wrong to condemn Rosebery as physically effeminate: his frame was too powerful, his voice too deep. But in his personality, contemporaries sometimes detected a certain unmanly streak. Typical was the statement of the Tory George Curzon, that Rosebery's 'two great faults are his tendency to treat grave matters frivolously and his feminine sensitiveness to criticism'.[44] Henry Massingham wrote in the *Nineteenth Century* magazine in November 1899 that 'his later appearances on the stage of politics have been of the character of the entrances of the prima ballerina'. On his early travels in the United States he apparently gave this feminine side free expression when he appeared in full drag one evening in New York. Staying at the home of the lawyer Samuel Barlow, he found himself without a formal suit because of a delay in the arrival of his baggage from England. So Barlow's daughter 'dressed him in her own skirts and other necessities and presented him to a few accidental callers as an elderly aunt – with entire success.' Rosebery claimed that, without his evening clothes, 'he could only be respectable in this costume'.[45]

Some of Rosebery's friendships might also seem to point to a degree of sexual ambiguity. Though he was always too reserved for true intimacy, it is interesting that of his few close relationships, one was with Eddie Hamilton, a life-long bachelor, and another with Regy Brett, married but with paedophile tendencies. He certainly never shunned the company of homosexuals. Thus in the 1870s he was on good terms with the Italian caricaturist Carlo Pellegrini, who won fame as 'Ape' in *Vanity Fair*. An ugly, impecunious but amusing individual, Pellegrini openly flaunted his pederasty, yet Rosebery was happy to meet him often. In his scandalous autobiography *My Life and Loves* Frank Harris wrote, 'The best thing I can say of the English aristocracy is that this member of it and that remained Pellegrini's friend throughout his career and supplied his needs time and again. Lord Rosebery was one of his kindliest patrons.'[46] In his later life he was friendly with Horatio Brown, historian, poet, and former lover of John Addington Symonds. Brown lived in Venice, where he delighted in the attentions of muscular gondoliers, but visited Scotland regularly, partly to see Rosebery. Brown's correspondence with Rosebery gives no hint of anything beyond affection, though it is peppered with risqué observations. Thus when he was staying in a hotel in Peeblesshire in 1910, he wrote excitedly to Rosebery of the way his landlady had been 'expatiating on the good looks of the kilted territorials and their manly march. She said, "Aw!

Mr Brown, it was just one lift" – very graphic.'[47]★ Rosebery thought so much of Brown that in 1916 he pressed for the Government to award him an honour of some sort as a tribute to his historical work on Venice. 'If a point is ever stretched, this one of the cases where it might be,' he wrote to Lord Hardinge, referring to the problems inherent in bestowing a decoration on an overseas resident like Brown. With Britain in the middle of the Battle of the Somme, recognition for a homosexual writer living in Italy can hardly have seemed a priority. Rosebery's request was refused.

Diana Mosley used to say she knew Hitler was not homosexual because he preferred to surround himself with bluff, middle-aged men rather than attractive young officers. On that basis, there could be cause for suspicion about Rosebery. A fetching appearance and bachelor status seemed to be two of the prerequisites for employment as his private secretary. When the editor of the *Scotsman* Charles Cooper was pressing the claims of Thomas Gilmour in 1884, he told Rosebery that Gilmour was 'a young, good-looking fellow'.[48] In 1906 Rosebery needed another secretary, and the society hostess Lady Colebrooke arranged for him to meet a certain Arthur Guise. 'If you liked his looks, I hope you will not give up the idea of taking him.'[49] Rosebery's longest-serving private secretary was Neville Waterfield, a graduate of New College, Oxford who went to work for him in 1890 after a spell at the International Investment Trust, and stayed with him for fourteen years. A man of notable charm if not political insight, Waterfield effectively became part of Rosebery's family, adored by the children and admired by their father. But it was his physical qualities that struck others. In a revealing letter written during a visit to Dalmeny in October 1898, Raymond Asquith opined that 'Rosebery's secretary Waterfield must have been very handsome when he first took the post eight years ago. He inclines one to believe the worst of his illustrious master.'[50]

There are several other factors to be considered in the argument for Rosebery being homosexual. One was his fondness for company less socially elevated than himself, as Cabinet colleague Arthur Acland noted, or, as Lady Raleigh put it more delicately, 'his taste for the society of his intellectual inferiors'.[51] Another was his misogyny, a common enough trait in Victorian England but more pronounced in Rosebery than in many. 'Mixed bathing is questionable, but mixed dinners are abhorrent,' he told

---

★ In this spirit, Brown also told Rosebery a good joke about a French lady and a Highlander. 'He is proceeding with such vigour and violence that she, fearing too speedy a termination, kept murmuring, "Doucement, doucement" (gently, gently). Whereupon he retorted, with an indignant snort, "Too sma, is it? I'd have ye ken yon's pride of the Highlands."' Brown to Rosebery, 16 February 1920.

his son-in-law, the Marquess of Crewe, in 1913. He also explained to Crewe that the virtue of the Jockey Club was that 'it affords a refuge at Ascot from intriguing dowagers and speculative virgins'.[52] In this context, John Morley has an interesting note of a meeting with Rosebery at Euston Station in November 1893, before he caught the boat-train to Dublin. They talked about Princess Hélène, the pretty daughter of the Comte de Paris, whom they had just met at an official luncheon: 'Rosebery, as it happens, was loud in her praises, rather remarkable in him, who seldom shows any interest in women, least of all a friendly and winning one.'[53]

Rosebery's vacations at his villa in Posillipo near Naples, bought in 1897, also led to insinuations. This part of Italy was renowned as a Uranian paradise where English homosexuals could indulge their passions with young Neapolitans without any risk of prosecution, Italy having legalised sexual relations between men in 1891. Among those drawn to the area was the writer Norman Douglas, who by coincidence also bought a villa in Posillipo in 1897. According to the historian James Money, the delights of Naples and Capri 'demolished any thoughts Douglas may have had of leading a conventional life. Not only did they induce a desire to be free of social constraints but they also encouraged his, so far latent, pederasty.'[54] Some suspected the same was true of Rosebery. In his book *The Intersexes*, published in 1908, the pseudonymous 'Xavier Mayne' dropped a heavy hint about the former Prime Minister's activities: 'One eminent personage in British political life, who once reached the highest honours in a career that has appeared to be taken up or thrown by with curious capriciousness or hesitancy, is a constant absentee in his beautiful homeland in Southern Europe, whence only gentle rumours of his racial homosexuality reach his birth-land.'[55] But such rumours were not confined to Rosebery's visits to Italy. The author George Ives wrote in his diary that Rosebery was 'said by almost everyone to have been a homosexual. I was told by a deputy coroner, that one of the chiefs of CID, Dr McNaughton, told him that the Hyde Park Police had orders never to arrest Lord Rosebery on the principle that too big a fish often breaks the line.'[56]

'All this does not amount to much,' wrote Rosebery at the conclusion of a passage about William Pitt's childhood in his biography of 1891. Exactly the same could be said of the claims of Rosebery's homosexuality. All is based on speculation. The case is built on weak foundations which begin to crumble immediately they are subjected to examination. Take the charge about a furtive double life in Italy centred on his villa at Posillipo: in truth, Rosebery had coveted the Villa Delahante since the 1870s, and had dreamt about purchasing it with Hannah – hardly the behaviour of one who is planning a gay retreat. Once he bought it he only stayed there for short periods each year, and in 1909 handed it over to the British Government. While he was away it was looked after by the British Consul in Naples, Eustace Neville-Rolfe, whose family and children were allowed to use it, sometimes for months on end. Moreover, he took his own children to the villa, encouraged his mother to stay, and in 1900 offered the use of it to Joseph Chamberlain. Such openness contradicts the image of 'Rosebery's reclusive annual holidays at Posillipo'.[57] Norman Douglas is said to have 'circulated circumstantial stories'[58] about him, yet the only mention of Rosebery in Douglas's fulsome diaries records the time Douglas and his fellow Scot Arthur Conan Doyle called at the villa for tea in 1902.

The point about Rosebery's private secretaries is similarly unconvincing. There is nothing incriminating in any of their correspondence with him: the letters of Waterfield – who went on to lead a quiet, blameless, and married life as head of the Oxford University careers office – are jocular but not intimate; those of Gilmour are studiously business-like; as for Arthur Guise, his manner was soon found to be intolerable and he had to resign. Rosebery wanted bachelors not for amorous reasons, but because they were more likely to give him the undivided loyalty he demanded. But this was not an iron principle, as he explained to Sir George Murray* when seeking to make a new appointment in 1903: 'It is important, but not indispensable, that my PS should be single.' Indeed, when Rosebery told Winston Churchill of his need to find a replacement for Waterfield in 1903, he made no mention of matrimony: 'There are only two indispensable requisites – he must be a gentleman and must write shorthand. But do not let it slip out, even in your sleep, or I shall have my hall door forced by a hungry crowd.'[59] Nor do the other arguments stand up. No homophile pattern is discernible in Rosebery's friendships; in fact he rather wearied of Brett, who was inclined to hero-worship, and liked to exaggerate their intimacy. 'He was almost universally unpopular and distrusted. His besetting sin, as with most of us, was vanity,' Rosebery once wrote.[60] Men like Brett and Ferdy Rothschild may have expressed their devotion to him, but Rosebery's response was always to shudder and withdraw. If he was said to have a feminine side, so was John Morley, more often and more pointedly, and no one questioned his inclinations. The dressing-up as a maiden aunt was probably nothing more than a youthful prank, which was never repeated.

---

*Murray was knighted in 1899.

Rosebery was certainly aware of the realities of the homosexual under-world of nineteenth-century England. When the Prince of Wales stayed at Dalmeny in March 1890 to open the Forth Rail Bridge he and Rosebery discussed the Cleveland Street scandal in which several aristocrats were accused of liaisons with male prostitutes in a London brothel; the Prince's son Albert Victor, known as Eddy, was implicated in the affair, though this never became public. After the opening ceremony Rosebery showed Barnbougle to the Prince. 'He was very civil and confidential. He hoped he might consider me a friend and told me all about his Cleveland Street troubles. He showed me a very disparaging letter from the Empress Frederick about his son,' wrote Rosebery in his diary. Another time he recorded a talk with Gladstone about the alleged pederasty of George Canning, Whig Prime Minister under George IV. Rosebery did not believe it, but Gladstone, who was 18 when Canning died in 1827, said he 'was much struck by Canning's devotion to his brother Robertson, then a handsome boy of 16'.

And there is a plausible case for saying that Rosebery, under the tute-lage of William Johnson, may have had some homosexual experiences at Eton and Oxford, possibly with Frederick Vyner. But there is nothing to say that they continued in adulthood. For all his easy friendliness with homosexuals themselves, Rosebery seems genuinely to have been repelled by actual manifestations of homosexuality. In 1879 a member of the Jockey Club, the Marquis de Talon, was accused of 'vile and unnatural practices' in sharing a bed with a friend. Rosebery called a meeting of stewards to ensure that Talon, who claimed he had been drunk, was fined and forced to apologise, Rosebery drew up the statement which Talon signed: 'I regret exceedingly that I have transgressed in any way the rules of God and man.'[61] When Gladstone told him he had been moved to tears by a Howard Sturges novel about the love of a small boy for a strong one, Rosebery pro-nounced the book 'distasteful'. It should be remembered that though he struggled with his faith, Rosebery was a deeply religious man who took the moral edicts of Christianity seriously. And his devotion to Hannah cannot be questioned; a homosexual in a sham marriage would surely not have felt the burden of genuine grief that Rosebery carried to his grave. To see his secretiveness as a sign of sexual duality is to misunderstand his character. His mystery was largely a consequence of his abnormal shyness, which made him shrink from company. Feeling socially awkward, after Hannah's death he descended into solitude. He was leading not a double life, but a lonely one. 'I have been alone so long,' he wrote in 1904.[62] And it was to overcome this loneliness that twice in his later life he sought companionship not through some clandestine, criminal affair but through marriage. For too long the fixation with the idea of his homosexuality has caused Rosebery's romantic interest in women to be overlooked and ignored.

What is really striking is how little sound evidence there is in support of the charge of homosexuality. In all the many political diaries of the time, not a single salacious rumour about Rosebery is mentioned. More tellingly, Rosebery's sworn enemy Loulou Harcourt makes no specific allegation against him. He mentions twice the different moral atmosphere of Downing Street under Rosebery, but this could be a reference to his belief that Rosebery was involved in corruption at the Bank of England and bribery at the *Daily Chronicle*. Had Loulou discovered any damaging information about Rosebery, he would not have hesitated to include it in his journals, not least because his fellow conspirator Henry Labouchere was an aggressive campaigner against homosexuality.★ After all, his diaries were startlingly candid. He even recorded Commons gossip that his own father was 'in the habit of frequenting Mrs Jeffries' brothel' – which he said was 'not true'.[63] He also confessed his own devotion to one of his Etonian favourites, Francey Egerton, whom he wanted to be his private secretary: 'He is a very charming boy. If I can once get hold of him I shall not let him go in a year.'[64] (Wisely, Egerton's father objected.) Loulou's letters to Regy Brett and to Oscar Browning – the pederast King's College history don – contain no insinuation against Rosebery. Nor is there any such material in Rosebery's papers or diaries, or in Rosebery's correspondence in other archives.

The supposition that Rosebery was a homosexual really begins to fall apart when it comes to the Oscar Wilde scandal. According to the most favoured theory, Rosebery had in the early 1890s embarked on an affair with one of his secretaries, Lord Drumlanrig, heir to the 9th Marquess of Queensberry, who was enraged by their intimacy and vowed to take his revenge on Rosebery. His anger was only compounded by the discovery that his third son, Lord Alfred Douglas, universally known as 'Bosie', was involved with Oscar Wilde. Having seen one son embroiled in a homosexual scandal, he was determined to save another from the same fate. When threats and persuasion failed to separate Bosie and Wilde, Queensberry goaded Wilde into suing him for libel by publicly accusing him of

★Labby was responsible for the section in the 1885 Criminal Law Amendment Act which made illegal any form of homosexuality in private. Until then, the law had only been concerned with sodomy, public indecency and the corruption of youths.

sodomy. Wilde's legal action collapsed after just two days, for Queensberry had hired private detectives to amass a wealth of evidence about his pro-clivities. Under pressure from Queensberry, who threatened to expose Rosebery if no action were taken, the Government hounded Wilde through two more criminal trials until a guilty verdict was achieved. Wilde was sentenced to two years' hard labour, went into exile on his release, and died a broken man in 1900.

More than a century later, when Oscar Wilde is regarded as a martyr to the cause of sexual liberation, there is an obvious attraction in the idea of a Government plot led by a hypocritical Prime Minister anxious to cover up his own propensities. But the theory does not stand up to scrutiny, being largely based on the outpourings of two diseased minds, one belonging to a violent, unbalanced homophobe, the other to a pathological sexual fan-tasist and fraudster. The homophobe was Lord Queensberry, an eccentric Scottish nobleman who loathed Christianity, homosexuality and Judaism in equal measure. Ill-tempered, coarse, and perhaps clinically insane, he devoted much of his time to heckling church sermons and bullying his family. He was also a keen sportsman, and one of his few productive achievements was to codify the rules of boxing. His brutish ways led to the dissolution of his first marriage; his second was annulled within a year on the grounds of non-consummation due to impotence – a severe embar-rassment for someone who made such a fetish of masculine prowess. The fantasist was Sir Edmund Backhouse, an Oxford-educated Chinese scholar who lived as a recluse in Peking. During his lifetime he was respected as a distinguished historian of the Chinese Empire; after his death, it was revealed that much of his work was based on his own forgeries. Even stranger were his extraordinarily detailed but unpublishably obscene mem-oirs, which related a tale of unbridled bisexual lust stretching across decades and continents, featuring not only himself but a galaxy of celebrated part-ners, including the elderly but enthusiastic Dowager Empress of China.

What united these two peculiar men was their assertion that Rosebery was an active homosexual whose seduction of Lord Drumlanrig had had fatal consequences. Queensberry – who 'saw homosexuals everywhere', in the words of Wilde's great biographer, Richard Ellmann – convinced him-self that Rosebery was 'a snob queer', and an unhealthy influence on his son. Backhouse, in his secluded, make-believe world of erotomania, claimed that as one of Rosebery's lovers he had enjoyed nights of 'linger-ing and protracted copulation' at Barnbougle Castle. His memoirs then describe, with the same relish, the relationship between Rosebery and Drumlanrig. The possibility that there was any shred of veracity in

Backhouse's work was demolished by Hugh Trevor-Roper in his biography *The Hermit of Peking* (1976), which described the memoirs as a 'pornographic novelette'. It is scarcely credible that Backhouse's work should ever have been regarded as an authoritative source rather than an outlandish work of priapic fiction. To cite just one obvious error, Backhouse in his lurid reference to his carnal visit to Barnbougle in September 1893 describes Rosebery as the Prime Minister, when Gladstone still had six months left in office. Needless to say, there is no mention of Backhouse in any of Rosebery's diaries or correspondence.

Queensberry's congenital instability – one of his eighteenth-century ancestors, known as 'the cannibalistic idiot', killed a boy and roasted him on a spit – suggests that he was no more reliable than Backhouse. His links with Rosebery dated from 1879, when he made a friendly approach just after the first Midlothian campaign. Queensberry's letter shows that he was not the rabid Tory often portrayed by historians: 'As to my politics, I should think that if I was to speak out my opinions, I should be set down by the world as the most out and out radical,' he wrote, adding, 'I should like very much some day to get to know you better.'[65] But two years later, Queensberry's outspoken atheism led to his expulsion from the Lords. Since his title was a Scottish rather than a British one, he sat in the Upper House not as of hereditary right but as an elected representative peer. In 1880, however, he refused to take the Oath of Allegiance to the Sovereign, describing it as a piece of 'Christian foolery', and was denied his place. He made several attempts at re-election, at one stage trying to enlist Rosebery's help: 'May I ask you to give me your vote at the ensuing election of peers as a great injustice has been done not only to myself but to the phase of thought I represent?'[66] Queensberry's efforts were to no avail, and, feeling ostracised, he began to turn against Rosebery: 'As for you Scottish peers, you are all tarred with the same brush. I don't recognise much manliness in any of you,' Queensberry wrote to him on 30 January 1886.

By one of those twists which litter the Wilde scandal, Queensberry had been, through marriage, distantly related to Rosebery, for his first wife Sybil was Lord Leconfield's niece. But, as the saga unfolded, this connection only fuelled Queensberry's burning hatred of Rosebery. It was in 1892, when Rosebery took on Lord Drumlanrig as one of his official secretaries at the Foreign Office, that the fire really started to smoulder. The unorthodoxy of the appointment has been exaggerated. The frequently-quoted description of Drumlanrig by one of his nephews – 'a highly nervous boy, with considerable charm but no great intelligence'[67] – was not based on any personal knowledge. Educated at Harrow and a former lieutenant in the Coldstream Guards, Drumlanrig was perhaps not an intellectual but, unlike his father, he was a committed Liberal, amiable, diligent and popular, virtues that impressed not just Rosebery, who described him to the Queen as 'a most excellent young man', but also the wider political establishment. A civil servant as solid as Murray was moved to write of him: 'I do not think I have often come across anybody to whom I got attached in so short a time. Brightness and good temper like his are all the more attractive because so few have such a stock of them,' he told Rosebery.[68] Moreover, the Leconfield tie meant he was hardly a stranger to Rosebery. As early as 1891, when he was still in the Guards, he had borrowed a set of documents on Irish Home Rule from Rosebery's office, which contradicts the myth that he was a political illiterate. In the spring of 1893, with the Liberals anxious to swell their ranks in the Upper House, Drumlanrig was offered promotion to the junior ministerial position of Lord-in-Waiting.

According to Rosebery's account, it was Algy West, not himself, who put forward this idea: 'Algernon West came to the Foreign Office saying that the Government had been unable to complete the lordships-in-waiting and suggested Drumlanrig be called up to the House of Lords. The idea took me entirely by surprise but I felt bound not to conceal the proposal from Lord Drumlanrig.' So Rosebery mentioned it, though in the most negative way: 'I urged him strongly not to accept it. I pointed out that it was a dreary fate to be buried in the House of Lords and that it was impossible to predict what line his father might take. But after two days' reflection, he said he was strongly minded to accept because he wanted to enter on a political life.'[69] Knowing how sensitive Queensberry was about the Lords, Rosebery insisted that Drumlanrig gain his father's formal approval. At first Queensberry maintained that the 'decision would revive the memory of the insult he had received from the Scottish peers', but after some further persuasion from Drumlanrig he gave his written consent to the elevation. In June 1893 Drumlanrig was created Lord Kelhead.

Yet Queensberry was always a man of extreme volatility. Within a month he had changed his mind. Still excluded from the Lords, he persuaded himself that he had been deliberately snubbed by Rosebery. As he descended into paranoia, he fired off letters to Rosebery, Gladstone and the Queen, complaining of the insult he had suffered and alleging that Rosebery's Leconfield relatives were behind the move. 'Lord Rosebery has evidently made himself the instrument of family spite against myself and strives by the most unjustifiable means to bring about a state of things which not only constitutes a serious slight to myself but will continue, I fear, to be a subject of discord and disturbance between me and my son,' he told the Queen.[70] At first Rosebery did not treat any of this nonsense seriously, even when one of Queensberry's offensive letters to Gladstone was read out to the Cabinet. He wrote to the Queen, 'It is doubtless unnecessary to warn Your Majesty that the Nobleman does not appear to be in complete possession of his senses on all occasions.'[71]

Such mocking indifference only heightened the turbulence of Queensberry's mind. He was now gripped by a new, more horrible fear: that Drumlanrig's peerage was not simply a calculated insult to himself but was designed by Rosebery as a means of enticing Drumlanrig into his sexual embrace. Here again he detected the influence of his ex-wife Sybil's family, for he had always suspected her suave, lisping father Alfred Montgomery to be a homosexual. In his unhinged state, Queensberry sensed that his father-in-law must have somehow colluded with Rosebery in the corruption of his son. It was therefore his duty to save Drumlanrig from the web of degradation spun by those two inverts. A former amateur boxing champion, Queensberry now decided to take action by personally confronting the Foreign Secretary.

On 6 August 1893 Rosebery travelled to Bad Homburg. Before leaving England he had received several messages from Queensbery, each warning of an impending assault. By now Rosebery realised he was dealing with 'a lunatic', as he put it to Munro-Ferguson, who travelled with him to Germany. That analysis was confirmed on 11 August when another letter from Queensberry reached him, this one even more explicit. 'Cher fat boy' began two pages of anti-Semitic, homophobic, viciously insulting rants. 'I always thought you the King of snobs and prigs and now I know you are a coward and a liar as well', it said in one place; 'I presume the savory odour of your Jew moneybags has too delicious a fragrance to allow me to achieve any justice', in another; 'It is not necessary for me to hide myself behind the bulwarks of effete customs which enable a coward like yourself to insult a man', in a third. Throughout the letter Queensberry warned of an impending fight: 'Oh fat boy, keep yourself fit. Use a skipping rope mightily, man of valour. You will find it good for your fat carcass. I have a punching ball here on which I am having inscribed in black letters "The Jew Pimp". I shall daily punch it to keep my hand in until we meet once more.' After further references to 'this dirty Jewry business', he concluded by describing Alfred Montgomery as 'a pimp of the first water and quite fitted by nature to run in double harness with yourself'.[72]

When he wrote that rancorous letter, Queensberry was in the south of France. By 19 August he was in Homburg, stomping through the town and, according to Rosebery's own account, 'informing everyone, even ladies, of the direful things that he was going to do that boy pimp and boy lover Rosebery.'[73] The German authorities recognised that they would have a serious problem on their hands if the British Foreign Secretary were to be attacked by a deranged Scot in one of their most popular and tranquil resorts. The police placed Queensberry's quarters under surveillance, while Rosebery was given a bodyguard. The local chief of police also called on Queensberry who, rather shaken by this intervention, 'gave his word of honour to commit no assault and offer no insult while in Homburg'. That evening, temporarily chastened, Queensberry had an interview with the Prince of Wales, who told him, 'We are quiet people in Homburg and don't like disturbance.' At seven o'clock the next morning Queensberry was on a train for Monte Carlo.

But once away from the German police and the Prince of Wales he grew defiant once more, and began to repeat his threats. 'If Lord Rosebery fancies he has done with me,' he told a reporter from the *New York Herald* based in southern France, 'he is vastly mistaken. I went to Homburg to give him "one in the eye" and I believe I succeeded in a measure. But I am not yet satisfied and I am going to London to see this matter through. I will not rest until I have brought it to a head and if an assault on the person of Lord Rosebery is necessary – why, I am prepared to commit that assault. You see my intention is to show up Lord Rosebery publicly, and possibly my only chance of doing so is to force him to bring me up before the law courts for assault.' Brandishing a bundle of letters which he said 'contained the full proof of the moral obliquity' of Rosebery, he warned, 'If his Lordship likes to continue to play the waiting game in the hope of tiring me out – well, he can, but I don't think in the long run he will find it pays.' Throughout Rosebery maintained an air of heroic scorn, undermining Queensberry's accusation of cowardice. 'It is a material and unpleasant addition to the labours of Your Majesty's service to be pursued by a pugilist of unsound mind,' he wrote to the Queen after the incident.[74]

All this bluster was of course a poor attempt to disguise the fact that Queensberry had been humiliated in Bad Homburg. For several months afterwards he was quiet. Then, in early 1894, he burst on the scene again, this time with Oscar Wilde as well as Rosebery in his sights. In April he wrote to his son Bosie begging him to end his friendship with 'this man Wilde'. When that approach failed he turned up at Wilde's home in Tite Street and accused him of sodomy; Wilde threw him out. The Douglases were terrified of Queensberry's unpredictability, and Alfred Montgomery wrote to him to suggest a meeting. Queensberry replied in a more frenzied tone than ever, describing Wilde as 'a damned cur and coward of the Rosebery type' and saying he wished he could 'shoot the fellow [Wilde] on sight'. Further, he blamed Montgomery's daughter Sybil for the growing scandal: 'Your daughter's conduct is outrageous and I am now fully convinced that the Rosebery–Gladstone–Royal insult came through my other son [Drumlanrig], that she worked that.'[75] When Wilde's lawyer threatened a libel action, Queensberry was only too pleased. A courtroom duel was precisely what he wanted.

As the shadow of the mad Marquess loomed over Oscar and Bosie through the late summer and early autumn of 1894, there was a tragic development involving his eldest son. On 18 September Drumlanrig announced that he was engaged to be married to Alexandra – Alix – Ellis, daughter of Major-General Arthur Ellis, equerry to the Prince of Wales. 'I hope you will not consider that marriage is likely to impair the efficiency of a private secretary or that it is a crime to be visited with as heavy a penalty as lack of moustache on a military attaché,' he joked to Rosebery.[76] But he faced the awkward hurdle of having to tell his father, from whom he had been so tempestuously estranged since his elevation to the House of Lords. 'What the result of the interview will be I don't know, and I feel it is not exactly an auspicious moment! However, that cannot be helped and of course I know in any case that I shall have to look forward to considerable difficulties.' Before father and son could meet, Drumlanrig's life came to a sudden and violent end. In early October he went to stay at Quantock Lodge in Somerset, the home of Edward Stanley, MP. There he met Alix's family, including her brother Gerald and her father, the General; they were all impressed by the 27-year-old peer. On the afternoon of 18 October Drumlanrig, Gerald Ellis and three other men formed a shooting party, while the women went for a drive.

At about four o'clock, after a 'goodly number of pheasants and partridges had been killed on the estate and lunch had been partaken picnic-fashion',[77] the men moved on to a turnip field about two miles from the lodge. There, disappearing into another field to look for a bird he had apparently winged, Drumlanrig became detached from the rest of the party. Suddenly, during a lull in the firing, a single, strangely muffled shot rang out across the countryside. Sensing something was amiss, one of the keepers asked anxiously, 'Where is his lordship?' Half in jest, half in fear, another of the party said 'I hope he hasn't shot himself.'[78] The search began, and soon Drumlanrig was found, lying on the ground beside a hedge. His head was covered in blood; his gun lay across his stomach. He had died from a single shot through his mouth. At an inquest five days later, the jury reached a verdict of accidental death. The coroner suggested that Drumlanrig, having failed to find his wounded bird, had heard the wheels of a carriage on the nearby road. Thinking it was the ladies returning he had run forward to greet them, only to discover the vehicle belonged to a stranger. He then turned round, saw the shooting party, and tried to rejoin it by crawling through the hedge beside the stump of a tree, during which manoeuvre he set off his loaded gun.

Both Drumlanrig's family and Alexandra's were grief-sticken by the event. General Ellis wrote to Rosebery on 22 October: 'His mother, poor woman, is broken-hearted and poor old Alfred Montgomery [Drumlanrig's maternal grandfather] is prostrate. Drummy was devoted to you – as well you know – and so proud to serve you and to earn your good opinion. I quite think I shall never see his like again. The most lovable youth I ever met. No wonder my poor child was fond of him. They would indeed have been a bright and happy couple and quite devoted to each other. She is just now stunned by the news and turned into stone by the sudden shock.'[79] The funeral was held in Scotland, at Annan, on Friday 26 October, and despite his atheism Queensberry attended. A memorable picture of the Marquess was left by Neville Waterfield, who was representing Rosebery and sent him this report: 'Suddenly there emerged a jaunty figure, clad in a darkish grey frock coat and trousers, brown boots and gloves, a large white fox-hunting neck-cloth and a top hat on the side of the head. You can believe that a clown could not have stepped more incongruously into that dismal circle . . . When the coffin appeared Lord Queensberry, who had hitherto preserved a more or less self-satisfied air, was forsaken by his bravado and, breaking down, shambled tearfully away at the head of the procession which followed the choir and coffin down the glen. The whole ceremony was very simple and sincere and rendered, if possible, the more sad by the grotesque misery of the principal mourner.'[80]

Queensberry took his 'groteque misery' out on Rosebery. Just two days after the tragedy he wrote another of his vitriolic, incoherent, almost indecipherable letters, attacking Rosebery for his 'silly servile ramblings in the cause of the Jewish lie'. He continued, 'My boy has gone to his rest, where, in the course of nature, such as you will shortly go and a good job too . . . It is a gruesome event whichever way you look at it. All that I deplore is the way my son and I have parted without reconciliation. He has gone to his rest but for a year or more we have neither spoken nor met. This bad blood between us was made by you.'[81] At the beginning of November he wrote in the same vein to Alfred Montgomery: 'Now that the first flush of this catastrophe and grief is passed, I write to tell you that it is a judgement on the whole lot of you. Montgomerys, The Snob Queers like Rosebery and certainly Christian hypocrite Gladstone, the whole lot of you! . . . What fools you all look, trying to ride me out of the course and trim the sails and the poor boy comes to this untimely end. I smell a Tragedy behind all this and have already got wind of a more startling one.'[82] Queensberry's belief that he had lost his eldest son to a homosexual scandal now intensified his mission to save Bosie and destroy Wilde.

But was there any truth in Queensberry's suspicions about Rosebery and Drumlanrig? The conspiracy theory is that Drumlanrig tried to avert revelations of his affair with Rosebery by proposing to Alexandra Ellis; when the whispers – and perhaps even blackmail – continued, he nobly decided to take his own life in order to protect Roseberry.[83] For this theory to be credible two conditions must be satisfied: first, that Drumlanrig himself was homosexual; and second, that he committed suicide. A number of stray pieces of evidence are often cited in support of the last. It is said that his school, Harrow, like Eton, was notorious for its tolerance of vice, though this is hardly proof of Drumlanrig's own sexual preferences. The often-quoted remark from Loulou Harcourt's journal, that the news of Drumlanrig's engagement made 'the institution of marriage ridiculous', might be founded on a variety of circumstances apart from Loulou's spite – the brevity of the courtship, Queensberry's eccentricity, Drumlanrig's perceived frivolity, or the couple's financial prospects, since Queensberry was notoriously mean, and General Ellis had no private income. Equally open to misinterpretation is a passage in a letter written to Rosebery by Henry Foley, a civil servant, who is quoted as having called the marriage 'terrible news'.[84] And so he did – but in affectionate mockery, as the context of the phrase makes clear: a fuller quotation suggests that Drumlanrig was in the highest spirits about his engagement. 'The ex-military attaché [Lord Drumlanrig] arrived in London yesterday,' wrote Foley on 21 September, 'and communicated to me under the seal of the deepest secrecy the terrible news that he is contemplating matrimony. He will doubtless wish to be the first to break cover in the matter with his chief, so I will only add that his inamorata is a daughter of Arthur Ellis (who alas cannot subscribe much towards the operation) and, as he rapturously exclaimed, "simply fizzes like champagne, dear old chap, don't you know!"'[85] It is clear from General Ellis's letter to Rosebery that Alix was in love with Drumlanrig, and he was certainly attractive to women. On his death Lady Monkswell wrote her diary, 'He had a particularly charming way of speaking and a bright and delightful smile. He was very good looking with fair hair and blue eyes. It was quite pretty to hear him. I met him once or twice at dinner – the sort of dear little fellow you could not help loving.'[86]

It is not possible to rule out suicide completely. There was something decidedly odd about the way death occurred, for the single bullet fractured Drumlanrig's jaw, passed through his mouth and shattered his skull, with some of the shot exploding through his right eye. For this to have happened Drumlanrig would have had to be holding the gun pointing upward – not the most natural way to hold a gun when trying to climb through a hedge. Just days after the incident the ever-reliable George Murray met his cousin H.J. Mordaunt, who had been a member of the shooting party. Murray subsequently reported to Rosebery: 'To add to the mystery, he was shot through the mouth upwards, a circumstance almost impossible to produce by accident. On the other hand, the hypothesis of suicide is almost equally improbable, for want of motive. He seems to have been in his usual spirits all through the week and no reason is known why he should have been otherwise. The whole thing to my mind is inexplicable; but Mordaunt told me that his own opinion, which is shared by the doctor and by the two other guns, is that it was suicide.'[87] Yet as the letters from Murray, Ellis and Foley all indicate, Drumlanrig showed no sign of depression or anxiety in the days or hours preceding the shooting. And if he had really wanted to kill himself, it was a strangely public and contrived way to do so, particularly as he might easily have been seen by one of the keepers. He left no suicide note, nor any letter that might point to blackmail.

More importantly, Rosebery himself was inclined to believe that accident was the most likely explanation. His thoughts on the event, never before revealed, are contained in two letters, one to Murray, the other to Queen Victoria. On 23 October he told Murray that 'the hypothesis of suicide is inconceivable. It is, however, so much in the family★ that one feared it at first. Arthur Ellis' account excludes such a possibility. What can one think?'[88] Drumlanrig having been a Lord-in-Waiting on the Queen, she immediately wrote to Rosebery, questioning the inquest verdict: 'There seems a strong impression from the Coroner's inquest that he [Drumlanrig] committed suicide.'[89] Rosebery replied, giving a rather distorted summary of the coroner's theory: 'His fiancée had driven out to join him shooting and had returned to luncheon. In the afternoon, he heard wheels again, thought it was her, ran forward, stumbled and let his gun off.'[90] If Rosebery had been in a scandalous relationship with Drumlanrig,

★Drumlanrig's grandfather, the 8th Marquess of Queensberry, had died in 1858 in a similar shooting accident, leading to the same mutterings about suicide.

he might have been expected to give the Queen a sanitised version of the event, avoiding any incriminating reference to suicide. The interesting point is that in none of his papers, including these two letters, is there the smallest indication that he felt any guilt about or involvement in the tragedy. His air is that of a detached observer, not a heartbroken lover. When Frederick Vyner was murdered by Greek brigands he had been disconsolate, experiencing a telepathic, almost physical pain. There was nothing of the sort with Drumlanrig; his diary for 19 October has the single line, 'news of poor Drumlanrig's death'. After Vyner's death, he had unsuccessfully pressed the University to put up a plaque in his friend's memory at Oxford; within just two months of Drumlanrig's death, having given a donation in his name to a children's hospital, he almost seemed bored with the whole business: 'Will you inform privately whomsoever is responsible for the Drumlanrig memorial that I will not subscribe to it?' he instructed his sister.[91] His political work seemed to be unaffected. In the week of the funeral he was on rare fighting form, travelling to Yorkshire to deliver a speech at a Sheffield banquet and his famous address at Bradford on House of Lords reform, before going south again to Bristol to accept the Freedom of the City. Most tellingly of all – if Rosebery had a secret to hide, would he have treated Drumlanrig's father with such humorous contempt? And would such a shy and private man have recorded the incident at Bad Homburg in such unblushing detail if any of Queensberry's taunts had contained a vestige of truth? It seems unlikely.

Queensberry's battle with Oscar Wilde reached its climax in early 1895, when he left at the Albemarle club the famous 'somdomite'* card addressed to Wilde. Disastrously, Wilde decided to sue. To those who suspected Rosebery's involvement, his depressive illness at this time seemed born of fear that Wilde's legal action would result in his own exposure. A leading racing man and friend of Rosebery, Lord Durham, wrote to Regy Brett in April, reflecting such rumours: 'The Newmarket scum say that Rosebery never had influenza and that his insomnia was caused by terror of being in the Wilde scandal.'[92] But again, this shows no understanding of political and chronological reality. Rosebery's nervous collapse had begun before Queensberry delivered his card at the Albemarle. It was at its peak before Wilde received it. There was simply no parallel between the fluctuations of his illness and Wilde's fortunes in the witness box. Rosebery himself said during this period that he was 'very much up and down',[93] but

---

* The 'hideous words' in Queensberry's scrawled card have been alternatively read as 'posing as a Somdomite' or 'Ponce and Somdomite'.

these peaks and troughs bore no relationship to anything that was happening in court. 'He is certainly better,' wrote Hamilton of Rosebery on 25 April, before Wilde's first criminal trial had begun. In his book *The Trials of Oscar Wilde* Michael Foldy triumphantly cites an entry in Hamilton's diary for 28 May, 'Rosebery seems better', which he links to Wilde's departure for Reading Gaol on the 27th. Yet on 20 May, before the second criminal trial had even begun, Loulou Harcourt had written that 'Rosebery is said to be much better'. The fact is that Rosebery's life-long insomnia, dating from his childhood, is well documented, and it is clear that the savage bout of 1895 was brought on not by Wilde but by the unique pressures of his post as Prime Minister, combined with other worries. Perhaps most convincingly of all, Loulou Harcourt, who would have been only too delighted to be able to pin the Wilde scandal on Rosebery, thought that financial troubles accounted for his insomnia.[94]

Rosebery's name was dragged into the Wilde case quite inadvertently, when Sir Edward Clarke, Wilde's solicitor in his libel action, quoted from Queensberry's letters to Alfred Montgomery of 1894 – in which he had lashed out at Rosebery and called Wilde 'a damned cur and coward of the Rosebery type'[95] – in an ill-conceived attempt to prove the insanity of the Marquess. All Sir Edward succeeded in doing was to fan sensationalist gossip in the press and public, thereby ensuring that the Government would be compelled to deal vigorously with Wilde. When the jury in Wilde's first criminal trial failed to reach a verdict, there were moves behind the scenes to persuade the Government to drop the case. Some felt Wilde was being mercilessly hounded, others that too much filth was being paraded in public. Queensberry's successful barrister in the libel case, the Dublin lawyer Edward Carson, went to see the Solicitor-General Sir Frank Lockwood to ask, 'Can you not let up on the fellow now? He has suffered a great deal.' Lockwood replied, 'I would, but we cannot, we dare not. It would at once be said both in England and abroad that owing to the names mentioned in Queensberry's letters, we were forced to abandon it.'[96] The Irish nationalist Tim Healey also begged Lockwood to halt the prosecution: 'I would but for the abominable rumours against Rosebery,' said the Solicitor-General.[97] This cannot be taken to imply any suspicion of guilt on Rosebery's part: Clarke's error simply made it imperative for the Crown to quell any suspicions of a cover-up. Rosebery's detractors are fond of quoting part of an entry in Hamilton's diary for 21 May which seems to hint at a sinister desire to protect him. Oscar Wilde's second criminal trial for indecency was about to start, and Hamilton wrote: 'A verdict of guilty would remove what appears to be a wide-felt impression that the Judge and

Jury were on the last occasion got at, in order to shield others of a higher status in life.' What is almost always ignored is the next part of Hamilton's entry, which firmly points to Rosebery's complete innocence of anything to do with the scandal: 'I asked Ham Cuffe (the Public Prosecutor) the other day whether there was a grain of reason for this suspicion; and he said positively, No. He had read through every word of the case; and there was not a name mentioned of anybody not only of whom he had ever heard, but of whom nobody else would have ever heard.'[98]

After Wilde's conviction Lord Alfred Douglas used an obscure French magazine, La Revue Blanche, to peddle accusations of an intrigue involving Roseberry. 'I would wish to ask Mr Asquith, the then Home Secretary and an old friend of Oscar Wilde, if he was not threatened by Lord Rosebery that if a second trial was not instituted and a verdict of guilty obtained against Mr Wilde, the Liberal party would be removed from power.'[99] Neurotic and selfish, Bosie was no more a credible witness than his father. The idea that the Liberal Government was terrified of losing power because of the Wilde scandal is absurd. With their programme in tatters and their majority dwindling, they were resigned to defeat long before Queensberry ever set foot in the Albemarle Club. Most of the Cabinet, including the triumvirate of Rosebery, Morley and Harcourt, actually relished the thought of leaving office. Nor was the Government willing to give Queensberry any help in his vendetta. When he asked the Treasury for assistance towards the costs of his investigation, Harcourt refused, on the grounds that many of Queensberry's payments 'were in the nature of bribes to blackmailers'.[100]

There was no state conspiracy against Wilde, because there no need for one. Like Sir Charles Dilke, he had brought himself down through his own reckless and self-destructive behaviour. His addiction to working-class male prostitutes made his doom inevitable, as he recognised when he talked of 'feasting with panthers'. In fact, given the weight of evidence against him, Wilde was fortunate not to face a more serious indictment: had he been charged with sodomy rather than mere gross indecency, he would have faced ten years in prison. He later admitted himself that he was 'not an innocent man'.[101]

One postscript to the Wilde saga did involve Rosebery. In 1897, after his release from prison, Wilde travelled to Italy with Lord Alfred Douglas and ended up in Posillipo, where they rented a small villa. The local English community was scandalised: 'It is very curious that none of the English colony have left cards upon us – fortunately we have a few simple friends among the poorer classes,' wrote Wilde to his friend Robbie Ross in

October.[102] At this time Rosebery had just completed the purchase of his villa, for £16,000, and had not yet stayed there. In late December he was alarmed to learn from the Prince of Wales the rumour of Wilde's presence in the vicinity. Immediately he wrote to the British Consul in Naples, Eustace Neville-Rolfe: 'A letter I received this morning from the Prince makes me fear that the villa will be uninhabitable. "I am told that Oscar Wilde himself is next door (if there is such a door) to your villa." I don't believe it, but it would be terrible if true.'[103] Three days later Rolfe confirmed the news, but told Rosebery he had little to fear: 'Oscar Wilde calling himself Mr Sebastian Nothwell★ is in a small villa at Posillipo fully two miles from you. He and Alfred Douglas have definitely parted and Wilde lives a completely secluded life. He came here as Mr Nothwell for some business and I let him suppose I did not know him by sight. He looks thoroughly abashed, liked a whipped hound. He has written a volume of poems, but no one in London would publish them and I hear he is printing them at his own expense. I really cannot think he will be any trouble to you, and after all the poor devil must live somewhere.'[104] Three months later, Neville-Rolfe gave Rosebery the reassuring news that Wilde 'has left Naples for good. He said he was getting demoralized here!'[105]

But even after Wilde was dead, the ghost of his scandal returned to haunt Rosebery one last time, at a moment of great personal tragedy.

★ Neville-Rolfe may have misheard the alias used by Wilde, who travelled in Europe after his release from Reading jail under the name Sebastian Melmoth.

13

'Purged as with fire'

———

'THE NEW YEAR is pretty certain to see a change in Government,' Edward Hamilton, now Sir Edward,★ wrote in his diary for 1 January 1895. 'I would lay even money that the change will come about halfway – probably on some unforeseen contingency.'

From the beginning of the year, the stench of decay emanating from the Rosebery government was inescapable. As in all dying administrations, its members abandoned any attempt to deal with grand political themes. Instead they concentrated on petty disputes over territory and personality. 'I saw John Morley today,' Murray told Rosebery on 2 January. 'He poured out all his little grievances, as usual, on the principle, I suppose, that 20 black rabbits make a white horse.' One of his grievances was the omission from the New Year's Honours of a baronetcy for a particular Irish doctor: 'I drew a touching picture of your having spent the last month being torn to pieces by wild doctors, musicians, politicians, etc., but he said that was what Prime Ministers are for.'[1]

Rosebery own incapacity at this time contributed to the disastrous situation. His mental and physical decline, his petulance and flippancy, his feud with Harcourt and his shyness with colleagues all rendered him a force for fragmentation rather than unity. In a reflection of the widespread gloom, Henry Massingham of the *Daily Chronicle*, a keen Rosebery supporter in March 1894, now wrote privately to Haldane: 'I shall pursue a quietly critical and merciless campaign. There is no great man at the head of affairs from whom we can expect initiative. Therefore we must fend for ourselves. One doesn't want to do endless mischief but even the fighting spirit is wanting and no great intellectual or moral influence is available.'[2] Haldane himself wrote in despondency to his sister, 'Things are looking very bad politically and the situation has not been grappled with. I have seen Lord Rosebery but it is no good. We are all in low spirits.'[3]

In this political quagmire the Government staggered from one crisis to

———

★ Appointed KCB 1894.

another. Typical was the predicament that arose in early March when Arthur Peel suddenly announced his resignation as Speaker of the House of Commons. The quest to fill the vacancy soon became another drain on the Cabinet's time and energy, as ministers were torn between the needs of the House and the demands of party loyalty. Authoritative and popular, the Secretary of State for War Henry Campbell-Bannerman would have been an ideal choice, and actually wanted the job; 'My nomination would be more acceptable to the opposition than that of any other man of our own,' he rightly told Rosebery on 9 March.[4] But Rosebery's rocky administration could not afford to lose one of its most capable members, as he explained in his reply: 'No Minister, least of all you, can be spared to fill the Speakership. The fabric of our Government is delicate enough; it cannot now be touched without risk of ruins. Please, therefore, do not further press or entertain an idea which I sincerely believe to be disastrous on this score alone.'[5] Campbell-Bannerman, whose loyalty and unselfishness far outstripped those of any of his colleagues, gracefully withdrew. The problem now was to find an alternative candidate. The independent-minded Liberal Unionist Leonard Courtney was favoured by many in the Cabinet, including Harcourt, but attracted little support from Tories, who wanted to run their own candidate, Sir Matthew White Ridley. Rosebery, showing much more commitment to his party than Harcourt, always opposed Courtney, on the grounds that it would be a humiliation for the Government to fail to find a suitably qualified Liberal. 'We should have a score of Speakers among our party,' he told Harcourt. One of the men he suggested was Haldane, who instantly rejected any such idea: 'I felt the life would be an artificial one and mean a complete break,' he told his mother.[6] Another name Rosebery came up with was that of William Gully, QC, the obscure Member for Carlisle. For someone so anonymous, Gully had a surprisingly colourful background: his father, a doctor, had been mixed up in the infamous poisoning in 1876 of the barrister Charles Bravo. Dr Gully had enjoyed an intimate friendship with Mrs Bravo, who was strongly suspected of murdering her husband, but never charged. It was a fabrication, however, that William Gully's grandfather was a professional boxer.*

Gully, regarded as 'absurd and out of the question' by Harcourt, appeared to have little chance. But on 25 March Courtney was forced to withdraw from the race when the Liberal Unionists joined the Tories in withholding

---

*A champion boxer named Jack Gully (1783–1863) went on to become Liberal MP for Pontefract; in 1975 he was portrayed by Henry Cooper in the film *Royal Flash*. But he was no relation.

their backing from him. Unless the Liberals fell in behind Gully, the Conservative Sir Matthew White Ridley would be unopposed. Harcourt was so contemptuous of Gully that he declared himself indifferent to such an outcome, in direct contrast to Rosebery who, showing some resilience despite his illness, was determined to see a Liberal victory, and insisted on Gully's candidature. 'It would be an intolerable humiliation to have to acknowledge that we had in our ranks no man fit to be Speaker,' he told Ellis, the Chief Whip. On 10 April the Commons met to decide the Speakership in the first contested election for the post since 1839. Ridley seemed the clear favourite, but his chances were undermined when Balfour, the Tory Leader in the Commons, made an ill-judged attack on Gully and on Liberal partisanship. Harcourt replied in his most crushing style, rallying the Liberals with the blunderbuss of his invective. The result was that Gully, against all odds, won by 285 votes to 274. It was also a victory of sorts for Rosebery, who had for once proved himself a better judge of Liberal backbench feeling than Harcourt. The Queen, who thought the label of impartiality was only applicable to Tories, quivered with predictable outrage: 'He is a man utterly unknown <u>except</u> for being the <u>son</u> of a <u>doctor</u> mixed up in a disgraceful poisoning case and the grandson of a prize fighter . . . The Queen cannot believe Lord Rosebery can approve it . . . The Queen thought Lord Rosebery used to say that the *best man* should be chosen for important posts and not <u>merely</u> because he belongs to the party who were in office.'[7] By now heartily weary of the Queen's incessant sniping at the Liberals, Rosebery replied in spirited vein. 'All Speakers are highly successful, all Speakers are deeply regretted and are generally announced to be irreplaceable. But a Speaker is soon found and found, almost invariably, among the mediocrities of the House.' Yet Gully was 'no mediocrity', continued Rosebery; he was a 'polished and refined gentleman, a counsel who would have been a judge.'

The Queen proved less difficult over the struggle to remove her cousin George, the exuberantly whiskered and fiercely traditionalist Duke of Cambridge, from his post as Commander-in-Chief of the British Army. She agreed it was desirable that the Duke, aged 76 and holder of the post for the past 39 years, should soon retire, not least because Campbell-Bannerman was planning a thoroughgoing organisational reform of the army. But, as she explained in her diary, 'what the Duke wishes is not to be kicked out by those violent radicals who have made such attacks on him. I assured him it would not be. He was ready to resign but could not allow himself to be turned out.'[8] When she saw Rosebery on 9 May, she said she did not like 'the haste exhibited', but did admit that George was 'too old'. The plan drawn up by the Queen, Rosebery and Henry Campbell-Bannerman was that the Duke should leave with dignity in November 1895. As pressure mounted, however, the Duke became more stubborn, a mood exacerbated by the Prince of Wales, who clumsily told the Duke, in a 'casual, pick tooth manner'[9] on his way to the races, that the sooner he went, the better. His resentment was reflected in the hysterical outpourings of Lady Geraldine Somerset, who had been a Lady-in-Waiting to his mother and even at an advanced age remained deeply though unrequitedly in love with him. In her diary she wrote, 'The whole thing is an intrigue, it is perfectly clear, between the Prince and Lord Rosebery, two beastly opportunists! Lord Rosebery, thinking to avoid difficulties for his government, is ready to throw the Duke as a sop to the radical wolves.'[10] Campbell-Bannerman found that Cambridge was growing more obstinate than ever, telling Rosebery on 17 May, 'He says he will not go at any price. The Queen is much disturbed and sees no way out of the impasse.'[11]

Yet the Duke was not as iron-willed as he pretended, and his temper fluctuated wildly. Within two days his defiant façade had collapsed, and he told the Queen that he was 'willing to accept the inevitable, though I deeply regret it'.[12] Having conceded the principle, he then tried to postpone his retirement as long as possible by quibbling over his date of departure and demanding a pension of £2000 a year, on top of the £12,000 he received annually as a Royal personage. These delaying tactics sapped the patience of Rosebery, Campbell-Bannerman and the Queen, who called the Duke 'undignified' in the way he clung to office. On 17 June Rosebery, having fully recovered from his illness, had the Duke in for an interview in which, according to the account his secretary Neville Waterfield recorded, he did not mince his words. The Duke began by speaking 'with great vehemence and at great length on the subject of his services and the abominable way in which it was proposed to treat him', claiming that Rosebery would have shown more consideration for 'a footman'. Rosebery stoutly responded, 'You are a Prince of the Blood and I am bound to say that the effect of your coming to ask for £2000 a year as compensation for retirement would be deplorable. If that sum were awarded, a debate of the most painful kind would ensue and I should be sorry to see such a result incurred for £2000 a year.' The Duke replied, 'I am not a rich man but a very poor one. I will have to curtail my expenses. I will lose my occupation and position. And for what? Because the Government thinks a change is necessary. The Queen sent me a patent in 1887 giving me the office for life and I have done nothing discreditable since then. As to the question of my age, it is an unmerited insult.' Again Rosebery exhibited no cowardice in the face of the Duke's effrontery: 'If you had been an ordinary officer, you would have retired years ago.' He stressed that reorganisation of the army was vital, and could not happen without the Duke's retirement. And he warned that 'there are only two courses open. We must either state that the Duke has retired or we must state that the Duke declined to retire without an allowance.' The Duke went away muttering that 'no one would treat a shoe-black so'.[13]

The next day the Cabinet discussed the Duke's proposed pension, and agreed unanimously to refuse it. Rosebery communicated this decision to the Duke, who said he was 'filled with grief and sorrow' and now looked upon himself 'as absolutely disgraced'.[14] Even so, bereft of support and under the threat of public humiliation, the Duke had no alternative but to resign without his pension. The next day, 20 June, his retirement was announced in the House of Commons. The mission had finally been accomplished. Campbell-Bannerman has been rightly praised for his firmness and tact in handling this difficult situation, but Rosebery also deserves credit for confronting the Duke about his unreasonable demands. Interestingly, the Duke never bore Campbell-Bannerman any ill feeling, reserving his resentment for Rosebery, whom he called 'a regular cur' and 'that blackguard', and his cousin the Queen, 'the worst of all'. Nor was the Duke's successor as Commander-in-Chief, Lord Wolseley, an ultra-Tory, much impressed with Rosebery: 'when he roars like a lion, he brays like an ass,' he told the Duke.[15]

As the spring unfolded, the Government was plagued by other difficulties. By-elections went against the Liberals. The Bill to Disestablish the Welsh Church, announced by Rosebery with such fanfare in his Cardiff speech in January, was bogged down in the Commons by skilful Tory delaying tactics. Ministers all but gave up making public speeches across the country. There were the usual rows in Cabinet over foreign policy. On 28 March the Under-Secretary at the Foreign Office, Sir Edward Grey, caused consternation to the Little Englanders when he warned in the House that, since the entire Nile basin was within the British and Egyptian sphere of influence, any French encroachment would be regarded as 'an unfriendly act'. Although the contrary has been suggested, his inflammatory remarks − prompted by reports of a French expedition from west Africa − were made without premeditation or any prior discussion with Rosebery, as Kimberley's journal reveals: 'Grey had no written speech, as was generally supposed, only some rough notes. Grey and I had some conversation on the subject in the afternoon . . . But he did not feel sure anything would be said.'[16] The undiplomatic language in which Grey's impromptu statement was couched provoked an outcry both in France and at home. Rosebery however gave the declaration his full backing, for it was in line with his own imperial thinking on Africa, as he explained to Kimberley: 'It is true that Grey made his statement without consultation from me. But that was unnecessary as he knows the views I hold and the policy I maintain, and has known them for two years past.'[17] Grey was grateful for this prime ministerial vote of confidence: 'I am so glad to know you approved of what I said. It seemed to me at the time that it was necessary to speak clearly and, if I did not, things with France must go from bad to worse.'[18] Morley and Harcourt – described by Edward Hamilton as 'the solitary Dodos of Cobdenism'* – were far less approving and caused a stir in Cabinet on 30 March with complaints about unnecessary provocation of the French. Rosebery, though he had just risen from his sick-bed and 'trembled from head to foot like an aspen,'[19] was absolutely firm in his defence of Grey. To the Queen he spoke of his contempt for that 'small but powerful section of the Cabinet which advocates an attitude of unbounded deference to all foreign nations, more especially France.' Short of resignation or a public disavowal of Grey, the Little Englanders had no option but to accept the policy, however reluctantly. Morley as usual talked of quitting, but as usual remained. Privately, however, he was filled with such bitterness against Rosebery that it lasted well beyond the end of the Government. 'Rosebery and I have had little communication since, save a few words in Cabinet. I fear the wound is deep. He is aggrieved and so am I. His insomnia may be some excuse but I have excuses too; my health is not much better than his. God knows when he and I shall sit together again,' Morley wrote in his diary.

The divide between the imperialists and the Little Englanders only widened in the following months. There was a further Cabinet clash over Uganda, when Rosebery pressed strongly for the building of a railway to the coast, a project Harcourt regarded as one of jingoist extravagance. But once more, after a further round of bluster and threatened resignation, he gave way. He mounted his high horse again in April, when Rosebery and Kimberley took vigorous action against the Nicaraguan government for expelling the British Vice-Consul; they sought an indemnity of £15,000 and sent three Royal Navy warships to enforce their demand. Harcourt called for arbitration but was over-ruled, a British force occupied the port of Corinto, and the Nicaraguans agreed to pay.

Rosebery's will may have prevailed in these incidents, largely because Harcourt and Morley were too exhausted and disunited to translate their

---

*A reference to Richard Cobden, MP (1804–65), the great radical campaigner for Free Trade whose energy and oratory ensured the repeal of the Corn Laws in 1846.

own menacing words into action, but in the domestic arena he was in worse trouble than ever. Economic problems abounded as unemployment in the skilled work-force reached 8 per cent, and agriculture remained sunk in depression. There was the stink of financial scandal in the air when the possibility emerged that the former Liberal Chief Whip Edward Marjoribanks, now Lord Tweedmouth, had given bribes to Irish MPs to encourage their attendance at the House of Commons, and the Government was further attacked for delays in securing the extradition from Argentina of the corrupt Liberal MP Jabez Balfour.* More serious for Rosebery was the decision by the Lord Chancellor, Lord Herschell, to remove Justice Vaughan Williams from the Bankruptcy Court and return him to circuit duties. Williams had been investigating corruption in the City, and in the feverish atmosphere of the time it was rumoured that he was downgraded in order to protect the Rothchilds and Rosebery. Even Loulou Harcourt, as keen to sniff out any scandal against Rosebery as a pig on a truffle hunt, admitted there was nothing in this, but it shows how mud, however unfairly thrown, seemed to stick to him.

Rosebery was perhaps more complicit in a row over the sale of political honours, when, late in his premiership, he felt compelled to award peerages to a pair of rich industrialists, James Williamson and Sydney Stern, who had made substantial donations to the Liberal party. Initially Rosebery had opposed these honours, having pledged himself not to create any more peers, but he was told by the former Whip Arnold Morley that he had little choice because Gladstone pledged his word to Stern and Williamson. Rosebery later said that 'after some hesitation' he gave way in order 'to save' Gladstone's reputation. The whole sordid affair remained a controversy for years, and was even raised by Lloyd George in 1927 when he was engulfed in his own scandal over party corruption. Rosebery felt he was acting chivalrously in upholding Gladstone's 'solemn obligation',[20] but in truth it merely revealed his naivety about party management, and his inability to set his own stamp on his premiership. 'Rosebery ought to have put his foot down and declined point-blank to fulfil any pledge of so disgusting a kind,' wrote Hamilton.[21] In the same way, Hamilton was troubled by Rosebery's decision to award a baronetcy to the former Tory MP for Colchester, Captain Naylor-Leyland, whose sole qualification appeared to be his willingness to cross the floor of

---

*A nonconformist politician and, according to *The Times*, 'the greatest scoundrel' of his age, Balfour had made a fortune through the fradulent expansion of the Liberator Building Society. In 1892, after the Liberator had collapsed, he resigned his Burnley seat and fled to Argentina. It was three years before he was brought home and put on trial at the Old Bailey. Found guilty, he was sentenced to 14 years.

the House to the Liberal side. 'I believe that here again, the responsibility rested mainly on Arnold Morley but I think Rosebery might fairly have declined to have had anything to do with so discreditable a bargain.'[22] Regy Brett told Rosebery that his awarding of honours showed a lack of 'consistency and firmness' – 'I cannot understand how your bravery, so conspicuous and attractive when you are face to face with your adversaries in the House of Lords, fails you sometimes in the secrecy of your study.'[23]

Other aspects of prime ministerial patronage proved just as irksome during these difficult months of 1895. Regy Brett placed Rosebery in an awkward dilemma when he asked for the vacant secretaryship of the Office of Woods and Forests. Rosebery was surprised at the self-seeking nerve of this request, especially because Regy had no qualifications for the post. 'He particularly resents suggestions and applications. He likes to make appointments of his own creation. He is more sensitive of this than most Prime Ministers,' Hamilton confided. Rosebery did not, however, like to refuse a friend out-of-hand, so he dithered for some time, putting the Office of Woods through 'great inconvenience in consequence'.[24] Eventually, after more than three weeks, Rosebery decided to give the post to Sir John Horner, a Somerset squire and friend of the Asquiths. Regy went into the kind of sulk that seemed to be infecting Government circles at this time, and refused an invitation to visit Rosebery at The Durdans. Rosebery then tried to make amends by offering him the secretaryship of the Office of Works, which had just fallen vacant through the promotion of Rosebery's cousin Henry Primrose – rejected for a CB a year earlier – to the chairmanship of the Board of Customs. Regy gleefully accepted, but the appointment of this plausible but unpopular schemer caused a storm among the Liberal faithful. The Chief Whip Tom Ellis fumed at Murray, 'Brett's appointment is simply *execrable*. I have already received a very hot letter about giving such an appointment to a man with about £6000 a year, with fine houses in town and country, who has always left his party in the lurch. It will do Lord Rosebery and the party an immense injury. See how the whole thing looks. A Primrose is promoted and a rich personal friend – who has never done the party a good turn – is placed in his stead. It will be looked upon as Whiggery with a vengeance. Ugh!'[25]

Rosebery's mismanagement was equally evident in the fiasco of the Cromwell statue. The proposal for a monument to the Protector at the Palace of Westminster was first mooted in August 1894 by Herbert Gladstone, the Commissioner for Works, who infuriated Rosebery by announcing it without consulting him. 'No harm has been done that I know of but had the Queen objected I should have been in an awkward position as I must have told her that I knew nothing of the matter until I read the announcement in *The Times*. This could scarcely have produced a good effect. I hope in future you will keep me informed,' wrote Rosebery to Gladstone.[26] Nevertheless, the Cabinet approved the project in December and the distinguished sculptor Hamo Thornycroft was then chosen to carry out the work. But a government so addicted to quarrelling could never let anything happen smoothly. In April 1895 ministers fell into a heated argument over the site of the statue. Harcourt, in a characteristic sneer at Rosebery, demanded that it be put in Westminster Hall between Charles I and Charles II rather than 'amongst a ruck of Prime Ministers'; Rosebery thought there would be 'something of an outrage in placing Cromwell between two men, one of whom he tried to execute, the other of whom he executed'. Instead, he suggested a space immediately in front of the Palace, a location Harcourt described as 'a ditch'.[27] Before the matter could be settled there was another embarrassing setback on 17 June, when a Commons resolution to provide £500 for the statue had to be withdrawn in the face of angry opposition from the Irish members, who had a near-visceral loathing for the memory of Cromwell. Unfortunately, Rosebery had not been informed of the decision to withdraw the motion. Aggrieved by his Cabinet's failure in communication he spluttered about resignation, though Hamilton warned him the next morning that it would be absurd to step aside over such a minor issue. The Chief Whip Tom Ellis also thought Rosebery was being self-indulgent and unreasonable, and spoke his mind directly: 'In all essentials of foreign and domestic policy, your views and decisions have prevailed. The circumstances of our position in the House of Commons make it necessary to come to prompt decisions as to business procedure and announcements.' With a mixture of bitterness and defensiveness Rosebery replied that 'what occurred was only the outward and visible sign of what has been going on for the last fifteen months and which has long been intolerable.'[28] It was not until 1899, long after Rosebery's government had fallen, that the statue was finally erected in the place Rosebery had earlier advocated, on the sunken ground beside the main entrance to the Houses of Parliament. Under the cloak of anonymity, Rosebery met the £3000 cost himself.

There was a crumb of comfort when on 29 May Rosebery's horse Sir Visto unexpectedly won the Derby. 'Damn the fellow. He is invincible – *on the turf*,' wrote Loulou Harcourt. But there was little public enthusiasm about this victory, as Hamilton noticed: 'Rosebery did not get anything like the reception he got last year; and people will say that this is evidence of his dwindled popularity.'[29] Nor could Sir Visto lift the spirits of a man reduced to political impotence by his own illness and the divisions in his

Cabinet. The Harcourt feud ran as deep as ever, Rosebery privately describing Loulou as 'a serpent' and a 'baleful influence'. Kimberley regularly complained about the impossibility of working with Harcourt as a colleague, a problem Rosebery fully understood. 'I agree with you that the position with regard to foreign affairs is almost intolerable. Had it not been on the whole that we have had our way, I should have thought it my duty to make way patriotically for a homogenous government that could carry out an efficient foreign policy,' he wrote to Kimberley.[30] Since the Grey declaration, his relations with Morley had been almost as bad. Straight after the Cabinet meeting of 28 May Rosebery made a friendly approach, saying to Morley, 'Well, if we are obliged to differ now, we shall I hope be as good friends as ever when we are no longer colleagues in the Cabinet.' In response, Morley uttered the single word 'Perhaps', then flounced out of the room. Later that day he wrote to apologise: 'I hope you will forgive that careless word "perhaps" with which I left your room. It did not come from my heart. I live in profound dejection just now and I should say a mournful "perhaps" to any word promising happiness some future day.'[31] But they remained unreconciled, and Rosebery referred to the Irish Secretary as 'a petulant spinster'.

Rosebery complained that his other colleagues 'hardly ever volunteered to come and see him', yet as Hamilton noted, this was partly his own fault: 'Charming and winning as he can be, if he likes, he is often rather standoffish and does not always like.'[32] But there was little point in ministers visiting Downing street or The Durdans for long political discussions, since Rosebery's ministry was so obviously doomed: the Cabinet had lost any sense of direction. Gladstone, who in his retirement in Dollis Hill was kept informed of events by Morley and Lord Tweedmouth, left this assessment of the miserable state of the Government: 'an anarchical cabinet, abundant pledges, obstructive opposition, complete acquiescence in small achievement and an apathy and languor in the general mind curiously combined with a decided appetite for novelties and for promises apart from the prospect of performance'.[33] It was dispiriting for all concerned, not merely the Prime Minister. And it lingered in the memory: 'Is there any member of Rosebery's Cabinet, in either House, who wishes to see it assembled again for any purpose under heaven?' asked Asquith in 1899.[34]

On the evening of 21 June there was a debate in the Commons about the army. Harcourt, in his capacity as Leader of the House, was in jovial form as he chatted to MPs on the terrace overlooking the Thames. 'Thank heaven there is one night on which we need not fear a crisis,' he said.[35] In the chamber itself, the Secretary of State for War Henry Campbell-

Bannerman was under attack from the Unionists over his alleged failure to ensure that the Army had sufficient reserves of the new explosive cordite – a rather trumped-up charge since the Unionist front bench had been privately assured that there were adequate supplies; in any case there was no need to keep large stocks, as cordite could be manufactured quickly. It was a relatively minor issue, but Campbell-Bannerman, inadequately briefed and never a master of detail, made a hash of his answer. Moments later the bell sounded as the Opposition called a snap division to reduce the War Secretary's salary by £100. Ill-prepared, the Liberals lost by 7 votes. 'It is a chance blow, but in my view a fatal one,' wrote Harcourt to Rosebery that night. Campbell-Bannerman felt he had no alternative but to offer his resignation, since the vote 'amounted to a censure upon myself'.[36]

The Cabinet met at eleven the next morning to discuss the crisis. For the first time in three years Rosebery and Harcourt were united in their views, both urging the immediate resignation of the Government. Other ministers argued for a dissolution; only two wanted to remain, supported by the Chief Whip Tom Ellis, who hoped to hang on as long as possible since he feared the party was not ready for an election and claimed, rather unconvincingly, that 'every 12 hours gained was worth a seat'.[37] It would have been possible to put a new motion asking the House of Commons to rescind the cordite vote, but by now most ministers were sick of office and longed for release. Moreover, it was felt that the loss of Campbell-Bannerman, by far the most popular member of the Cabinet, would be an overmastering blow. 'You were right to offer your resignation,' wrote Rosebery to him, 'but no earthly reason would have induced me to separate myself from you.'[38] This first meeting was inconclusive, but at another held at four in the afternoon it was agreed that the Government should go at once.

Rosebery travelled to Windsor by the 6.30 train to deliver his resignation to the Queen. 'To him personally it would be an immense relief if the Government were to go out as the scenes in the Cabinet must have been quite dreadful,' she recorded in her journal after seeing him. In his own account of the audience, Rosebery noted: 'the Queen said, "I shall be very sorry to lose you", and I bowed deeply. She said that she dreaded the work of change, that she could not read her own letters and that writing had become difficult to her. I suggested dictation but she said she could not dictate. When she talked of the new Government, she said, "Chamberlain has always been loyal." I replied that the drawback to his great and brilliant qualities and talents was that he was not quite a gentleman. The audience was not above half an hour, much shorter than usual.'[39] Ever changeable, the Queen suddenly warmed again to Rosebery at the moment of his leaving; their relationship had indeed improved once it became plain that his government was incapable of passing any Liberal measures. She not only bestowed upon him a large marble bust of herself – Gladstone had received two halfpenny photographs on his resignation in 1894 – but also offered him a vacant knighthood in the Order of the Thistle, telling him that 'as a Scotsman, he ought to prefer this to the Garter'.[40] She wrote to her daughter Empress Frederick, 'The change of Government was not such a satisfaction as perhaps it might have been for I lose some people I was very fond of and who were very able: Lord Spencer, Campbell-Bannerman and Mr Fowler were terrible losses. And personally I am very fond of Lord Rosebery and prefer him in certain respects to Lord Salisbury. He is much attached to me personally.'[41]

Rosebery professed himself delighted to be at the end of his painful labours. 'I am ready to jump out of my skin and feel like Harry or Neil on the sudden proclamation of a whole holiday,' he told his sister.[42] Such feelings were natural, yet Rosebery was also haunted by a sense of failure. For the rest of his life he brooded on the events of 1894–5, often stating that he wished he had never accepted office. To Regy Brett he said in 1898 that he had been 'deluded by his colleagues' and had 'made a mistake'; he would have 'done better to go out on the predominant partner speech'.[43] He had been 'grieved' to learn that 'private friendship was incompatible with political loyalty'.[44] His experience only deepened the repugnance he had always felt for traditional party politics, that 'evil-smelling bog from which I was always trying to extricate myself'.[45] To Murray in 1901 he recalled with pain 'the disabling' severity of his insomnia, which left him 'half prostrate, and wholly nervous, irritable and on edge'.[46] Rosebery had faced enormous difficulties in his premiership, and there were those who were surprised that he had lasted more than a year. Yet, as in other aspects of his discordant life, there was a glaring contrast between his brilliance as Foreign Secretary and his incapacity as Prime Minister. In effect, the responsibilities of the post had found him out. In her *Autobiography* Margot Asquith wrote, 'Lord Rosebery was too thin-skinned, too conscious to be really happy. He was not self-swayed like Gladstone, but he was self-enfolded. He came into power at a time when the fortunes of the Liberal party were at their lowest; and this, coupled with his peculiar sensibility, put a strain upon him.' As Henry Labouchere wrote cruelly, but for once not unjustly, 'By universal consent, Lord Rosebery would have been fitted for the highest place in the land – if only he had never occupied it.' It was a view echoed by Haldane, who said that Rosebery 'wished to be a Pitt but ended up in being a Goderich'.[47]★

The Unionists under Salisbury came into power and quickly dissolved Parliament. The subsequent General Election was a disaster for the Liberals, the Unionists gaining an overall majority of 152, the greatest defeat of a government since the 1832 Reform Act. If the Liberal record in office was weak, its campaign was pure farce, with the leading figures fighting on different platforms. Harcourt stressed temperance reform, Morley spoke solely on Home Rule. Rosebery, as a peer, was barred from electioneering, but at the Albert Hall just before the dissolution of Parliament he had made one of his great radical orations, taking the iniquities of the House of Lords as his theme. 'We are told that any violent demonstrations of popular will will always be obeyed by the House of Lords. But you cannot legislate by a succession of hurricanes' was one of his resounding lines. The Lords was the question 'on which I am pledged to fight the election of 1895', he said. And he compared the 'fresh breath of freedom and independence' in America with the way the Upper House had made 'a mockery of freedom' in Britain. Rosebery was probably correct in his instinct that the Lords was a far stronger issue for Liberals than the divisive questions of Irish self-government and restrictions on the alcohol trade, but yet again he failed to bring his two most important colleagues into line. The triple-headed nature of the Liberals' tactics only emphasised the disunity of the party, as Tweedmouth reported to Gladstone: 'Our weak spot is the want of one leader and one policy to conjure by.'[48] And Rosebery himself proved not to be the electoral asset with the working classes that his party had hoped when he was propelled into the leadership and won the Derby in early 1894. 'He may make himself the leader we want. But, so far, his name has apparently taken little or no hold on English electors, however well he may stand in Scotland,' wrote the former junior minister Sir Ughtred Kay-Shuttleworth just after the election.[49]

As if to reinforce this ineffectuality, Rosebery went on a yachting trip around Scotland with Neville Waterfield during the campaign, a gesture that smacked of astonishing disdain for the Liberal cause. 'I have slept like a hibernating animal since embarking on this yacht last Friday,' he wrote to his sister from Orkney.[50] Party leaders are not usually expected to hibernate during elections. Ellis, the Chief Whip, once more expressed his exasperation: 'It is a thousand pities that you cannot proceed with your Lords campaign. It is

★Viscount Goderich, that 'transient and embarrassed phantom', was Prime Minister from 1827–8. Lord Ripon, Rosebery's Colonial Secretary, was his son.

my deliberate conviction that we should win the election hands down if you had been in a position to carry the spirit of your speech at the Albert Hall,' he wrote to Rosebery at the start of the contest. Rosebery's response was to blame his colleagues for not supporting him over Lords reform: 'I have done all I could; but, single-handed and ill, I could do no more.' This did nothing to mollify Ellis. At the election's close he was frankly censorious, comparing Rosebery's inactivity with the energy displayed by the Tory leader. 'I think it was a calamity that you were away at sea with an injunction – so the newspapers said – that letters were not to reach you. All that time encouraging messages from you to our victors would have been a fillip to our workers and evidence of the reality of your leadership. Salisbury seems to have simply sat at the tape machine and despatched stirring messages to every centre of fierce activity in the country. I know they had a very palpable effect.'[51]

Rosebery's voyaging meant that during the election huge backlogs of correspondence built up; arriving at the small port of Oban, for instance, he found more than three hundred letters waiting for him. The one moment of real pleasure he derived from the campaign was the news of Harcourt's defeat in his Derby constituency, where the former Chancellor's anti-drink message went down like a glass of stale beer. His pleasure was shared by George Murray, who wrote, 'the event at Derby happened just before I left town and filled me with delight. I just caught sight of Loulou in the street, looking like a piece of blotting paper that had been rained upon for a week.'[52] Overall, Rosebery viewed the election with an almost philosophical detachment, showing more interest in the 'stink of herrings' in the Orkneys than in Liberal losses. Even when the full scale of the disaster became apparent, he appeared unconcerned. Writing to Canon Scott Holland he struck a somewhat incendiary note. 'I do not need consolation with regard to this general election. It was inevitable and it can scarcely fail to do good. The Liberal Party had become all legs and wings, a daddy-long-legs fluttering amongst 1000 flames; it had to be consumed in order that something more sane, more consistent, more coherent could take its place. The Liberal Party is purged as with fire. It sees in its purgatory that it must concentrate itself and that it cannot gain victories as a mad mob of dervishes, each waving his own flag and howling curses on everyone else's.' Unless the Liberals changed, he argued, they would soon be obliterated by another movement from the left. 'It is always possible that that may happen which has happened in Belgium – the elimination of Liberalism, leaving the two forces of reaction face to face. Whether that shall happen here depends on the Liberal Party.'[53]

The concern in Liberal circles was that Rosebery, having take so little interest in the election, might now indulge in one of his periodic retirements, leaving the party completely rudderless. Munro-Ferguson therefore wrote him a frank letter, setting out his faults and his duties.

> The late Government was regarded as a weak government; it was thought that from one cause and another you had not exerted sufficient authority, that Harcourt was disloyal, that you spoke too much as an individual and not enough as Head of State . . . You have heavy work before you and not only amongst your colleagues but you will have to be very accessible to the political world and very kind to it, doing a great deal which may be very irksome as if you liked it. There is nothing you can't do if you have recovered your strength and if you mean business, especially with Harcourt. He was beaten at his game 20 years ago and I am perfectly certain he can be beaten now and that you will do it. The whole organisation is perfectly loyal to you.[54]

Regy Brett, with more candour than tact, also warned Rosebery that he would have to change his methods. 'Mystery and aloofness are the chief ones. If you are going to carry on the fight, it can only be by conquering first the sympathies and hopes of the rank and file of our party and grouping round you a faithful and intimate guard of Praetorians.'[55] Such words might have angered Rosebery only a few months earlier but now, refreshed from his sailing and his freedom from office, he was ready to rejoin the fray. When Sir Edward Hamilton dined with him at Brooks's on 31 July, he found him in good spirits. 'He made no allusions to "cutting and running" as I feared might be the case. On the contrary, he said he should make a point of showing himself on the meeting of Parliament.'[56]

But Rosebery insisted that if he were to remain the Parliamentary leader of the Liberals, he would have to end his co-operation with Harcourt. 'It is not possible that the sham of a partnership can be carried on any longer,' he told Campbell-Bannerman soon after the General Election.[57] The animosity between the two men stretched back more than a decade, and after his experience in Cabinet and of Loulou's intrigues Rosebery found the idea of continuing to work with Harcourt intolerable. Throughout his premiership the two men had scarcely been on speaking terms. As Rosebery put it to Gladstone, 'if co-operation between us was impracticable when we were bound by the strictest official ties and living under the same roof in Downing Street, it was obviously impossible in opposition when every man is too apt to be a law unto himself.'[58] To the editor of the *Leeds Mercury*, Wemyss Reid – who was to become one of Rosebery's most trusted advisers over the next eight years – he said that 'no earthly power will induce me to take part in the dishonest hypocrisy of the last year or two. Nothing will lead me again to consent to anything like a dual leadership between myself and a man I cannot trust.'[59] Harcourt's customarily bullish behaviour gave Rosebery the opportunity to strike. Unchastened by his defeat in Derby and subsequently elected for Monmouth, Harcourt remained the Leader of the Opposition in the House of Commons. In this capacity he called a meeting of the Liberal front-benchers from both Lords and Commons, to be held at Lord Spencer's London home on 14 August. And, provocatively, he did so without consulting Rosebery, who consequently felt that once more Harcourt was trying to claim for himself the prerogative of party leader. Having been informed by Spencer of the planned joint meeting, Rosebery replied on 12 August declaring the end of his political connection with Harcourt: 'In no shape or form can it be renewed. One plain lesson we have learned from our experience, which is that that connection was essentially unreal, was injurious to the party and irksome (to say the least of it) to each other. It is in the interest of the party and of Harcourt and myself that it should never be renewed. Nor can any member of the late Cabinet be surprised at the decision.'[60] A copy of this letter was also sent to Harcourt, who told Spencer 'it was a damned piece of impertinence' and subsequently wrote to Rosebery expressing his 'pain and surprise'. In a memorandum Lord Spencer drew up of his interviews with Harcourt at the time, he recorded that 'Harcourt assumed the air of absolute ignorance that any serious disagreement had existed between him and R. Personal differences he deprecated as far as they interfered with political action. In old days, as in the case of Canning and Castlereagh, these ended in a duel. The letter would have had this effect and he [Rosebery] might have been shot in the buttocks!!'[61]

In practice, Rosebery's declaration made little difference to the running of the Parliamentary party. His letter was shown only to members of the late Cabinet, who decided that nothing needed to be done in response, a tactic reinforced by a further note Rosebery sent Spencer in which he said, rather defensively, 'my declaration does not involve any immediate action on the part of anybody'. So Rosebery remained titular leader and Harcourt in charge in the Commons. It was a fatuous arrangement, but the members of the former Cabinet – and Rosebery himself – preferred it to an open, public breach which might have split the party in two. In his journal Kimberley expressed approval both for Rosebery's action and for the impassivity of the front bench: 'I think Rosebery is quite right after all that passed in the late Government. If he had let Harcourt quietly assume the leadership of the Opposition in the Commons without saying anything, it would have been answered that he acquiesced. By entering a decisive caveat at once, he has prevented this. Nothing further can or ought to be done now. The party must decide and it would be premature to consult them now. Probably we shall drift on with two "leaders" who have no communication with each other!'[62]

Those on the front bench might have been relieved that a public rift was avoided, but by failing to act resolutely Rosebery had only weakened his position. He had declared the dual leadership to be an impossibility, yet had allowed it to remain in place. Instead of forcing his party to choose between himself and Harcourt, he had opted for continuing paralysis. He complained – with some justice – of Harcourt's lack of consultation, but this was also his own biggest failing: he had told none of his colleagues before writing to Spencer. The outcome was that he merely succeeded in casting Harcourt as an innocent victim of his own pique. Lord Ripon, a good judge of this awkward situation, analysed it thus: 'It is to me unintelligible that a man should inform his enemy that it is his irrevocable intention never to meet him again in Council and should then in a few months quietly resume relations with him as if nothing had happened. If Rosebery does so it will be the best thing for the Party but it will be fatal to his ever exercising any control over Harcourt, who will for the future be justified in despising his threats.'[63] Munro-Ferguson pointed out another vulnerability in Rosebery's stance: 'You are not in a strong position to establish discipline because it is not long since you had your own way with the Foreign Office against Mr Gladstone and against the strongest of your colleagues. Any immediate and open rupture must I think do harm to your reputation as well as to the country.'[64]

Over the coming months many of the late Cabinet tried to reconcile Rosebery and Harcourt, but to no avail. Harcourt adopted a posture of benign indifference, Rosebery one of icy aloofness. 'I will never again be party to perpetrating that fraud on the public. I will gladly retire to facilitate unity but I will have nothing to do with a sham, painted unity or with crying unity when there is none,' he wrote.[65] Before the new session of Parliament opened in January 1896 efforts were made by Asquith and Ripon, but they found that 'Mentmore is unyielding'. Tweedmouth also tried his hand but got nowhere. 'The fact is that things are hopeless, so long as these personal difficulties exist, and they will I am afraid continue to exist,' noted Hamilton.[66] In early February Rosebery held a gathering of leading Liberals at Mentmore, omitting to invite Harcourt. 'The breach remains unhealed,' wrote Kimberley. Five months later, on 7 July 1896, Hamilton dined with Rosebery: 'There is no chance of bringing him near to Harcourt. I told him that rumours reached me that Harcourt was not unfavourable to some improved relationship and pointed out how awkward it would be if Harcourt put out his hand and Rosebery refused to take it. But Rosebery said that such movement on Harcourt's part was very unlikely.' In fact,

Rosebery did exchange an ostentatious handshake with Harcourt, at a purely social, not a political gathering, but Harcourt was left unmoved by this gesture. The incident took place at a reception in February held by Fanny Tweedmouth, as Morley described: 'Rosebery insisted on making his way up to Harcourt and shaking his hand with much *impressment*. The party looked on, and held its breath. I am not sure that the great man did not regard it as "a damned impertinence" and I am not sure it was not.'[67]

Morley's relations with Rosebery were almost as bad. They had never recovered from the nadir of Rosebery's inflexibility in giving the Foreign Office to Kimberley in March 1894, and Morley had then become thoroughly disillusioned with the behaviour of his chief as premier. In January 1896 he saw Hamilton, who questioned him about his coldness towards Rosebery. In response, Morley launched a swingeing attack in which he condemned Rosebery's policies on Ireland and in foreign affairs and his entire conduct of business. According to Hamilton's account, 'he had never given Morley a helping hand while he was Chief Secretary for Ireland; had never said a word about Home Rule in his speeches; and when the Arrears Bill came before the House of Lords, Rosebery never got up his case. The fact was, Morley said, Rosebery was – he did not wish to use a hard term – so he would not say – "cunning", but Rosebery was too *deep*; and sensible as Morley was of Rosebery's trueness as a personal friend, he felt he was a political colleague with whom he had little in common, and whom he could not properly understand.' Morley further thought that it was 'not generous of Rosebery' to refuse to make any concession over the Harcourt difficulty.[68]

After an initial burst of enthusiasm in the new parliamentary session, including a powerful speech on the Address, Rosebery soon relapsed into his diffident ways. Even his most supportive colleagues were offended by his inapproachability. At a dinner in October 1895 Margot Asquith complained to him – without much elegance of expression – that 'you don't see enough people and you don't seem glad to see the few that you do see'. Her husband backed her up: 'I think the social side of things has been considerably neglected.'[69] After talking to Arthur Acland, one of the most moderate and least sensitive among the former ministers, Hamilton told Rosebery that 'Acland was very sore about a note he had received from [you] which he regarded as very cold – indeed chilling. As he had been one of your most loyal supporters, he thought he might have had somewhat warmer an expression of recognition.'[70]★

★ Acland later told Margot Asquith that it was 'a late and chilly business reply which Marshall and Snelgrove might have spawned.'

The truth was that Rosebery was thoroughly disenchanted with politics. Whatever ambition he had had for the leadership had been destroyed by the events of 1894–5. He was weary of the compromises and clashes, the lack of power and purpose. From the beginning of 1896 he began to return to his favourite political sport, contemplating his resignation. When he saw Haldane on 15 January 1896 he said that, rather than reach an agreement with Harcourt, 'what I should much prefer is that I should retire and leave the opposition without what is practically an element of division – myself'.[71] In a letter of 20 January 1896 to Lord Tweedmouth, who was also pushing for a reconciliation with Harcourt, Rosebery clearly spelt out his desire for retirement. Tweedmouth had written to suggest that 'if Pitt and Fox could consent to sit the in same cabinet, you, Harcourt and Morley should not find it difficult to arrive at common ground'. In his reply Rosebery said, 'I adhere to every syllable of my letter of the 12th of August. That letter was not written on impulse but on conviction burnt deep into my nature by bitterest experience: a conviction as deep and vivid now as it was then, for the impression of the 16 months of office after Mr Gladstone's resignation is one I can only lose with life itself. I am not prepared to disregard the lessons I learned so painfully and I am afraid that for good and for evil my colleagues must reckon with the resolution that I announced on the 12th of August 1895 as an irrevocable and ineffaceable fact.' Rosebery then asked what was to be done? He could come to some 'makeshift' arrangement with Harcourt – but he had a far better solution, 'not distasteful to Harcourt and which would be infinitely agreeable to me. It is that I should retire from the leadership and, for the present at any rate, from politics. I cherished the hope of being able to do so in 1890 and have never lost it since.' Rosebery explained that he had wanted to leave immediately after the 1895 General Election, but that was not possible 'without incurring the reproach of deserting the party at a period of unusual depression'. He then spelt out the advantages of his immediate retirement:

a. My colleagues would find no difficulty in acting together in opposition if I was out of the way.
b. It would cause infinite gratification to myself and I should be able to lead the life that for many reasons I prefer.
c. My colleagues agree on foreign policy more with Harcourt and Morley than with me.
d. I have recovered my sleeping power since I left office. But I think that it is likely that if I had to go through the same experiences as I had in 1894 and 1895 it might again leave me and so disable me.
e. I do not flatter myself that I lend any strength or popularity to the party to compensate for the obstacle to political harmony that I represent.

Concluding that he felt he should imminently retire from the leadership 'and so secure the unity which you feel is so essential at this juncture', Rosebery urged Tweedmouth to inform his colleagues of his offer to resign.[72] Tweedmouth was aghast, and refused to accept 'the part which you wish to impose upon me'.

Rosebery did not press the point at the time. But rumours of his departure abounded during the course of the spring and summer, as evidenced by this comic verse which appeared in the Birmingham press in June 1896:

> Here lies a Premier who
>> Perhaps belied prophetic rumour.
> His early death was owing to
>> A rather fatal gift of humour:
> Your perfect radical should ever be
>> In awful, deadly earnest.

Yet it was more than just humour that had alienated the Liberal rank and file. Since March 1894 Rosebery's stock with the Party had plummeted because of his poor performance in office. All the worst fears about his amateurism, his instability and his lack of vision had been confirmed. At a meeting of the National Liberal Federation in late March there was a move by a group of radicals to submit a resolution declaring No Confidence in the party leader. This was ruled out of order by the NLF Executive, yet the very fact that such feelings were being expressed by Liberal members demonstrated the extent of their disillusion with Rosebery. The mood was summed up by a letter to *The Times* of 25 March 1896 from A.O. Hume, President of the Radical and Liberal Association of Dulwich, who claimed that more than a third of Liberal supporters in the area had refused to vote in the 1895 General Election because they did not want 'the re-establishment as Premier of Lord Rosebery, to whose bad tactics, faint-heartedness and want of vigour we owe the disasters of the last Parliament'. Hume's letter amounted to a comprehensive attack on Rosebery's political character. With heavy irony, Hume described him as a 'most amiable and accomplished gentleman, with a well-marked, if somewhat dilettante, leaning towards Liberalism and possessed of a gift for elegant chaff and graceful persiflage, endowing him with a perfect mastery of the art of post-prandial oratory.' But, he claimed, through Rosebery's leadership, 'disaster on disaster followed faster and faster' because of his 'total want of dash and daring'. If he stayed in the post, there would be 'a continued paralysis' in the party. Rosebery was, thought Hume, utterly devoid of that holy enthusiasm in the cause of man which can alone invest anyone with the power of a true leader in our crusade against the privileged classes. In a cold, intellectual fashion he sympathises in abstract and theoretic views of reform and progress. Sandwiched in between literature and horse-racing, he holds politics as a gentlemanly and creditable recreation. His oratory smacks of unreality. In what heart has it awakened one single spark of holy enthusiasm for good? To us, it is but as the phosphorescent sparkles on a gloomy tropical ocean when a cyclone impends – attractive for the moment as the pyrotechnic coruscations are wont to be, but fatuous, devoid of solid basis, throwing no light on national troubles and difficulties, bringing no warmth to people's hearts, only presaging danger, if not disaster and destruction. It is only disaster to which his fecund tongue has led us, and it is only further disaster that the retention of this will-o-the-wisp leader can ever bring us.

Rosebery was only too aware of the discontent. Part of him even welcomed it, so deep was his alienation from politics. Indicative of this scorn was his decision, exactly a year after the cordite vote, to have a celebratory dinner on the verandah of The Durdans, thus establishing a tradition he maintained for the rest of his life. By the autumn he was ready to grasp at any pretext for resignation. And one soon arose – through the return to the political arena of his predecessor as Liberal leader. Gladstone had remained outside politics since his retirement in March 1894 and had refused to become involved in the spat between Rosebery and Harcourt. But a growing outcry over Turkish massacres in Armenia moved him to consider a return to the public platform, in an echo of his great Bulgarian crusade of the 1870s. The Armenia question was a difficult one for Rosebery, whose approach to foreign policy was always driven more by realism than by moral posturing. On the one hand, like the rest of the Liberal party he was genuinely disturbed by the scale of the suffering of the Armenians, who had 'been plundered, murdered and ravished by their hundreds and thousands', as he wrote in December 1895.[73] On the other, the only credible option for Britain, he believed, was to back her protests with the threat of military action against Turkey through the Concert of Europe: as he saw it, if the Liberals were not willing to go to war, then their outrage was nothing more than hollow rhetoric. But war carried with it the potent risk of spreading the conflict across eastern Europe. In any case, he thought the problem was one for the Tory Government rather than the Opposition: 'I must decline to grope in the dark in this powder magazine. While the responsibility of silence on this question is great, the responsibility of speech at the moment is still greater,' he wrote to Sir Edward Russell.[74]

This was not the view of a large section of Liberals, who thought their leader should be speaking out against international injustice, not hiding behind the substantial figure of Salisbury. By September 1896 the clamour against Turkish barbarity had grown too loud for Gladstone to ignore. 'My father is greatly stirred on Armenia and we shall be very glad if he speaks out,' Helen Gladstone wrote to Rosebery.[75] He did just that, at Liverpool on 24 September, in what proved to be the last public performance of his career. From his eyrie at Barnbougle Rosebery watched events with some anxiety, telling the journalist Charles Geake that 'If Mr Gladstone is simply going to lash up the anger of the nation without proposing any substantive policy, he will be incurring a great responsibility, and in my opinion he cannot know enough of the facts of the case to propose such a policy.'[76] Rosebery's prediction was correct: recapturing the fire of old, Gladstone launched into a scorching denunciation of the Turkish Empire, demanding that Britain take some decisive – but unspecified – action in response to the atrocities.

Rosebery, due to clarify his own stand on foreign policy in an eagerly-awaited speech in Edinburgh on 9 October, regarded Gladstone's intervention as an act of disloyalty. In his agitated state, the abusive newspaper coverage he had received played on his mind. The Liberal Unionist *Spectator* described his stance on Armenia as 'ridiculously inadequate', while a series of articles in the *Daily Chronicle* argued that he was so weak he should make way for Harcourt. Only eighteen months earlier Henry Massingham, the *Chronicle*'s editor, had been Rosebery's strongest supporter in the press, so strong that Loulou suspected he had been bribed by the Rothschilds. Now, his loyalties completely reversed, he worked in league with Loulou to persuade Sir William to adopt a pro-Armenian policy as a means of undermining Rosebery. 'If you were to take the head of a movement of this kind you would greatly strengthen your position – only to do this you must do it before Rosebery has come into the field,' Loulou told his father.[77] Massingham also wrote directly to Sir William, urging him to come out in favour of unilateral action by Britain against Turkey without reference to the Concert of Europe. Unhappily for his two supporters, Sir William shared Rosebery's opinions on Armenia, believing that coercion on the part of Britain was 'out of the question', and therefore refused to commit himself. He spelt out this line in a speech to his constituents on 5 October, when the only action he urged was a new diplomatic understanding with Russia on the Eastern Question. Massingham, with the true editor's gift for distorting the message to match his own ideological agenda, represented Harcourt's bland remarks as a powerful attack on Turkey, and glowingly compared his robustness with Rosebery's insipidity.

This was all too much for Rosebery. Haldane, who visited Dalmeny at the beginning of October, found him full 'of vague mutterings and gloom' as he 'walked up and down to Barnbougle in the wet gravel in his evening pumps for ages'. On the day of Harcourt's speech to his constituents Rosebery was alerted by William Benn, a leading member of the National Liberal Club, of the activities of Massingham and Loulou: 'I need hardly inform you that the cruel attacks made upon you over Armenia are part of a plot to espouse the cause of Harcourt. Morley has been assailed by a certain group ever since he supported your leadership and is now doing penance in order to put himself right with Harcourt's friends. The present crisis is declared "a convenient moment for getting rid of Rosebery". The thing is so overdone that the malice is apparent.'[78]

The following day, 6 October, Rosebery decided on his course. He sat down in his study to write to Tom Ellis, the Liberal Chief Whip. It was probably the most important letter of his political life. Several drafts were necessary before he arrived at a text that satisfied him. He then wrote out, in his own hand, a copy for the press. But he spoke to no one as he crafted his words, not even his devoted secretary Neville Waterfield, who was present at Dalmeny. On 7 October, in mid morning, he sent for the Edinburgh representative of the Press Association,★ Mr A. Eddington, who later left this account of what happened:

> I had a letter from Lord Rosebery asking me to come that evening to Dalmeny station, where a carriage would be waiting to take me to the House. On arrival there, the secretary handed me the letter and I had just finished reading it when Lord Rosebery entered the room. No doubt he observed my dismay at its contents and I had the courage to ask him to reconsider the matter as it would be a great blow to the country and the party. Lord Rosebery said the letter would that evening be in the possession of Ellis and his decision was irrevocable. He said he wanted me to take every precaution that the letter should not appear in any of the clubs that night but be reserved for the morning papers. I told him that his wishes would be complied with. On returning to Edinburgh I saw the telegraph superintendent and asked him to put the letter in the hands of a trustworthy operator and to see that no knowledge of its contents leaked out. These conditions were strictly observed.[79]

On the 8th, Britain awoke to the sensational news: Rosebery had resigned as leader of the Liberal party. In his official letter to Ellis he stated:

★ Not the Central News Agency, as Rosebery himself claimed.

The recent course of events makes it necessary to clear the air. I find myself in apparent difference with a considerable mass of the Liberal party on the Eastern question and in some conflict of opinion with Mr Gladstone, who must necessarily always exercise a matchless authority in the party; while scarcely from any quarter do I receive explicit support. This situation, except as regards Mr Gladstone, is not altogether new, but in saying this I complain of no one. I regret only that I should appear to divide the energies and faith of Liberals. This question, however, is above and beyond personal considerations. When I speak, which I do this week, I must speak my mind, and speak it without reference to party. Under these circumstances it is the best for the party and myself that I should do so, not as leader, but as a free man. I consequently beg to inform you that the leadership of the party, so far as I am concerned, is vacant, and that I resume my liberty of action.

This was a public declaration, but Rosebery also sent a private note to Ellis which contained a veiled reference to the Loulou–Massingham plot. Expressing sorrow for his 'scurvy' message, he said, 'it had to be done. The condition of the Liberal party is a scandal and so far as I am concerned must be terminated. Mr Gladstone's appearance, affording as it does a rallying point and a shelter for the disloyal, of which he is quite innocent and unconscious, is the last straw.'[80]

On 7 October Rosebery also despatched three other letters giving personal notice of his resignation. Two were to his former Cabinet colleagues H.H. Asquith and Earl Spencer, repeating the claim that Gladstone's move had united 'all the elements of hostility and intrigue against me'.[81] To Asquith, he said with some sincerity: 'From the bottom of my heart I can say that one of my deepest regrets in coming to that decision is the political severance with yourself for your loyalty and friendship are one of the few bright associations with the last two years. I hope that, very soon, you will replace me.'[82] The third letter was to Gladstone himself: 'I will not disguise that you have, by again coming forward and advocating a policy which I cannot support, innocently and unconsciously dealt the *coup de grâce*; by enabling discontented Liberals to pelt me with your authority. But, as you well know, the situation has long been impossible and almost intolerable, and I for one am glad that it should cease.' Gladstone replied by return of post in equable fashion: 'Your letter is an acknowledgement of receipt for a stab under the fifth rib: and regarded in that view it is not only kind, but kindness itself. I can desire nothing more than to follow it. Our political relations have been tragical enough, but you have prevented their carrying any infection into the personal sphere.'[83]

Despite Rosebery's professed faith in his prospects, Asquith was unimpressed, as Margot's diary reveals. They happened to be playing golf with Balfour in Dunbar at the moment of the resignation.

I had been talking about Rosebery and Henry said he was in a stronger position now than he had ever been for he had shown a good deal of independence and even Mr Gladstone's rather inopportune appearance on a platform had not rallied Liberals around him on the Armenian question. Henry's only fear was that Rosebery, in his coming speech, might from too much confidence say something injudicious. But later Henry called me up to his dressing room and he threw into my lap a black-edged letter from Rosebery . . . I could hardly believe my eyes and could only say, 'Quick, Henry, wire to him to say you will go to Dalmeny tomorrow and to Tom Ellis to publish nothing till he hears from you.' Which he promptly did. The next day he went to Dalmeny but the *Scotsman* was put into his hand with 'Resignation of Leadership' in huge letters. It was too late. When Frances★ flourished this paper before Arthur's eyes, he merely said, 'Bloody fool.' I felt deeply angry with Rosebery for saying he had scarcely from any quarter received explicit support. It was such a lie for in his Armenian policy *everyone* except a few priests and women were on R's side. Mr Gladstone's influence I consider absolutely dead and for once even Harcourt agreed with him – the old cry of disloyal colleagues and private intriguing would begin again. There never had been a worse moment for Rosebery to have made his coup and at the same time in a momentary and personal way he was making for himself a great occasion for his speech tomorrow.

Asquith's luncheon at Dalmeny on the 8th was enlivened by the presence of Alfred Harmsworth, who had started the *Daily Mail* just six months earlier and had come to interview Rosebery. In his diary, Rosebery referred to Harmsworth as 'an interesting young man' – rather an understated description of someone who went on to build one of Britain's biggest and most controversial newspaper empires. In return, Harmsworth in the *Daily Mail* described a jovial peer released from his cares: 'The man who had this morning startled the world appeared as merry and sunburned as though he had just returned from the moors or the links.' Asquith, though courteous as always, was less pleased with his host and complained to Rosebery of not having been consulted. According to Margot's account, 'Henry returned to dinner pale. He had given it hard to Rosebery for single-handed action and denounced him as selfish and disloyal for his "no explicit support" sentence. I read out loud a virulent article against Henry in the *Evening News*: it was his personal ambition and cold intriguing that had ousted Rosebery and a lot of venomous lies in the same vein which

★Lady Frances Balfour, A.J. Balfour's sister-in-law.

made my blood boil. Dinner was dull and I could see Henry was worried by his talk with Rosebery and the whole situation.'

The next evening, 9 October, Rosebery was due to speak at the Empire Theatre in Edinburgh. The announcement of his resignation had created about the meeting an atmosphere of almost intoxicating excitement. People gathered in their masses around the Empire, as the old Scottish cry of 'Rozbury, Rozbury' filled the mellow autumn air. Rosebery left Dalmeny at around six o'clock, and was still scribbling his notes as the carriage drew up outside the theatre. 'The scene was memorable from the obvious, almost palpable tension of everybody there. I never saw a political gathering like it,' Lord Crewe★ wrote to his sister.[84] As he walked in, Algy West – who was among the guests at Dalmeny – thought he looked 'ashy pale, with that unseeing look I know so well'.[85] Rosebery's family, including Constance Leconfield and his two girls (the two boys being at Eton), sat in the best box, along with Margot Asquith, who left this wonderfully vivid record of Rosebery's speech.

> He rose, very pale, highly nervous. He stood quite motionless for what seemed an eternity of cheering. We all stood up and waved our handkerchiefs and I felt tears rise in my throat. Edinburgh is usually a hard audience but the whole occasion had roused them to boiling heat and the quieter he stood, gazing icily down, the more violently the people yelled and clapped until, with the faintest movement, Rosebery gave an acknowledgement and the whole house was hushed as if in sleep. He spoke for an hour and fifty minutes but it was not long; it was a very finely arranged speech beautifully said and well-expressed – the best he has ever made. It had its indiscretions but on the whole everyone said he had made the most of a very big and significant occasion. It wants a good deal of personality to impress a large, uncertain and inquisitive company – this Rosebery has got. He has a great sense of the dramatic and a mask-like face. He is sentimental also which is dear to the Scotch and he himself, above and beyond all, was deeply moved.[86]

In the first half of his speech Rosebery dealt thoroughly with the Armenian question, warning of the danger of Britain being dragged into a conflict: 'You know what a European war means. It means the massacre, the slaughter of hundreds of thousands of people; it means the ruin and devastation of the regions it invests.' And he took a swipe at those Liberals gripped by moral indignation over Turkey: 'It is against a solitary and feverish interest in the East that I enter my protest. Some persons, some guides

★ In 1896 he was not yet Rosebery's son-in-law.

of public opinion, are trying to work up in this country the sort of ecstasy which precedes war, even if it does not intend war.' Then, with the words 'Now I have done with public affairs', he turned to his own position. 'It would be affectation to deny that you expect from me some sort of personal statement' – at which, noted Margot Asquith, 'the excitement was intense and I felt my heart tighten.' Rosebery referred to the constant barrage of newspaper criticism, the difficulties of a peer leading the Liberal Party – 'he is, parliamentarily speaking, almost impotent and helpless'– and the lack of loyalty displayed by his followers. He concluded, 'I have gladly come forward on this occasion to lay down the proud post of leader of the Liberal party with one object alone – in order to promote unity. Let me beg, then, whatever else may be the result of my action, that my resignation may produce unity among you. If it does not unite you, the sacrifice has been in vain.'

Relieved that his ordeal was over, Rosebery was on his best conversational form that evening as he entertained his dinner guests at Dalmeny with talk of history and literature. In the coming weeks his air was that of a man freed from his chains. 'I am 20 years younger. That is the net result of my emancipation. The position was hypocrisy and intolerable and I had to clear the air,' he told Herbert Bismarck on 23 October. When he spoke at the annual Oyster Festival in Colchester on the 21st, *The Times* noted that he seemed 'exhilarated by his release from leadership. His speech was remarkable for its note of confidence and hilarity, which is significant in a statesman who has just been hustled out of the most prominent position in his own party. He spoke with a sense of deliverance from the dictation of the small-minded wire-pullers.'

Rosebery was buoyed up by the flood of support that followed his momentous decision. At one stage he was receiving more than a hundred letters and telegrams a day, most of them favourable. That from Arthur Godley, Gladstone's former secretary, was typical: 'I rejoice in the step you have taken. Nothing under the circumstances could have been done better.'[87] William Benn of the National Liberal Club, who had alerted Rosebery to the Loulou conspiracy, wrote: 'You have done the right thing. It was no longer possible to fight these treacherous ruffians in the dark. The fight must be in the open. You have the pick of the party still with you.'[88] Ben Tillett, the dockers' leader and one of those working-class radicals so often drawn to Rosebery, said: 'I see no other course open to you than the one you have adopted. While Mr Gladstone lives, I see no possibility of any Liberal Leader's position being anything but intolerable and impossible.' The journalist J.A. Spender assured Rosebery that 'the striking support you have had from the country Liberals (whom your opponents presumed to be against you) has, I am sure, very much strengthened your hold upon the party and removed a great many misconceptions and prejudices which were started in 1894.' And Dr Spence-Watson of the National Liberal Federation, once so dismissive of Rosebery as a potential premier, hoped that Rosebery was now 'aware of how deep a hold you have taken upon the affectionate respect of a large part of the Liberal party. I must tell you how grateful I am for your Edinburgh speech. You have raised politics to a true noble platform.'[89] That was the opinion, too, of the Royal Household. Lord Carrington, former Lord Chamberlain of the Household, reported that the Queen and her entourage were thrilled: 'There is only one opinion at Balmoral about your speech: they say it is the finest you have ever made and they all applaud the stand you have made.'[90]

Yet the voices of Rosebery's senior Liberal colleagues were almost unanimous in their disapproval. They were irritated that he had consulted no one and felt betrayed by his accusations of disloyalty. His resignation had been, they thought, a selfish, impulsive gesture, and thus in keeping with his behaviour in office. 'I am vexed beyond words at what has occurred,' wrote Lord Spencer to his brother. 'I knew that some day Rosebery would escape his more prudent colleagues and take some step to create a crisis by himself, I little thought he would have selected the present moment for this. I think that a man in his position ought not to act precipitately.'[91] Lord Tweedmouth thought Rosebery had 'failed to show any plausible reason in his Edinburgh speech for resigning office',[92] while Ripon believed that the effect of Rosebery's letter 'must be deeply injurious and I am forced to the conclusion that it establishes his unfitness for the position he has filled. He hands us over body and soul to Harcourt: it is a strange return for the support we gave him in the struggle with his rival.'[93] Some protested directly to Rosebery. Acland, who feared that the leadership question would obscure the need for reform in the party, called his move 'a thunderbolt of disaster', and Sir Ughtred Kay-Shuttleworth said that his 'resignation has filled me with dismay. I for one cannot accept your decision as final. Your object is the unity of the party and my first impression is very decided, namely that few things could be more fatal to the union and strength of the party than your retirement.'[94] Asquith told Hamilton that 'in taking the step he had, Rosebery had acted selfishly; he had no doubt improved his personal position for the moment, but in doing so he had sacrificed the interests of his colleagues and friends. What Rosebery lacked was the primary qualification for statesmanship, which Pitt had emphasized – that is patience.'[95]

Gladstone called Rosebery's move 'disastrous and deplorable'.[96] That was also the view taken by many outside the party who had been close to Rosebery. George Murray, for instance, accused him of being 'rather hard on your colleagues. None of them have said anything inconsistent with your lead and, however strong your case, are they not entitled to some sort of warning instead of a bolt out of the blue shot onto their breakfast tables? With the best of intentions, I am afraid I cannot conceal that I am in rather low spirits.'[97] Nor was Edward Hamilton particularly sympathetic, confiding to his diary that the resignation was 'a symptom of impatience and impetuosity, calculated to give the idea that he has gone off in a huff, and is too thin-skinned for political warfare'.[98] Rosebery's own mother, not one to miss a chance of criticising her son, joined in the chorus: 'I only hope and trust that you have not acted in a hurry or from momentary feelings of irritation but have fully thought out and weighed all the consequences of your retirement.'[99]

Perhaps the most poignant letter came from Tom Ellis himself: 'Fourteen days have passed by since you wrote to me the two letters which filled me with pain and sadness. I have been finding it more and more difficult to give any adequate expression to the keenness of regret I feel at the circumstances which drove you to the decision and at the momentous decision itself. I had nursed the hope that it could be warded off . . . Every hour's reflection upon the new situation created by the decision only serves to emphasize my regret and sadness. The sense of desolation grows on me . . . And now we have to strive to put the best face on things, to work without devotion and without much hope. We have to try and assume that all will go well with the Party when in our inmost hearts we are depressed and torn with doubts and misgivings.'[100]

Harcourt and Morley were the two Liberals who had most to gain from Rosebery's exit, since it was they who would now have to establish some form of leadership. But if they gained politically, they had nothing but contempt for Rosebery personally. That old bruiser Sir William thought Rosebery had run away from the fight: 'I believe that he funked the future which he saw before him – that he felt called upon to say something on politics in general and give a lead and that he did not know what to say and so he took up his hat and departed.'[101] Of Loulou he demanded, 'Was there ever such a childish fool as Rosebery?'[102] Harcourt had been so annoyed by Rosebery's complaints about consultation and disloyalty that, he informed Morley, if Rosebery were to repeat them he would reveal to the public the truth about the Congolese treaty and the Bradford speech. Morley, the destroyer of Harcourt's premiership ambitions, was fully in agreement with him as to the 'unjustifiable' nature of Rosebery's conduct. His rage bursts forth from the pages of his diary:

> *Thursday, 8 October*   Rosebery resigns. The reasons given were quite inadequate. 1. *Apparent* difference with considerable mass of party. If only apparent, he should have waited to see if it was real. How does he know what this considerable mass really think? 2. Some conflict of opinion with Mr Gladstone. But the party is not responsible for this. Why should the party be embarrassed because Mr Gladstone says something to which Rosebery does not assent? He has not had 'explicit support'. This last is an old story and recalls the foolish resignation when he was Prime Minister. What will follow? Infinite damage to the party and the fermentation of endless intrigue.

> *10 October*   I cannot express the intolerable disgust which possesses me when I survey the scene.

> *14 October*   Spencer to lunch. He thinks just as I do about Rosebery's proceeding and much the same about his character, so wanting in straightness.

> *21 October*   Saw Fowler who had been to Dalmeny. The topic is becoming more wearisome. The more I hear, the less amiable, the less *gentil*, must the whole proceeding be counted. It is the work of a concentrated egotist with few principles and little scruple.[103]

Within barely a year, all the worst fears about Harcourt's inadequacy as leader were realised, leading to a new bout of speculation about Rosebery's return.

14

'I must plough my furrow alone'

O N 29 DECEMBER 1895 Dr Leander Starr Jameson led a motley band of
adventurers on an invasion of the Boer republic of the Transvaal. The
aim was to provoke a rising among the *Uitlanders* or outsiders who claimed
to be suffering discrimination under the anti-British regime of President
Kruger. According to Jameson's plan, in the revolution that followed Kruger
would be overthrown and the Transvaal brought under the British flag. But
Jameson's Raid was a reckless, hopeless fiasco characterised by incompetence,
amateurism, and wishful thinking. The Uitlanders proved far less rebellious
than Jameson had hoped, his troops far less able. Almost as soon as he had
crossed the border, he was forced into a humiliating surrender.

It quickly emerged that Jameson, a Scottish-born doctor, soldier, and
colonial politician, had not been acting on his own. The real master-mind
was Cecil Rhodes, the ruthless and romantic millionaire Prime Minister of
the Cape Colony, who was filled with grandiose dreams of a British empire
stretching from the Cape to Cairo and had been locked in a struggle with
Kruger for supremacy in south-east Africa. Like so many of the grandest
Victorian imperialists, Rhodes was both a racist and a Liberal. He passionately believed in the superiority of the Anglo-Saxon people, and once said:
'If there be a God, I think that what he would most like me to do is to
paint as much of the map of Africa British as possible and to do what I can
elsewhere to promote the unity and extend the influence of the English-
speaking race.'[1] Yet this belief in racial destiny was combined with social
reform, support for colonial self-government, and a mystical empathy with
Africa. He despised reactionary, centralist rule from London, and so favoured
the concept of Irish autonomy that he gave heavy financial backing to
Parnell's nationalist party. In 1891 he also made a donation of £5000 directly
to the Liberal party. Despotic, tough and impatient, Rhodes could also be
curiously naïve and idealistic, perhaps a reflection of his origins as the son
of a country parson. For all his unrivalled wealth and power in southern
Africa, based on the fortune he had made in diamonds, he dressed shabbily,
spoke with a squeaky voice, and remained a bachelor all his life.

Unsurprisingly, given the similarity of their political outlook, Rosebery was the statesman Rhodes most admired. They corresponded regularly, and met on terms of genuine warmth when Rhodes made his periodic visits to England. At Rosebery's instigation, at the beginning of 1895 he was appointed to the Privy Council, an honour he was keen to accept; he felt it carried the implication that one day the Council might develop into a representative body for the empire, the sort of institution that imperial federationists had long advocated. Rhodes also had some influence on Rosebery's thinking about Britain's role in Africa. 'I feel very confident about the ultimate success if the English people do not scuttle out of Uganda and Egypt, for I feel certain that with increased and increasing prosperity here – almost certainly due to our own rule – settled government will steadily spread up the Nile to Khartoum,' he wrote to Rosebery in June 1893, just at the time when Portal was undertaking his mission.[2] The closeness between the two men was symbolised several years later, when on a visit to England in May 1899 Rhodes offered Rosebery the extraordinary sum of £50,000 to fight a national political campaign on an imperial platform;[3] Rosebery, who had lost none of his hatred for anything that might compromise his independence, turned it down. The affinity that prompted Rhodes's generosity in 1899 had also given rise four years earlier to allegations that Rosebery was complicit in the Jameson Raid.

In Britain, news of the failed coup was greeted initially with incredulity and anger, a mood that soon changed to jingoistic support for Jameson when the public learnt of the telegram sent by the German Kaiser to Kruger congratulating him on foiling the Raid. In the storm of conflicting emotions, one question stood out: how much did the Colonial Office, headed by Joseph Chamberlain, know about the Raid? Within two days of Jameson's arrest, Rhodes had resigned as Prime Minister of the Cape Colony, which was tantamount to an admission of guilt. Chamberlain, however, roundly denounced the invasion, calling it a 'flagrant piece of filibustering for which there is no justification', agreed to a public inquiry, and ensured that Jameson and his fellow conspirators, who had been handed over to the British authorities by President Kruger, were put on trial.* All this bustle, which won him lavish praise both in the Commons and from the press, could not obliterate the suspicion that Chamberlain had something to hide. Rosebery himself, still leader of the Liberal party at the

* They were found guilty of an offence against the Foreign Enlistment Act and sentenced in July 1896 to 15 months. Jameson's barrister was Sir Edward Clarke, who only two years earlier had represented Oscar Wilde. Jameson's health broke down in prison, and he was released in December 1896.

time, saw nothing fine in his actions. 'What else could he have done?' he asked Sir Edward Russell. 'The whole Liberal press is tumbling over each other to adore Mr Chamberlain: they might as well deify a policeman for walking the beat.'[4] And he later told Edward Hamilton that he had 'the best reason to believe that there was truth in the rumours that in the Transvaal business, culminating in the Raid, Chamberlain's hands were not clean.'[5]

He was right. In the memorable phrase of Cecil Rhodes, Chamberlain was 'up to his neck in it', and through his friendship with Rhodes Rosebery was aware of the Colonial Secretary's involvement. Indeed, there is some evidence that Chamberlain may even have tried to orchestrate the timing of the Raid and the Uitlander rising, by means of a telegram he sent Rhodes in November 1895: 'You must allow decent interval and delay fireworks for a fortnight.'[6] Whatever favourable interpretation Chamberlain and his apologists might try to put on these words, nothing could disguise the fact that 'fireworks' must, in the context, have referred to military intervention. Yet none of this came out during the official Parliamentary inquiry into the Raid, which began its work in the summer of 1896 and published its report in July 1897, with a complete exoneration of Chamberlain and condemnation of Rhodes. Dismay in the Liberal party and among the public greeted this vapid report. Arnold Morley called it the 'Lying-in-state at Westminster' and W.T. Stead described the inquiry committee as 'The Worshipful Company of Whitewashers'. Convinced of Chamberlain's guilt, Rosebery was even more brutal: 'I have never read a document at once so shameful and so absurd. One would laugh, did not one cry.'[7]

What made the inquiry all the more embarrassing for the Liberals was that the driving force on the Committee was Sir William Harcourt, by now Party Leader following Rosebery's resignation. Instead of trying to expose Chamberlain, he appeared only to be interested in assisting the cover-up. Harcourt's excuse for his strange conduct, which outraged a large section of the Liberal Parliamentary Party, was that his primary goal was to ensure that blame fell on Rhodes. Because he instinctively disliked imperial adventurism, he had come to regard Rhodes as a menace, and was there-fore disinclined to trust anything he said. Never for a moment did he believe in Chamberlain's guilt. Besides, he feared that to heap blame on the Colonial Office would damage Britain's prestige, undermine Parliament and stir up further divisions in South Africa. It was therefore his patriotic duty, as he saw it, to ensure that Chamberlain was proclaimed innocent. Wemyss Reid gave Rosebery this summary of Harcourt's approach and its consequences: 'The South African Committee report has been a mortal blow to Harcourt, whose warmest friends at the beginning of the session are now his bitterest foes. Harcourt's explanation is very lame. He believed the Boers would be satisfied if Rhodes was censured with sufficient severity. He confessed that he did not realize the strength of feeling in the House of Commons about Chamberlain. He thought the agitation was confined to the newspapers.'[8] Sir Frank Lockwood, the former Solicitor-General, was in despair. 'What a devil of a mess we are in over this report,' he wrote to Rosebery. 'I can't understand what made Harcourt take the line he did. Bob Reid says "He loves intrigue". But at any rate we're in a tight place now. Harcourt's position is a hot one. Morley does nothing but throw his eyes up to heaven, not that he will find much comfort there.'[9]

It must be said that other factors conspired against Harcourt. In the middle of the inquiry he suffered a bad bout of influenza. The Jameson conspirators cleverly managed to drag out proceedings by focusing on irrelevancies such as the Uitlander grievances, aided in this process by the chairman of the inquiry, the Tory MP W.L. Jackson,[*] who was so weak that to call him a lightweight would have been a compliment. Harcourt's fellow Liberals on the committee gave him no support. Campbell-Bannerman, utterly bored by the whole affair, was at his indolent worst, while Labouchere, enveloped in his fanatical left-wing anti-Semitic loathing of capitalism, was obsessed with the idea that a Jewish financial conspiracy of some description lay behind the Raid, which caused him to send the committee up endless blind alleys. 'Labouchere has done more to render the committee abortive than any other man. He was continually running about declaring that he had got wonderful evidence in the pocket which when it was examined always came to nothing,' wrote Campbell-Bannerman.[10]

There have always been suspicions that another, darker force was at work, driving the Liberals to collude in a cover-up. The theory was that Rosebery, through his friendship with Rhodes, knew almost as much about the Raid as Chamberlain, and so was just as guilty; Chamberlain, all too aware of this, intimated to the Liberals that if he were pushed too far he would reveal the extent of this knowledge. An informal deal was therefore struck, whereby the Liberals would exonerate Chamberlain in return for his silence about Rosebery. On the surface this theory seems ludicrous,

[*] His son was the great England cricket captain F.S. Jackson who won the Ashes in 1905 and later became chairman of the Conservative party under Baldwin. As a Yorkshire cricketer, F.S. Jackson played regularly against Rosebery's son Lord Dalmeny, Captain of Surrey in the Edwardian age.

Rosebery as Prime Minister in June 1895, still recovering from the nervous illness which left him 'a physical and moral wreck'. The effects of the heavy doses of morphine used to combat his chronic insomnia can be seen in his startled, exhausted eyes

Rosebery in 1896, by F.C. Gould. 'Sometimes his mind seemed to be far away, and he had to make an effort to pull it back again'

Rosebery at the Devonshire House fancy dress ball in 1897. Having gone as an unnamed 18th-century gentleman, he was aggrieved to be likened to the 'effeminate gossip' Horace Walpole

Daisy, Countess of Warwick, was smitten with Rosebery following the end of her affair with the Prince of Wales. 'Far too much fuss, in my opinion, is made by women about personal morality,' she told Rosebery

Princess Victoria, daughter of Edward VII. 'I know I have a real, true friend in you,' she said to Rosebery. But the Royal family disapproved of her fondness for him and she died a spinster

The American actress Maxine Elliott, 'ebony, ivory and roses'

William Gladstone, who sometimes doubted whether Rosebery had 'any common sense'

Sir William Harcourt, who described Rosebery as a 'liar and a rogue' after losing the battle for the premiership

John Morley, Liberal intellectual. He once said that Rosebery was 'the most natural-born leader I have ever met'

Henry Campbell-Bannerman, whose authority as Liberal leader in the early Edwardian age was powerfully challenged by Rosebery

Above: Rosebery opening Colchester Town Hall in May 1902. 'Without doubt, the greatest living orator,' said the author John Buchan

Right: 'They listen and accept his mastery.' Rosebery at Chesterfield in December 1901, giving one of the most brilliant and controversial speeches of his life

A nightmare in Downing Street, as Rosebery is beset by crisis in every quarter. 'I am crucified to my place and it is damnable'

Sir Charles Dilke, whose career was destroyed by a notorious divorce case, always believed he had been the victim of a conspiracy instituted by Rosebery, a claim undermined by his own record of epic promiscuity

Cecil Rhodes, imperialist visionary, capitalist and adventurer. How much he told Rosebery about the Jameson Raid of 1895 has long been the subject of intense speculation

Right: Lord Drumlanrig, secretary to Rosebery and son of the unbalanced Marquess of Queensberry. His relationship with Rosebery, clouded by parental vitriol and scandalous insinuations, ended in tragedy

Below left: Lord Alfred Douglas, Drumlanrig's younger brother, with his lover Oscar Wilde. Queensberry called Wilde 'a damned cur and coward of the Rosebery type', words that were to drag the Prime Minister's name into one of the most famous trials of the 19th century

Below right: 'A delicious embodiment of lust.' Maud Allan in her daring costume as *Salome*. Her performance in the role brought her to the libel court in 1918, causing more anguish to Rosebery in the twilight of his life

Above: Rosebery as Chancellor of the University of London, towards the end of his public life

Left: Rosebery, in retirement, at his desk. 'I am too accustomed, I am afraid, to solitude'

since the most important Liberal player on the committee, Sir William Harcourt, was a sworn enemy of Rosebery. Surely he would have been delighted to humiliate his foe? But it should be remembered that in doing so Harcourt would have been hurting his own party, and giving ammunition to the Unionists. His spat with Rosebery had never been made public, and any revelations at this time would have detracted from his own central purpose: to attack Rhodes. Harcourt may have behaved badly in Cabinet, but he was not so disloyal as to use the vehicle of the Jameson Raid to destroy one of Liberalism's most senior figures.

Far from this story being just another unsubstantiated smear on Rosebery, like the Dilke and Wilde scandals, the probability is that Rhodes had indeed told him something of his scheme for a takeover of the Transvaal, and that Chamberlain planned to use this potentially incriminating fact if he came under assault from the Liberals. Like most other imperially-inclined politicians, Rosebery had long been concerned about the situation in the Transvaal, where the discovery of gold in the 1880s had attracted an influx of foreigners. Inevitably tensions arose between the Boers and these Uitlanders, who were excluded from the franchise and generally treated as aliens. Throughout the early 1890s, as the numbers of Uitlanders grew, there was speculation about the possibility of violent conflict in the republic; one rumour held that British loyalists in the Transvaal possessed no fewer than 7000 rifles and were ready to seize the capital of Johannesburg. For Rhodes, the threat of armed insurrection was an ideal way of hitting at Kruger and thereby seizing control of the territory. The imperial administration in London could not, of course, lend direct support to violence against a sovereign state which was nominally under British suzerainty. But the government could order a military or police intervention under the pretext of quelling anarchy and preventing loss of life, as Gladstone had in Egypt in 1882. As Rosebery put it to the then Colonial Secretary Lord Ripon in September 1894, 'We could not be unconcerned if British settlers should be shot down in conflicts caused by a persistent denial of their civil rights.'[11] A few months later Rhodes travelled to England to be sworn into the Privy Council. Before the ceremony he went to stay at Mentmore, and there, according to his own account, he gave Rosebery some sort of outline of his plan to support a Uitlander uprising in Johannesburg. Rhodes said later that he felt it only fair to give Rosebery this information in case it might affect the decision to appoint him to the Privy Council. Apparently Rosebery allayed his fears on that score: 'Oh, that's all right, I'm a bit of a filibuster myself.'[12]

A heavy douche of cold water has been poured on Rhodes's story,* yet there is no reason why he should have made it up. After all, Rosebery was his political ally, and Rhodes had nothing to gain by undermining him. In Rosebery's papers are number of cryptic notes from Rhodes dating from the time of his admission to the Privy Council which hint at deep discussions between the two men about the Transvaal. 'I understand your difficulty. Whatever you decide, nothing has or will cross my lips, not even to Jameson,' reads one. 'Your gift [of membership of the Privy Council] will please the people at the Cape. I believe my thoughts are in some way similar to yours. The enclosed cables, which when read please tear up, will explain how anxious I was for your answer,' reads another, which could refer to reports of impending trouble in Johannesburg.[13] Despite Rhodes's professed discretion, it seems that he relayed the substance of his Mentmore conversation to at least three other people: one of his secretaries, Dr Hans Sauer; the correspondent of *The Times*, Flora Shaw; and, most importantly of all, Sir Graham Bower, the official secretary to the British High Commission in the Cape. Bower, who was eventually made one of the scapegoats for the fiasco of the Raid, was an austere, meticulous administrator who applied a rigid set of ethics in both his professional and his private life. Teetotal and vegetarian, he never took a holiday, was scrupulous about public money and, according to his daughter, 'fanatically honest'.[14] It is unlikely that he exaggerated or misinterpreted what Rhodes had told him. But it was his honesty that landed him in difficulty. During a visit to London in early 1896 he had called at the Colonial Office and mentioned Rhodes's story about his Mentmore visit. Later in the year, in October, as the inquiry was proceeding, Chamberlain decided to use this information to protect himself. Through the Colonial Office he explicitly ordered Bower to 'put down on paper' a report of what Rhodes had said about his talk with Rosebery, laying particular emphasis on Rosebery's phrase that he was 'a bit of a filibuster' himself. In his instruction, Chamberlain explained the purpose of his demand: 'I desire a full statement in writing from Sir Graham Bower as to this interview or interviews if there were two of them, with dates and any confirmatory particulars or further details which he can supply. I have no intention of using this unless attacks are made upon Sir Graham Bower or the Colonial Office by Mr Rhodes but it is necessary that I should have them for defensive purposes.'[15]

Bower was shaken by this order from Chamberlain, as he recorded in

*Robert Rhodes James, in his 1962 biography of Rosebery, described it as 'extremely flimsy'.

his diary. It was 'ostensibly a request for a letter to be used as a shield against Rhodes,' he wrote. 'But, on reading it, the thought occurred to me that it might be used to coerce the opposition members on the South Africa committee.'[16] Bower, being a dutiful civil servant, did as he was told by his political master and to Sir Robert Meade, the Permanent Under-Secretary at the Colonial Office, sent a full reply, which contained these passages: 'During the interview with Mr Rhodes, he told me that he had told Lord Rosebery his plans and that he thought it right to do so as the latter was making him a Privy Councillor. Later on, after the Raid, Mr Rhodes told me that Lord Rosebery had warned him that the police must not move till after the rising . . . I desire to add that Lord Rosebery's name was given to me in the strictest confidence and that in communicating the conversation to you in so far as it affects Lord Rosebery it is on the honourable understanding that it will only be used confidentially.' Sir Robert Meade told Bower he could give no such assurance: 'There can be no obligation of secrecy between a public official and a Secretary of State. Mr Chamberlain does not propose to use the communication you make except in his and your defence, but if either is attacked he must, of course, have a free hand to do what is necessary for his and your protection. For myself, I do not believe that the attack will be made but we must provide against all possible contingencies.'[17] It appears, incidentally, that Rhodes would have been prepared to use the Mentmore conversation in his own defence, had he come under heavy fire from the Liberals. Years later, his secretary Hans Sauer revealed that Rhodes had explained to him why he did not fear the Liberals' cross-questioning: 'We also have a cat in the bag which, if let out, would show that one of their big men knew all about it.' The big man in question, Rhodes said, was Lord Rosebery.[18] It is also interesting to note that, although he regarded the Raid as a blunder, Rosebery had personally a great affection for Dr Jameson. He wrote years later to Jameson's brother: 'When one knew the man one realized at once the noble and generous character which has fascinated so many thousands. I was most impressed by him when I went to see him in prison and found him the same cheerful, unchanged, unsubdued "doctor". One would have trusted him readily with one's life or anything else.'[19]

The inquiry was so ineptly handled that neither Chamberlain nor Rhodes had to resort to the last-ditch measure of using Rosebery's name. Rhodes, from his fondness for Rosebery, was anxious to avoid doing so. Harcourt came to the inquiry with his mind made up that Rhodes was the culprit, and he allowed nothing to alter that. Sir Graham Bower did not believe Harcourt's approach to be dishonourable, for 'an exposé would have exploded not one but several powder magazines and caused a sacrifice of life which would, ultimately, run into the hundreds of thousands.'[20] It seems certain, however, that Chamberlain would have used Bower's letter if he had found himself in a tight corner.

Rosebery must bear some of the blame for the farcical way the Liberals handled the committee of inquiry. His innate distrust of Chamberlain led him to think that the party was walking into a trap by co-operating so enthusiastically with the Colonial Secretary, yet his isolation from Harcourt meant that he had no influence over the Committee's establishment and terms. When in June 1896 he privately urged the Liberals not to take part, he was blithely ignored. While Rosebery sulked, Harcourt acted – disastrously – on his own authority. It says something for the depth of Harcourt's hatred for Rosebery that he preferred to work with Chamberlain than with his own party leader.

Rosebery's behaviour in the wake of the Raid has often been cited as evidence that the Mentmore conversation with Rhodes was no more than fantasy. If he was guilty, why did he condemn Chamberlain more fiercely than any other Liberal did? Why did he call for a public and not a narrow Commons inquiry? Why was he so dismissive of the report? Why did he tell friends of Chamberlain's guilt? The reality is that Rosebery felt he had done nothing wrong in speaking to Rhodes about the possible consequences of a putative rising in Johannesburg. Everyone in political circles thought some sort of conflict between Kruger and the Uitlanders was inevitable, and that it would require a response from the British authorities. Furthermore, Rhodes had given him few details of the operation, so Rosebery could with conviction and honesty say he knew nothing beforehand of the Jameson plan; indeed, in December 1894 Rhodes himself was not sure how the crisis might develop. In any case, since the Mentmore discussion was a private one, Rosebery could readily deny its alleged substance; he actually did so in June 1896 when Lord Ripon asked him about it, claiming that 'there is no truth in the story'. At the time of the Raid, Rosebery was out of office, so he believed he bore no taint of responsibility for the fiasco. And, above all, he despised Chamberlain's brand of impulsive, aggressive, 'wild-cat' imperialism, which he contrasted with his own more cohesive, less destructive Liberal Imperialism. He was therefore genuine in his revulsion at the Colonial Secretary's inept handling of the Raid, which caused such damage to the prestige of the empire. When Margot Asquith visited Dalmeny in November 1897 she recorded, 'I can see Rosebery thinks Joe [Chamberlain] very lucky to get off so well in the South African affair. Harcourt muddled it all famously.'[21]

Chamberlain escaped from the inquiry without a single word of con-demnation, which was all reserved for Rhodes. In another absurdity, he was even asked by Harcourt to help draft the final report. When the shame-ful document was published on 20 July 1897, a large number of Liberal MPs were so infuriated that in the subsequent Commons division they voted against their own front bench. Harcourt was seen to have received a crippling blow to his authority, in dominating a committee that 'was from the beginning to end a disaster', in the words of the Liberal journalist J.A. Spender. Labouchere had been made to look a fool, Campbell-Bannerman an idler, the Whips incompetent. From the uproar emerged a mounting pressure on Rosebery to return to politics and take back the leadership of the party. Many of his supporters felt sure his resignation had only been a temporary move, designed to force Harcourt's hand. Now that Harcourt's ineffectiveness had been so mercilessly exposed, it was time for Rosebery to take up the reins again. Over the coming months, the calls grew ever louder for his return. 'For the moment, there is no one else whose name is very generally acceptable, let alone a rallying-cry for a broken army,' wrote Asquith.[22] In July 1898 Sir William Benn told Rosebery that he was 'the only possible solution' to the leadership crisis: 'Wherever Liberals gather, you are the topic of conversation.' Harcourt was 'finished', Labby 'diminished', Asquith 'a little too high and mighty', said Benn. The result was that 'no Liberal leader who is alive is so discussed as yourself.'[23] Such sentiments were also reflected in the press. As the radical writer W.L. Stobart explained in the *Fortnightly Review* in June 1898, when calling for Rosebery's return, 'his name has been received with marked approval at Liberal gatherings. We somehow realize the difference between a party politician and a statesman. Liberals feel that, so far as foreign affairs are con-cerned, Lord Rosebery is the only man amongst them to whom the nation will pay attention.' A more objective but still favourable profile had appeared in *The Outlook* in March 1898, in which Rosebery was described as 'far and away the most interesting personality in politics – puzzling, if you will, unaccountable often, beyond a doubt, but none the less who, even when he does not convince, always has the supreme merit of inter-esting the public.' After referring to Rosebery's record in foreign affairs, his 'passion for Empire', and his gift of political prescience, the magazine con-tinued: 'Lord Rosebery is in many ways a lonely figure. In temperament and taste, and in worldly circumstances, he is very unlike the great mass of his party. Will he lead the Liberals again? At the moment it can only be affirmed that no man stands higher in public estimation than he does.'

But Rosebery was adamant in his refusal to abandon his retirement. He said that little had changed since his Edinburgh speech, and his return would only spell the revival of divisions within the party. Besides, he was enjoying the other aspects of his life outside politics: travel, his children, literature. He appeared to take more interest in the education of his offspring than in the future of the Liberal party. 'My first thought is for the happiness and welfare of the girls,' he told his sister Constance as they discussed the appointment of a new governess. 'Fraulein Geister will never do. I want an English lady and if I can't get one, I don't want a foreigner at all.'[24] He also fretted about the dangers of bad influences on his sons, still at Eton. 'I wish the boys to be as much as possible with Eddy Hamilton and their uncle. The society of emancipated youths is not good for them,' he said to Constance. But he once claimed to be philosophical about their future: 'We cannot shape these boys, beyond a limited extent. If they grow up to be healthy English gentlemen in the best sense, and not without intellect or intellectual tastes, we should thank God and not ask for more.'[25]

Rosebery's disgust with politics ran deeper than ever. In a personal memorandum written in Naples in February 1897 he noted: 'I am bound to say that I have had a revolting experience of the higher positions in British government and that it will take some time to wash out of my mouth the taste of the last administration.'[26] A month later, when E.T. Cook, editor of the Liberal *Daily News*, asked him to speak out on foreign policy, claiming that he was the 'de facto leader of the Liberal party', Rosebery replied: 'Last October I laid down the leadership. I retained and reserved nothing. Such a course involves a sacrifice – to some men a great sacrifice. In exchange I obtained absolute liberty of action or of inaction. No one has any claim now, except that of personal attachment, to press me or ask me to do anything.' Far from persuading him to return, the South African inquiry's ineptitude only strengthened his determination to keep out. To Gibson Carmichael of the Scottish Liberal Association he wrote in May 1897: 'Since my October speech, much has happened that has moved me strongly but I have kept my silence rather than disturb that unity or seem to put myself forward. Now at the 11th hour, when all possible blunders have been committed and at least one crime, I am less than ever likely to break my silence.'[27] He took the same theme – that his absence had helped to promote Liberal party unity – with Wemyss Reid of the *Leeds Mercury*: 'Why should I emerge from my retirement? Two observations occur to me. In the first place, if I spoke, I should disturb the unity. Secondly, if I emerged for one purpose, I should have broken the spell. I could hardly return into retirement. I cannot be retired for one purpose and active for another. I cannot be kept like a fire engine in a shed and brought out to play upon the occasional conflagration.'[28]

Rosebery adhered to his self-denying ordinance on politics throughout 1897, but he could not extend it to ceremonial occasions. That summer witnessed Queen Victoria's Diamond Jubilee, an event which was turned into a extravagant celebration of Britain's imperial grandeur. Rosebery spoke at the banquet given for the Colonial premiers at the Imperial Institute, and at the National Liberal Club, as well as attending the Jubilee Service on 20 June in St George's Chapel, Windsor, of which he left this description in his diary: 'The Queen came in leaning on an oriental★ at 11. She sat quietly through the short service (about half an hour), wiping her eyes occasionally and toying with her spectacles. At the end she whispered something to the Empress Frederick and all the family came and kissed her hand and face and she embraced them. Princess Louise† received the coldest greeting. All were moved. I never saw anything more perfectly pathetic.'[29] On the 22nd, Jubilee Day itself, he went to the service of thanksgiving at St Paul's and then in the evening joined the crowds thronging the streets of central London, where he delighted in the role of anonymous celebrant. 'Not a drunkard or a word of ill-temper. The police wonderful. The best illuminations were outside the Bank of England. Got home at 2.30, having walked four and a half hours.' Other Jubilee events provided less happy memories. Travelling to a reception at Buckingham Palace, his 'unoffending brougham' collided with the Speaker's four-ton carriage and lost a wheel. On 2 July he went to the Devonshire House fancy-dress ball as a gentleman of the eighteenth century. 'I was described, greatly to my disgust, as that effeminate gossip Horace Walpole. If challenged for a name I should have said the Duke of Devonshire of that time, but I had no idea of anybody.'

In 1898, while many Liberals continued to press for his return, Rosebery was still playing the familiar tune about his retirement. In January, in response to a request from the Liberal Party for a donation, he wrote to Munro-Ferguson: 'I have formally retired from public life. I have cut myself off from all connection with the Liberal party and have left it under the *apparent* guidance of the politician I profoundly mistrust. Under these circumstances, it is scarcely logical to subsidize the party.'[30] Six

---

★ The Queen's Indian Secretary, Munshi Abdul Karim, who taught her Urdu. Her fondness for him caused jealousy and disputes in the Royal Household.

† The Marchioness of Lorne, soon to be the Duchess of Argyll. The fifth and youngest daughter of Queen Victoria, she offended her mother by complaining about what she alleged was the Munshi's insolent behaviour.

months later he asked Sir Edward Russell, 'Why should I leave my life of happiness with my friends and children in my home? There is no vacancy, no summons, no call of duty. Even were it otherwise, my latest experience of politics and politicians has given me a scorn of politics and politicians . . . Leave me then, my dear Sir Edward, in my tranquillity and let the good and great men in active political life still bandy their sonorous charges of inconsistency and folly.'[31] In the same week William Jacks, the ironmaster and Liberal supporter, was told by Rosebery that 'the leadership cannot be doffed and donned like a great-coat. As to the people who, as you say, wish for my return to express confidence in me, they may be numerous but they are certainly dumb. Glad am I that they are so for I have never of late years been so happy as since my abdication.'[32]

A wonderfully rich picture of Rosebery in his semi-retirement at this time comes from the pen of Raymond Asquith, who died in the First World War. He visited Dalmeny in October, and sent his Oxford friend H.T. Baker these impressions of the master of the house: 'Rosebery is quite admirable – my ideal of what a man of 50 should be – clever, cynical, sensual and wonderfully witty and ready; he improves with keeping. I had a delightful walk and talk with him this afternoon, about Jowett, the Union and Oxford in general. I have studied him somewhat closely this time and I must say I am not surprised that he is abhorred by the nonconformist conscience. He is a spoilt child, and gives that impression more than anyone else I know. He is frankly cynical about politics and completely disillusioned about everything else in the world. He has rooms full of the most priceless bibliological treasures but he has forgotten where to find things and almost what they are and doesn't care twopence now about the whole collection which he has taken infinite pains to amass.'[33]

But Rosebery was not quite the political Trappist he pretended. In his brilliant essay on Rosebery A.G. Gardiner described him as 'a lonely man, full of strange exits and entrances, incoherent, inexplicable, flashing out in passionate, melodramatic utterances, disappearing into some remote fastness of his solitary self.'[34] This was precisely his behaviour from early 1898 as he alternated between book-lined retirement and sudden public appearances, with the result that his real political intentions were wreathed in mystery. There was no consistency about his actions. He again threatened to resign as President of the Scottish Liberal Association because, he said, he was 'in silence and in retirement',[35] yet he happily became an Epsom district councillor, a position which he claimed was infinitely preferable to that of an MP. He would not donate to the Liberal cause, yet became

President of the Liberal Eighty Club.* He refused to speak on behalf of the Liberal party, yet in the London County Council elections of March 1898 he made a stirring oration on behalf of the much more left-wing Progressive Party. Beatrice Webb, soon to become an influential figure in Rosebery's life, was on the platform with him and was struck by his mixture of charisma and peevishness.

> I sat behind him and watched him narrowly. He has lost that drugged look – heavy eyes and morbid flesh – that he had as Premier. He is at once older, healthier and better looking. His speech had vigour, astuteness and flashes of dramatic genius. But he was woefully full of himself. His whole expression and attitude was concentrated self-consciousness and sensitiveness – not sufficient of an actor to lose himself in his part, not sufficient of a patriot to lose himself in his cause. Throughout there was an undercurrent of complaint, of personal grudge against the political world. He is not a leader. Outside foreign politics, he has no creed and only a scrappy knowledge. His very egotism is ineffective egotism: an egotism that shrinks from the world's touch, not the egotism that forces itself on the world. For my part, if a man is to be full of himself, I like him to have the will and capacity to make the world full of him also.[36]

In May 1898 Rosebery had a more melancholy public duty, acting as one of the pall-bearers at the funeral of William Gladstone, with whom he had experienced such a long, complex and often troubled relationship. In his diary he described the 'noble sight and ceremony', Mrs Gladstone 'a figure of sublime, unspeakable woe. Supported by her two sons, she knelt at the head of the coffin and, when it was covered, seemed to wish to kiss the ground, saying "once more, only once more".'[37] Paying tribute in the House of Lords to 'the pure, the splendid, the dauntless figure of William Ewart Gladstone' he honoured the Liberals' late leader as 'the bravest of the brave. There was no cause so hopeless that he was afraid to undertake it; there was no amount of opposition that would cow him when once he had undertaken it; it was faith, manhood and sympathy that formed the triple base of Mr Gladstone's character.'

Gladstone had been Liberal leader for almost a quarter of a century. Neither of his successors lasted much more than a couple of years. Harcourt staggered on through 1898, but in the autumn two events persuaded him to resign. The first was the engagement of his son Loulou to the daughter of an American banker. Without Loulou by his side, Harcourt lost not only his greatest ally, but also much of his personal

---

*Set up in 1880 to celebrate the Liberals' crushing triumph at the General Election.

ambition.★ The second was an explosive intervention by Rosebery in the field of foreign policy which reopened all the old wounds connected with African imperialism that had so disfigured the government of 1892–95. Sir Herbert Kitchener, marching heroically through the Sudan, had achieved a string of victories against the native forces, culminating in his triumph at Omdurman on 2 September. He then took his army further down the Nile to confront a French expedition, under Major Marchand, which had planted the tricolour at Fashoda. Kitchener and Marchand met on 19 September; fortunately, both were cool-headed enough to avoid an immediate outbreak of hostilities. But under the terms of the Grey Declaration of 1895 which had proclaimed the whole Nile basin to fall within Britain's sphere of influence, there was a real danger of war unless the French withdrew. As elements of the British public, fired up by Omdurman, grew increasingly bellicose, a serious crisis developed between the two nations. Into this tense atmosphere stepped Rosebery. On 12 October, at a dinner held by the Surrey Agricultural Association, he threw all his oratorical weight behind Kitchener and the Tory Government: 'If the nations of the world are under the impression that the ancient spirit of Great Britain is dead, or that her resources are weakened or her population less determined than ever it was to maintain the rights and honour of its flag, they make a mistake which can only end in disastrous conflagration.' His rhetoric was greeted with rapturous enthusiasm and, emboldened by this response, Rosebery spoke in still more fiery vein ten days later at Perth, where he urged that the humiliation of Gordon's fall 'must be wiped out'. Following his example other Liberal Imperialists, including Asquith, Grey and Haldane, came out strongly for a resolute policy against the French. On 4 November, at a Mansion House banquet in honour of the newly ennobled Lord Kitchener of Khartoum, Rosebery was given an ardent ovation after another barnstorming performance. Then Salisbury, the principal speaker of the evening, gained yet wilder cheers with his announcement that the French had withdrawn from Fashoda. The crisis was over.

Rosebery's speeches had perfectly captured the defiant, imperialist mood that seized Britain after the Jubilee celebrations. By giving such powerful expression to the wave of support behind the Government, Rosebery enabled Salisbury to be absolutely resolute in his stand against the French. In the process, he strengthened his image as the great patriotic

---

★Rosebery telegraphed his congratulations to Sir William but sent not a word to his son. 'I doubt if he will ever forgive Loulou,' wrote Hamilton.

statesman, a leader who put Empire above party. More popular now than he had been as Prime Minister, he was hailed by the *Fortnightly Review* as 'the most effective influence since Palmerston upon that middle mind of politics which is the maker of majorities'. Rosebery had also put heart back into his Liberal Imperialist followers, those same men who had been so disappointed by his resignation and retirement. 'We are proud of our chief today,' Haldane wrote, while Ferguson thought the speech 'just what we wanted'.[38]

If Rosebery had found Gladstone's Armenian speech of two years earlier intolerable, Harcourt now felt exactly the same about his predecessor's intervention over Fashoda. He was convinced, incorrectly, that there was a plot afoot with Rosebery behind it, and he was also piqued that Rosebery had so comprehensively upstaged him at Kitchener's Mansion House banquet – where, speaking last, Harcourt had been received with bored impatience. In addition, there were mutterings against him among the Liberal rank-and-file, as illustrated by a resolution passed by the Home Counties Liberal Federation demanding 'an early settlement of the question of the Leadership of the Liberal party'.[39] On 14 December, in a public letter to Morley, he formally declared his resignation as Liberal leader. Morley responded by also withdrawing from the opposition front bench. If the two men thought this would prompt a reaction in the party against Rosebery, they were badly mistaken. 'The announcement about Harcourt and John Morley has created very little excitement – much less than one might have expected – and much less I imagine than they expected themselves,' wrote Hamilton.[40] Earl Spencer, however, like Sir William, saw Rosebery at the centre of the trouble: 'It may strengthen Rosebery's position, which I confess I regret, as I think he is much to blame and responsible for a great deal that has happened and is now happening within our ranks,' he wrote.[41]

Asquith was probably Harcourt's most likely successor, but he did not want to give up his legal practice, so the shrewd, imperturbable but unglamorous Scot Sir Henry Campbell-Bannerman became the fourth Liberal leader in the space of five years. For those who wanted Rosebery, Campbell-Bannerman was little more than an acceptable stop-gap until their hero could be persuaded to resume his rightful place; or, as the *Manchester Guardian* later put it, 'here was an easy-going creature that would keep the nest warm for a bird of more brilliant plumage to be welcomed back to its natural home in good time.' Sir Edward Grey argued that 'the more things are knocked about, the more things will tend to a more normal balance of parties, and in the Liberal party towards the ascendancy of Rosebery.'[42] But Rosebery, ambivalent as always about his own position, warned against any intriguing to undermine the new leader. 'Remember that he is thoroughly straight, a gentleman, a friend of yours, a Scot, and do not be hasty to despair of him or criticise him,' he adjured Munro-Ferguson.[43] And Rosebery also sent Campbell-Bannerman a warm letter of support. 'For the first time in years there will be a handful on the front bench working like a good team, unjealous with real, friendly and eager co-operation. The Liberal Party have not had such a chance for a long time.'[44]

But Campbell-Bannerman could not begin to compete with Rosebery in popularity. The extent of the Earl's hold on the British public was revealed in April 1899, when his daughter Peggy, the first of his children to leave the family home, married the Marquess of Crewe at Westminster Abbey. Predictably, Rosebery's mother did not approve of the match – because of the age gap, Crewe being a widower of almost 41 and Peggy only 18. Equally predictably, Rosebery disagreed with the Duchess. He told the Queen, 'I like him very much and he is all that I could wish for, for I think nothing of the obvious difference in age, as it seems to me that such marriages are often the happiest.'[45] With his blessing, therefore, the wedding went ahead on 20 April, inspiring an outburst of public enthusiasm such as only the late Jubilee could be said to rival. Indeed, one paper held the scenes to prove that 'Lord Rosebery was the most popular of all the Queen's subjects and attained the prestige of Royalty itself.' From early in the morning, sightseers gathered around the Abbey and in Parliament Square in their thousands, most of them wearing primroses as a tribute to the bride's family name. Such was the throng that the police had to halt all traffic around Westminster, while inside the Abbey the crush was said to be 'unbearable'.[46] It was even feared that the crowd was so densely packed, some spectators might suffocate. 'Peggy's wedding grew into a kind of popular demonstration,' wrote the Duchess. 'I hardly ever saw a greater crowd. The police were unprepared for it and scarcely able to cope.'[47] At half past one, Rosebery and Peggy drew up in their carriage outside the Abbey, to be greeted by 'roar upon roar of cheering'.[48] In another homage to Rosebery, the London *Evening News* appeared that afternoon printed on primrose-yellow paper. Margot Asquith wrote after the wedding: 'I have never seen such a crowd. It was national and showed what I have felt about Rosebery, that he has the stars on his side and a way of impressing the public. He is quite an extraordinary man in this way and not to be lightly brushed aside . . . The Abbey was beautiful and the company distinguished. All the world seemed to be there. When the Prince of Wales went up the aisle, he was a nobody compared to Rosebery.'[49]

To the frustration of his friends, Rosebery still refused to exploit his

indisputable popularity by making a full return to politics. He was compared by the writer Goldwin Smith to a revolving light, now flashing out
brilliantly, now lost in complete darkness.[50] Just three days after Peggy's
wedding, Edward Hamilton spent an afternoon at The Durdans and noted
later that 'Rosebery won't give any hint as to his intentions about the
future. He fairly puzzles me. Does he intend to return to active politics? If
so, he might at any rate be frank about it with his intimate friends. If he
does not intend to come back, why should he continue to take such an
interest in party developments and party concerns? And is he not, by maintaining his public character, rather posing as a possible leader under false
pretences?'[51] Such puzzlement only increased when Rosebery made
another of his controversial interventions, this time at the City Liberal
Club in May, when he demanded that the Liberals modify the old policy
of Irish Home Rule and instead adopt a new 'Imperial spirit'. For some
time he had been moving away from his previous adherence to the traditional emerald-green flagship of Liberalism. Nearly a year earlier, in a personal memo of July 1898, he had set out three reasons why he felt a new
Irish policy was needed: 'the British constituencies have consistently
shown their aversion to Home Rule'; the Irish party had become increasingly independent and disloyal; and reform of local government needed to
be given a chance to work.[52] The 1898 Irish Local Government Act had
created elected county and district councils throughout Ireland; Rosebery
personally felt that this reform 'cannot soon or hastily be encumbered or
overshadowed by an Irish Parliament'. But such were the sensitivities of the
Irish question that his attempt at the City Liberal Club in 1899 to set out
a new route for Liberalism only provoked more anger, even among his supporters, as Hamilton recorded in his diary for 8 May: 'I had a long talk with
Lady Tweedmouth yesterday; and she said that her husband, C. Bannerman
and others were all equally concerned about it. They regard it as disappointing and inconsiderate – disappointing because it produces the impression that he is not a genuine Liberal and that he does not wish to assume
the lead again; inconsiderate because it makes the position of his late colleagues which is difficult enough as it is still more difficult.'

Margot Asquith's diary reflected her bitterness: 'Rosebery's speech was
astonishingly stupid. Henry said to me, "He has learnt nothing and forgotten nothing." Henry has thought for a long time that Rosebery would
surely make some awful mistake in his later role of critic, prophet and
highly isolated statesman avoiding and courting the public. His attack on
the decay of Parliamentary Liberalism does not come well from a man who
does nothing for the party and everything for himself.'[53] Asquith himself

wrote to Rosebery in the frankest terms, calling the effect of his speech 'very depressing'. He regretted the way Rosebery had sneered at those 'fighting against overwhelming odds' and warned that 'what will be said – and not without plausible reason – is that you are seeking to reconstruct the Liberal Party and to create its succession on the basis of unionism and jingoism. This seems to offer the doubting middle voter the maximum inducement to remain or become Tory and the minimum of motive to join our ranks.'[54]

Other attempts were made to persuade Rosebery to take on the political responsibilities implicit in his speeches. In June Wemyss Reid wrote him a letter that smacked of hero-worship: 'There was a time when we who believed in you and clung to you were comparatively few in number. Now we are a great army. If you could mix, as I do, among all sorts and conditions of men you would know what you really are to your fellow-countrymen and how strong is the compulsion which duty lays upon you to fulfil the hopes and anticipations which they formed upon you. It is a cause I shall never abandon till I have seen its full and assured triumph.'[55] But Rosebery would not make a definite move. The *Daily Mail* compared him to 'a coy lover with no ardour for office who leaves the maiden to propose to him but at each proposal raises his terms.' In more sober vein Herbert Gladstone, now Liberal Chief Whip following the death of Tom Ellis, travelled to The Durdans in July 1899 to persuade Rosebery to return. The venture had the blessing of Campbell-Bannerman, but that made little difference to Rosebery's stubbornness. After dining on the lawn in perfect summer sunshine, the two men went for an evening drive through the Surrey countryside. According to Herbert Gladstone's account, Rosebery admitted that 'the basis of his Edinburgh speech was not as final as he wished, but he could make it so. He could not take any part without committing himself altogether. His only defence to appeals was in complete abstention.' Rosebery further claimed that his City Liberal Club speech had been misunderstood, and that it would be wrong to return 'just when C.B. was pulling everything together. If he came back he would alienate as much as he would attract.' Rosebery also expressed the fear that 'if he took any part, Harcourt and Morley would at once be at him.' After returning from their drive they went for a brief walk in the woods, then carried on talking in the house. It was only when Gladstone asked whether he intended to speak in the House of Lords that Rosebery finally said, 'I'm going to bed.' Altogether, their conversation about Rosebery's position had lasted more than four hours. 'The impression on my mind', wrote Gladstone, 'is that he is *fighting* to keep out for the present but contemplates coming back in the event of a national crisis or the party going wrong on the FO or when Harcourt disappears.'[56]

In 1873 Rosebery had been warned by his uncle Bouverie Primrose against the danger of making himself 'incomprehensible' through excessive pride – and 'incomprehensible' was certainly the word for his current position. On the one hand, he claimed he would not be disloyal to Campbell-Bannerman. On the other, 'he had said nothing which precluded his ultimate return to power'. His resignation of 1896 had been 'sincere and solemn' – but he would come back if there were 'an emphatic call'. He said he was under no obligations to his former colleagues, and then complained when they 'rarely came near him'.[57] At heart, Rosebery had no desire to be involved with the hard, dirty work of political management, trying to build coalitions and negotiate compromises. His experiences of the previous two decades had given him a profound distrust of party politics. As J. A. Spender put it, 'To Lord Rosebery, politics were always half a dream and half a nightmare. A party was at best an unpleasant necessity and at worst an odious kind of tyranny. He seemed to have all the gifts of a great public man combined with the artist's distaste for public life and especially for that part of it which requires the taste and judgement of the individual to be deferred to the rough necessities of organised team-work. To the official leaders he was an unceasing perplexity; they demanded he should come in or stay out and he would do neither.'[58] In one of his own notes expressing just these antipathies noted by Spender, Rosebery referred to the 'pervading squalor of politics. They are all rotten from top to bottom. No real patriotism, no independence of thought, only the craving for office and honours and the blind, unscrupulous worship of party.'[59] What he really sought was power untrammelled by the despised party system. His hope was to be swept back to the leadership through public acclaim on receipt of a 'distinct call' of national duty, rather than be manouvred back through the machinations of 'hack politicians', as he called them. Until he received that call, he would remain in semi-retirement. The protestations of his friends and allies would avail nothing unless they were backed by evidence of an overwhelming demand for his return such as would make his position unassailable.

Realistically, a popular summons was only likely to occur at a time of national crisis. And in the autumn of 1899 just such a crisis arose, when the long-simmering hostility between the Boers and the British Empire finally boiled over into war. Both sides had proved intransigent. For Chamberlain and the British High Commissioner in South Africa, Sir Alfred Milner, war was inevitable and even desirable, the only way of ensuring British domination of the region. For President Kruger there could be no compromise. 'I am not ready to hand over my country to strangers,' he said.[60] Rosebery thought that through inept diplomacy the Tory Government had grossly mishandled its dealings with South Africa and its nominal suzerainty over the Transvaal, but he also felt that 'it is impossible for Britain to tolerate within her territories a state of things which is not merely a constant source of irritation and unrest but also an imminent danger.'[61] Just as war was becoming inevitable, Dr Jameson made a surprising secret approach to Rosebery see whether he might use his independent position to broker a peace. The South African journalist Charles Boyd reported to Rosebery in August having received the following message from Jameson, who had been talking to Milner: 'Things are now so much hanging on the brink, so much is at stake and Milner is so strong but at the same time so much in want of support that I felt that I must stick at nothing to help. And Milner fairly jumped at your suggestion of an appeal to the Big Liberal as the very thing that might bring matters right. Both Milner and I will do our best to cable begging Lord Rosebery's intervention.'[62] In England at the same time, Edward Hamilton had had exactly the same idea. Citing his settlement of the coal strike in 1893, Hamilton wrote to Rosebery saying he should offer his services 'to go out as a Plenipotenary to the Cape' to negotiate a peace.[63] But Rosebery said he 'did not see how he could now be any good or how he could offer his services. It would be quite another matter if the Government approached him but he could not see very well how they could at this eleventh hour.'[64]

Once war began, Rosebery believed that all sides had a duty to rally behind the nation and 'relegate party controversy to a more convenient season', as he put it in a letter to *The Times*.[65] That was not the way the majority of Liberals viewed the conflict. They regarded it as a jingoistic and ill-conceived adventure, while many on the left of the party saw a parallel between the struggles of the Boers and of the Irish people against the British yoke. This difference of opinion led to a bloody split in the party, and Rosebery was the proud, enigmatic figure at the centre of the row. From his carefully cultivated position of independence he was determined not to let the Little Englanders over-ride the Imperialists. 'The Liberal Party is nearing the final cataclysm,' he wrote to Sir Edward Grey on 21 October. 'The Rump will break with the Imperialist section and ally itself with the Irishry. All this in the long run will tend to the good.' In a speech he made in Bath on 26 October 1899 when he accepted the Freedom of the City, he declared boldly, 'I believe that the party of Liberal Imperialism is destined to control the destinies of this country.' Harcourt, after reading the speech, derided Rosebery's idea. 'His hold on our people is too limited,' he wrote to Loulou. 'I doubt whether even in ten years he will be capable of leading a party. He is too selfish, too trivial, too much a poseur.'[66] Harcourt's prediction seemed to be borne out when, in the first test of opinion in the new Parliamentary session, 94 Liberals voted in favour of a pro-Boer amendment on the Loyal Address to the Queen's Speech and just 15 voted with the Tory Government. It was a severe embarrassment for the Liberal Imperialists. The *Daily Chronicle*'s editor Henry Massingham, a fanatical pro-Boer, argued that Rosebery's resumption of the leadership would be a disaster: 'Lord Rosebery may still possess, inside the House of Commons and out of it, a small personal following, clinging to him for the sake of his personal grace and distinction and other admirable qualities of which he has somehow failed to give his country their full advantage. But a party leader, according to all the rules of the game, he cannot be. He has contributed little to Liberalism's past and promises nothing for its future.'

Rosebery, who had never tried to understand the complexities of the Commons, was still confident of victory for his cause. 'I think the Liberal Imperialists should unfurl their flag. The name alone will purge the Liberal party of the ranker elements which have done so much harm,' he told Haldane.[67] The leading Liberal Imperialist MP Thomas Brassey reported Rosebery's optimism to Milner at the end of November: 'Rosebery says in a letter I had from him two days ago, "the Liberal Party, which is Imperialist in the truest sense, has got to fight against the Rump or Little Englanders. The fight is one of a giant against a dwarf and therefore should not be very formidable." '[68] Rosebery's spirits were raised all the higher by his victory in the election for the Rectorship of Glasgow University, when he overwhelmingly defeated the Conservative candidate Lord Kelvin. The atmosphere was so tense that during the contest one student, Carlo La Torre, an Italian and a keen Rosebery supporter, allegedly challenged the honorary secretary of the University's Conservative Association, Robert Begg, to a duel. Sadly, according to a contemporary report which appeared in the Glasgow University magazine, La Torre's fencing skill did not match his courage; his cheek was slashed by Begg's blade and the contest was brought to an immediate end. The event has gone down in history as the last duel fought on Scottish soil; the University fencing club even stages an annual 'Last Duel' competition. But the veracity of this much-loved tale has recently been challenged by the Glasgow University Archive Service, which points out that there is no mention of the incident in any other records. In contrast Gerald Warner, author of a history of the University, is 'convinced that there was a scuffle with swords'.[69] Whatever the truth, the very existence of the story again demonstrates Rosebery's unique gift for provoking controversy and creating drama.

By the start of 1900 both Rosebery and the Liberal Imperialists appeared to be gaining ground. A new body, the Liberal Imperialist Council, was set up to provide some cohesion in the fight against the Little Englanders. Although the front-benchers like Grey stayed aloof, having condemned internal party groupings on the pro-Boer side, the Liberal Imperialist Council soon attracted more than 220 members. The driving force behind the organisation was the Liberal MP for Louth, Robert Perks, a Methodist solicitor who had made a fortune in railway finance and had already proved his managerial skills by establishing, with Lloyd George, the powerful lobby group known as the Non-Conformist Parliamentary Council. Like many Methodists he was an eager imperialist, seeing the Empire as an instrument for the spread of Christian civilisation. This love of Empire drew him to Rosebery, and he soon created for himself the role of Rosebery's chief advocate. Many found it incongruous that such a fiercely committed, self-made nonconformist should be so closely allied to the Derby-winning plutocratic grandee. Yet Rosebery's racing image belied a far more serious and religious side, while Perks, without ambition for office himself, was keen to invest all his energy in the man he saw as the saviour of Liberalism. Despite his organisational skills, Perks probably did Rosebery more harm than good in the long term, for he was an unpopular, scheming, divisive individual. In her diary Beatrice Webb called him a 'repulsive being, hard, pushing, commonplace, with no enthusiasms except his desire to have his knife into the Church – a combination of Gradgrind, Pecksniff and Jabez Balfour, and the choice of this man as his first lieutenant throws an ugly light on Lord Rosebery.'[70]

For all his faults, Perks was invaluable in bringing a greater unity to Liberal Imperialism in 1900. 'My notion has always been to secure sufficient power to capture and control the old,' he wrote to Rosebery of the battle against the Little Englanders.[71] The rising strength of the Imperialists was shown in a Commons division in July on a motion put by Sir Wilfred Lawson, an extreme pro-Boer, when 38 Liberals voted with the Government and just 30 with Lawson – a clear reversal of the previous autumn's humiliation. Grey and Haldane felt it was only a matter of time before Rosebery would be able to take over from Campbell-Bannerman. Grey wrote to him on 26 July: 'If you were to make the great sacrifice of coming out as leader of the party, with Asquith as leader in the House of

Commons, I think a strong and successful opposition would be built up. All I need say for the moment is that if you take the lead I shall recognise an obligation to make more sacrifices for politics than I have done since you retired.'[72] Rosebery's growing stature as potential leader was boosted by the disastrous start to the war, when daring, unorthodox Boer tactics inflicted a string of humiliating defeats on the British, most notably at the Battle of Spion Kop in January 1900, when 30,000 troops under General Sir Charles Warren were forced to retreat under heavy fire; 1,750 of Warren's men were killed, wounded or captured, while the Afrikaners lost only 300. The Boer sieges of the towns of Ladysmith, Mafeking and Kimberley heightened the mood of crisis and gloom. The faltering campaign reflected badly both on the quality of British leadership under General Sir Redvers Buller, who quickly won the soubriquet 'Sir Reverse', and on the competence of the Government. Salisbury, one of whose speeches in the Lords was described as 'simply deplorable' by the Prince of Wales, turned seventy in February 1900 and was in visible decline. Meanwhile Balfour was too much the cynic to be able to provide inspirational guidance to an anxious nation; he appeared to look on the military setbacks with the philosophic detachment of a bored academic examining a mediocre undergraduate essay. By contrast, Rosebery was in his finest oratorical form, his instinctive imperialism and sense of Britain's historical destiny perfectly suited to the moment of peril. In a much-admired speech at Chatham in January he demanded that the Government use scientific methods to ensure that Britain's navy and capital were employed to the fullest effect. Soon afterwards Albert Beneke, a Liberal Unionist barrister, wrote him a letter which reflected a widespread feeling: 'Our country wants a man and it is because I think you are the man she needs that I write to you. What the country wants is a great Whig leader who thinks more of her than of his party. The nation is intensely dissatisfied with the Tory democratic alliance and still more disgusted with the Radicals.'[73] Similarly, in his book *The Lessons of War*, published in 1900, Henry Spenser Wilkinson wrote that 'there is no other public man who commands such general confidence and it is practically certain that if the Cabinet were compelled to resign by an adverse vote in the House of Commons, Lord Rosebery would be the first statesman to be consulted by the Queen.'[74] He was right, for Rosebery had also become the darling of the Court, as Marie Adeane, one of the Queen's Maids-of-Honour, noted: 'The Queen is rather disgusted with Lord Salisbury and Balfour; the tone is quite changed. I bet on Rosebery; I cannot admire his character but I do recognise his genius and I feel certain he is the coming man.'[75] In the House of

Lords in January, Rosebery launched another attack on the Government's lack of vigour in the prosecution of the war. Regy Brett, now 2nd Viscount Esher, was impressed: 'Rosebery made an unpremeditated and extraordinarily good speech. I had not heard him for a long time and the improvement was very marked. He spoke with much fire and his gestures, which were so awkward, have got quite good. His voice is strong and clear. It was really a first-rate performance. If his character has strengthened as much as his speaking, he is fit to be Prime Minister.'[76]

The problem was that Rosebery's character had not changed. He remained beset by doubts and hesitations. As so often in the past, his platform appearances were followed by strange, brooding silences which left his friends in despair. After his speech in the Lords he performed no other public duties for three months, apart from attending a meeting of the Water Committee of Epsom Urban District Council. 'Party politics seem remote and even repugnant. I can feel no interest in them,' he wrote in February.[77] He turned down the post of Chairman of the Port of London Commission, offered him by the Unionist government: 'I will not deny that just now I prize my liberty and that, having severed the last ties of a public nature which forced me to remain in England, I should feel great reluctance in submitting to another at this time,' he told C.T. Ritchie, the President of the Board of Trade.[78] When Raymond Asquith asked him to speak at the Oxford Union in April 1900, Rosebery wrote back saying he was 'too old and stiff to take part in sham fights'. On seeing this letter, H.H. Asquith remarked, 'A sham fight is just the thing that ought to suit him, seeing his extraordinary disinclination for real ones.'[79] He finally carried through his threat to resign from his presidency of the Scottish Liberal Association, explaining that he needed to resume 'his absolute independence unfettered even by the slightest bonds of nominal office'.[80] For most of May he worked on the final chapters of his *Napoleon* biography. In June, he disappeared to Bad Gastein. 'I must report to you', wrote Wemyss Reid in June, 'of the growth of a feeling of impatience with regard to your return to the scene.' The next month Reid was repeating this theme in even stronger terms: 'You are the only possible saviour. Patriotism itself demands your return to the helm in the great crisis through which we are passing. If you do not come back you will have missed your chance. When a man means to cross a stream it will not do for him to sit on the bank until all the water has run past. Sooner or later he must wet his feet.'[81] Rosebery's unwillingness to declare his intentions was becoming almost as great a topic of national conversation as the war itself. 'Lord Rosebery is the Sphinx of politics, if he has not, indeed, outsphinxed the Sphinx,' wrote *The Young Man* magazine in July 1900.

Deliberately or unconsciously he has placed himself on a pedestal in an environment of mystery and attracted to himself the steadfast gaze of England. What will he do? Where is he going? The future of Lord Rosebery is one of the things which all England is unanimous in caring about . . . Lord Rosebery has a golden opportunity, such as come to few men in our time. He may be the greatest man in England or a man of no account. He may make himself a great figure in history, the Statesman of the 20th century, or he may be satisfied to spend his unrivalled gifts on unworthy causes and shine as a patron of the Turf. He may make himself a name which will live in the heart of England when the Turf and the tipster have passed away or he may be content to be a name in the society columns of the *Morning Post*. The key to the future of Lord Rosebery is in Lord Rosebery's hand. Which way will he turn it?

Torn between his dreams of imperial greatness and his hatred of politics, Rosebery himself did not know. Lunching with Edward Hamilton in July he repeated that 'he would stand by his resignation which was perfectly genuine, and he would not come forward as a political leader, unless the circumstances were very extraordinary, or unless he received the most distinct and emphatic recall from a sufficient number of people, or representatives thereof, to form a party.'[82] What Rosebery appeared to resent was that the acclaim for his return had not been sufficiently loud or unanimous. To Reid, he complained that talk of his leadership was based on 'the whispers of half-a-dozen friends'. In other letters he struck a similarly querulous, self-centred note: 'For the past four years, the Liberal Party has got on very well without me. Not a word or scarcely a word has been uttered in public of regret at my departure. The Liberal Party has no claim on me any more than I have a claim on the Liberal Party. We bade each other adieu four years ago, for better or worse. If the party felt any concern, it did not show it,' he wrote from Bad Gastein to one Liberal member.[83] 'I have retired publicly from party politics. Nothing but an irresistible call of duty would make me return to them. My experience of office would make me especially distrustful of any promises of support,' he told the Congregational cleric Dr Guinness Rogers.[84]

The clamour against the Unionist Government had quietened by the summer of 1900, following a succession of victories by General Roberts that included raising the sieges of Kimberley and Ladysmith. Seizing his opportunity, Salisbury sought to exploit this turn in the tide and the schisms in the Liberal party by calling a General Election in October. There were hopes that Rosebery might come out of his seclusion to invigorate the Liberal campaign, and H.H. Asquith travelled to Mentmore in late

August to urge him 'to take the bull by the horns'. But Rosebery agreed to only the most half-hearted gesture, writing a public letter of support to Hedworth Lambton, hero of the siege of Ladysmith and the Liberal candidate for Newcastle. Perks had no fewer than a million copies of this letter printed and circulated in every constituency. But it made no difference to Lambton's fortunes: he finished bottom of the poll in Newcastle, more than four thousand votes behind the second-placed Tory.

Elsewhere, the Liberals did not fare badly in the highly-charged, often squalid 'Khaki Election', in which the Unionists, said Campbell-Bannerman, 'had reached a depth of infamy in party malice'. Salisbury increased his majority by only four seats. Rosebery, however, was shaken by the ineffectiveness of his letter to Lambton. It appeared to confirm all his worst fears about his lack of influence on the political scene, contrary to what his supporters had been saying. He wrote angrily to fellow Liberal Imperialist Henry Fowler, 'If the Liberals wanted me back they should have taken steps to make their wishes known. They would have either obtained the object of their desires or would have thrown upon me the responsibility of refusing them. The only interference in party politics of which I have been guilty in the past four years was my letter to Lambton. Its general effect (i.e., that on the country) was nil.'[85]

Its personal effect on Rosebery was to increase his instability. For a month he retreated from the public gaze, ignoring all the entreaties of his friends. Fowler told him there was a 'universal belief' that he was 'the only possible leader'. His words were brushed aside. J.A. Spender warned that his followers were upset: 'What are they to do when the potential object of their affection withdraws into the wilderness and apparently doesn't think them worth cultivating?'[86] Rosebery did not care. Herbert Samuel, a rising star of Liberalism, told him conspiratorially that 'a movement may possibly be set afoot before long relating to the leadership of the Liberal party'.[87] He was indifferent to the news. Earl Spencer thought this kind of conduct showed Rosebery at his worst: 'Whatever one may feel about Rosebery as Prime Minister – and personally I do not feel admiration or confidence in him in that capacity – one must admit that he is a considerable power in the country and we cannot afford to lose his help. As long as he remains in the selfish, miserable attitude he has assumed, he indirectly fans and encourages cabals. There is this, moreover, to be remembered. Rosebery has done nothing for the party since he retired.'[88]

A profile of Rosebery in *Vanity Fair*, describing him as 'Little Bo-Peep', also expressed a sense of disappointment: 'He has never redeemed his early promise. For just as he is at the moment a Leader of no Party, so he has been a statesman full of possibilities but without that balance which is needed for really great success. He is a clever fellow who is often called able but with all his cleverness, his brilliance and his wit, he reminds one of a man with ten talents who does nothing with them. He has won two Derbys running, yet in the great affairs of Empire, he seems to let his chances – and there have been many – slip. He is supposed to know all about Foreign Affairs but, like a brilliant meteor, he has left no mark on the shifting sands of time. He still has a future before him, for he is but 53. Will he ever overtake it?'

'He was afraid to plunge and yet not resolute enough to hold to his determination to keep aloof,' said H.H. Asquith soon after the election.[89] The truth of those words was demonstrated when suddenly, in the middle of November, Rosebery blazed out in characteristic style with a magnificent Rectorial Address at Glasgow University. In the middle of an imperial war, his speech was a defence of the nobility of the British Empire, delivered with an uplifting eloquence which no other politician of the time could have matched. The Empire, he declared, was 'built not by saints and angels, but the work of men's hands; cemented with men's honest blood and with a world of tears, welded by the best brains of centuries past; not with the taint and reproach incidental to all human work but constructed on the whole with pure and splendid purpose. Human, and yet not wholly human, for the most heedless and the most cynical must see the finger of the divine.' Rosebery had proved he could still be a powerful force when he wished. Once more his supporters were encouraged. Haldane called the speech 'simply admirable'. The Liberal Imperialist MP Reginald McKenna felt 'it is now or never. We want him back; if we are to do any good in the immediate future it must be under his leadership. The party, with the exception of Labby and Co., is prepared to follow him.'[90] *The Times* called it 'a remarkable speech which stamps Rosebery as the most advanced Liberal of the day. He has a wider knowledge of facts, a firmer grasp of their bearings upon national life and a more profoundly reasoned conception of the conditions on which the Empire has to hold its place in the world than have been displayed by any other man occupying the same position in the country.'

Even Campbell-Bannerman, under formidable pressure from both the Radical and the Liberal Imperialist wings of the party, felt that Rosebery should come back, partly because, as he put it, 'as long as he is merely looking over the wall, there will be no peace for us'.[91] In public, Campbell-Bannerman said that 'we should welcome him and rejoice to see him standing among his own comrades'; in private, he was a little less genial: 'I will hold the door wide open, but I shan't ring the dinner bell or hang out the flag of distress.' Nevertheless, according to Perks – perhaps not the most impartial judge – Campbell-Bannerman recognised Rosebery's unique appeal. On 5 December Perks gave Rosebery this account of a conversation he had recently held over dinner with Campbell-Bannerman. With his usual offensive tactlessness, Perks had opened by saying, 'Rosebery is the only possible leader of the Liberal Party. He is the only man to whom the country looks.'

> c.b.: It is so and no one could be better pleased than I should be. He is head and shoulders above everyone else and it is his right position.
> perks: You are old friends. Why don't you go and see him and say so?
> c.b.: I don't believe he would see me. I tried to see him a year ago and failed. Rosebery should make more speeches, then he would fall into his old and right position.
> perks (concluding, in his letter to Rosebery): I feel certain that C.B. spoke from the heart.[92]

It is a measure of Campbell-Bannerman's patience and imperturbability that he was willing to tolerate such a belittling intervention.

The two men did eventually meet, on 9 February 1901, when Campbell-Bannerman called at 38 Berkeley Square, as he reported wryly to James Bryce. 'I lunched yesterday with the Cardinal Prince himself. There was not much in it at all. Perfectly friendly, deeply interested, but immovably aloof.' To Lord Ripon, Campbell-Bannerman said he found Rosebery 'not steadfast and unmovable, but unmovable without being steadfast'.[93] Rosebery's followers were by now thoroughly exhausted by his waywardness. Asquith told Hamilton, at the end of February, that 'people were getting tired of the game Rosebery was playing which nobody could understand; and they would soon be bound to look elsewhere for a leader.'[94] The new King, Edward VII, who had succeeded to the throne in January on the death of Queen Victoria, was so disturbed by Rosebery's aloofness that he contemplated making a direct approach to beg him to return to the forefront of politics. Fortunately, Salisbury dissuaded him from such an unwise, potentially unconstitutional, course.

Part of the explanation for Rosebery's perversity throughout this period was physical. The intense speculation about his position had brought on a series of psychosomatic attacks, and he dreaded a return to the months of insomnia that had so crippled his premiership. In May 1900 he apologised to Haldane for the poor quality of a speech he made at London University – 'I was as dull as 300 owls' – by explaining that 'for some reason or another

I have for some time past been run down to zero. To do the slightest thing has been an effort against the grain. Broadbent is puzzled and murmurs "influenza poison".[95] Also in the spring of that year he suffered an attack of lumbago. During a visit to Sandringham in November 1900 – that month, significantly, saw the tenth anniversary of Hannah's death – he was so unwell that he thought he had contracted typhoid. Even more worryingly, he complained to Hamilton on 18 March 1901 that 'he had lately had threats of a return to sleeplessness and he thought that any additional strain upon him might bring the trouble back. Of course any failure of his sleeping power may disqualify him from ever resuming office in a Liberal or any other administration. He swore me to secrecy on this point which is not unnatural. His continuing to hold aloof will be attributed to other causes – selfishness, cowardice and the absence of a proper sense of what is due from him to the country and his former party.'[96]

But there were also political factors holding him back from full involvement in party politics. His disillusionment with traditional Liberalism, which he regarded as hopelessly unsuited for the needs of twentieth-century Britain, led him to consider moving in two new directions. One was towards a centrist non-party government, the idea first put to him by Lord Randolph Churchill in 1887 as a way of breaking though the Irish difficulty. It was for this reason that he steadfastly refused to take on the Liberal leadership of the House of Lords in March 1901 when Kimberley announced his wish to retire because of ill-health, as Hamilton again recorded: 'The fact is, he does not want to commit himself politically. His sympathies are undoubtedly Liberal; but he can see no real future for a Liberal party freed from Irishmen.' Hamilton's account then relates Rosebery's suggestion that on the retirement of Salisbury 'the only alternative then would be, not a Liberal government, but a sort of coalition government, formed of the best men of both parties who might perhaps unite under him, because he had taken no side decidedly.' Possibly it was with the idea of working more closely with Chamberlain that in November 1900 he had offered him the use of his Italian villa. It was in fact an extraordinary move, for not only had he always disliked Chamberlain personally, but the Colonial Secretary was loathed within the Liberal party. Chamberlain had thanked him, and turned down the offer.

The other direction in which Rosebery looked was far more radical, and once again must undermine any notion of his innate Toryism. From the middle of 1900, mainly under the influence of Haldane, he became involved with the Fabian socialists, the group led by Sidney and Beatrice Webb which aimed to replace Gladstonian laissez-faire Liberalism with state collectivism as the doctrine of the left. The early Fabians are usually seen as worthy, gradualist reformers, keen on the minutiae of local government and trade unionism; in reality, they were far more sinister. A key part of their ideology was an obsession with the vitality of the Anglo-Saxon race, which they feared was being undermined by destitution, ignorance, alien immigration, and individualism. 'The country is gradually falling to the Irish and Jews,' warned Sidney Webb,[97] while H.G. Wells wrote in *Anticipations* that in British southern Africa 'the nigger squats and multiplies' in 'stagnant ponds of population'.[98]

The Fabians were heavily influenced by such thinkers as Karl Pearson, a socialist who believed the Empire should be a breeding-ground for the British race, and Francis Galton of the University of London, who coined the term 'eugenics' and urged Government action 'against customs and prejudices that impair the physical and moral qualities of our race'.[99] It is no exaggeration to describe the Fabians, under the sway of such thinking, as Britain's first national socialists, contemptuous of liberty and dedicated to the worship of state control, racial predominance, and eugenics. Typical of their philosophy was the statement made in 1910 by one of their leading members, the writer George Bernard Shaw, that 'a part of eugenic politics would finally land us in the extensive use of lethal chambers. A great many people would have to be put out of existence simply because it wasted other people's time to look after them.' Similarly, H.G. Wells, raging against 'ill-bred, ill-trained swarms of inferior citizens', called for the 'sterilisation of failures'.[100]

The harshness of the Fabian tenets was exemplified by the tragic life of beautiful Beatrice Webb, who suppressed her passionate nature in her crusade for socialism and in the process became a bitter, prudish, crabbed and humourless martinet. Born into a privileged family, in her twenties she renounced wealthy society to work as a social investigator among the poor of the East End. In the 1880s she was deeply in love with Joseph Chamberlain, then a widower, and when he became engaged to another woman she contemplated suicide and took to her bed in a state of nervous collapse. In 1892 she married the dull, prosaic municipal activist and writer Sidney Webb. It was a political partnership rather than a normal marriage, for Sidney Webb was 'very small and ugly', in Beatrice's own words, and, as she told him, 'I do not love you.'[101] Having met Beatrice and Sidney at dinner, George Murray, in a letter to Rosebery in 1895, poked fun at the void in the centre of their life: 'The Webbs made a strong attack on all aspects of capitalist society. Mrs Webb was charmingly frank, especially on the hedonistic and utilitarian aspects of the procreation of children. I gathered from her that Webb, having carefully balanced the two, has decided not to run the risk of having any – in which (purely from a hedonistic point of view) I must say I think he does well.'[102] It is perhaps not surprising that a woman whose own personal life was based on repression for the sake of ideology should later have become a propagandist for Stalin's Soviet Union.

That Rosebery could be mixed up with a group like this seems almost incredible, but throughout his life he had a fondness for mavericks and unorthodox alliances, his relationship with Robert Perks being a good example. And in his constant search, after his resignation, for an alternative to the two parties, he was not averse to contemplating extreme political solutions. What Britain needed, he said in 1899 during the Cromwell Tercentenary celebrations, at a time when the South African war was in severe trouble, was 'a dictator, a tyrant, a man of large mind or iron will who would see what had to be done and do it.' Another time, his loathing for conventional politics led him to advocate a Cabinet made up entirely of businessmen, 'in which no member of an existing or former Government should be included'. In one coruscating assault on the Parliamentary system he expressed the hope that 'future generations will nerve themselves without regard to those persisting Shibboleths for some great national effort in which party machinery will be both useless and forgotten.'[103] At times Rosebery's hatred of parliamentary governance appeared to be making a revolutionary of him. 'What power London could exert if it chose to put it out! Five millions of people surrounding the Parliament and the centre of the Empire!' he told Shoreditch electors in 1900.[104]

In terms of ideology, Liberal Imperialism, with its emphasis on social reform to improve the quality of the British stock, had much in common with Fabian socialism. Rosebery often talked of the need for 'a model race' or 'an imperial race'; in Glasgow in 1902, in a reference to the fashionable concept of social Darwinism, he called for 'a condition of national fitness equal to the demands of our Empire – administrative, parliamentary, commercial, educational, physical, moral, naval and military fitness – so that we should make the best use of our admirable raw material.'[105] The Fabians too put forward the idea of a 'national minimum' of standards for housing, education, sanitation, and wages, 'a minimum necessary for breeding an even moderately imperial race', in the words of Sidney Webb. In their imperialist fervour the Fabians had the same contempt as Rosebery for the Little Englanders of Liberalism. George Bernard Shaw's 1900 tract *Fabianism and Empire*, which Rosebery read and admired, was a direct

attack on those Liberals who 'still cling to the fixed-frontier ideals of indi-
vidualist republicanism, non-interference and nationalism, long since
demonstrated by experience and theory to be inapplicable to our present
situation.'[106]

The problem for the Fabians was that they had no political leader, for
Sidney Webb was little more than a hack writer and bureaucrat, devoid of
any magnetism. They therefore fixed on Rosebery, not only because of his
imperialism but also because, in his war with the LCC and the settlement
of the coal strike, he had shown his willingness to embrace collectivist ideas
beyond Gladstonianism. Though the Webbs and Rosebery knew one
another a little through the LCC, he first met them properly at a dinner in
March 1900 organised by Richard Haldane, who believed that the fusion
of Rosebery's charisma and the Fabians' radical ideas would turn Liberal
Imperialism into a potent force. Initially the dinner was not a success, as
Beatrice Webb recorded: 'Haldane sat me down next to Lord Rosebery
against the will of the latter. At first he avoided speaking to me. But feeling our host would be mortified if his little scheme failed utterly, I laid out
myself to be pleasant to my neighbour, though he aggravated and annoyed
me with his ridiculous airs.' By the end of the evening, however, some of
Rosebery's iciness had thawed. As he left, he called out to Sir Edward Grey,
another guest, 'Don't tell the world of this new intrigue of Haldane's', and
then winked at Beatrice, 'which at least showed he had a sense of humour,'
she wrote. After he had gone, she said to Haldane, 'I feel deeply honoured
at the place you gave me, but if I were four-and-twenty hours in the same
house as that man, I should be rude to him.'[107] There were further meetings over the course of the year, but Beatrice continued to find Rosebery
difficult. After another dinner at Haldane's in February 1901 she wrote to
her sister, 'Lord Rosebery is the most confirmed poseur and it is impossible to get on natural terms with him. It would certainly not do to count
on him, as he has no sooner undertaken to do something than he wants to
get out and by the time one has acquiesced in that, he suddenly reappears
again on the scene.'[108]

Just as the chances of co-operation appeared to be fading, a renewed
split in the Liberal party over South Africa supplied a fresh impetus. In the
summer of 1901 the Boer War had reached a dangerous stage, as the British
forces resorted to primitive 'concentration' camps, where women and children were herded, and to the destruction of homesteads, as a means of
countering the guerrilla warfare of the Boers. Such tactics caused widespread revulsion in Liberal ranks, a reaction shared by Sir Henry Campbell-
Bannerman, who had received direct reports of the inhumane conditions

in the camps from the campaigner Miss Emily Hobhouse, of the South African Women and Children Distress Fund. On 14 June at a dinner in Holborn hosted by the National Reform Union, Campbell-Bannerman, almost red with anger, spoke out: 'When is a war not a war? When it is carried on with the methods of barbarism in South Africa.' This utterance caused a sensation, and was portrayed by his opponents as a treacherous attack on the British army. Kipling wrote of the

> Mildly nefarious
> Wildly barbarous
> Beggar that kept the cordite down.

Liberal Imperialists found their leader's remark intolerable, and saw it as a deliberate attempt to drive them out of the party. Asquith, who until this point had been semi-detached from the Liberal Imperialist group, publicly condemned Campbell-Bannerman in a speech in Essex a week later; the Liberal Imperialists were so delighted with Asquith's intervention that they decided to organise a dinner in his honour, to be held in London on 19 July. It was, said the journalist Henry Lucy, 'war to the knife and fork'.

Rosebery was abroad at the time of this storm, taking the cure in Bad Gastein. His feelings about politics are clear from his diary entry for 21 June: 'I love this longest day, not least because it is the anniversary of the fall of the last government. And tonight how I enjoyed my after-dinner walk on the Kaiser promenade, the dark silk of the mountains, the pure air of heaven itself.' From his isolation in Austria, Rosebery foresaw the total collapse of unity within the Liberal party. 'I do not see how a schism can be avoided,' he wrote to Spender.[109] But, having little interest in reviving the cause of Liberalism, Rosebery refused to lend his assistance to the Imperialists. 'I am convinced that for the present, the less you have to do with me, the better for you (I mean by "you" the party). If I appear on the scene, you will be blighted by the old cry of a Rosebery intrigue,' he told Munro-Ferguson. He further explained why he would refuse the invitation to preside at the dinner for Asquith on the 19th: 'My presence might be taken to mean that I wished to profit by what he has done and associate myself with his success. That would be very repugnant to me.'[110] Once more, there was exasperation at his silence. Moberley Bell of *The Times* wrote to him with brutal candour. 'When it goes down to posterity that this man, occupying a perfectly unique position for good or evil in the Empire, endowed with exceptional position, wealth, ability and influence over men, recognising that he lived in exceptionally critical times, in times when (as he said himself), it was the duty of every Englishman to strain every nerve to resist the decadence of Empire, that this same man said, "No, I have tried it once and thrown it off like an old shoe, I won't try it again," what would your verdict on him be if you could write 40 years hence?' Through his silence, he told Rosebery, he was 'bidding for the power of impotence and putting yourself not on the fence but astride it.'[111] Rosebery later told Bell, rather flippantly, that this 'was the earnest letter of a serious parent entreating his son to finish sowing his wild oats.'[112]

On his return to England in July, far from lending his support to Asquith, Rosebery deliberately poured more salt on the gaping wound in the Liberal party. On 17 July, just two days before the Asquith dinner, he wrote an inflammatory letter to *The Times* in which he announced that he had no desire 'to re-enter the arena of party politics, far from it; I shall never voluntarily return to it.' He then went on to attack the pretence that there could be unity in the party, because there was 'a sincere, fundamental and incurable antagonism of principle with regard to the Empire at large and our consequent policy. One school or the other must prevail if the Liberal party is once more to become a force.' The effort to paper over the cracks, he warned, was nothing more than 'organised hypocrisy'.★ At a time of such party discord, Hamilton regarded the letter as an act of extreme self-ishness: 'There is a great want of consideration towards his former col-leagues about the promulgation of it . . . It is a great concern to me. For I am beginning to think R. will now never occupy the position for which I believe he is destined by his brilliant talents.'[113] And Haldane could not refrain from a word of reproach: 'The uncertainty as to what can and cannot be avoided in the future is trebled by your withdrawal from any sort of candidature for the nation's leadership.'[114]

Having announced his retirement from party politics, Rosebery then dramatically appeared at a luncheon held at the City Liberal Club on the very day of the Asquith dinner, causing more consternation to the Imperialists, who, predictably, had not been informed of this step. In his speech he uttered a passage that was to be forever associated with his career. Reflecting on his own position he said, 'I must plough my furrow alone. That is my fate, agreeable or the reverse; but before I get to the end of that furrow, it is possible that I may find myself not alone.' Inevitably, this performance overshadowed the Asquith dinner, which fell rather flat. Rosebery's fitful behaviour was castigated on many sides, *The Times* calling

★ Taken from Disraeli's cynical description of the Tory party, uttered in the Commons in 1845.

it 'not worthy of a statesman'. Herbert Gladstone said that Rosebery's description of Liberalism as an 'organised hypocrisy' could 'never be forgiven', and he thought the City Liberal Club speech was 'a slur upon the honest middle party which, sympathising with neither extreme, is striving hard to keep the party together as a whole. Those are the men who have always looked to you as the leader and now they are deeply offended.'[115] Sir Almeric Fitzroy, the Clerk of the Privy Council, remarked in his diary, 'Lord Rosebery has destroyed the carefully constructed paradise of Liberal unity in one blow . . . and laid bare the deep-seated cause of disintegration.'[116] Asquith himself proved remarkably tolerant, though in an interview with Rosebery at Dalmeny in September 1901 he admitted – according to Rosebery's account – that what annoyed him was 'my not saying a word of encouragement. He and his friends were all fighting my battle and I ought in a sentence to have supported them.' In reply Rosebery explained rather feebly that 'I feared to compromise him by associating myself with him. That was the sole reason I did not mention him at the lunch. It was to serve and not to injure him. My allusion to my lonely furrow was to separate my responsibility from him.'[117] Even Sir Edward Grey, while promising Rosebery to 'plough a furrow which goes in the same direction', admitted that 'the situation needs delicate handling and for the present there is some soreness'.[118] Writing to others, Grey warned that Rosebery was in danger 'of becoming an astral body outside the planetary system of party politics'.[119]

That is exactly why the Fabians were delighted. With Rosebery so publicly freed from the chains of Liberalism, he could now become the leader of a new radical cause. 'We did not take the tragic view of Rosebery's intervention taken by the little set of his immediate followers,' wrote Beatrice Webb. 'If Lord Rosebery really means business, really intends to come forward with a strong policy, then he has done a good service by stepping boldly out of the ranks of obsolete Liberalism. Rosebery's business is to destroy Gladstonianism. Whether or not he is to become a real leader depends on whether he has anything to put in place of defunct Liberalism.'[120] The Fabians now took on the self-appointed task of supplying him with a new policy, based on their concept of a interventionist state providing a national minimum. George Bernard Shaw, declaring that 'our policy must be to back him for all we are worth',[121] seemed excited by the prospect of assuming control of Rosebery. He wrote to Sidney Webb, 'Rosebery, being a peer and a political pillar, is necessarily a political tool. He is at present screaming for somebody to come and handle him, exactly like the madman in *Peer Gynt*, who thinks he is a pen and implores people to write with him. Your strength has always been in your willingness and your capacity to be the tool wielder.'[122] Together, Webb and Shaw then wrote a magazine article which was, in effect, a draft manifesto. Entitled 'Lord Rosebery's Escape From Houndsditch', it appeared in the September edition of *The Nineteenth Century* under Sidney Webb's name. Its central theme was a call for the British state to abandon Victorian individualism and adopt a programme of 'National Efficiency' in every area of public administration. In the article, the Liberal leaders were portrayed as a set of tailors working in Houndsditch, the centre of the clothes trade, 'piecing together Gladstonian rags and remnants' to make 'patched up suits'. Lord Rosebery was the only one who had 'turned his back on Houndsditch' and had 'called for a new outfit'. Webb proposed that Rosebery's new approach should include such measures as municipal enterprise, a minimum wage, poor law reform, and a national state education system.

The goal of an efficient, powerful, well-regulated public sector, guiding the life of the nation, has been the elusive dream of progressive politicians for more than a hundred years. Indeed, there are striking similarities between Webb's vision of 'National Efficiency' and both Harold Wilson's emphasis on state planning in the 1960s and Tony Blair's focus on 'modernisation' in this century.* Searching for a light to guide him out of the fog of Gladstonian Liberalism, Rosebery was another who was drawn the idea, telling Beatrice Webb that her husband's article was 'the most brilliant I have read for many a day'.[123] Nor were the Webbs and their collaborator Haldane the only ones pushing Rosebery in the direction of 'Efficiency'. Dismayed by the evidence of bureaucratic mismanagement during the Boer War, he had lent his support to the Administrative Reform Association, a body set up by James Knowles, editor of *The Nineteenth Century*, to campaign for public bodies to be run on business lines. The cult of the businessman was a particular enthusiasm of Arnold White, the proto-fascist author of *Efficiency and Empire*, published in 1901, which warned that without a radical overhaul of her institutions, the Empire was doomed. Rosebery told White that he was 'in substantial agreement' with much of the book, and White's complaint that British rulers were chosen for their debating skills rather than their practical abilities was often

---

*New Labour's fixation with targets and league tables has an uncanny parallel in Webb's call for the Government to put all state bodies 'into honorary competition with one another by an annual investigation of municipal efficiency, working out their statistical excellence in drainage, water supply, paving, cleansing, watching and lighting, housing, and hospital accommodation, and publicly classifying them all according to the results of the examination.'

repeated by Rosebery; 'I'm afraid Rosebery had got the businessman fad on the brain,' said the Tory Lord Northbrook in 1901.[124] Rosebery also eagerly swallowed reports from his outspoken friend Admiral Lord Fisher on waste in the Royal Navy. 'The £31 million of Navy estimates is ample if properly administered,' Jacky Fisher told him in 1901, but the problem was that the Government were squandering this resources: 'We are weak everywhere and strong nowhere.'[125] The real solution was to be utterly ruthless in dealing with incompetence, said Fisher. In an ideal system, he would be permitted to take out any admiral who had shown the 'slightest deficiency' and 'shoot him like a dog'.

Rosebery's role as an independent statesman, separated from his party, was further demonstrated by a secret approach he made to Salisbury in July, at the time of the 'knife and fork' crisis. For all his criticisms of Campbell-Bannerman, Rosebery had never been as jingoistic about the war as Chamberlain's supporters, and he had a particular dislike of Alfred, now Lord, Milner, not just for his botched, intransigent diplomacy but, retrospectively, for his role at the Treasury in formulating Harcourt's 1894 Death Duties Budget. On 9 July Sir Arthur Markham, a leading member of Perks's Liberal Imperial Council, wrote to Rosebery explaining that through a contact in the Transvaal he had learnt that Kruger might be willing to accept him (Rosebery) as an intermediary for peace negotiations with the British Government. In response Rosebery invited Markham and his Transvaal contact, Edouard Lippert, to Berkeley Square, where they discussed a possible peace initiative. Lippert explained that the real stumbling-block to negotiations was the Boers' lack of trust in Milner. 'If he could be removed, everything would be comparatively easy,' he said. The solution, suggested Rosebery, might be to appoint a separate British negotiator to explore peace terms.[126] Rosebery then went to the House of Lords to tell Salisbury of the meeting, urging him to consider talks led by an independent figure. But the Prime Minister was unenthusiastic, saying it would be impossible for negotiations to be held without Milner and Chamberlain. Nor had Lippert provided Rosebery with any specific terms for a settlement. 'In matters of such delicacy, where criticism is so vehement, it is wisest to adhere to the beaten road of negotiations,' Salisbury wrote.[127] Rosebery tried again, adding the suggestion that the Liberal Unionist Lord Goschen might be a possible British representative. 'Forgive my troubling you, but in view of the terrible drain of the war I do not like to neglect the chance of ending it,' he said.[128] Once more the Prime Minister showed himself obdurate. 'My conclusion is that the risks of such a course as you sketch would outweigh the advantages it would bring,' he warned, the main reason being that the Boers would see such negotiations 'as proof that we are exhausted and disposed to give in'.[129] Although this particular initiative failed, in Rosebery's mind the need for a negotiated settlement of the war had been strengthened.

Inspired by his recent burst of activity and the Webbs' support, Rosebery was in much more productive form than usual in the summer of 1901. He worked closely with Perks to try to build up the management of the Liberal Imperial Council, donating £1000 to a fund to sponsor candidates and recruiting an able Liberal agent, William Allard, to assist Perks. To improve the organisation's image he effected both a change of name, to the Liberal Imperial League, and of President, with Sir Edward Grey replacing Lord Brassey, who was wealthy and conscientious, but unglamorous. Yet even with its new name, staff and money, the Liberal Imperialist League attracted few followers and little attention. Perks was distrusted, Grey lacked inspiration, and Haldane was seen as no more than an intriguer. Disunity and accusations of treachery had badly damaged the Imperialist cause over the previous two years, while Campbell-Bannerman appeared to have been strengthened by his ordeals.

To turn the ebbing tide, some sensational event which would capture the public imagination was needed. And the Liberal Imperialists knew that Rosebery, for all his peculiarities, was the only man who could orchestrate one. It was therefore with relief and excitement that they greeted his announcement at the beginning of November that he had accepted an invitation to speak at Chesterfield on 16 December. The news of the forthcoming speech caused a ferment, not just in the Liberal party but across Britain. To a country tired by the continuing war, enraged by the failures of Government and the military, mourning the loss of Victorian certainties and confidence, Rosebery's imminent pronouncement suddenly appeared as a beacon of hope. Standing above the internecine party strife, he was looked upon as the one figure who could provide the answers to the nation's deepening problems.

As Rosebery's Chesterfield appearance grew nearer, anticipation reached fever pitch. His gifts for the 'dramatic and conspicuous' were never on fuller display. Henry Massingham once complained that the press always treated Rosebery 'as if he were a new soap or a member of the Royal Family'. That kind of interest was never more intense than in the build-up to Chesterfield. Newspapers were filled with speculation over what he would say, and with profiles of the Great Man. In Derbyshire, extra telephone and telegraph lines had to be installed by the Post Office to relay reports. A vast railway shed beside Chesterfield station was converted into a public hall, yet the demand for tickets exceeded fivefold the number of places available. 'The whole human race are writing me letters,' Rosebery complained.[130] Perks, who revelled in intensifying this frenzy, ordered a number of special trains to convey politicians, reporters and celebrities to the meeting, and also arranged with Harmsworth's *Daily Mail* for millions of copies of the address to be printed. As Edward Hamilton wrote on 19 November, 'I doubt if the prospect of any speech ever created more excitement. It is striking testimony to the immense interest taken in the man. There is no one else on whom people hang in the same way.' Campbell-Bannerman took a more cynical view when he reported to James Bryce on the political situation: 'Outside Potentate says he must save the country – urgent and critical – hang the plough; can no longer stand aside; will in six weeks be ready to utter the words which will save us from ruin. Takes some time, naturally, to think what will be most popular. Dec 13. Six weeks not yet up: still thinking. General fuss: importance of position greatly relished by potentate.'[131]

Rosebery's followers kept cranking up the pressure. 'There is an almost universal feeling that what you have to say next Monday will have a momentous bearing not only on your own future but on the fortunes of the country. The civilized world is waiting anxiously,' claimed Wemyss Reid.[132] Joseph Pease, a future Liberal Chief Whip, wrote from Saffron Walden, 'Feverish anxiety exists in this part of the country as to what you are going to say. There is an intense longing to again lean upon you as leader of the party.'[133] Perks managed to strike a note simultaneously both intimidating and reassuring: 'You have never failed in a speech and you won't do so on Monday. We have great faith in you. You will have a splendid band of men around you and all the country wants to know from your own lips that in this crisis you mean to respond to the country's call.'[134] From the Chief Whip's Office, predictably, Herbert Gladstone urged Rosebery to make unity his central theme: 'We're at an impasse. C.B. doesn't have a hold over the leading men of the party and Asquith and Grey have failed to attract the support of the rank and file so we await your speech with hope. I do say with all the insistence in my power that sections will give way to you when they give way to no one else.'[135] But Rosebery, as he explained to Hamilton, had no interest in party unity: 'He did not care much about putting himself out to rehabilitate the Liberal party. That party was nothing to him now and it was in such a hopeless condition that it was past praying for.'[136]

By 16 December Chesterfield was a bubbling cauldron of expectation. The railway shed, bedecked with patriotic banners of red, white and blue, was packed to capacity, with more than four thousand people inside. Even larger crowds gathered in the surrounding streets and at the station, despite the bitingly cold weather. As Rosebery's train from London arrived at five o'clock, there was a loud chorus of 'For Auld Lang Syne', repeated again and again while he walked to his carriage. Preceded by a brass band, he then made a slow progress to the Portland Hotel, where he washed and changed before travelling with a bodyguard to the hall. Dressed in black with a bunch of violets in his buttonhole, he calmly stepped onto the platform to a huge roar of welcome. According to the *Daily Mail's* account, 'At first Lord Rosebery struggled with the acoustics and both he and the Chairman had to appeal for silence. Eventually Lord Rosebery, after a strenuous few minutes, found the range. He spoke with effort, his voice strained and tired by great difficulties, but he spoke with effect.'

In this speech Rosebery abandoned the humour which was his trademark. Instead, he spoke with 'sustained seriousness' about South Africa, attacking the Government for its heavy-handed diplomacy and its policy of demanding unconditional surrender from the Boers. In line with the policy he had suggested to Salisbury in July, he advocated that negotiators from each side should meet 'at a wayside inn' to reach a settlement. He then turned to the Liberal crisis and demanded that the party free itself from the Irish alliance and adopt a new set of principles to regain the confidence of the public. His imagery was striking: in Liberal circles, he declared, 'there are men who sit still with the fly-blown phylacteries of obsolete policies bound round their foreheads, who do not remember that while they have been mumbling their incantations to themselves, the world has been marching and revolving, and that if they are to have any hope of leading it or guiding it they must march and move with it too. I hope, therefore, that when you have to write on your clean slate, you will write on it a policy adapted to 1901 or 1902, and not a policy adapted to 1892 or 1885.' Rosebery expounded his policy of 'National Efficiency', exactly on the lines set out in Sidney Webb's 'Houndsditch' article, calling for radical improvements in the war office, the navy, the promotion of commerce, and the running of Parliament, in order to halt 'the physical degeneracy of our race'. And he ridiculed the idea that there was no alternative to the present failing Unionists: 'If it were true, put up the shutters, forswear your empire, and go and dig in your cabbage gardens. The nation that cannot produce an alternative government to this one is more fit to control allotments that an Empire.'

After a performance lasting two hours, Rosebery sat down to resounding cheers. Soon a chant of 'For He's A Jolly Good Fellow' was ringing round the hall. In the heat of this moment, Rosebery appeared to be unstoppable. 'He has cleared the air with a vengeance and in such sort that there is nothing remaining for Liberalism but complete submission to his leadership,' wrote the *Daily Telegraph*.

I5

'Was there ever such a man?'

R OSEBERY'S STANDING WITH most of the British public had never
been higher than it was in the immediate aftermath of Chesterfield.
He had lived up to extravagant expectations and emerged with his reputation as both orator and statesman enhanced. 'The only really disgusting
thing about your speech,' wrote Sir George Murray, his old Downing
Street secretary, 'is that it seems to have satisfied everybody. Devout men
out of every party under heaven say they heard you speaking in their own
tongue.'[1]

The Liberal Imperialists, especially Grey and Haldane, were naturally
overjoyed at the combative return of their hero. Grey, who had been on
the platform at Chesterfield, told Rosebery, 'I admired it immensely, even
down to the physical triumph of carrying it through in the most awful
place to speak which I ever beheld. There was nothing to which I don't
give a whole-hearted assent.'[2] Grey felt so moved that he even wrote to tell
Campbell-Bannerman that Chesterfield had forced him to follow
Rosebery as leader. 'Egotism masquerading as patriotism! The whole thing
is utterly odious for honest people to have to deal with,' was Campbell-
Bannerman's response to this letter.[3] Haldane was quite as ecstatic as Grey,
telling Rosebery: 'I feel like those at Kimberley when General French with
his ten thousand cavalry suddenly appeared on the horizon and swept in to
the relief of the besieged.★ Charles Trevelyan said to me when you sat
down – his eyes were full of tears – "You all told me he had genius. Now
I know it." You stood before us once more as a leader. From Asquith downwards, you could not make one of us believe you are not so. There it stands
written by the Eternities.'[4] Writing to John Buchan, Raymond Asquith
gave the reaction of his family: 'The old funk is coming back at last. My
father says it was the best speech he ever made in his life, delivered in a railway shed full of snow and Derbyshire miners and as long as the Manchester

---

★ This refers to an incident late in 1899; French had pretty well cleared the Cape of invad-
ing Boers by the time Lord Roberts arrived in January 1900.

Ship Canal. The whole thing was wonderfully stage-managed by Perks.'[5] Not surprisingly, the Webbs were thrilled to see their concept of National Efficiency emblazoned across the papers. 'The speech seems to us almost perfect,' Beatrice told Haldane. And in some Tory quarters there was praise for Rosebery. Winston Churchill, the young MP for Oldham and a Boer war hero himself, proclaimed in a speech in Blackpool in early January 1902: 'Lord Rosebery possesses the three requirements which an English Prime Minister must have. He must have a great position in Parliament, he must have popularity in the country and he must have rank and prestige in the great circle of European diplomacy, and I know of no other man than Lord Rosebery on the opposition side who possesses those three qualifications.'*

All but the most extreme jingoes and Milner supporters agreed with Rosebery's call for peace negotiations to end the Boer War, and his resonant 'wayside inn' phrase helped create the climate which led to the Vereeniging agreement of May 1902. 'It is to you and Lord Kitchener that we owe this blessed peace,' wrote Wemyss Reid to him, with some justification.[6] But if Chesterfield led to a solution in one direction, it created problems in another, for it further divided the Liberal Party. Many rank-and-file members, particularly on the radical wing, were incensed to be told that their most cherished beliefs were nothing more than 'fly-blown phylacteries', that 'a clean slate' meant the abandonment of all that Gladstone had held dear, including Irish Home Rule. 'The speech is more likely to end in further dispersion of our party than in its unity,' John Morley told Robert Spence Watson of the National Liberal Federation. 'Rosebery has no intention whatever of rejoining the party or doing anything to contribute to its reunion. He does not believe that on the old lines it has any future.'[7] Locked in their cocoon of Liberal Imperialism and contempt for Campbell-Bannerman, many of Rosebery's followers did not appreciate the offence he had caused to those who did not share their views. Revealingly, Wemyss Reid admitted that he was 'thunderstruck' when, speaking in January 1902 to a reliable back-bench MP, he was told that 'the great majority of the party in the Commons was anti-Rosebery'. The MP went on to say that the activities of Perks and Haldane on behalf of Rosebery 'put up the backs of the moderate and sensible Liberals of the centre'.[8] This was confirmed by a *Manchester Guardian* poll of Liberal MPs which showed the majority of them still to be behind Campbell-Bannerman. Lord Spencer, usually a good barometer of mainstream opinion in the party, told his brother that he 'did

---

*From R. Churchill and M. Gilbert, *Winston S. Churchill*.

not like Rosebery's references to general policy, especially discarding the policy of 1886 and 1892. It is not loyal to Mr G., it is unfair to his own policy and that of his colleagues. I shall certainly stick to C.B.'[9]

The *Westminster Gazette*, edited by Spender, also believed that Rosebery's speech showed a fundamental disloyalty to Campbell-Bannerman: 'He stabbed the Liberal Leader under the fifth rib. The truth of the matter is that Lord Rosebery will never allow any man to sit unmolested upon the throne which he abdicated. If Lord Rosebery is not to rule, there shall be no King of Israel.' That was exactly how Campbell-Bannerman felt. 'It leaves things no better than before: the same mystery, the same underground enmity, the same unsettled uncomfortable position,' he wrote on the day after Chesterfield.[10] To Herbert Gladstone, attempting emollience with his claim that the speech might offer a chance to 'sink differences' in the party, Campbell-Bannerman poured out his anger and puzzlement: 'All he said about the clean slate and efficiency was an affront to Liberalism and was pure claptrap – Efficiency as a watchword! Who is against it? This is all a mere *réchauffé* of Mr Sidney Webb who is evidently the chief instructor of the whole faction.'[11]

Campbell-Bannerman decided to confront Rosebery directly. Often portrayed as a plodding if honest politician, the Liberal leader displayed unwonted cunning and ruthlessness in the way he handled their meeting and its aftermath, outmanoeuvring his far more brilliant but less pragmatic rival. On 23 December he saw Rosebery at Berkeley Square. The records the two men left of their conversation are very different. According to Rosebery, they concentrated entirely on the issues of South Africa and Irish Home Rule. He attacked Campbell-Bannerman over the phrase 'the methods of barbarism', to which 'he said nothing and offered no explanation. He gave me the impression of not being very proud of it.' On Ireland, 'I said I could have nothing further to do with Mr Gladstone's policy, that much had happened since 1892 including the Irish Local Government Bill and my experience at the FO . . . He tried to soften down my declaration but I was emphatic.' The meeting then ended abruptly: 'In the midst of the conversation he said that he must catch his train and hurried off.'[12] In his account Rosebery makes no reference, apart from the one noted regarding Irish policy, to his own position or to his relationship to the Liberal party, yet these are the very points stressed by Campbell-Bannerman. After leaving Berkeley Square he wrote immediately to Lord Spencer: 'One object of mine in going was that it is alleged that we (perhaps I must say I) stand in the way of a grand conciliation: the truth being that he is the impediment, though his speeches do not disclose it. I told him that this was what I wanted to clear up.' But Campbell-Bannerman informed Lord Spencer that Rosebery was unco-operative: 'Will he join? Impossible. Has been five or six years out of the party; is not (in ecclesiastical phrase) "in communion" with it. Besides is debarred by Irish policy. Is against Home Rule in any form.' According to Campbell-Bannerman's version, Rosebery was disingenuous about his programme of efficiency, reportedly saying that 'if his theory coincided with the recommendations of Sidney Webb, it was pure accident.' Campbell-Bannerman summarised the situation: 'We were entirely friendly, and I did not at all urge him, only enquired and asked for an explanation. The great point is that *he won't join in*. I never thought he would but I have it flat from him.' Campbell-Bannerman then added a vital conclusion: 'I thought I had better let you know at once. I think it would be very desirable somehow to let the world at large know. It is very unfair that we should be blamed for being irresponsive to his seductions, when it is he that won't play.'[13]

Campbell-Bannerman did all he could to give 'the world at large' his own interpretation of the Berkeley Square meeting. From the Lord Warden Hotel in Dover he wrote to most of his senior colleagues, including Ripon, Gladstone, Bryce, Fowler, Tweedmouth and Harcourt, informing them of Rosebery's decision to maintain his independence. 'He declined to come into consultation even on South Africa because he is not, as he said, "in communion" with us,' Campbell-Bannerman told Fowler.[14] The Liberal leader also cultivated sympathetic voices in the press to ensure that his message was heard. Thus on Boxing Day he wrote to C.P. Scott of the *Manchester Guardian*: 'I am constrained to give you in the strictest secrecy a hint. You are all on the wrong track: there has been no offer of help to the Party – it was to the Country. He will not join in, even on the War. There has never been any unwillingness on our part for his return: this is absolute. The impediment is that he won't.' To Spender, he claimed that Rosebery 'won't rejoin; won't consult; won't do nuffin'.' Just as he had hoped, Campbell-Bannerman's own version of the meeting soon found its way into the newspapers. Within a week of his visit to Berkeley Square the *Dundee Advertiser* carried a report – probably provided by Harcourt – identical to the one he had given his colleagues.[15] The rest of the Liberal press followed, and Rosebery found himself portrayed as the arrogant recalcitrant who had rejected a friendly approach from the Liberal leader.

Feeling himself the victim of a carefully-worked intrigue, Rosebery first complained to the Liberal Chief Whip, Herbert Gladstone: 'I think it a great pity that C.B. should apparently have talked so much about an informal chat between two old friends. There is a great deal of inspired rubbish visible in the newspapers – notably the *Dundee Advertiser* – which I cannot believe to have come from him and certainly does not come from me. Yet there was no one else present. This sort of thing destroys all confidence in communication and renders it indeed impossible.'[16] He then tackled Campbell-Bannerman personally, condemning him for giving his colleagues reports of their meeting which 'do not materially differ from those in the newspapers . . . it never occurred to me that our private, confidential (and interrupted) chat, as between two old friends and colleagues, was in any sense formal or intended for communication to others.'[17] Campbell-Bannerman, scenting victory in this struggle, was unapologetic in his reply, and not entirely truthful: 'Although we talked as friends, I cannot leave out of sight my responsibility as leader of the party in the Commons and I was *bound* to report the gist of our talk, of course in strict confidence, to my Cabinet colleagues. That is all I have done. For what appeared in the press I am in no way responsible.'[18]

Only a month earlier, in the frenzy surrounding Chesterfield, to the public Rosebery had looked the inevitable leader of the Liberal party. Even Labouchere had written, 'Rosebery has the greatest opportunity that ever befell a statesman. It seems to me that he has the ball at his feet.'[19] Yet suddenly he was on the defensive, battling to explain his position to a hostile Liberal press and party. Within just three weeks of Chesterfield, Rosebery's name was roundly booed at a meeting of the London Liberal Federation, while Campbell-Bannerman was cheered when he said of Rosebery, 'I do not know how it is elsewhere, but it is hard to see in this country how a public man can take an effective part in public life in detachment from all political parties.' Rosebery's supporters had been guilty of two fundamental misconceptions after Chesterfield. One was that the sheer magnetic force of his personality would overwhelm any opposition and compel the party to rally around him: he would not have to fight for the leadership, since the mass of Liberalism would instantly respond to the exhilaration of his cry. Yet to their disappointment, the call from the party never came. As Perks confessed four years later, 'The mistake was made when the party did not rally to him as we expected after Chesterfield.'[20] Rosebery claimed never to have believed the wilder dreams of his followers. As he put it to Arthur Godley in January 1902, 'When my speech was first delivered, one might have thought that the Liberal Millennium was at hand. I was not so simple and the old gang has been at work, with some success.'[21] Later, in November 1902, looking back on Chesterfield, he said to Wemyss Reid, 'I was told that if I came out, I should have an enormous following. I was absolutely convinced that I should have hardly any. But I thought it my duty to come out at a national crisis and I soon found that I was right and my friends were wrong.'[22]

The second mistake was to underestimate the tenacity and shrewdness of Campbell-Bannerman himself. Some, like Grey, naively thought the cautious old Scot would simply be blown away by Rosebery's oratory. But Campbell-Bannerman, backed by the party machine, was determined not to yield to the challenge. Resentment at the disloyalty of the Liberal Imperialists, opposition to their views, and a growing personal dislike of Rosebery, whom he privately nicknamed 'Baron Barnbougle', all had their part in building his resilience. And after Chesterfield he played his hand far more adroitly than the Roseberyites, of whom Morley had written pre-sciently in December, 'They are such babies in intrigue that they may be on the rocks before they know it, and without intending it.'[23]

The split between the leadership and the Liberal Imperialists grew wider as both Rosebery and Campbell-Bannerman went on the offensive. At Liverpool on 14 February Rosebery again called for a 'clean slate' in Liberal domestic policy, and for the abandonment of Home Rule. Haldane remained in his state of rapture: 'It needed strength and courage to say what you said. As a member of this great historic party, I feel that I now have something to fight for, that I can be proud of.'[24] But Herbert Gladstone, when he saw Rosebery just after the Liverpool speech, found him 'very restless' and agitated, full of talk about the dangers of the Irish alliance and his own doubts about taking office again. 'I have resigned; I am not in the party,' he told Gladstone.[25] And that was the issue on which Campbell-Bannerman now sought a very public clarification. Addressing the National Liberal Federation in Leicester on 19 February he made a direct attack on Rosebery and on the programme outlined at Chesterfield. 'I do not know down to this moment of my speaking to you whether Lord Rosebery speaks to us from the interior of our political tabernacle or from some vantage ground outside. I practically put that question publicly to him a month ago, but he does not answer it. Gentlemen, I am no believer in the doctrine of the clean slate. I am, in fact, wholly opposed to the doc-trine of the clean slate. I am equally opposed to the practice and penance of the white sheet. I am not prepared to erase from the tablets of my creed any principle or measure or proposal or ideal or aspiration of Liberalism.' Rosebery's reply was instantaneous and clear. In a letter to *The Times* he declared, 'My friend Sir Henry Campbell-Bannerman anathematised my declarations on the "clean slate". It is obvious that our views on the war and its methods are not less discordant. I remain therefore outside his taber-nacle, but not, I think, in solitude.' As usual, in taking this step – what he described as a 'definite separation' – Rosebery had acted without informing his supporters.

The breach was formalised three days later, on 24 February, with the creation of a new body, the Liberal League, which Rosebery and Perks had been planning since the Liverpool speech as part of 'the long campaign' against the Little Englanders. The League was launched at 38 Berkeley Square, with Grey, Perks, Haldane, Asquith and Munro-Ferguson in attendance. Presiding over this small gathering was Rosebery, who warned his colleagues that they could be undermining their careers by association with him. He further explained that there were three courses open to him: to act in isolation, to retire into private life, or to act in communion with a group of MPs. But in view of his rejection of Home Rule and his support for Empire there was the risk, if he chose the third, that there might be little to separate the League from the Liberal Unionists, especially if the latter were to support a more liberal domestic policy. The other members were willing to accept this danger, and it was unanimously agreed that the new League should be established, with Rosebery as President and Grey, Asquith and Henry Fowler as vice-presidents. It was stated at the launch that the twin purposes of the League were, first, to promote the programme Rosebery had set out at Chesterfield, especially with regard to Imperialism and Efficiency, and, second, to ensure that 'MPs who agreed with Lord Rosebery should not allow themselves to be drummed out of the Liberal Party by Sir Henry Campbell-Bannerman', to use the words of Asquith.[26] Perks concentrated on the organisational practicalitics, renting an office in Victoria, hiring an able young staff (they included William Allard and Freeman Freeman-Thomas, later Marquess of Willingdon and Viceroy of India), and quickly raising a fund of £6000, including donations of £1000 each from Alfred Harmsmorth and his brother Harold, another £1000 from Rosebery himself, and £500 from Sir Charles Tennant, father of Margot Asquith.

Despite Perks's undoubted managerial skills, the Liberal League had a difficult start. Its establishment was formally announced in *The Times* on 26 February to little fanfare and amid much confusion. There was no sign of mass movement of either MPs or peers to Rosebery's banner; even his own son-in-law, the Marquess of Crewe, refused to join the League. As Hamilton put it on 3 March, 'He has the quality, no doubt – Asquith, E. Grey, Fowler and Haldane; but he has not got quantity; and quantity helps to form a party better than quality.'[27] The Liberal Party machine worked energetically to keep it that way; one potential candidate was firmly told by Herbert Gladstone that 'it would be altogether wrong for you to join a sectional organisation like the League'.[28] Many senior figures viewed the new body with something approaching disgust. 'I dislike extremely groups in Liberal ranks,' Earl Spencer told Asquith, 'and this last group is not one to promote one special policy, such as Imperialism, but to lay down the whole policy of the Liberal Party which I for one do not wish to remodel and I therefore cannot possibly approve of the formation of the new Liberal League even with its eminent leaders among whom I regret you are one.'[29] Campbell-Bannerman himself took this line: 'For the present the new League is laughed at in the House of Commons, except the half-dozen who have got the whole thing up. Rosebery seems universally condemned and it is fully expected that a few speeches will finish him. In the meantime I shall take a quiet, unaggressive line.'[30] In addition, several leading members of the Liberal Imperialist League (LIL) were annoyed that their own band had suddenly been superseded without any notice. W.S. Robson, the Vice-President of the League, attacked Rosebery's 'impetuous letter of separation', saying that it 'shows an astounding want of appreciation of the conditions of modern party organisation.'[31] In reality, however, most members of the old LIL ended up joining the new League.

In March the prospects of the League briefly improved, with indications of powerful support for Rosebery in certain constituencies, especially in Scotland. When he spoke at Glasgow City Hall on 10 March, there was a renewal of the excitement that had illuminated Chesterfield. Students from the University dragged his carriage through the streets, while the crowds were so dense that, as Rosebery wrote, 'I feared to see a policeman crushed to death.'[32] In his speech, he stressed the importance of his 'Efficiency' programme, which would ensure that the League reached out to those 'who have not touched politics for many years'. More good news came in the promise from the Harmsworths that their provincial press would 'work assiduously' for Rosebery; they also talked of establishing a specific League newspaper in Edinburgh.[33] Under Perks's influence the nonconformists too appeared to be moving in Rosebery's direction. Robertson Neil, editor of *The British Weekly*, told Rosebery that he had attended a conference of Free Church Ministers where 'I was simply amazed by the meeting's practical unanimity in favour of your leadership. It was proposed in the end to adopt a resolution in favour of unity under your leadership of the party and C.B's leadership in the House of Commons.'[34]

But this optimism soon began to fade as the League failed to make any decisive impact on the Liberal Party. Partly it was a question of timing. On 31 May, little more than two months after the launch of the League, the Boer War was finally brought to an end. At a stroke, the primary cause of the split in the Liberals' ranks had been removed. Once South Africa was no longer a dominant issue, there was far greater interest in party unity and far less in any separate organisation. On the Unionist side, the resignation of Salisbury and his replacement as Prime Minister by A.J. Balfour gave the Government a new lease of life, weakening the potential appeal of the League to disgruntled moderates. Meanwhile Rosebery, after his burst of activity, was slipping back into his isolationist ways, disappointed that the glory of Chesterfield had proved so fleeting. Throughout much of March and all of April he was in Europe, visiting Cannes, Naples, Sicily and Paris – just at the time when the infant organisation was looking to him to provide a lead.

The Webbs had joined the League, inspired by the hope that 'Efficiency' would become the dominant policy of the left, but soon became disenchanted with Rosebery. Before Chesterfield, Beatrice's sister Kate Courtney had spoken of her doubts that 'you will catch that bird effectively at all. I think you will want a more inspiring and inspired personality to draw the Liberal Imperialists in your net.'[35] That was what Beatrice now felt, writing of the 'mysterious Rosebery' in her diary: 'At present he is an enigma. Whether on account of his social position or of his brilliancy or because of his streaks of wit and original thought, he can make all the world listen. He has imagination and sensitiveness and he is a "born actor". His is first rate at "Appearances". But, as yet, he shows no sign of capacity for co-operation or even for leadership of a group of subordinates. All he has done is *strike attitudes* that have brought down the house at the time and left a feeling of blankness a few days later.'[36] In the summer she expressed frustration that he had made little effort to draw any trade unionists into the League: 'He wants strengthening on the democratic side and it would have cost him so little.'[37]

And Beatrice Webb's disappointment was echoed by several of those at the top of the League. Grey wrote to his wife early in the year, 'He has a habit of hiding his light, and making it seem as if the light that was in him was darkness. I am all for letting him go his own way, but I don't think I can help him much to play his game at present. It is an underground game, which is all right for him; but for us, who are in the House here, it is difficult to take part in it without playing the underhand game.'[38] In July Edward Hamilton dined with Rosebery, and confessed in his diary, 'I am beginning to see no future for him, so far as turning his position and his talents to practical account is concerned. His own party does not grow; the Liberal party is in a hopeless condition.'[39] In October, Lord Carrington warned that 'Rosebery's supporters won't stand this attitude of shilly-shallying much longer. Many are already dubbing Rosebery "a rotter".'[40] But Rosebery was weary of these constant demands for action. He had sounded his trumpet at Chesterfield, and few had responded. When Hamilton charged him with not doing enough to build on his support, he broke out angrily, 'It is all very well for you to talk of my many friends. But as far as I can see, they don't come tumbling over one another. There is no proof of their longing to support me. If they do, why don't they join the Liberal League?'[41] Still in this spirit of grievance, on 14 November Rosebery drafted a long response to Wemyss Reid, who had complained of the 'ostentatious attitude of detachment you have assumed'. It was never posted, Rosebery preferring to send Reid a much shorter, less agonised version a week later. Yet the original draft is more revealing of Rosebery's innermost thoughts than the later document; it is a classic example of his uniquely personal blend of self-deception, self-pity and self-deprecation:

> We seem to be in a vicious circle, for it is clear that Lord Rosebery must be worn out or beaten down before his ardent supporters are satisfied by his stamina to back him up. I remember we had a head gardener here many years ago whose defect it was not to be a good manager of men. He used to be seen with his coat off digging fanatically while his subordinates stood around and sympathetically watched him. That is the position which the mass of the Liberal Imperialists have generously marked out for me, until I find myself digging my own grave. The question, put plainly, is: am I to spend the few remaining years of my life in fagging for gentlemen whose delicacy and diffidence compel them to be mere spectators.

Most of the League's vice-presidents would have described this as an exact reversal of the real situation.

In a revealing summary of his own outlook, he continued,

> I am practically alone. If fifteen members of the House of Commons and fifteen members of the House of Lords do not constitute political loneliness, I do not know what does. The sympathy of the gentlemen outside is an elegant figment which is its own reward and does not deceive for a moment. Nor have I any other illusions. Long ago I renounced any idea of office. I have held office for a short time in my life but never power. I would never hold office again without power and it is, humanly speaking, impossible that I should hold it with power. If I did it would come too late. So in what I have been doing, I have been working for others without any idea of any personal object. I hope that Asquith and Grey may yet lead the Liberal party with the policy which we hold in common, for I rely on their comparative youth and vigour. That is the extent of my ambition.

Rosebery explained that he had only spoken out to combine 'sane imperialism with sane liberalism' and thereby land Grey and Asquith in power. 'Duty, however, does not prescribe that I shall do this to my grave. There are many honourable and useful employments which I can fill and retain my true friends like yourself without filling the functions of a political target for all parties. I consider myself to be failing in many ways – the powers of memory, work and speech are lessening; no one knows the misery of a long speech of mine, and it will be well when I retire for good. But when I retire, it will be mainly due to those who have pushed me forward and returned home.'[42]

The problems of the Liberal League went much deeper than the President's waywardness. The fact was that the cry of 'Efficiency' had little public appeal. It was too nebulous, too uninspiring. It seemed to offer not so much a political ideology as a method of administration. Raymond Asquith epitomised the cynicism with which the concept was generally viewed: 'Rosebery continues to prance on the moonbeam of efficiency and makes speeches on every street corner: but he might as well call it the Absolute at once for all the meaning it has to him or anyone else: no one has the least idea what he wants to effect and beyond a mild bias in favour of good government and himself as premier, nothing can be gleaned from his speeches.'[43] G.K. Chesteron was another who enjoyed poking fun at Rosebery: 'I am not very certain of the secret doctrine of the sect in this matter. As far as I can make out "efficiency" means that we ought to discover everything about a machine except what it is for. There has arisen in our time a most singular fancy: the fancy that when things go very wrong we need a practical man. It would be far truer to say that when things go very wrong we need an unpractical man. Certainly, at least, we need a theorist.'[44]

The hollowness of the doctrine of 'Efficiency' was soon exposed by the Liberal League's response to Arthur Balfour's 1902 Education Bill, one of the biggest domestic reforms of the early twentieth century. If 'Efficiency' meant anything, then the League should have given the measure its full backing, for its aim was to rationalise the education system by putting local authorities in charge of schools, in place of myriad school boards. But the Liberal nonconformists were fiercely opposed to the scheme because it meant that Anglican and Catholic voluntary schools could be subsidised from the local rates. They argued that under the proposed legislation dissenters would not only have to give financial support to sectarian teaching but, even worse, some of them – especially in the remoter parts of Wales and the north of England – might be forced to send their children to an Anglican or Catholic school if that were the only one in their local area.

The Bill was, in the words of Perks, 'a threat to civil and religious free-dom'.[45] As the dominant organisational force in the League, Perks was able to ensure that his narrow view prevailed, claiming that there was 'a torrent of popular hostility against the Government'.[46] Under such pressure, Rosebery was persuaded to come out against the Bill, and attacked it for 'undermining our constitutional structure' – this from a politician who had spent the previous three years condemning the rottenness of Britain's 'con-stitutional structure'. And Rosebery's assertion, in a speech made in London, that the Bill would 'do more to stunt the educational develop-ment of the country than almost any measure we can conceive possible', was nothing short of cant. Thanks to Perks – and Rosebery's weakness in failing to stand up to him – the League had failed its first challenge. Coherence of policy had been sacrificed to political opportunism. The 'fly-blown phylacteries' of traditional Liberalism had remained in place. Bravely, a few members of the League, led by Haldane and Munro-Ferguson, tried to adhere to the doctrine of 'Efficiency' rather than sur-render to Protestant sectarianism, but they were heavily outnumbered. While Haldane expressed his annoyance to Rosebery, warning that his action 'has cost you in central support',[47] the Webbs and other Fabians abandoned the League altogether, seeing no hope for its future. 'Rosebery is so intent on trying to find out which course will *appear right* to the ordin-ary men of affairs that he forgets altogether which course will work out best in social results. He seems positively frightened at the thought of any such enquiry,' wrote Beatrice Webb.[48]

The next challenge on policy arose in May 1903, when Joseph Chamberlain, with breathtaking audacity, launched his campaign for Tariff Reform in a speech at Birmingham. His demand that the Government drop free trade in favour of a system of imperial preference had the effect of a shattering explosion on the political landscape, for he had dared to question the most basic assumptions about the governance of Britain. The Unionists were torn apart, the Liberals united for the first time in a decade. 'Free Trade' was more than just an economic theory – it was the very bedrock of the civic order, the system that made Britain prosperous and powerful. As Campbell-Bannerman put it, 'To dispute Free Trade, after fifty years' experience of it, is like disputing the laws of gravitation.'[49] Chamberlain's argument was that the world had changed in those decades since Cobden's crusade. Britain was now facing severe economic compe-tition overseas, especially from Germany and the USA, and her industries needed protection. And by adopting a preferential tariff on imports from the colonies, Britain would strengthen the bonds of Empire.

451

It was this imperialist message that initially put Rosebery in a quandary over his response to Chamberlain's declaration. Although he no longer believed in imperial federation with the same passion as he had in the 1880s, he was still the best-known advocate of imperialism in the country. In his first public utterance on the subject, at the Burnley Chamber of Commerce on 19 May, he struck a hesitant note: it was not right, he said, 'to reject, hastily and without mature consideration, any plan offered on high authority and based on large experience, for really cementing and uniting the British Empire,' yet he doubted if imperial preference would bind the colonies closer to the Mother Country. So balanced was his speech that the *Daily News* remarked, 'Is it possible that Mr Chamberlain is looking to Lord Rosebery for assistance in pushing the new gospel?'

In the ferment created by Chamberlain there was little place for such public philosophising. The Liberals had been galvanised into action, with Asquith leading the charge, and Rosebery would be left in utter isolation if he did not join the battle. 'Surely this astonishing move of Chamberlain's offers a wonderful chance of showing what Imperialism really means, by enabling you and the others to define the true proportions of the various parts of the Empire,' wrote Crewe to him on 29 May. 'It would be a great misfortune if the defence of Free Trade were to fall into the hands of those whose Imperial imagination is as defective on one hand as Chamberlain's is excessive on the other.'[50] Grey wrote in similar vein, urging Rosebery to 'speak out strongly' to eliminate the danger of 'letting it be thought your own part is to be one of detachment'.[51] Of perhaps more importance – in light of Rosebery's fondness for businessmen – was a letter from the great Scots-born American steel magnate, Andrew Carnegie, who had been a friend since the 1880s. Carnegie warned that 'tinkering with tariffs' would divide Britain and the USA, cause endless problems for Canada, and ultimately lead to 'the disunion' of the Empire.[52] On 12 June Rosebery came out unequivocally against Chamberlain's scheme at a great Liberal League dinner in London, demolishing every one of the Colonial Secretary's arguments. Having demonstrated that Britain's trade was expanding rather than contracting, he pointed out that the introduction of tariffs would lead to dearer food, restrict the economies of the Dominions, increase the costs of raw materials, and raise the price of British exports. Finally, he expressed the fear that 'the delicate, world-wide organisation of the British Empire' might be imperilled by Chamberlain's imperial zollverein.★

★ The *Zollverein*, or customs union, was formed by the states of the German confederation in 1834 to improve internal trade.

Rosebery's speech contradicted his statement of the previous November to Wemyss Reid, for both his intellectual and his oratorical powers appeared to be undiminished. Henry Fowler said afterwards that he had sounded 'a trumpet note to which the whole party can respond'.[53] Superficially, his attack on Chamberlain could be viewed as another example of an opportunistic desire to fall in with the Liberal mainstream, as in the case of the Education Bill of 1902. After all, much of his rhetoric about Empire, efficiency and the British race was very similar to that uttered by enthusiasts for tariff reform. Lord Milner, for instance, came out strongly for imperial preference because 'if the nation was weak, unhealthy and impoverished, the very foundations of the Empire must crumble' – exactly the sort of language Rosebery had used in Glasgow in 1900.[54] Some of the nonconformist members of the Liberal League, still obsessed with education, were so certain Rosebery would back tariff reform that, in a bizarre initiative, they secretly made overtures to Chamberlain. Lady Edward Cecil gave Milner the story on 24 June after a conversation with Chamberlain himself: 'Joe told me that scouts from the Liberal League had immediately approached him to offer him the leadership of their party if he would give them some hope on the Education Bill. "I told them not to talk nonsense, I was as responsible for the Bill as my colleagues, and that I did not mean to lead." Then one of Rosebery's henchmen came in and said, "Do you want Rosebery to join you?" and Joe answered, "If you mean, do I want him to make a speech as an outsider backing my idea up, of course I do, but not as a colleague."'[55] Rosebery, with his dislike of both Chamberlain and anything that threatened to compromise his independence, certainly knew nothing of this clandestine manoeuvre.

In any case, he had strong and sincerely-held objections to tariff reform which made it impossible for him to consider any co-operation with Chamberlain. At the heart of the economic debate over Chamberlain's plan were two different visions of imperialism. On one side was the Imperialism of Protection, led by industrial entrepreneurs who felt themselves under threat from international trade and sought to build captive markets in the colonies. It is no coincidence that Chamberlain, who had made his fortune in screw manufacturing and whose political base was centred on industrial Birmingham, should have taken this gloomy, defensive view. On the other side was the Imperialism of Free Trade, which held that the power of capital was more important than productive capacity to the British economy. Finance, banking, the City, and overseas investments had all prospered under free trade, and built Britain's imperial greatness. Protection would only damage such interests. In the light of his City and

Rothschild connections it was perhaps understandable that Rosebery should take this view; for him, capital was one of Britain's 'supreme assets'. In a speech made in 1905 he said: 'The unity of the Empire is very largely cemented by free trade. I believe freedom, in all its essentials, for every part of it, is the essence of the Empire and therefore I for one am not prepared to enter into a course of policy which would fetter that freedom both in the Colonies and at home.' In this context, an important influence on Rosebery's thinking and that of the other Liberal Imperialists was Halford Mackinder, a geography lecturer from Oxford who claimed that increasing economic competition would actually strengthen Britain's role as the financial power-house of the world. In a series of lectures given in 1899 he had declared that the more industrial and commercial activity became dispersed, 'the greater will be the need of a controlling centre to it. Though in the human frame there are many muscles, there is only one brain.'[56]

Rosebery's hostility to tariff reform appeared to present him with a golden opportunity to re-establish his claims to national leadership. His imperialism and patriotism could have made him the dominant figure of the campaign for free trade, since Campbell-Bannerman was too much of a Little Englander to be able to provide any reassurance for those dissident Unionists who opposed Chamberlain. 'The crisis is so grave that no self-respecting public man can decently hold aloof. There is a great opening for Rosebery. Let him throw himself into the battle and with his eloquence and his talents he may come out of it our unquestioned leader,' wrote Ripon to Spencer.[57] But, as so often before, Rosebery refused to seize the moment, held back by diffidence, pride, scruple, and his continuing revulsion from politics. Throughout the summer of 1903, when his supporters felt he should have been heading the charge, he was wrapped in introspection. When Hamilton wrote to him in June, begging him to be more active, 'I got a chilling, heart-breaking note from him. He says that I need not trouble myself about him: he had led the Liberal party once, and never again! It is hopeless, evidently: and one must most reluctantly give up the idea of his ever being of any real use to his country. So all those splendid talents are to be thrown away; and all one's cherished hopes dashed to the ground. I feel somehow or other I have failed in my endeavours to see Lady Rosebery's last wishes carried out.'[58]

Rosebery infuriated Grey and Asquith by his refusal to join the Free Trade Union, the main all-party campaign body against tariff reform, because he saw it as a rival to the Liberal League. Grey warned him that just the opposite was the case: 'If the President of the Liberal League withholds his support from the Free Trade Union, the League itself will be prejudiced and those whose work is specially connected with it will be handicapped and discouraged.'[59] When Asquith begged him to reconsider his decision, saying 'we do not wish even to appear to be isolated from you', Rosebery replied, 'When I resigned in 1896, I quite made up my mind to have nothing more to do with party organisations or party politics. Circumstances, as you know, compelled me temporarily to break that resolution more than eighteen months ago and also to connect myself with the political organisation which we know as the Liberal League. The last was a matter of sheer necessity in my judgement but nothing would induce me to go a step further in party politics. I am pledged to the Liberal League and there I will do what I can. But more than that I cannot undertake.' Asquith denied that the Free Trade Union was a party organisation, saying he wanted it 'as catholic as possible' and pointing out that 'the absence of your name would be a very serious setback.'[60] Rosebery eventually relented, joining the Union in late July, but contributed little beyond his name.

Another more unorthodox approach came from Winston Churchill, who had inherited his father's dream of a grand centrist coalition with Rosebery at its head. Never one to be unduly concerned about party loyalties, Winston Churchill had lost his faith in Unionism long before Chamberlain fired his protectionist rocket. A romantic imperialist and radical aristocrat, steeped in history and literature, a man whose father had been one of Rosebery's closest friends, at the start of his long career in politics Winston Churchill was bound to be an admirer of the 5th Earl. After Rosebery's resignation as Liberal leader in 1896 Churchill, then twenty-one years old, had written to his mother, 'Rosebery is a great man and one of these days he will lead a great party.' His friendship with Rosebery had begun in 1900, when he first visited The Durdans. Rosebery had been impressed with the young man's energy, if not his diction: 'I will take your advice about elocution lessons, though I fear I shall never learn to pronounce my S properly,' Churchill said when thanking Rosebery for his hospitality.[61] Churchill took to motoring over to The Durdans, sometimes with worrying results: 'I am afraid I disturbed your horses with my motor car yesterday. I am learning to drive so this is a rather dangerous period.' In August 1901 Rosebery hosted a dinner at Mentmore for Churchill and several other members of his boisterous Commons club, the Hooligans, named after its most prominent member Lord Hugh Cecil. To Churchill, Rosebery was full of charm: 'I cannot tell you how much I enjoyed the Hooligan visit. It rejuvenated me.'[62] But he soon began to find the group rather puerile: 'Not very amusing,' he confessed in his diary after another visit.[63]

It was at the time of Chesterfield that Winston Churchill, still nominally a Tory, grew excited by the idea of a new Rosebery movement. Just before the speech he wrote to Rosebery, 'People are restless and anxious and they look to you for guidance.'[64] Afterwards, Churchill expressed his delight at Rosebery's achievement: 'I am so glad it has been a splendid success. I was so afraid, as you know, that nothing could realise the anticipations of the country, but you certainly sustained the occasion and it is equally certain no one else in England could have done so.'[65] His friend Hugh Cecil warned him not to be too carried away by fantasies of his role in an imminent Rosebery premiership. 'Whatever might be wise for you to do, if for instance you were offered office in a Rosebery administration, now it would be madness not to remain unequivocally Unionist.'[66] But in the following year, as the Liberal League took its first tentative steps, Churchill felt ever-increasing enthusiasm for the idea of a new centrist grouping which could change the entire structure of British politics. He told Rosebery, on 10 October 1902, that he envisaged 'a party which shall be free at once from the sordid selfishness and callousness of Toryism on the one hand and the blind appetites of the Radical masses on the other', with Rosebery 'upholding the flag for which my father fought so long and so disastrously.' His suggested name was 'Tory-Liberal', which he preferred to 'Tory-Democrat' or 'Liberal-Imperialist'.[67] Predictably, Rosebery gave little encouragement: 'You must not compromise your career by premature action. Some day, perhaps not long hence, the psychological moment may come for a new departure but it is not yet. The fact is that people in this country fight about names and not kings. Their first object is to enfold as many people as possible behind some crumbling, obsolete ramparts on which they have hoisted a pole which once held a flag. Why the people are there they can scarcely say themselves. As for me, I am fighting the machine, and the machine will probably win.'[68] Despite this negative response, the tariff reform controversy gave fresh impetus to the hopes of Churchill, who was an ardent supporter of free trade. 'I am absolutely in earnest in this business and if, and by the aid and under the aegis of Beach★ we cannot save the Tory party from Protection, I shall look to you.'[69] That autumn, as he told Rosebery of his idea for an all-party campaign against Chamberlain's plans, he warned: 'The odds against us are very heavy. Beach and Goschen are old and husky. No one pays any attention to Asquith. We are children. Joe's electric strength carries all before it. You alone can

---

★ Sir Michael Hicks-Beach, the former Conservative Chancellor of the Exchequer, who had left the Government in 1902 and was also strongly opposed to tariffs.

counter him and stem the tide.'[70] Yet even Winston's eloquence was in vain. Rosebery refused to move. As J.A. Spender once said of Rosebery, 'he was the most uninfluenceable of men'.[71] Rather than joining a coalition, Churchill ended by crossing the floor of the House, without any help from Rosebery.

Such was Rosebery's sense of his own dignity that attempts to influence him could indeed be counter-productive, as St Loe Strachey, editor of the *Spectator*, was perceptive enough to recognise. He told the author John Buchan, who was planning to send Rosebery a letter asking him to return to the fray: 'In many people such a letter would do good. But I am doubtful about Lord Rosebery. To a man so intensely proud and sensitive as he is, with all the feelings of the grand seigneur abnormally developed, it might seem a little patronising.'[72] This was certainly the case when Alfred Harmsworth, rapidly becoming the greatest press baron of his age, attempted to entice Rosebery into leading a crusade against Chamberlain and for 'Efficiency'. Harmsworth's politics were always fluid but, as he had demonstrated in making such a success of the *Daily Mail*, he possessed an intuitive understanding of the public mind. Aware of Rosebery's unique popularity and of the widespread public antipathy to tariff reform – which was seen as the precursor to food taxes – Alfred Harmsworth and his brother Harold had been talking for months to Perks about an autumn campaign to be backed by their publications, which would include the already promised new pro-Liberal League paper produced in Edinburgh, to be launched in October. By September Alfred Harmsworth was willing to put the resources of his press empire behind Rosebery. In a letter exuding presumption he wrote directly to the Earl, setting out his detailed plans: 'I am enclosing a list of the speeches already arranged, a list we understand to be by no means complete. It is obvious from this programme that unless you enter upon a series of meetings calculated to attract attention equal to that of Mr Gladstone's Midlothian campaign, it will be impossible for any press organisation to achieve a possibility of success.' Harmsworth went on to tell Rosebery that it was 'absolutely essential' he should make at least two speeches in September, with another eight to follow by 15 December. 'We would therefore, with the utmost respect, suggest that you consent to the arrangement of a series of speeches which will allow us the chance – by no means a sure one under the circumstances – of carrying our press campaign to a successful issue by giving us the support we ask.' Allard, Secretary of the Liberal League, was to arrange some suitable dates. Harmsworth concluded, 'we feel there is not a moment to be lost. I am therefore remaining in London in order to organise our staff in the hope of success.'[73]

Rosebery was sitting with the journalist J.A. Spender in a tent on the lawn at Mentmore when he received this letter from the hands of Harmsworth's courier. Spender recorded that Rosebery 'laughed but was visibly angry'. The next day, 2 September, Rosebery replied to Harmsworth, complaining that he had been given an ultimatum without any warning: 'It appears that you are carrying on a press campaign against overwhelming odds and that unless I at once fix the dates for at least ten speeches to be delivered by me, it will be impossible for you to carry the contest and so pressing is the emergency that you cannot leave London to keep an appointment with me tomorrow. I do not gather the cause on behalf of which this desperate contest is being waged nor why it depends on me. Is it the cause of Liberal Imperialism? Surely that is healthy enough. Is it the cause of Free Trade? Surely that is not desperate. Nor can I see the connexion between either and the vital necessity of at least ten speeches to be disclosed by me. I doubt if such a letter as this was ever addressed to a public man in this country.' Rosebery said he would write again when he had reflected more on Harmsworth's demands.

Later that day Rosebery saw Perks, who reported the gist of their conversation to Harmsworth. 'As the former leader (and in my judgement the future leader also) of a great political party, it would be impossible for Lord Rosebery to enter into a compact with a vast journalistic combination which might seriously fetter him, as well as possibly his political associates, in the inception and practical application of his policy. Lord Rosebery spoke, as he always does, most kindly of you. But I may say *very privately* that he said he had not seen in the *Daily Mail* much evidence of the support you led him to think he would receive if he "came out" as he has done.'[74] On 5 September Rosebery sent Harmsworth an outright rejection:

> I am not ambitious as you know and even if I were I could not sacrifice my liberty of action or, I must add, my self-respect . . . I am quite aware of the value of the support of your journalistic system to the causes I have at heart and I would be glad to acquire it. But there is something I value more which I should forfeit if I handed over to you the arrangement of my campaign as if I were a lecturer or a singer. Nor do I know, in any case, how far or how long we should agree on policy. You have never consulted me as to the policy of your papers . . . I am sure you have made your proposal – strange and unprecedented as it is – in the friendliest spirit. But I am equally sure that it is impossible that I should hand over the planning of my future course to anyone whatsoever. I think you must realize what would be felt if it was understood that I had assigned this charge to a great newspaper proprietor. It would be said, not unnaturally, that I was being 'run' by him.[75]

The relationship between tycoon and statesman swiftly became acrimonious. Harmsworth told Spender he had been 'insulted' by Rosebery and was therefore abandoning his plans for an Edinburgh-based pro-Liberal League newspaper. He also refused to provide any more funding to the Liberal League. 'It does not require much knowledge of the world', he wrote to Perks, 'to know that the present lamentable inactivity is weakening the public respect for our friend to a degree he possibly does not understand. I cannot set in motion a machine of the magnitude of our business without corresponding activity on his part . . . I do not like Lord Rosebery's letter to me because he suggested I had endeavoured to impose a policy on him. There was no mention of policy in my letter to Lord Rosebery.'[76] In his turn, Rosebery again expressed a sense of betrayal rooted in Harmsworth's failure to back him vigorously enough after Chesterfield: 'Is it wonderful if, under these circumstances, disliking politics as I do and having come forward from purely public and patriotic motives, I "gang warily" now? If the promises of support I had received before Chesterfield had been fulfilled afterwards, I should willy-nilly have been at the head of an overwhelming political force.'[77] Writing to Harold Harmsworth, Rosebery even claimed that the promise of a new Scottish newspaper had been 'one of the material considerations which induced me to come forward in the winter of 1901. I should only blame myself . . . I should have remained in retirement.'[78] But for once Perks dared to utter some implicit criticism of his hero's aloofness and inaccessibility: 'I wish you could have got the chance of talking with Alfred because I feel that with a little careful handling they would not drift away and the influence of their papers is very great indeed.'[79]

With no grasp of Rosebery's character, Alfred Harmsworth always remained astonished that the Earl had turned down his offer. He wrote to Winston Churchill on 14 September 1903: 'Lord Rosebery does not realize how much his lack of activity injures him in the country and specially in the provinces. I almost despair of politics as the present time.'[80] More than a year later, in December 1904, he told Perks, 'Rosebery might have had *The Times* under his control, to say nothing of other papers. Now they don't even report him.'[81] The following December he was still finding Rosebery's attitude incredible: 'What a chance Lord Rosebery lost! Was there ever such a man? Did ever such a statesman have such an offer as I made him – the other people offered me what I have since got. I wanted to serve Rosebery. No man ever had such journalistic support before him. I took care my offer should go into his own hands. He rejected it and I don't mind telling you that the very next day I made an offer to the other people and they took it. These politicians don't understand business. I am a businessman and I don't like to see my practical suggestions rejected.'[82] By 'the other people', Harmsworth meant the Tariff Reform League. Within barely a month of his offer to Rosebery, he was expressing his public support for Chamberlain, and for imperial preference.

Such bare-faced inconsistency and lack of principle – hallmarks of Harmsworth throughout his career – showed that Rosebery was probably wise to have rebuffed him. Indeed, Lord Hugh Cecil had warned Winston Churchill of the dangers of submitting of Harmsworth's influence: 'I should not advise taking Harmsworth too far into confidence. He is not a very trustworthy man.'[83] Yet Rosebery's decision, however just, also marked his growing isolation and waning influence. It was not only Harmsworth who felt disheartened. Many of Rosebery's followers, including those in the League, believed they could no longer rely on him. His absences were too long, his appearances too sporadic. 'I see less of him than I ever did,' wrote Hamilton. 'He does not volunteer my company as he used to; and when I propose myself he is apt to make excuses. It may be merely that love of isolation is growing upon him.'[84] Rosebery could still blaze forth, as he did at Sheffield in October in a brilliant attack on Chamberlain, declaring that 'a great commercial country like ours cannot reverse a commercial system, on which so much prosperity has been built, purely on hypotheses. I would rather take a sound policy from a recumbent or even bed-ridden statesman than an unsound policy from the most energetic and enthusiastic statesman that ever lived.' But an occasional speech was not enough. Sir Edward Russell's *Liverpool Post* summed up the frustration of his supporters after Sheffield: 'Lord Rosebery has again shown that in him the nation has a leader, an incomparable leader, if only he would once and for all make up his mind to lead.'

Instead of taking the lead, Rosebery sank further into his solitary, melancholic ways, preferring to write long private memoranda about his own position than speeches or articles for the Liberal cause. Typical was one produced in August 1903, in which he said he would 'unhesitatingly' refuse to join a Liberal government: 'Personally my wish to have done with the contentions of public life has never wavered since 1896, on the contrary it has strengthened. Politically, it would not be possible to join a hierarchy of which the only positive or distinctive note has been proscription of my policy and a reiterated attachment to the policy of Gladstone's Home Rule.'[85] In another document, produced in September, he claimed it would be 'impossible' for him to form a future Liberal government; he would divide the party; his peerage meant he could never possess the confidence of the House of Commons; he could not sit 'with honour' in a Cabinet containing Harcourt and Campbell-Bannerman; he was 'not a party man', and he had only a score of followers in Parliament.[86] When the Liberal churchman George Potter begged him in October 1903 to take up the leadership, he wrote back frankly, 'Let me give you the true picture: a man with a natural distaste for politics and strong aversion to party, who dislikes office and has a bitter recollection of it, who suffers on any occasion of pressure from insomnia, can only engage in politics under an imperative sense of duty. Were he to follow his bent and desire he would withdraw altogether and never see Parliament or platform again. To my mind such a man is more deserving of commendation than the bustling politician who cares for nothing else, lives for nothing else.'[87]

Rosebery was still in his mid fifties at the time of the tariff crisis, an age when most political leaders are reaching their peak. But he had talked himself into premature retirement and old age. He complained that his memory, hearing, vigour and powers of application 'were all impaired', and feared that if he were to return to office 'I should once more be sleepless. My occasional speaking experiences make this evident. Now there would be no harm in this if it only meant death, for there could be no better death. But the horror is that it means life and office and total incapacity in both.'[88] He was withdrawing, not just from politics but from wider society, retreating into his libraries to ponder his books and his painful memories. His loneliness was exacerbated by the departure of his children from his domestic circle: Harry was in the Grenadier Guards, Neil at Oxford, where his idleness was a cause of concern to his father. 'I shall be satisfied and relieved if Neil gets a degree at all, for he has no idea of continuous work,' he told the historian Herbert Fisher.[89] His daughter Sybil, always the liveliest, most emotional of his four children, married Charles Grant of the Coldstream Guards in March 1903. Of her wedding, Rosebery wrote in his diary: 'She was wonderfully cool and held my hand all the way to church.' A melancholy, self-absorbed figure, he could see no future role for himself on the national stage. With increasing vehemence, he rejected all overtures from his former colleagues. In January 1904 he refused Earl Spencer's request that he should give a dinner for the Liberal peers at the opening of Parliament. He also declined to attend a meeting of front-benchers to discuss the party's attitude to the Unionist dissidents – or 'free fooders', as they were known. 'My attendance would be, in appearance at any rate, a renewal of those official relations which I deliberately severed when I resigned the leadership in 1896,' he told Spencer.[90] This was a stance confirmed by Winston Churchill, who saw him in March

1904 and wrote to Lord Hugh Cecil: 'I found him very frank and more friendly than ever before. SECRET. He told me that he would not join a C.B.–Spencer government and that he had conveyed to the King his own inability to form one and had recommended His Majesty to send for Spencer and C.B. jointly in the event of a change. He thought the outlook very obscure and said that nearly all the people who were worth anything were getting into impossible relations with either party.'[91] Distraught at Rosebery's attitude, Haldane temporarily lost his faith in Liberal politics: 'Liberalism, in the hand into which it is passing away from yours, is not longer the cause with which much of my life has been associated. And there comes in most heavily of all the sense that there is passing from the ship the pilot who understands and for whom I care most deeply,' he wrote to Rosebery.[92] Margot Asquith had little sympathy for him, however, quoting Curzon's description of him as 'an incorrigible rotter'. After a visit to Dalmeny she wrote, 'He is selfish, as cowardly and conventional as he thinks himself undaunted. He is terrible only to country neighbours and servants. His political outlook just now is about as bad as Napoleon's in Moscow and yet it ought to have been better than any man's in England if he hadn't muffed all his chances. "Forward my man and I will follow!" has been his political war cry and being unable to compel an army he consoles himself by a small bodyguard of volunteers with whom he is quite at ease and who applaud all his psychical moments or what in stage language are called "wrong entries".'[93]

Several other contemporaries were struck by how dejected, almost physically broken, he seemed. Beatrice Webb confided to her diary following a reception at the University of London in April 1904: 'The man was clearly not at ease. He seemed worried by a hankering after us, yet he is not willing to be friends or even friendly acquaintances. And politically I think he is past praying for. For all that, I feel sorry for the man. He suffers and is not ennobled by his suffering. Has he written himself down as a failure? I suppose so.' Edmund Gosse set down this macabre description after seeing him in early 1905: 'His appearance is now becoming very extraordinary. The flesh is so puffy and thick on his cheeks, and his eye-orbits so deep, that it looks as if he had a face over his face. His colour is unhealthy, a dull, deep red.'[94]

A banquet at Windsor Castle in November 1904 revealed Rosebery's increasingly morose and distracted state. Strangely for one so well versed in social etiquette, he failed to read his invitation carefully and appeared in black tie rather than full evening dress. Dreadfully embarrassed, he tried to stay on the fringes of the gathering, but was summoned before the King:

'I see you have come in the train of the American ambassador,' said Edward VII disapprovingly. During the course of the banquet Rosebery talked to H.O. Arnold-Foster, the Unionist War Secretary, who left this vivid account: 'He asked me how I was and I said I was very well but that I did not know that I had any right to be alive. He took this very seriously and with a face like an undertaker, he asked me, "Is life worth living?" I said on the whole it was but he was not at all content and kept repeating his question with great solemnity. He had evidently been thinking a great deal about it.' The conversation then shifted to the Liberals, and Arnold-Foster expressed the hope that they were committed to reform of the War Office. '"What about C.B.?" growled his Lordship and then spoke the most concentrated bitterness about C.B. whom he called "the greatest conservative in the House".' Later, Arnold-Foster travelled back to Windsor railway station in a carriage with Campbell-Bannerman: 'C.B. unconsciously repaid Rosebery in kind by making some very sniffy remarks about him and his coming in the wrong costume. There is certainly no love lost between those two great men.'[95]

Rosebery's political isolation was further emphasised in 1904, when he was a lone voice of opposition to the Anglo-French agreement known as the Entente Cordiale which Edward VII had played a key role in securing. The treaty was welcomed by the public and political parties alike, as it seemed to put an end to centuries of enmity. Rosebery courageously took a very different view. Lloyd George happened to arrive at Dalmeny on the very day of the signing of the treaty. 'Well, I suppose you are just as pleased as the rest of them with this French agreement,' were Rosebery's first words of greeting. Lloyd George assured him that he was. 'You are all wrong. It means war with Germany in the end!'[96] He spoke out in public in similar terms, warning that 'this unhappy agreement is much more likely to promote than to prevent unfriendliness'. At the time Rosebery – who admitted, with some pride, that he was a 'well-known and conspicuous heretic on the question' – was accused of being an anti-French Germanophile, but this was a distortion of the truth. He much preferred France to Germany as a country, as demonstrated by his regular visits to Paris, his love of French literature and his fascination with Napoleon, while he was also deeply suspicious of the Kaiser, whom he regarded as a 'dangerous fool'. Ironically, it was Rosebery's own biography of Napoleon that had helped to create a pro-British mood in Paris, according to the historian Sir George Prothero, who was in Paris at the time: 'Your book had more effect in preparing the way for the present Entente than any other single event,' he told Rosebery in 1912.[97] But Rosebery always clung to the traditional nineteenth-century view that Britain should avoid entanglement on the Continent: 'I am not a believer in durable friendships between nations,' he said.[98] Moreover, he feared that the French alliance would prove ineffectual in holding back an ever more powerful Germany: 'You are leaning on an aspen and the German Emperor has four millions of soldiers and the second best navy in the world,' he told Sir Edward Grey.[99] In this Rosebery was far more prescient than his fellow politicians. As J.A. Spender told him in 1927, 'You were the only man who rightly interpreted the Entente and saw its meaning and consequences and again and again in after years I wished that I had listened to you more.'[100] At the time, his opposition was regarded by friend and foe alike as another example of his eccentricity. Edward VII was particularly annoyed, as Rosebery explained to his former secretary Thomas Gilmour in 1905: 'The King was very angry with me and I had to tell him that it was to me a novel and I also thought a dangerous doctrine that the Sovereign should take the responsibility of arranging treaties with foreign countries out of the hands of Ministers. It is all very well now, when everybody but myself and the *Morning Post* appears satisfied with the French entente, but if things go wrong it may have serious consequences for the Sovereign.' Rosebery added, rather disparagingly, 'The worst of it is that the King thinks now he is a great statesman.'[101]

For all the popularity of the Entente, it was obvious towards the end of 1904 that the Unionist Government was crumbling, racked by divisions over tariff reform and hit by public anger about education and the importation of Chinese 'coolie' labour into South Africa. As the Liberals' fortunes rose, some still clung to the possibility that Rosebery might become Prime Minister when Balfour fell. Robertson Nicholl, editor of *The British Weekly*, told Perks in December that 'we want Rosebery very badly and for my part I cannot see how on earth we can get on without him.'[102] William Allard, the Secretary of the Liberal League, urged him to make more speeches to strengthen his influence, and *The Times* called on him to embark on a new Midlothian campaign for free trade, to 'force himself on the country and the Liberal party'. Interestingly, one of those who wished for a Rosebery premiership was Lloyd George. He told Perks that 'Rosebery is the only possible man', but claimed to be too 'nervous and shy'[103] to approach him directly, a reflection of how awe-inspiring Rosebery remained even in his isolation. The Welsh radical had admired the Chesterfield speech, which he said had shown that Rosebery was 'a statesman who had the courage to tell the truth about South Africa',[104] but there was also a much more Machiavellian reason for his support: Lloyd George reckoned that if Campbell-Bannerman became Prime Minister, the need for political balance would require him to place the Liberal Imperialists Asquith, Grey, Fowler and Haldane in prominent posts; whereas if Rosebery were Prime Minister, then the Little Englanders, including himself, would have to come to the fore. Through Perks Lloyd George was invited to Dalmeny, but nothing came of the visit; several inconsequential conversations left him 'with the conclusion that Rosebery was a very solitary man and out of touch with the trends in the party'.[105]

The journalist J.A. Spender, editor of the *Westminster Gazette*, also made another attempt. In a letter of 22 October 1904 he told Rosebery, rather extravagantly, that his 'position with the public and the rank and file of the Liberal party is stronger than at any time during the last nine years'. But Rosebery, he said, could not continue to make occasional attacks on Chamberlain and then 'step aside and decline responsibility. Hasn't the time come for some plain intimation that you accept the responsibility, such as Mr Gladstone gave in the last month of the Midlothian campaign? When you are taking the most effective lead and making the best speeches, it is absurd to have to treat you as detached from the main army.'[106] Rosebery drafted a lengthy response but did not send it, and instead invited Spender to lunch at Berkeley Square. 'He was quite uncompromising,' wrote the journalist afterwards. 'He denies my premises, rejects my conclusions.' Rosebery showed Spender his draft letter:

> the substance of it was that he was without support in the country and in the House of Commons had only 26 members behind him. The press, with the solitary exception of the *Leeds Mercury*, was hostile, whether Liberal or Conservative. The *Westminster Gazette* was cold-bloodedly neutral. In such circumstances he could not form a Government which would live or do him any good. Being in the House of Lords, he could only be Prime Minister if he had in an *exceptional degree* the support of the party and there was not the smallest ground for supposing it would be given to him. As to his responsibility, he was absolved by the action of the Liberal leaders themselves. He had made his overtures at the time of the Chesterfield speech and later and they had been rejected. The next Government would no doubt be a Government for the defence of free trade but it must also have a positive policy and the Liberal leaders had declared their dissent from his ideas on that subject. His position would be worse than in 1894 if he attempted to form a Government in these circumstances. Therefore he would make no such declaration as I suggested.[107]

In another private memorandum dated October 1904 Rosebery frankly admitted it was the fear of taking on political responsibility that inhibited him: 'So strange is my position, that I dare not speak often for, if I did, I might find myself called upon to take the responsibility attaching to a very active part and undertake a leading share in a new administration which I know would be doomed to a speedy catastrophe.'[108]

As Rosebery had ruled out taking on the premiership, it seemed almost certain that the King would send for Campbell-Bannerman if the Liberals regained power. But there was also the remote possibility that Earl Spencer, the Party leader in the Lords, would become Prime Minister, in which case Rosebery, it was said, might be persuaded to serve as Foreign Secretary. The King visited Mentmore in February 1905 and expressed the hope that Rosebery would take part in a Liberal government. 'I told him that I was not in favour with the Liberal party, when he interrupted and said that I was the one thing they wanted very much. He knew more about it than I did. Later I said I had nothing to do with the Liberal party, that I did not even sit among them, to which he responded, "Yes, that's just the pity".'[109] Rosebery reinforced the point in a letter to the King: 'There are circumstances under which association with a Government is inconsistent with personal honour and would do more harm than good to the public service. That is certainly the case when one is aware that one is at most only in partial agreement with its chief or principal members. The Liberal party has had the opportunity of adopting the policy in which I believe and has determined otherwise. That it was free to do but its freedom gives me mine.'[110] Despite what he said to Rosebery's face, the King was not in truth enthusiastic about him becoming Foreign Secretary: later in 1905 the Duchess of Sutherland reported Edward VII as having said to her, 'in a whisper of mysterious emphasis', that Rosebery 'is a Francophobe and in the present condition of affairs that would be most dangerous.'[111]

Throughout the first half of 1905, as he wandered from one of his great houses to another or ventured to the Continent, Rosebery was preoccupied with the question of whether he would serve in a Liberal government. The answer was usually in the negative. 'After ten years of comparative freedom I should ill accommodate myself to official bonds,' he wrote in one memorandum of 2 March. 'Nor am I any longer fit for it, according to the high standards which I conceive to be necessary.' If Rosebery was reluctant to serve at all, why had he bothered with that speech at Chesterfield, and the Liberal League? The answer he found for himself: to prevent moderate men leaving the Liberal party, and thereby to halt the drift to Little Englander extremism which would have stopped a Liberal victory. There was some justification in this. If Rosebery's Liberal League had not been formed, there is little doubt that much of the money and imperialist talent it attracted would have been lost to the Liberal cause.

Rosebery confessed that 'I could have done much more had I thrown myself headlong into the fray', but the result would have been that 'I should have been compelled to take office, which has never been in my contemplation.'[112] Never can there have been a modern politician who was more devoted to introspection than to action. He travelled to Naples in May, and with Mount Vesuvius erupting in the background indulged in yet another bout of self-communing: 'My best course would be total and final retirement,' he wrote on the 3rd. Because of his loathing for the party machine, the only alternative would be to speak as an independent. But, he asked, 'Is it worth while to spend the few remaining years of one's life in embarrassing one's friends in office by maintaining an independent political position and raising the voice of one crying in the wilderness? The question answers itself.' In conclusion, he felt he was 'near the time at which I shall bid a final farewell to the political scene'.[113]

Not surprisingly, his erstwhile political allies in the Liberal League had already given up on him, worn out by waiting and wondering. Margot Asquith, who had long since decided that Rosebery did not have 'the public spirit or unselfishness' to lead the party, told St Loe Strachey of the *Spectator* in January 1905 that 'he was definitely not going back into political life', and therefore 'I want you in your paper not to talk of a Rosebery administration but an Asquith one.'[114] In July Grey, Asquith and Haldane dined at Berkeley Square in one last half-hearted attempt to persuade Rosebery to return. Rosebery himself wrote to Haldane the following morning, 18 July, that 'our dinner and discussion [was] singularly futile and hopeless. I think in some way I must have been responsible for this; if so, I am sorry. But the fact is that the situation does not in any way clear up and my political vision is clogged and dim.'[115]

After this, the three men decided to act on their own, without consulting Rosebery. A couple of months later they met at Relugas, Grey's fishing lodge in Morayshire, where they drew up a private compact by which they pledged to refuse to serve under Campbell-Bannerman unless he agreed to accept a peerage and to give Asquith the Chancellorship of the Exchequer, Grey the Foreign Office and Haldane the Woolsack. None of this was conveyed to Rosebery, either at the time or when Asquith visited Dalmeny in October. Instead Haldane, who had been discreetly cultivating a strong relationship with the Palace, informed Sir Francis Knollys, the King's private secretary, of the Relugas plan. 'One longs for Rosebery,' wrote Haldane, explaining the compact. 'Had he been coming in to his right place at the head of affairs, we could have gone anywhere with confidence. But it seems now as if this were not to be and we have to do the only thing we can do, which is to follow resolutely a plan of concerted action.'[116] Four days later Knollys replied pointing out how disastrous it would be if the trio refused office: the King would be forced either to accept Campbell-Bannerman without the moderates, or to look for an alternative Prime Minister. 'I grieve to say that I look upon Rosebery as being out of the question for reasons you and I know only too well. The King will be in a most unfortunate position if you do not accept,' he said.[117]

Once more, just as at the time of Chesterfield, the senior Liberal Leaguers were to find that they had severely underestimated Campbell-Bannerman's resilience. Before he dealt with them, however, he considered it was time to bring down the curtain on that long-running farce, the speculation over Rosebery's position. In August Earl Spencer had visited Mentmore; as he should have expected, when he raised the subject in the billiard room just before dinner he received no clear answer about the future, as Rosebery's account reveals: 'As I moved to the door, Spencer said, "I hope you will be with us when we come in," or some such words. So I murmured something about all that having passed by for me, that I had resigned in 1896 and that was a definite act. Then he said something – I know not what exactly – about my powers of speaking but I did not and do not understand what that had to do with the question. So I replied, "Oh, you will have plenty of speakers without me", and by that time had gone into the hall, where the conversation had to drop which I had been eluding all day.'[118] To his brother, Spencer wrote that Rosebery had said 'You must know that I am not to be considered any more in such matters.'[119] When Spencer reported to Campbell-Bannerman what had happened, the Liberal leader replied, 'It is a miserable mistake for him to cut himself off from the party and from active public life but he has gone so far it must be taken as final.'[120] Privately, Campbell-Bannerman was only too relieved, telling J.A. Spender he had been 'not very anxious' that Spencer's mission should succeed.

The final separation was confirmed in the late autumn of 1905, when the issue of Irish Home Rule arose once again. In his speeches since 1899, particularly at Liverpool in 1902, Rosebery had moved away from the traditional Gladstonian policy, largely because the Irish nationalists under John Redmond now sought an 'independent Parliament' rather than simply devolution within the United Kingdom. Apart from Perks, most of the other Liberal Imperialists still adhered to the principle of Home Rule; they believed, however, that it should be achieved by gradual stages rather than by a single legislative onslaught, and only on the condition that throughout the process the supremacy of the Imperial Parliament at

Westminster was maintained. This 'step by step' approach, as it was called by Asquith, involved such measures as stronger local government, reforms of the British administration at Dublin Castle, and executive devolution before the creation of an Irish legislative assembly. They also argued that the Liberal party should work in sympathy with British public opinion rather than allow the Irish nationalists to dictate policy. 'If we are to get a majority in the next House of Commons, it can only be by making it perfectly clear to the electors that it will be no part of the policy of the new Liberal government to introduce a Home Rule Bill in the new Parliament,' wrote Asquith to the Chief Whip, Herbert Gladstone, on 22 October.[121]

Rosebery's distance from his colleagues now worked disastrously against him. With his usual inconsistency he contradicted his pledges of imminent retirement by embarking on a speaking tour of the West Country. Adopting the role of outside spectator, at Stourbridge on 25 October he called for a definitive statement on Home Rule from the Liberal party, telling his audience, 'Any middle policy – that of placing Home Rule in the position of a reliquary and only exhibiting it at great moments of public stress, as Roman Catholics are accustomed to exhibit the relics of a saint – is not one which will earn sympathy or success in this country.' Unknown to Rosebery, a 'middle policy' was exactly what the Liberals and the Irish were now planning. At the beginning of November Campbell-Bannerman held detailed negotiations with Asquith and the Irish leaders, as a result of which he committed his party to the 'step by step' policy. In discussions with Redmond and T.P. O'Connor he assured them that he was personally 'stronger than ever' on Home Rule, though he had to be realistic about what he could achieve. It was rumoured that another item may have featured on the agenda of these talks: the future of Rosebery. According to a report in the *Daily Mail*, Redmond extracted a pledge from Campbell-Bannerman that the Earl would not serve in his government. There is no evidence of this in the Campbell-Bannerman papers, nor is it mentioned in the account of the meeting left by Redmond – but the Rosebery papers contain an intriguing note from Perks, who saw Alfred Harmsworth at the beginning of December and asked him about the *Daily Mail*'s story: 'He said he has an Irishman on his staff who is "close" to the Irish leaders. This was the source and Harmsworth was certain it was correct.'[122]

Soon after these negotiations, in a speech at Stirling on 23 November, Campbell-Bannerman outlined his Irish policy. Attempting to encompass both Irish nationalism and Asquithian gradualism, he was deliberately ambiguous. Having promised that 'the opportunity of making a great advance on this question of Irish Government will not be long delayed', he urged the Irish to accept any instalment of devolution 'provided it was consistent with and led up to the larger policy'. Though this was in line with the agreed 'step by step' approach, many newspapers, particularly the Irish *Freeman's Journal*, chose to interpret Campbell-Bannerman's vague remarks as a declaration in favour of Home Rule. As he read the press coverage while travelling between speaking engagements in Cornwall, Rosebery took the same view. He regarded the Stirling speech as a direct personal challenge, and determined to counter it. At a well attended meeting at Bodmin on 25 November, he denounced the way Campbell-Bannerman had 'hoisted once more, in its most pronounced form, the flag of Irish Home Rule'. He objected to that flag because 'it impairs the unity of the free trade party and it indefinitely postpones legislation on social and educational reform on which the country has set its heart. I, then, will add no more on this subject, except to say emphatically and explicitly and once and for all that I cannot serve under that banner.'

Like so many of his important speeches, Rosebery's Bodmin outburst caused a sensation. Most of the Liberal party saw it as an act of cruel disloyalty, just when the party had revived under Campbell-Bannerman's leadership. Winston Churchill, now firmly in the Liberal camp, told Lord Hugh Cecil: 'Rosebery indeed has broken his own crockery. Was there ever such an unrelated, reckless and ill-judged pronouncement? How he could! Not one single friend was consulted with and he has continued to irritate the whole party by sticking it at a critical moment. I am really very sorry about it, for you know how much I like him and how kind he has always been to me. That he should stand apart from a Liberal government is not serious – for that he always intended to do. But the purposeless sacrifice of his influence is a new and ugly feature in a situation already complex.'[123] John Morley's comment was that 'the lonely furrow will be lonely indeed. A pity!' The Liberal Imperialists were particularly embittered by the threat to their carefully developed Irish scheme – for Rosebery, as President of the League, was seen by many as speaking on their behalf. Grey, usually the most loyal of Roseberyites, wrote to him in distress: 'C.B's Stirling speech wasn't intended as you take it. Asquith discussed Ireland with him in London; got an assurance that C.B. agreed with Asquith's Irish declaration and Asquith has now telegraphed to me that he regards the sense of C.B's speech, which you have denounced, to be quite innocuous. This is a pleasant situation for me! If it wasn't for feelings of personal friendship I should not mind. But, as it is, I feel full of strange oaths. I can't desert Asquith and I want to defend you. I feel dead beat at that.' Asquith himself was furious, as Harry Poulton, the Liberal League

MP, reported to Rosebery two days after Bodmin: 'I called at Asquith's chambers in the Temple and was never more taken aback in my life. I found him, so far from being pleased as I expected, very much put out and indeed angry. He has interpreted C.B's speech in an entirely opposite sense and says that everyone has done so including Haldane. They regard your utterance as a positive disaster. To me this came as a shock indescribable. Asquith said you had damned the whole lot with the charge of officially raising the Home Rule flag. He claimed that attacks on C.B. were natural from the Irish and the Tories but wrong and unjustifiable from one in your position.'[124] In his rage, Asquith told Morley: 'never was anything so disloyal. It is us – his own friends – whom he forces into humiliation and capitulation.' Asquith then ridiculed 'the notion of Rosebery now being able on any terms to come into the Liberal Government'.[125]

Rosebery had to face up to the enormity of the error he had made. As Spender warned him on 29 November, 'The blame is put on you. The Tories will not spare you but will use you as a gift from the Gods to them and as a scourge for the unhappy Liberal party. The weakness of the position from your point of view is that there is no possible alternative to C.B.' Spender even feared the Tories would ruthlessly use Rosebery's speech in the imminent election, foreseeing every hoarding placarded with big posters: 'Lord Rosebery's advice to electors: "Don't fight under the Bannerman Banner." What isn't good enough for Rosebery to fight for isn't good enough for you to vote for.'[126] Shocked by the reaction to his speech, Rosebery retreated to The Durdans, and there sank further into depression. What made him particularly bitter was that neither Asquith nor Grey had consulted him. Though they knew he was speaking in Cornwall, they had failed to send him any communication informing him of Asquith's discussions with Campbell-Bannerman, as he complained to Grey on 28 November: 'How could I guess that conference? How could I divine it? Is it not a pity that I should be kept entirely in the dark with regard to a matter of such supreme importance, particularly when I was on a speaking tour?'[127] When Spender dined with Rosebery that night, he found him 'in a savage and despairing temper. He denounced Asquith and Grey in unmeasured terms, accusing them of having abandoned him, saying he had done with public life, having no party and no friends. He had consulted those with him in Cornwall and they all agreed the Stirling speech meant Home Rule. His brain was not good enough to interpret the language of a speech, and he was not fit therefore to take a leading part in politics. Of course now he is "sorry he spoke" but he sees no way of unsaying it.'[128]

Rosebery had only himself to blame. He was the one who had rejected attempts at co-operation over the previous two years, claiming to have retired from politics and to have no interest in taking office. And as he ploughed his lonely furrow he had rarely consulted colleagues about his own actions, so it was somewhat hypocritical of him to attack others for behaving the same way. Once his anger had cooled, however, Rosebery was clear-sighted enough to recognise that his own diffidence was part of the problem. In a revealing letter to Asquith of 28 December, he said that before Bodmin 'I knew you were overwhelmingly busy and did not like to trouble you. Moreover, there was a certain shyness on my part, and reluctance to appear to interfere too much in a political future in which I had renounced any official share. You, I think, have much the same shyness, and even in conversation we waited for the other to begin.' But he still expressed regret that Asquith had failed to send him so much as a telegram about Ireland: had he done so, then 'I would gladly have been silent. For during two years I have been sweating (there is no other word) for unity in the Free Trade party.'[129]

In his letter to Asquith Rosebery kept repeating that he had no desire for office, while in his own personal memorandum about the Bodmin fiasco he asserted that the Liberal Imperialists had failed to consult him because 'they were well aware that I was not prepared to accept office in any shape, and so communication with me would have only compromised them needlessly.'[130] But Rosebery's statements should never be taken at face value. For all his protestations about retirement, there undoubtedly still lurked within him a yearning to be the centre of attention. Even if he genuinely did not want to hold office, he would have liked to be made an offer. The actor in him would have enjoyed the melodrama, the grand seigneur in him would have relished the entreaties. The idea that Rosebery had not entirely ruled out office is given some credibility by a letter J.A. Spender – who saw more of him at this time than anyone else – wrote to Lord Crewe in 1930: 'Up to the time of the Bodmin speech, Rosebery had by no means made up his mind to stand out from the Campbell-Bannerman Government and he felt somewhat aggrieved at being kept out of the counsels of the party while his particular friends, Asquith and Grey, had been consulted about everything. If there was this exclusion, Spencer, I think, was responsible for it. Spencer told me that he had put the question direct to Rosebery in August and had received a flat refusal to join. No doubt, Spencer reported this to C.B. However, in a later conversation, Rosebery said that "no proposal had been made" to him and he had declined nothing.'[131] This contradicts the impression he had given everyone else, Lord Spencer included, but simply proves how oddly the mind of 'The Great Sphinx' worked.

Campbell-Bannerman was only too pleased with Rosebery's Bodmin outburst, for it freed him from any possibility of having to negotiate with him. As his friend T.R. Buchanan recorded, 'C.B. came to the conclusion that Rosebery's step had cleared the air, delivered him from the difficulty of having to ask Rosebery to join, and that those most embarrassed would be Rosebery's own friends in the party, the Leaguers, particularly Asquith, Grey and Haldane.'[132] To Asquith he wrote, 'My only complaint against our friend is his saying that "I raised a banner". It was he who stirred the waters at Stourbridge by challenging us either to put Home Rule away altogether or make it our foremost object. I am bound to say that was nothing but mischief. However, I do not think any harm has come of the episode. One effect, it seems to me, is to clinch the argument in favour of the broad course.'[133] Against this background, the question arises: did Campbell-Bannerman deliberately use his Stirling speech to goad Rosebery into that self-destructive statement? Both the *Daily Mail* story and Harmsworth's letter to Perks carry a suggestion of some sort of deal between Campbell-Bannerman and Redmond, and certainly the Stirling declaration had a nationalist tinge to it; it is interesting that in all his welter of vague language Campbell-Bannerman never once used the phrase 'step by step'.

Certainly Rosebery always believed he had been the victim of a calculated act, writing to Spender on 19 December, 'I cannot modify my interpretation of the Stirling speech. The *Daily Mail* argues that the speech of C.B. was made with the intention of excluding me. If that is so, it was superfluous.'[134] Several others believed Campbell-Bannerman had indeed subtly manipulated Rosebery into his rashness at Bodmin. Hudson Kearley, a Liberal League member who was soon to serve in Campbell-Bannerman's Government and accompanied Rosebery on his speaking tour, later wrote in his memoirs that Stirling was 'a master stroke. Rosebery made the fatal mistake of many clever men: he had underestimated his adversary. C.B. had laid a very simple trap and Rosebery had walked into it.' The journalist Henry Lucy recorded in his diary in December 1905 that 'C.B., not being disposed to have two kings on the Cabinet throne, threw a fly with an eye to Lord Rosebery's whereabouts. The bait being taken, he was the last man inclined to relieve the fish of the consequent embarrassment.'[135] On the other hand, Campbell-Bannerman seems to have been taken aback by the ferocity of Rosebery's reaction to his Stirling speech. 'What a bombshell in a certain camp (not ours) is Barnbougle's public repudiation of Home Rule. I think he is off his head,' he told James Bryce – not exactly the words of someone involved in trying to manipulate the situation.[136] And Buchanan recorded that Campbell-Bannerman was initially annoyed by the Bodmin speech, hardly the reaction of a leader who has laid a successful trap. There was certainly no collaboration with Asquith, as Margot's diary for 26 November seems to make clear: 'I cursed both Rosebery and C.B. in the train to London to Henry, who said he would like to knock their heads together.' A few days later she was cursing again, this time 'the cruel fate of Henry having to work with a cur like Rosebery and a blunderer like C.B.'[137]

What is certain is that the Unionists, in desperate straits, hopelessly divided and the losers of 22 by-elections in the previous three years, took heart from Rosebery's speech, imagining that it signalled a fatal schism in the Liberal party over Ireland. 'The squall has given us hope,' Lord Hugh Cecil told Margot Asquith.[138] Balfour had been considering resignation since 2 November, when he told Joseph Chamberlain that he was tired of office and wanted to give the Liberals the awkward task of trying to form a government before the General Election which had to be held soon. On 4 December, as the ructions over Bodmin continued, he finally resigned, and the King decided to send for Campbell-Bannerman. J.A. Spender still held out the remote hope that, despite everything, Rosebery might be part of the new administration. He had been to The Durdans and found the Earl in a contrite mood, apparently willing to be supportive and perhaps, he thought, even prepared to consider office. Putting his most optimistic interpretation on these facts he rushed to Campbell-Bannerman's London home. But he found that the Liberal leader was not to be denied his moment of triumph. According to Spender's account,

> He was in the highest spirits and overflowing with the little quips which never failed him in good times and bad. He said he was expecting a summons from 'Jupiter' (he nearly always spoke of King Edward as 'Jupiter') and it might cause him to get up and leave me abruptly at any moment, but in the meantime he was very glad to have news of 'the Lord' ('Barnbougle' or 'the Lord' were his usual designations for Rosebery). Did he come this time with a sword or an olive branch? I made my unauthorised communication and left him to judge, saying what I could for the expediency of letting the Bodmin quarrel rest, even if he could not see his way to saying anything soothing. Then he twinkled all over, as only C.B. could twinkle, and after some moments of apparent reflection delivered his ultimatum, 'Will you please tell Lord Rosebery that within two hours from now I expect to have accepted the King's commission to form a Government, and that being so,

I can obviously say no more about the Irish question until I have an opportunity of consulting my colleagues in the Cabinet.' There could scarcely have been a more skilful answer or the closing of a chapter with a more deadly politeness.[139]

But Rosebery always denied that he had given any positive message to Spender, or was willing to make any overture to Campbell-Bannerman, and in a letter to Rosebery of 30 September 1927 Spender admitted that he had had 'no authority' when he went to the Liberal Leader.[140]

As soon as Campbell-Bannerman accepted the King's commission, the Relugas compact collapsed. Asquith, who had been at best half-hearted about the plan, immediately accepted office as Chancellor of the Exchequer. Intriguingly, one of his private reasons for doing so was to avoid giving any succour to Rosebery, so disillusioned was he with his former ally. 'The worst feature of standing out is that it plays into Rosebery's hands,' he told Margot after Relugas.[141] Haldane soon followed, as War Secretary. Grey's loyalty to Rosebery caused him to hold out for a time. As Regy Esher recorded, 'Grey feels that Rosebery gave him his first chance in politics and he cannot, he thinks, properly desert him' – a position Margot found incomprehensible: 'I am so amazed at Grey's feeling for Rosebery and his really thinking – as he undoubtedly does – that Rosebery is a man worth making sacrifices for. That such a wise, steadfast brave man as Edward Grey should love Rosebery is a problem I cannot attempt to unravel.'[142] But his loyalty to the party and to his friends Asquith and Haldane eventually persuaded him to accept the Foreign Office. To Munro-Ferguson he explained his thinking: 'Rosebery's outburst about Home Rule has had a bad effect on our prospects for the Election, and we cannot stand them being made any worse by any of us standing out. That is the deciding factor as I know it.'[143]

Rosebery wrote affectionate letters to his League vice-presidents, and at a meeting of the League on 11 December praised them for their patriotism. He maintained that one of the central purposes of the League had been to secure office for those Imperialists who might otherwise be kept out by the Radicals. 'The League must feel that it has not lived and worked in vain when it sees its vice-presidents in positions of high and conspicuous trust,' he said. But privately he was distraught over the way 'C.B. has won all along the line', to use Esher's words. For the last four years he had been locked in an epic struggle with Campbell-Bannerman. He had lost comprehensively, and had been deserted by all but a straggling band of devotees. In all his political life he had never been so irrelevant, so sidelined. As a mere youth he had been courted by Gladstone and Disraeli. Now he was ignored. On 12 December the Asquiths met Spender at a luncheon. 'He told us he had been with Lord Rosebery, who was really unhappy and bitter that he had been told nothing and knew nothing. He spoke with a good deal of feeling for Rosebery, whose failure he looks on as tragic,' recorded Margot in her diary. That sense of Rosebery's irrelevance was confirmed in January 1906, when the Liberals enjoyed the greatest landslide victory in their history and sent the Tories to the worst defeat they were to know until 1997. Rosebery's Bodmin speech had not affected the outcome in the slightest.

Rosebery had often threatened to commit political suicide in the past. The irony of Bodmin was that it was all a terrible accident.

16

'What a wicked, clever woman'

JUST BEFORE THE Chesterfield speech in December 1901, the *Daily Mail* carried a profile of Rosebery. After praising his political achievements, the article went on: 'Underlying all this scintillating surface there is a grim and terrible pathos in his life – the pathos of utter solitude. Unseen by the crowd of admirers who worship and envy him in his proud supremacy, unrecognised by those who write and speak of him as a well-known friend, there is an almost tragic loneliness in his position. He has not a single intimate; there is not a living creature with whom he can entirely throw off the garment that hides his inner self. He is, even in the midst of the applauding multitude at a reception or at his own dinner table, always alone. This seclusion is extraordinary in so prominent a man.'

Even as a child Rosebery had been self-contained. As an adult, he spent days at a time with only his books and thoughts for company. Those who stayed as his guests in his various homes were often surprised by how little they saw of him, since he often remained in the privacy of his own rooms. On one occasion at Dalmeny he ignored a house party for an entire weekend, except for a brief visit to the library to pick up a penknife. But although solitude was a habit of long standing Rosebery had missed the warmth of genuine intimacy since Hannah's death, while doubting that he could ever recapture the companionship he had once experienced with her. 'Rosebery is not cheerful. He complains of loneliness. Marriage frightens him. He cannot believe in a fresh, disinterested affection. As if that mattered to anyone who understands love,' wrote Regy Brett to his friend the Reverend C.D. Williamson in 1895. 'I disapprove of second marriages but I suppose the Prime Minister cannot these days have a mistress. Certainly he requires an intimate friend. Or he will die.'[1] Rosebery had so far managed to survive without an 'intimate friend', but the pain of his solitude had not eased. Again it was Regy who in 1902 recorded Rosebery talking of his 'great loneliness at Dalmeny. All his family are scattered. Peggy is married. Sybil is unable to live in the north since her illness. Neil is at Oxford, Harry in London. He is to be pitied. Rosebery has sacrificed too much to ambition, a fatal thing for happiness – unless it really fills a man's life. And this only happens to Napoleon natures when success is achieved.'[2]

During the years after Hannah's death there were many women who would have been only too glad to help Rosebery end his solitude, whether as his second wife or even as his mistress. Behind a façade of strict morality extra-marital affairs were widely tolerated among the aristocracy, provided that they were conducted with mannerly discretion. Indeed, in the set that revolved around the substantial figure of the pleasure-seeking King, adultery was almost a social convention. Some eager attempts were made to entice Rosebery into this world of deliciously furtive liaisons. The Liberal supporter Lady Colebrooke, wife of one of the King's Lords-in-Waiting, who called herself 'the Vyper', was obviously smitten with Rosebery, as her flirtatious letters to him reveal. In October 1906 she invited him to join a house party hosted by the Earl of Home: 'It's so good for you instead of dining tête-à-tête with your secretary and we want you so badly. This is not gush but everybody loves meeting you which you probably know. It's always such fun when you are there. I have tried every bed in the house and found a comfortable one for you.' In another letter, after a visit to Dalmeny, she wrote, 'I was shocked to hear that I behaved in such an undignified fashion at Dalmeny. I run after you in a disgusting fashion and quail before you – such an odd combination.'[3] It was the Vyper who informed Rosebery that Ishbel Aberdeen, wife of the 7th Earl, was in love with him, and had been distressed when he rejected her: 'She told me with tears in her eyes that you were the one man she loved (next to Lord Aberdeen) and you had dropped her. How cruel of you to play fast and loose with her,' wrote the Vyper in her teasing manner.[4]

Another who made advances both amorous and political was the beautiful blue-eyed and tempestuous Countess of Warwick, who never allowed herself to feel inhibited by her wedding vows. As the heiress Frances Maynard with an income of more than £30,000 a year she had been marked down by Queen Victoria as a possible bride for Prince Leopold, the Duke of Albany. But Daisy, as she was always known, was not one to bow to the dictates of others, even the Queen, and she refused Prince Leopold's offer. Instead, in 1881 she gave her hand to Lord Brooke, son and heir of the Earl of Warwick. Within five years she had embarked on her first affair, with the dashing naval officer Lord Charles Beresford. So explosive was their relationship that the Prince of Wales, a friend of Beresford, felt compelled to intervene to ensure it did not become a public scandal. The Prince in his turn soon fell in love with Daisy, who was delighted to play the role of Royal favourite. The affair, perhaps the most intense of the Prince's many romances, lasted throughout the early 1890s, and Princess Alexandra confessed to Rosebery that during this time she 'hated Lady Warwick'.[5] But 'Darling Daisy', who had become Countess of Warwick on the death of her father-in-law in 1893, was no orthodox aristocratic hostess. Within her burned not just physical passion but also a growing anger at injustice and poverty. These feelings were greatly sharpened in 1895 when the left-wing *Clarion* newspaper savagely attacked her for organising a luxurious fancy-dress ball at a time of high unemployment. In a rage, she tore up to London to challenge the editor, Robert Blatchford. Unperturbed by the irruption into his office of a famous and wrathful society beauty, Blatchford stood his ground and calmly gave Daisy an hour-long lecture on socialist economics. In the train on the way home, Daisy recorded, 'I thought and thought about all that I had been hearing and learning. I knew my outlook on life could never be the same as before this incident.'[6]

Daisy's growing radicalism spelt the end of her affair with the Prince, who was bored by her philanthropy and abhorred the very word 'socialism', but it drew her towards the greatest name in progressive politics. She had met Rosebery in 1894 at Dunrobin Castle, and from 1896 they became close friends, so close that Rosebery agreed to stand godfather to her son Maynard, born in 1898. Daisy quite openly assured Rosebery that he was 'what schoolgirls call "an ideal"', but whether he returned her devotion remains a matter of conjecture, since almost all his letters to her were burnt in a serious fire at her Essex home, Easton Lodge. Her own correspondence conveys a sense of a woman deeply in love, but often exasperated by the aloofness shown her by the object of her desire. Ignored by historians until now, these letters are some of the most revealing ever written to Rosebery. The first inkling of her admiration appears in an invitation to Warwick Castle in February 1895, in the course of which she told him that 'your own personality teaches a lesson of strength and courage and sorrows overcome'.[7] She invited him to Warwick again in May 1896: 'It will be a real pleasure if you can come for a quiet talk – and perchance there will be a nightingale.'[8] Writing in September from Dunrobin, where Rosebery had just been staying, she dared a new level of endearment and veneration.

> The party here is very commonplace now that you have left but my compensation has been to dream of you for three consecutive nights, giving me, I think, some sort of right to send you a letter, although such a course would break the spell. I would like to give such poor service as I can render to your interests if you will give me your friendship and trust me. Your career has

always been to me the subject of the keenest admiration and interest. Most women have ideals of great men and you have been mine. This is not written hastily but since we met here I have had two years to 'consider' you and to pluck up the courage to tell you that I should be proud to be of some use to you – ever! I don't mean that I could ever be the 'political platform' woman but there are other quiet ways in which one can work and influence. I have a true sympathy with your ambitions. It would be unbecoming and unnecessary to allude to the keen attraction of your personality but I may add that your friendship would be my most valued possession.[9]

Flattered but claiming to be a little overwhelmed, Rosebery wrote back two days later:

My personality has not attracted many people in my life so at this time of day a spontaneous offer of help from a brilliant and beautiful woman comes as a sort of miracle. What can I give you in return? My friendship in the usual sense is worth very little. I am a wretched correspondent; a solitary being, more and more rooted in loneliness and destined, it seems, to be more and more solitary. I need not draw the contrast with yourself. If you accept my friendship, you must know the worst or at least what I believe to be the worst. As to the power of a woman like yourself, I hold the strongest views. It is not the 'political platform' woman that exercises power I mean. It is social charm and insight that turns all men topsy turvey and has a force in these days that is almost alarming. You yourself are an instance. When feminine fascination and spirit are thrown in the balance against a man, that man is doomed. I do not think this is right or fair, but it is so. Is this power to be wielded on my side? It seems almost too much to hope.[10]

Daisy, overjoyed by such a positive response, replied in the most forward terms, hinting at the ease with which they might meet secretly in London. 'Of woman's powers, such as mine are are laid at your feet. I know more of your thoughts than you think. I have taken a house in London as an "office", having much in hand that can only be realized in London. If you ever want to see me or send for me, I shall be there. If, however humbly and before the sun sets, I can ever feel I have been of some slight use to the man who shadows all public men in my thoughts, I shall be rewarded.'[11] The friendship blossomed, and Rosebery saw her both in Colchester, which he visited for the annual oyster festival, and in Paris. Yet an element of frustration began to creep into the correspondence, perhaps because Rosebery was not fulsome or forward enough in reciprocating Daisy's feelings. At Christmas 1896 she flirtatiously expressed her 'heartfelt wishes' that 'all your desires be fulfilled (or at least as many as are good for you)', then added, 'Have you been to Paris again? I found myself accused of *pursuing you* to Oyster feasts and then to Paris. The former I certainly plead guilty to. My subsequent pursuit was hardly so successful. Perhaps my stay in Paris would have been pleasanter had I seen you more than *once*.'

Over the following years Daisy kept striving for a greater intimacy. In 1899 she told him she 'would like to see inside your house, which I have never yet done', adding provocatively that after reading about Rosebery in William Cory's journal, 'I know he and I would have an understanding.'[12]★ For all the apparent distance Rosebery maintained, it would be wrong to dismiss the possibility of some dalliance between them. He certainly felt more towards her than most women, as is plain from this note of 1897, accompanying a birthday present: 'I send you a little umbrella to shield you from the weather when you listen to the nightingales.' In early 1900 during the Boer War Rosebery travelled incognito to Paris, where he met Daisy for a few days. She recorded that they dined tête-à-tête, and he also invited her to share his box at the theatre. Unfortunately, anti-British feeling was at its height, and as soon as the former Prime Minister was recognised by the audience, 'a menacing growl' went round the theatre. 'Very soon there was a tap on our box door and the Chief Inspector of the Paris Police came to warn us that it would not be safe for us to leave the theatre by the usual way. He had brought with him an escort of police to protect us while we escaped by a back way before the crowd could realize we had gone. By this time the whole theatre was calling out: "A bas les Anglais! Vive les Boers!"'[13] The following words about her attitudes to infidelity and sex, written to Rosebery after Paris, are perhaps significant: 'My conscience is never troubled save if I have been mean or unjust or hurt someone in deed. Far too much fuss, in my opinion, is made by women about personal morality which, after all, is entirely a matter for the individual. I have very high ideals and up to the present they are not satisfied so that truly Diana is more appropriate to my mode of life (even in Paris!) than Catharine II. Please let me meet you *alone* when I next see you.' She also expressed a longing to be with him 'on the marble terrace of the Naples villa or any-where else'.[14] In October she went up to Dalmeny, a visit she 'truly enjoyed' – but, as always, she wanted to be closer: 'Let me dine alone with you (it won't compromise either of us). You can send me a telegram and I can always come up for a night.'[15]

Daisy continually urged Rosebery to re-establish himself on the national stage of politics and thereby fulfil his destiny to be 'the greatest statesman of them all'. In the same letter of May 1900 in which she referred to the

---

★A reference to *The Letters and Journals of William Cory*, edited by F.W. Cornish (1897).

Roman goddess Diana, she told Rosebery, 'I don't believe you realize all your name means in this country today. You say people do not tell you of it but they are afraid of you and of intruding upon you. Most of the young Conservatives and enthusiastic ones would break with the present state of affairs and throw in their lot with you. I hear it every day. I know them and they want to throw their lot in with you. Lord Salsibury's days are closing in. You cannot leave a Balfour or a Chamberlain to take the lead. You and you alone are the man. You shut yourself up and you don't know your own popularity – or you pretend you don't.' But sometime during 1901 her ardour cooled. Perhaps she wearied of his insensitivity: after Chesterfield, she confessed that though she was 'full of the hero-worship that you know is inherent in me', she would say little because 'last time we met you hurt me by your flippancy and I was, I fear, somewhat discourteous.'[16] There was another reason for her coldness, however: her new lover, Captain Joseph Laycock of the Queen's Guards, ruggedly masculine and one of the richest men in England. From 1901 onwards her letters to Rosebery express only regrets about the past and his failure to take a real political lead. In one, undated but probably from sometime in 1902 or 1903, she is fascinating on the subject of her own and the King's opinions of Rosebery:

> The country wants you and won't wait. I know you have no incentive to work. You have got everything and had everything in the world. But surely a great opportunity like the present is given to few? . . . I can't write to you as I want and wish. I seem to see your cynical smile as you read. But I don't care. I wish I lived in your house as a secretary or a charwoman and could give you a good talking to at least twice a week. You must do something for us all who spend our lives in 'hero-worship' and you've got to justify it. The King is as anxious about you as I am. He implores you to reconstruct the Liberal party. The King said, 'How can I send for C.B.? I shall have to if Rosebery *will* not take his opportunity and I *can't* do that!' He added, 'Why does Rosebery hang back? I think I know *why*. He is a *Conservative* at heart!!' This was too much for me! I plainly said that you are a Liberal of the very best and strongest type and clearest conscience. Oh say they are not true. Prove they are not true.

In 1904 Joe Laycock, now a major, ended his affair with Daisy in order to look after his wife, who had been horribly injured in a car accident in which she lost both a leg and an arm. Distraught, Daisy threw herself into her political work, becoming ever more left-wing and joining the Marxist Social Democratic Federation. Writing to Rosebery she set out her new political vision, and her sadness at the way his prospects had faded. 'I once longed to see you in the forefront of the great reform movement. And you told me you didn't care and I wanted to be your close friend – to encourage, inspire and serve you with such wits and brains as I have. But you *wilfully* dropped behind and I had to go on. And a wide river rolls between us now and neither of us can ever bridge it. It is unlikely I shall ever see you again.' She hoped that socialism would create a new world, 'setting men free from the money greed and the money terror, from the need to struggle to deprive other men of the necessities of life. You know I always put love first in all things and gave all in my love – now the belief is the same, only it has merged into love of humanity.'[17] Her love of humanity led to debts of £90,000, the transformation of Easton Lodge into a trades union college and animal sanctuary, the letting of Warwick Castle to an American family and, eventually, standing as a candidate for the Labour party, with Communist support, against a young Anthony Eden in the 1923 General Election. Just before that contest, in 1922, she sent Rosebery a final, poignant letter. 'Perhaps you have forgotten me. Please believe me that I never forget you – in our short intimacy, your kindness to me and all the dreams that I built up around your political career that you were too indifferent to grasp. I have had a wonderful and interesting life – but how I wish that fate had made me a man.'[18]

Daisy was never able to offer Rosebery the prospect that she would become his wife. Yet ever since Hannah's death rumours had persisted about his remarriage. His name was linked with a host of eligible women, including Princess Maud, youngest daughter of the Prince of Wales, and Georgiana, the majestic Dowager Countess of Dudley. In 1898 the Unionist MP Lord Balcarres noted excitedly in his diary after seeing the *Times* journalist Perceval Landon, 'It is interesting to learn that Lord Rosebery is most anxious to marry Lady Egmont, widow of Lord Egmont who died quite recently . . . according to Landon's judgement she is somewhat vulgar and would ruin a Foreign Office party.'[19] Rosebery hated gossip on the subject of his remarriage, and when in January 1892 a *Telegraph* reporter quizzed him about his intentions, recorded in his diary that he 'nearly suffocated'. He was particularly annoyed by the announcement that he was to become engaged to Margot Tennant (who married Asquith in 1894), and never completely forgave her for not publicly contradicting the report, as she found when she met him in London soon afterwards: 'I was greeted with such frigid self-suppression that I felt quite exhausted.'[20] She had of course been strongly attached to Rosebery in her youth. 'I was vastly impressed by him and even rather in love,' she wrote in 1904. 'He had about him the look of authority. I did not distinguish between independence and independability.'[21] Towards the end of Rosebery's life she made this confession to him when asking for a signed copy of one of his books: 'I am a very old friend and you are my *first* love. This you did not know but it is true.'[22] If he had known it would have made little difference, for he found Margot far too loud and domineering, and had tried to dissuade Henry Asquith from marrying her. During a long talk at Dalmeny early in 1894 he told him that 'she was quite beautiful but a bad influence'.[23] He also urged Henry, before he went through with the marriage, to read E.F. Benson's novel *Dodo*, whose braying, pretentious heroine was supposed to be modelled on Margot. When Henry reported this remark to Margot, as she later admitted, 'it hurt me profoundly'. Soon afterwards, when the couple visited The Durdans, she took the opportunity to confront Rosebery. 'When I asked him if he would not have prevented my marriage if he could, he did not deny it. He said that he was the only one of my friends who had been doubtful as to my future happiness; to which I replied that if it was *my* happiness over which he was concerned *I* was the person to whom he should have gone, instead of giving oracular warnings to my finacé. I did not want fair-weather friends to stand by me when I was on the top of the wave, and added that if in future I had any matrimonial troubles, he would be the last man I would go to for sympathy or advice.'*

If most of the speculation in the press about Rosebery was nonsense, one story had more than a grain of truth. On 12 November 1892 the *New York Times* carried this report: 'Rumours that Lord Rosebery and Princess Victoria are betrothed have been discussed in the society papers for some time past. While discredited in well-informed circles, no absolute denial has been obtained and consequently credence has been added to them.' Rosebery was indeed attracted to Victoria, the middle of the Prince of Wales's three daughters, because of her looks but also for her shyness and sensitivity, which matched his own. Born in 1868 and known as 'Toria' in the Royal family, she was described by one of the ladies-in-waiting as a 'very sharp, quick, merry, and amusing' child.[24] By her early twenties she had grown into an accomplished, intelligent and graceful young woman who closely resembled her mother in both face and figure. Sadly for her, the Princess of Wales, denied fidelity in her husband, was extremely possessive of her daughters, especially Toria, whose allotted role in life was to serve as her mother's companion. Toria had already bestowed her affections on one socially unsuitable man, the equerry Sir Arthur Davidson, and Princess Alexandra was determined to prevent any other unacceptable liaisons.

During the early 1890s Rosebery came frequently within Princess

---

*From Margot Asquith, *More Memories*.

Victoria's orbit. Both were lonely, Rosebery the temperamental widower, Toria the young romantic trapped in her gilded cage and denied the chance of love. It was perhaps inevitable that a sympathy should develop between them. It appears that in the mid 1890s Rosebery let it be known in Royal circles that he was willing to press his suit. But the Princess of Wales was dismayed at the thought of Toria marrying not merely a non-Royal but a Radical politician, and 'would not hear of it'.[25] The Prince of Wales too was horrified by the idea of becoming the father-in-law of the leader of the Liberal party. Toria's own feelings were entirely ignored, and the possibility of marriage to Rosebery was never raised again. The two remained close over the subsequent years, however, and the tenderness between them is reflected in several of Toria's letters to the Earl. 'It sounds so monotonous & cold each time to say thank you for the lovely present,' she wrote in December 1902, 'but one can't always put in light words what one really feels or wishes to express. I think this broach quite exquisite in every way and shall value and treasure it always. You spoil me dreadfully with these continual & beautiful gifts.'

Three years earlier, in April 1899, Princess Victoria had been one of a Royal party that paid him a visit in Naples, and she obviously delighted in his company, though – as seems to have been the case in all Rosebery's relationships – his reserve managed to inspire an element of fear. On 4 April she sent him a note to ask if he would like to join her for shopping in Naples: '<u>Do</u> come . . . if <u>really</u> it does not <u>bore</u> you. I feel I must be getting on your <u>nerves</u> now! I did enjoy my afternoon <u>so</u> much yesterday.' On the 5th she was due to leave, and Rosebery had given her a memento of her visit, prompting her to write 'One line of goodbye & to tell you once again how <u>much</u> I enjoyed these last two days. You were so kind and sympathetic & it has done me <u>so</u> much good. I shall <u>never</u> forget these days I spent at Naples . . . I cannot tell you how much I shall treasure that lovely pin.' For weeks afterwards she repeatedly told him how enchanted she was with her stay, sent him photographs of her visit, and expressed the hope that nothing should 'interfere with our friendship. May God keep you and bless you forever.' The degree of their familiarity is revealed in a further letter of 25 June 1899 in which she complains about the gossip their relationship inspired: 'I know quite well everything I have written to you is safe . . . Nevertheless, there are always some who insinuate unkind things . . . Some of my relations were not so very nice. But I know I have a true, real friend in you and nowadays there are not so many about either.' Then, perhaps in a reference to the dashed hopes of marriage, she continues: 'I [have] talked [to] no one as I have to you and, as to thinking of dreams or illusions, surely you must think very badly of me should

I insinuate that. On the contrary, it is more than I can ever understand why you should deign to speak to me at all. So how could you possibly offend me in anything you say or do? How I envy you going off yachting. I am sure you will remember our day on board.' She also sends him a present: 'Will you think it <u>very</u> forward of me if I ask you to accept this in remembrance of Naples?'

Princess Victoria's emotions were troubled by the frustrations of their star-crossed affair, as extracts of two letters from 1899 reveal: 'I shall <u>never</u> forget anything of what you said. You must have thought me a fool but I could <u>not</u> answer. You have no idea how difficult it is. So excuse me and try to understand me without words . . . I am <u>proud</u> of the Christian and true friendship you have shown me and I do pray that <u>nothing</u> may change it. You have certainly not added to my troubles and worries. On the contrary, it has been a <u>blessing</u> and help to me to feel I have such a friend.'[26] Sir Francis Knollys, private secretary to Edward both as Prince of Wales and as King, took a vicarious pleasure in his involvement in the couple's friendship. In January 1897, for instance, he wrote to Rosebery from Sandringham, 'Princess Victoria looks a little better and her spirits have improved. She wishes me to tell you she was delighted to hear you were unwell as you always accuse her of being ill whenever you come here and appear to think it is a sham.'[27]

Unmarried and lonely, Princess Victoria grew increasingly embittered by her fate, and sometimes took out her resentment on Rosebery: 'When you are somewhere in my neighbourhood you do not seem to be very enthusiastic about wishing to speak to me,' she wrote in December 1904. In 1905 she was angered by what she saw as Rosebery's disloyalty in dining at Buckingham Palace with the King's lover, Alice Keppel; Rosebery, no moraliser, took 'a charitable view' of the relationship, feeling that 'rightly or wrongly, here was someone who cared for him for himself and to whom he could talk absolutely at ease and in confidence'.[28] In her turn, Princess Victoria offended Rosebery by teasing him for absenting himself from a Royal banquet in November 1908, unaware that it was the sacred anniversary of Hannah's death: 'I am so <u>distressed</u> at having chaffed you about coming to the banquet! I never thought at the time to what anniversary you alluded. Please <u>forgive</u> me for saying anything about it before the others.' In her later years, according to her Russian cousin the Grand Duchess Olga, she was treated as little more than 'a glorified maid' by her selfish mother, who used a handbell to summon her to her side.[29] Not surprisingly, Toria fell prey to maudlin hypochondria and depression. Her delicate features became cold and plain, her eager intelligence gave way to a cruel sarcasm. Through it all, it seems she never forgot Rosebery. A friend later recounted a conversation that took place towards the end of her life: 'Princess Victoria told me that there had been someone perfect for her but they would not let her marry him, and if you could have heard her voice break when she said, "We could have been so happy".'[30] She died a spinster in 1935.

Around 1895, when Rosebery was considering marriage to Victoria, Regy Brett – Lord Esher – referred several times in his journal to his friend's complaints about his loneliness. The same reference occurred again in Esher's journal in 1902, precisely at the moment when Rosebery may have been contemplating another and even more incongruous marriage. The woman he had allegedly fallen for was the American actress Maxine Eliot, a ravishing 34-year-old who entranced not just Rosebery but a phalanx of other British statesmen including Lord Curzon, Lord Birkenhead, and Winston Churchill. 'That beauty! How can one describe that beauty?' asked her fellow actress Constance Collier. 'Her head was small and crowded with great braids of coal-black hair. Her eyes were a sort of violet and I have never seen such big ones, or with such a soft, tender look in them. The colour varied as she talked and gave a feeling of the sea. Her skin was cream-coloured, like a camellia, with a glow behind it, and her lips were very red. She was ivory, ebony and roses.'[31] The King himself was taken with her, and years afterwards, in September 1909, he and Lord Esher 'both agreed that if Rosebery had had any pluck he would have married her'.[32] What they did not know was that – according to the account left by Maxine's niece, Diana Forbes-Robertson – Rosebery had in fact proposed to her seven years earlier. Maxine, on a visit to England, had charmed her way into the Prince of Wales's social circle. At Christmas 1901 she received an invitation from 'the Vyper', Lady Colebrooke, to dine and meet Rosebery. Rosebery, probably the most famous man in England, was flushed with the success of Chesterfield; determined to claim his attention, Maxine learnt most of his speech by heart. On the appointed evening she arrived in Lady Colebrooke's drawing room to be presented to the great man. As Diana Forbes-Robertson tells the story in *Maxine*,

> She addressed him in the fashionable drawl of the day accompanied by the smile of glowing eyes and brilliant white teeth that seldom failed.
>
> 'I'm so happy to meet you. Your speech at Chesterfield has impressed me most deeply. I declare I nearly know it by heart, I think.'
>
> 'Oh really?' said Rosebery, his drawl surpassing hers, and went on to the next guest.
>
> She raged with fury. He was insolent and intolerable . . . She took her place at the table, far down in rank from Rosebery, and could hardly eat from anger.

After dinner, when the guests had reassembled in the drawing room, Lady Colebrooke privately asked Maxine to provide some entertainment. At first she refused and then, seeing Rosebery slumped on a sofa, looking his most bored, she whispered to the Vyper that she would after all do an act. She stood up, went to the centre of the room, and started to perform an American comic ballad, 'Lasca the Cowboy', complete with clownish gestures and rolling eyes. Within minutes the whole room was convulsed in laughter. When she finished, Rosebery raised himself ponderously from his recumbent position and walked over to shake her hand.

> 'Miss Elliott, that was a joy. What a wicked, clever woman you are. And how beautiful. I would be delighted to take you to supper one night.'
>
> 'Oh, really?' she replied in a perfect imitation of his drawl, before turning to another guest.[33]

Rosebery was captivated rather than insulted. Supper à deux did soon follow, and when she went back to the United States, he sent flowers and letters after her.

At the time Maxine was married to her second husband, the comedian Nat Goodwin, but because of his drunken, philandering ways they effectively led separate lives. It is said that on her return to England in the spring of 1902, Rosebery suddenly asked her to get a divorce so she could marry him. In her niece's account, she refused him, 'to his vast astonishment'. Apparently her two experiences of matrimony had put her off making a third trial, and she had decided she preferred to win fame on the stage as Maxine Eliott, rather than in society as the Countess of Rosebery. Apart from the oblique evidence of the Esher journals, Diana Forbes-Robertson's account is uncorroborated by other sources. Her book is in other respects thoroughly researched, however, and based partly on the first-hand testimony of Maxine herself. And Rosebery, with his artistic spirit and his gambler's streak, was certainly given to dramatic, impulsive gestures. If the story of his proposal to Maxine is true, it is interesting that all the three women he wooed – a Jewess, a Royal Princess and an American actress – were far from being conventional, aristocratic choices. Each was in some sense both a society outsider and a star; such a duality may have had some appealing resonance for Rosebery, whose conception of his own character placed him apart from other men, whether as brooding, sensitive, bookish loner or as magnificent, visionary, independent statesman. Maxine was later rumoured to be engaged to Lord Curzon, that 'most superior person'. When asked by the American Associated Press whether it was true she replied, 'I would not marry God.'

A still more unobtainable woman who inspired in Rosebery distant fantasies of marital happiness was the writer George Eliot. They met when he was a young man, she in late middle age. Again, she was not conventionally beautiful but, as Rosebery told Herbert Fisher: 'She was a woman one could have married. She had such a loving voice and such beautiful eyes.'[34] Remarks like that, allied to the web of Rosebery's romantic interests, put the weak and nebulous allegations about his homosexuality into perspective. It is further possible that during the 1890s he had a mistress, Miss Bailey, who tried to make money by reporting their affair to the press. Both Herbert Bismarck and W.T. Stead asked him about a woman of that name, and Regy Brett, rather bravely, wrote to him in 1896 to say that 'the lady we spoke of claims that you have allowed her £4000 a year; that you have furnished her home; that she has heaps of letters, passages of which she has read out to certain persons; that when you went to Windsor to see Her Majesty on becoming Prime Minister you went straight to her house in Ascot; and that she used to lunch and dine with you in a private room at Vesey's.'[35] All such enquiries were countered by Rosebery with the bland assertion that he knew 'absolutely nothing on the subject'.[36] His straightforward masculine impulses were also revealed at a dinner party given by Jennie, Lady Randolph Churchill: according to one guest, 'he spent most of the evening examining the footmaids', who wore alluring, tightly-fitted uniforms specially designed by Jennie.[37] He may have found another outlet in the collection of pornography given to him by his old American friend Sam Ward, which included illustrations for the Marquis de Sade's work.[38]

Lacking the comfort of a wife, disappointed in politics and in love, after 1905 Rosebery became ever more introverted, forbidding and eccentric. The intensity of his craving for solitude comes across in the rather mournful experience of a new resident secretary, Arthur Guise, who took up his post at Dalmeny full of optimism in July 1906, and gushingly assured Rosebery that, 'I would do anything in the wide world for you.'[39] Sadly for him, within little more than a year the only thing Rosebery wanted Guise to do was leave him alone. As he explained in a frank letter, he had begun to find the young man's presence intensely annoying: 'I require more freedom and independence than are consistent with a permanent inmate of my house. I am not accustomed to it and am too old to get accustomed to it. It is intolerable to me that I cannot eat alone or with my sister or my children as I may wish, but that I have a permanent companion, however agreeable and pleasant he may be; it is a compulsory marriage against which my soul rebels and a bondage both for you and for me. This system must terminate.' Rosebery suggested that Guise should move out and carry on his duties from either Edinburgh or London. 'I will not be chained to anyone. Royalty is trained to be so chained. But I am not Royalty!'[40] Understandably wounded, Guise soon handed in his notice. Rosebery tried to reassure him that it was nothing personal: 'It is purely a question of the irksomeness of compulsory companionship into which confidence does not enter. I am too accustomed, I am afraid, to solitude.'[41] But Guise could not see himself as anything but a failure: 'If I could have won the trust and affection of such a chief it would have been an ideal life and to perform the meanest duty a pleasure and an honour. I suppose I have been spoilt and become unduly sensitive but it is humiliating to have failed where I started with such proud confidence.'[42] After this painful experience, he told Rosebery, he planned to return to his native Ireland, and become a farmer.

A portrait of Rosebery, isolated and intimidating, was left by Violet Asquith, Henry's daughter, who visited Dalmeny with her family in 1905. On Sunday morning they went to the local Presbyterian Church, and Violet recorded in her diary: 'From time to time I shot a sideway glance at our host, who sat at the further end of the pew seat, solid and inscrutable. Everyone seems to tremble before him from Lady Leconfield downwards – I *can't* understand it. I feel if I stayed here long I should too – there is nothing so infectious as fear. I felt quite funky sitting next to him at dinner on Sunday night – I needn't have as we got on quite well but he makes one feel that possessing such a mind, all others must seem dull and trite and commonplace, mere intellectual pygmies.'[43] The poet Henry Newbolt felt just as uneasy at one of Rosebery's all-male dinners at Berkeley Square. 'I had slipped that morning and cut my face deeply, so that my left cheek – the one towards my host – was conspicuously bound up in black plaster. All through dinner, I was aware of Rosebery's wide and curious eye fixed upon my patch and of his still more curious mind silently conjuring in what sort of affair I came by it.' On another occasion, Rosebery showed Newbolt a drawing of himself as a young man, 'a brilliant mind looking out from a beautiful and almost eager face. He stood close to it and stared at it with an expression of great sadness.'[44]

As he withdrew further into his chosen seclusion, Rosebery's anxieties about his health multiplied. He took to calling himself a 'well-preserved corpse' and complained of failing eyesight, piles and, despite having freed himself from political pressures, the return of insomnia. 'How odd it is to be old,' he said to Mary Gladstone Drew when he was only 56; at that age, Mary's father had yet to form his first government.[45] Never the most stoical of individuals, he told his sister in February 1907 that a raging toothache had caused him to spend 'the most wretched night of my life' in 'misery and agony'.[46] Rosebery's great-nephew Lord Egremont, writing many years later, recalled that when his grandfather, Constance's husband, was bitten by a dog and sat up all night worrying whether he was going to get hydrophobia, the incident annoyed Rosebery, 'who resented other people in his circle being as neurotic as he was.'[47] On 19 November 1907 he wrote himself this typically morbid note: 'I am now sixty and have probably not much to look to in life. This may be the last anniversary of my wife's death. At Sandringham ten days ago, I felt an unwonted weakness in my arms and legs when shooting. I have become an old man in many ways. Still it was time, I suppose and it is best to recognise the fact.'[48] In the same month, when doctors told him that sugar had been found in his urine but it was 'not serious', he wondered melodramatically in his diary, 'Is this the end?'[49] His sense of his own mortality was heightened by the loss of friends and relatives. His mother the Duchess of Cleveland died in May 1901, though as he told Haldane it was not an event that caused him too much anguish: 'Death is so universal, so inevitable, that one should not grieve too much in a case like this when it comes, after a life of 82 years of vivid enjoyment prolonged to the last, and puts a painless term to what must probably have otherwise ended in irksome and long-drawn sorrow.'[50] Herbert Bismarck died in 1904, and four years later Sir Edward Hamilton, probably his closest friend, succumbed to the circulatory disease that had crippled him for more than a decade. One of the last letters Rosebery sent to him, in June 1906, reads: 'It is with me half pain as well as half pleasure to see you now and to look back over the long vista of the happy, healthy years during which I knew you, beginning with the school ground when we were quaking little boys. My dear Eddy, my eyes are full of tears as I write.'[51]

His physical decline may have hindered his shooting, but Rosebery still enjoyed his horseracing. In 1905 his colt Cicero won the Derby in what he described as a 'a close and exciting race'. At the Jockey Club dinner after his victory, the King proposed his health, to which Rosebery said in reply that he was ashamed to win the Derby thrice when so many of his colleagues had never won it all, a remark that was greeted with a cheer by the Duke of Devonshire* – 'the only cheer he ever gave me', noted Rosebery.[52] One new pastime he took up during these years was motoring, inspired by his neighbour in Berkeley Square, Alfred Harmsworth, who was a car fanatic. He did not drive himself, relying instead on a

---

*He had succeeded as 8th Duke in 1891, but remained best known to Rosebery and in racing circles as 'Hartington'. Of his enthusiasm for the turf the *DNB* says that 'His success in racing was . . . hardly equal to his zeal for it and expenditure upon it.'

chauffeur,★ but he enjoyed the sensation of travelling at speed and came to believe that a ride in the car at night, like a carriage drive, was helpful for his insomnia. Because drivers were so inexperienced and vehicles so experimental, car ownership was beset with problems. Punctures, crashes and breakdowns were frequent occurrences on unsuitable roads: 'I had a smash in my new motor. We shall all be killed in them,' he told Hamilton.

The chauffeurs could present difficulties too. One day in December 1905 he wanted to go for a drive at Dalmeny but 'my chauffeur Chambers was not to be found. It turned out he was in the habit of absenting himself in this way and spending the night in some low haunt in Queensferry.' Also in 1905 another of his drivers accidentally killed a girl near King's Cross station, and Rosebery, as a witness, had to attend the coroner's inquest. Less serious but perhaps more terrifying was an incident in October 1906. Driving from Douglas back to Edinburgh on a cold after-noon after lunching with the King, he and his chauffeur were crossing bleak moorland when suddenly they were caught in a snow storm. Within minutes the moor was blanketed in snow more than a foot deep. They tried to turn around, but the car had become completely snow-bound. Attempting to push it they only managed to send it down a bank. A grip-ping passage in Rosebery's diary continues the story:

> There was nothing to do but abandon it. So I took the Life of Durham (two volumes) and off we marched on our own tracks, the driver Edmunds cheer-fully observing that it was many miles since we passed the last cottage. We set off at 5.30 in the dark in deep snow, but I felt it a walk of life or death, as if the fast falling snow obliterated the track we should probably have had to lie down for the night and should probably not rise again. The driver soon lagged hopelessly and I had to go back two or three times till I got an answer to my yell. I walked for dear life and came suddenly on a low, lightless roof. It turned out to be the lodge of Kerswall House, where I was kindly received by the tenants. Two reflections occurred to me on my trudge. The first was the strangeness of the contrast – one and half hours after lunching with the King and 40 people to be walking for dear life on a waste of snow. The second was that, had I one million sterling in each pocket, they would not have been the least use to me. So ended a gruesome adventure.[53]

He later estimated that they had walked more than four miles through the snow.

Rosebery continued to travel extensively, particularly to Bad Gastein

★Rosebery disliked the word 'chauffeur', preferring the term 'motor-driver', for as he told John Buchan in 1920, '"Chauffeur" is the name of a French robber who extorts money by roasting feet on a charcoal fire.' (Rosebery to Buchan, 7 June 1920, Rosebery NLS Acc 6975)

where he returned annually to take the cure, and to his villa in Posillipo, often with his children. His ownership of the villa did not make life easy for the British Consul in Naples, Eustace Neville-Rolfe, who paid for Rosebery's generosity in letting him use it by being bombarded with demands about everything from the storage of pictures to the building of a new lavatory. 'I want you to draw up a rough list of requirements for the villa. Cutlery is the first that occurs to me,' ran one characteristic letter.[54] Rosebery's sometimes dismissive attitude to servants is illustrated in this recollection of Neville-Rolfe's: 'On one of Rosebery's early visits, a butler whom he had brought complained that there was no place in which the footmen could do their work. "I was not aware", said Rosebery, "that foot-men ever did any work."'[55] It was discourtesy like this that so grated on Neville-Rolfe's daughter Amy, who met the Earl several times in Posillipo: 'Lord Rosebery has been distinguishing himself by his speeches lately. They are nicer than he is or rather than his manners are. He didn't impress one pleasantly.'[56] His English neighbour in Naples, the author Norman Douglas, later included this profile of him in his autobiography:

> I think he was happy during the short time he spent at this place. Yet he struck me as not exactly harassed but pre-occupied, or at least absorbed. I should also have called him a shy man. 'Shy' is an odd term to apply to a person like Lord Rosebery; such was the impression I always had of him. He was not taciturn or reserved, he was ready to laugh or talk; he relapsed easily into silence. One felt a little awkward at times, not knowing when the conversation would start again. 'Do you like these glasses?' he once asked at dinner. They were old Murano goblets, with citron-tinted beads. 'Very much, but not exactly for drinking wine out of. Rather too much colour for my taste.' 'Now that's just what I was thinking.' I wondered: was he really thinking about them? Sometimes his mind seemed to be far away, and he had to make an effort to pull it back again.[57]

Visiting him in April 1901, Edward VII was rather perplexed by the way Rosebery lived at the Posillipo villa. Resentful at being asked to give a luncheon party at short notice, Rosebery put the arrangements in the hands of a Neapolitan caterer, who produced an embarrassingly sub-stan-dard meal. Later the King asked his travelling companion Sir Charles Hardinge how he thought Rosebery could entertain himself for weeks on end in such a place. 'He is a strange, weird man, Sir,' was Hardinge's reply.[58] Five years later, staying again in Naples, the King asked Rosebery to dine, having heard he was at Posillipo. To the wrath of the King, who was fas-tidious about dress, Rosebery breezily turned up attired in a Yacht Squadron mess jacket and white tie. Sir Frederick Ponsonby, the King's assistant secretary, later recalled, 'Most people would not have even remarked this, and if they had would never have given it a second thought. But for King Edward this entirely spoilt the whole evening and he eyed Rosebery angrily all through dinner. To make matters worse Rosebery made a joke about his tie and became rather offhand about what was really in the King's mind a serious matter.' Later that night, when Rosebery asked leave to be excused to return to Posillipo, the King begged him to stay, claiming to have something he wanted to tell him. He then disappeared to play 'an interminable' game of cards, while Rosebery was kept waiting. Finally emerging, at nearly midnight, all the King did was bid Rosebery good night, retiring without another word. 'Rosebery was very angry and showed it,' according to Ponsonby.[59]

Those two incidents are indicative of the occasionally prickly relationship between Rosebery and his Sovereign. He often found the King tiresome, as this diary entry made after his Derby victory suggests: 'He took me off to his luncheon room where he gave me a glass of champagne, then sat down and talked *de omnibus rebus* till I thought I should never get away.' And he was both bored and exhausted by all the palaver that went with entertaining Royalty. When the King visited Mentmore in 1905 he brought with him two valets, an equerry, seven constables, two chauffeurs, one private detective – and a telegraphist, for a special wire and post office had to be installed in the house. The Princess Victoria affair and Rosebery's own shyness necessarily contributed to the strains between them. At one stage they were barely on speaking terms, as Ponsonby revealed in his memoirs. Rosebery had been invited to Windsor Castle for Ascot, but he 'sulked and became impossible practically the whole week. If anyone tried to draw him into conversation he turned an eye like a fish on them and withered them with biting sarcasm. So everyone avoided him. After dinner he would get a book and read, but he never joined in any of the jokes such parties produce.' On the last night he thawed a little, and ended by talking tête-à-tête with Ponsonby on the terrace. All the wit Rosebery had been suppressing during the week now came tumbling out, and it was not long before Ponsonby was weeping with laughter. So loud was the noise that other guests came over. 'Soon there were a dozen or more standing round our basket arm-chairs and Rosebery, liking an audience, became wittier and wittier.' The King, who was playing bridge, came out to see what was the commotion; the moment he appeared, Rosebery stood up and fell silent. 'There was an awkward pause and King Edward remarked that he must go back to his bridge. Rosebery then quietly followed and went back to his book.'[60] In a note written on the occasion of the King's death in May

1910, Rosebery reflected his decidedly mixed feelings towards his late Sovereign. 'He was impossible to understand, a verdict that Knollys agreed with. The day before he died, he saw Mrs Gordon. I record this to illustrate the fact that to the last moment of his life his greatest pleasure was to flirt with a pretty woman. He did not confide in men; he preferred to quarrel with them.'[61]

This is not the full picture, however, for King Edward retained a fondness for Rosebery, their friendship dated back to the 1870s, and in lighter moments the antagonism between them was replaced with humour. The King, for example, took to calling himself 'Haggis' when he visited Rosebery in Scotland. His mistress Alice Keppel told Lady Colebrooke that during a stay at Dalmeny 'she had never seen the King so pleased about anything. Rosebery is the one man he really cares about.'[62] At a dinner given by Lord Crewe in 1907 she told Rosebery directly, according to his own account, that 'the King and Queen were so fond of me, that the King was so devoted to me and I did not realize it and so the King sometimes had difficulty in talking to me about politics. I said that it was difficult for me to talk to him about politics and about C.B's government as it might be supposed to be animated by pique.'[63] The King was a great admirer of Rosebery's political talent, if not of his application, and repeatedly beseeched him to return to the arena. Seeing him at the Epsom Derby in 1907, the King made a telling slip of the tongue in urging him 'to rise like a sphinx from your ashes and take the lead again'.[64] In a candid letter of 21 October 1906 Rosebery analysed his relationship with the King, writing freely of both his personal and his political conduct.

> Your Majesty's kindness to me extends over 40 years and has been great and constant. It has always been met on my side by unbounded attachment and devotion – I would venture to say affection. But I am very awkward, when I feel deeply, at expressing myself in words and therefore I cannot resist the impulse to write, more especially as from that awkwardness I am sometimes afraid lest Your Majesty should not be aware of how warmly I appreciate your goodness to me. There are often long intervals when I do not see Your Majesty and after that my awkwardness is redoubled. I will try and overcome it. I am especially grateful for your confidence. I am worthy of it in the sense of being discreet. But of course on political matters I find it difficult to speak freely as my position is so strange and exceptional that I think it best to be altogether silent.[65]

The King replied generously, 'I can assure you that nothing gives me greater pleasure than to be in your society, whether we discuss political or social matters. My only regret is that you live so much the life of a recluse.'[66] The more chivalrous, non-censorious side of Rosebery was uppermost when, after the King's death, he went to see Alice Keppel because 'I thought I should show my sympathy.' During their intriguing conversation, Mrs Keppel told him that for twelve years 'the King showed her every letter he received within minutes of receiving it', though she had now burnt all her correspondence from him. She further explained that 'for the last two years the King did not confide in Knollys for he was afraid that everything he told Knollys went straight to Esher, who was a good man in his way but not the repository of confidences.' She concluded with the King's complaint that 'Queen Alexandra never addressed a word of endearment to him. He used to say that he had not been a good husband in point of fidelity but that he had always put the Queen first.'[67]

As he retreated into seclusion, Rosebery's relationships with his own children became less and less easy. 'They are devoted to him but are a good deal frightened,' wrote Hamilton after a drive with Sybil less than six months before her marriage. 'They find him so difficult to deal with. They can never ascertain what his plans and wishes are. He is too horribly restless and he never gives a thought to the convenience of others.'[68] The idleness he detected in his sons was a frequent subject of complaint. Of Neil's Oxford days he said, 'He has no idea what work is! He considers term a period of vacation and vacation a holiday.'[69] Yet he soon came to admire his younger son's intelligence and political acumen. Neil won the seat of Wisbech in 1910, before he was 30. Rosebery contrasted Neil and his smooth assurance with his less intellectually accomplished, more sporting elder son Harry. Indeed, he was particularly hard on his heir, who celebrated his coming of age in 1903 with a large ball in Edinburgh; his father did not bother to attend. He was also reluctant to allow Harry to go into politics. When the sitting Liberal MP for Midlothian, Alexander Murray, the Master of Elibank, decided before the 1906 election to switch to another Scottish constituency, the local Liberal Association thought Lord Dalmeny would be the ideal replacement, given the resonance of the family name. Rosebery, inevitably, proved difficult and urged that Harry remain in the Grenadier Guards; he only relented when he heard that the Liberals' alternative candidate was likely to be a supporter of Campbell-Bannerman. So Harry was selected, and in the landslide of 1906 became the country's youngest MP. Afterwards the Prime Minister, in a gesture of reconciliation to Rosebery, asked Lord Dalmeny to second the motion on the Royal Address, the task Rosebery himself had performed 33 years earlier in the Lords. But Rosebery told Harry, 'If you accept Campbell-Bannerman's invitation, you are no son of mine.'[70] It was, said Harry later, 'very embarrassing'. In yielding to his father's wishes, he sounded the death-knell of his political career before it had properly begun. He stood down at the next election. Harry's emotional distance from his father was reflected in the way he did not inform Rosebery until the last minute of his engagement in 1909 to Lady Dorothy Grosvenor, the 18-year-old sister of the Duke of Westminster. 'The news came on me so like a bombshell,' Rosebery told the Prince of Wales (later George V), 'never having seen or even heard of the young lady or had an idea that anything of the kind was in contemplation, that it took my breath away.'[71]★

Rosebery's involvement with Liberal politics had apparently come to a sour conclusion with the appointment of Campbell-Bannerman as Prime Minister. In the House of Lords he now sat ostentatiously on the cross-benches, and failed to give the new ministers any support. Winston Churchill, the new Colonial Under-Secretary, complained to Perks, 'I have frequently tried to see him but he is never able to see me.'[72] In November 1906 Sir Edward Grey offered him the British Embassy in Washington, but Rosebery refused on the grounds that 'the ambassador who goes to Washington without a wife would be mad'. The King tried to persuade him, but to no avail. 'The want of a hostess was so insuperable an obstacle that it was unnecessary to go further into the business,' argued Rosebery.[73] By 1907 his sense of disillusion with Liberalism was even greater. At a meeting of the Liberal League in March he announced that he owed the Government 'neither allegiance nor confidence – perhaps not even the common courtesies of life'; in future his intervention would be as 'the croaking of a retired raven on a withered branch.' His anti-Government croaking was particularly loud in August, when he launched a savage assault on their Scottish land reform bill, which he regarded as socialistic because it aimed to introduce fair rents and compulsory purchase.

In another move distancing himself from the Liberals, in April 1907 he met his old political colleague the Duke of Devonshire to talk about cross-bench co-operation. 'I said that I loathed politics and office but that I thought the present majority was dangerous and uncontrolled,' he recorded.[74] He put it to the Duke that they agreed on most issues, except perhaps education, and suggested that a new centrist movement might rally opinion. But the Duke felt he was too old and exhausted for another initiative; nor was he convinced as to Rosebery's commitment, a fear Rosebery had to confess was justified. 'I told him that the Liberal League

---

★The marriage was not successful, and ended in divorce in 1919. In 1924 he married, far more happily, Eva Lady Belper, also divorced, the artistic daughter of Lord Aberdare.

would have been a great success had I not always told them that I would not take office.'

As ever, there was inconsistency between Rosebery's words and his deeds. Despite his protestations about hating office and responsibility, in March 1907 he had made a bid for the Chancellorship of Oxford University, but was soundly beaten by Lord Curzon, 1101 votes to just 440, his humiliation increased when in one of Curzon's first acts as Chancellor he awarded Campbell-Bannerman an honorary degree. Disclaiming any connection with Liberalism, Rosebery nevertheless remained President of the Liberal League, which staggered on after the 1906 election without either purpose or popular support. So many of the League's senior members were now in Government that Perks thought it should be wound up, since it could no longer credibly claim to have an independent voice. 'The League has become an association of timid men pledged to political self-abnegation,' he informed Rosebery in November 1907. 'Personally I do not feel the League can continue to be of much use and I shall not regret its dissolution.'[75] Rosebery did not agree. For all his semi-detachment from politics, he was growing increasingly concerned by the rise of socialism, which he feared was taking over the Liberal party. He therefore came to see the League as a possible bulwark against this movement. As he put it to the Secretary of the League, William Allard: 'Now that we find ourselves between the devil of Socialism and the deep sea of Protection, the League seems to me more necessary in some form or another than ever before. Perhaps the country as a rule does not realize this, but it must soon, as the socialistic forces within and behind the permanent majority begin to assert themselves more openly.'[76]

It was the 'socialistic and anti-Imperial' drift of Liberalism which led Rosebery to so despise the party after 1906. Allard, however, professed himself to be 'shattered' after Rosebery told him, in the course of a private conversation in November 1907, that he felt no loyalty to the cause or to the Government. In the over-blown language Rosebery so often seemed to provoke in both men and women Allard wrote him a fourteen-page letter of distress, explaining, 'I felt that after locking-up the League offices and throwing the keys into the Thames, I could welcome the end of the world and the day of judgement as a highly appropriate sequel to the morning's talk.' He said he was 'filled with dismay', had gone home 'to sit and sulk' but could see no alternative to a Liberal government, particularly since the Tories had 'lost all sense of decency and veracity'.[77] Rosebery professed himself wounded by this, replying on 21 November: 'I boil with indignation at the impression produced by our conversation. I still hold that

"Liberal" is the noblest word in the English language. But the noblest word may be prostituted. The new Liberalism is in reality largely directed against liberty; the old Liberalism was meant to promote it. I maintain my independence of thought and action in support of the Liberalism I knew and practised.'[78]

It is easy to sneer, as many did at the time, that Rosebery had merely descended into a reactionary old age. In his fulminations against socialism he appeared to be offering proof of what many had long suspected – that beneath a shallow veneer of radicalism, he was nothing more than a traditional Tory aristocrat. But this is an over-simplified view. What Rosebery had recognised was that the Liberal party had no future if it succumbed to the ideology of socialism. In a class-led political structure the Liberals could never survive in competition on the left against the nascent Labour party and increasingly powerful trade union movement. An ever expanding state spelt doom for the Liberals, thought Rosebery, and he was a man of remarkable prescience. It was perhaps his second greatest political gift, after his oratory. Before any of his Liberal colleagues, for instance, he understood the importance of the force of imperialism; in the 1880s, he saw that there was no alternative to Irish Home Rule; he was the only politician to predict that the Entente Cordiale would result in conflict with Germany; he also said, in 1904, that war on the eastern front would lead to revolution and chaos in Russia; he regarded India not as the jewel in the Imperial Crown but rather as a threat to the Empire's existence. Even in the short term, he seemed to have almost uncanny powers of foresight. The diary of his secretary Thomas Gilmour records this conversation of April 1905, a time when politics appeared to be in a state of flux because of Chamberlain's tariff campaign and the stance adopted by the Liberal League:

GILMOUR: Nobody seems to know what will happen.
ROSEBERY: I know exactly what will happen. C.B. will form a Government and his greatest wrench will be having to find places for Asquith, Grey and Haldane. Asquith and Grey can have any places they want, but there will be much more difficulty in putting Haldane on the Woolsack.

And this was more than five months before Relugas.

Rosebery's predictions about socialism were equally to the point. Within his own lifetime, the Liberals were utterly obliterated as a political force. Amid all the euphoria in the Liberal party following the 1906 landslide, he was exceptional in seeing its demise: 'The old Liberal party is drawing to its end,' he wrote to Sir George Murray in 1907. 'These last two elections, particularly the last, are the Mene Mene Tekel Upharsen of the Liberal banquet. The socialist does not indeed get a majority but while the two old parties are cutting each other's throats, he slips in and will continue to slip in and the encouragement to his party is great. The Liberal party will lose their industrial seats, while the Conservative party, the natural refuge in times of trouble, creams off all who will accept protection.'[79] Some of this might smack of hypocrisy, for Rosebery had built his name as a radical, had been a pioneer of progressivism on the LCC, had flirted with the Webbs. But his radicalism was, as he said to Allard, mainly of a liberating kind – extending democracy and devolution, expanding free trade and the free market; unlike some of his colleagues, he had actually read Adam Smith's *Wealth of Nations*. Many of his interventions, as in the coal dispute, or his support for municipal enterprise, were chiefly aimed at halting the abuses of monopolistic contractors. As his private criticisms of Harcourt's 1894 Budget show, he was suspicious of State interference in private property; similarly, one of the main reasons he was so opposed to protection was that he believed a tariff system would greatly expand the role of government in business. Like his mentor Gladstone, he loathed the socialist vision of dependency on the State. In a richly prophetic speech made at Glasgow University in June 1908, he warned of the 'despotism exercised in the name of liberty and adorned by the word benevolence'. He told his audience, 'the lesson of our Scottish teaching was "level up"; the cry of modern teaching is "level down"; "let the Government have a finger in every pie", probing, propping, disturbing. Every day the area of initiative is being narrowed, every day the standing ground for self-reliance is being undermined; every day the public infringes – with the best intentions no doubt – on the individual; the nation is being taken into the custody of the state.'

Rosebery's anti-socialism sent a few wheezing breaths of life into the Liberal League, but by 1908 it was almost moribund. Several of its members thought it should be put out of its misery, but at a meeting on 12 March, Rosebery urged the League to 'rally' to a programme which put at its centre hostility to socialism and an independent Irish Parliament, and support for imperialism, free trade and Lords reform. He confided to his diary that his speech had been 'even worse than usual, partly from trying to put too much into it, partly from using notes, partly from a clammy afternoon audience, partly from my being out of touch with politics.'[80] It was agreed that the League should not only relaunch itself politically on the basis of the President's manifesto, but that it should make itself more socially attractive by renting a new central London headquarters complete with bedrooms and a restaurant – in effect, by becoming a political club. There was little real excitement behind these moves, however. One of those attending the meeting described it as 'the most dismal gathering he had ever attended; Lord Rosebery's audience was obviously ill at ease.'[81]

Meanwhile, the League's President was involved in another political scheme, chairing a House of Lords select committee into the composition of the Upper House. The role of the Lords had become increasingly contentious since the 1906 election as the peers blocked a number of vital Liberal measures, including a Licensing Bill, an Education Bill and a Plural Voting Bill. The Tories' misuse of the House for party ends was encapsulated in the notorious declaration by A.J. Balfour that 'the great Unionist party should still control, whether in power or opposition, the destinies of this great Empire'. Even some Unionists were troubled by the naked bias of the peers, and in 1907 one of their number, Lord Newton, introduced a reform bill. Although this attempt failed, a committee was established to study the question and Rosebery, after some predictable dithering and anguished correspondence, agreed to chair it. The cause was, after all, one dear to his heart: in both 1884 and 1888 he had urged the creation of just such a committee of inquiry. Yet he proved a poor chairman, over-sensitive to criticism and unable to establish any spirit of cohesion between his members. After attending a committee meeting on 4 February 1908, Lord Newton observed: 'Rosebery was in the chair. I was not at all impressed, as he indulges in soliloquies and allows speakers to talk irrelevantly without check. Somehow I got the impression that he was not comfortable when presiding over men more or less of his own calibre and wondered whether he had kept order in his own cabinet.'[82] In another critical judgement, Newton said that Rosebery appeared to be 'physically unequal to the moderate strain of the work involved. He was also liable to fits of discouragement.'[83] Lord Esher was surprised at the way Rosebery was so 'fussed' by the committee. 'It is packed with people who agree with him and not a single opponent of his view has been put upon it. He is a queer fish.'[84] There were other problems too, quite apart from Rosebery's weak guidance. Lord Halsbury, leader of the Tory ultra-traditionalists, announced that he violently objected to the very principle of reform, while the Government, preferring a more radical plan, took no interest in the committee's proceedings. Its Report, which proposed a reduction in the hereditary element and the loss of any automatic right to sit in the Upper House, made so little impact when it was published in late 1908 that it was not even debated on the floor of the House. Rosebery himself, instead of battling for the report, was only lukewarm about it. 'It is not my report and I am not paid to defend it,' he told Sir George Murray. 'It is, after all, only a record of willingness to be reformed and has no practical bearing, if even it ever be destined to have any.'[85]

By the time Rosebery's committee reported, the Government was under the new leadership of H.H. Asquith. Sir Henry Campbell-Bannerman had died on 22 April, from heart failure after a long illness.* He had become, after Sir William Harcourt – who predeceased him by four years – and Loulou, probably Rosebery's greatest enemy in the Liberal party, an odd achievement for one who was so essentially affable and unambitious. Asquith's succession to the premiership made Rosebery feel no warmer towards the Government, and his attempt to build bridges by inviting Rosebery to dine at Downing Street in June 1908 to celebrate the King's birthday earned him a frosty reply: 'I am so completely free of party ties that I am anxious not even to appear to resume them. I am on the cross-benches for life and I have always refused Ripon's sessional dinners, though he is a very dear old friend. As I suppose your dinner has a party complexion, I should prefer not to buckle on my uniform but to wish you well from the country.'[86]

Rosebery's political career seemed definitely at an end. The raven's croak would soon be heard no more. 'You must not waste regrets on me, for they are misplaced. I am as happy as possible,' he wrote to Mary Gladstone Drew towards the end of 1908. 'You see I have lost the party spirit, mainly from disuse, perhaps, and when a man can no longer make his conscience square with party, he is better off out of politics; better and purer and happier.'

In a memorable conclusion to his superb essay on Rosebery written in 1909, A.G. Gardiner said: 'The light has vanished from the morning hills, the vision has faded in grey disenchantment. He is the Flying Dutchman of politics – a phantom vessel floating about the wide seas, without an anchor and without a port. It is significant that his latest work should deal with "The Last Phase" of Napoleon, for it is that solitary figure standing on the rock of St Helena and gazing over the sea at the setting sun of whom he most reminds us. Behind, the far-off murmur of the great world where he was once the hero, now lost to him for ever; before, the waste of lonely waters and the engulfing night.'

But Gardiner was premature in this valediction. Before the final fall of night, a grave political crisis blew up that revived excited talk of Rosebery's return to Downing Street.

---

*By a doleful coincidence, the Duke of Devonshire had died just weeks earlier.

17

'A helpless monster'

~

'THERE IS NO question of a change of party for me. I am only, as I have been for years, a cross-bench man,' Rosebery wrote to John Morley in September 1909. 'If I dip into theology for my metaphor, I should say that the analogy is not between an Anglican becoming a Roman but rather a Roman declaring himself, like Dollinger, an old Catholic. I am where I have been any time in the last 13 years. But no doubt the Liberal Party has marched on with seven league boots and I, with my painful pumps, am left in the mud.'[1]

It is the eternal cry of ageing politicians that it is their party that has changed, not them. But it was certainly true in Rosebery's case. Under Asquith and his lieutenant Lloyd George at the Treasury, the Liberal Government had embarked on a programme of radical social reform which was utterly alien to the Gladstonian vision of the minimalist state. Old age pensions, a network of labour exchanges, a Rural Development Commission, trade boards to regulate labour in certain industries and an extensive scheme of compulsory national insurance against sickness and unemployment were among the elements of this programme, leading to the creation of the first modern welfare system. The approach was known as the New Liberalism, to distinguish it from the party's more cautious nineteenth-century past. Rosebery might have been expected to welcome this change in policy. Had he not famously demanded 'a clean slate', an end to 'the fly-blown phylacteries' of traditional Liberalism? But Rosebery's alternative, as set out at Chesterfield, did not call for an expansion in the role of government: 'Efficiency' sought to bring business into the running of the State, not the State into the running of business. What he saw now was burgeoning socialism, not 'New Liberalism'. His great fears were that in a political order based on welfare, the two parties would soon be competing against one another with extravagant promises of increased public expenditure, and that government paternalism would sap the resilience of the people. 'The State invites us every day to lean upon it. I seem to hear the wheedling and alluring whisper, "Sound you may be;

we bid you to be a cripple" . . . The soundest man if encouraged may soon accustom himself to the methods of the invalid; he may train himself to totter or be fed with a spoon,' he said at Glasgow University in 1908.

For Rosebery, the measures in themselves were bad enough, but he was equally disturbed by the way the Government planned to pay for its social reforms, and also to meet the costs of naval re-armament. Lloyd George's so-called 'People's Budget' of 1909 proposed large increases in death duties, a rise in basic income tax, the introduction of a 'super tax' on incomes above £3000 and, most importantly of all, new land taxes – a duty of 20 per cent on the unearned increment in land values, to be paid when the ownership of the land changed hands, together with a duty of a halfpenny in the pound on the capital value of undeveloped lands and minerals. The outrage felt at these proposals among most of the land-owning classes and in the City of London found expression in a chorus of disapproval which Rosebery joined with a letter to *The Times* on 21 June 1909: 'This is not a Budget but a revolution, a social and political revolution of the first magnitude.' As the Finance Bill made its passage through the Commons, the Unionists began to consider using their majority in the Lords to reject the Bill. Such a drastic step had not been taken for 250 years. It would threaten the very fabric of the British constitution, which held that the Lords had no right to interfere with a Finance Bill.

While public speculation mounted as to the Unionists' likely course and a mood of extremism descended on the Opposition benches, Rosebery began to re-emerge as a potential national leader, the man above party who could guide the country through its crisis, 'an unused asset in the national locker' in the words of W.T. Stead.[2] Just as during the Boer War and the Tariff Reform controversy, there was again talk of a Rosebery-led centrist movement, this time standing against both Socialism and Protection. Indeed, even before the 'People's Budget' clandestine attempts had been made to bring Unionist free traders and moderate Liberal Leaguers into a new alliance under Rosebery's leadership. 'I should like to tell you in confidence of a curious little dinner at Rosebery's to which I went,' St Loe Strachey of the *Spectator* told the Unionist MP Arthur Elliot in July 1907. 'The only other person there was Lord Hugh Cecil. We had a very interesting talk as to the possibility of moderate men on both sides acting together and getting more representation in the press.' On 23 February 1908 Strachey organised a meeting at his London flat to discuss more formal, organised co-operation under Rosebery. Those attending included the Unionists Lord Hugh Cecil and Arthur Elliot, the former Egyptian pro-consul Lord Cromer, and the League member F.W. Maude. The negotiations went nowhere because the Unionists did not think the time was ripe for such a move, and Rosebery professed himself only too pleased by this failure. 'It is personally a great relief to me as it frees me from the necessity of examining the question as regards myself,' he told Strachey. But he was not completely dismissive: 'When the time comes, as come it probably will some day, I think "Central League" would be as good a name as any.'[3]

The Budget crisis brought a renewed sense of urgency to this activity. In the wake of Rosebery's letter of protest to *The Times* of 21 June Strachey wanted to organise a banquet in Rosebery's honour, intended as 'a striking proclamation of the fact that the Liberal Party on the whole is by no means unanimous about the Budget,' he explained to Eddie Tennant, MP.[4] The Liberal League might have been supposed to be the obvious vehicle for another Rosebery-centred campaign, but that body had grown suspicious of its President because of his past waywardness. At a pivotal League meeting on 25 June, described as 'unpleasant and unsatisfactory' by Perks, opinion was divided over whether to protest against the Budget. The MP Harry Poulton spoke for many when he said, 'We should not follow Rosebery's advice unless he is ready to lead and take the consequences of leading. Some of us have made great sacrifices by following him.'[5] At a further meeting of the League's executive on 28 June, reported Allard, 'more than one speaker commented on the disappointment' caused by Rosebery's reluctance 'to lead or undertake the responsibilities of leadership.'[6]

Inundated with demands for action during the summer, Rosebery remained undecided as to how he would respond. The Duke of Northumberland wrote asking for advice on how the Lords should deal with the Budget; 'I mean to keep an open mind as to what the House of Lords ought to do till the time comes,' he grandly replied.[7] Then, at the end of August, he announced that he would set out his views in a speech to the Glasgow Chamber of Commerce on 10 September. If the excitement did not quite match the build-up to Chesterfield, still there was nationwide interest in what he might say, especially among politicians on both sides. Lord Lansdowne, the Unionist leader of the Lords, told him, 'Your attitude will be an important factor in the calculations which it will be our business to make . . . I hope you will say nothing which might enable people to invoke your high authority against us.'[8] Even Lloyd George believed Rosebery's speech would affect his Budget's future, 'Everything depends on what Rosebery says tomorrow,' he told Robertson Nicholl of the *British Weekly*. 'If he indicates that the Bill ought to be submitted to the judgement of the country, the Tory leaders will be stampeded by the wild men behind them.'[9]

For a politician who had not held office since 1895, Rosebery's platform oratory had proved remarkably influential. Now, in Glasgow, in front of an audience of more than 3000, his wide-ranging assault on the Budget severely exacerbated the constitutional crisis. He said that landowners were being treated unfairly, as if they were 'part of the criminal class', that the Budget was 'a revolution without the mandate of the people'. Invoking the memory of his first leader, he claimed that Gladstone would not have tolerated this measure 'because in his eyes, and in my eyes, too, his humble disciple, Liberalism and Liberty were cognate terms; they were twin sisters.' As to the position of the Lords, in effect he dared his fellow peers to reject the Bill, but did not do so explicitly: 'It is my duty to show why I believe it not to be in the best interests of the nation that this financial measure should become law.' And he concluded that the 'deep, subtle, insidious danger which underlies it all is the danger of Socialism.' This, he proclaimed, was 'the end of all, the negation of faith, of family, of property, of monarchy, of Empire.'[10]

As he drove away from the hall Rosebery was loudly booed as well as cheered, something that had not happened to him after his previous great platform speeches. On this issue he was, despite his magnetism, a much more divisive figure, for the Budget was popular with the working classes, who saw its opponents as the self-interested rich. Senior Liberals and the Liberal press were unanimous in their contempt. 'What poor stuff!' Winston Churchill said to his wife, 'and so inaccurate in fact – over and over and over again he betrays an almost childish unacquaintance with the common details of the Budget. He does not urge the Lords to reject it. On the other hand, he warns them against it. But the execution of the speech, its argument, its phrasing, seem to me feeble beyond words.' Clementine thought waspishly that Rosebery's attitude derived from his aristocratic upbringing: 'His delicate and refined nature has been kept aloof since early youth (by a thrifty marriage) from the sordid consideration of how to make ends meet.'[11] Dripping with mock regret, the left-wing *Daily Chronicle* stated, 'Lord Rosebery's speech marks the parting of the ways between him and Liberalism. He ceased years ago to march breast forwards in the van of the army of progress. He has preferred to lag in the rear. We have long lost him from our fighting ranks and now that he has passed over into the opposition camp, Liberalism is conscious only of a sentimental not an actual loss. His speech yesterday was that of a great landowner, not a great Liberal. The entire speech is coloured by the prejudices and prepossessions of landlordism.'

To symbolise his final rupture with Liberalism, the day before his

Glasgow speech Rosebery had resigned both as President of the League and as a member of the National Liberal Club. Had he retained the presidency of the League, Asquith, Haldane and Grey, still nominally vice-presidents, would have instantly departed. As it was, the Prime Minister could hardly contain his anger when writing to Rosebery on 11 September: 'I read your speech with the most profound regret. It marks the parting of the political ways between every one of your old colleagues who have in the past fought under you or by your side. It may be that we are all wrong and you alone are right. In the meantime anything in the nature of political co-operation becomes (by your own showing) the hollowest of pretences and it is quite impossible for myself and my colleagues to serve under your Presidency.'[12] Rosebery replied three days later, explaining that he had already resigned: 'I think that you have left me rather than I have left you, but were it otherwise I hope we shall give each other credit for acting conscientiously. All my old political friendship is locked up in your Cabinet. I doubt if any of you realize the painful struggle I had before speaking.'[13] Without Rosebery the League staggered on for a few more months, but was finally wound up in May 1910.

The Unionists were delighted by Rosebery's powerful rallying cry against the Government. 'Lord Rosebery's epoch-making speech last Friday at Glasgow has produced an enormous effect in the country,' wrote Lady Knightley, the wife of a Midlands Tory MP, in her diary.[14] 'Your speech was excellent,' said Lansdowne.[15] 'It seems to me that more than any statesman now living you have got the true understanding of national finance,' proclaimed Strachey.[16] Lord Hugh Cecil was so excited that he began to dream of an anti-socialist coalition, led by Rosebery, which would embolden the Lords to throw out the Budget and drive the Liberals from power: 'I cannot recall any speech equally powerful in its influence. It shows how weighty your authority is with the public. It is not too much to say that that authority strongly exerted might well determine the issue of the conflict that apparently awaits us.' Cecil then outlined his plan, whereby the King would induce Asquith to resign in advance of a dissolution and would then send for Rosebery to form a 'Ministry of Constitutional Defence', comprising all the leading opponents of the Budget, to carry the country over the elections. 'I think all moderate men would rally to your leadership and that your Ministry would excite real enthusiasm.'[17] Thrilled with the prospect of a Rosebery premiership, Cecil even wrote to the King's secretary, Sir Francis Knollys: 'It seems to me certain Lord Rosebery is more likely to lead the electors against the Budget and in defence of the House of Lords than any other man.'[18]

Knollys showed Cecil's letter to the King, but neither was taken with the imaginative plan. They both felt it would disastrous to dismiss a Prime Minister who had a large majority in the Commons, and doubted, because of 'his want of nerve', whether Rosebery was the man to lead a nation in the depths of a constitutional crisis. Nor was Rosebery persuaded. Replying to Cecil on 9 October, he said that he saw 'three serious obstacles' to the plan: the King would not countenance it; there would be no ministers willing to serve in such a government; and his own influence in the country was far weaker than Cecil recognised. In addition, there was his own 'abhorrence of office. But I acknowledge that I have always thought that the right outcome was a united, anti-socialist government, but I could never name its components.' He then turned to the Lords, claiming to be in a dilemma about what the House should do: 'It is, I admit, difficult for the House of Lords to pass the Budget without some disparagement of itself. It is, on the other hand, not less difficult for an unreformed House of Lords to reject it, especially without a clear support from the country, which, visibly and audibly, is at present lacking.'[19]

This sort of ambivalent language was not what the Unionists wanted to hear. They had seen the Glasgow speech as a clarion trumpet-call for a rejection of the Budget; now it seemed that Rosebery wanted to sound the drumbeat of retreat. 'People are already betting he will vote in favour of the Bill. What a rotter the man is when character comes to be tested,' Lord Balcarres confided in his diary.[20] His worst fears were confirmed during the Lords debate on the Finance Bill at the end of November, when Rosebery announced that, despite his opposition to this 'iniquitous and dangerous' measure, he would not vote against it. This speech caused deep indignation among the Opposition peers, who felt that he had betrayed them. It was, said Sir Almeric Fitzroy, the Clerk of the Privy Council, 'an unpleasant surprise for the Tory party and in leaving the House I heard denunciation of it in many quarters.'[21] In a later intervention in the debate, Lord Curzon accused Rosebery of having misled the public with his Glasgow performance. 'The impression produced on us was as though some great and famous commander had left us in the breach after he himself had taken us up to the walls and had fired the powder in the train.' The high Tory Leo Amery descended to personal abuse in writing to the journalist Leo Maxse, editor of the *National Review*: 'Rosebery, as always, fails at the moment of crisis. I knew it was exactly what was coming. If I ever wrote in the style of the editor of the *National* I should say, "the performances of this highly gifted political eunuch arouse interest but produce neither satisfaction nor concrete result. The creature has no guts." '[22]

It must be admitted that Rosebery was in an unenviably difficult position. However much he might dislike the Budget, he could not have supported the Unionists' unprecedented strategy for defeating it. It would have been absurd of him, as a renowned champion of Lords reform, to defend the most unconstitutional misuse of the Upper House's powers in centuries. He feared the peers were playing straight into the hands of those radicals who wanted to abolish the second chamber altogether. Unfortunately, his Glasgow speech had raised so many false expectations that he was now despised on both sides of the political divide, taunted as a reactionary by the Liberals and as a coward by the Tories. As he put it plaintively to Perks on 5 December, 'It brings home to me once more the dirt and squalor of party politics . . . The situation is the gravest in my lifetime but at this moment I do not see how I, distrusted and detested by both parties, can usefully intervene.'[23] And once more, lurking in the back of his mind, was the terror of being asked to take office if he put himself at the political forefront. The historian Algernon Cecil once wrote that Rosebery, after his experience of the premiership, was like 'a burnt child dreading the fire', and Rosebery almost confessed as much to John Buchan in December 1909: 'As for taking part in the fight, I cannot. For years, I have deliberately kept out of political controversy and have only intervened on rare occasions, like the present, when I could not help myself. If I were to join the battle, I should find myself back again where I will not be and indeed might find myself on the very verge of responsibilities I would not undertake.'[24]

Rosebery's advice to his fellow peers had no effect. On 30 November they rejected the Budget by 350 votes to 75. Two days later the House of Commons passed a resolution declaring the action of the Upper House to be 'a breach of the constitution'. Parliament was then dissolved and in the subsequent election in January 1910 the Liberals lost their overall majority, gaining 275 seats to the Unionists' 273, but Asquith remained in power with the support of the Irish and Labour members. The immediate consequence of the Unionists' defeat was that some form of legislation would certainly be introduced to deal with the Lords.

This should have been Rosebery's finest hour. At last, 36 years after his first public attack on the Lords and after decades of preaching in the wilderness, circumstances had finally conspired to make the role of the House of Lords the burning political issue of the day. Sadly, Rosebery was by now so isolated that he carried little weight with either the Government or the Opposition. The Liberal ministry was interested only in destroying the Lords' veto, not in reconstituting the second chamber; the hard core of

Unionists only in defending their vested interests. In March Rosebery introduced into the House a trio of resolutions which together would establish the principle of reform. He spoke with his usual eloquence, telling his fellow peers that the only alternative to change was 'to cling with enfeebled grasp to privileges which have become unpopular, to powers which are verging on the obsolete, shrinking and shrinking, until at last, under the unsparing hands of the advocates of single-chamber Government, there may arise a demand for your own extinction, and the second chamber, the ancient House of Lords, may be found waiting in decrepitude for its doom.' His speech fell flat, and he found his audience 'very chilly'. Sir Almeric Fitzroy described the scene in his diary: 'He had an immense audience but somehow failed, with all his earnestness and rhetorical skill, to produce an effect commensurate with the pitch to which expectation had been carried.'[25] Rosebery's three resolutions were passed, but were no more than an irrelevant sideshow to the real business – the Government's determination to end the veto by means of a Parliament Bill; and the Lloyd George Budget, which still awaited completion of its passage through both Houses.

At the end of April, amid a few grumbles, the Budget was finally passed in the Upper House; at the same time, the Commons gave a first reading to the Parliament Bill, under the terms of which the House of Lords would lose any right to interfere with a Money Bill, and retain only limited powers to delay other legislation. This measure signalled that the Commons was determined never again to allow its will to be frustrated by the Lords. The scene was now set for a titanic clash between the two Houses. As with the 1832 Reform Act, the only way to ensure that the Commons would prevail was by the threat of creating a flood of new peers to drown the Tory opposition. In December 1909 Sir Francis Knollys had warned Rosebery that in such an eventuality as many as three hundred peers might be required. 'The King, I imagine, will decline to agree to any such increase, which would practically destroy the House of Lords as a second chamber, would moreover make the House and also himself the laughing stock of the Empire, without another dissolution.'[26] Lord Hugh Cecil, still fantasising about his centre coalition government, thought that if the King were to refuse there might be a renewed opening for a Rosebery premiership: 'If I may say so, to steer the country through a great crisis does seem to be your vocation and duty.'[27] But Edward VII was not called upon to make the decision: on 6 May 1910 he died suddenly, 'the most cruel blow the country could sustain at this moment,' wrote Rosebery in his diary. The accession of George V led to a brief suspension of political hostilities, out of respect for the difficulties of his position, and during the lull the two warring factions agreed to hold a round-table conference in an attempt to settle the controversy over the Lords. It was a further indicator of Rosebery's isolation that he was not asked to play any part in these negotiations.

The talks dragged on for months, eventually breaking down on the issue of Irish Home Rule. The drama now shifted back to Westminster, as Parliament reassembled on 15 November after the long recess. Still eager to push the issue of reform, Rosebery introduced two further, more detailed, resolutions. The first argued for a tripartite Upper House consisting of hereditary peers, those who sat by virtue of their office, and those chosen from outside. After a brief debate the resolution was passed without a division, although Rosebery was criticised for the vagueness of his scheme. The second resolution, dealing with terms of tenure for ex-officio peers, was withdrawn by Rosebery on the rather eccentric grounds that 'it went too far in details' – precisely the opposite of the complaint made about the first.

Once more Rosebery's action was of little consequence. On 23 and 24 November Lord Lansdowne moved his own resolutions, providing for a reconstituted Upper House and for the settlement of differences by joint sittings or, in the last resort, by public referendum. While these were certainly radical proposals, they smacked of eleventh-hour opportunism in the face of impending emasculation by the Commons and the King's Prerogative. They also failed to address the most important point: how the Unionists would respond to the Parliament Bill, which had been brought into the Lords that same week. Before the Lords debated the measure Parliament was again dissolved, to enable the electorate to give its verdict on the question. If the public backed the Liberal Government again, the King would find it impossible to resist Asquith's demand for the creation of enough peers to pass the Parliament Bill.

The two elections of 1910 were the first in which peers were officially allowed to campaign. Throughout the nineteenth century they had been barred from doing so, and this had undoubtedly hindered Rosebery's career. An Amendment to Commons Standing Orders liberated them, but for Rosebery the change came too late; his oratory was sought by neither party. Not that he wished to contribute to the fight in any way: when asked to make a donation to the local Liberal campaign in Musselburgh, he replied, 'I have no connection with and no faith in either party and therefore no desire to maintain a communication through the medium of party funds.'[28] There was, however, one Primrose attached to the Liberal cause,

his second and favourite son Neil, who had been first elected MP for
Wisbech in January 1910 and retained his seat in December. Many were
struck by Neil's resemblance to the Earl in his manner. In her diary Margot
Asquith noted that he had 'inherited that glacial and slow voice' and
'acquired posing'.[29] Like Neil, almost all other Liberals kept their seats in
the second election, for the result was much the same as in January, leaving the combined Liberal, Irish and Labour members with a majority of
126 over the Unionists. The public had spoken. The King knew that his
duty was to accede to whatever might be Asquith's demands for new peers.

Even now, a large number of Unionists refused to give in. Led by the
elderly, energetic and extreme former Lord Chancellor, Lord Halsbury,
they were known as the 'Die-hards' or the 'Ditchers' because of their professed willingness to 'die in the last ditch' rather than surrender. As the
Parliament Bill made its stormy passage through both Houses over the
summer of 1911, the Ditchers' very public defiance put the new King in a
position of painful responsibility and awkwardness. In his perplexity,
George V turned to the one man he felt could assist him in his hour of
need: on 8 August, the night before the critical debate in the Lords which
would decide the fate of the Parliament Bill, he asked Rosebery to dine at
Buckingham Palace. According to the account left by Lord Esher, who was
on intimate terms with the King,

> He reminded Lord Rosebery of his having said he would render the King
> any service in his power, and then he added, 'I am now going to ask you to
> fulfil your promise.'
> 'What can I do?' Rosebery enquired.
> 'You must speak and vote for the Bill.'
> Rosebery threw up his hands and said, 'I cannot do that. I should be stul-
> tified.' The King said not another word and passed on to other topics and
> they had a most agreeable evening. The next day, he had a short note from
> Rosebery to say that he would do as the King wished.[30]

Typically, Rosebery did not go about his duty in a straightforward way.
As the crisis over the Bill reached its final climax in the House of Lords, no
one could be confident of the outcome. The weather, the hottest yet
recorded in Britain, only added to the nerve-shredding excitement. So high
were temperatures that roads melted, railway lines buckled and a serious fire
broke out in the Carlton Hotel near the Houses of Parliament. In all this
boiling tension, the stance taken by Rosebery would be vital, for he still
retained some influence over the centre ground. When he stood up to
speak, on the second day of the debate, the atmosphere was electric. In a
packed House, all eyes turned to the diminutive, white-haired figure of the

man who had once governed the Empire and who might still govern the destiny of the Lords. Yet he made a poor speech, lasting just fifteen minutes, another demonstration of his diminishing powers. Simultaneously theatrical and incoherent, he refused to disclose which way he would vote, implying that he might abstain. His old friend Arthur Godley, now Lord Kilbracken, felt that 'he rather overdid the dramatic business, inflections of the voice and something of the style of a mid-Victorian tragic actor.'[31] After this embarrassing performance Rosebery disappeared to one of his Pall Mall clubs to sulk. But he returned to the debate in the evening to take his place on the cross-benches, sitting with that 'curious, impassive stare – a sphinx no man can read', as he had been described by A.G. Gardiner. At half-past ten that night Lord Curzon, who had emerged as the key Unionist supporter of the Government, appeared to be making the final speech. Then Halsbury felt compelled to speak again, and was immediately followed by Rosebery, who, in the words of Kilbracken, 'darted forward with lightning speed from the cross-benches and in melodramatic fashion announced his intention of voting with the Government.' This provoked a bitter retort from Lord Selborne, one of Halsbury's Ditchers, who threw back in Rosebery's face a speech he had made in May in which he had warned that the Parliament Bill would turn the Upper House into a 'useless sham', 'a mere fantasy from which all substance has been stripped'.

The spirit of the Halsburyites rose at this crushing demolition of Rosebery, but sank again when the division was taken soon afterwards: the Government had won by 131 to 114, a majority of 17. The struggle was over. The King would not have to take the step he had dreaded. Rosebery's interventions, for all their obtuse theatricality, had been decisive in securing the passage of the Bill. By his own estimate, the number of peers who followed him narrowly exceeded the Government's majority, as he recorded in his diary. 'On my return to the House, I was assured that the issue was very doubtful and that twenty peers would vote for the Government if I declared in favour of the Bill. So I did.'[32] Emotionally drained, Rosebery staggered home to Berkeley Square and went straight to bed, only to be roused at half past midnight by a messenger from the King, delivering a generous note of thanks. Rosebery replied the next morning: 'I should never have forgiven myself if I had abstained and in consequence the large creation of peers had taken place. It is clear that the Government votes alone would have been insufficient to defeat Halsbury, so that it is lucky that we voted. I voted and should have said so – only I was hurried – to protect the Crown from outrage and the Empire from the scandal of this vast creation.'[33] Contradictory to the end, Rosebery voted for the Bill

– then the next day lodged a 'solemn protest' against it in the ancient and rarely used journal kept in the House of Lords for such purposes.

During his second intervention in the debate Rosebery had announced that he was 'speaking in the Lords for the last time'. In this at least he was consistent: after lodging his written protest, he never set foot in Parliament again. At 63, an age at which Churchill had yet to become Prime Minister for the first time, and 25 years younger than Halsbury, Rosebery's strange political career, so full of brilliance and dashed hopes, had finally come to an end. Not that his contemporaries ceased to dream that he might return. It is a tribute to the remarkable magnetism of his personality that long after 1911 he continued to be seen as the potential saviour of the nation. Thus, during the coal strike of 1912 Alfred Harmsworth, now ennobled as Lord Northcliffe, urged him to intervene, as he had so successfully in 1893. Rosebery declined, pointing out that he was no longer a minister, had not the confidence of the governing party, knew 'nothing of the negotiations', and was 'an obscure and unpopular individual'.[34] Northcliffe apologised for having bothered him: 'I would not have worried you had I not received so many suggestions from the public that you should undertake this great national work. Unfortunately, John Bull does not by any means regard you as a statesman in complete retirement.'[35] As the political crisis of 1912 worsened in consequence of a dangerous combination of industrial unrest, militant Suffragette protests, Ulster's paramilitary opposition to Irish Home Rule, and the looming threat of conflict with Germany, Harold Cox, editor of the *Edinburgh Review*, told Rosebery he had a duty to give the nation a lead: 'The battle is only just beginning. You are badly wanted and badly wanted now. You can make people listen as no other man in England can. It is more than ever important that you speak (or write) now for there is otherwise no really effective criticism of the government.'[36] Rosebery replied with the kind of letter he seemed to have been writing for almost a decade: 'From the public point of view I see nothing to be gained from my returning to public life. The battle may be beginning but you do not want Chelsea pensioners in the services. I agree with neither party. And the result is that I am obnoxious to both. I am desirable to nobody and can be of no assistance to the country which recognises only two parties and considers any other views those of an intruder.'[37]

When the crisis over Ireland deepened in 1913 as Ulster descended into open rebellion and the two parties were deadlocked over the Home Rule Bill, there was renewed talk of Rosebery taking on the national leadership. Arthur Balfour, who had been replaced as Unionist leader in 1911 by the far more partisan figure of Andrew Bonar Law, wrote to the King and to Bonar Law suggesting that, instead of trying to coerce Ulster, the Government should agree to a dissolution of Parliament. In these circumstances, either Rosebery or himself should be asked to form a caretaker government until the new Parliament was returned, a similar scheme to the one outlined by Lord Hugh Cecil in 1909: 'I'm not sure that it would not be better for Rosebery, if he would consent, to act alone for I'm still identified with the party of which I was once the Leader and this cannot be said of Rosebery. His "lonely furrow" would, after all, enable him to play an important role in public affairs.'[38] Again, in December 1913 Esher wrote to King George's private secretary, Lord Stamfordham, urging the King to 'insist on dissolution and, if refused by Asquith, he should send for a neutral statesman such as Rosebery to form an interim Government for the purpose of appealing to the country.'[39] As the impasse continued into 1914, the King's assistant secretary Sir Frederick Ponsonby went to Mentmore to discuss the possibility of a round-table conference on Ireland. In his memoirs Ponsonby recorded this description of dinner at the Buckinghamshire 'palace': 'It was tête-à-tête between Lord Rosebery and myself. The house was like the British Museum, full of art treasures: every picture was priceless, every piece of furniture had a history. We dined in a dining-room of the rococo style with heavy gilt carvings and looking-glasses and were waited on by a butler and three ponderous footmen. Remembering that I was very fond of claret, he had a magnum of Lafitte '75, specially selected from his cellar.' Conversation over dinner was frivolous – 'He was in a delightful, irresponsible mood, very witty and amusing'; after the coffee and cigars, Rosebery became serious and suggested they go for a drive to talk about the political situation. For one and a half hours, in the darkness, they were driven in a carriage through the grounds. Ponsonby set out the idea for a conference, but Rosebery said it would never work because the Unionists had nothing to gain, and Asquith could offer nothing that Ulster would accept. Ponsonby was less impressed by Rosebery than by the magnificence of his surroundings; he felt that Rosebery seemed 'to have lost touch with the political world and that he was unwilling to rouse himself to take any serious view of the problem. We returned to the house about eleven o'clock and at once Lord Rosebery went to bed, as he said if he began talking he would lose that sleepy feeling one gets from driving.'[40] The fact was that by this time Rosebery's hatred of politics had become almost pathological: 'Politics, always dirty and debasing, are dirtier than ever. I honestly feel grateful to the persons who take part in politics and who have the morbid taste of washing their hands always in dirty water. A gentleman will likely do in politics what he would kick a man downstairs for doing in ordinary life. And so I endeavour to shut my eyes to them.'[41]

One sorry consequence of Rosebery's contempt for politics was a rupture with Munro-Ferguson. After Edward Hamilton, Ronald Munro-Ferguson had been his most loyal confidant during the peak of his career, but for a number of years Rosebery had sensed him trying to distance himself, and in July 1912 he expressed his feelings of hurt: 'When I consider our former relations and that you have not come near me for some years, I am forced to the conclusion that your friendship with me is at an end. I do not complain in the least. You are in politics and I am out of them. But somehow I always hoped that ours was not a political friendship.' Rosebery then asked for the return of all his letters. 'They can be of no interest or value to you, nor are they to me, but I wish to have them at my disposal.'[42] Munro-Ferguson replied that while it was true they had not met for some years, 'this had to be if I was to move on a course of my own. For the effect of our friendship on my public life was to put an end to my individuality. Anything I did or said was taken to represent your views, so much so that as I grew older it became humiliating and deprived me of all power of initiative.'[43] Rosebery complained in return that Munro-Ferguson was treating him 'as if I were a leper', adding that if his wife had been alive 'you would not have shunned this house'.[44] Munro-Ferguson, in the final letter of this painful exchange, agreed that Lady Rosebery's loss was 'a great calamity' which had changed both their lives; nevertheless, 'were I to be seen walking with you in the park it would destroy the belief in my independence which I have at last established and which is the sole source of my strength.'[45] To this rebuff Rosebery appended a note: 'What a strange idea of friendship and a strange friend.'

Outside politics, Rosebery did not avoid all civic responsibilities. In the summer of 1911 he travelled to Vienna as Ambassador Extraordinary charged with formally announcing the accession of King George V, but later in the year turned down a request that he should travel with the Royal Family as Lord High Steward on a state visit to India, pleading his physical infirmities. 'I am not fitted by experience or manners or appearance for court functions,' he told the King, 'Moreover I am afraid from want of habit that I should commit disastrous blunders. Since 1907 I have been subject to a number of little infirmities and one rather grave one, which are irksome in various ways. If I were by any chance disabled on such a voyage I should never forgive myself.'[46] It was a wise decision. His place was taken by the Earl of Durham, who wrote to Rosebery from the ship describing the rocky voyage: 'We've had a beastly time and half the human souls on board succumbed. The Queen's room was flooded and she had to be carried to another cabin on a litter by two large marines.'[47]

His natural dignity and wit meant that Rosebery continued to be in demand for other public duties. Banquets were hosted and school prizes given away, memorials unveiled and Royal occasions marked. He inaugurated libraries across the country, and fought for the creation of a National Library of Scotland. In June 1911 he was the chief speaker at a dinner given in Westminster Hall to representatives of the Dominion Parliaments; 'I bellowed unsuccessfully for 25 minutes,' he recorded. Sir Robert Baden-Powell persuaded him to join the Scouts Advisory Council. Elected Rector of St Andrews University, in 1911 he gave the address for the five-hundredth anniversary of its foundation, a sparkling speech full of historical allusions. When Lloyd George's secretary, later his mistress, Frances Stevenson, graduated from Royal Holloway College in 1910, she had found Rosebery presiding over the rowdy event: 'I was "capped" by Lord Rosebery, a dignified, handsome figure who resented the ragging indulged in by the attendant students and at one point sat down and refused to proceed with the ceremony until the noise ceased.'[48]

Such activities could not however hide the fact that the twilight was starting to descend on his life. His health was becoming poor. 'I find increasing digestion difficulties in speaking after dinner and must give up that gloomy diversion,' he noted in November 1911. As a remedy, Margot Asquith briskly recommended that he 'take pure liquid paraffin every day'.[49] During a dinner at Buckingham Palace during the war he suffered a violent attack of hiccoughs from drinking ginger beer – alcohol having been banished from the Royal table – and could not speak a word to the Queen on his left. Most of his teeth had disappeared, and in 1917 the last one fell out. His eyesight and memory were in decline, severe blows for someone whose life revolved around the written word. A serious bladder problem in 1914 required a prostate operation, 'a strange and painful experience' which he described in ghoulish detail in one of his betting books. The surgical procedure involved the insertion of a catheter morning and evening, causing him such agony the first time it was done that he was subsequently injected with cocaine to numb the pain, though the catheter remained an 'object of horror'. For 24 hours after the operation 'I was in such torture as I never imagined. Every few minutes there was a spasm. Opium and every sort of alleviating potion was administered. And indeed throughout my illness opiates of all kinds had no effect on me whatsoever.' He refused food for nine days, and also suffered his usual insomnia. 'When the nurse fell asleep, I would bellow out a hymn tune, as I could not bear to hear signs of that repose I could not obtain.' Perhaps worst of all was the arrival of the King to see him, 'on a horrible day of sickness'. On his release from hospital he wrote to Mary Gladstone Drew, 'Surgical operations are no doubt blessings in disguise, but the disguise is so complete that one fails to discover the blessing.'[50]

His depression was only heightened by the outbreak of war in August 1914. As the black clouds gathered over Europe he derived no satisfaction from the fact that he had long predicted such a disaster, and his innate gloominess meant he did not share the national optimism about its brevity or favourable outcome. 'War with Germany, by sea or land, is a tremendous affair for any two nations to undertake; if we won, we should gain little but a bloody nose and two black eyes,' he had said to J.A. Spender in 1907.[51] Once the war began, he confessed he was 'petrified and in my stoniness am best left alone, reading.'[52] When his beloved Dalmeny was requisitioned for military purposes, the house to serve as a hospital, the shore-side at Hound Point as a gun emplacement, he wrote to his sister, explaining that he planned to move south for the duration of the war: 'This means, of course, the introduction of a formidable co-proprietor with all his rounds, approaches and common, indeed, superior rights besides the wreckage of that beauty spot and much besides. I am not the King of Spain and could not endure such a Gibraltar. And so that beautiful home of 250 years comes to an end and all our happy associations are in dust. It is a mortal blow to me. The only comfort is that it is a sacrifice to the country in her hour of stress.'[53] With a little more enthusiasm he tried to do his duty in other ways, donating money for patriotic causes, speaking at recruitment rallies, drafting messages for the King to send to the troops, serving as the Vice-President of the National Patriotic Organisations Central Committee and as Lord-Lieutenant in several counties. He declined, however, the post of Military Deputy for Scotland: 'I have never had any connection with military matters. It is 20 years since I held office and I am at least 10 years older since my operation last year and so I could not undertake novel and arduous duties with any hope of efficiency.'[54] In the same vein he refused Asquith's offer of the post of High Commissioner of the Church of Scotland: 'I suppose that if at this time of stress I was required to sweep a crossing and I could do it efficiently, I might attempt it. But there is no call of patriotism to go and entertain the General Assembly at Holyrood and being single, I am ill-fitted to meet it if there were. No one indeed would be the worse if the office were suspended during the war or altogether abolished.'[55]

Rosebery was often accused of being a Germanophile on the basis of his distrust of the French, his friendship with Bismarck, and his admiration for Teutonic organisation, which played such a part in the 'Efficiency' movement at the beginning of the century. He was, however, profoundly suspicious of German aggression, and once described their methods as 'notorious'; moreover, though like most Victorians he believed in Anglo-Saxon superiority, he loathed the violent racism of German colonialists, as this extract from a letter written to the Colonial Secretary Lord Ripon in June 1893 makes clear: 'We should not be associated in any way with the Germans in their proceedings in South Africa. They are a brutal people in their treatment of the natives.'[56] What Rosebery derided, at the start of the war, was the atmosphere of mob hysteria against the enemy. 'I strongly agree with you in what you say about the denunciations of the Germans,' he told Constance. 'They seem to have behaved vilely and no doubt it is the popular thing to trounce them. But though I do not like or admire him, I am convinced the German Emperor did not want war. I grieve for that noble gentleman, Francis Joseph of Austro-Hungary, who seems to be crowning a life of misfortune by a supreme catastrophe. One can be as zealous about the war as I am without blackguarding the enemy.'[57] Yet once the horrors of the Belgian conquest emerged and the war became bogged down on the Western Front, he was as fiercely anti-German as anyone. In the spring of 1916, in his role as a Fellow of Eton,★ he demanded the expulsion of a boy named Schroeder who was found to be of German parentage; only Lord Halsbury agreed with him, and Schroeder was allowed to stay.[58] He was more successful in securing the resignation of the Head Master, the Reverend Edward Lyttelton, for the offence of delivering an anti-patriotic address at St Margaret's, Westminster in 1915. There was certainly an air of hand-wringing about Lyttelton's opening words: 'We have to remember that so great a war cannot be laid to the charge of any one nation. It is the result of blind misunderstanding of each other and we English have taken very little trouble to be understood. If strife is to be avoided hereafter, we must learn to see what is good in the aims of others and help them.' At a time when hundreds of thousands of young Britons were dying in Gallipoli and Flanders, Rosebery found these sentiments intolerable. 'I regard the present headmastership as distinctly detrimental to the school and could not be responsible for prolonging it a day longer than is necessary,' he told one of the other fellows.[59] His view prevailed, and Lyttelton soon departed. As the slaughter mounted, Rosebery grew still more vehement in his anti-German feelings. In 1917 he wrote, 'What we

★A governor of the College.

all wish is to bring the war to an end. That is why I am in favour of reprisals; not for vengeance but for a practical purpose. Nothing can more conduce to this purpose than making Prussian citizens, now gloating over reports of the outrages committed in their name, realize by experience the nature of those methods. I should be sorry if reprisals brought about the death of Prussian babies, wholly innocent of the crimes of their Government. But I am infinitely more concerned for British babies and am convinced that the surest way of protecting them is to make Prussia endure what she inflicts.'[60]

Rosebery's bitterness arose partly from his dismay at Britain's conduct of the war. He was kept informed of the Government's inadequacies by his old friend Admiral Fisher, the First Sea Lord. Lord Fisher was optimistic at the start of the war – 'Jellicoe★ is full of spirit. It's all too splendid', he told Rosebery[61] – but soon changed his view, especially after clashing with Winston Churchill over the Dardanelles campaign, which he regarded as a terrible drain on naval resources. 'Winston, like every genius (and he really is a genius), will brook no criticism and idolizes power and so has surrounded himself with third-class sycophants.'[62] In May 1915 Fisher resigned his post, causing Rosebery to splutter, 'Every German from the Emperor to the cabin boy will rejoice.' In 1916, with no prospect of victory in sight, he wrote to Fisher, 'Fortunate indeed is the country and opulent in high capacity that is able to dispense with Lord Fisher in a gigantic war. I wish I could think that embarrassment of riches was the cause.'[63] When Sir Oliver Lodge, the Principal of Birmingham University, told him that the country needed a dictatorship and the shooting of a few war officials, Rosebery's response was not encouraging: 'The late and present Government have had a dictatorship ever since the beginning of the war and see what they have made of it. Rarely have I felt less confidence in a Government than I do in this.'[64]

Rosebery also received news from the front through his son-in-law, Sybil's husband Charles Grant, a soldier of outstanding courage and unflappability. Injured in the first fighting in France in September 1914, he wrote to Rosebery, 'Reassure Sybil when you see her about my wounds. They were not at all severe, one only a scratch . . . I think the war will be a long and tiring one as I do not see we can allow the Germans to sack the world. I must say their organisation is a wonderful one and they have some fine leaders.'[65] A year later he was complaining to Rosebery about the lack of resources in the British army. 'To my mind the Germans are beaten already,

---

★The Commander of the Grand Fleet.

that is to say that I do not for a moment suppose they can obtain a victory here, but that is not enough. We must have enough forces to break their line and drive them back to their own country.'[66] Like Fisher, Grant despaired of Winston Churchill's leadership: 'The difficulty of men of genius is that they may sweep away the opposition of men of lesser qualities against their better judgement.'[67]

The cheerless news from the battle fronts sank Rosebery further into his despondency. He refused to see friends, on the ground that he was 'suffering from melancholia and wished to be alone'.[68] At the height of the Dardanelles campaign he wrote this private note: 'An awful darkness, a darkness that can be felt, has overspread the world. Its inhabitants are all prostrate with terror.'[69] When Margot Asquith asked about some roses at Dalmeny, he replied with bitterness, 'I have nothing to do with Dalmeny now and I know nothing about roses.'[70] In this climate of despair he meditated endlessly on his past life, gripped by a sense of failure and loneliness, barely able to see any light in the Stygian gloom. On the eve of his seventieth birthday, on 6 May 1917, he penned these lines: 'When I look back on my life, as I do tonight, I can see only the blackness of sorrows; that, no doubt, is morbid and I can scarcely account for it myself but so it is. It seems strange that all one's joys should have faded like dreams and have abandoned the theatre to misery. In vain do I conjure up the credit account: my wife, my children, my friendships. The debit account glares stonily at me.' Rosebery's thoughts reached such morbid depths that sometimes he longed for the end of his own life, as Mary (Gladstone) Drew discovered when she dined with him in March 1916: 'He is terribly down over the war and the apparent bleeding to death of these mighty kingdoms. He would like to fall asleep and pass away but he dreads pain. He has not sufficient interest in coming events to desire life's continuance.'[71]

The woeful management of the war had made Asquith vulnerable. All his authority evaporated in the heat of conflict. In December 1916 he was driven from office in a daring manoeuvre by David Lloyd George, exuding the resolution and confidence Asquith so conspicuously lacked. Lloyd George created an inner War Cabinet made up of just four other men which met almost daily until the end of the war. Almost all the Asquithian Liberals refused to serve in his wider government. In an attempt to strengthen its prestige and balance, Lloyd George made an extraordinary move: he despatched his new War Secretary, the Earl of Derby, to call on Rosebery, that ageing recluse, to offer him the post of Lord Privy Seal. Although it was 21 years since he had last sat in government, Lloyd George knew Rosebery's name would add lustre – if not administrative dynamism

– to his ministry. However, it was also 44 years since Rosebery had first turned down the offer of a ministerial job, that of a post at the Board of Rating, and he was not ready to change the habits of a lifetime: the offer was instantly declined. He reflected privately a few months later,

> What a preposterous mission it was that Eddy Derby undertook in coming to urge upon me the Privy Seal in a 'consultative capacity' and pressing on me the great weight that my name would carry. What would a 'consultative capacity' amount to? There is no longer a Cabinet. Was I to sit at home till the seeker after advice should arrive, ignorant of when and why that might be? Again, there was not a word about policy. I was to give a blank cheque to a man whose policy I have disapproved of more often than most people. And whether consultative or not I should have to attend the House of Lords which I have not entered for five and a half years and which I hope never to see again. However, I was able to refrain from these aspects of the case by simply foundering myself on the impregnable fact of my physical and mental decrepitude.[72]

In another more imaginative note, Rosebery said that 'if Rip Van Winkle on emerging from his long sleep had been invited to become President of the United States, the invitation could hardly have been more misdirected or Rip more unfit for the place.'[73] Curzon also suggested that Rosebery might make 'a splendid ornamental figurehead' for the British mission to Russia in 1917, but after his last rebuff Lloyd George rightly felt it was not worth pursuing the idea.[74] As he watched from outside, Rosebery's faith in official wartime competence remained low despite the change in Government, and he regularly warned of the imminence of a 'Bolshevik revolution' and the 'dissolution of Empire'.[75]

Like almost every family in Britain, Rosebery's was touched by the carnage. In November 1914 his sister Constance lost her second son, Reginald Wyndham. Then, in 1917, a far crueller blow befell him. Both his sons were performing their military duties heroically. Harry had rejoined the Grenadier Guards, and rose to be General Allenby's military secretary in Palestine. Neil, who had served in France with the Buckinghamshire Yeomanry at the start of the war, married Lady Victoria Stanley, daughter of the Earl of Derby, in 1915. It was a match Major Grant approved of, as he told Rosebery: 'Sybil and I know Victoria very well and she is a dear little thing. I am afraid, however, you will miss Neil very much; he has been the most dutiful of sons.'[76] Neil had been due to go to the Dardanelles, a prospect which horrified his father: 'He is not the least military and has brains and was at the beginning of a happy, married life and seemed to have a future, if that be worth having. The war and its hereafter are nightmares and daymares.'[77] Instead, still MP for Wisbech, he was asked to join the Government as Under-Secretary for Foreign Affairs, and in 1916 became a Whip. An idealistic young man who preferred military operations to political manoeuvres, he then decided to return to the Bucks Yeomanry, and like Harry was posted to Palestine. Fighting against the Turks near Gaza on 17 November, he was hit in the head by a stray bullet, and died instantly. His cousin, Major Evelyn de Rothschild, was killed beside him.

For Rosebery, Neil's death was a calamity. Despite some political differences – for Neil had little enthusiasm for Imperialism – he had been more than just a son. In the recent dark days of Rosebery's loneliness, Neil had been one of his few sources of happiness. Lord Birkenhead wrote of 'the singular love and affection by which these two men were united. They were indeed more like brothers in their easy and affectionate intimacy than like father and son.'[78] In his grief, Rosebery filled pages of notebooks with memories of his beloved Neil – his christening at Barnbougle, 'the poor wee owl' on his first day at Eton, their travels together to Posillipo and Malta, his maiden speech in Parliament. He wrote to the King, who had sent a letter of sympathy: 'Neil was everything to me, not that he was a favourite, for favouritism in families breeds sorrow. But he had lived with me so much the longest and we had so many tastes in common that he had become my greatest friend and confidant. But I have no right to complain. Hundreds of thousands of others have borne and are bearing the same and I glory in his death for your and for his country.'[79]

To heighten Rosebery's anguish, a strange sequel to this tragedy dragged Neil Primrose's name into one of the most sensational trials of the war. In May 1918 a Canadian-born dancer named Maud Allan took the right-wing MP Noel Pemberton Billing to court over what she claimed were libellous allegations he had published in *The Vigilante* that her depraved activities were undermining the war effort. A monocle-wearing, swivel-eyed extremist, Billing claimed that Allan was at the centre of a cult of no fewer than 47,000 sexual perverts; the names of these deviants, he said, were in a black book which had fallen into the hands of German agents. This lurid, far-fetched tale was all too eagerly swallowed by the more credulous sections of the British public, fatigued by war and looking for explanations for military setbacks.

What made the case all the more thrilling was Maud Allan's reputation as a symbol of exotic sexuality. She had sprung to international fame in the Edwardian age performing in Oscar Wilde's notorious play *Salome*, dancing on stage in a costume consisting of little more than some strategically-placed beads and a transparent black chiffon skirt. An illustrated pamphlet distributed at the time of her first show in London in 1908 was explicit about her erotic appeal: 'Miss Allan is such a delicious embodiment of lust that she might win forgiveness with the sins of her wonderful flesh.'[80] Rosebery saw her in action at the Palace Theatre. With admirable restraint, he noted in his diary afterwards that she gave 'a strong performance'.

Maud's semi-nudity would not have been allowed in a music hall, but the biblical and classical allusions of her act served to elevate her to a higher artistic plane, and she became the darling of fashionable society. Having toured much of Europe and Russia with her risqué act, Maud Allan stayed in America during most of the war, making several Hollywood films. At the end of 1917 she returned to Britain to give another performance of *Salome*. This was too much for Billing, Independent MP for East Hertfordshire since 1916, who had taken on a self-appointed role as guardian of public morals. Obsessed with the idea of a sexual conspiracy spreading its tentacles through the Establishment, he decided to act against what he saw as Miss Allan's degeneracy. In February 1918 he publicly accused her of lesbianism and treachery, goading her to sue him. There was more than a touch of Lord Queensberry about Billing – both were unbalanced eccentrics with a passionate loathing of Jews and homosexuals, a neurotic fixation about Oscar Wilde, and an eagerness to use the courts against their enemies – but Billing was perhaps an even greater maverick than Queensberry. Before going into politics he had been a singer, theatre impresario, soldier, farmer, property developer, yacht dealer, journalist and publisher; his first magazine, *British South African Motor Car*, was doomed by the fact that there were no motor cars in South Africa when he launched it. His only enduring work was as an inventor and aviation pioneer. During his lifetime he took out more than 2000 patents, including one for self-lighting cigarettes and another for a clothes-measuring contraption; he also founded the aircraft factory in Southampton that eventually built the Spitfire.

There was one other parallel between Queensberry and Billing: a link with Lord Rosebery. At his trial Billing, who conducted his own defence, repeated his claims about a black book containing the records of 47,000 perverts under German influence. He then called his star witness, a woman named Eileen Villiers-Stuart, a private investigator who had once worked for the Government but now backed his purity campaign. In a testimony that riveted the court and caused uproar outside, she said she had been shown the black book by none other than Evelyn de Rothschild and Neil Primrose, with whom she had established a close friendship. The tome, 'about the size of a *Chambers Nineteenth Century Dictionary*', had come into

Neil Primrose's hands, she said, through his work as a Government Whip. Even more dramatically, she alleged that Primrose had left the ministry and rejoined the army because he wanted 'to get out of public life' so he could 'handle the whole book'. In her most explosive statement of all, she asserted that he and Major de Rothschild had been killed by their own side, because 'they both knew of the book'.

Society was outraged by Villiers-Stuart's sinister charges. 'The fantastic foulness of the insinuations that Neil Primrose and Evelyn de Rothschild were murdered from the rear makes one sick,' wrote Cynthia Asquith.[81] Rosebery himself was appalled, and made 'immediate representations' to the War Office and Lord Curzon, who raised the reporting of the trial in Cabinet on 4 June 1918. On the advice of the Home Secretary, Sir George Cave, it was decided that nothing could be done, apart from urging the press not to publish obscene material.[82] To have held the trial in secret would only have served to heighten public suspicions of an official cover-up. Billing's crude and paranoid theories were no more credible than those of Backhouse and Queensberry twenty years earlier; indeed, one of his other witnesses, a militant homophobe by the name of Harold Spencer, was almost certainly insane. But his case provided an emotional outlet for public anger against the government and, to the horror of the Establishment, Billing was acquitted by the jury. It appeared that Oscar Wilde and Maud Allan were to blame for the failures on the Western Front.

The mood of frustration did not last much longer. During the late summer the German lines finally started to crumble under the weight of a new Allied offensive, and on 11 November the Armistice was declared. Rosebery was barely aware of victory: earlier in the month he had collapsed with a stroke after a day's shooting at his lodge in Midlothian. He was immediately taken to the house in Randolph Crescent, Edinburgh which he had rented for the duration of the war. For a number of days it seemed the end had arrived, as he hovered between delirium and coma. On Armistice Night itself a large celebratory crowd gathered in Randolph Crescent, demanding a speech from the great orator and chanting the old Scottish cry 'Rozbury! Rozbury!' But sadly, as his sister Constance later recalled, 'it was one of Archie's worst days and he was unconscious at the time.'[83] Once the military hospital had vacated Dalmeny, Rosebery was able to return to his real home, and the change of surroundings appeared to lift his spirits. During the course of 1919 he gradually recovered, but remained partially paralysed for the rest of his life.

Rosebery regained his mental powers enough to begin reading again, though his eyesight was poor, and to consider the turbulent political situation in the aftermath of war. At first he was merely a distant spectator, as this extract from a letter of February 1919 to James Bryce shows: 'As to home politics, I can find no savour in them. They pass before me like a film and I wish those who are in them well out of them. It is strange to watch all this like a dead person or disembodied spirit but that is the pitch at which I have arrived.'[84] But soon he started to take a greater interest in public affairs. However profound his detestation of the Party game, the smell of politics was always in his nostrils, and he never ceased to think about statecraft, both past and present. Typical was this pragmatic note to Herbert Fisher regarding attempts to end the Anglo-Irish war by negotiations in late 1921 between Lloyd George's Government and the Irish nationalists: 'Here we are in the degraded but I suppose necessary position of having to negotiate with rebels and assassins in Ireland, but I suppose the whole affair may be safely put down as an odious necessity.'[85]

The writer John Buchan, who saw him frequently during these twilight years, thought that Rosebery had become more conservative in his crippled old age: 'In our talks he was deeply pessimistic. He had lost nearly all the aristocratic radicalism which had made him Mr Gladstone's chief lieutenant in Scotland and had adopted something very like old-fashioned Toryism. His creed was based largely on Burke, and like Burke, he distrusted everything in the nature of plebiscitary democracy.'[86] Rosebery argued that he was reverting to the Whig creed of his forebears, rather than embracing Toryism: 'I used to dislike the Whigs,' he wrote in 1921, 'but in my years of loneliness I have come to the conclusion that they governed England better than anybody else. They thought out their measures carefully and adapted them to their times and generation. They were not heroic but they were wise. In modern days we see much heroism but little wisdom.'[87] As John Buchan admitted, Rosebery had little faith in individual Tories. When Stanley Baldwin unexpectedly succeeded Bonar Law as Prime Minister in 1923, he remarked cruelly that it was 'a strange experience to realize that the Prime Minister of Great Britain is a man of whom one had never heard.'[88] He hated the rise of Ramsay MacDonald even more,* writing to King George's secretary Lord Stamfordham in February 1924: 'The Prime Minister . . . circulated pamphlets by the thousand in German against our contention. It is terrible to think that such a man should be in high office with the support of anybody in this country.'[89] And even in his decline, he retained his prescience. At the beginning of the General Strike in May 1926, he told Buchan, 'I do not think it will last

---

*The Labour leader had campaigned against the war and was widely accused of treachery.

long. I do not believe that half the men know what they are striking for.'[90] It was over in just ten days.

Rosebery also retained his acerbity. His correspondence with Mary Drew was littered with peppery judgements about his reading material. Of an autobiography by Ethel Smyth, the composer and suffragette, he said: 'I really think it is the silliest book I have ever read and that is saying much. I cannot understand how it is people persuade themselves, though they are perfectly insignificant, that their doings and even their nursery performances should interest the public. I think I have read more rubbish than any other human being ever created.' Again: 'I agree with you that the first volume of Byron's letters is unreadable. But I hoped that your devotion to the saintly and delicate Caroline Lamb would carry you through. To my mind she is simply repulsive.' And again, on the autobiography of his old Liberal Imperialist colleague R.B. Haldane, a prolific but often opaque writer with an interest in abstruse branches of philosophy: 'I do not propose to read Haldane's book. I have read his Secret Memorandum and that was enough.' He could feel every bit as annoyed with Mary Drew herself. He found her voice 'peculiarly rasping', her manner 'irritating' and 'aggressive', and he told his sister in 1923 that he 'did not feel equal to facing her alone'.[91]

This sharpness extended into other aspects of his life, and led to a number of typically 'Rosebery' rows. One was caused in 1920 when he complained peevishly to Hannah's cousin Lady Battersea that his old Liberal colleague Augustine Birrell 'never displayed the *least* interest in me'. The barb was relayed to Birrell, who wrote angrily to Rosebery, 'This gave me as keen a pang as I have ever lately felt – for there is no one, outside my own enchanted circle of my own loves and losses, in whom I have ever felt so keen an interest as you. To have it suggested that I never made my feelings known to you was a great grief.'[92] Rosebery's reply was emollient, but the harm was done. He also succeeded in offending the Vicar of Mentmore, Henry Skelton, who decided in 1920 that he wanted to leave the parish to work in the Anglican church's Magdalen Hospital Rescue Home for Fallen Girls. 'The Bishops are always trying to get him away from Mentmore,' Rosebery moaned to his estate manager. 'They apparently think that Mentmore souls are not worth saving in comparison to those of reclaimed harlots. I shall never see him again if he goes to Magdalen Hospital. I always looked on him as a friend and I really thought I had done all I could to satisfy him and so am disappointed.'[93] Skelton, when he heard this, thought Rosebery was being selfish, and told him he had to consider his own wife and children, who were lonely and isolated at Mentmore.

Skelton further complained that Rosebery seemed 'unwilling or unable to give' the testimonial he required before he could take up his new post at the Magdalen Hospital. In response, Rosebery sent a bald, bland three-line reference, which did not please Skelton at all: 'I must confess that I had hoped the testimonial would be a little less impersonal.' He also attacked Rosebery's argument that many other clergymen were in a similar position of isolation: 'It would be cold comfort to a starving man to be told that there must be hundreds of other people in the same case.'[94] Rosebery now felt aggrieved, and wrote to the Vicar, 'Nothing has hurt me more in all this painful affair than your want of confidence in me. That confidence has been given to others and yet I had some claims to it in various characters, as patron, as principal parishioner and as a friend.' But Skelton wanted to hear no more: 'I feel so upset by the whole miserable business and have been feeling so unwell that I have not the heart to attempt any further explanation.'[95]

Rosebery also embroiled himself in a lengthy row with the Duke of Atholl over plans to build a national war memorial at Edinburgh Castle. The Duke headed the committee which, from February 1919, drew up the plans and organised the funding. But Rosebery thought the whole idea grotesque, believing it would ruin the Castle. 'On the Castle Rock there is already a national memorial of a unique kind. I mean the Castle itself. That is a noble monument of all Scottish history and to bastardise this with a view to connecting it with the recent war would surely be a mistake from every point of view,' he wrote to the *Scotsman* in June 1919. In the years that followed he kept grumbling against the Duke and the proposed memorial. Having deplored the 'modern mania for adapting ancient buildings to modern requirements', he then attacked the design as resembling 'a huge jelly mould'. The committee members ignored what they came to call Rosebery's 'annual grouse', and in 1927 the memorial opened to much acclaim.

It was with considerably more justification that in November 1919 Rosebery had exploded with rage when he discovered that the Ministry of Munitions were planning to sell off 178 acres of his land in Edinburgh which had been commandeered during the war for the establishment of the Turnhouse aerodrome. With all the ferocity and sarcasm he could muster, he attacked the Ministry's action in a series of letters to the press. The sale was condemned as 'a lawless proceeding', the official in charge as either 'a pickpocket or a burglar'. 'You propose to sell a rich farm of mine against my will. It is unnecessary to repeat what honest men think of such conduct,' he fulminated.[96] Under this barrage the Ministry capitulated, though not before a junior minister, F.G. Kellaway, had used a public meeting to attack Rosebery for his selfishness and lack of patriotism. This provoked another salvo from Rosebery: 'I rejoice in the violence of his language, because that is always a sign of a weak case, which it is intended to obscure . . . I rejoice that he calls my letter waspish because a wasp implies a sting and I certainly meant to plant a sting to fill the void which ought to have been occupied by a conscience.'[97] After his victory he told Admiral Lord Fisher: 'It is the most extraordinary incident of my life and we could not be worse off under the Stuarts' – but part of him had derived an invigorating pleasure from the tussle. Years later, after his death, one of those involved in the dispute apologised to his son Harry for the Ministry's conduct. 'There is no need,' said the 6th Earl. 'Had it not been for Turnhouse my father would not have lived for another ten years.'[98]

Throughout this post-war decade Rosebery's mind remained alert, but his body was in cruel decline. He had once, at the peak of his powers, said to Margot Asquith that 'death should come to us suddenly before we feel the slow agony of decay. When I kick the bucket I should like to feel I had a kick in reserve.'[99] Sadly, for him this was not the case. The 'slow agony of decay' was all too apparent. In February 1919 the writer Edmund Gosse was walking down a street in London with the Liberal peer Lord Reay when a car drew up beside them.

> The next moment there emerged a little withered figure in a railway cap of cloth, who stood blinking in the sun. Snow-white hair, closely-shaven drawn parchment cheeks, dull eyes that gazed out blankly. I should, positively, not have known who it was. Lord Reay spoke cheerfully to him, and he shook hands with us both but said not a word; stood there, without a smile, then turned, still not speaking, and was pushed by two servants into the motor, which had blinds drawn down. Lord Reay, ten years his senior, very much animated by excitement and distress, looked quite young and turning to me said, 'We have seen a dying man! What a rapid and fatal change! We ought not to have stopped, not have spoken! Who could guess that he had suddenly come to that?' It was terrible.[100]

Incapacitated since his stroke, Rosebery grew weaker in his limbs and was inclined to accidents. 'Yesterday I went out, like a fool, and had a bad fall and today I am in great pain,' he said to Mary Drew after bruising his shoulder in December 1920.[101] Since he was unable to hold a pen, all his correspondence had to be dictated. In his state of 'lamentable decrepitude' he disliked receiving guests, fearing that he would be a bore to them. But in the early 1920s he still went heroically to meetings of the British Museum trustees and the Eton Fellows; the Fellows met for his convenience on the ground floor of the Great Western Hotel at Paddington, to spare him having to deal with stairs. And he still saw a few trusted friends, such as Buchan, Spender, the writer Frederic Harrison, an old colleague from LCC days, and Randall Davidson, the Archbishop of Canterbury, whose journal recorded his impressions of Rosebery. After a visit to The Durdans in March 1920, Davidson found him 'much less ill than I expected. He has largely lost the use of one side and completely of his left arm, but, barring this, one would have thought him very much as of old, only looking unkempt and as if he needed somebody to tidy him up – a rather melancholy condition. He wants a wife or a sister or a daughter. Solitary as his life has been, it is more solitary than ever now that he complains he cannot read the paper properly because he cannot turn it over with one hand and that his books tumble down when he tries to turn up things. He talked of the higher side of things and I tried to get in some helpful prods, for he is quite amendable to them for all his religious reserve.' Three years later, Davidson was 'touched to see how much he dwells on the religious side of things. It is all in his own cynical way but it is very real. He has a copy of the Revised Bible in large print, a several-volume edition, beside his chair and is clearly reading his Bible in the most simple-minded way. Before I left he asked for a prayer and blessing and altogether his attitude touched me considerably.'[102] Apart from religion Rosebery also derived comfort from his little granddaughter Ruth, Neil's only child, and she was a happy, innocent presence at the The Durdans or Dalmeny. 'I had a very happy birthday. Grandpa gave me some lovely books about birds and a scrapbook and then he sent to London for some people to come and show us some moving pictures, which were very funny,' Ruth wrote to Constance Leconfield in 1924. After 1922 Rosebery never again stayed at Mentmore, having handed it over to his heir Harry, Lord Dalmeny.

From 1925 Rosebery went into a steeper decline as his ailments multiplied. Confined to a wheelchair, he was almost completely blind, suffered long bouts of insomnia, and frequently complained of being tired and 'tortured by haemorrhoids'. Obliged by his sense of duty to attend a Royal function at Buckingham Palace in the summer of 1925, he wrote pathetically to Lord Stamfordham: 'I must explain that my legs have gone out of action completely. I cannot move or show the slightest sign of respect. I am very sorry because it is odious to me to receive Their Majesties in such a condition. Kindly prepare them for seeing a monster, and a helpless monster.'[103] Even sadder was a letter he sent his sister Constance in June 1926, which reveals a longing to be released from his physical torment. 'I am afflicted by every sort of complaint, the names of many of which cannot be communicated to ladies, so I must be silent about them. But I can assure you that I am a mass of diseases. I often think it would be better for all concerned if I disappeared and ceased to afflict my many attendants and relations with anxieties or at least troubles about me. When I think of the number of human beings whom I absorb, who might be doing more useful things, and when I think of myself lying like a toad in the hole, I am constantly under the impression that though I know a Higher Power orders it differently, it might be well if I disappeared.'[104]

One day in 1925 a doctor gave him one of his regular insulin injections but mistakenly doubled the dose. His family thought the end had arrived. He fell into a coma, and remained in this condition for several hours. His children were summoned urgently to his bedside at The Durdans – but when Peggy arrived from Paris, where she had been staying, she found to her surprise that her father had recovered. 'If this is Death, it is absolutely nothing,' he said.[105] But there was to be no immediate escape, and he was forced to continue with his dark and harrowing journey. 'You would not like to see me in pain – and such pain. I am brought very low,' he told Constance. There were occasional good days. 'Here the sun is shining and I am basking in it,' he said one August day in 1927, not long after his eightieth birthday. But despite an alert mind, life remained a weary struggle. Balfour called on him in September 1927: 'He was pleasant and interesting but with no other companion than a little grandchild whom he adores; to get to the dining room he had to be lifted bodily from his sofa onto his wheelchair and then again from his wheelchair to his seat at luncheon. I am afraid he is physically failing.'[106]

'How long, oh Lord, how long,' wrote Rosebery to Constance in August 1928, quoting the poem he had written as a child, which 'predicted exactly what I am suffering now'. John Buchan, who continued to visit him regularly, recalled that it was 'a melancholy experience for me to see this former Prime Minister of Britain crushed by bodily weakness, sorrowing over the departing world and contemptuous of the new.' In April 1929 Buchan went for a drive with him at The Durdans. 'I had never seen Surrey more green and flowery, but he was unconscious of the spring glories and was sunk in sad and silent meditations.'[107] It was obvious that death was near. In the early morning of 21 May Rosebery was granted his merciful release, with Harry and Constance by his side. In accordance with his last wishes, the 'Eton Boating Song', written by his tutor William Johnson, was played on a gramophone as he breathed his last. The music of his boyhood was the last sound he heard.

His body was taken from The Durdans through London to King's Cross to be put on a train for the long journey to Edinburgh. As the hearse travelled slowly through Berkeley Square a great, silent, mournful crowd gathered outside Number 38 to pay its last respects. From Edinburgh the oak coffin was taken to Dalmeny, where after a private funeral service he was buried in the family's stone vault in the pretty little village kirk. Soon afterwards a public memorial service was held at St Giles Cathedral in Edinburgh. In his oration the Very Reverend Charles Warr, Dean of the Order of the Thistle, described Rosebery as 'the most representative Scotsman of his times, raised to an unchallenged supremacy in his people's affection; for two generations he reigned among us as the recognised spokesman of our brave and rugged land; the alert and jealous guardian of its traditions, the indomitable champion of its interests. In death he comes back to his own people.'

The Archbishop of Canterbury, Randall Davidson, told Sir George Murray that Rosebery had at last reached the death 'for which his heart has been longing'. He then reflected on the departed's enigmatic character: 'You can't "fit" that most strangely shaped friend into any ordinary category. Angles and eccentricities at once emerge which make it a misfit. But he will hold for us, while life lasts, a treasured place in life's recollection.'[108]

It was precisely those 'angles and eccentricities' that made Rosebery such a unique and memorable character. For decades his defects, quite as much as his qualities, fascinated the political world and the public. 'There was something wistful in him, a sense of the unreached,' said another cleric, Bishop Pollock of Norwich, at the time of his death. Rosebery had always seemed destined to become Britain's Prime Minister. He had all the right gifts for a brilliant political career, a superb intellect combined with flowing eloquence and personal charisma. He could charm friends with his scintillating wit and captivate the masses with his powerful oratory. Rarely for a politician, he possessed both the popular touch and a natural air of authority. Lady Monkswell, LCC member and wife of a senior Liberal politician, echoed the thoughts of many when she wrote in her diary in 1890, having been present at a Rosebery speech, 'He looks to me like a man who fears neither God nor man, as clever as you please, knowing his own mind, perfectly determined to get on, hard, clear-headed and unremorseful. Nobody could be better fitted out than he for the nerve-destroying, heart-breaking work of political life.'[109]

She could not have been more wrong. Lord Rosebery might have attained the highest office, but he never fulfilled his promise. The greatness that appeared to lie within his grasp continually eluded him. His premiership, lasting just 18 months during 1894–5, was one of the shortest and most dismal in modern British history. Instead of living up to the expectation that he would prove himself a second Palmerston or Pitt, Rosebery was almost broken by the strain of his position. His Cabinet was gripped by division, his own body by illness and insomnia. It was with a sense of relief, not regret, that he gave up the premiership. Within little more than a year of leaving Downing Street he had also resigned the Liberal leadership. He never held political office again. Lord Birkenhead, the Unionist Lord Chancellor of the 1920s, later wrote, 'It is strange that a man of such brilliancy should have achieved, in a high perspective, so little.'

During his long years in the wilderness after 1896, Rosebery often brooded on the shadow of failure which appeared to hang over him. 'A man who has been more or less in public life for a quarter of a century, who has been Foreign Secretary and a First Minister, but who has never enjoyed an instant of power, and has now been long in seclusion without a follower and almost forgotten, what can be a greater failure?'[110] But he then went on to suggest that this was a superficial view. The concept of success, he argued, should not be seen purely in terms of realising the conventional aims of fame, power, honours, social distinction and wealth: 'The wise man, I think, does not consider these as the best purpose in life. What he wishes to achieve is happiness in the large sense of the word, a well-ordered life of work, friendship, family affection and, if possible, religious faith.'

Such modest goals, he felt, could never be reconciled with politics, which destroyed friendships and hindered real work. In 1917, in an interesting letter to his friend Lord Kilbracken, who as Arthur Godley had once been Gladstone's secretary, Rosebery set out his distrust of the 'vulgar and squalid impulse' of political ambition: 'Your ambition has been to lead a useful and happy life and that should be the true object of the wise. That you have brilliantly accomplished. You have honour and friends sufficient, you have three score years and ten, a full mind and an active body. Had you chosen a political career you might now be banging a table and denouncing all sorts of honest and respectable men and might hope to rest in the Abbey and be remembered more or less in fifty years. (I don't give more, for Gladstone is already fading fast).'[111] The tragedy of Lord Rosebery's life was that he could never resist the lure of politics, no matter how much revulsion he felt when confronted by the detail of their practice. He could perhaps have been a great writer, a successful journalist, a sportsman, or a society figure, but instead he chose a path that was bound to lead him into emotional and physical turmoil.

Not that Rosebery hated all politics – just the British Parliamentary version. He disliked what he saw as its sham principles and shabby deals, and complained repeatedly that throughout his career he never exercised real power. Instead of the Cabinet system, he preferred the idea of government through 'a man of large mind and iron will who would see what had to be done and do it'.[112] Rosebery would have liked to be that man, but his own character and the political structure of his time and place denied him the chance. He might have enjoyed being an absolute monarch, or an eighteenth-century premier like his hero William Pitt the Younger, standing above Party in guiding the nation, but he had to make do with the more limited role of a Victorian Cabinet minister – and at times even that was too compromising for him.

At the core of Rosebery's apparent failure was a personality unsuited to the tough world of politics. Thin-skinned, often neurotic, he lacked that relish for battle which characterised his arch rival Sir William Harcourt. A master of introspection and self-absorption, he was plagued by doubts about his fitness for office, endlessly clutching at excuses to evade ministerial responsibility. It is an indicator of his self-doubt that the area in which he most excelled, platform speaking, was the political activity he most despised. In her remarkably objective essay about her father Rosebery's daughter Sybil wrote: 'The keynote to his complicated character and indeed to many of his actions lay in a morbid streak which haunted him always and which is known under various names such as sensitiveness, self-depreciation and so on. Except when working in his library or when in the company of little children or in the act of making a speech, this dreadful companion haunted him always – amazingly enough. This spoiled pleasures which come as a matter of course to many who envied his gifts and advantages, was responsible for his stormy moods and recurrent bitterness and robbed him of any real joy in achievement.'[113] In a similar vein, the historian A.G. Gardiner claimed that Rosebery had the 'temperament of the artist, not of the politician', and it was that which led in the end to 'the tragedy of unfulfilment'. Such a temperament made him a 'creature of moods and moments' with a 'Byronic instinct for melodrama' which meant that 'political leadership was impossible'.

Rosebery himself said his greatest flaw was an over-developed sense of pride. Reflecting on his seventieth birthday in 1917 he wrote, 'What has been my besetting sin, I ask myself. Probing as deeply as I can, I answer Pride; a blight at the root of my life.'[114] A heightened awareness of his own dignity, a gift for taking extreme offence at the slightest affront, an obsession with maintaining his independence of action and an air of petulance were all damaging manifestations of this flaw which made him a difficult colleague and a poor leader. It was often said that they were a consequence of the ease with which he had reached the top, assisted by wealth, privilege and patronage. The Scottish radical aristocrat Ruaraidh Erskine of Marr wrote that 'his supreme misfortune was, I think, that almost from his cradle he was attended by the twin spirits of rank and fortune; and instead of correcting, they spoiled the child.' In particular, as a peer who succeeded in his early twenties he had no experience of either the House of Commons or a Parliamentary election, 'with its disorderly gatherings, its organised oppositions, its hostile little meetings, its jeering throng, its stream of disagreeable and often silly questions,' to quote Winston Churchill.[115] Because he had never had to struggle for anything in life, his character had little of the steel that is tempered in adversity. Some said he was no more than an egotist. In a scathing profile written in 1924, Philip Guedalla claimed that Rosebery's 'long career has been a painfully protracted adolescence. Sometimes he would play quietly with his toys for years together. But at intervals, swept by those dark impulses which devastate a nursery, he dashed them on the floor and went off to mutter in a corner.'[116] Though extreme in its vituperation, this assessment exemplifies a widely held view. A career that once promised so much, in the end bred feelings of despair. Even his closest political ally, the Liberal MP Ronald Munro-Ferguson, could not hide his frustration, writing to Rosebery in 1906, 'You will always confess the mind of the country but you will never undertake the continuous effort and drudgery which is an essential condition of success.'[117]

For all the exasperation he provoked in so many people, it would be unfair not to mark the more glorious side of Rosebery's career: his platform appearances which inspired such unique public excitement, his wonderfully rich language and humour, his superb performance as Foreign Secretary, which not only strengthened the Empire but also averted possible war in the Balkans, Afghanistan and Siam. He was a man of rare political insight, as his judgements regarding Ireland, Imperialism, the Entente Cordiale and the rise of the Labour Party demonstrate. It could be argued that, through the Liberal League, he kept his party together during the dark days of the Boer War when many moderates, denied an outlet for their views, might otherwise have left it. The influence of his oratory was prodigious; his famous speech at Chesterfield was vital in promoting a negotiated peace in the Boer War, while his address at Epsom in 1898 may have prevented war with France over Fashoda. Such phrases as 'the Gladstonian Umbrella' and 'the Commonwealth of Nations' became part of the political lexicon. Above all, his glittering, strange, compelling personality added to the richness and colour of late Victorian and Edwardian politics, while the legacy of that richness can still be enjoyed in his writings and in the treasures he left behind at Dalmeny.

Looking back on his contradictory, haunted life, often touched by tragedy but always fascinating, it seems appropriate to use the words he himself spoke with regard to human weakness when paying a tribute in 1896 to another great but flawed Scotsman, Robbie Burns:

> Mankind is helped in its progress almost as much by the study of imperfection as by the contemplation of perfection. Had we nothing before us in our futile and halting lives but saints and the ideal, we might well fail altogether. We grope blindly along the catacombs of the world, we climb the dark ladder of life, we feel our way to futurity, but we can scarcely see an inch around or before us. We stumble and falter and fall, our hands and knees are bruised and sore and we look up for light and guidance. Could we see nothing but distant unapproachable impeccability, we might well sink prostrate in the hopelessness of emulation and the weariness of despair. Is it not then, when all seems blank and lightless and lifeless, when strength and courage flag, and when perfection seems as remote as a star, is it not then that imperfection helps us? When we see that the greatest and choicest images of God have had their weaknesses like ours, their temptations, their hours of darkness, their bloody sweat, are we not encouraged by their lapses and catastrophes to find energy for one more effort, one more struggle? Where they failed we feel it a less dishonour to fail; their errors and sorrows make, as it were, an easier ascent from infinite imperfection to infinite perfection.

Notes

INTRODUCTION

1. Diary of Margot Asquith, 20 April 1899.
2. *The Young Man Magazine*, July 1900.
3. Sir Ian Malcolm, *Vacant Thrones*.
4. E.T. Raymond, *The Man of Promise*.
5. Diary of Margot Asquith, 23 October 1904.
6. Diary of Beatrice Webb, 16 May 1900, Passfield papers.

CHAPTER 1: 'ALMOST A GOOD GENIUS'

1. Dalmeny papers.
2. This unintentionally hilarious document is quoted in parts by Lord Crewe and Robert Rhodes James, but the fullest version is in Jane Stoddart, *The Earl of Rosebery*.
3. Note on the death of William Gladstone, 19 May 1898, Rosebery NLS 10111.
4. Robert Rhodes James, *Rosebery*.
5. Letter to H.A.L. Fisher, 29 December 1924, Fisher papers.
6. Thomas G. Coates, *Rosebery Life and Speeches*.
7. Coates, *op.cit.*
8. Rhodes James, *op.cit.*
9. G.W.E. Russell, *Portraits of the Seventies*.
10. Sybil Grant, 'A Great Scotsman', Rosebery NLS Acc 8365.
11. Rosebery to his sister Constance Leconfield, 29 May 1892, Petworth papers.
12. Raymond Asquith to H.T. Baker, 1 October 1898.
13. Edward Hamilton's Diary, 19 April 1890.
14. The Marquess of Crewe, *Lord Rosebery*.
15. *Ibid.*
16. Rhodes James, *op.cit.*
17. *Ibid.*
18. Letter from Lady Leconfield to Lord Crewe, 12 March 1930, Rosebery NLS 10195.

19. Rosebery NLS 10191.
20. Dalmeny papers.
21. Lady St Helier, *Memories of Fifty Years*.
22. Note, 21 August 1916, Dalmeny papers.
23. Letter to Eileen, Lady Stanhope, 4 July 1924, Stanhope papers, U1590/C645.
24. Memorandum entitled 'A Day At Battle', Rosebery NLS, Acc 8365/36.
25. Rhodes James, *op.cit.*
26. Sybil Grant, *op.cit.*
27. Letter to Lady Leconfield, 12 September 1905, Petworth papers 5577.
28. Rhodes James, *op.cit.*
29. Letter to the Revd George Renaud, 13 March 1895, Rosebery NLS Acc 7870.
30. Letter to his mother, Dalmeny papers.
31. Letter to Lady Rosebery, 27 October 1855, Rhodes James, *op.cit.*
32. Letter to Lady Leconfield, 22 August 1928, Petworth papers 5586.
33. Crewe, *op.cit.*
34. Recollection in a letter to Lady Stanhope, 15 December 1914, Stanhope papers, U1590, C587/2.
35. Crewe, *op.cit.*
36. Dalmeny papers.
37. Letter to George Dundas, Easter 1861, Rosebery NLS 10071.
38. James Brinsley Richards, *Seven Years at Eton*.
39. Lord Esher, *Cloud-Clapped Towers*.
40. John Chandos, *Boys Together*.
41. James Lees-Milne, *The Enigmatic Edwardian: The Life of Reginald, 2nd Viscount Esher*.
42. E.T. Raymond, *The Man of Promise*.
43. Crewe, *op.cit.*
44. Note from Lord Halifax to Lord Crewe, Rosebery NLS 10195.
45. Rhodes James, *op.cit.*
46. Letter from William Johnson to Lord Dalmeny, 18 August 1862, Rosebery NLS 10012.
47. Quoted in almost every biography and essay on Rosebery, including Winston Churchill's *Great Contemporaries*.
48. A.G. Gardiner, *Prophets, Priests and Kings*.
49. Rhodes James, *op.cit.*
50. Letter from Johnson to Lady Harry Vane, 6 May 1864, Rosebery NLS 10012.
51. Letter to Lady Leconfield, undated, Petworth papers 5570.
52. Crewe, *op.cit.*
53. Letter to William Gladstone, Gladstone papers, Add Ms 44290.
54. Eton Society Record Book, Eton College archives.
55. Rosebery NLS 10071.
56. Coates, *op.cit.*
57. Rhodes James, *op.cit.*

58. Letter to Lady Leconfield, 1 January 1861, Petworth papers 5570.
59. Letter to William Johnson, 5 May 1862, Rosebery NLS.
60. Coates, *op.cit.*
61. Sir Frederick Ponsonby, *Recollections of Three Reigns*.
62. All three letters: Rosebery NLS 10012.
63. Ian Anstruther, *Oscar Browning*.
64. James Lees-Milne, *op.cit.*
65. Tim Card, *Eton Renewed: A History from 1860 to the Present Day*.
66. Card, *op.cit.*
67. William Johnson to Lord Dalmeny, Midnight 23 March 1862, Rosebery NLS 10012.
68. William Johnson to the Duchess of Cleveland, Rhodes James, *op.cit.*
69. Letter to Lady Leconfield, sent from Eton, undated, Petworth papers 5570.
70. Dalmeny papers.
71. Letter from Frederick Wood to Lord Dalmeny, 2 February 1866, Rosebery NLS 10071.
72. Rosebery's obituary of Vyner in *Morning Post*, 19 May 1870.
73. Correspondence from Edward Cheney, Rosebery NLS 10071.
74. Letter from William Johnson to the Duchess of Cleveland, July 1864, Rosebery NLS 10012.
75. Edward Cheney to Lord Dalmeny, undated, Rosebery NLS 10071.
76. William Johnson to the Duchess of Cleveland, 7 May 1864, Rosebery NLS 10012.
77. Letter from William Johnson to Frederick Wood, quoted in Faith Compton Mackenzie, *William Cory*.
78. F. Warre-Cornish, *The Letters and Journals of William Cory* (1897).
79. Letter from William Johnson to Lord Dalmeny, January 1865, Rosebery NLS 10012.
80. Rhodes James, *op.cit.*
81. Lady Leconfield to Lord Crewe (undated), Rosebery NLS 10195.
82. Rhodes James, *op.cit.*
83. 12 June 1926, Eton Archives Col P6/4/63A.
84. Letter to Rosebery, 20 June 1870, quoted in Faith Mackenzie, *op.cit.*
85. Rosebery NLS 10098.

CHAPTER 2: 'THE EMPTINESS OF A LIFE OF PLEASURE'

1. The Marquess of Crewe, *Lord Rosebery*.
2. Jane T. Stoddart, *The Earl of Rosebery*.
3. Though it was the same sum his father had received as an undergraduate at Cambridge: Stanhope papers, U1590 C150.

4. Exodus, chapter 2, verse 14. The story is in Crewe, *op.cit.*
5. Dalmeny papers.
6. Letter from Charles Dodgson to Rosebery, 30 November 1893, Rosebery NLS 10091.
7. Undated letter, Rosebery NLS 10071.
8. Letter to Lady Leconfield, 17 December 1866, Petworth papers 5570.
9. Letter from S. James-Owen to Lord Crewe, 8 March 1938, Rosebery NLS 10195.
10. Letter from Henry Tollemache to Lord Crewe, 27 August 1929, Rosebery NLS 10195.
11. T.H.S. Escott, *Personal Forces of the Period.*
12. Lady Angela St Clair Ershine, *Memories and Base Details.*
13. J.A. Spender, *The Public Life.*
14. Churchill to A.G. Gardiner, quoted in *Prophets, Priests and Kings.*
15. Note by Lord Rosebery, 1 July 1915, Dalmeny papers.
16. A.R.C. Grant and Caroline Combe, *Lord Rosebery's North American Journal.*
17. Note in Betting Book during trip to Venice, 1873, Rosebery NLS 10191.
18. Robert Rhodes James, *Rosebery.*
19. William Johnson to Rosebery, 30 August 1868, Rosebery NLS 10012.
20. Bouverie Primrose to Lord Stanhope, 15 December 1865, Stanhope papers U1590 C510.
21. Gardiner, *op.cit.*
22. Dean Liddell to Rosebery, 26 February 1871, Rosebery NLS 10072.
23. Rosebery to J.A. Spender, 16 October 1916, Spender papers Add MS 46387.
24. Rhodes James, *op.cit.*
25. Diary of Rosebery, 15 and 16 September 1869, Dalmeny papers.
26. Quoted in E.H. Thruston, *The Earl of Rosebery: Statesman and Sportsman.*
27. Crewe, *op.cit.*
28. Betting Book, Rosebery NLS 10191.
29. *Ibid.*
30. Diary of Beatrice Webb, April 1904, Passfield papers.
31. Grant and Combe, *op.cit.*
32. *Ibid.*
33. Maud Elliott Howe, *Uncle Sam And His Circle.*
34. Lately Thomas, *Sam Ward: King of the Lobby.*
35. *Ibid.* There appears to be no written record of this bombastic prediction, and Robert Rhodes James has argued that Rosebery never said it. It has usually been ascribed to his time at Eton, but in view of the mutual admiration between Ward and Rosebery and Rosebery's growing self-confidence by the mid 1870s, the Mendacious Club would seem a much more likely venue.
36. Ward to Lawley, New York, 23 December 1873, Rosebery NLS 10074.
37. Grant and Combe, *op.cit.*
38. Lately Thomas, *op.cit.*

39. Diary of Rosebery, 19 February 1872, Dalmeny papers.
40. Hesketh Pearson, *Labby*.
41. Rosebery to Francis Knollys, 16 February 1873, Rosebery NLS 10190.
42. Margot Asquith's Diary, 5 December 1897.
43. Memorandum, Rosebery NLS 10177.
44. Mary Fox to Rosebery, undated, Rosebery NLS 10128.
45. Mary Fox to Mrs Grigg, undated, Rosebery NLS 10128.
46. Memorandum dated 10 October 1914, Rosebery NLS 10177.
47. Rhodes James, *op.cit.*
48. Rosebery to Ousley Higgins, 15 January 1873, Rosebery NLS 10073.
49. Diary of Lord Rosebery, 1 April 1874, Dalmeny papers.
50. All entries: Diary of Lord Rosebery, Dalmeny papers.
51. Bronwen Montgomerie to Rosebery, 12 May 1882, Rosebery NLS 10079.
52. Journal of trip to America 1874, Rosebery NLS 10192.
53. Romilly Jenkins, *The Dilessi Murders*.
54. Vyner to Muncaster, 21 April 1870, Crosby Stevens, *Lord Muncaster's Journal*.
55. Memorandum written by Rosebery, 21 April 1871, Rosebery NLS 10188.
56. *Lord Muncaster's Journal*.
57. Rosebery to Mary Gladstone, 10 May 1881, Mary Gladstone papers Add Ms 46,237.
58. Rosebery to Ousley Higgins, 21 October 1871, Rosebery NLS 10072.
59. Lord Randolph Churchill to Rosebery, 19 March 1871, Rosebery NLS Acc 8654.
60. 11th Marquess of Huntly to Rosebery, 27 August 1871, Rosebery NLS 10071.
61. Stoddart, *op.cit.*
62. Maud Elliott Howe, *op.cit.*
63. Rosebery memorandum (undated), Rosebery NLS 10191.
64. Grant and Combe, *op.cit.*
65. Rosebery Journal, February 1872, Rosebery NLS 10189.
66. Diary of Lord Rosebery, 23 May 1874, Dalmeny papers.
67. Rosebery Journal, 24 December 1874, Rosebery NLS 10192.
68. Rosebery Journal, April 1873, Rosebery NLS 10191; also quoted in Gordon Martel's excellent *Rosebery and the Failure of Foreign Policy*.
69. Note by Rosebery, undated, Rosebery NLS 10189.
70. Note by Rosebery, April 1873, Rosebery NLS 10190.

CHAPTER 3: 'I SHALL BE DEVOTED TO YOU, ARCHIE'

1. E.S. Hope to Rosebery, 12 November 1871, Rosebery NLS 10071.
2. William Johnson to Rosebery, 30 August 1868, Rosebery NLS 10012.

3. Crewe, *Lord Rosebery*, and Robert Rhodes James, *Rosebery*.

4. Crewe, *op.cit.*

5. W.F. Moneypenny and G.E. Buckle, *Life of Disraeli*.

6. Disraeli to Rosebery, 23 September 1868, Dalmeny papers.

7. Lord Randolph Churchill to Lord Dalmeny, 7 October 1867, Rosebery NLS 10009.

8. Rosebery Betting Book, 14 December 1870, Rosebery NLS 10188.

9. Diary of Lord Rosebery, 15 September 1875, Dalmeny papers.

10. *Ibid.*, 17 December 1876, Dalmeny papers.

11. William Johnson to Rosebery, 30 August 1868, Rosebery NLS 10012.

12. Rosebery to the Duchess of Cleveland, 27 October 1867, Dalmeny papers.

13. Catherine Gladstone to Rosebery, 21 October 1869, Rosebery NLS 10021.

14. Crewe, *op.cit.*

15. Crewe, *op.cit.* and Rhodes James, *op.cit.*

16. Granville to Rosebery, 13 February 1869, Rosebery NLS 10072.

17. Lord Birkenhead, *Contemporary Personalities*.

18. Rosebery, *Lord Randolph Churchill*.

19. Diary of Lord Rosebery, 7 February 1871, Dalmeny papers.

20. *Ibid.*, 28 January 1873, Dalmeny papers.

21. A.R.C. Grant and Caroline Combe, *Lord Rosebery's North American Journal 1873*.

22. Thomas Coates, *Rosebery Life and Speeches*.

23. Journal of Lord Kimberley, 8 May 1871.

24. Jane T. Stoddart, *The Earl of Rosebery*.

25. Coates, *op.cit.*

26. Letter to Charles Geake, undated but *circa* 1900, Geake papers.

27. Letter to the Duchess of Cleveland, 24 November 1871, Dalmeny papers.

28. Journal of Queen Victoria, 14 May 1870, Royal Archives.

29. Rhodes James, *op.cit.*

30. Frank Lawley to Ousley Higgins, 29 April 1872, Rosebery NLS 10073.

31. Frank Lawley to Ousley Higgins, 5 June 1872, Rosebery NLS 10073.

32. Diary of Lord Rosebery, 6 May 1872, Dalmeny papers.

33. Rosebery to Gladstone, 16 February 1872, Gladstone papers, Add Ms 44288.

34. Rosebery to Gladstone, 2 May 1873, Gladstone papers, Add Ms 44288.

35. Rosebery Betting Book, Rosebery NLS 10190.

36. Rosebery to Gladstone, 25 May 1873, Add Ms 44288.

37. Coates, *op.cit.*

38. Knollys to Rosebery, 10 October 1874, Rosebery NLS 10039.

39. Diary of Lord Rosebery, 30 September 1874, Dalmeny papers.

40. *Ibid.*, 9 March 1874, Dalmeny papers.

41. Frank Lawley to Rosebery, 31 October 1872, Rosebery NLS 10073.

42. Crewe, *op.cit.*

43. *Daily Telegraph*, 15 July 1876.

44. *Vanity Fair*, 3 June 1876.

45. Diary of John Bright, 11 February 1876.

46. Correspendence between Rosebery and Hope, Rosebery NLS 10074.

47. Rosebery to the Duchess of Cleveland, 30 July 1885, Dalmeny papers.

48. Rosebery note, *circa* 1872, Rosebery NLS 10189.

49. *Daily Mail*, 16 December 1901.

50. Journal of Lewis Harcourt, 5 December 1880, Vol. 347.

51. Unpublished manuscript by the Marchioness of Crewe, extract in *The Times*, 26 February 1977.

52. Niall Ferguson, *The House of Rothschild*.

53. Richard Davis, *The English Rothschilds*.

54. Diary of Lady Battersea (Mrs Cyril Flower), 19 November 1890, Battersea papers Add Ms 47,940.

55. Davis, *op.cit.*

56. Countess of Warwick, *Afterthoughts*.

57. Story told by Regy Brett and recounted in the Journal of Lewis Harcourt, 12 January 1887, Vol. 380.

58. Leon Edel, *Henry James: The Conquest of London*.

59. Sybil Grant, 'A Great Scotsman', Rosebery NLS Acc 8365.

60. Diary of Lord Rosebery, 31 March 1874, Dalmeny papers.

61. Journal of Lewis Harcourt, 5 December 1880, Vol. 347.

62. Letters from Hannah in Dalmeny papers, 9–042.

63. Hannah to Annie Yorke, 8 January 1878, Edward Hamilton papers, Add Ms 47963.

64. Rhodes James, *op.cit.*

65. Davis, *op.cit.*

66. Lucy Cohen, *Lady de Rothschild and her daughters*.

67. Hannah to Rosebery, 25 January 1878, Dalmeny papers, 9–042.

68. Hannah to Rosebery, 4 February 1878, Dalmeny papers 9–042.

69. David Feldman, *Englishmen and Jews*.

70. Cohen, *op.cit.*

71. Rhodes James, *op.cit.*

72. Richard Davis, *op.cit.*

73. Diary of Thomas Gilmour, 7 February 1885, NLS Acc 8989/3.

74. Memorandum by Sir Edward Hamilton, Add Ms 48,613.

75. Letter from Lady Rosebery to Sir Edward Hamilton, 17 September 1889, Hamilton papers Add Ms 48,613.

76. Journal of Lewis Harcourt, 26 March 1882, Vol. 350.

77. The story was told by Sir George Leveson-Gower, recounting a conversation with Rosebery. It is quoted in John Raymond, *The Doge of Dover*, and also in the Journal of Lewis Harcourt, January 1887, Vol. 381.

78. Letter to Hamilton, 25 September 1890, Add Ms 48,613.

79. John Vincent (ed.), *The Crawford Papers*.

80. Kenneth Young, *Harry, Lord Rosebery*.
81. Lady Battersea, *Reminiscences*.
82. *The Times*, 15 February 1882.
83. Haldane to his mother, 13 September 1899, quoted in H.G.C. Matthew, *The Liberal Imperialists*.
84. Letters to Mary Gladstone, 22 June 1880 and 13 January 1881, Mary Gladstone papers, Add Ms 46,237.
85. Rosebery to Munro-Ferguson, 5 August 1889, Rosebery NLS 10017.

CHAPTER 4: 'A CONCEITED LITTLE ASS'

1. Thomas F.G. Coates, *Rosebery Life and Speeches*.
2. Chamberlain to Rosebery, 27 January 1877, Rosebery NLS.
3. Rosebery to HM Queen Victoria (undated copy, *c.* 1885), Rosebery NLS 10106.
4. Rosebery to Gladstone, 2 October 1878, Add Ms 44288.
5. Reid to Rosebery, 24 December 1878, Rosebery NLS 10074.
6. Reid to Rosebery, 1 January 1879, Rosebery NLS 10074.
7. Richard Shannon, *Gladstone*.
8. Richardson to Rosebery, 3 January 1879, Rosebery NLS 10075.
9. Diary of Lord Rosebery, 8 January 1879, Dalmeny papers.
10. Colin Matthew, *Gladstone*.
11. Lord Crewe, *Rosebery*.
12. Lucy Masterman (ed.), *Mary Gladstone, Diaries and Letters*.
13. M.R.D. Foot and H.C. Matthew, *The Gladstone Diaries*.
14. Diary of Lord Rosebery, 24 November 1879, Dalmeny papers.
15. *Ibid.*, 25 November 1879, Dalmeny papers.
16. *Ibid.*, 29 November 1879, Dalmeny papers.
17. Sir Philip Magnus, *Gladstone*.
18. Agatha Ramm, *The Gladstone–Granville Correspondence*.
19. Mary Gladstone, *op.cit.*
20. Hannah Rosebery to Constance Leconfield, 4 December 1879, Petworth papers PHA 9680.
21. Colin Clifford, *The Asquiths*.
22. Masterman, *op.cit.*
23. Richardson to Rosebery, 22 February 1880, Rosebery NLS 10075.
24. Jane Stoddart, *The Earl of Rosebery*.
25. Robert Kelley, 'Midlothian: A Study in Politics and Ideas'. This article provides a superb commentary on Gladstone's political philosophy as outlined in the campaign.
26. Edward Hamilton's Diary, 30 August 1884.
27. Gladstone to Granville, 26 March 1880: Ramm, *op.cit.*

28. Ralph Richardson to Rosebery, 6 April 1880, Rosebery NLS 10075.

29. Robert Rhodes James, *Rosebery*.

30. Kelley, *art. cit.*

31. Rosebery to Queen Victoria, 26 July 1893, Royal Archives, RA VIC/N48/215.

32. Diary of Lord Rosebery, 24 April 1880, Dalmeny papers.

33. Rhodes James, *op.cit.*

34. Diary of Lord Rosebery, 24 April 1880, Dalmeny papers.

35. Rosebery to Gladstone, 25 April 1880, Gladstone papers, Add Ms 44288.

36. Granville to Rosebery, 25 April 1880, Rosebery NLS 10075.

37. Rhodes James, *op.cit.*

38. Hannah Rosebery to Constance Leconfield, 27 April 1880, Petworth Papers PHA 9680.

39. Edward Hamilton's Diary, 3 May 1880.

40. Mary Gladstone to Rosebery, May 1880, Rosebery NLS 10015.

41. Rosebery to Mary Gladstone, April 27 1880, Add Ms 46,237.

42. Edward Hamilton's Diary, 21 March 1890.

43. Diary of Lord Rosebery, 25 April 1880, Dalmeny papers.

44. Rosebery to Gladstone, 14 July 1880, Gladstone papers Add Ms 44288.

45. Diary of Lord Rosebery, 21 June 1880.

46. Rosebery to Mary Gladstone, 21 July 1880, Mary Gladstone papers, Add Ms 46,237.

47. Hartington to Rosebery, 9 August 1880, Rosebery NLS 10076.

48. Hannah Rosebery to Constance Leconfield, 12 August 1880, Petworth papers, PHA 9680.

49. Gladstone to Granville, 13 September 1880, Ramm, *op.cit.*

50. Rosebery to Mary Gladstone, 26 August 1880, Mary Gladstone papers Add Ms 46,237.

51. Donaldson to Rosebery, 6 October 1880, Rosebery NLS 10013.

52. Diary of Lord Rosebery, 18 June 1880, Dalmeny papers.

53. *Ibid.*, 12 June 1881, Dalmeny papers.

54. Sam Ward to Margaret Terry, 22 December 1882, quoted in Maud Elliott Howe, *Uncle Sam and His Circle*.

55. Journal of Lewis Harcourt, 5 December 1880, Vol. 347.

56. *Ibid.*, 13 April 1881, Vol. 347.

57. *Ibid.*, 27 August 1881, Vol. 348.

58. Masterman, *op.cit.*

59. Diary of Lord Rosebery, 7 and 10 April 1882, Dalmeny papers.

60. Leon Edel, *Henry James: The Conquest of London.*

61. Memorandum in Betting Book, Rosebery NLS 10190.

62. Cooper to Rosebery, 11 March 1881, Rosebery NLS 10010.

63. Rosebery to Godley, 5 February 1881, Rosebery NLS 10077.

64. A.G. Gardiner, *The Life of Sir William Harcourt.*

65. *Ibid.*
66. Granville to Gladstone, 16 April 1881, Ramm, *op.cit.*
67. Edward Hamilton's Diary, 22 April 1881.
68. Crewe, *op.cit.*
69. Journal of Lewis Harcourt, 30 April 1881, Vol. 348.
70. Diary of Sir Charles Dilke, 28 April 1881, Add Ms 43924.
71. *Ibid.*, 3 May 1881, Add Ms 43924.
72. Gladstone to Granville, 7 May 1881, Ramm, *op.cit.*
73. Diary of Lord Rosebery, 14 May 1881, Dalmeny papers.
74. Mary Gladstone to Rosebery, 12 May 1881, Rosebery NLS 10015.
75. Journal of Lewis Harcourt, 10 June 1881, Vol. 348.
76. Mary Gladstone to Rosebery, 11 May 1881, Rosebery NLS 10015.
77. Diary of Thomas Gilmour, 18 October 1885, Gilmour papers, Acc 8989/4.
78. Gladstone to Rosebery, 30 July 1881, quoted in Foot and Matthew, *op.cit.*
79. Rosebery to Gladstone, 1 August 1881, Gladstone papers, Add Ms 44288.
80. Edward Hamilton's Diary, 3 July 1881.
81. Dilke to Rosebery, 4 August 1881, Rosebery NLS 10077.
82. Frank Lawley to Rosebery, 5 August 1881, Rosebery NLS 10077.
83. Hamilton to Rosebery, 5 August 1881, Rosebery NLS 10031.
84. Journal of Lord Kimberley, 8 July 1895.
85. Gardiner, *op.cit.*
86. Rosebery to Ward, 12 November 1881, Maud Elliott Howe, *op.cit.*
87. Undated memo, but before May 1882, Rosebery NLS 10176.
88. Gladstone to Rosebery, 11 December 1882, Foot and Matthew, *op.cit.*
89. Crewe, *op.cit.*
90. Memorandum dated 6 May 1881, Rosebery NLS 10176.
91. Rosebery to Gladstone, 6 May 1881, Rosebery NLS 10176.
92. Crewe, *op.cit.*
93. Diary of Lord Rosebery, 7 May 1881, Dalmeny papers.
94. *Ibid.*, 15 July 1881, Dalmeny papers.
95. Rosebery to Ronald Munro-Ferguson, 20 August 1887, Rosebery NLS 10017.
96. Journal of Lord Esher, 27 November 1890.
97. Edward Hamilton's Diary, 10 February 1881.
98. Note of conversation with Anderson, 12 March 1908, Betting Book, Rosebery NLS 10185.
99. Sheila Goodie, *Mary Gladstone.*
100. Rosebery to Gladstone, 18 May 1882, Gladstone papers, Add Ms 44288.
101. Rosebery to Gladstone, 27 June 1882, Gladstone papers, Add Ms 44288.
102. Cooper to Rosebery, 14 June 1882, Rosebery NLS 10010.
103. Betting Book, Rosebery NLS 10176.
104. Rosebery to Gladstone, 6 December 1882, Gladstone papers, Add Ms 44288.
105. Gladstone to Rosebery, 10 December 1882, Gladstone papers, Add Ms 44288.

106. Cooper to Rosebery, 10 December 1882, Rosebery NLS 10010.
107. Quoted in Foot and Matthew, *The Gladstone Diaries*.
108. Rosebery to Gladstone, 22 December 1882, Gladstone papers, Add Ms 44288.
109. Edward Hamilton's Diary, 24 December 1882.
110. Journal of Lewis Harcourt, 23 December 1882, Vol. 352.
111. Edward Hamilton's Diary, 17 December 1882.
112. Rosebery to Hamilton, 12 December 1882, Hamilton papers, Add Ms 48,612A.
113. Granville to Gladstone, 23 December 1882, Ramm, *op.cit.*
114. Mary Gladstone to Rosebery, December 1882, Rosebery NLS 10015. This letter is wrongly attributed in Rhodes James's account to Catherine Gladstone.
115. Catherine Gladstone to Rosebery, 14 December 1882, Rosebery NLS 10021.
116. Gardiner, *op.cit.*
117. Sir Charles Mallet, *Herbert Gladstone*.
118. Diary of Lord Rosebery, 6 January 1883, Dalmeny papers.
119. Crewe, *op.cit.*
120. Journal of Lewis Harcourt, 6 February 1883, Vol. 353.
121. Edward Hamilton's Diary, 18 March 1883.
122. Rosebery to Granville, 8 March 1883, Rosebery NLS 10080.
123. Diary of Sir Charles Dilke, 12 April 1883, Add Ms 43,925.
124. Rosebery to Dilke, 15 April 1883, Harcourt papers Adss 14.
125. Dilke to Harcourt, 17 April 1883, Harcourt papers Adss 14.
126. Dilke to Rosebery, 19 April 1883, Rosebery NLS 10080.
127. Rosebery to Gladstone, 7 April 1883, Gladstone papers Add Ms 44288.
128. John Vincent (ed.), *Diaries of 15th Earl of Derby*, 5 May 1883.
129. Diary of Lord Rosebery, 5 May 1883, Dalmeny papers.
130. Edward Hamilton's Diary, 6 May 1883.
131. Cooper to Rosebery, 11 May 1883, Rosebery NLS 10010.
132. Diary of Sir Charles Dilke, 28 May 1883, Add Ms 43,925.
133. Gladstone papers, Add Ms 44288.
134. Gladstone to Donaldson, 6 April 1883, Gladstone papers Add Ms 44546.
135. Journal of Lord Esher, 7 June 1894.
136. Munro-Ferguson to Lord Crewe (undated, but *c.* 1930), Rosebery NLS 10195.
137. Edward Hamilton's Diary, 2 June 1883.
138. Journal of Lewis Harcourt, 7 June 1883, Vol. 355.
139. Vincent, *op.cit.*, *Derby Diaries*, 6 June 1883.
140. Memorandum 19 November 1910, Dalmeny papers.
141. The story is in T.H.S. Escott, *Personal Forces of the Period*, and is also alluded to in E.T. Raymond, *The Man of Promise*.

CHAPTER 5: 'A DARK HORSE'

1. Journal of Lewis Harcourt, 8 June 1883, Vol. 355.
2. 7 June 1883, in Vincent, *Derby Diaries*.
3. Rosebery to Gladstone, 30 July 1883, Gladstone papers, Add Ms 44288.
4. Hamilton to Rosebery, 31 July 1883, Rosebery NLS 10033.
5. Cooper to Rosebery, 12 August 1883, Rosebery NLS 10010.
6. Edward Hamilton's Diary, 24 August 1883.
7. Rosebery to Gladstone, 30 July 1883, Gladstone papers, Add Ms 44288.
8. Journal of Lewis Harcourt, 6 February 1883, Vol. 353.
9. Hannah Rosebery to Constance Leconfield, 20 October 1883, Petworth papers PHA 9669.
10. Rosebery to Mary Gladstone, 19 December 1883, Mary Gladstone papers, Add Ms 46,327.
11. T.G. Coates, *Rosebery Life and Speeches*.
12. Lord Crewe, *Lord Rosebery*.
13. Denis Judd, *Empire*.
14. A.P. Thornton, *The Imperial Idea and Its Enemies*.
15. E.T. Raymond, *The Man of Promise*.
16. Winifried Baumgart, *Imperialism*.
17. Speech to the Royal Colonial Institute, 1 March 1893, quoted in Thornton, *op.cit.*
18. Rosebery to Sir William Mackay, 26 December 1884, Rosebery NLS Acc 7628.
19. Rosebery to Sir William Mackay, 1 October 1887, Rosebery NLS Acc 7628.
20. Bernard Semmel, *Imperialism and Social Reform*.
21. Robert Rhodes James, *Rosebery*.
22. Quoted in Jeffrey Butler, *The Liberal Party and the Jameson Raid*.
23. Crewe, *op.cit.*
24. Rosebery to Gladstone, 24 April 1884, Gladstone papers Add Ms 44288.
25. Rosebery to Hamilton, 6 May 1884, Hamilton papers Add Ms 48612A.
26. Edward Hamilton's Diary, 6 May 1884.
27. Journal of Lewis Harcourt, 29 June 1884, Vol. 359.
28. Vincent, *op.cit.*, 8 July 1884.
29. Crewe, *op.cit.*
30. Lucy Mastermen (ed.), *Mary Gladstone, Diaries and Letters*.
31. Diary of John Morley, 18 March 1883, MS Eng.d.3437.
32. Journal of Lewis Harcourt, 24 March 1882, Vol. 350.
33. Quoted in Foot and Matthew, *The Gladstone Diaries*.
34. Rosebery to Gladstone, 24 September 1884, Gladstone papers, Add Ms 44,288.
35. A.B. Cooke and John Vincent (eds), *Lord Carlingford's Journal*.
36. Journal of Lewis Harcourt, 26 September 1884, Vol. 360.
37. Foot and Matthew, *op.cit.*

38. Spencer to Harcourt, 16 October 1884, P. Gordon (ed.), *Spencer Papers*.
39. Robinson and Gallagher, *Africa and the Victorians*.
40. Niall Ferguson, *The House of Rothschild*.
41. *Ibid*.
42. Rosebery to Granville, 12 November 1884, Rosebery NLS 10081.
43. Edward Hamilton's Diary, 12 November 1884.
44. Journal of Lewis Harcourt, 25 January 1885, Vol. 364.
45. Cooper to Rosebery, Rosebery NLS 10010.
46. Diary of Thomas Gilmour, Acc 8989/3.
47. Rosebery to Gladstone, 1 February 1885, Gladstone papers Add Ms 44288.
48. Catherine Gladstone to Rosebery, 4 February 1885, Rosebery NLS 10021.
49. Rosebery to Hamilton, 31 December 1884, Hamilton papers Add Ms 48612A; Hamilton to Rosebery, 26 January 1885, Rosebery NLS 10031.
50. Edward Hamilton's Diary, 31 January and 2 February 1885.
51. Rosebery to Gladstone, 8 February 1885, Gladstone papers, Add Ms 44288.
52. Rosebery to Constance Leconfield, 12 February 1885, Petworth papers 5572.
53. Journal of Lewis Harcourt, 12 February 1883, Vol. 364.
54. Diary of Thomas Gilmour, 12 February 1885, Acc 8989/3.
55. Chamberlain to Rosebery, Rosebery NLS 10082.
56. Quoted in Elizabeth Longford, *The Life of Wilfred Scawen Blunt*.
57. Diary of Thomas Gilmour, 14 September 1886, Acc 8989/4.
58. Diary of Lord Rosebery, 16 February 1885, Dalmeny papers.
59. Crewe, *op.cit*.
60. Cooke and Vincent, *Lord Carlingford's Journal*.
61. Rosebery to Stead, 24 April 1885, Stead papers, Churchill 1/62.
62. Granville to Gladstone, 29 May 1885, Ramm, *op.cit*.
63. Herbert Bismarck to Rosebery, 1 June 1885, Rosebery NLS 10201.
64. Diary of Lord Rosebery, 28 September 1885, Dalmeny papers.
65. Wolseley papers, Hove.
66. Rosebery to Herbert Gladstone, 22 April 1885, Viscount Gladstone papers, Add Mss 45,986.
67. 'Bon mot', recorded in the Journal of Lewis Harcourt, 13 December 1885, Vol. 374.
68. Diary of Lord Rosebery, 20 April 1885, Dalmeny papers.
69. Chamberlain to Rosebery, 17 May 1885, Rosebery NLS 10083.
70. Diary of Lord Rosebery, 2 May 1885, Dalmeny papers.
71. A.B. Cooke and John Vincent, *The Governing Passion*.
72. Diary of Lord Rosebery, 5 June 1885, Dalmeny papers.
73. Note by Rosebery, 22 June 1885, Betting Book, Rosebery NLS 10177.
74. Journal of Lord Kimberley, 28 June 1885.
75. Edward Hamilton's Diary, 13 May 1885.
76. Gladstone to Rosebery, 13 November 1885, Gladstone papers, Add Ms 44,288.

77. Rosebery to Brett, 25 December 1885, Esher papers.

78. Rosebery to Munro-Ferguson, 4 May 1886, Rosebery NLS 10017.

79. Diary of Thomas Gilmour, 14 September 1886, Acc 8989/4.

80. Rosebery to Spender, 15 November 1898, Spender papers, Add Ms 46,387.

81. Rosebery to Knollys, 15 November 1885, Rosebery NLS 10039. ·

82. Jane Stoddart, *The Earl of Rosebery*.

83. Edward Hamilton's Diary, 28 November 1885.

84. *Ibid.*, 24 November 1885.

85. Masterman, *op.cit.*

86. Rosebery to Mary Gladstone, 30 December 1885, Mary Gladstone papers, Add Ms 46,237.

87. Journal of Lewis Harcourt, 30 December 1885, Vol. 375.

88. Lady Spencer to her husband, 21 November 1885, Gordon *op.cit.*

89. Agatha Ramm, *The Gladstone–Granville Correspondence*.

90. Healey to Labouchere, 7 December 1885, copy in Rosebery NLS 10041.

91. Rosebery, NLS 10041.

92. Diary of Lord Rosebery, 12 December 1885, Dalmeny papers.

93. Rosebery to Gladstone, 12 December 1885, Gladstone papers, Add Mss 44,288.

94. Spencer to Rosebery, 30 December 1885, Gordon, *op.cit.*

95. Rosebery to Spencer, 31 December 1885, Gordon, *op.cit.*

96. Labouchere to Rosebery, 16 December 1885, Add Mss 10041.

97. Rosebery to Hamilton, 22 December 1885, Hamilton papers, Add Mss 48,612A.

CHAPTER 6: 'YOU HAVE A GREAT POLITICAL FUTURE'

1. Chamberlain to Rosebery, 3 January 1886, Rosebery NLS 10085.

2. Journal of Lewis Harcourt, 15 January 1885, Vol. 376.

3. *Ibid.*, 8 March 1886, Vol. 405.

4. Agatha Ramm, *Darling and Beloved Child*.

5. F.E. Hames (ed.), *Personal Papers of Lord Rendel*.

6. Edward Hamilton's Diary, 31 January 1886.

7. Journal of Lord Kimberley, 3 February 1886.

8. F.E. Hames, *op.cit.*

9. Journal of Lewis Harcourt, 11 January 1886, Vol. 377.

10. Edward Hamilton's Diary, 20 September 1885.

11. Elizabeth Longford, *Victoria RI*.

12. Lady Spencer's diary, 12 December 1884, Gordon (ed.), *Spencer Papers*.

13. Diary of Lord Rosebery, 12 December 1884, Dalmeny papers.

14. *Ibid.*, 27 September 1885, Dalmeny papers.

15. A.B. Cooke and John Vincent, *The Governing Passion*.
16. Hannah Rosebery to Hamilton, 29 January 1886, Hamilton papers Add Ms 48613.
17. Diary of Lord Rosebery, 2 February 1886, Dalmeny papers.
18. Rosebery to Ronald Munro-Ferguson, 20 August 1887, Rosebery NLS 10017.
19. Journal of Lewis Harcourt, 2 February 1886, Vol. 377.
20. Rosebery to Constance Leconfield, 3 February 1886, Petworth papers, 5572.
21. Rosebery to the Duchess of Cleveland, 3 February 1886, Rosebery NLS 10085.
22. Rosebery to Dilke, 3 February 1886, Rosebery NLS 10085.
23. Robert Rhodes James, *Rosebery*.
24. Ralph Martin, *Lady Randolph Churchill*.
25. Hannah Rosebery to Hamilton, 16 December 1885, Hamilton papers, Add Ms 48,613.
26. Diary of Thomas Gilmour, 14 September 1886, Acc 8989/4.
27. Rosebery to Bismarck, 8 September 1885, Rosebery NLS 10201.
28. Diary of Lord Rosebery, 20 and 28 July 1885, Dalmeny papers.
29. Smalley to Rosebery, 3 August 1885, Rosebery NLS.
30. Roy Jenkins, *Dilke* and Rhodes James, *op.cit.*
31. Jenkins, *op.cit.* and Rhodes James, *op.cit.*
32. Jenkins, *op.cit.*
33. Hammond to Crewe, 12 August 1936 and Crewe to Hammond, 17 August 1936, Rosebery NLS 10195.
34. Journal of Lewis Harcourt, 29 March 1894, Vol. 406.
35. Edward Hamilton's Diary, 2 June 1886.
36. Rendel, *op.cit.*
37. James Lees-Milne, *The Enigmatic Edwardian*.
38. Labouchere to Rosebery, 13 February 1885, Rosebery NLS 10041.
39. Memorandum (undated), Dalmeny papers.
40. Winston Churchill, *Great Contemporaries*.
41. Rhodes James, *op.cit.*
42. Frank Hardie, *The Political Influence of Queen Victoria*.
43. Thomas Coates, *Rosebery Life and Speeches*.
44. Bismarck to Rosebery, 31 January 1885, Rosebery NLS 10201.
45. Gordon Martel, *Imperial Diplomacy*.
46. Rosebery to Queen Victoria, 26 March 1886, RA VIC/H29/133.
47. Lord Crewe, *Rosebery*.
48. Rosebery to Queen Victoria, 28 March 1886, RA VIC/H29/139.
49. Rosebery to Queen Victoria, 28 April 1886, RA VIC/H29/168.
50. Ripon papers, Add Ms 43,516.
51. Rosebery to Gladstone, 25 April 1886, Add Ms 44,289.
52. Journal of Lewis Harcourt, 9 January 1886, Vol. 376.

53. Gladstone to Rosebery, 28 April 1886, quoted in Foot and Matthew, *The Gladstone Diaries*.
54. Diary of Thomas Gilmour, 17 April 1886, Acc 8989/4.
55. Edward Hamilton's Diary, 24 April 1886.
56. Rosebery to Queen Victoria, 3 July 1886, RA VIC/H29/181.
57. Martel, *op.cit.*
58. Trevor Royle, *The Kitchener Enigma*.
59. Rosebery to Bismarck, April 1886, Rosebery NLS 10201.
60. Journal of Lewis Harcourt, 14 March 1886, Vol. 378.
61. Cooke and Vincent, *op.cit.*
62. Journal of Lewis Harcourt, 26 January 1886, Vol. 377.
63. Brett to Rosebery, 19 February 1886, Rosebery NLS 10006.
64. Note of conversation, Rosebery NLS Acc 8654.
65. Diary of Lord Rosebery, 7 July 1886, Dalmeny papers.
66. *Ibid.*, 31 March 1886, Dalmeny papers.
67. Rodd to Lord Crewe, 23 July 1929, Rosebery NLS 10195.
68. Stephen Gwynn, *The Letters and Friendships of Sir Cecil Spring-Rice*.
69. *Ibid.*
70. Rosebery to Gladstone, 29 June 1886, Gladstone papers Add Ms 44,289.
71. Diary of Thomas Gilmour, 6 July 1886, Acc 8989/4.
72. Diary of Lord Rosebery, 7 July 1886, Dalmeny papers.
73. Rosebery to Herbert Bismarck, 16 October 1886, Rosebery NLS 10201.
74. Note dated 19 November 1886, Betting Book, Rosebery NLS 10177.
75. Rosebery to Gladstone, 12 November 1886, Gladstone papers Add Ms 44,289.
76. Crewe, *op.cit.*
77. Rosebery to H.A.L. Fisher, 20 May 1914, Fisher papers Ms 57.
78. Rosebery's note of conversation with Lord Randolph Churchill, 1887, Rosebery NLS Acc 8654.
79. Diary of Lord Rosebery, 3 July 1887, Dalmeny papers.
80. Memorandum, 1917, Dalmeny papers.
81. Rosebery to Ronald Munro-Ferguson, 23 March 1887, Rosebery NLS 10017.
82. Ferguson to Rosebery, 1 April 1887, and Rosebery to Ferguson, 5 April 1887, Rosebery NLS 10017.
83. Ferguson to Rosebery, 22 March 1887 and Rosebery to Ferguson, 23 March 1887, Rosebery NLS 10017.
84. R.T. Robertson, 'Lord Rosebery and the Imperial Federation League, 1884–1893' (*New Zealand Journal of History*, Vol. 13, October 1979).
85. 'Lord Rosebery's Apostasy', in *The Fortnightly Review*, December 1897.
86. Lady Aberdeen to Rosebery, 8 November 1888, Rosebery NLS 10087.
87. G.M. Trevelyan, *Grey of Fallodon*.
88. Rosebery to Bismarck, 24 August 1894, Rosebery NLS 10201.

89. Margot Asquith's Diary, 9 October 1896.
90. John Buchan, *Comments and Characters*.
91. Jane Stoddart, *The Earl of Rosebery*.
92. Augustine Birrell, *Things Past Redress*.
93. Robartes to Neil Primrose, 8 December 1905, Rosebery NLS 10119.
94. E.F.C. Collier (ed.), *A Victorian Diarist*, entry for 1 March 1892.
95. Sir Ian Malcolm, *Vacant Thrones*.
96. Rosebery to W.T. Stead, 19 October 1888, Stead papers.
97. Smalley to Rosebery, 9 November 1885 and 14 October 1888, Rosebery NLS.
98. Lord Rosebery, *The Earl of Chatham*.
99. Sybil Grant, 'A Great Scotsman'. Rosebery NLS Acc 8365/38.
100. Diary of Lord Rosebery, 30 March 1883, Dalmeny papers.
101. Sir Almeric Fitzroy, *Memoirs*.
102. Diary of Margot Asquith, 17 February 1905.
103. Malcolm, *op.cit.*
104. Diary of Thomas Gilmour, 26 October 1885, Acc 8989/4.
105. Rosebery to Reid, 14 November 1902, Rosebery NLS 10058.
106. Sybil Grant, *op.cit.*
107. The Countess of Warwick, *Afterthoughts*.
108. J. Lee Thompson, *Northcliffe: Press Baron in Politics*.
109. The phrase used by Rosebery's friend Evan Charteris in his entry for the *DNB*.
110. Journal of Lord Kimberley, 20 May 1898.
111. Edward Hamilton's Diary, 18 July 1890.
112. Richard Shannon, *The Crisis of Imperialism*.
113. Ken Young and Patricia Garside, *Metropolitan London: Politics and Urban Change, 1837–1981*.
114. *The Times*, 17 October 1885.
115. Rogers to Rosebery, 7 December 1888, Rosebery NLS 10060.
116. Stoddart, *op.cit.*
117. Brett to Rosebery, 26 January 1889, Esher papers 2/8.
118. William Saunders, *The History of the First London County Council, 1889–91*.
119. Morley to Rosebery, 19 January 1889, Rosebery NLS 10046.
120. Edward Hamilton's Diary, 11 January 1889.
121. Saunders, *op.cit.*
122. Andrew Saint (ed.), *Politics and the People of London*.
123. Sir Harry Haward, *The London County Council From Within*.
124. Recollection of Charrington, given to Lord Crewe, Rosebery NLS 10195.
125. Monkswell papers, Dep d.837.
126. Sir John Robinson, *Fifty Years of Fleet Street*.
127. Diary of Sir John Lubbock, 2 April 1889, Avebury papers Add Ms 62,683.
128. Rosebery to Bismarck, 17 March 1889, Rosebery NLS 10201.
129. Rosebery to Bismarck, 2 April 1889, Rosebery NLS 10201.

130. Hannah Rosebery to Hamilton, 20 October 1889, Hamilton papers Add Ms 48613.
131. Saunders, *op.cit.*
132. Edward Hamilton's Diary, 18 April 1889.
133. Monkswell papers, Dep d.837.
134. Rosebery to Stead, 31 January 1895, Rosebery NLS 10101.
135. Brett to Rosebery, and Sandhurst to Brett, 16 January 1892, Rosebery NLS 10006.
136. Frederic Harrison, 'Lord Rosebery and the London County Council', in *The Nineteenth Century*, June 1890.
137. Justin McCarthy, *British Political Leaders.*
138. Recollection of Sir Henry's grandson who, much to his grandfather's disgust, joined the Liberal Party in 1890. Recorded by Lord Crewe, Rosebery NLS 109195.

CHAPTER 7: 'OUR HAPPY HOME IS A WRECK'

1. Rosebery to Cooper, 18 April 1887, Rosebery NLS 10010.
2. Rosebery to Ronald Munro-Ferguson, 17 October 1887, Rosebery NLS 10017.
3. Margot Asquith, *Autobiography.*
4. Profile of Rosebery in the *Glasgow Herald*, 22 May 1929.
5. Diary of John Morley, 16 November 1894.
6. Sybil Grant, 'A Great Scotsman', Rosebery NLS 8365/38.
7. Peter Gordon, *The Spencer Papers.*
8. Diary of Margot Asquith, 9 November 1897.
9. Diary of Beatrice Webb, 16 March 1900, Passfield papers.
10. Sir Ian Malcolm, *Vacant Thrones.*
11. Diary of Lord Rosebery, 9 May 1875, Dalmeny papers.
12. Note by Rosebery, October 17 1874, Rosebery NLS 10192.
13. Diary of Margot Asquith, 28 October 1905.
14. Charles Geake, *Lord Rosebery.*
15. Told to Loulou Harcourt by Sir George Murray, Journal of Lewis Harcourt, 14 June 1894, Vol. 409.
16. George Plumptre, *The Fast Set.*
17. Rosebery to Peck, 23 September 1913, Rosebery NLS 10124.
18. *The Nineteenth Century*, October 1894.
19. Rosebery to Herbert Bismarck, 30 April 1904, Rosebery NLS 10201.
20. Sybil Grant, *op.cit.*
21. Note in Dalmeny papers.
22. Rosebery to Mary Gladstone Drew, 20 August 1920, Mary Gladstone papers Add Ms 46,327.

23. E.T. Raymond, *The Man of Promise*.
24. Quoted in Percy Colson, *Lord Goschen and his Friends*.
25. Rosbery to Drummond-Woolf, 3 August 1887, Rosebery NLS 10087.
26. Rosebery to Hartington, 7 November 1890, Rosebery NLS 10088.
27. George Cornwallis-West, *Edwardian Hey-Days*.
28. Edward Hamilton's Diary, 20 April 1889.
29. Journal of Lewis Harcourt, 26 January 1886, Vol. 377.
30. Rosebery to Countess Stanhope, 21 June 1911, Stanhope papers U1590, C587/2.
31. Letter by Rosebery, 17 December 1925, Petworth papers PHA 5610.
32. Journal of Regy Brett, 21 March 1895, Esher papers.
33. Rosebery to Stead, 21 May 1893, Stead papers.
34. Rosebery to Margot Asquith, 3 May 1918, Margot Asquith papers MS Eng c. 6680.
35. Harry Graham to Rosebery, 30 December 1905, Rosebery NLS 10115.
36. Journal of Lewis Harcourt, 3 February 1895, Vol. 414.
37. Hamilton papers, Add Ms 48,626.
38. Esme Howard, *Theatre of Life*.
39. Rosebery to Constance Leconfield, 26 December 1891, Petworth papers 5573.
40. Rosebery to Constance Leconfield, 17 October 1891, Petworth papers 5573.
41. Rosebery to Lord Randolph Churchill, 30 June 1886, Lord Randolph Churchill papers.
42. Rosebery to Margot Asquith, 17 July 1916 and 4 May 1919, Margot Asquith papers, MS Eng c.6680.
43. Rosebery to Earl Stanhope, 7 February 1903, Stanhope papers U1590 c587/1.
44. Dalmeny papers.
45. Diary of Sir John Lubbock, 3 and 4 March 1892, Avebury papers, Add Ms 62,683.
46. Rosebery to Hamilton, 6 March 1892, Hamilton papers Add Ms 48,612A.
47. Diary of Lord Rosebery, 13 August 1890, Dalmeny papers.
48. Journal of Regy Brett, 13 August 1892, Esher papers.
49. Rosebery to Munro-Ferguson, 28 March 1888, Rosebery NLS 10017.
50. Note by Rosebery, Betting Book, Rosebery NLS 10177.
51. Note by Rosebery, 1918, Betting Book, Rosebery NLS Acc 8365/53.
52. Rosebery to Canon of Christ Church, 25 February 1901, Rosebery NLS 10114.
53. Rosebery to Mary Gladstone, 27 October 1881, Mary Gladstone papers Add Ms 46,237.
54. Rosebery to Brett, 29 November 1894, Esher papers.
55. Lord Crewe, *Rosebery*.
56. Lord Ronald Gower, *Old Diaries*.

57. Lucy Cohen, *Lady de Rothschild and Her Daughters*.

58. John Colville, *Footprints in Time*.

59. Rosebery to Sir George Murray, 3 December 1895, Murray papers.

60. Journal of John Morley, 5 August 1892, Morley papers, d 3450.

61. Dated 1 April 1891, Petworth papers 5573.

62. Kenneth Young, *Harry, Lord Rosebery*.

63. Rosebery to Munro-Ferguson, 13 November 1890, Rosebery NLS 10017.

64. Journal of Regy Brett, 30 April 1899, Esher papers.

65. Diary of Margot Asquith, 9 November 1897.

66. Edward Hamilton's Diary, 18 April 1890.

67. Gladstone papers, Add Ms 44,289.

68. Rosebery to Catherine Gladstone, 25 October 1890, Catherine Gladstone papers, Add Ms 46,226.

69. Rosebery to Earl Stanhope, 31 October 1890, Stanhope papers U1590, c.587/1.

70. Note in Dalmeny papers.

71. Hannah Rosebery to Edward Hamilton, November 1890, Hamilton papers Add Ms 48,613.

72. Rosebery to Gladstone, 17 November 1890, Gladstone papers, 44,289.

73. Diary of Constance, Lady Battersea (Mrs Cyril Flower), 25 November 1890, Add Ms 47,940.

74. M.R.D. Foot and H.C. Matthew, *The Gladstone Diaries*.

75. Royal Archives, RA VIC/F39/62.

76. Rosebery to Ferdinand Rothschild, 22 November 1889, Rosebery NLS 10088.

77. Edward Hamilton's Diary, 12 October 1890.

78. *Ibid.*, 19 November 1890.

79. Petworth papers, 5573.

80. Rosebery to Sir William Harcourt, 28 December 1890, Harcourt papers Adss 14.

81. Rosebery to Brett, 15 December 1890, Esher papers.

82. Rosebery to Bismarck, 19 and 24 of January 1891, Rosebery NLS 10201.

83. Diary of Lord Rosebery, 8 March 1891, Dalmeny papers.

84. Edward Hamilton's Diary, 7 April 1891.

85. Diary of Lord Rosebery, 13 March 1891, Dalmeny papers.

86. *Ibid.*, 13 and 14 March 1891, Dalmeny papers.

87. Crewe, *op.cit.*

88. Diary of John Morley, 7 December 1891.

89. Hamilton to Rosebery, 29 November 1891, Rosebery NLS 10031.

90. Rosebery to Munro-Ferguson, 26 April 1891, Rosebery NLS 10017.

91. Rosebery to Constance Leconfield, 12 December 1891, Petworth papers 5573.

92. Diary of John Morley, 4 August 1892.

93. Munro-Ferguson to Rosebery, 28 July 1912, Rosebery NLS 10120.
94. E.F.C. Collier (ed.), *A Victorian Diarist.*
95. Rosebery to Constance Leconfield, 13 January 1915, Petworth Papers, 5581.
96. Augustine Birrell, *Things Past Redress.*
97. Diary of Margot Asquith, 23 October 1904.
98. Rosebery to Buchan, 10 May 1926, Buchan NLS Acc 6975.
99. Rosebery to Godley, 7 July 1907, Kilbracken papers, Add Ms 44,902.
100. Sybil Grant, 'A Great Scotsman', Rosebery NLS Acc 8365/38.
101. Note (undated) in Dalmeny papers.
102. Note, November 1914, Dalmeny papers.
103. Rosebery to Morley, 1 September 1908, Morley papers Mss Eur D573.
104. Winston Churchill, *Great Contemporaries.*
105. Rosebery to Hamilton, 4 November 1891, Hamilton papers Add Mss 48,612.
106. Crewe, *op.cit.*
107. John Powell, *Liberal by Principle.*
108. Diary of John Morley, 7 December 1891.
109. W. Robertson Nichol, *A Bookman's Letters.*
110. Philip Guedalla, *A Gallery.*
111. Rosebery to Oscar Browning, 24 July 1890, Browning papers, 1/1313.
112. Norman Hapgood, *Literary Statesmen and Others.*
113. Rosebery to Earl Stanhope, 26 June 1920, Stanhope papers U1590 c.587.
114. Rosebery to H.A.L. Fisher, 4 January 1911.
115. Rosebery to Brett, 11 October 1891, Esher papers.
116. Rosebery to Geake, 1 April 1899, Geake papers.
117. *Sunday Times*, 11 September 1921.
118. Sybil Grant, *op.cit.*
119. Colville, *op.cit.*
120. Rosebery NLS, 10116.

CHAPTER 8: 'IT IS PRETTY FANNY'S WAY'

1. Diary of Beatrice Webb, 31 December 1890, Passfield papers.
2. Morley to Rosebery, 27 January 1890, Rosebery NLS 10045.
3. A.G. Gardiner, *The Life of Sir William Harcourt.*
4. R. Robinson and J. Gallagher, *Africa and the Victorians.*
5. Rosebery to Brett, 11 October 1891, Esher papers 10/9.
6. Joyce Marlow, *The Oak and the Ivy.*
7. D.A. Hamer, *Politics in the Age of Gladstone and Rosebery.*
8. Edward Hamilton's Diary, 25 November 1890.
9. Rosebery to Harcourt, 21 March and 28 May 1891, Harcourt Adss 14.
10. Edward Hamilton's Diary, 9 April and 29 May 1891.

11. Note dated 27 October 1891, Dalmeny papers.
12. Rosebery NLS 10031.
13. Arnold Morley to Rosebery, 10 March 1892, Rosebery NLS 10090.
14. Brett to Rosebery, 16 January 1892, Esher papers.
15. Dalmeny papers.
16. Frank Hardie, *The Political Influence of Queen Victoria*.
17. Gardiner, *op.cit.*
18. Edward Hamilton's Diary, 12 March 1892.
19. *Ibid.*, 24 June 1892.
20. Diary of John Morley, 23 June 1892.
21. Diary of Lord Rosebery, 8 July 1892.
22. Hamilton papers, Add Ms 48,612.
23. Journal of Lewis Harcourt, 19 July 1892, Vol. 383.
24. Diary of John Morley, 2 July 1892.
25. *Ibid.*, 1 to 4 July 1892.
26. Horace G. Hutchinson, *The Private Diaries of Sir Algernon West*.
27. Diary of John Morley, 12 to 14 July 1892.
28. F.E. Hames (ed.), *Personal Papers of Lord Rendel*.
29. Acton to Murray, 20 December 1892, Murray papers.
30. Letter in Dalmeny papers.
31. H.C.G. Matthew, *Gladstone 1875–1898*.
32. Edward Hamilton's Diary, 19 July 1892.
33. Hamilton to Rosebery, 21 July 1892, Rosebery NLS 10032.
34. Diary of John Morley, 22 July 1892.
35. Rosebery to Hamilton, 3 August 1892, Hamilton papers, 48,612A.
36. Gardiner, *op.cit.*
37. Ferguson to Rosebery, 27 July 1892, Rosebery NLS 10018.
38. Journal of Lord Kimberley, 13 July 1892.
39. Lord Crewe, *Rosebery*.
40. Rhodes James, *Rosebery*.
41. Rosebery to Gladstone, 31 March 1892, Gladstone papers Add Ms 44,289.
42. Diary of John Morley, 4 August 1892.
43. Edward Hamilton's Diary, 4 August 1892.
44. *Ibid.*
45. D.A. Hamer, *John Morley*.
46. Gladstone to Rosebery, 4 August 1892, Rosebery NLS 10024.
47. Catherine Gladstone to Rosebery, 4 August 1892, Rosebery NLS 10021.
48. Diary of Lord Rosebery, 5 August 1892, Dalmeny papers.
49. The description of Morley's visit to Dalmeny is taken largely from his diary.
50. Journal of Lewis Harcourt, 6 August 1892, Vol. 384.
51. *Ibid.*
52. Note of conversation with Gladstone on 16 August 1892, Rosebery Betting Book, NLS 10176.

53. Diary of John Morley, 10 August 1892.
54. Edward Hamilton's Diary, 11 August 1892.
55. This account is in Rosebery Betting Book, NLS 10176.
56. Richard Shannon, *Gladstone, Heroic Minister*.
57. Elizabeth Longford, *Victoria RI*.
58. Hamilton to Rosebery, 12 August 1892, Rosebery NLS 10032.
59. Journal of Lewis Harcourt, 13 August 1892, Vol. 384.
60. Diary of John Morley, 13 August 1892.
61. Journal of Lewis Harcourt, 14 August 1892, Vol. 384.
62. Albert, Prince of Wales to Rosebery, 14 August 1892, Rosebery NLS 10016.
63. Brett to Rosebery, 14 August 1892, Rosebery NLS 10006.
64. Rosebery's report of conversation given to Regy Brett, 7 September 1892, Esher papers.
65. Buckle to Rosebery, 14 August 1892, Rosebery NLS 10090.
66. Edward Hamilton's Diary, 13 August 1892.
67. Gladstone to Rosebery, 15 August 1892, Gladstone papers Add Ms 44,289.
68. Edward Hamilton's Diary, 15 August 1892.
69. Diary of John Morley, 15 August 1892.
70. Journal of Lewis Harcourt, 18 August 1892, Vol. 385.
71. Edward Hamilton's Diary, 15 August 1892.
72. Gardiner, *op.cit.*

CHAPTER 9: 'THE IDEAL MASTER TO SERVE'

1. Agatha Ramm, *Darling and Beloved Child*.
2. Diary of Lord Rosebery, 18 August 1894, Dalmeny papers.
3. Ramm, *op.cit.*
4. Horace Hutchinson (ed.), *The Private Diaries of Sir Algernon West*.
5. Gladstone to Rosebery, 18 August 1892, Gladstone papers, Add Ms 44,289.
6. Journal of Lord Kimberley, 1 December 1892.
7. Rosebery to Gladstone, 14 December 1892, Gladstone papers, Add Ms 44,290.
8. J. Saxon Mills, *Sir Edward Cook*.
9. Journal of Lewis Harcourt, 19 August 1892, Vol. 385.
10. Edward Hamilton's Diary, 22 August 1892.
11. Hesketh Pearson, *Labby*.
12. Report of conversation with Labouchere, given by Reid to Morley, 23 September 1892, Rosebery NLS 10041.
13. Rosebery's note of interview with Henrietta Labouchere, 24 November 1892, Rosebery NLS 10041.
14. Rosebery NLS 10041.
15. Henry Labouchere to Rosebery, 25 January 1893, Rosebery NLS 10041.

16. Journal of Lewis Harcourt, 30 January 1893, Vol. 390.
17. Rosebery NLS 10041.
18. Previously unpublished note (undated), Rosebery NLS Acc 8365/42.
19. Bernard Semmel, *Imperialism and Social Reform*.
20. T.G.F. Coates, *Rosebery Life and Speeches*.
21. Margery Perham, *Lugard*.
22. Thomas Pakenham, *The Scramble for Africa*.
23. A.G. Gardiner, *The Life of Sir William Harcourt*.
24. Gordon Martel, *Imperial Diplomacy*.
25. Gladstone to Rosebery 17 September 1892, Rosebery NLS 10024.
26. Spencer to Rosebery, 23 September 1892, in P. Gordon, *The Spencer Papers*.
27. Record of conversation, Esher journal, 5 October 1892, Esher papers.
28. Queen Victoria to Lord Rosebery, 28 September 1892, RA VIC/B45/42a.
29. Hutchinson, *op.cit.*
30. Richard Shannon, *Gladstone: Heroic Minister*.
31. Gladstone to Rosebery, 17 September 1886, Rosebery NLS 10024.
32. Robert Rhodes James, *Rosebery*.
33. Shannon, *op.cit.*
34. Rosebery NLS 10024.
35. Gladstone papers, Add Ms 44,289.
36. Rosebery NLS 10045.
37. Gladstone to Harcourt, 24 September 1892, quote in Foot and Matthew, *The Gladstone Diaries*.
38. Gladstone to Rosebery, 25 September 1892, Gladstone papers Add Ms 44,289.
39. Foot and Matthew, *op.cit.*
40. Asquith to Rosebery, 22 September 1892, Rosebery NLS 10001.
41. Rosebery to Gladstone, 29 September 1892, Gladstone papers Add Ms 44,289.
42. Kimberley to Harcourt, 6 October 1892, quoted in John Powell, *Liberal by Principle*.
43. Rosebery to Queen Victoria, 3 October 1892, RA VIC/B45/44.
44. Rosebery NLS 10018.
45. Journal of Lord Kimberley, 1 December 1892.
46. Hutchinson, *op.cit.*
47. Asquith to Rosebery, 6 November 1892, Rosebery NLS 10001.
48. Munro-Ferguson to Rosebery, 12 October 1892, Rosebery NLS 10018.
49. Hutchinson, *op.cit.*
50. Martel, *op.cit.*
51. Anthony Low, 'British Public Opinion and the Uganda Question', *Uganda Journal*, 1954.
52. Rosebery to Gladstone, 4 February 1893, Add Ms 44,290.
53. Diary of John Morley, 6, 7, 8 February 1893.

54. *Ibid.*, 20 February 1893.
55. Martel, *op.cit.*
56. Perham, *op.cit.*
57. Journal of Lewis Harcourt, 20 July 1893, Vol. 394.
58. R. Robinson and J. Gallagher, *Africa and the Victorians*.
59. Edward Hamilton's Diary, 4 October 1892.
60. John Marlowe, *Cromer in Egypt*.
61. Lord Cromer, 'Egypt', manuscript in British library, Add Ms 44,906.
62. Martel, *Imperial Diplomacy*, has a superb analysis of the European implications of Rosebery's foreign policy.
63. Wilfred Scawen Blunt, *My Diaries*.
64. Rosebery to Queen Victoria, 12 May 1893, Royal Archives RA VIC/ B46/50.
65. Blunt, *op.cit.*, 11 May 1893.
66. Hutchinson, *op.cit.*
67. Gladstone to Rosebery, 1 November 1892.
68. Rosebery to Gladstone, 4 November 1892, Gladstone papers, Add Ms 44,290.
69. Rosebery to Dufferin, 1 November 1892, Dufferin papers D 1071.
70. Dufferin to Rosebery, 2 November 1892, Dufferin papers D 1071.
71. Journal of Lewis Harcourt, 9 November 1892, Vol. 387.
72. F.E. Hames (ed.), *Personal Papers of Lord Rendel*.
73. *Ibid.*
74. Waddington to Rosebery, 3 November 1892, Dufferin papers D 1071.
75. Gladstone to Rosebery, 4 November 1892, Rosebery NLS 10025.
76. Rosebery to Gladstone, 7 November 1892, Gladstone papers, Add Ms 44,290.
77. Lord Cromer, 'Egypt', Add Ms 44,906.
78. Marlowe, *Cromer*.
79. Lord Cromer, 'Egypt', Add Ms 44,906.
80. Martel, *op.cit.*
81. Queen Victoria to Rosebery, 18 January 1893, RA VIC/O28/9.
82. Rosebery to Queen Victoria, 18 January 1893, RA VIC/O28/10.
83. Rosebery to Queen Victoria, 24 January 1893, RA VIC/O28/45.
84. Marlowe, *Cromer*.
85. Edward Hamilton's Diary, 20 January 1893.
86. Diary of John Morley, 20 January 1893.
87. Marlowe, *Cromer*.
88. Journal of Lewis Harcourt, 20 January 1893, Vol. 390.
89. Lord Cromer, 'Egypt', Add Ms 44,906.
90. *Ibid.*
91. Journal of Lewis Harcourt, 23 January 1893, Vol. 390.
92. Niall Ferguson, *The House of Rothschild*. In this epic work Professor Ferguson

writes, 'The question remains whether the Rothschilds got anything material out of their relationship with Rosebery. The answer is that by and large they did not.'

93. Lord Cromer, 'Egypt', Add Ms 44,906.
94. *Ibid.*
95. Robert Rhodes James, *Rosebery.*
96. Corbett to Rosebery, 27 March 1893, Rosebery NLS 10091.
97. Hamilton to Rosebery, 10 September 1893, Rosebery NLS 10032.
98. Sir Rennel Rodd, *Social and Diplomatic Memories.*
99. Ramm, *Darling and Beloved Child.*
100. Note, 3 August 1893, Betting Book, Rosebery NLS 10176.
101. Stanley Weintraub, *Victoria.*
102. Rosebery to Constance Leconfield, 21 January 1893, Petworth papers 5574.
103. Journal of Regy Brett, 12 January 1893, Esher papers.
104. Rosebery to Dufferin, 22 August 1892, Dufferin papers D 1071.
105. Dufferin to Rosebery, 25 December 1892 and 21 March 1893, Dufferin papers D 1071.
106. Edward Hamilton's Diary, 4 July 1893.
107. Journal of Lewis Harcourt, 20 February 1893, Vol. 391.
108. 'The Foreign Policy of Lord Rosebery', in *Contemporary Review*, July 1901.
109. Martel, *op.cit.* Professor Martel's excellent revisionist study demolishes many of the myths about Rosebery's foreign policy.
110. *Ibid.*
111. Rosebery to Queen Victoria, 26 July 1893, RA VIC/N48/215.
112. Dufferin papers D 1071.
113. Dufferin to Rosebery, 27 July 1893, Dufferin papers D 1071.
114. Rosebery to Gladstone, 30 July 1893, Gladstone papers Add Ms 44,290.
115. Dufferin papers, D 1071.
116. Journal of Lewis Harourt, 31 July 1893, Vol. 394.
117. Hutchinson, *op.cit.*
118. F.E. Hames (ed.), *Personal Papers of Lord Rendel.*
119. Rosebery to Gladstone, 6 October 1892, Gladstone papers Add MS 44,290.
120. Note by Gladstone, 25 July 1894, quoted in Foot and Matthew, *op.cit.*
121. Diary of John Morley, 29 December 1893.
122. *Ibid.*, 11 August 1893.
123. Rosebery to Queen Victoria, 9 June 1893, RA VIC/B46/58.
124. Lord Randolph Churchill to Rosebery, 2 September 1893, Rosebery NLS 10009.
125. Journal of Lord Kimberley, 5 September 1893.
126. Diary of John Morley, 19 September 1893.
127. Diary of Lord Rosebery, 7 September 1893, Dalmeny papers.
128. Henry Pelling, *A History of British Trade Unionism.*

129. David Powell, 'The Liberal Ministries and Labour 1892–1895', in *History*, October 1983.
130. Acland to Rosebery, 10 November 1893, Rosebery NLS 10091.
131. Rosebery to Queen Victoria, 14 November 1893, Royal Archives, RA VIC/B4/85.
132. Mundella to Rosebery, 17 November 1893, Rosebery NLS 10091.
133. *The Times*, 16 November 1893.
134. 'Foreign Views of Lord Rosebery', in *Fortnightly Review*, 1 December 1894.
135. Rosebery to Queen Victoria, 15 November 1893, RA VIC/B46/86.
136. Rosebery to Spencer, 20 December 1893, quoted in Peter Gordon (ed.), *The Spencer Papers*.

CHAPTER 10: 'I MUST BE A REAL PRIME MINISTER'

1. Horace Hutchinson, *The Private Diaries of Sir Algernon West*.
2. Diary of John Morley, 16 February 1894.
3. *Ibid.*, 29 December 1893.
4. *Ibid.*, 4 January 1894.
5. *Daily Chronicle*, 3 March 1894.
6. Agatha Ramm, *Darling and Beloved Child*.
7. Note of conversation with Queen Victoria, 20 May 1899, Betting Book, Rosebery NLS 10183.
8. Diary of John Morley, 11 August 1893.
9. F.M.G. Wilson, *A Strong Supporting Cast*.
10. Angus Hawkins and John Powell, *Journal of 1st Earl of Kimberley*.
11. Hutchinson, *op.cit.*
12. Undated note in Dalmeny papers.
13. A.G. Gardiner, *The Life of Sir William Harcourt*.
14. Diary of John Morley, 3 August 1892.
15. Peter Stansky, *Ambitions and Strategies*.
16. Diary of John Morley, 4 August 1893.
17. *Ibid.*, 5 August 1894.
18. Edward Hamilton's Diary, 31 March 1894.
19. J.A. Spender and C. Asquith, *The Life of Lord Oxford and Asquith*.
20. D.A. Hamer, *John Morley*.
21. Conversation with Harold Laski, 1922; quoted in Hamer, *op.cit.*
22. Journal of Lewis Harcourt, 20 February 1894, Vol. 402.
23. Journal of Regy Brett, 14 January Esher papers.
24. Diary of Sir Charles Dilke, November 1880: 'Loulou Harcourt caught misbehaving with two other boys. The other two boys were flogged; he was let off but eventually had to leave.' Add Ms 43924.
25. Matthew Parris, *Great Parliamentary Scandals*.

26. Journal of Lewis Harcourt, 10 January 1894, Vol. 398.

27. *Ibid.*, 11 January 1894, Vol. 399.

28. Diary of John Morley, 12 January 1894.

29. Journal of Lewis Harcourt, 12 January 1894, Vol. 399.

30. Diary of John Morley, 12 January 1894.

31. Journal of Regy Brett, 7 September 1892, Esher papers.

32. Edward Hamilton's Diary, 17 April 1887.

33. Journal of Regy Brett, 5 April 1891, Esher papers.

34. Note in Crewe papers, Crewe NLS 10195.

35. Edward Hamilton's Diary, 30 January 1894.

36. Immediately after the event, Rosebery wrote a memorandum giving his side of the leadership story. Now in the Dalmeny archives, it was printed in two parts in *History Today* in December 1951 and January 1952, later in the appendix of Robert Rhodes James's biography.

37. Edward Hamilton's Diary, 15 January 1894.

38. Memorandum in Dalmeny papers, reprinted in *History Today*.

39. *Ibid.*

40. Journal of Lewis Harcourt, 22 January 1894, Vol. 399.

41. Edward Hamilton's Diary, 11 February 1894.

42. Diary of John Morley, 17 February 1894.

43. Diary of Lord Rosebery, 17 February 1894, Dalmeny papers.

44. Memorandum in Dalmeny papers, reprinted in *History Today*.

45. Diary of John Morley, 11 February 1894.

46. Journal of Lewis Harcourt, 11 February 1894, Vol. 401.

47. *Ibid.*, 12 February 1894, Vol. 401.

48. Diary of John Morley, 20 February 1894.

49. Journal of Lewis Harcourt, 20 February 1894, Vol. 401.

50. *Ibid.*, 21 February 1894, Vol. 401.

51. Asquith, Earl of Oxford and, *Fifty Years of Parliament*.

52. Diary of John Morley, 21 January 1894.

53. Edward Hamilton's Diary, 21 January 1894.

54. Journal of Lewis Harcourt, 22 February 1894, Vol. 402.

55. *Ibid.*, 28 February 1894, Vol. 403.

56. Diary of John Morley, 23 February 1894.

57. Rosebery to Gladstone, 24 February 1894, Gladstone papers Add Ms 44,290.

58. Diary of Lord Rosebery, 24 February 1894, Dalmeny papers.

59. Journal of Lewis Harcourt, 26 February 1894, Vol. 403.

60. Hawkins and Powell, *op.cit.*, Kimberley's journal for 28 February 1894.

61. Memorandum in Dalmeny papers.

62. Journal of Lewis Harcourt, 23 February 1894, Vol. 403.

63. Acland to Rosebery, 2 March 1894, Dalmeny papers.

64. *Daily Chronicle*, 1 and 3 of March 1894.

65. Journal of Lewis Harcourt, 17 April 1894, Vol. 407.

66. Edward Hamilton's Diary, 31 August 1887.
67. Journal of Regy Brett, 7 June 1894, Esher papers.
68. Colin Matthew, *Gladstone*, 1875–1898.
69. Diary of John Morley, 1 March 1894.
70. Edward Hamilton's Diary, 2 March 1894.
71. Memorandum in Dalmeny papers, reprinted in *History Today*.
72. Reid to Rosebery, 2 March 1894, Dalmeny papers.
73. Memorandum in Dalmeny papers, reprinted in *History Today*.
74. Foot and Matthew, *The Gladstone Diaries*.
75. Diary of John Morley, 2 March 1894.
76. Journal of Lewis Harcourt, 3 March 1894, Vol. 404. Morley saw Loulou the next morning to report this conversation.
77. Peter Stansky, *op.cit.*
78. Journal of Lewis Harcourt, 2 March 1894, Vol. 404.
79. Queen Victoria to Rosebery, 3 March 1894, RA VIC/A69/92.
80. Memorandum in Dalmeny papers, reprinted in *History Today*.
81. Diary of John Morley, 3 March 1894.
82. Harcourt's note of this meeting, quoted in A.G. Gardiner, *op.cit.*
83. Memorandum in Dalmeny papers, reprinted in *History Today*.
84. Journal of Lewis Harcourt, 3 March 1894, Vol. 404.
85. Gardiner, *op.cit.*
86. Memorandum in Dalmeny papers, reprinted in *History Today*.
87. Journal of Lewis Harcourt, 5 March 1894, Vol. 405.
88. *Ibid.*
89. Bryce to Rosebery, 7 March 1894, Mss Bryce 121.
90. Edward Hamilton's Diary, 7 March 1894.
91. Queen Victoria's Journal, 5 March 1894 (Royal Archives).
92. Journal of Regy Brett, 4 March 1894, Esher papers.
93. Edward Hamilton's Diary, 3 March 1894.
94. Rosebery to Herbert Bismarck, 26 March 1894, Rosebery NLS 10201.
95. Rosebery to Munro-Ferguson, 6 February 1894, Rosebery NLS 10019.
96. Rosebery to Buckle, 23 December 1895, Rosebery NLS 10106.

CHAPTER 11: 'YOU HAVE CHOSEN BARABBAS'

1. Knollys to Rosebery, 21 March 1894, Rosebery NLS 10039.
2. Diary of John Morley, 16 March 1894.
3. Journal of Regy Brett, 1 April 1894, Esher papers.
4. Edward Hamilton's Diary, 8 March 1894.
5. Journal of John Morley, 16 March 1894.
6. Journal of Lewis Harcourt, 4 March 1894, Vol. 404.
7. Sir Charles Mallet, *Herbert Gladstone*.

8. Austen Chamberlain to Leo Maxse, 9 March 1894, Maxse 443.

9. Report of conversation with the Duchess; Canon Rogers to Rosebery, 19 July 1895, Rosebery NLS 10060.

10. Rosebery to Gladstone, 18 March 1895, Gladstone Add Ms 44,290.

11. Sir John Robinson, *50 Years of Fleet Street*.

12. Charles Eyre Pascoe, *Number 10 Downing Street*.

13. Acton to Murray, Whit Sunday 1894, Murray papers.

14. Acton papers, Add 8119 (1) M354.

15. Journal of Lewis Harcourt, 27 March 1894, Vol. 406.

16. *Ibid.*, 8 March 1894, Vol. 405.

17. Rosebery to Murray (undated), Murray papers.

18. Reported by Hamilton to Rosebery, 11 March 1894, Rosebery NLS 10133.

19. Giles St Aubyn, *Queen Victoria*.

20. Reid to Rosebery, 9 March 1894, Rosebery NLS 10092.

21. Rosebery to Queen Victoria, 9 March 1894, Royal Archives, RA VIC/D11/169.

22. Journal of Lewis Harcourt, 9 March 1894, Vol. 405.

23. Queen Victoria to Rosebery, 4 March 1894, RA VIC/A70/6.

24. Queen Victoria to Rosebery, 9 April 1894, RA VIC/A70/23.

25. Diary of John Morley, 16 March 1894.

26. Edward Hamilton's Diary, 16 March 1894.

27. Queen Victoria to Lord Rosebery, 17 March 1894, RA VIC/A70/17.

28. Morley to Rosebery, 16 March 1894, Rosebery NLS 10045.

29. Ellis to Rosebery, 19 March, Rosebery NLS 10092.

30. J. Saxon Mills, *Sir Edward Cook*.

31. Edward Hamilton's Diary, 11 November 1894.

32. Rosebery to Bismarck, 14 and 26 March 1894, Rosebery NLS 10201.

33. A.G. Gardiner, *The Life of Sir William Harcourt*.

34. Edward Hamilton's Diary, 29 March 1894.

35. Robert Rhodes James, *Rosebery*.

36. Journal of Lewis Harcourt, 4 April 1894, Vol. 407.

37. Edward Hamilton's Diary, 7 April 1894.

38. Gardiner, *op.cit.*

39. Diary of John Morley, 5 April 1894.

40. Rosebery to Queen Victoria, 13 July 1894, RA VIC/A70/21.

41. Edward Hamilton's Diary, 26 April 1894.

42. Keith Robbins, *Sir Edward Grey*.

43. Note of conversation with Rosebery, 21 May 1894, Fisher papers 1/62.

44. H.C.G. Matthew, *The Liberal Imperialists*.

45. John Powell, *Liberal by Principle*.

46. Gardiner, *op.cit.*

47. *Ibid.*

48. Gordon Martel, *Imperial Diplomacy*.

49. *Ibid.*
50. Powell, *op.cit.*
51. *Ibid.*
52. A.J.P. Taylor, 'Prelude to Fashoda: The Question of the Upper Nile 1894–95', in *English Historical Review*.
53. Diary of John Morley, 7 June 1894.
54. Angus Hawkins and John Powell, *The Journal of the 1st Earl of Kimberley*.
55. A.J.P. Taylor, *art.cit.*
56. F.E. Hamer (ed.), *Personal Papers of Lord Rendel*.
57. Rosebery to Portal, 10 August 1894, Dalmeny papers.
58. Edward Hamilton's Diary, 21 May 1894.
59. Diary of John Morley, 11 June 1894.
60. Journal of Regy Brett, 27 September 1894, Esher papers.
61. Rosebery to Russell, 8 May 1895, Russell papers.
62. Rosebery to Queen Victoria, 7 May 1894, RA VIC/A70/32a.
63. Edward Hamilton's Diary, 21 June 1894.
64. Journal of Lewis Harcourt, 29 May 1894, Vol. 408.
65. *Ibid.*, 24 July 1894, Vol. 410.
66. Buckle to Brett, 13 June 1894, Esher papers.
67. Journal of Lewis Harcourt, July 10 1894, Vol. 410.
68. Diary of John Morley, 3 July 1894.
69. Edward Hamilton's Diary, 6 May 1894.
70. Rhodes James, *op.cit.*
71. Journal of Regy Brett, 7 June 1894.
72. Rosebery to John Hawke, Secretary of the National Anti-Gambling League, 23 June 1894, Rosebery NLS 10095.
73. Rosebery to the Gimcrack Club, 1897, quoted in Charles Geake, *Lord Rosebery*.
74. Rosebery to Stead, 20 June 1894, Stead papers.
75. Stephen Koss, *Asquith*.
76. Kenneth Bourne, *The Foreign Policy of Victorian England, 1830–1902*.
77. F.E. Hamer, *op.cit.*
78. Journal of Lewis Harcourt, 24 July 1894, Vol. 410.
79. Harcourt to Spencer, 21 September 1894, in Peter Gordon (ed.), *The Spencer Papers*.
80. Diary of John Morley, 14 September 1894.
81. Russell to Rosebery, 20 September 1894, Russell papers.
82. Diary of Beatrice Webb, 1 December 1903, Passfield papers.
83. Haldane to Rosebery, 6 June 1894, Rosebery NLS 10029.
84. Edward Hamilton's Diary, 1 October 1894.
85. Rosebery to Brett, 23 October 1894, Esher papers.
86. Queen Victoria to the Empress Frederick, 28 March 1894, in Agatha Ramm, *Darling and Beloved Child*.

87. Salisbury to Queen Victoria, 27 October 1894, RA VIC/A70/77.
88. Fletcher to Crewe, 7 October 1931, NLS Crewe 10195.
89. Queen Victoria to Rosebery, 30 October 1894, RA VIC/A70/78.
90. Frank Hardie, *The Political Influence of Queen Victoria*.
91. Arthur Bigge, on behalf of Queen Victoria, to the Prince of Wales, 16 November 1894, RA VIC/A71/4A.
92. Edward Hamilton's Diary, 5 September 1905.
93. Chamberlain to Devonshire, 13 November 1894, quoted in Peter Fraser, *Joseph Chamberlain*.
94. Note of audience, 7 December, Rosebery NLS 10174.
95. Peter Stansky, *Ambitions and Strategies*.
96. Journal of Lewis Harcourt, 19 February 1895, Vol. 415.
97. Edward Hamilton's Diary, 4 November 1894.
98. Rosebery to Mary Gladstone Drew, 7 December 1894, Mary Gladstone papers, Ms Add 46,237.
99. Bernard Palmer, *High and Mitred*.
100. Murray to Bigge, 16 April 1895, Rosebery NLS 10103.
101. Browning to Rosebery, 16 January 1895, Rosebery NLS 10151.
102. Helen Gladstone to Rosebery, 20 January 1895, Rosebery NLS 10151.
103. Journal of Lewis Harcourt, 24 July 1894, Vol. 410.
104. Diary of John Morley, 5 January 1895.
105. Michaela Reid, *Ask Sir James*.
106. Diary of Margot Asquith, 16 January 1895.
107. Kenneth Young, *Balfour*.

CHAPTER 12: 'A DAMNED CUR AND COWARD OF THE ROSEBERY TYPE'

1. Diary of Beatrice Webb, 20 January 1895, Passfield papers.
2. Rosebery to Constance Leconfield, 13 January 1895, Petworth papers 5575.
3. Murray to Rosebery, 16 January 1895, Rosebery NLS 10049.
4. Note on his letters, Haldane NLS 5923.
5. Journal of Lewis Harcourt, 17 of February 1895, Vol. 415.
6. Memorandum by Rosebery, 19 February 1895, Rosebery NLS 10146.
7. Journal of Lewis Harcourt, 19 February 1895, Vol. 415.
8. Tweedmouth to Rosebery, 19 February 1895, Rosebery NLS 10102.
9. Angus Hawkins and John Powell, *The Journal of the 1st Earl of Kimberley*.
10. Journal of Lewis Harcourt, 20 February 1895, Vol. 415.
11. A.G. Gardiner, *The Life of Sir William Harcourt*.
12. Robert Rhodes James, *Rosebery*.
13. Note in Rosebery NLS 10146.
14. Journal of Lewis Harcourt, 23 February 1895, Vol. 416.

15. Diary of Lord Rosebery, 22 February 1895, Dalmeny papers.
16. Broadbent to Reid, 27 February 1895, Rosebery NLS 10102.
17. Broadbent to Reid, 3 March 1895, Rosebery NLS 10102.
18. Diary of Lord Rosebery, 11 March 1895.
19. Brett to the Revd C.D. Williamson, 14 March 1895, Esher papers.
20. Journal of Regy Brett, 14 March 1895, Esher papers.
21. Edward Hamilton's Diary, 17 March 1895.
22. *Ibid.*, 18 March 1895.
23. Murray to Bigge, 19 March 1895, RA VIC/A71/27.
24. Journal of Lewis Harcourt, 20 March 1895, Vol. 416.
25. Broadbent to Reid, 21 March 1895, Rosebery NLS 10120.
26. Journal of Lewis Harcourt, 20 March 1895, Vol. 416.
27. Edward Hamilton's Diary, 12 April 1895.
28. Rosebery to Stead, 17 April 1895, Stead papers.
29. Peter Gordon (ed.), *The Spencer Papers*.
30. Note written at The Durdans, 30 September 1903, Dalmeny papers.
31. Richard Davenport-Hines, *The Pursuit of Oblivion*.
32. Sybil Grant, 'A Great Scotsman', Rosebery NLS 8365.
33. Diary of Lord Balcarres, 3 August 1924, in John Vincent (ed.), *The Crawford Papers*.
34. John Wilson, *A Life of Sir Henry Campbell-Bannerman*.
35. Edward Hamilton's Diary, 8 March 1895.
36. Note written in 1917, Dalmeny papers.
37. Words of James Thomson, 19th-century poet, quoted in Hilary Rubinstein, *The Complete Insomniac*.
38. Note on Biography, 1872, Rosebery NLS 10189.
39. Diary of Beatrice Webb, 9 February 1901, Passfield papers.
40. Diary of Margot Asquith, 26 June 1905.
41. Edmund Bergler, *Homosexuality*.
42. Diary of Margot Asquith, 17 April 1899.
43. Peter Thompson and Robert Macklin, *The Man Who Died Twice*.
44. Journal of Lord Esher, 23 July 1908, Esher papers.
45. The correspondence about this escapade is in the papers of Lord Crewe, who understandably did not refer to it in his 2-volume Life. The story was recalled for Crewe by Paul Dana of New York, a friend of Miss Barlow's, in November 1929.
46. Frank Harris, *My Life and Loves*.
47. Brown to Rosebery, 5 August 1910, Rosebery NLS 10122.
48. Cooper to Rosebery, 15 September 1884, Rosebery NLS 10010.
49. Lady Colebrooke to Rosebery, February 1906, Rosebery NLS 10120.
50. Asquith to H.T. Baker, 1 October 1898, quoted in John Jolliffe (ed.), *Asquith, Life & Letters*.
51. Quoted in Max Egremont, *Balfour*.

52. Rosebery to Crewe, 4 February 1913 and 27 April 1895, Crewe papers, CUL.
53. Diary of John Morley, 13 November 1893.
54. James Money, *Capri*.
55. Neil McKenna, *Secret Life of Oscar Wilde*.
56. *Ibid*.
57. J.O. Baylen and Robert L. McBath, 'A Note on Oscar Wilde, Alfred Douglas and Lord Rosebery, 1897', in *English Language Notes*, 1895.
58. Hugh Trevor-Roper, *The Hermit of Peking*.
59. Rosebery to Murray: 15 October 1903; Rosebery to Winston Churchill: 19 August 1903, Churchill Archive Char 2/8/63.
60. Note in Dalmeny papers, 1915.
61. Statement by Talon (in Rosebery's hand), October 1879, Rosebery NLS 10075.
62. Rosebery to Harry Graham, 7 July 1904, Rosebery NLS 10118.
63. Journal of Lewis Harcourt, 6 August 1885, Vol. 371.
64. *Ibid*., 29 March 1893, Vol. 406.
65. Queensberry to Rosebery, December 1879, Rosebery NLS 10075.
66. Queensberry to Rosebery, 23 November 1885, Rosebery NLS 1.
67. Lord Queensberry and Percy Colson, *Oscar Wilde and the Black Douglas*.
68. Murray to Rosebery, 19 October 1894, Rosebery NLS 10049.
69. Rosebery memorandum, Rosebery NLS 10176.
70. Queensberry to Queen Victoria, 17 July 1893, Rosebery NLS 10065.
71. Rosebery to Queen Victoria, 12 June 1893, Royal Archives, RA VIC/D42/104.
72. Queensberry to Rosebery, 6 August 1893, Rosebery NLS 10176.
73. Rosebery memorandum, August 1893, Rosebery NLS 10176.
74. Rosebery to Queen Victoria, 29 October 1893, Royal Archives, RA VIC/Y60/234.
75. H. Montgomery Hyde, *Lord Alfred Douglas*.
76. Drumlanrig to Rosebery, 18 September 1894.
77. Report in the *Bridgewater Mercury*, 24 October 1894.
78. *Ibid*.
79. Ellis to Rosebery, 22 October 1894, Rosebery NLS 10098.
80. Waterfield to Rosebery, 27 October 1894, Rosebery NLS 10098.
81. Queensberry to Rosebery, 20 October 1894, Rosebery NLS 10098.
82. Richard Ellman, *Oscar Wilde*.
83. Michael Foldy, *The Trials of Oscar Wilde*, an entirely derivative volume, is typical of this approach.
84. Neil McKenna, *op.cit*.
85. Henry Foley to Rosebery, 21 September 1894, Rosebery NLS 10097.
86. E.F.C. Collier (ed.), *A Victorian Diarist*.
87. Murray to Rosebery, 22 October 1894, Rosebery NLS 10049.
88. Rosebery to Murray, 23 October 1894, Murray papers.

89. Lord Rosebery to Queen Victory, 22 October 1894, RA VIC/A70/68.
90. *Ibid.*
91. Rosebery to Constance Leconfield, 10 December 1894, Petworth papers.
92. Durham to Brett, 21 April 1895, quoted in James Lees-Milne, *The Enigmatic Edwardian.*
93. Rosebery to Sir Edward Russell, 26 March 1895, Russell papers.
94. Journal of Lewis Harcourt, 14 May 1895.
95. A full transcript of the trial is published in Merlin Holland, *The Irish Peacock and the Scarlet Marquess.*
96. Trevor Fisher, *Oscar and Bosie: A Fatal Passion.*
97. Ellman, *op.cit.*
98. Edward Hamilton's Diary, 21 May 1895.
99. H. Montgomery Hyde, *op.cit.*
100. Journal of Lewis Harcourt, 31 May 1895.
101. Neil McKenna, *op.cit.*
102. Queensberry and Colson, *op.cit.*
103. Rosebery to Neville-Rolfe, 26 December 1897, Neville-Rolfe papers, GUN 71.
104. Neville-Rolfe to Rosebery, 30 December 1897, Rosebery NLS 10098.
105. Neville-Rolfe to Rosebery, 9 March 1898, Dalmeny papers.

CHAPTER 13: 'PURGED AS WITH FIRE'

1. Murray to Rosebery, 2 January 1895 Rosebery NLS.
2. Massingham to Haldane, 14 January 1895, Massingham MC41/98/33.
3. Haldane to his sister Elizabeth, 31 January 1895, Haldane Mss 6010.
4. Campbell-Bannerman to Rosebery, 9 March 1895, Rosebery NLS 10002.
5. Rosebery to Campbell-Bannerman, 11 March 1895, Rosebery NLS 10002.
6. Haldane to his mother, 15 March 1895, Haldane Mss 5951.
7. Queen Victoria to Lord Rosebery, 11 April 1895, RA VIC/A71/43.
8. Giles St Aubyn, *The Royal George.*
9. Campbell-Bannerman to Rosebery, 15 May 1895, Rosebery NLS 10002.
10. St Aubyn, *op.cit.*
11. Campbell-Bannerman to Rosebery, 17 May 1895, Rosebery NLS 10002.
12. St Aubyn, *op.cit.*
13. Note taken by Rosebery, 17 June 1895, Rosebery NLS 10105.
14. John Wilson, *Life of Campbell-Bannerman.*
15. *Ibid.*
16. Angus Hawkins and John Powell, *Journal of the 1st Earl of Kimberley*, 28 March 1895.
17. Rosebery to Kimberley, 6 April 1895, quoted in John Powell, *Liberal by Principle.*

18. Grey to Rosebery, 30 March 1895, Rosebery NLS 10028.

19. Journal of Lewis Harcourt, 30 March 1895

20. Taken from Rosebery's letter to the *Banker Journal*, 7 September 1927, responding to Lloyd George's allegations of selling honours.

21. Edward Hamilton's Diary, 7 July 1895.

22. *Ibid.*, 30 June 1895.

23. Brett to Rosebery, 26 July 1895, Rosebery NLS 10006.

24. Journal of Lewis Harcourt, 3rd April 1895

25. Ellis to Murray, 6 June 1895, Rosebery NLS 10105.

26. Rosebery to Gladstone, 23 August 1894, Viscount Gladstone papers, Add Mss 45,986.

27. Note by Rosebery, 13 May 1895, Rosebery NLS 10146.

28. Ellis to Rosebery, 18 June 1895, Rosebery NLS 10105; Rosebery to Ellis, 19 June 1895, T.E. Ellis papers.

29. Edward Hamilton's Diary, 29 May 1895.

30. Rosebery to Kimberley, 7 April 1895, quoted in Powell, *Liberal by Principle*.

31. Morley to Rosebery, 28 May 1895.

32. Edward Hamilton's Diary, 25 April 1895.

33. From Gladstone's *Autobiographica*, quoted in Richard Shannon, *Gladstone*.

34. Wilson, *op.cit.*

35. A.G. Gardiner, *The Life of Sir William Harcourt*.

36. Campbell-Bannerman to Rosebery, 22 June 1895, Rosebery NLS 10002.

37. Peter Stansky, *Ambitions and Strategies*.

38. Rosebery to Campbell-Bannerman, 24 June 1895, Rosebery NLS 10002.

39. Note in Betting Book, Rosebery NLS 10176.

40. Queen Victoria to Rosebery, 27 June 1895, RA VIC/A71/69a.

41. Agatha Ramm, *Darling and Beloved Child*.

42. Rosebery to Constance Leconfield, 7 July 1895, Petworth papers 5575.

43. Journal of Regy Brett, 10 May 1898, Esher papers.

44. *Ibid.*, 8 February 1898, Esher papers.

45. Crewe, *Lord Rosebery*.

46. Rosebery to Murray, 15 December 1901, Murray papers.

47. Horace Hutchinson, *The Private Diaries of Sir Algernon West*.

48. Peter Stansky, *op.cit.*

49. *Ibid.*

50. Rosebery to Constance Leconfield, 18 July 1895, Petworth papers 5575.

51. Ellis to Rosebery, 7 July and 14 August 1895, Rosebery NLS 10105; Rosebery to Ellis, 7 July 1895, T.E. Ellis papers.

52. Murray to Rosebery, 7 August 1895, Rosebery NLS 10049.

53. Rosebery to Holland, 21 August 1895, Crewe papers.

54. Munro-Ferguson to Rosebery, 27 July 1895, Rosebery NLS 10019.

55. Brett to Rosebery, 24 June 1895, Rosebery NLS 10006.

56. Edward Hamilton's Diary, 31 July 1895.

57. Rosebery to Campbell-Bannerman, 27 July 1895, Campbell-Bannerman papers, Add Ms 41,226.

58. Rosebery to Gladstone, 25 August 1895, Gladstone papers, Add Mss 44,290.

59. Peter Stansky, *op.cit.*

60. *Ibid.*

61. Peter Gordon, *The Spencer Papers.*

62. Hawkin's and Powell, *op.cit.* 15 August 1895.

63. Peter Stansky, *op.cit.*

64. Munro-Ferguson to Rosebery, 3 October 1865, Rosebery NLS 10019.

65. Rosebery to Munro-Ferguson, 2 October 1895, Rosebery NLS 10019.

66. Edward Hamilton's Diary, 19 January 1896.

67. Morley to Spencer, 13 February 1896, in Peter Gordon, *op.cit.*

68. Edward Hamilton's Diary, 24 January 1895.

69. Diary of Margot Asquith, 30 October 1895.

70. Hamilton to Rosebery, 15 November 1895, Rosebery NLS 10031.

71. Diary of Lord Rosebery, 15 January 1896, Dalmeny papers.

72. Rosebery to Tweedmouth, 20 January 1896, Dalmeny papers. This letter contradicts the claim in Rhodes James' biography, p. 388, that 'throughout 1896 Rosebery gave no hint that he was awaiting his opportunity to retire from the leadership.'

73. Rosebery to Corrie Grant, 24 December 1895, Rosebery NLS 10106.

74. Rosebery to Sir Edward Russell, 9 December 1895, Russell papers.

75. Helen Gladstone to Rosebery, 17 September 1896, Rosebery NLS 10108.

76. Rosebery to Charles Geake, 24 September 1896, Geake papers.

77. Peter Stansky, *op.cit.*

78. Benn to Rosebery, 5 October 1896, Rosebery NLS 10108.

79. Eddington to Crewe, 10 December 1931, NLS Crewe 10195.

80. Rosebery to Ellis, 6 October 1896, Rosebery NLS 10108.

81. Peter Stansky, *op.cit.*

82. Rosebery to Asquith, 6 October 1896, Rosebery NLS 10001.

83. Both letters in the Gladstone papers, Add Ms 44,290.

84. Crewe to Florence Henniker, 18 October 1896, Crewe (CUL) P/4.

85. Hutchinson, *op.cit.*

86. Diary of Margot Asquith, 9 October 1896.

87. Godley to Rosebery, 9 October 1896, Rosebery NLS 10108.

88. Benn to Rosebery, 10 October 1896, Rosebery NLS 10108.

89. Letters from Tillett, Spencer and Spence Watson in Rosebery NLS 10109.

90. Carrington to Rosebery, 13 October 1896, Rosebery NLS 10008.

91. Lord Spencer to C.R. Spencer, 12 October 1896, in Peter Gordon, *op.cit.*

92. Note of conversation with Lord Monkswell, Monkswell papers Dep d. 837.

93. Ripon to Spencer, 8 October 1896, quoted in Peter Stansky, *op.cit.*

94. Acland and Kay-Shuttleworth's letters in Rosebery NLS 10109.

95. Edward Hamilton's Diary, 3 November 1896.

96. Sir Charles Mallet, *Herbert Gladstone*.

97. Murray to Rosebery, 8 October 1896, Rosebery NLS 10049.

98. Edward Hamilton's Diary, 8 October 1896.

99. The Duchess of Cleveland to Rosebery, 8 October 1896, Rosebery NLS 10108.

100. Ellis to Rosebery, 20 October 1896.

101. Harcourt to Morley, 26 October 1896, Gardiner, *op.cit.*

102. Peter Stansky, *op.cit.*

103. Diary of John Morley, 8, 10, 14 and 21 October 1896.

CHAPTER 14: 'I MUST PLOUGH MY FURROW ALONE'

1. Elizabeth Longford, *Jameson's Raid*.

2. Rhodes to Rosebery, 22 June 1893, Dalmeny papers.

3. Note of conversation in Betting Book, 12 May 1899, Rosebery NLS 10183.

4. Rosebery to Russell, 14 January 1896, Russell papers.

5. Edward Hamilton's Diary, 16 October 1896.

6. Longford, *op.cit.*

7. *Ibid.*

8. Reid to Rosebery, 23 July 1897, Rosebery NLS 10156.

9. Lockwood to Rosebery, 20 July 1897, Rosebery NLS 10110.

10. Jeffrey Butler, *The Liberal Party and the Jameson Raid*.

11. Rosebery to Ripon, 2 September 1894, Ripon papers Add Ms 43,516.

12. Butler, *op.cit.*

13. Rhodes to Rosebery, 19 and 22 December 1895, Dalmeny papers.

14. Deryck Schreuder and Jeffrey Butler, *Sir Graham Bower's Secret History*.

15. Chamberlain to Sir Robert Meade, Permanent Under-Secretary at the Colonial Office, quoted in Schreuder and Butler, *op.cit.*

16. Schreuder and Butler, *op.cit.*

17. *Ibid.*

18. Longford, *op.cit.*

19. Lord Crewe, *Lord Rosebery*.

20. Schreuder and Butler, *op.cit.*

21. Diary of Margot Asquith, 9 November 1897.

22. Robert Rhodes James, *Rosebery*.

23. Sir William Benn to Rosebery, 31 July 1898, Rosebery NLS 10111.

24. Rosebery to Constance Leconfield, 12 July 1897, Petworth papers 5575.

25. Rosebery to Herbert Fisher, 16 June 1905, Fisher papers.

26. Memorandum dated 26 February 1897, Betting Book, Rosebery NLS 10177.

27. Rosebery to Gibson Carmichael, May 1897, Rosebery NLS 10110.

28. Rosebery to Wemyss Reid, 11 March 1897, Rosebery NLS 10156.

29. Diary of Lord Rosebery, 20 June 1897, Dalmeny papers.
30. Rosebery to Munro-Ferguson, 10 January 1898, Rosebery NLS 10019.
31. Rosebery to Sir Edward Russell, 27 July 1898, Rosebery NLS 10111. This letter has been wrongly attributed to Edward Cheney in previous biographies.
32. Rosebery to Jacks, 23 July 1898, Rosebery NLS 10111.
33. Rosebery to H.T. Baker, 1 October 1898, in John Joliffe, *Asquith: Life and Letters*.
34. A.G. Gardiner, *Prophets, Priests and Kings*.
35. Rosebery to Gibson Carmichael, 19 October 1898, Rosebery NLS 10111.
36. Diary of Beatrice Webb, 2 March 1898, Passfield papers.
37. Diary of Lord Rosebery, 28 May 1898, Dalmeny papers.
38. H.C.G. Matthew, *The Liberal Imperialists*.
39. Peter Stansky, *Ambitions and Strategies*.
40. Edward Hamilton's Diary, 16 December 1898.
41. Spencer to Horace Seymour, 15 December 1898, quoted in Peter Gordon (ed.), *The Spencer Papers*.
42. Matthew, *op.cit.*
43. Munro-Ferguson to Rosebery, 14 March 1899.
44. Rosebery to Campbell-Bannerman, 8 January 1899, Rosebery NLS 10002.
45. Rosebery to Queen Victoria, 15 February 1899, Royal Archives, RA VIC/F40/114.
46. James Pope-Hennesey, *The Likeness of a Liberal*.
47. Duchess of Cleveland to Eustace Neville-Rolfe, 25 April 1899, Neville-Rolfe papers.
48. Pope-Hennesy, *op.cit.*
49. Diary of Margot Asquith, 20 April 1899.
50. Jane Stoddart, *The Earl of Rosebery*, quoting Goldwin Smith.
51. Edward Hamilton's Diary, 23 April 1899.
52. Memorandum 26 July 1898, Betting Book, Rosebery NLS 10177.
53. Diary of Margot Asquith, 6 May 1899.
54. Asquith to Rosebery, 6 May 1899, Asquith papers MS Asquith 46/10.
55. Reid to Rosebery, 9 June 1899, Rosebery NLS 10156.
56. Note by Herbert Gladstone, 26 July 1899, Viscount Gladstone papers, Add Ms 45,986.
57. Quotations from Edward Hamilton's Diary, 8 May 1899, and Crewe, *Lord Rosebery*.
58. J.A. Spender, *The Public Life*.
59. Undated note, around 1900, Dalmeny papers.
60. Richard Shannon, *The Crisis of Imperialism*.
61. Memorandum on the South African Crisis, October 1899, Betting Book, Rosebery NLS 10177.
62. Boyd to Rosebery, 6 August 1899, Rosebery NLS 10112.
63. Hamilton to Rosebery, 3 October 1899, Rosebery NLS 10133.

64. Edward Hamilton's Diary, 6 October 1899.

65. Matthew, *op.cit.*

66. A.G. Gardiner, *The Life of Sir William Harcourt.*

67. Rosebery to Haldane, 21 November 1899, Haldane papers.

68. John Wilson, *Life of Campbell-Bannerman.*

69. Report by Lynn Morgan, Glasgow University Archives, 16 November 2000; *Scotland on Sunday*, 22 Feb. 2004; Gerald Warner, *Conquering by Degrees; Glasgow University Union, A Century History* (1985).

70. Diary of Beatrice Webb, 19 May 1902, Passfield papers.

71. Stephen Koss, *Asquith.*

72. Grey to Rosebery, 26 July 1900, Rosebery NLS 10028.

73. Beneke to Rosebery, 18 February 1900, Rosebery NLS 10156.

74. G.R. Searle, *The Quest for National Efficiency.*

75. Victor Mallet, *Life with Queen Victoria.*

76. Regy Brett to his son Maurice, 31 January 1900, Esher papers.

77. Rosebery to Albert Beneke, 26 February 1900, Rosebery NLS Acc 7628.

78. Rosebery to Ritchie, 23 March 1900, Ritchie papers Add Ms 53,780.

79. Raymond Asquith to H.T. Baker, 17 April 1900, in Joliffe, *op.cit.*

80. Searle, *op.cit.*

81. Reid to Rosebery, 14 June and 5 July 1900, Rosebery NLS 10156.

82. Edward Hamilton's Diary, 26 July 1900.

83. Rosebery to Richard Johnson, 27 June 1900, Rosebery NLS 10113.

84. Rosebery to Dr Guinness Rogers, 28 July 1900, Rosebery NLS 10113.

85. Rosebery to Fowler, 14 October 1900, Rosebery NLS 10113.

86. Spender to Rosebery, 27 October 1900, Rosebery NLS 10113.

87. Samuel to Rosebery, 23 October 1900, Rosebery NLS 10113.

88. Earl Spencer to Kimberley, 8 November 1900, quoted in Gordon, *op.cit.*

89. Asquith to Herbert Gladstone, quoted in Sir Charles Mallet, *Herbert Gladstone.*

90. Report of conversation with McKenna, given by Wemyss Reid to Rosebery, 17 November 1900, Rosebery NLS 10157.

91. Wilson, *op.cit.*

92. Perks to Rosebery, 5 December 1900, Rosebery NLS 10050.

93. Wilson, *op.cit.*

94. Edward Hamilton's Diary, 24 February 1901.

95. Rosebery to Haldane, 24 May 1900, Haldane NLS 5903.

96. Edward Hamilton's Diary, 18 March 1901.

97. Bernard Semmel, *Imperialism and Social Reform.*

98. H.G. Wells, *Anticipations* (1901).

99. Semmell, *op.cit.*

100. *Ibid.*

101. Carole Seymour-Jones, *Beatrice Webb.*

102. Murray to Rosebery, 3 October 1895, Rosebery NLS 10049.

103. Matthew, *op.cit.*
104. Speech in Shoreditch, 27 October 1900, quoted in H.G.C. Matthew, *The Liberal Imperialists.*
105. Winifried Baumgart, *Imperialism.*
106. Semmel, *op.cit.*
107. Diary of Beatrice Webb, 16 March 1900, Passfield papers.
108. Beatrice Webb to her sister Mary Playne, 10 February 1901, quoted in Norman Mackenzie, *The Letters of Sidney and Beatrice Webb.*
109. Rosebery to Spender, 20 June 1901, Spender papers, Add Ms 46,387.
110. Rosebery to Munro-Ferguson, 28 June 1901, Rosebery NLS 10019.
111. Moberly Bell to Rosebery, 11 July 1901, Rosebery NLS 10114.
112. E.H.C. Moberly Bell, *Life and Letters of C.F. Moberly Bell.*
113. Edward Hamilton's Diary, 17 July 1901.
114. Haldane to Rosebery, 17 July 1901, Haldane NLS 5903.
115. Reid to Rosebery, 24 August 1901, Rosebery NLS 10156.
116. Sir Almeric Fitzroy, *Memoirs.*
117. Memorandum of conversation, 28 September 1901, Dalmeny papers.
118. Grey to Rosebery, 20 July 1901, Rosebery NLS 10028.
119. Matthew, *op.cit.*
120. Diary of Beatrice Webb, 26 July 1901, Passfield papers.
121. Norman and Jeanne Mackenzie, *The First Fabians.*
122. Seymour-Jones, *op.cit.*
123. N. and J. Mackenzie, *op.cit.*
124. Searle, *op.cit.*
125. Fisher to Rosebery, 22 May 1901, Fisher papers (Churchill).
126. Note of conversation taken by Rosebery, 18 July 1901, Rosebery NLS 10114.
127. Salisbury to Rosebery, 25 July 1901, Rosebery NLS 10115.
128. Rosebery to Salisbury, 25 July 1901, Rosebery NLS 10115.
129. Salisbury to Rosebery, 31 July 1901, Rosebery NLS 10115.
130. Rosebery to Spender, 13 November 1901, Spender papers MS Add 46,387.
131. Wilson, *op.cit.*
132. Reid to Rosebery, 10 December 1901, Rosebery NLS 10157.
133. Pease to Rosebery, 23 November 1901, Rosebery NLS 10015.
134. Perks to Rosebery, 14 December 1901, Rosebery NLS 10050.
135. Herbert Gladstone to Rosebery, 13 December 1901, Viscount Gladstone papers, Add Ms 45,986.
136. Edward Hamilton's Diary, 4 December 1901.

CHAPTER 15: 'WAS THERE EVER SUCH A MAN?'

1. Murray to Rosebery, 31 December 1901, Rosebery NLS 10049.
2. Grey to Rosebery, 17 December 1901, Rosebery NLS 10028.

3. John Wilson, *Life of Campbell-Bannerman.*
4. Haldane to Rosebery, 17 December 1901, Rosebery NLS 10029.
5. John Joliffe, *Asquith Life and Letters.*
6. Reid to Rosebery, 2 June 1902, Rosebery NLS 10157.
7. Morley to Robert Spence Watson, 25 December 1901, Spence Watson papers, 1/344.
8. Reid to Rosebery, 28 January 1902, Rosebery NLS 10158.
9. Earl Spencer to C.R. Spencer, 18 December 1901, in Peter Gordon (ed.), *The Spencer Papers.*
10. John Wilson, *op.cit.*
11. *Ibid.*
12. Memorandum by Rosebery, 23 December 1901, Dalmeny papers.
13. Campbell-Bannerman to Lord Spencer, 23 December 1901, quoted in Gordon, *op.cit.*
14. Edith Henrietta Fowler, *Life of Lord Wolverhampton.*
15. There is an excellent account of the way Campbell-Bannerman manipulated the press against Rosebery in David Gutze's article 'Rosebery and Campbell-Bannerman: The Conflict over Leadership Reconsidered', in *The Institute of Historical Research Bulletin,* November 1981, Vol. 54.
16. Rosebery to Herbert Gladstone, 10 January 1902, Viscount Gladstone papers, Add MS 45,986.
17. Rosebery to Campbell-Bannerman, 13 January 1902, Campbell-Bannerman papers, Add Ms 41,226.
18. Campbell-Bannerman to Rosebery, 14 January 1902, Campbell-Bannerman papers Add Ms 41,226.
19. Labouchere to Reid, 22 October 1901, Rosebery NLS 10041.
20. Perks to Alice de Rothschild, 17 December 1905, Rosebery NLS 100052.
21. Rosebery to Arthur Godley, 11 January 1902, Kilbracken papers, Add Ms 44902.
22. Rosebery to Reid, 14 November 1902, Rosebery NLS 10157.
23. H.C.G. Matthew, *The Liberal Imperialists.*
24. Haldane to Rosebery, 16 February 1902.
25. Note of two conversations with Rosebery, 18 and 19 February 1902, Viscount Gladstone papers, Add Ms 45,986.
26. Note on foundation of Liberal League, taken by Neville Waterfield, Rosebery NLS 10168.
27. Edward Hamilton's Diary, 3 March 1902.
28. Allard to Rosebery, 25 June 1902, Rosebery NLS 10168.
29. Spencer to Asquith, 3 March 1902, quoted in Gordon, *op.cit.*
30. John Wilson, *op.cit.*
31. Matthew, *op.cit.*
32. Diary of Lord Rosebery, 11 March 1902, Dalmeny papers.
33. Harold Harmsworth to Rosebery, 12 June 1902, Rosebery NLS 10050.

34. Robertson Nicholl to Rosebery, 5 March 1902, Rosebery NLS 10168.

35. Carole Seymour-Jones, *Beatrice Webb*.

36. Diary of Beatrice Webb, 28 February 1902, Passfield papers.

37. *Ibid.*, 21 July 1902.

38. Sir Edward to Lady Grey, 28 January 1902, in G.M. Trevelyan, *Grey of Fallodon*.

39. Edward Hamilton's Diary, 16 July 1902.

40. *Ibid.*, 14 October 1902.

41. *Ibid.*, 12 October 1902.

42. Rosebery to Reid, 14 November 1902, Rosebery NLS 10058.

43. Raymond Asquith to Buchan, 2 March 1902, quoted in Joliffe, *op.cit.*

44. G.K. Chesterton, *What's Wrong With the World*.

45. *Methodist News*, 13 January 1903.

46. Perks to Rosebery, 24 July 1902, Rosebery NLS 10052.

47. Haldane to Rosebery, 4 November 1902, NLS Haldane 5904.

48. Diary of Beatrice Webb, 10 November 1902, Passfield papers.

49. John Wilson, *op.cit.*

50. Crewe to Rosebery, 29 May 1903, Rosebery NLS 10117.

51. Grey to Rosebery, 11 June 1903, Rosebery NLS 10028.

52. Carnegie to Rosebery, 14 June 1903, Rosebery NLS 10117.

53. E.T. Raymond, *The Man of Promise*.

54. Bernard Semmel, *Imperialism and Social Reform*.

55. G.R. Searle, *The Quest for National Efficiency*.

56. Semmel, *op.cit.*

57. Lord Ripon to Lord Spencer, 30 May 1903, in Gordon, *op.cit.*

58. Edward Hamilton's Diary, 11 June 1903.

59. Grey to Rosebery, 13 July 1903, Rosebery NLS 10028.

60. Asquith to Rosebery, 9 and 10 July, Rosebery to Asquith 10 July 1903, Rosebery NLS 10001.

61. Winston Churchill to Rosebery, 31 July 1900, Rosebery NLS 10009.

62. Rosebery to W.S. Churchill, 6 August 1901, Churchill archives CHAR 1/29.31.

63. Diary of Lord Rosebery, 15 August 1901, Dalmeny papers.

64. W.S. Churchill to Rosebery, 15 November 1901, Rosebery NLS 10009.

65. W.S. Churchill to Rosebery, 17 December 1901, Rosebery NLS 10009.

66. Lord Huge Cecil to W.S. Churchill, 28 December 1901, in Churchill and Gilbert, *Winston S. Churchill*.

67. Churchill to Rosebery, 10 October 1902, Rosebery NLS 10009.

68. Rosebery to W.S. Churchill, 12 October 1902, Churchill archives CHAR 2/2/20.

69. W.S. Churchill to Rosebery, 29 May 1903, Rosebery NLS 10009.

70. W.S. Churchill to Rosebery, 9 October 1903, Churchill and Gilbert, *op.cit.*

71. J.A. Spender, *Life, Journalism and Politics*.

72. St Loe Strachey to Buchan, July 1903, Strachey papers STR/3/2/26.
73. Harmsworth to Rosebery, 1 September 1903, Northcliffe papers Ms Add 62,154.
74. Perks to Harmsworth, 3 September 1903, Northcliffe papers Ms Add 62,154.
75. Rosebery to Harmsworth, 5 September 1903, Northcliffe papers Ms Add 62,154.
76. Harmsworth to Perks, 10 September 1903, Dalmeny papers.
77. Rosebery to Perks, 14 September 1903, Dalmeny papers.
78. Rosebery to Harold Harmsworth, 27 October 1903, Dalmeny papers.
79. Perks to Rosebery, 8 September 1903, Rosebery NLS 10051.
80. A. Harmsworth to W.S. Churchill, 14 September 1903, CHAR 1/39/19.
81. Perks to Rosebery, 12 December 1903, Rosebery NLS 10051.
82. Report of conversation given by Perks to Rosebery, 13 December 1905, Rosebery NLS 10052.
83. Lord Hugh Cecil to W.S. Churchill, 31 August 1903, Churchill and Gilbert, *op.cit.*
84. Edward Hamilton's Diary, 1 March 1904.
85. Rosebery memorandum, August 1903, Dalmeny papers.
86. Rosebery memorandum, 30 September 1903, Dalmeny papers.
87. Rosebery to George W. Potter, 30 October 1903, Rosebery NLS 10118.
88. Rosebery memorandum, 30 September 1903, Dalmeny papers.
89. Rosebery to Fisher, 16 June 1905, Fisher papers.
90. Rosebery to Spencer, 6 January 1904, quoted in Gordon, *op.cit.*
91. W.S. Churchill to Lord Hugh Cecil, 26 March 1904, Churchill and Gilbert, *op.cit.*
92. Haldane to Rosebery, 23 March 1904, Haldane NLS 5906.
93. Diary of Margot Asquith, 23 October 1904.
94. John Wilson, *op.cit.*
95. Gordon, *op.cit.*
96. David Lloyd George, *War Memoirs.*
97. Prothero to Rosebery, 29 June 1912, Rosebery NLS 10123.
98. Rosebery to Fisher, 12 September 1915, Ms Fisher 57.
99. Trevelyan, *Grey of falloden* .
100. Spender to Rosebery, 15 September 1927, Rosebery NLS 10127.
101. Diary of Thomas Gilmour, 8 April 1905, Acc 8989/5.
102. Nicholl to Perks, 12 December 1905, Rosebery NLS, 10051.
103. Lloyd George to Perks, 25 July 1904, Rosebery NLS 10051.
104. B.B. Gilbert, *David Lloyd George.*
105. Lloyd George to Herbert Lewis, 20 December 1904, in Peter Rowland, *Lloyd George.*
106. Spender to Rosebery, 22 October 1904, Spender papers, Add Ms 46,387.
107. Note of conversation, 2 November 1904, Spender papers, Add Ms 46,387.
108. Private memorandum, 10 October 1904, Dalmeny papers.

109. Memorandum of King's visit, 7 February 1905, Dalmeny papers.
110. Rosebery to King Edward VII, 11 February 1905, Dalmeny papers.
111. Note taken by Rosebery of conversation in December 1905 with the Duchess of Sutherland, Betting Book, Rosebery NLS 10184.
112. Memorandum, 2 March 1905, Dalmeny papers.
113. Memorandum written in Naples, 3 May 1905, Dalmeny papers.
114. Margot Asquith to Strachey, 3 January 1905, Strachey papers STR 11/7/7.
115. Rosebery to Haldane, 18 July 1905, Haldane NLS 5906.
116. Haldane to Knollys, 12 September 1905, Haldane NLS 5906.
117. Knollys to Haldane, 16 September 1905, Haldane NLS 5906.
118. Note of conversation, 6 August 1905, Betting Book, Rosebery NLS 10184.
119. Lord Spencer to C.R. Spencer, 8 August 1905, quoted in Gordon, *op.cit.*
120. Campbell-Bannerman to Spencer, 26 August 1905, quoted in Gordon, *op.cit.*
121. H.W. McCready, 'Home Rule and the Liberal party, 1899–1906', in *Irish Historical Studies*, Vol. 13, 1963.
122. Perks to Rosebery, 13 December 1905, Rosebery NLS 10052.
123. Quoted in Churchill & Gilbert, *op.cit.*
124. Poulton to Rosebery, 27 November 1905, Rosebery NLS 10170.
125. John Wilson, *op.cit.*
126. Spender to Rosebery, 29 November 1905, Rosebery NLS 10170.
127. Trevelyan, *op.cit.*
128. Sir Charles Mallet, *Herbert Gladstone.*
129. Rosebery to Asquith, 28 December 1905, Rosebery NLS 10170.
130. Memorandum, January 1906, Dalmeny papers.
131. Spender to Crewe, 2 February 1930, NLS Crewe 10195.
132. John Wilson, *op.cit.*
133. Campbell-Bannerman to Asquith, 1 December 1905, quoted in the Diary of Margot Asquith.
134. Rosebery to Spender, 19 December 1905, Spender papers, Add Ms 46,387.
135. Kearley and Lucy quotations in David Gutze, *art.cit.* n. 15.
136. John Wilson, *op.cit.*
137. Diary of Margot Asquith, 5 December 1905.
138. *Ibid.*
139. J.A. Spender, *Life, Journalism and Politics.*
140. Spender to Rosebery, 30 September 1927, Rosebery NLS 10128.
141. Diary of Margot Asquith, 11 September 1905.
142. *Ibid.*, 6 December 1905.
143. Trevelyan, *op.cit.*

CHAPTER 16: 'WHAT A WICKED, CLEVER WOMAN'

1. Brett to Williamson, 14 March 1895, Esher papers.
2. Esher to his son Maurice, 9 December 1902, Esher papers.
3. Lady Colebrooke to Rosebery, 11 and 19 October 1906, Rosebery NLS 10120.
4. Lady Colebrooke to Rosebery, December 1905, Rosebery NLS 10120.
5. Diary of Lord Rosebery, 5 January 1898, Dalmeny papers.
6. The Countess of Warwick, *Life's Ebb and Flow*.
7. Lady Warwick to Rosebery, 18 February 1895, Rosebery NLS 10102.
8. Lady Warwick to Rosebery, 1 May 1896, Rosebery NLS 10107.
9. Lady Warwick to Rosebery, 14 September 1896, Rosebery NLS 10108.
10. Rosebery to Lady Warwick, 16 September 1896, Rosebery NLS 10108.
11. Lady Warwick to Rosebery, 6 October 1896, Rosebery NLS 10108.
12. Lady Warwick to Rosebery, 8 June 1898, Rosebery NLS 10112.
13. The Countess of Warwick, *op.cit.*
14. Lady Warwick to Rosebery, May 1900, Rosebery NLS 10113.
15. Lady Warwick to Rosebery, 7 October 1900, Rosebery NLS 10113.
16. Lady Warwick to Rosebery, 18 December 1901, Rosebery NLS 10115.
17. Lady Warwick to Rosebery, 23 November 1904 (?), Rosebery NLS 10128.
18. Lady Warwick to Rosebery, 16 May 1922, Rosebery NLS 10127.
19. John Vincent (ed.), *The Crawford Papers*.
20. Margot Asquith, *Autobiography*.
21. Diary of Margot Asquith, 23 October 1904.
22. Margot Asquith to Rosebery, 15 September 1927, Rosebery NLS 10127.
23. Kenneth Young, *Harry, Lord Rosebery*.
24. Anita Leslie, *Edwardians in Love*.
25. *Ibid.*
26. All letters, Princess Victoria to Rosebery, on microfilm in Royal Archives, now catalogued: RA GV/DD2/39, GV/DD2/7, GV/DD2/8, GV/DD2/13, GV/DD2/40, GV/DD2/43, GV/DD2/61A.
27. Knollys to Rosebery, 13 January 1897, Rosebery NLS 10039.
28. Note in Betting Book, 26 February 1905, Rosebery NLS 10176.
29. Christopher Hibbert, *The Royal Victorians*.
30. Leslie, *op.cit.* The woman to whom Toria said this was Leslie's great-aunt, Mary Crawshay.
31. Diana Forbes-Robertson, *Maxine*.
32. James Lees-Milne, *The Enigmatic Edwardian*.
33. Forbes-Robertson, *op.cit.*
34. Note of conversation with Rosebery, 4 September 1909, Ms Fisher 59.
35. Regy Brett to Rosebery, 24 March 1896, Rosebery NLS 10006.
36. Rosebery to Stead, 30 April 1896, Stead papers.

37. Ralph G. Martin, *Lady Randolph Churchill*.
38. 'One night on board the yacht *Vesta*, Mr Ward told us that he had given his erotic library to Lord Rosebery': Paul Dana to Lord Crewe, 1 November 1930, Crewe NLS 10195.
39. Guise to Rosebery, 7 January 1906, Rosebery NLS 10120.
40. Rosebery to Guise, 3 November 1907. Rosebery NLS 10120.
41. Rosebery to Guise, 28 November 1907, Rosebery NLS 10120.
42. Guise to Rosebery, 29 November 1907, Rosebery NLS 10120.
43. Diary of Violet Bonham-Carter, 24 October 1905, in Mark Bonham-Carter and Mark Pottle (eds), *Lantern Slides*.
44. Susan Chitty, *Playing the Game*.
45. Rosebery to Mary Gladstone Drew, 23 December 1903, Mary Gladstone papers, Add Ms 46,237.
46. Rosebery to Constance Leconfield, 14 February 1907, Petworth papers.
47. Lord Egremont, *Wyndham and Children First*.
48. Note, Dalmeny papers.
49. Diary of Lord Rosebery, 16 November 1907, Dalmeny papers.
50. Rosebery to Haldane, 24 May 1901, Haldane NLS 5905.
51. Rosebery to Hamilton, 29 June 1906, Hamilton papers, Add Ms 48,612B.
52. Diary of Lord Rosebery, 31 May 1905, Dalmeny papers.
53. Diary of Lord Rosebery, 9 October 1905, Dalmeny papers.
54. Rosebery to Neville-Rolfe, 30 July 1897, Neville-Rolfe papers.
55. Note by Neville-Rolfe, 8 March 1898, Neville-Rolfe papers.
56. Amy Neville-Rolfe to Robert Gunther (her future husband), 1 November 1898, Neville-Rolfe papers.
57. Norman Douglas, *Looking Back*.
58. Philip Magnus, *Edward VII*.
59. Sir Frederick Ponsonby, *Recollections of Three Reigns*.
60. *Ibid*.
61. Note, 17 May 1910, Dalmeny papers.
62. Lady Colebrooke to Rosebery, 19 October 1906, Rosebery NLS 10120.
63. Note of conversation with Alice Keppel, 14 June 1907, Betting Book, Rosebery NLS 10184.
64. Betting Book, Rosebery NLS 10184.
65. Rosebery to King Edward VII, 21 October 1906, Rosebery NLS 10016.
66. King Edward VII to Rosebery, 22 October 1906, Rosebery NLS 10016.
67. Note of conversation with Alice Keppel, 13 May 1910, Dalmeny papers.
68. Edward Hamilton's Diary, 12 October 1902.
69. Rosebery to H.A.L. Fisher, 15 December 1905, Ms Fisher 57.
70. Young, *op.cit.*
71. Rosebery to Prince George, 9 February 1909, Royal Archives, GV/AA 53/33.
72. Churchill to Perks, 13 January 1907, Rosebery NLS 10053.

73. John Wilson, *Life of Campbell-Bannerman*.
74. Note of conversation, 2 April 1907, Betting Book, Rosebery NLS 10184.
75. Perks to Rosebery, 26 November 1907, Rosebery NLS 10053.
76. Rosebery to Allard, 16 May 1907, Rosebery NLS 10171.
77. Allard to Rosebery, 16 November 1907, Rosebery NLS 10171.
78. Rosebery to Allard, 21 November 1907, Rosebery NLS 10171.
79. Rosebery to Murray, 27 July 1907, Murray papers.
80. Diary of Lord Rosebery, 12 March 1908, Dalmeny papers.
81. Sir Almeric Fitzroy, *Memoirs*.
82. Lord Newton, *Retrospection*.
83. Lord Newton, *Lord Lansdowne: A Biography*.
84. Esher to his son Maurice, 25 June 1907, Esher papers.
85. Rosebery to Sir George Murray, 8 January 1909, Murray papers.
86. Diary of Margot Asquith, June 1908.

CHAPTER 17: 'A HELPLESS MONSTER'

1. Rosebery to Morley, 13 September 1909, Morley Mss Eur D573.
2. Stead to Rosebery, 12 March 1909, Rosebery NLS 10121.
3. Rosebery to Strachey, 27 February 1908, Strachey papers STR 12/7.
4. Strachey to Tennant, 12 August 1909, Strachey papers STR 16/3.
5. Perks to Rosebery, 25 June 1909, Rosebery NLS 10053.
6. Allard to Rosebery, 28 June 1909, Rosebery NLS 10172.
7. Rosebery to Northumberland, 3 September 1909, Rosebery NLS 10172.
8. Lansdowne to Rosebery, 3 and 6 September 1909, Rosebery NLS 10172.
9. Cameron Hazelhurst and Christine Woodland, *A Liberal Chronicle*.
10. *The Times*, 10 September 1909.
11. Mary Soames (ed.), *Speaking for Themselves*.
12. Asquith to Rosebery, 10 September 1909, Ms Asquith 46.
13. Rosebery to Asquith, 14 September 1909, Rosebery NLS 10001.
14. Peter Gordon (ed.), *Politics and Society*.
15. Lansdowne to Rosebery, 12 September 1909, Rosebery NLS 10168.
16. Strachey to Rosebery, 11 September 1909, Strachey STR 7.
17. Lord Hugh Cecil to Rosebery, 8 October 1909, Rosebery NLS 10121.
18. Giles St Aubyn, *Edward VII*.
19. Rosebery to Lord Hugh Cecil, 9 October 1909, Rosebery NLS 10121.
20. Diary of Lord Crawford, 5 October 1909, in John Vincent, *The Crawford Papers*.
21. Sir Almeric Fitzroy, *Memoirs*.
22. Amery to Maxse, 26 November 1909, Maxse papers.
23. Lord Crewe, *Lord Rosebery*.
24. Rosebery to Buchan, 23 December 1909, Rosebery NLS Acc 6975 (13).

25. Fitzroy, *op.cit.*
26. Knollys to Rosebery, 21 December 1909, Rosebery NLS 10039.
27. Lord Hugh Cecil to Rosebery, 1 February 1910, Rosebery NLS 10122.
28. Rosebery to Charles Dalrymple, 17 December 1910, Rosebery NLS 10122.
29. Diary of Margot Asquith, 16 November 1909.
30. Journal of Lord Esher, 4 October 1911, Esher papers.
31. Lord Kilbracken, *Reminiscences*.
32. Diary of Lord Rosebery 10 August 1911, Dalmeny papers.
33. Rosebery to King George V, 11 August 1911, RA PS/GV/O912/17.
34. Rosebery to Northcliffe, 18 February 1912, Northcliffe Add Ms 62,154.
35. Northcliffe to Rosebery, 20 February 1912, Northcliffe Add Ms 62,154.
36. Cox to Rosebery, 1 April 1912, Rosebery NLS 10123.
37. Rosebery to Cox, 10 April 1912, Rosebery NLS 10123.
38. Kenneth Young, *Balfour.*
39. James Lees-Milne, *The Enigmatic Edwardian.*
40. Sir Frederick Ponsonby, *Recollections of Three Reigns.*
41. Note by Rosebery, 19 September 1914, Rosebery NLS 10124.
42. Rosebery to Munro-Ferguson, 20 July 1912, Rosebery NLS 10120.
43. Munro-Ferguson to Rosebery, 22 July 1912, Rosebery NLS 10120.
44. Rosebery to Munro-Ferguson, 26 July 1912, Rosebery NLS 10120.
45. Munro-Ferguson to Rosebery, 28 July 1912, Rosebery NLS 10120.
46. Rosebery to King George V, 8 September 1911, Rosebery NLS 10123.
47. Durham to Rosebery, 11 November 1911, Rosebery NLS 10123.
48. Frances Lloyd George, *The Years That Are Past.*
49. Michael and Eleanor Brock (eds), *H.H. Asquith: Letters to Venetia Stanley.*
50. Rosebery to Mary Gladstone Drew, 26 February 1914, Mary Gladstone papers Add Ms 46,237.
51. Rosebery to J.A. Spender, 24 January 1907, Spender papers 46,387.
52. Rosebery to Constance Leconfield, 11 October 1914, Petworth papers 5580.
53. Rosebery to Constance Leconfield, 20 August 1914, Petworth papers 5578.
54. Rosebery to the Earl of Derby, August 1915, Rosebery NLS 10125.
55. Rosebery to Asquith, 10 March 1915, Asquith MS Eng c 6716.
56. Rosebery to Lord Ripon, 7 June 1893, Ripon papers Add Ms 43516.
57. Rosebery to Constance Leconfield, 14 September 1914, Petworth papers 5580.
58. Tim Card, *Eton Renewed.*
59. Rosebery to Cecil Lubbock, March 1916, Rosebery NLS.
60. Letter by Rosebery to press, May 1917, Rosebery NLS 10125.
61. Fisher to Rosebery, August 1914, Rosebery NLS 10124.
62. Fisher to Rosebery, 13 October 1914, Rosebery NLS 10124.
63. Rosebery to Fisher, 16 March 1916, Fisher papers.
64. Rosebery to Lodge, 4 July 1915, Rosebery NLS 10125.
65. Grant to Rosebery, 24 September 1914, Liddell Hart Archives, 2/1/2.

66. Grant to Rosebery, 9 June 1915, Liddell Hart Archives, 2/1/8.

67. Grant to Rosebery, 17 June 1915, Liddell Hart Archives, 2/1/9.

68. Quoted in letter from Horatio Brown, 17 November 1914, Rosebery NLS 10125.

69. Dalmeny papers, May 1915.

70. Rosebery to Margot Asquith, 10 November 1915, Ms Eng d.3273.

71. Lucy Masterman, *Mary Gladstone Diaries and Letters*.

72. Note 1916, Dalmeny papers.

73. Note 1917, Dalmeny papers.

74. Curzon to Lloyd George, undated, Lloyd George papers F/11/8/3.

75. Rosebery to Northcliffe, Northcliffe papers Add Ms 62, 154.

76. Grant to Rosebery, 7 March 1915, Liddell Hart Archives, 2/1/4.

77. Rosebery to H.A.L. Fisher, 12 September 1915, Fisher 57.

78. Lord Birkenhead, *Points of View*.

79. Rosebery to King George V, 20 November 1917, RA GV/AA 48/144.

80. Philip Hoare, *Wilde's Last Stand*.

81. Lady Cynthia Asquith, *Diaries*.

82. Hoare, *op.cit.*

83. Constance Leconfield to Lord Crewe, 22 August 1931, NLS Crewe 10195.

84. Rosebery to Bryce, 11 February 1919, Mss Bryce 121.

85. Rosebery to Fisher, 11 October 1921, Ms Fisher 57.

86. John Buchan, *Memory-Hold-The-Door*.

87. Rosebery to Strachey, 19 October 1921, Strachey STR 12/7.

88. Kenneth Young, *Harry, Lord Rosebery*.

89. Rosebery to Stamfordham, 20 February 1924, RA PS/GV/O912/51.

90. Rosebery to Buchan, 10 May 1926, Rosebery NLS Acc 6975.

91. Rosebery to Constance Leconfield, 6 December 1924, Petworth papers 5584.

92. Birrell to Rosebery, 23 June 1920, Rosebery NLS 10126.

93. Rosebery to Charles Edmunds, 18 December 1920, Rosebery NLS 10126.

94. Skelton to Rosebery, 31 December 1920, Rosebery NLS 10126.

95. Skelton to Rosebery, 12 January 1921, Rosebery NLS 10127.

96. Robert Rhodes James, *Rosebery*.

97. *Ibid.*

98. Young, *op.cit.*

99. Rosebery to Margot Asquith, 1 December 1887, Asquith papers, MS Eng d.3273.

100. Evan Charteris, *The Life and Letters of Sir Edmund Gosse*.

101. Rosebery to Mary Gladstone Drew, 13 December 1920, Mary Gladstone papers, Add Ms 46,237.

102. Journals of Randal Davidson, 2 March and 4 February 1924, extracts in Crewe papers, NLS Crewe 10203.

103. Rosebery to Stamfordham, 24 June 1925, RA PS/GV/O912/57.

104. Rosebery to Constance Leconfield, 26 June 1926, Petworth papers 5585.
105. Winston Churchill, *Great Contemporaries*.
106. Balfour to Joan Lascelles, 24 September 1927, quoted in Young, *Balfour*.
107. Buchan, *op.cit.*
108. Davidson to Murray, 28 May 1929, Murray papers.
109. Journal of Lady Monkswell, 14 July 1890, quoted in Collier, *A Victorian Diarist*.
110. Crewe, *op.cit.*
111. Letter to Lord Kilbracken, 11 August 11, 1917, Kilbracken papers.
112. Speech in London, 14 November 1899, Matthew, *Liberal Imperialists*.
113. Sybil Grant, 'A Great Scotsman', Rosebery NLS, Acc 8365.
114. Dalmeny papers.
115. Winston Churchill, *Great Contemporaries*.
116. Philip Guedalla, *A Gallery*.
117. Rosebery NLS, 10019.

Bibliography

Archives

Acton, 1st Baron (Cambridge University Library)
Alverstone, 1st Baron (R.E. Webster) (British Library)
Asquith, H.H. (Bodleian Library, Oxford)
Asquith, Margot (Bodleian Library, Oxford)
Avebury, 1st Baron (Sir John Lubbock) (British Library)
Battersea, 1st Baron, and Constance, Lady Battersea (previously Flower) (British Library)
Browning, Oscar (King's College Library, Cambridge)
Bryce, James (Bodleian Library, Oxford)
Buchan, John (National Library of Scotland)
Campbell-Bannerman, Sir Henry (British Library)
Carnarvon, 4th Earl of (British Library)
Chamberlain, Joseph (Birmingham University Library)
Churchill, Lord Randolph (Cambridge University Library)
Churchill, Winston S. (Churchill Archives, Cambridge)
Conway, 1st Baron (W. Martin) (National Library of Scotland)
Crewe, 1st Marquess of (Cambridge University Library and National Library of Scotland)
Cromer, 1st Earl of (British Library and Public Record Office)
Dilke, Sir Charles (British Library)
Dodgson, Charles (British Library)
Douglas, Norman (Beineke Library, Yale)
Dufferin and Ava, 1st Marquess of (Northern Ireland Public Record Office)
Drew, Mary (Mary Gladstone) (British Library)
Edward VII, HM King (Royal Archives, Windsor)
Ellis, T.E. (National Library of Wales)
Escott, T.H.S. (British Library)
Esher, 2nd Viscount (Regy Brett) (Churchill Archives, Cambridge)
Eton Society (Eton College Library)
Evans, Sir Edward (Liverpool Record Office)
Fisher, 1st Baron (Admiral Sir Jacky Fisher) (Churchill Archives, Cambridge)

588

Fisher, H.A.L. (Bodleian Library, Oxford)

Galway, 7th Viscount (Nottingham University Library)

Geake, Charles (Bristol University Library)

George V, HM King (Royal Archives, Windsor)

Gilmour, Thomas Lennox (National Library of Scotland)

Gladstone, 1st Viscount (Herbert Gladstone) (British Library)

Gladstone, W.E. (British Library)

Gladstone, Catherine (Mrs W.E. Gladstone) (British Library)

Grant, Sir Charles (Liddell Hart Archives, King's College, London)

Haldane, 1st Viscount (National Library of Scotland)

Hamilton, Sir Edward (British Library)

Harcourt, Sir William (Bodleian Library, Oxford)

Harcourt, 1st Viscount (Loulou Harcourt) (Bodleian Library, Oxford)

Hardinge of Penhurst, 1st Baron (Charles Hardinge) (Cambridge University Library)

Headlam, Cuthbert (Durham Record Office)

Kilbracken, 1st Baron (Arthur Godley) (British Library)

Kimberley, 1st Earl of (John Wodehouse) (Bodleian Library, Oxford and National Library of Scotland)

Knollys, 1st Viscount (Sir Francis Knollys) (Royal Archives, Windsor)

Leconfield, Constance, Lady (Lady Constance Primrose) (Petworth House, courtesy of West Sussex Record Office)

Lee, Sir Sidney (British Library)

Lloyd-George, 1st Earl (David Lloyd George) (House of Lords Record Office)

London County Council (London Metropolitan Archive)

Massingham, Henry (Norfolk Record Office)

Maylock, Sir Willoughby (London Metropolitan Archive)

Maxse, Leo (West Sussex Record Office)

Milner, 1st Viscount (Bodleian Library, Oxford)

Monkswell, 2nd Baron (Bodleian Library, Oxford)

Morley, John (Bodleian Library, Oxford and India Office Collection, British Library)

Murray, Sir George (Blair Castle, Pitlochry)

Murray, 1st Baron and Master of Elibank (National Library of Scotland)

Neville-Rolfe, Eustace (Norfolk Record Office)

Northcliffe, 1st Viscount (Alfred Harmsworth) (British Library)

Passfield, 1st Baron and Beatrice, Lady Passfield (Beatrice and Sidney Webb) (London School of Economics)

Playfair, 1st Baron (Imperial College Library, London)

Queensberry, 9th Marquess of (private collection)

Reading, 1st Marquess of (India Office Collection, British Library)

Ripon, 1st Marquess of (British Library)

Ritchie, 1st Baron (British Library)

Rosebery, 5th Earl of (National Library of Scotland and private collection, Dalmeny)

Russell, Sir Edward (Liverpool University)

St Aldwyn, 1st Earl (Sir Michael Hicks Beach) (Gloucestershire Record Office)
St Loe Strachey, John (House of Lords Record Office)
Saunders, David (Churchill Archives Centre)
Spence Watson, Robert (House of Lords Records Office)
Spender, J.A. (British Library)
Stanhope Family (Centre for Kentish Studies, Maidstone)
Stead, W.T. (Churchill Archives Centre)
Victoria, HM Queen (Royal Archives, Windsor Castle)
Wolseley, 1st Viscount (General Sir Garnet Wolseley) (Hove Central Library)
Wyndham, George (Duke of Westminster's private collection)

Contemporary Newspapers and Magazines

The Annual Register
Baily's Monthly Magazine
Blackwood's Edinburgh Magazine
Bridgewater *Mercury*
The Contemporary Review
Daily Chronicle
Daily Mail
Daily Telegraph
Edinburgh Evening News
The Fortnightly Review
The Illustrated London News
Methodist News
The Morning Post
The New York Times
The Nineteenth Century
The North American Review
The Outlook
The Pall Mall Gazette
The Review of Reviews
The Saturday Review
The Scotsman
Sheffield Telegraph
The Spectator
The Sunday Sun
The Times
The Times Literary Supplement
Truth
Vanity Fair
Westminster Review
The Young Man Magazine

Cardiff Central Library

029 2038 2116

Renewed Items 19/02/2013 13:40

XXXX3779

Item Title	Due Date
* Rosebery : statesman in tu	12/03/2013

* Renewed today

Thank you for renewing

www.cardiff.gov.uk

BIBLIOGRAPHY

Published Sources

Anstruther, Ian, *Oscar Browning: A Biography* (1983)

Argyll, Duke of, *Autobiography and Memoirs* (1906)

Armytage, W.H.G., *A.J. Mundella 1825–1897: The Liberal Background to the Labour Movement* (1951)

Asquith, Lady Cynthia, *Diaries 1915–1918* (1968)

Asquith, Earl of Oxford and, *Fifty Years of Parliament* (1926)

Asquith, Margot, *Autobiography* (2 vols, 1920, 1922)

—— *More Memories* (1933)

Auchincloss, Louis, *Persons of Consequence: Queen Victoria and her Circle* (New York, 1979)

Bahlman, Dudley (ed.), *The Diary of Sir Edward Walter Hamilton* (2 vols, 1972, 1993)

Balfour Browne, J.H., *Recollections Literary and Political* (1917)

Barker, Michael, *Gladstone and Radicalism: The Reconstruction of Liberal Policy in Britain 1885–1894* (1975)

Barnes, John and Nicholson, David, *The Leo Amery Diaries 1896–1929* (1980)

Barrie, James, *An Edinburgh Eleven* (1889)

Basset, A. Tilney, *Gladstone to His Wife* (1936)

Battersea, Constance, *Reminiscences* (1920)

Baumgart, Winfried, *Imperialism: The Idea and Reality of British and French Colonial Expansion 1880–1914* (1982)

Bennet, Daphne, *Margot: A Life of the Countess of Oxford and Asquith* (1984)

Bentley, Michael, *Politics Without Democracy, 1815–1914* (1984)

—— *The Climax of Liberal Politics: British Liberalism in Theory and Practice 1868–1918* (1987)

Bergler, Edmund, *Homosexuality: Disease or Way of Life?* (1956)

Bernstein, George, *Liberalism and Liberal Politics in Edwardian England* (1986)

Betts, Raymond, *The False Dawn: European Imperialism in the Nineteenth Century* (1976)

Birkenhead, Lord, *Points of View* (1922)

—— *Contemporary Personalities* (1924)

Birrell, Augustine, *Things Past Redress* (1937)

Black, Eugene C., *The Social Politics of Anglo-Jewry, 1880–1920* (1988)

Blunden, Margaret, *The Countess of Warwick* (1967)

Blunt, Wilfrid Scawen, *My Diaries* (2 vols, 1919–20)

Bonham Carter, Mark and Pottle, Mark (eds), *Lantern Slides: The Diaries and Letters of Violet Bonham Carter 1904–1914* (1996)

Bourne, Kenneth, *The Foreign Policy of Victorian England 1830–1902* (1970)

Brent, Peter, *The Edwardians* (1972)

Brett, M.V. (ed.), *Journals and Letters of Viscount Esher* (1934)

Brock, Michael and Eleanor (eds), *H.H. Asquith: Letters to Venetia Stanley* (1982)

Brooks, David, *The Destruction of Lord Rosebery* (1986)

Buchan, John (ed.), *Lord Rosebery: Miscellanies Literary and Historical* (2 vols, 1921)
—— *Memory-Hold-The-Door* (1940)
—— *Comments and Characters* (1940)
Butler, David and Butler, Gareth, *British Political Facts 1900–1994* (1994)
Butler, Jeffrey, *The Liberal Party and the Jameson Raid* (1968)
Cannadine, David, *Aspects of Aristocray* (1994)
Card, Tim, *Eton Renewed: A History from 1860 to the Present Day* (1994)
Cassar, George H., *Kitchener: Architect of Victory* (1977)
Cecil, Algernon, *British Foreign Secretaries 1870–1916* (1927)
Chandos, John, *Boys Together: English Public Schools 1800–1864* (1985)
Charmley, John, *Splendid Isolation: Britain and the Balance of Power 1874–1914* (1999)
Chesterton, G.K., *What's Wrong With The World* (1910)
Chitty, Susan, *Playing the Game* (1997)
Churchill, Winston, *Great Contemporaries* (1937)
Clifford, Colin, *The Asquiths* (2002)
Coates, T.G.F., *Lord Rosebery: His Life and Speeches* (1900)
Cohen, Lucy, *Lady de Rothschild and Her Daughters, 1821–1931* (1935)
Collier, E.C.F. (ed.), *A Victorian Diarist: Extracts from the Journals of Mary, Lady Monkswell, 1873–1895* (1944)
Collin, A.M., *Proconsul in Politics: A Study of Lord Milner in Opposition and in Power* (1964)
Colson, Percy (ed.), *Lord Goschen and his Friends* (1946)
Colville, John, *Footprints in Time* (1976)
Compton Mackenzie, Faith, *William Cory* (1950)
Cook, E. Thornton, *What Manner of Men* (1934)
Cooke, A.B. and Vincent, John (eds), *Lord Carlingford's Journal* (1971)
Cooke, A.B. and Vincent, John, *The Governing Passion: Cabinet Government and Party Politics in Britain 1885–886* (1974)
Corder, Percy, *The Life of Robert Spence Watson* (1914)
Cornwallis-West, George, *Edwardian Hey-Days* (1930)
Crane, Denis, *The Life Story of Sir Robert Perks* (1909)
Craton, Michael and McCready, H.W., *The Great Liberal Revival* (1966)
Cregier, Don, *The Bounder from Wales: Lloyd George's Career Before the First World War* (1976)
Crewe, Lord, *Rosebery* (2 vols, 1931)
Dasent, Arthur Irwin, *Piccadilly in Three Centuries* (1920)
Davenport-Hines, Richard, *The Pursuit of Oblivion: A Global History of Narcotics 1500–2000* (2001)
Davis, Richard, *The English Rothschilds* (1983)
Douglas, Norman, *Looking Back* (1934)
Dowling, Linda, *Hellenism and Homosexuality in Victorian Oxford* (1994)
Dugdale, Blanche, *Family Homespun* (1940)
Dunlop, Ian, *Edward VII and the Entente Cordiale* (2004)

Edel, Leon (ed.), *The Selected Letters of Henry James* (1956)

—— *Henry James: The Conquest of London, 1870–1883* (1962)

Egremont, Lord (1st Baron), *Wyndham and Children First* (1968)

Egremont, Max (2nd Baron), *Balfour* (1980)

Ellman, Richard, *Oscar Wilde* (1987)

Enry, H.V., *Liberals, Radical and Social Politics 1892–1914* (1973)

Ensor, R.C.K., *England 1870–1914* (1936)

Erskine, Lady Angela St Clair, *Memories and Base Details* (1922)

—— *Fore and Aft* (1932)

Erskine of Marr, Ruaraidh, *King Edward VII and Some Other Figures* (1936)

Escott, T.H.S., *Personal Forces of the Period* (1898)

Esher, Lord, *Cloud-Clapp'd Towers* (1927)

Feldman, David, *Englishmen and Jews: Social Relations and Political Structure 1840–1914* (1994)

Ferguson, Niall, *The House of Rothschild: The World's Banker 1849–1999* (1991)

Fisher, Trevor, *Oscar and Bosie: A Fatal Passion* (2002)

Fitzroy, Sir Almeric, *Memoirs* (1925)

Flint, John, *Cecil Rhodes* (1974)

Foldy, Michael, *The Trials of Oscar Wilde: Deviance, Morality and Late Victorian Society* (Yale, 1997)

Foot M.R.D. Foot and Matthew, H.C.G., *The Gladstone Diaries* (1978–1994)

Forbes-Robertson, Diana, *Maxine* (1964)

Fowler, Edith Henrietta, *The Life of Lord Wolverhampton* (1912)

Fraser, Peter, *Joseph Chamberlain: Architect of Democracy* (1966)

Freeden, Michael, *The New Liberalism* (1978)

Fry, Michael, *The Scottish Empire* (2003)

Gann, L.H. and Duignan, Peter, *Burden of Empire* (Stanford, 1967)

Gardiner, A.G., *Prophets, Priests and Kings* (1909)

—— *The Life of Sir William Harcourt* (2 vols, 1923)

Geake, Charles, *Lord Rosebery: Appreciation and Addresses* (1899)

Gibbon, Sir Gwilym and Bell, Reginald, *History of the London County Council 1889–1939* (1939)

Gilbert, Bently, *Lloyd George: A Political Life, 1863–1912* (1987)

Gilmour, David, *Curzon* (1931)

Gladstone, Herbert, *After Thirty Years* (1928)

Gladstone, Mary, *Diaries and Letters*: see Masterman, Lucy (ed.)

Gooddie, Sheila, *Mary Gladstone: A Gentle Rebel* (2003)

Gordon, Peter (ed.), *The Red Earl: The Papers of the 5th Earl Spencer* (2 vols, 1981, 1986)

—— *Politics and Society: The Journals of Lady Knightley of Fawsley, 1885–1913* (1999)

Gordon-Lennox, Lady Algernon, *The Diary of Lord Bertie of Thame* (1924)

Gower, Lord Ronald, *Old Diaries, 1881–1901* (1902)

Grant, A.R.C. and Combe, Caroline (eds), *Lord Rosebery's North American Journal* (1967)

Grant Duff, M.E., *A Victorian Vintage* (1930)

Grey of Falloden, Viscount, *Twenty-five Years* (1925)

Grigg, John, *The Young Lloyd George* (1973)

—— *Lloyd George: From Peace to War, 1912–1916* (1985)

Guedalla, Philip, *A Gallery* (1924)

Gwynn, Stephen, *The Letters and Friendships of Sir Cecil Spring Rice* (1929)

Haldane, Richard Burdon, *An Autobiography* (1929)

Hall Tharp, Louise, *Three Saints and a Sinner* (1956)

Hamer, D.A. *John Morley: A Liberal Intellectual in Politics* (1968)

—— *Liberal Politics in the Age of Gladstone and Rosebery* (1972)

Hamer, F.E. (ed.), *Personal Papers of Lord Rendel* (1931)

Hamilton, Arnold, *A Selection from Goldwin Smith's Correspondence* (1913)

Hamilton, Lord George, *Parliamentary Reminiscences and Reflections, 1886–1906* (1922)

Hapgood, Norman, *Literary Statesmen and Others* (1897)

Hardie, Frank, *The Political Influence of Queen Victoria 1861–1901* (1963)

Hardwick, Molly, *Mrs Dizzy* (1972)

Harris, Frank, *My Life and Loves* (1922)

Hattersley, Roy, *The Edwardians* (2004)

Haward, Sir Harry, *The London County Council From Within: Forty Years of Official Recollections* (1932)

Hawkins, Angus and Powell, John (eds), *The Journal of John Wodehouse, 1st Earl of Kimberley for 1862–1902* (1997)

Hazelhurst, Cameron and Woodland, Christine, *A Liberal Chronicle: The Journals and Papers of J.A. Pease 1908–1910* (1994)

Heffer, Simon, *Power and Place: The Political Consequences of King Edward VII* (1998)

Hibbert, Christopher, *The Royal Victorians: King Edward VII, His Family and Friends* (1976)

—— *Queen Victoria: A Personal History* (2000)

Hoare, Philip, *Wilde's Last Stand: Decadence, Conspiracy and the First World War* (1997)

Holland, Bernard, *Life of the Duke of Devonshire* (2 vols, 1911)

Holland, Merlin, *The Irish Peacock and the Scarlet Marquess: The Real Trial of Oscar Wilde* (2003)

Holloway, Mark, *Norman Douglas* (1976)

Houseman, Laurence, *Palace Scenes* (1937)

Howard, Esme, *Theatre of Life* (1935)

Howe, Maud Elliott, *Uncle Sam Ward and His Circle* (1938)

Hudson, Roger, *The Jubilee Years* (1996)

Hutchinson, Horace, *The Life of Sir John Lubbock* (1914)

—— *The Private Diaries of Sir Algernon West* (1922)

Hyde, H. Montgomery, *The Trials of Oscar Wilde* (1962)

—— *Henry James at Home* (1969)

—— *Lord Alfred Douglas* (1984)

Hynes, Samuel, *The Edwardian Turn of Mind* (1991)

Jackson, Patrick, *The Last of the Whigs: A Political Biography of Lord Hartington, 8th Duke of Devonshire* (1994)

Jalland, Pat, *Death in the Victorian Family* (1996)

James, Lawrence, *The Rise and Fall of the British Empire* (1994)

James, Robert Rhodes, *Lord Randolph Churchill* (1959)

Jenkins, Romilly, *The Dilessi Murders: Greek Brigands and English Hostages* (1961)

Jenkins, Roy, *Mr Balfour's Poodle* (1954)

—— *Sir Charles Dilke: A Victorian Tragedy* (1958)

—— *Rosebery* (1963)

—— *Asquith* (1964)

—— *Gladstone* (1995)

—— *Churchill* (2001)

Jenkins, T.A., *Gladstone, Whiggery and the Liberal Party 1874–1886* (1988)

Jeyes, S.H., *Lord Rosebery* (1906)

Johnson, Nancy E., *The Diary of Gathorne Hardy, later Lord Cranbrook, 1866–1892* (1981)

Johnston, James, *Westminster Voices: Studies in Parliamentary Speech* (1928)

Joliffe, John (ed.), *Raymond Asquith: Life and Letters* (1980)

Judd, Denis, *Radical Joe: A Life of Joseph Chamberlain* (1977)

—— *Empire* (1996)

Kent, William, *John Burns: Labour's Lost Leader* (1950)

Kilbracken, Lord, *Reminiscences* (1931)

Kochanski, Halk, *Sir Garnet Wolseley: A Victorian Hero* (1999)

Koss, Stephen, *Lord Haldane: Scapegoat for Liberalism* (1969)

—— *Asquith* (1976)

Lang, Theo, *My Darling Daisy* (1966)

Lees-Milne, James, *The Enigmatic Edwardian: The Life of Reginald, 2nd Viscount Esher* (1986)

Leslie, Anita, *Jennie: The Life of Lady Randolph Churchill* (1969)

—— *Edwardians in Love* (1972)

Levenson-Gower, Sir George, *Years of Endeavour, 1886–1907* (1942)

Levine, Naomi B., *Politics, Religion and Love* (New York, 1991)

Lloyd George, David, *War Memoirs* (1993)

Lloyd George, Frances, *The Years That Are Past* (1966)

Longford, Elizabeth (writing as Elizabeth Pakenham), *Jameson's Raid: The Prelude to the Boer War* (1970)

Longford, Elizabeth (ed.), *Louisa, Lady-in-Waiting* (1979)

—— *A Pilgramage of Passion: The Life of Wilfred Scawen Blunt* (1979)

—— *Victoria R.I.* (1998)

Lowe, C.J., *The Reluctant Imperialists: The Foreign Policies of the Great Powers, 1878–1902* (2 vols, 1967)

McCallum, R.B., *The Liberal Party from Earl Grey to Asquith* (1963)

McCarthy, Justin, *British Political Leaders* (1904)

Mackay, Ruddock F., *Balfour: Intellectual Statesman* (1985)

McKenna, Neil, *The Secret Life of Oscar Wilde* (2003)

Mackenzie, Norman and Jeanne, *The First Fabians* (1977)

Magnus, Philip, *Gladstone* (1954)

—— *Kitchener: Portrait of An Imperialist* (1958)

—— *King Edward VII* (1964)

Malcolm, Sir Ian, *Vacant Thrones* (1931)

Mallet, Sir Charles, *Herbert Gladstone: A Memoir* (1932)

Mallet, Victor (ed.), *Life with Queen Victoria: Marie Mallet's Letters from Court* (1968)

Marlowe, John, *Cromer in Egypt* (1970)

—— *Milner: Apostle of Empire* (1976)

Marlow, Joyce, *The Oak and the Ivy: A Biography of William and Catherine Gladstone* (1977)

Marsh, Peter, *Joseph Chamberlain: Entrepreneur in Politics* (1994)

Martel, Gordon, *Imperial Diplomacy: Lord Rosebery and the Failure of Foreign Policy* (1986)

Martin, Ralph, *Lady Randolph Churchill: A Biography, 1854–1895* (1969)

Masterman, Lucy, *Mary Gladstone: Her Diaries and Letters* (1930)

Matthew, H.C.G., *The Liberal Imperialists* (1973)

—— *Gladstone 1875–1898* (1995)

—— and Foot, M.R.D., *The Gladstone Diaries* (1978–1994)

Matthews, Roy, and Mallini, Peter, *Vanity Fair* (1982)

Mills, J. Saxon, *Sir Edward Cook, KBE: A Biography* (1921)

Milne, James, *The Romance of a Pro-Consul: Being the Life and Memories of Sir George Grey* (1899)

Minnery, R.J., *Number 10 Downing Street: A House in History* (1963)

Moberly Bell, E.H.C., *The Life and Letters of C.F. Moberly Bell* (1927)

Money, James, *Capri* (1986)

Moneypenny, W.F., and Buckle, G.E., *Life of Disraeli* (1929)

Monkswell, Lady, *A Victorian Diarist: see* E.F.C. Collier (ed.)

Montgomery, John, *1900: The End of an Era* (1968)

Morley, John, *Recollections* (1917)

Murray, Douglas, *Bosie: A Biography of Lord Alfred Douglas* (2000)

Newton, Lord, *Lord Lansdowne: A Biography* (1929)

—— *Retrospection* (1941)

Nicholl, W. Robertson, *A Bookman's Letters* (1915)

Nicholls, David, *The Lost Prime Minister: A Life of Sir Charles Dilke* (1995)

O'Brien, Terence, *Milner* (1979)

O'Connor, T.P., *The Memoirs of an Old Parliamentarian* (2 vols, 1929)

O'Donnell, C.J., *The Failure of Lord Curzon: A Study in Imperialism* (Delhi, 1903)

Owen, Frank, *Tempestuous Journey: Lloyd George, His Life and Times* (1954)

Owen, Roger, *Lord Cromer: Victorian Imperialist, Edwardian Proconsul* (2004)

Paget, Lady, *In My Tower* (1924)

Pakenham, Thomas, *The Boer War* (1979)

—— *The Scramble for Africa* (1999)

Palmer, Bernard, *High and Mitred: Prime Ministers as Bishop-Makers, 1837–1977* (1992)

Parris, Matthew, *Great Parliamentary Scandals* (1995)

Parry, Jonathan, *The Rise and Fall of Liberal Government in Victorian Britain* (1993)

Pascoe, Charles Eyre, *Number 10 Downing Street: Its History and Associations* (1908)

Pearson, Hesketh, *Labby, The Life of Henry Labouchere* (1936)

Perham, Margery, *Lugard: The Years of Adventure, 1858–1898* (1956)

Petre, Sir Charles, *A Historian Looks At His World* (1972)

Plumptre, George, *The Fast Set: The World of Edwardian Racing* (1985)

Ponsonby, Sir Frederick, *Recollections of Three Reigns* (1951)

Pope-Hennessy, James, *Lord Crewe: The Likeness of a Liberal* (1955)

Porter, Bernard, *The Absent-Minded Imperialists* (2004)

Porter, Roy, *London: A Social History* (1994)

Powell, John, *Liberal by Principle: The Politics of John Wodehouse, 1st Earl of Kimberley* (1996)

Queensberry, Marquess of and Colson, Percy, *Oscar Wilde and the Black Douglas* (1949)

Radziwill, Princess Catherine, *Memories of Forty Years* (1914)

Ramm, Agatha (ed.), *The Gladstone–Granville Correspondence* (1962)

—— *Darling and Beloved Child: The Last Letters between Queen Victoria and Her Eldest Daughter, 1886–1901* (1990)

Raymond, E.T., *The Man of Promise: Lord Rosebery* (1923)

Raymond, John, *The Doge of Dover* (1960)

Reid, Michaela, *Ask Sir James* (1987)

Reid, Stuart, *Memoirs of Sir Wemyss Reid: 1842–1885* (1905)

Ribblesdale, Lord, *Impressions and Memories* (1927)

Richards, James Brinsley, *Seven Years of Eton* (1883)

Robbins, Keith, *Sir Edward Grey* (1971)

Roberts, Andrew, *Salisbury: Victorian Titan* (1999)

Robinson, Sir John R., *Fifty Years of Fleet Street* (1922)

Robinson, Ronald and Gallagher, John, *Africa and the Victorians* (1961)

Rodd, Sir Rennell, *Social and Diplomatic Memories* (1922)

Rosebery, Lord, *Pitt* (1891)

—— *Napoleon: The Last Phase* (1900)

—— *Lord Randolph Churchill* (1906)

—— *Chatham: His Early Life and Connections* (1910)

Rowland, Peter, *Lloyd George* (1975)

Royle, Trevor, *The Kitchener Enigma* (1985)

Rubinstein, Hilary, *The Complete Insomniac* (1974)

Russell, Alice, *Political Stability in Later Victorian England* (1992)

Russell, G.W.E., *Portraits of the Seventies* (1916)

Saint, Andrew (ed.). *Politics and the People of London: The London County Council 1889–1965* (1989)

St Aubyn, Giles, *The Royal George: The Life of HRH Prince George, Duke of Cambridge* (1963)

—— *Edward VII: Prince and King* (1979)

—— *Queen Victoria* (1991)

St Helier, Lady, *Memories of Fifty Years* (1909)

Samuel, Viscount, *Memoirs* (1945)

Saunders, William, *History of the First London County Council* (1892)

Schreuder, Deryck and Butler, Jeffrey (eds), *Sir Graham Bower's Secret History of the Jameson Raid and the South African Crisis, 1895–1902* (Cape Town, 2002)

Seaman, L.C.B., *Victorian England: Aspects of English and Imperial History, 1837–1901* (1973)

Searle, G.R., *The Quest for National Efficiency: A Study in British politics and British political thought, 1899–1914* (1971)

Seeley, J.R., *The Expansion of England* (1888)

Semmel, Bernard, *Imperialism and Social Reform* (1960)

Seth-Smith, Michael, and Mortimer, Roger, *Derby 200: The Official History of the Blue Riband of the Turf* (1979)

Seymour-Jones, Carole, *Beatrice Webb: Woman of Conflict* (1992)

Shannon, Richard, *The Crisis of Imperialism, 1865–1915* (1976)

—— *Gladstone: Heroic Minister, 1865–1898* (1999)

Soames, Mary (ed.), *Speaking for Themselves: The Personal Letters of Winston and Clementine Churchill* (1998)

Southgate, Donald, *The Passing of the Whigs: 1832–1886* (1962)

Southwark, Lady, *Social and Political Reminiscences* (1913)

Spender, J.A. and Asquith, Cyril, *Life of Lord Oxford and Asquith* (1932)

Spender, J.A., *Life of Sir Henry Campbell-Bannerman* (1923)

—— *The Public Life* (2 vols, 1925)

—— *Life, Journalism and Politics* (1927)

Spinner, Thomas J., *George Joachim Goschen: The Transformation of a Victorian Liberal* (1973)

Stansky, Peter, *Ambitions and Strategies: The Struggle for the Leadership of the Liberal Party in the 1890s* (1964)

Stevens, Crosby, *Ransom and Murder in Greece: Lord Muncaster's Journal 1870* (1989)

Stoddart, Jane, *The Earl of Rosebery: An Illustrated Biography* (1900)

Street, G.S., *The Ghosts of Piccadilly* (1907)

Strong, Sir Roy, *Diaries* (1987)

Sturgis, Matthew, *Passionate Attitudes: The English Decadence of the Eighteen Nineties* (1995)

Summer, Dudley, *Haldane of Cloan: His Life and Times* (1960)

Sylvester, Christopher, *The Pimlico Companion to Parliament* (1996)

Taylor, A.J.P. (ed.), *Lloyd George: A Diary by Frances Stevenson* (1971)

Thomas, Lately, *Sam Ward: King of the Lobby* (Cambridge, Mass. 1965)

Thompson, J. Lee, *Northcliffe: Press Baron in Politics, 1865–1922* (2000)

Thompson, Paul, *Socialists, Liberals and Labour: The Struggle for London, 1885–1914* (1967)

Thompson, Robert and Macklin, Robert, *The Man Who Died Twice: The Life and Adventures of Morrison of Peking* (2003)

Thomson, Malcolm, *David Lloyd George: The Official Biography* (1948)

Thornton, A.P., *The Imperial Idea and Its Enemies: A Study in British Power* (1966)

Tillett, Ben, *Memories and Reflections* (1931)

Trevelyan, G.M., *Sir George Otto Trevelyan: A Memoir* (1932)

—— *Grey of Fallodon* (1937)

Trevor-Roper, Hugh, *The Hermit of Peking: The Hidden Life of Sir Edmund Backhouse* (1976)

Thruston, Edmund Heathcote, *The Earl of Rosebery: Statesman and Sportsman* (1928)

Tuchman, Barabara, *The Proud Tower* (1966)

Vanderbilt, Consuelo, *The Glitter and the Gold* (1973)

Vincent, John (ed.), *The Crawford Papers: The Journals of David Lindsay, 27th Earl of Crawford and 10th Earl of Balcarres during the years 1871 to 1940* (1984)

—— *The Diaries of Edward Henry Stanley, 15th Earl of Derby, 1878–1893* (2003)

Walling, R.A.J. (ed.), *The Diaries of John Bright* (1930)

Ward, Mrs Humphrey, *Marcella* (1894)

Warwick, Frances, Countess of, *Life's Ebb and Flow* (1929)

—— *Afterthoughts* (1931)

Webb, Beatrice, *My Apprenticeship* (1926)

—— *Our Partnership* (1948)

Weintraub, Stanley, *Victoria: Biography of a Queen* (1986)

—— *The Importance of Being Edward: King in Waiting, 1841–1901* (2000)

Weller, Philip, *The Hound of the Baskervilles: Hunting the Dartmoor Legend* (2001)

Wilson, A.N., *The Victorians* (2002)

Wilson, F.M.G., *A Strong Supporting Cast: The Shaw Lefevres, 1789–1936* (1993)

Wilson, John, *CB: A Life of Sir Henry Campbell-Bannerman* (1973)

Wilson, Trevor (ed.), *The Political Diaries of C.P.Scott, 1911–1928* (1970)

Wolf, Lucien, *Life of Lord Ripon* (1921)

Young, Ken and Garside, Patricia, *Metropolitan London: Politics and Urban Change 1837–1981* (1982)

Young, Kenneth, *Arthur James Balfour* (1963)

—— *Harry, Lord Rosebery* (1974)

Zeigler, Philip, *Diana Cooper* (1981)

Zetland, Marquess of, *The Letters of Disraeli to Lady Bradford and Lady Chesterfield* (1929)

Articles

Atherley-Jones, L.A., 'Lord Rosebery's Enterprise against the House of Lords' (*Nineteenth Century*, December 1894)

Baylen, J.O. and Robert McBath, 'A Note on Oscar Wilde, Lord Alfred Douglas and Lord Rosebery 1897' (*English Language Notes*, Vol. XXIII, September 1985)

Burgess, M.D., 'Lord Rosebery and the Imperial Federation League 1884–1893' (*New Zealand Journal of History*, Vol. 13, October 1979)

Dicey, Edward, 'Lord Rosebery's Resignation' (*Fortnightly Review*, November 1896)

Dilke, Sir Charles, 'The New Prime Minister' (*North American Review*, May 1894)

Fahey, David M., 'Rosebery, *The Times* and The Newcastle Programme' (*Institute of Historical Research Bulletin*, Vol. 45, May 1972)

Filon, Augustus and Delbruck, Hans, 'Foreign Views of Lord Rosebery' (*The Fortnightly Review*, December 1894)

Gutze, David, 'Rosebery and Ireland 1898–1903' (*Institute of Historical Research Bulletin*, Vol. 53, May 1980)

—— 'Rosebery and Campbell-Bannerman: The Conflict over Leadership Reconsidered' (*loc. cit.*, Vol. 54, November 1981)

Harrison, Frederic, 'Lord Rosebery and the London County Council' (*The Nineteenth Century*, Vol. XXVII, June 1890)

Kellas, James, 'The Liberal Party and Scottish Church Disestablishment' (*English Historical Review*, Vol. 79 1964)

—— 'The Liberal Party in Scotland 1876–1895' (*Scottish Historical Review*, Vol. 44, April 1965)

Koss, Stephen, 'Morley in the Middle' (*English Historical Review*, Vol. 82, 1967)

Kelley, Robert, 'Midlothian: A Study in Politics and Ideas' (*Victorian Studies*, Vol. 4, December 1960)

Low, Anthony, 'British Public Opinion and the Uganda Question' (*Uganda Journal*, Vol. 18, 1954)

McCready, H.W., 'Home Rule and the Liberal Party 1899–1906' (*Irish Historical Studies*, Vol. 13, 1963)

—— 'Sir Alfred Milner, The Liberal Party and the Boer War' (*Canadian Journal of History*, March 1967)

Mackenzie, Kenneth, 'Some British Reactions to German Colonial Methods 1885–1907' (*Historical Journal*, Vol. 17, 1974)

Massingham, H.W., 'The Future of Lord Rosebery' (*The Nineteenth Century*, November 1899)

Meelboom, John. A., 'Lord Rosebery: The Shattered Idol' (*Westminster Review*, May 1902)

Miller, T.B., 'The Egyptian Question and British Foreign Policy 1892–1894' (*The Journal of Modern History*, Vol. XXXII, March 1960)

Penson, Lillian, 'The New Course in British Foreign Policy 1892–1902' (*Transactions of the Royal Historical Society*, 4th series, Vol. 25, 1943)

Powell, David, 'Liberal Ministries and Labour 1892–1895' (*History*, Vol. 68, October 1983)

Stobart, W.L., 'Lord Rosebery and His Followers' (*Fortnightly Review*, June 1898)

Strachey, St Loe, 'The Seven Lord Roseberys' (*The Nineteenth Century*, October 1894)

Taylor, A.J.P., 'Prelude to Fashoda: The Question of the Upper Nile 1894–95' (*English Historical Review*, Vol. 66, January 1950)

Trainor, Luke, 'The Liberals and the Formation of Imperial Defence Policy 1892–95' (*Bulletin of the Institute of Historical Research*, Vol. 52, 1969)

Tyler, J.E., 'Campbell-Bannerman and the Liberal Imperialists' (*History*, Vol. 23, December 1938)

Sidney Webb, 'Lord Rosebery's Escape from Houndsditch' (*Nineteenth Century*, September 1901)

Unsigned Articles

'Lord Rosebery's Soliloquy' (*Saturday Review*, January 1897)

'Lord Rosebery's Apostasy' (*Fortnightly Review*, December 1897)

'A Palmerston with Nerves' (*Fortnightly Review*, July 1899)

'Lord Rosebery's Chance' (*Fortnightly Review*, December 1900)

'The Foreign Policy of Lord Rosebery' (*Contemporary Review*, July 1901)

Index

Abbreviations are used as follows: CB = Campbell-Bannerman; G = Gladstone; HR
= Hannah Rosebery (*née* de Rothschild); R = Lord Rosebery; QV = Queen
Victoria
Titles are generally the latest used in the text.